C0-AWZ-370

# A HISTORY OF RUSSIAN PHILOSOPHY

VOLUME ONE

# A HISTORY

## OF

# RUSSIAN PHILOSOPHY

by

## V. V. ZENKOVSKY

*Professor of Philosophy and Psychology,*
*Russian Orthodox Theological Seminary, Paris*

*Authorized translation from the Russian*

*by George L. Kline*

*Ph.D., Visiting Assistant Professor of Philosophy, University of Chicago*

VOLUME ONE

Columbia University Press, New York

First published in England 1953
by Routledge & Kegan Paul Ltd
Broadway House 68-74 Carter Lane
London E.C.4

Published in the U.S.A. 1953
by Columbia University Press
Columbia University, New York

Library of Congress Catalog
Card Number 53-12113

Second Printing 1954
Third Printing 1967

Printed in Great Britain

# AUTHOR'S PREFACE
## TO THE RUSSIAN EDITION

I FEEL that a few prefatory remarks are called for in connection with the publication of the present work, upon which I have been occupied for many years.

It has long been my aim to write a history of Russian philosophy. I began gathering material for such a history in 1910, continuing this work after I moved to Western Europe. The lectures in the history of Russian philosophy which I gave on several occasions to the senior class of the Theological Institute in Paris were especially important to me in this connection. These lectures gave me numerous opportunities to verify the basic conception which had taken shape during my studies. In the process of preparing this book for publication I have once more studied all of the source material that was available to me carefully; and these detailed and painstaking studies have further reinforced my basic point of view with respect to the development of Russian philosophic thought.

Certain readers may criticize me because I do not simply expound and analyse the theoretical constructions of Russian philosophers but also relate these constructions to the general conditions of Russian life. However, this is the only valid procedure for an historian, especially an historian of philosophic thought. Russian philosophy, despite its unquestionable connection with, and even dependence upon, Western European thought, has produced original theoretical constructions, and these constructions have been related to the needs and conditions of Russian life as well as to the logic of ideas. I have attempted in this book to exhibit the internal unity and dialectical connectedness in the development of Russian philosophy—to the extent that I have been able to discover such unity and connectedness—with the greatest possible objectivity.

I am profoundly grateful to the Y.M.C.A. Press of Paris for having undertaken the publication of my book.

V. ZENKOVSKY

*Paris, June 1948*

# AUTHOR'S PREFACE
## TO THE ENGLISH EDITION

I AM highly gratified by the appearance of my book in English, and I hope that it may contribute to a better understanding of the Russian spirit and of Russian intellectual and spiritual searchings. My book was written primarily for Russian readers; it thus presupposes a certain acquaintance with Russian creative work and Russian culture generally. But I venture to hope that, thanks to the skill of the translator, it will prove accessible in its present form to my English and American readers.

V. ZENKOVSKY

*Paris, August 1952*

# TRANSLATOR'S NOTE

I T has seemed most convenient in preparing this book for the use of English readers to omit bibliographical references to primary or secondary works which are available only in Russian. Consequently, only works available in either English, French, or German have been included. Readers interested in Russian sources are referred to the original Russian edition of the present work (two volumes, Paris, 1948, 1950).

Translated titles of works published in Russian are printed in Roman type, e.g. Chernyshevski, The Anthropological Principle in Philosophy. Italics are used only where the title is given in a language in which the work in question has been published, e.g. Solovyov, *La Critique des principes abstraits*, Lenin, *Materialism and Empiriocriticism.* Russian names and titles are reproduced according to the transliteration system shown in the table on p. 925.

In general, Christian names are given in their English equivalent rather than simply transliterated, e.g. Peter rather than Pyotr, Theodore rather than Fyodor. Exceptions are made in the case of one or two Russian thinkers whose names have become well known to English readers in the Russian form, e.g. Fyodor Dostoyevsky, Nikolai Gogol.

Square brackets are used (sparingly) in the text to enclose material added by the translator; they are used within quotations to enclose material added by the author.

This translation has been made from the original Russian text as revised by the author to include a number of additions and corrections. Thus, in the case of discrepancies between the Russian and this English edition, the latter is to be regarded as authoritative.

To avoid possible misunderstanding I should like to make it clear that, while I hold Professor Zenkovsky in the highest esteem as a scholar and historian, I do not share his theological or metaphysical views. I have undertaken the arduous task of making his monumental work available to an English-speaking public because, quite simply, I believe it to be the most complete and readable as well as the fairest and most reliable history of Russian philosophy that has appeared to date in any language.

GEORGE L. KLINE

*Orangeburg, New York, September 1952*

# CONTENTS

## VOLUME I

## CONTENTS

# INTRODUCTION

## I. THE SCOPE OF THIS BOOK

THE aim of this book is to acquaint the reader with the history of Russian philosophy, including all relevant material and exhibiting its inner dialectical connectedness and historical continuity. There are many works in our literature devoted to individual Russian thinkers or to tendencies in Russian thought, but there is as yet no history of Russian philosophy, in its full scope, in the Russian language. The present book is intended to fill this gap and at the same time to provide a reliable guide to the study of Russian thought.

## 2. HISTORICAL CONDITIONS OF THE DEVELOPMENT OF PHILOSOPHY IN RUSSIA

Independent creative work in the field of philosophy, or rather, the first germs of such work, did not appear in Russia until the second half of the eighteenth century. The nineteenth century inaugurated a period of intensive, rapidly growing philosophic activity, which was to define the career of philosophy in Russia. However, it would be a serious error to conclude that, before the first half of the eighteenth century, philosophic needs were alien to the Russian mind. In fact, they appeared quite frequently; but, with rare and insignificant exceptions, they found their resolution in a religious world-view. In this respect Russian culture up to the second half of the eighteenth century was very close to that of the Middle Ages in the West, with its basic religious orientation. The birth of philosophy, as a free and independent form of intellectual creativity, from the womb of a religious world-view is a general fact in the history of philosophy (it was thus in India, Greece, and medieval Europe). The religious consciousness, if it fecundates all of the mind's energies, inevitably generates philosophic creativeness. It is not the case that philosophic thought is always and everywhere born from doubt. To a much greater extent philosophic thought is set in motion by primitive intuitions which, although

I

rooted in a religious world-view, carry their own specific motivations and inspirations. But the essential point is that philosophic
thought grows only in conditions of free inquiry—and inner
freedom is here no less important than external freedom.

In Western Europe these two sources of philosophic creativity
were supplemented by an enormous philosophic heritage from the
ancient world. The West naturally considered itself an *heir* of
ancient philosophy, connected to it by living bonds—especially
since Latin was the language of the Church. This put at the dis-
posal of the early Middle Ages a finished philosophic terminology
(although, on the other hand, this terminology was often a source
of philosophic error).

We find an entirely different situation in Russia: when philosophic thought began to awaken there, it found an intense and
active philosophic life already present in the West. Not only a rich
*past* but also a vital philosophic *present* stood before Russian minds
in such strength and abundance that it repressed and hampered
philosophic interests at the same time that it aroused them.
Enormous efforts were required to combine in oneself the necessary
scholarship with free creative activity.

As a result, the combination of these three elements of philosophic creativity was different in Russia and in the West. On the
one hand, Russian thought remained at all times connected with
*its own* religious elementality, its own religious soil; this was, and
is, the chief root of its specific quality, but also of various complica-
tions in the development of Russian philosophic thought. On the
other hand, freedom was always dear to the Russian mind: almost
always it was the state rather than the Church which introduced
oppressive censorship in Russia—and, if oppressive tendencies
arose within the Church which gained great strength because of
the pressure of the state, the spirit of freedom was never extinguished in the ecclesiastical consciousness. Both of the factors
necessary for philosophic creativity (a religious world-view and
intellectual freedom) were present in Russia when, after suffering
the Tartar yoke and passing through the 'time of unrest' at the
beginning of the seventeenth century, Russia started on a path of
independent cultural activity. But the third factor—the presence
of a rich and creative philosophic life in the West—had a negative
as well as a positive significance. On the one hand, in uniting
themselves to the philosophic culture of the West, Russians seemed
to block their own ascent to the heights of philosophic thought,
and rapidly lost themselves in the complex philosophic problems

of the time. In this respect, it is amazing how rapidly Russian scientists reached the heights of contemporary culture (Lomonosov in the middle of the eighteenth century, Lobachevski in the early nineteenth century, and many others). But, in philosophy, original creative work was very much hindered in Russia by what Russians found in the West. Whole generations were captured by the West, following its creation and quests with warmth and passion. In general, Russia answered with a living echo to whatever took place in the West. It was in the sphere of literature that the strength of its own genius first appeared. After several decades of imitation of the West, after Derzhavin and Zhukovski, came Pushkin, in whom Russian creativity found its own path—not alienating itself from the West, indeed, responding to the life of the West, but freely embracing the elemental depths of the Russian spirit. Other forms of art followed after literature (the theatre, painting, and, later, music), and soon philosophy too found its career in Russia—also without alienating itself from the West, indeed, learning constantly and diligently from the West, but at the same time living by its own inspirations, its own problems. The nineteenth century revealed philosophic talent among Russians. Russia entered on the path of independent philosophic thought.

### 3. THE CONCEPT OF PHILOSOPHY IN GENERAL

We must consider here a misunderstanding which is frequently found in modern histories of philosophy and which may have very unfavourable consequences for the study of philosophy in Russia. I have in mind the opinion which holds that *theory of knowledge* is an indispensable and basic part of philosophy. This opinion has become especially strong in the history of philosophy since Kant, and it has frequently been said that where there is no theory of knowledge there is no philosophy. Of course, no one to-day would deny the paramount importance of theory of knowledge for philosophy—in fact, all of modern philosophy in the West moves under this sign. However, such *decisive* importance should not be attached to theory of knowledge in determining what is and is not philosophy. It is sufficient to recall two geniuses who stood on the threshold of modern philosophy in the West—Giordano Bruno and Jakob Böhme—to recognize that it is not merely the presence of a theory of knowledge which guarantees the philosophic character of thought. Sometimes metaphysics is put forward instead of theory of knowledge as a necessary part of philosophy, and yet such decisive significance should not be ascribed to it either. Philosophy has not *one* but *several* roots, and this is precisely what determines its uniqueness. Philosophy is present wherever there is *an attempt to unify the spiritual life by rational means.* Various forms of experience (not only sensory—external, psychic, social—but also nonsensory—moral, aesthetic, religious) set problems for our thought and demand their solution by rational means. These solutions may be present at the level of intuitive insight; but philosophy, although it is set in motion and nourished by intuitions, arises only where rational energies are operative in clarifying intuitions. Philosophy cannot be 'prophetic'; that is a misuse of the term. 'Prophetic' writings may have great importance for philosophy; they may open up new eras. But philosophy does not prophesy, it convinces. It seeks forms of rationality and 'convincing grounds' (at the level of the logos) not only for the hearer or reader but for itself. Experience itself, in all its diversity, and the description of experience *do not make up philosophy*—experience only sets problems for the philosophizing consciousness; philosophic creativity merely *takes its departure* from experience. And, of course, this creative activity is itself a problem. Thus with logical inevitability the critical analysis of knowledge, of its means and possibilities, is generated.

It is extremely important to note that philosophic creativity always moves toward the building of *systems.* This is the 'level of the logos', where everything which is born in the depths of spirit, which arises without asking leave of anyone, must be 'made to fit' into a system, to find its place in it. In this (psychological) sense philosophic creativity is 'monistic'. But, of course, the point is not whether the system is constructed from a single basic proposition, or from many, but whether 'systematic form' is given to the *whole* content of spiritual life. If philosophic creativity does not always achieve system, it nevertheless always moves toward it.

#### 4. GENERAL FEATURES OF RUSSIAN PHILOSOPHY

These considerations are essential for us when we turn to the study of Russian philosophy and particularly to its *historical* investigation. Students of Russian philosophy have often seen an essential deficiency in its relatively slight interest in questions of theory of knowledge; this charge, as we shall see presently, is unfounded. But, even if the situation were such as certain historians characterize it, are we to conclude that an undeveloped interest in theory of knowledge is a sign of philosophic immaturity? As we have already indicated, there are definitely no grounds for this: theory of knowledge is not the central philosophic discipline. It may be deliberately placed at the centre of philosophy and taken as a point of departure (as has been the case in Western Europe during the last two centuries), but careful historical research shows that in almost all philosophers *primitive intuitions* operate at the heart of creative activity—these, and not theory of knowledge, determine the course of their thought, the logic of their theoretical constructions. I do not mean to belittle the importance of theory of knowledge, nor its enormous influence on the critical spirit which, especially since Kant, has reigned in philosophy. Nevertheless, theory of knowledge has a *negative*, not a *positive*, significance—it merely frees us from philosophic naïveté, from an uncritical transfer of generalizations or theoretical constructions from one field of philosophy to another. I mention this here not in order to polemicize with the adherents of 'epistemologism'—but in the name of historical sobriety and justice. Who would deny the fundamental importance of *moral* themes in Fichte during all periods of his philosophic activity—despite his painstaking work on the theoretical constructions of pure transcendentalism? And Fichte was in fact occupied with the construction of a theory of knowledge which would be free from the contradictions of Kant's system! Another example: are we to deny Kierkegaard the title of philosopher? Are we to consider Nietzsche merely a writer on social and political themes?

In Russian philosophy—so far as one can judge from its century and a half of development—there are certain specific characteristics which in general relegate theory of knowledge to a secondary place. With the exception of a small group of orthodox Kantians, Russian philosophers have tended in the solution of epistemological problems to *ontologism*, i.e. the recognition that cognition is not the primary and defining principle in man. In other words, knowing is recognized as only a part and function of our activity in the world; it is a certain event in the life-process, and thus its meaning, its tasks, and its possibilities are determined by our general relation to the world. This need not be interpreted in the spirit of that primitive pragmatism which was expressed with such seductive naïveté by William James. As we shall see presently, the 'ontologism' of Russian philosophic thought has a different meaning. Anticipating our future analysis, we may say briefly that Russian ontologism expresses not the priority of 'reality' to knowledge, but the inclusion of knowledge in our relationship to the world, our 'activity' in it.

### 5. THE ANTHROPOCENTRISM OF RUSSIAN PHILOSOPHY

I have touched on the question of the ontologism of Russian philosophy only in order to show the groundlessness of the opinion which holds that Russian philosophy has not yet attained maturity, because questions of theory of knowledge have not been sufficiently elaborated by Russian philosophers. However, I do not mean to assert that 'ontologism' is a characteristic feature of Russian thought (although many writers have held this). If I were to offer a general characterization of Russian philosophy—which, of course, cannot pretend to precision or completeness—I should emphasize the *anthropocentrism* of Russian philosophic thought. Russian philosophy is not *theocentric* (although many of its representatives have been deeply and essentially religious); it is not *cosmocentric* (although problems of nature-philosophy very early attracted the attention of Russian philosophers)—it is above all occupied with the *theme of man*, his fate and career, the meaning and purpose of history. This is especially evident in the predominance of a *moral* orientation, even in abstract problems. This is one of the most active and creative sources of Russian philosophy; the 'panmoralism' which Leo Tolstoy expressed with such extraordinary force in his philosophic writings may be found, subject to certain limitations, in almost all Russian thinkers—even in those who have not written on specifically moral problems (for example, Kireyevski). This moral orientation also includes an intense interest in social problems, but it is revealed most clearly in the extraordinary and decisive attention which is given to problems of *historiosophy*.[1] Russian thought is *historiosophical through and through*; it is concerned constantly with questions of the 'meaning' of history, the end of history, etc. The eschatological conceptions of the sixteenth century were echoed in the utopias of the nineteenth century and in the historiosophical reflections of the most

1. This word (which translates the Russian *istoriosofiya*, modelled on the German *Historiosophie*) is somewhat awkward in English, although it has been current in German philosophic literature since Hegel. It means 'philosophy of history', and connotes a Hegelian view of the historical process as organic and rational. 'Historiosophy' and 'historiosophical', both of which occur frequently in this work, are compact and convenient terms, which it seems undesirable to paraphrase. *Trans.*

diverse thinkers. This extraordinary, one might say excessive, attention to the philosophy of history is not, of course, accidental and is clearly rooted in those spiritual orientations which derive from the Russian past, from the national peculiarities of the 'Russian soul'. This circumstance was not especially favourable to the development of 'pure' philosophy in Russia; an interest in problems of the philosophy of history involves a thinker in extremely complex, intricate, and difficult material. On the other hand, the so-called 'subjective method' (a term which was adopted by a school of Russian historiosophy headed by N. K. Mikhailovski—see Ch. XII) operates most easily in historiosophy. A valuational element is introduced into the analysis of historical reality. Unless one is extremely careful, a kind of internal censorship intrudes upon philosophic creativity, rejecting whatever is considered 'dangerous' in the practical sphere or might 'justify' a given harmful trend in social life. This inner censorship, of course, obstructs free philosophic inquiry and brings about a most dangerous accommodation of theory to the 'needs of the day'. Throughout the whole period of philosophic activity in Russia—from its beginnings in the late eighteenth century to our own day—this danger has often made itself felt. But it would be superficial to dismiss this 'accommodation' to contemporary issues—an accommodation unworthy of philosophy—without noting its deeper aspect. The anthropocentrism of thought has a profound motivation—the impossibility of 'separating' the theoretical and practical spheres. This was very well expressed by N. K. Mikhailovski when he called attention to the uniqueness of the Russian word '*pravda*'. 'Every time the word "*pravda*" comes into my mind,' he wrote, 'I cannot help admiring its astonishing inner beauty . . . ; only in Russian, it seems, are "truth" and "justice" designated by the same word, fusing as it were into one great whole. "*Pravda*"—in this vast meaning of the word—has always been the goal of my searchings. . . . ' The inseparability of theory and practice, of abstract thought and life—in other words, the ideal of 'wholeness'— is one of the chief inspirations of Russian philosophic thought. Russian philosophers, with rare exceptions, have sought wholeness, a synthetic unity of all aspects of reality and all impulses of the human spirit. And in historical being—more than in the study of nature or in the pure concepts of abstract thought—'wholeness' is an indispensable byword. The anthropocentrism of Russian philosophy constantly impels it toward the discovery of wholeness, both as actually given and as ideally envisioned.

## 6. THE INDEPENDENCE OF RUSSIAN PHILOSOPHY

Russian philosophy has more than once been charged with a lack of 'originality'.[1] 'Everything that Russia contributed in philosophy,' writes one historian of Russian philosophy, 'was born either from direct imitation or unconscious subjugation to foreign influences, or from an eclectic striving to fuse several foreign ideas into a single whole.'[2] If this charge were true, it would of course be impossible to speak seriously of 'Russian philosophy', and it would be pointless to investigate its history. In the cultural history of all peoples there are always works marked by imitation or foreign influences; however, they are mentioned in scholarly studies only so that history's dark pages may not be forgotten. The charge that Russian philosophy lacks originality, unless it is made simply for rhetorical purposes, rests on deliberate malevolence toward Russian thought, a deliberate wish to degrade it. I am not going to refute this charge—this whole book should prove the groundlessness of such a judgment. Nevertheless, I consider it necessary in this introductory chapter to clear up certain misunderstandings which, although not in such an acute form as the charges above quoted, do appear among students of Russian thought, especially those who first studied the subject.

I do not propose to treat of what has been written in Russia in mere 'imitation of the West'; student exercises are not worth discussing. Nor do I propose to consider the alleged 'eclecticism' of Russian thinkers. This charge indicates a complete misunderstanding of the *synthetic* intentions of Russian thinkers: unsuccessful or incomplete attempts at synthesis may appear as eclecticism to a superficial observer. I shall put all this aside, and treat only the question of the 'influences' of Western philosophers on Russian thought.

The concept 'influence' may be applied only where there is at least some measure of *independence* and *originality*; unless this is present one cannot speak of influence: it is impossible to influence a vacuum. Therefore, historians study the influences on those thinkers who are distinguished by their independence: thus, a study of Aristotle makes it possible to establish that his own theories

1. This point of view is expressed very sharply by B. V. Jakovenko, who has written a large book on the history of Russian philosophy [published only in Czech; Prague, 1938].

2. Jakovenko, *Ocherki russkoi filosofi* [Outlines of Russian Philosophy], Berlin, 1922, p. 5.

grew out of his discussions with Plato. Historians attempt to find a link with medieval philosophy in Descartes's basic propositions, which were the beginning of the idealistic tendencies of the modern period. In Boutroux's original theories they see the influence of Comte, etc.

Even where a 'school' grows up around a great thinker, it is not possible to resolve the work of this school completely into the 'influence' of the founder of the school. The Academy after Plato, which went through several periods of development, is a good example of this. 'Academic scepticism', although it deviated from Plato's basic teaching, remained essentially true to it. However, one must not confuse the concepts 'Platonism' and 'school of Plato'; the philosophy of Plotinus may be included in the school of Plato merely by using the new term 'Neo-Platonism', but patristic Platonism, enriched and creatively transformed by Christian dogmatics, cannot be fitted into the concept of the 'school of Plato'. Similarly, the extraordinary closeness of Thomas Aquinas to Aristotle's philosophy does not give us the right to include Thomism in the 'school of Aristotle'. To take an example from modern philosophy, the whole Marburg school (Cohen, Natorp, *et al.*), and Rickert's trend, may be included in the 'school of Kant' (as tendencies in 'Neo-Kantianism'). But Schelling and especially Hegel are not in any case to be included in the 'school of Kant', despite the rooting of their transcendental idealism in Kant's philosophy.

All of this complicates the question of 'influence'. There are various degrees, various levels of influence; but none of them excludes independence or originality; all of them *infallibly presuppose it*. Epicurus cannot be historically separated from Democritus, Spinoza from Descartes, Fichte from Kant; but who can doubt their independence and originality? Originality, in the strict sense —as complete novelty of ideas—is so rare in the history of philosophy that, if only 'original' theories were studied, the history of philosophy could be written in eight or ten paragraphs. But in real historical life 'interdependence', the combining of influences, and the effect of the entire philosophic culture of a given period on individual thinkers, are so strong that the significance and historical effectiveness of given thinkers are not annulled or reduced by the fact that they are subject to various influences. The whole question is: whether to regard a given thinker as simply a 'writer' on philosophic themes, who reproduces the results of others, or a real thinker, i.e. one who thinks for himself and does not merely select from the works of other authors. Of course, there are always doubtful cases: to one historian a given philosopher may appear 'sufficiently' independent to be called a philosopher; for another the same writer may not deserve the title of philosopher. In Russian philosophy there is a striking example of such a divergence of opinion—I have in mind Belinski (see Ch. VIII). No one disputes his literary talent; but his place in the history of Russian *philosophy*, in the opinion of many historians, is only that of a 'popularizer' of the philosophic tendencies of his time in Russia. Others consider him a genuine philosopher.

All of these considerations have special application to the history of Russian philosophy. We have already mentioned that Russian thinkers were for many decades 'students', in the true sense, of Western philosophers, and that it was not without effort and even torment that they cleared their own path for philosophic work. Therefore the history of Russian philosophy is much concerned with the 'influences' of Western philosophy. Despite this, Russian thinkers began early to clear their own path (not always bringing their projects to completion), and thus dialectically prepared for the appearance in a later period of original philosophic systems. This means, of course, that there is *dialectical and historical unity* in Russian philosophic thought; and, by the same token, it provides ample evidence of its independence and hence originality.

Certain historians prefer to speak not of 'Russian philosophy' but of 'philosophy in Russia', meaning by this to emphasize that there is nothing 'specifically Russian' in Russian philosophic theories, that Russian philosophy has not yet become national, i.e. has not succeeded in revealing or expressing the fundamental searchings of the Russian soul. This, of course, is untrue, as we shall amply convince ourselves in our detailed study of various thinkers.

### 7. IMPOSSIBILITY OF ELIMINATING VALUE JUDGMENTS IN HISTORICAL RESEARCH

From these considerations it is quite clear that the historian cannot dispense with *valuations* in his research. It is not necessary for him to be a 'judge', to make gratuitous and belated 'remarks' concerning individual thinkers. But he cannot avoid value judgments. The historian's 'objectivity' does not consist in eliminating valuations from his exposition. Rickert and his followers are right in their theory of historical knowledge when they emphasize the significance of the element of value in historical research. However, to accept and justify the element of valuation in the historian's work is not to endorse arbitrariness of valuation: every valuation aims essentially at acceptance by others; it thus testifies to its supra-individual nature. The roots of our valuations, of course, are deeply subjective, but their intention is definitely supra-individual —and each of us both in life and in historical judgments should free himself from prejudices, from casual and unexamined valuations, from those hidden impulses of the spirit, for example, which are connected with 'partisanship'—in general, from the psychology of *sectarianism*. The breadth and justice of our valuation lends strength to our judgments, and sooner or later others will accept them.

In writing this book, the author has often had to rely on his value judgments, in so far as they were necessary for the research itself. The author hopes that the reader, if he will read this book without prejudice, will acknowledge the author's impartiality and his real desire to present the development of Russian philosophy in its original guise, although this may not always be clearly and convincingly expressed.

## 8. DIVISION INTO PERIODS OF THE HISTORY OF RUSSIAN PHILOSOPHY

Nothing gives such definite evidence of the independence and originality of Russian philosophy as its *development*. Development can only be organic, i.e. a matter of *dialectical connectedness*, not mere historical succession. Strictly speaking, the development of Russian philosophy did not begin until the nineteenth century (including the last two decades of the eighteenth), but these first manifestations of independent philosophic activity were preceded by a rather long period which may be called the 'prologue' to Russian philosophy. I have in mind the entire eighteenth century, when Russia began with extraordinary impetuosity and ardent enthusiasm to absorb into itself the fruits of European civilization. This enthusiasm for the West (which became at times a real 'bondage' to the West) applied to both the external and internal forms of European life. There was particular enthusiasm for the rich spiritual world of the West, with its divergent tendencies and searchings. The second half of the eighteenth century in Russia presents us with the picture of a widespread and feverish assimilation of Western culture, in part superficial, but in part more profound. There was simple imitation, to be sure, but there was also a passionate fervour, a kind of creative enthusiasm, and there was also an awakening of Russian creative energies. A whole galaxy of gifted men strove to stand 'at the level of the century', in Pushkin's phrase. The eighteenth century was the real springtime of the Russian enlightenment, impelling Russians above all to 'learn' from the West. It is interesting to note that, despite the brilliant development of Russian creative activity in the nineteenth century, this feature of sincere 'discipleship' has remained with Russians up to our own time, testifying not only to praiseworthy modesty but perhaps also to what Russian writers during the first half of the nineteenth century called 'universally-human aspirations'. The development of the Russian genius did not lead to isolation, to a closing in upon itself. For example, the intensive programme of translation which developed in Russia toward the middle of the eighteenth century (although its beginnings must be placed several centuries earlier—see below, Ch. I) not only did not slacken in the nineteenth and twentieth centuries, at a time when many original Russian works were appearing in all realms of culture, but became even more intensive—and, what is most important, more systematic. But this is no reason for regarding the eighteenth century in Russia as a period devoid of manifestations of independent creative activity. On the contrary, we assert that everything which reached maturity in the nineteenth century had *begun to manifest itself in the eighteenth century*. Of course, to show this fully we should have to go far beyond the limits of pure philosophy—but we cannot permit ourselves to digress from our task.

We should like to make one more remark. In all spheres of culture, including that of philosophic thought, the eighteenth century in Russia was not wholly isolated from the preceding periods. Of course, the reforms of Peter the Great constituted a clear boundary between the seventeenth and eighteenth centuries, but historical research has long since made it clear that there was intensive development in Russia even before the eighteenth century. In fact, beginning with the middle of the fifteenth century, various creative movements began to develop in Russia; there was the beginning of a *rapprochement* with the West, relations with which had been interrupted by two centuries of the Tartar yoke. In the field of philosophic thought there was also a certain fermentation—at first within the framework of the religious world-view, but gradually becoming independent of it.

For the purposes of our research, it is necessary to familiarize ourselves briefly with events prior to the eighteenth century.

Therefore, the 'prologue' to Russian philosophy is divided into two parts: (A) the entire period from the middle of the fifteenth century to the time of Peter the Great, and (B) the eighteenth century. When the period of independent philosophic thought began, philosophic activity was at first limited to clarifying its own problems, its own independent path. Even the most powerful philosophic mind of the first half of the nineteenth century, I. V. Kireyevski, stood only on the threshold of the creation of a philosophic system —as a result, it is true, of a number of unfavourable external circumstances. He wrote a series of sketches, but did not carry his projected works to conclusion. This situation lasted for more than half a century, but beginning with the 1870's (when the first works of Vladimir Solovyov appeared) Russian philosophy started on the construction of systems. This is the first period in the development of Russian philosophy: we consider that it lasted until the end of the nineteenth century. In the twentieth century, Russian philosophy has not only developed beside Western European philosophy but has gradually begun—especially since the Russian revolution—to achieve world-wide influence.

## 9. SURVEY OF PRINCIPAL WORKS IN THE HISTORY OF RUSSIAN PHILOSOPHY

It remains to make a brief survey of basic works in the history of Russian philosophy.[1] [Only works available in English, French, or German are included. *Trans.*]

1. N. Berdyaev, *The Russian Idea* (tr. from the Russian by R. M. French, New York, 1948), offers a survey of special problems in Russian thought. This book contains many brilliant characterizations, but it *presupposes* a thorough knowledge of Russian thinkers.

2. D. I. Chizhevski, *Hegel in Russland* (Veröffentlichungen der slavistischen Arbeitsgemeinschaft an der deutschen Universität in Prag, Series I, No. 9), Reichenberg [Czechoslovakia], 1934. Although this work is devoted to a special theme, it touches upon almost everything of importance in the history of Russian thought. [A revised and enlarged Russian version of Chizhevski's book was published in Paris, in 1939 (*Gegel v Rossi*); since it contains some material not included in the German edition, references will

---

1. In this chapter we offer a *general* bibliography of Russian philosophy. Special bibliographies (on individual thinkers) are given separately in each chapter.

occasionally be made to it rather than to the German edition. *Trans.*]

3. J. Kolubowskij, 'Die russische Philosophie', in F. Ueberweg, *Grundriss der Geschichte der Philosophie*, 12th ed., Berlin, 1928, Pt. V, pp. 335–48. This essay, following the style of Ueberweg's text, is highly compressed, and is provided with a full bibliography.

The works of the following two French writers should be taken together:

4. Ferdinand Lannes, 'Coup d'oeil sur l'histoire de la philosophie en Russie', and 'Le Mouvement philosophique en Russie', *La Revue Philosophique*, XXXII (1891), pp. 17–51, and XXXIV (1892), pp. 561–89. G. Seliber, 'La Philosophie russe contemporaine', *ibid.*, LXXIV (1912), pp. 27–64, 243–75. Lannes's two articles treat the late eighteenth century briefly and give a substantial outline of Russian philosophy up to the 1840's (ending with Bakunin). Lannes's exposition is very precise and provides a good orientation. Seliber's two articles are much briefer; he begins with Vladimir Solovyov and ends with Berdyaev. Seliber's characterizations are quite apt, but brief. Both of these writers, taken together, offer a great deal of material on Russian philosophy, despite the omission of many authors.

5. J. A. Lappo-Danilevski offers much of value on the history of Russian philosophy in his study 'The Development of Science and Learning in Russia', published in the anthology *Russian Realities and Problems*, Cambridge, 1917. Lappo-Danilevski's article contains many masterly, if brief, characterizations, and covers the whole period of the development of Russian philosophy.

6. Thomas G. Masaryk's two-volume work *The Spirit of Russia; Studies in History, Literature, and Philosophy* (translated from the German by E. and C. Paul, New York, 1919), although devoted to the philosophy of history in Russia, provides a great deal of factual material on Russian philosophy in general, up to the beginning of the twentieth century. Masaryk has made a thorough study of Russian history; and he tries to be objective in his exposition, but unfortunately does not always succeed. Nevertheless Masaryk's book is very useful.

The publications mentioned thus far deal, more or less completely, with the history of Russian philosophy as a whole. We pass now to works which treat individual periods or trends:

7. Alexandre Koyré, *La Philosophie et le problème national en Russie au début du XIXᵉ siècle*, Paris, 1929. Koyré's work is a very thorough and thoughtful study of Russian philosophy from the beginning

of the nineteenth century to the late 1840's. Its chief value lies in the detailed exposition and careful analysis of the works treated.

8. Osip Lourié, *La Philosophie russe contemporaine*, Paris, 1892. This is a work of limited value, devoted to a few Russian philosophers (Vladimir Solovyov, Leo Tolstoy, *et al.*) of the late nineteenth century.

9. P. N. Milyukov, *Outlines of Russian Culture*, ed. by Michael Karpovich, translated from the Russian by V. Ughet and E. Davis, Philadelphia, 1948. In this, as in his other works on Russian history, Milyukov constantly touches upon themes connected with philosophy. (See especially Parts II and III.)

1. Our survey makes no claim to completeness. It is possible that new studies in the history of Russian philosophy have appeared in Soviet Russia. New material that was accessible to us has been noted.

# PART ONE
## On the Threshold of Philosophy

# CHAPTER I

## Up to the Time of Peter the Great

### I. THE INFLUENCE OF BYZANTIUM

W E have already mentioned that prior to the eighteenth century we do not find in Russia any independent works, or even sketches, of a philosophic character. In view of this, the historian of Russian philosophy should begin his study with the eighteenth century. However, it would be a serious mistake to assume that before this time Russians got along without philosophy, or that they experienced no philosophic needs. In fact, we find various traces—fragmentary, to be sure—of this awakening of philosophic interests; but they were all contained within the framework of a *religious world-view*, and therefore did not bring intellectual activity to the point of independent philosophic thought. The 'secularization' of philosophy and its separation from the religious consciousness took place in Russia much later than in Western Europe and—what is more important—in a quite different way. This secularization was already taking place, in a sense, within the ecclesiastical consciousness itself, as well as outside of it—but *not in opposition to it*, not as a struggle against the Church (which was the case in the West). The 'anthologies', which had such wide circulation in ancient Russia, contained excerpts from the philosophic writings of the Church Fathers as well as the ancient philosophers. Though this material was fragmentary, it was not superficial, as is evidenced by the large proportion of the extant copies of such anthologies which emphasize philosophic problems.[1] Christianity came to Russia not only as a religion but

1. See, for example, the Diopter anthology, the earliest copy of which dates from 1305. In the Rumyantsev Museum in Moscow there are nine copies of this anthology made at different periods. This anthology (which was translated from Greek into Church Slavonic, probably in Bulgaria) contains, in addition to its theological sections, elements of cosmology and very detailed elements of anthropology. The general conception is close to Aristotle; the doctrine of the

also as a world-view, in its full scope, embracing the most varied
themes. Much non-Christian or apocryphal material also penetrated to us from Byzantium and the Slavic lands. The Apocrypha
and legends—a variety of Christian mythology—brought with them
various 'occult sciences'. Astrology became especially widespread
at this time (as it was in Western Europe during the same period).[1]
But, although the Christian world-view penetrated very deeply
into the Russian soul, historians have frequently been puzzled by
the fact that, despite an indubitable religious animation in ancient
Russia, this religious energy—which produced countless monasteries
and enormous numbers of saints and righteous men—did not
awaken the *religious Logos* to creative activity, did not develop theological thought. 'In the history of Russian thought', one scholar
remarks, 'there is much that is enigmatic and incomprehensible.
And above all—what is the meaning of this centuries-long, unduly
protracted Russian silence? How are we to explain this tardy and
belated awakening of Russian thought?' [2] The harsh judgment of
P. Ya. Chaadayev, one of the leading philosophers of the nineteenth century, is widely known: 'Standing as it were outside of
time', he wrote, 'we [Russians] have not been touched by the
universal education of the human race.' [3] Does not the feeble
development of Christian enlightenment (its complete absence,
according to Chaadayev) mean that Russia was outside of history?
'We have not brought one idea into the mass of human ideas,' he
wrote; 'we have not furthered in any way the progress of human
reason.' 'Looking at us, one might say that the general law of mankind had been abrogated with respect to us. In any case, we
constitute a gap in the moral order of the world. . . .' [4]

significance of the human *body* for the soul is especially interesting ('without the
body the soul is powerless', etc.). Studies of the 'Judaizing heresy' have revealed
much evidence of familiarity with Aristotle. Kurbski was also very much
interested in Aristotle. Shakhmatov has written a paper on 'Plato in Old
Russia', and Raikov has studied the history of the heliocentric system in Russia.

1. See especially Ye. V. Anichkov, *Old Russian Pagan Cults*. Next to the Holy
Scriptures, the favourite reading in ancient Russia was the Apocrypha, with
which the so-called 'spiritual poems' are associated. In both the Apocrypha and
the spiritual poems religio-philosophic problems are raised, in the solution of
which Christian and non-Christian motifs are fancifully interwoven. This whole
question has been insufficiently investigated from a philosophic point of view.

2. G. Florovsky, *Puti russkovo bogosloviya* [Paths of Russian Theology], Paris,
1937, p. 1.

3. See his first 'Philosophical Letter' (*Sochineniya* [Works], Moscow, 1913,
I, 77).

4. *Ibid.*, p. 84. Concerning Chaadayev, see Ch. V below.

Chaadayev's extreme scepticism remained an isolated phenomenon in Russian literature, but it is interesting because it exhibits clearly an erroneous presupposition which leads to a false judgment of the spiritual life of nineteenth-century Russia. Those who ponder the fact of the 'late awakening of Russian thought' are continually led astray by the sharp contrast between Russia in the thirteenth to seventeenth centuries and Western Europe during the same period; as a result they evaluate the historical facts quite incorrectly. To overcome this temptation and to evaluate soberly the history of Russian spiritual development, it is necessary to keep clearly in mind the difference between the paths of Russia and Western Europe during these centuries, as well as to renounce the idea that the history of Western Europe is the only form of 'progress', both as to type and tempo of development.

In the West, Christianity spread from Rome, which was not separated from the peoples of Europe by barriers of any kind, but on the contrary was very closely connected to them—whereas Christianity came to Russia from a *distant and alien country*.[1] Rome was a *solicitous mother* to the peoples of the West; furthermore, the ecclesiastical unity of the West found expression and substantial supplementation in the fact that the Latin language was common to all of the West, both ecclesiastically and culturally, and at the same time formed a *direct connection to antiquity*. Ancient culture, in so far as it was assimilated, was felt in the West to 'belong'.

Everything was different in Russia. Politically Russia lived entirely apart from Byzantium, but ecclesiastically it was dependent on Byzantium. The Russian Church began very early to strive for canonic emancipation from the Greek Church; and after the fall of Constantinople [1453], which was a great shock to Russia, this repulsion from Byzantium became even stronger. When Ivan IV told the Papal Legate: 'Our faith is Christian but not Greek'—he was giving precise expression to the Russian ecclesiastical consciousness of the time. Greek did not become the liturgical language in Russia,[2] and this *linguistic isolation* of the

1. I cannot go into the dispute concerning the source from which Christianity came to ancient Russia, a dispute which is being carried on with such warmth and partiality by Jugie and others. All the Russian historians reject Jugie's theoretical constructions.

2. Certain historians see in this the chief cause for the 'belated awakening of Russian thought', for example, Shpet (*Ocherki razvitiya russkoi filosofi* [Outlines of the Development of Russian Philosophy], p. 12) speaks of the 'fatal' significance of this fact.

Russian world had enormous significance for the development of Russian culture, dooming it in advance to 'backwardness'. However, this circumstance was modified to a certain extent by the fact that the southern and western Slavs, who were linguistically and ethnically related, experienced during this period a flowering of spiritual culture—hence Russia, as a result of its connection with them, was never wholly isolated from the West. However, in addition to linguistic isolation the destiny of Russia was also influenced by a religious watchfulness toward the West, which was especially intensified after the Council of Florence [1439] and the 'union' concluded there, which was rejected by the Russian people. This watchfulness, which Byzantium continually implanted in Russia, for a long time hindered Russians in their spiritual searchings and shackled freedom of thought. Is this not the reason why so many Russians fell into blind captivity to the West, when intensified communication with the West began?

The influence of Byzantium on Russia was, of course, very significant and profound; it has not as yet, by the way, been thoroughly investigated or impartially evaluated. We must not forget that Byzantium, at the time when Russia was accepting Christianity, was at the acme of its cultural creativity—but soon after this it unquestionably began to decline. Its gaze, its hopes, were then wholly turned toward the West, where Byzantium hoped to find support in its struggle against the Turks—and how characteristic it is that after the fall of Constantinople all of the Greek cultural leaders fled to the West, to which they contributed their brilliant culture—and no one emigrated to Russia, which was akin in faith, and always generous and hospitable! The marriage of Ivan III to Sophia Palaeologus united Russia, not with the Greek, but with the Western world. And yet Russians, who found in the Church a source of spiritual activity, continued to gravitate toward the Greek tradition.

## 2. CREATIVE MOVEMENTS IN RUSSIAN CULTURE

However essential what we have said may be for understanding why and to what extent Russian historical development differs from that of the West, this alone does not explain the enigma of the 'belated awakening of Russian thought'. Florovsky has justly remarked in this connection that, 'It is not possible to explain the difficulty of ancient Russian development by lack of culture: this crisis was a crisis of culture, not one of lack of culture; . . . it was a consequence and expression of inner difficulties or aporias.'[1] Florovsky himself adds rather enigmatically that this was 'a crisis of Byzantine culture in the Russian spirit'—which evidently is to be understood as meaning that Byzantine culture did not liberate or awaken Russian creative energies but on the contrary hampered them. This is perhaps true in part, but only in part—for nowhere do we find signs of a significant opposition to Byzantinism on the part of the Russian spirit. I think that there was, in addition to linguistic isolation, the lack of direct ties with antiquity, and the centuries-old suspicion of a West which constantly attempted to subordinate Russia ecclesiastically to Rome—an additional reason for the slow awakening of the 'Logos' in the Russian ecclesiastical consciousness in that consciousness itself, in the type and style of 'Russian faith'. It is very characteristic in this connection that the Schism [*Raskol*]—which separated from the Church a large group of conservative-minded, although very brilliant and spiritually strong, people—liberated *creative energies* in the Russian Church. In the eighteenth century we note a genuine renaissance of the ecclesiastical spirit (although it was precisely in the eighteenth century that the state began to apply pressure to the Church). The Schism channelled off the conservative forces of the Church—but, even in the Schism, creative searchings began to manifest themselves, giving evidence of the great accumulation of spiritual energies in the Russian people. This indicates to us that the period of 'silence' (although this characterization as a whole is incorrect, as we shall see below) was a period of *accumulation of spiritual energies* and not a spiritual slumbering. The historical development of Russian *icon-painting* during this period is a strange and enigmatic contrast, and for that very reason an eloquent one, to the slow development of independent thought in Russia. The great creations of Rublev (late fourteenth and early fifteenth centuries) are, of course, intimately connected with Byzantine icon-painting; but they testify to the awakening and development of native Russian creative energies. We find in these creations such artistic depth, such flashes of insight into what lies beyond the boundaries of religious consciousness (Rublev's most remarkable work is the icon of the Holy Trinity), that it is impossible not to agree with Prince Eugene Trubetskoi, who characterizes these icons as a 'meditation in colours'.[2] Such work is a manifestation of the Logos; the icons are

1. Florovsky, *op. cit.*, p. 2.
2. See his *Umozreniye v kraskakh* [Meditation in Colours], Moscow, 1916. Unfortunately the enormous theme touched upon by Pr. Trubetskoi in his

permeated with theological intuitions.[1] One historian has justly pointed out that the acceptance of Christianity evoked in Russians an enormous spiritual uplift, a genuine animation.[2] Of course, the penetration of Christianity into Russia took place slowly outside of the cities, but this did not diminish the fact of creative animation, which was not at all sterile and did not fail to touch the Logos. In any case, the Christian consciousness of old Russia exhibits that pre-eminence of the moral and social principle of which we shall see an extreme expression in nineteenth-century Russian philosophy. The Christian world-view fecundated creative movements in this specific direction, and at the same time Russians (from the very beginning) perceived the *beauty* of Christianity with particular force. What is now considered a legend—the chronicle story of how the ambassadors of Saint Vladimir were captivated by the beauty of the Byzantine liturgy—is especially characteristic of the aesthetic sensitivity which accompanied the appearance of Christianity in old Russia. The chronicle story may be a legend, but the very fact that it arose is valuable evidence of what Christianity brought to the Russian soul. The assimilation of Byzantine icon-painting awakened such creative energies that Rublev's works of genius became possible. The development of icon-painting in old Russia, the literature of the subject, the disputes, the passionate defence of religious 'truth' in the icons (versus external 'realism'), and finally the anxious guarding of this marvellous art in the Russian Schism —the penetration of religio-aesthetic contemplation into the very marrow of the Russian people—this alone is sufficient evidence that the religious consciousness of old Russia did not live *outside the Logos.* And the fact that Christianity appeared in old Russia at a time when Byzantium had already seen the end of the period of dogmatic movements explains why the Russian religious consciousness accepted Christian doctrine as something finished and not subject to analysis.

study is merely noted, but not developed by him. Cf. the histories of Russian art, especially P. P. Muratov, *Les Icones russes*, Paris, 1929, pp. 153–94. 'Nothing', Muratov remarks, 'disturbs the musical unity of the icon, nothing weakens o obscures its mystical force.'

1. In Vladimir Solovyov and his followers, 'Sophiology' is very closely connected with the interpretation of icons consecrated to Sophia, the Divine Wisdom (see Pts. III and IV).

2. P. N. Milyukov, *Outlines of Russian Culture*, Philadelphia, 1942, pt. I, p. 3.

### 3. MYSTICAL REALISM

The question which we have just brought up is extremely important for a correct understanding of philosophic culture in Russia, and we must explore this theme further in order to make clear why the paths of Russian thought were, and are, different from those in the West. Russian philosophic creativity—we shall be persuaded of this more than once in the sequel—struck such deep roots in the religious soil of old Russia that even those tendencies which broke decisively with religion in general, remained attached (if only negatively) to this religious soil.

One frequently encounters the opinion that there was at the foundation of Russian Christianity from the very beginning an exaggerated asceticism which concealed an abhorrence of the world. Although asceticism did penetrate deeply into the Russian psychology (one critic wrote an entire article on 'The Ascetic Infirmities of the Russian Intelligentsia'[1]), this opinion is erroneous. Asceticism among Russians was always a *derivative* phenomenon. I consider as extremely characteristic, even decisive (for an historical appraisal of 'Russian faith'), the fact that the *Bogomilian* sect, with its sharp dualism and intense preoccupation with the problem of evil, left the Russian religious consciousness almost entirely unaffected —despite its geographical proximity to Russia, despite constant and abundant connections with Bulgaria, and the very important influence of the Southern Slavs on the Russian ecclesiastical consciousness. Russian asceticism did not aspire to *rejection* of the world or disdain for the flesh, but to something quite different—to that clear vision of heavenly truth and beauty which by its radiance makes the injustice which reigns in the world irresistibly clear, and thus summons us to emancipation from the world's bondage. At the basis of asceticism lies a positive, not a negative, element: It is a means and a path to the transformation and sanctification of the world. The vision of heavenly truth and beauty inspires to asceticism. This explains why the image of 'light' is such a favourite in the Russian ecclesiastical consciousness; the people love to call their faith 'shining Orthodoxy'. Here is the root of the *cosmic* motif which connects Russian religiosity with that of the Church Fathers: the world is seen as wholly illuminated and permeated by divine light. It is not accidental that the Easter holiday, the triumph of light over darkness, has received such an important place in the liturgy of the Russian Church. What Gogol once

1. A. M. Skabichevski, *Sochineniya* [Works], St. Petersburg, 1903, Vol. II.

emphasized is true—that nowhere, even in the Orthodox East, is this holiday celebrated as it is in Russia. A perception of the world in the light of the Easter experience lies at the very centre of the Russian religious consciousness; apart from this it cannot be understood. The unmasking of life's injustices, which is the principal concern of the ecclesiastical literature of the twelfth to fourteenth centuries, never leads to a renunciation of life, but is always conjoined to a faith in the transfiguration of life through divine power. How interesting in this connection are the religious verses in which a humble awareness of human sinfulness, and at the same time the bright hope of divine grace, is so clearly expressed! In the religious poem 'The Lamentation of the Earth', the Lord *consoles the earth* (which 'had burst out crying' before the Lord, depressed by the sins of men):

> The Lord himself spake unto the moist earth:
> 'Be thou patient, Mother, moist earth,
> Be thou patient yet a little time, moist earth!
> Come not the sinful slaves to God himself
> In pure repentance?
> If they come, I shall add the heavenly kingdom to
>      the light of their freedom;
> If they come not to me, to God, I shall take away
>      the light of their freedom.'

The doctrine of the Last Judgment, of the eventual unveiling of all injustice and sin before the face of God, was the firm basis of Russian religious and philosophic thinking; it precluded confusion of earthly and heavenly justice, of the human and the divine. But in preventing their *confusion*, the idea of the last judgment did not lead to their *separation*. Therefore, the Russian ecclesiastical consciousness did not depart from the fundamental theocratic conception of Christianity, but it interpreted this conception quite differently from the West. We shall consider this in greater detail below; for the present we shall simply emphasize that nowhere in the Russian religious consciousness do we encounter the perversion of Christian doctrine which results from a one-sided asceticism. Even the extreme forms of asceticism, which led in the Schism to frequent burnings, did not result from a renunciation of the world but from an obsessive idea that the Antichrist had come.

Essential to the Russian form of Christianity is a sober sense of the 'inseparability', but also the 'non-fusibility', of the divine and human worlds, which defined the ecclesiastical attitude toward state power—an attitude that is not yet fully understood. We shall speak of the problem of power in the ecclesiastical consciousness when we come to characterize the *historiosophical* problem (§§ 6–8). I should like for the moment to return to Russian icon-painting and its significance for an appraisal of the spiritual life of Russia in the fourteenth to seventeenth centuries. It has been justly noted by one historian that 'the Russian icon provides incontrovertible evidence of the complexity and profundity, the genuine and exquisite beauty of old-Russian *spiritual experience*'.[1] In fact, not only was iconolatry very dear to Russians; it preserved in itself and imprinted upon human consciousness the mystery of Godmanhood. 'There is not a single Russian theologico-polemical treatise', Tsvetayev remarks, 'in which iconolatry, which was so dear to the Russian, was not defended.'[2] The opinion, once expressed, that 'there is temptation in the beauty of holy images', drew a heated rejoinder from Joseph 'Isographus'. We should note in this connection the unhappy fate of a certain Viskovatov who, as a political figure (he served as a 'clerk' under Ivan IV ['The Terrible']), intervened with unusual warmth in the dispute concerning the new trend in icon-painting. Iconolatry, which was so dear to the heart and mind of churchmen, was a form of *God-thinking*, in which the aesthetic element was submerged in a 'rapture of the mind'. One must read, for example, the life of the Reverend Sergius, with its complete and childlike submissiveness to God, to touch those chords of the soul which are so characteristically Russian. Here one grasps intuitively what may be expressed discursively as follows: All material things serve as means for expressing a higher truth, a higher beauty. In philosophic terms, this is a *mystical realism*, which recognizes empirical reality, but sees *behind* it another reality; both spheres of being are real, but they are of hierarchically different value; empirical being is sustained only through 'participation' in a mystical reality. The theocratic idea of Christianity amounts to asserting the need to illuminate all that is visible, all that is empirical, by relating it to a mystical sphere; the whole of history, the whole life of the individual, must be sanctified through the transforming activity of divine power in the empirical sphere.

1. Florovsky, *op. cit.*, p. 1.
2. D. V. Tsvetayev, *Protestanty i protestantizm v Rossi do epokhi preobrazovani* [Protestants and Protestantism in Russia up to the Period of the Reforms], Moscow, 1890, p. 520.

### 4. CHARACTERISTIC FEATURES OF RUSSIAN RELIGIOSITY

Let us return for a moment to the general theme of Russian religiosity; this will be very important for us in our further study. First of all, we should make special note of the Russian 'maximalism', which runs like a red line through the whole history of Russian spiritual life. Without doubt this maximalism is not in itself of religious origin—it is connected with the 'native' peculiarities of the Russian soul, formed during the whole course of Russian history. The immensity of the Russian spaces, the absence of high mountains in Russia—all of the 'geopolitical' influences have determined the peculiarities of the Russian soul. But while they are 'native' and have determined the style and forms of spiritual life, these peculiarities of the Russian soul have found special support in certain basic features of Christianity, with which they grew deeply together. I have in mind the motif of 'wholeness' which gives Christianity a radical colouring: It teaches us to fear all 'mediocrity' and moderation, all luke-warmness. Christianity by its very nature is directed to *every* human being; it wants to embrace him completely, to enlighten and sanctify his entire soul. Of course, this motif played, and continues to play, an enormous rôle in Western Christianity too (in both Catholicism and the Protestant faiths), since it is connected with the very essence of Christianity. But in the Russian soul it gained a special force. The alternative: 'all or nothing', unrestrained by everyday prudence, uninhibited by concern for practical results, leaves the soul a stranger to everyday sobriety. *Spiritual* sobriety, on the other hand, is highly valued by the Russian religious consciousness. This spiritual sobriety sharply restricts the scope of *imagination* in the spiritual life. Religious daydreaming and the attainment of 'delight' through the power of the imagination are equally alien to it. It is interesting to note that Russian saints, who were not afraid of the most difficult undertakings, did not practise those forms of spiritual life which in the West led to the 'stigmata', to unusual visions, to mystical cults (of the 'heart of Jesus'), to the 'imitation' of Christ. All of this was definitely alien to the Russian saints and ascetics. Although they shunned the power of the imagination in the spiritual life and observed a strict spiritual sobriety, the Russian saints and ascetics did not reject the idea of an 'embodiment' of spiritual energies; in the subtle question of the relation of spiritual and material, of divine and earthly principles, they avoided both extremes—the merging, as well as the separation, of the two realms of being. Everything which might give even a slight preponderance to the material principle (i.e. might further their illicit merging) was regarded as a *coarsening* of spiritual being —hence, for example, the refusal to use sculpture in the churches and, on the other hand, the unreserved worship of icons. The opposition to instrumental music in the church and the gradual development of church singing is to be interpreted in exactly the same way. These phenomena of Russian religiosity may be interpreted differently, but all of this, of course, comes *from the Logos and is not outside of it*; it is permeated with deep and fructifying intuitions. The disdain for an everyday sobriety which might have restrained this natural maximalism, was supplemented by the principle of 'spiritual tact', which clearly exhibits an aesthetic element.

But in all of this there were, and are, temptations. Mystical realism, which seeks a fitting equilibrium in a combination of the spiritual and material, may submit to the temptation of seeing such an equilibrium where it does not exist. The mind may be captured by some utopia; thus, for example, we are to understand the passionate searching of Russians within the Church for a sacred meaning in the power of the Tsar. As we shall see below, the political ideology of the sixteenth and seventeenth centuries was wholly created by ecclesiastical circles—not in order to 'aid' the state, but from motivations within the Church, in its search for the sacred quality of historical being. The premature ascription of sacred meaning to the power of the Tsars, the astonishing 'poem' of 'Moscow—the Third Rome', was a flowering of utopianism on the theocratic level. It grew out of a passionate longing to draw nearer to the embodiment of the Kingdom of God on earth. It was an astonishing myth, which grew out of the need to combine the heavenly and the earthly, the divine and the human, in a concrete reality. From the depths of mystical realism, ecclesiastical thought proceeded directly to meditations on the *secret of history*, the mysterious and sacred aspect of external historical reality.

We shall turn in a moment to the concrete forms in which these ecclesiastical searchings were cast, but before doing so, we must pause to consider one other characteristic of Russian religiosity, *viz.* ascetic and devout 'folly' [*yurodstvo*] for Christ.

## 5. ASCETIC AND DEVOUT 'FOLLY' AND ITS PLACE IN THE RELIGIOUS LIFE OF OLD RUSSIA

Ascetic and devout 'folly' was (and to a certain extent still is) widely practised in Russia; not all such devotees achieved sainthood, but all or nearly all of them were striking manifestations of Russian religious life. It is true that there were ascetic and devout 'fools' in the Greek Church too, but compared to the Russian Church they were rare occurrences.[1]

The ascetic and devout 'fools' scorned all earthly comforts; they often acted against common sense in the name of a higher truth. They took upon themselves the heroic task of deliberate insanity, in order to attain freedom from the world's temptations; but there is no shade of contempt for the world or rejection of the world in their attitude. They placed a low value on the vain outward aspect of life and scorned petty self-gratification. They feared everyday comforts and wealth, but they did not scorn man or tear him away from life. There was a striving in ascetic and devout 'folly' toward the higher truth and justice which is usually obscured by the trivialities of every day. Nevertheless, this is not metaphysical spiritualism, but a mystical realism which sacrifices the earthly for the sake of the heavenly. Such devotees longed for truth, justice, and love, and for this reason they inevitably proceeded to unmask all injustice among men. They have always attacked state power with particular harshness, and the latter has bowed submissively before the spiritual greatness of the ascetic and devout 'fool' (this is especially evident in the example of Ivan IV). This devotion is not, in its essence, *hysterical*; on the contrary, there is in it an unquestioned high sobriety. But it feels crowded within the limits of the earthly principle alone; it hungers to assert, both in the individual human being and in the world, the pre-eminence of spiritual truth. It is radical and bold, and it radiates a genuine religious inspiration before which everyone bows.

Ascetic and devout 'folly' is an expression of the fact that no combination of divine and human, of heavenly and earthly, should subordinate the heavenly to the earthly. The divine may remain unexpressed; but there should be neither sanctimoniousness nor rapture over the poetry of the world to the forgetfulness of the heavenly beauty which can find no place in our life. This is not

1. According to Fedotov, the Greek Church had in all only six ascetic and devout 'fools' (*Svyatyie drevnei Rusi* [The Saints of Old Russia], Paris, 1931, p. 105).

Platonism, but an assertion of the hierarchical principle, i.e. the subordination of the earthly to the heavenly. The ascetic and devout 'fools' felt an intuitive aversion to the temptation of every false or partial or nominal 'embodiment' of Christianity. Its specific development coincides with the origin of the passionate utopian poem of 'Moscow—the Third Rome', with its naïve identification of Russian reality and 'Holy Russia'. The ascetic and devout 'fools' were also inspired by the *ideal* of Holy Russia, but they were soberly aware of all the injustices of Russian reality.

## 6. FUNDAMENTAL IDEOLOGICAL SEARCHINGS UP TO THE SIXTEENTH CENTURY

After this brief outline of Russian religiosity, let us return to our basic theme—to an elucidation of those factors within the framework of the ecclesiastical consciousness which led to a development of philosophic thought.

The great dogmatic themes, and the philosophic problems connected with them, had not yet awakened activity in Russian minds, not because of *indifference* but because of the *absolute firmness* of these doctrines. When, at the end of the seventeenth century, an itinerant follower of Jacob Böhme, Quirin Kuhlman (a German from Breslau), appeared in Moscow and began to preach his doctrines—in the spirit of the chiliastic tendencies which were then very widespread in Western Europe—he was seized and died a martyr's death. In the Russian ecclesiastical consciousness it was not the *general principles* of Christianity which called forth lively and intense intellectual work (because of the absolute firmness of these principles for those within the Church), but problems of *concrete* Christianity in its individual and historical manifestations. Concerning the first, i.e. the realization of Christianity in individual life, these problems were connected with the idea of a Last Judgment where everyone would have to answer for his deeds and intentions. At this level, the vanity and cares of the world were thought of as a difficult obstacle in the way of the realization of Christian truth and justice. Hence the idea was often found among Russians that genuine Christianity can be realized only in monasticism, i.e. in the renunciation of worldly vanity and cares. But in this tendency toward monasticism, as the only path to a Christian life, there was no contempt for, or abhorrence of, the world but merely an acute awareness of the sinfulness which prevails in it. Russian monasticism in fact provided unrivalled examples of spiritual strength, purity of heart, and freedom from the bondage of the world. The Russian monasteries were the focus of the spiritual life of old Russia. They constantly reminded men of that heavenly truth and justice which must be added to the world from within, while the world must be purified and sanctified, in order—thus transformed—to become the Kingdom of God. 'The true life', the people were convinced, was lived in the monasteries, and it was for this reason that Russians were so fond of 'visiting the holy places', to which they were attracted by the longing to share in the Kingdom of God 'manifested' on earth. In the monasteries there burned a light not of this earth, by which the earth itself was to be illuminated if it would only discard the excrescence of sinfulness.

These are the same tendencies of 'mystical realism' with which we are already familiar. But in the monasteries themselves, in their spiritual activity, not only was there no forgetfulness of the world but, on the contrary, meditations on the world developed more clearly and strongly. The monasteries did a great work of charity, constantly remembering the needs and miseries of the people; yet it was in the monasteries specifically that the *national ideology* was formed. An ecclesiastical culture developed which centred about them. Icon-painting developed and flourished in the monasteries; they were also the centre of historical writing. Russians were educated in the monasteries, and all the ideological disputes in Russia from the fifteenth to the seventeenth century were connected directly or indirectly with the monasteries. One historian of Ivan IV (second half of the sixteenth century) has justly remarked that 'the ecclesiastical disputes and interests clearly reflect the wealth of spiritual life, the abundance of talents among the intelligentsia which surrounded Ivan IV during the first years of his reign.'[1] This intelligentsia was theologically educated and thought along theological lines; we need only mention Prince Kurbski, the brilliant writer of that period. The principal theme of the ideological searchings of Russian ecclesiastical circles was an *historical* theme, which grew out of the general theocratic principle of Christianity and was understood in the spirit of mystical realism—as a doctrine of the dual structure of the world and of history.

Of course, the foundations of this whole ideology, which was constructed by churchmen, were already present in Byzantium; but they struck living roots in the Russian soul, and Russians applied themselves warmly and passionately to historical themes.

1. Yu. Vipper, *Ioann Grozny* [Ivan the Terrible], 1922, p. 35.

The Logos of the Church tended in this direction, and at this level it was manifested with genuine feeling, boldly and radically.

The theocratic theme of Christianity was developed in Russia not as a pre-eminence of spiritual over secular power, which was the case in the West, but as an imputing to state power of a *sacred mission*. This was not a movement toward caesaropapism, for the Church itself came to the state in order to give it the strength of grace through sanctification. State power was the point at which divine Providence entered into history. This was the 'mystery' of power, its connection with the mystical sphere. For this reason the ecclesiastical consciousness, in developing the theocratic idea of Christianity, strove to find a way to sanctify power. Power was to assume ecclesiastical functions, and ecclesiastical thought occupied itself in constructing a national ideology. Later the state power was to accept this ideology, which had been created by the Church, and make it an official creed; but the whole ideology was ecclesiastical, both in *origin* and *content*. The ecclesiastical Logos applied itself with warmth and intensity to the themes of historiosophy, and bequeathed them to future Russian philosophy, which to the present time has not abandoned historiosophical themes.

### 7. THE DOCTRINE OF MOSCOW—THE THIRD ROME

The special conception of state power which we have been discussing matured first in Byzantium and then sent up shoots among the Southern Slavs. In Russian ecclesiastical circles the idea of the 'sacred mission' of power flamed up with particular force after the fall of Constantinople (1453). The idea had already developed in Byzantium that there should be a single Emperor for the whole Christian world; this doctrine sprang from the general conviction among Byzantine thinkers that *Constantinople* would have a central place in the Christian world as a '*second Rome*', replacing the earlier Rome. When, at the end of the fourteenth century, Grand Prince Vasili I of Moscow refused to pay allegiance to the Byzantine Emperor, he received a very characteristic retort from the Patriarch of Constantinople:

'It is impossible', the Patriarch wrote, 'that Christians should have a church without having an emperor, for empire and church exist in close union and communion, and cannot be separated one from the other. The Holy Emperor occupies a high place in the church; he is something quite different from local lords and princes.'

This whole doctrine was closely connected with the prophecy of

Daniel concerning the four kingdoms—a prophecy which had exceptional influence in the development of the philosophy of history in both East and West. It includes such words as these: 'And in the days of these kings shall the God of heaven set up a kingdom, which shall never be destroyed; . . . it shall break in pieces and consume all these kingdoms, and it shall stand forever' (Daniel, ii. 44). Among Byzantine writers the idea of an eternal kingdom (understood, following the early commentators, as the Roman Empire), an idea applied to Byzantium, had a permanent place; but during the closing centuries of the Byzantine Empire this conception began to lose ground. When Byzantium fell, the idea that henceforth the 'God-chosen' kingdom was to be the Russian Empire found insistent expression in the Russian ecclesiastical consciousness. After the Union of Florence (1439), Russian ecclesiastical circles evidenced definite mistrust toward the Greeks, who had entered the Union. The Russian Church began to consider itself the only guardian of the truth of Christ in its purity. This same period saw the rise of the remarkable legend of the 'white cowl',[1] which affirmed that the Russian Church had been elected from above as the guardian of Christ's truth. At the end of the fifteenth century the well-known theory of Moscow as the 'Third Rome' was developed in the epistles of the monk Philotheus.[2] This theory is a complete historiosophical conception, which introduces us directly into the field of philosophy. For us, in our study of the ecclesiastical roots of later philosophic searchings, there are a number of elements in this theory which are obviously close to the eschatological expectations of the time (the end of the world, according to contemporary calculations, was expected in 1492). The end of the world is at the same time the end of history, i.e. the beginning of the Kingdom of God. This idea had a firm place in the Russian ecclesiastical consciousness of the time (as in the Christian world generally). But when the year 1492 came, this eschatological conception was forced to assume a new form. On the one hand, thinkers still strove to fix a definite date for the end of the world; thus the theory had arisen that the end of the world was to come after 7000 years, i.e. in the eighth millennium [after the creation of the world—*viz*. the fifteenth century A.D. *Trans*.].[3] Another

1. See any standard history of Russian literature.
2. See H. Schäder, *Moskau der dritte Rom*, Hamburg, 1929.
3. Metrop. Zosima in composing an Easter service for the year 8000 wrote: 'In that year we expect the universal coming of Christ'. We find the same thoughts in Prince Kurbski and in Maximus the Greek [died 1556].

turn of thought which tried to find a way out of the historiosophical impasse was broader, and opened up a wide field for meditation and new ideas. It rejected the *knowability* of the ways of Providence in history. General providentialism was not weakened, but the assertion was made that we cannot know accurately how Providence will be realized in history. This proposition, which tore men's thinking away from the oversimplified schemes of providentialism, led at the same time to a recognition that what is 'sacred' in history—its mysterious logic—is *not parallel to its empirical aspect*. Providence in history is a greater mystery than at first appears. In other words, the general foundations of providentialism are correct, but Providence is hidden from us in the concreteness of history.

Among the general propositions of providentialism, ecclesiastical thought emphasized especially the idea that the ultimate destiny of the world is bound up *only* with what takes place among the *Christian* peoples. For *Starets* Philotheus [1] the pulse of history beats only in the relationship between God and the 'chosen people'.[2] Not all Christian peoples are chosen, and in the determination of this choice the idea of a 'Christian Emperor' plays a decisive part. With the fall of Byzantium the idea of a 'wandering kingdom' began to be asserted with special force: The first two Romes (Rome and Constantinople) had fallen. Where was the third, the new one? Russian thinkers firmly and confidently accepted Moscow as the third Rome, for only in Russia, it was felt, had the Christian faith been preserved in its purity. In line with the earlier eschatological ideas, it was further asserted: 'There will not be a fourth Rome', i.e. the Russian Empire is to stand until the end of the world.

1. The Russian term *Starets* (plural: *Startsy*) (literally, 'Elder') is retained in this translation to avoid the misleading connotations of the English word 'Elder'. '*Starets*' is a title which signifies not age or ecclesiastical authority but wisdom and 'spiritual authority'. Western readers will recall, for example, *Starets* Zosima in Dostoyevsky's *Brothers Karamazov. Trans.*

2. This is essentially the biblical conception. See Malinin, *Starets Filofei i yevo poslaniya* [*Starets* Philotheus and His Epistles], Kiev, 1901, p. 315. Is this not the basic source of the later historiosophical theories which divide all nations into 'historical' and 'nonhistorical'? These theories were especially widespread toward the end of the eighteenth century both in the West and among Russian thinkers.

8. THE PROBLEM OF THE STATE IN THE ECCLESIASTICAL
CONSCIOUSNESS; INTERNAL DIFFERENTIATION
IN THE LATTER

Among these historiosophical propositions it is important to note
the idea of the special mission of the Russian people and the
Russian Empire. It was in the sixteenth century that the doctrine
of 'Holy Russia' and of Russia's universal, world-wide significance
was first put forward.[1] On the other hand, the ecclesiastico-
political ideology connected with another favourite Russian idea—
the ideology of 'autocracy' and the theory of the relationship of
church and state—was closely bound up with this historiosophical
conception. Russian ecclesiastical circles took from Byzantium the
idea of the sacred mission of imperial power; in the seventeenth
century the eastern patriarchs asserted that the Russian Tsars had
received their power by succession from the Byzantine Emperors.[2]
Joseph Volokolamski (whose views on another question we shall
discuss below)—an outstanding ecclesiastical figure and writer of
the late fifteenth and early sixteenth century—was a brilliant
theorist of the sacred ministry of the Tsar. 'The Tsar's nature is
like that of every man,' he wrote, 'but his office and his power are
like those of the most high God.' The Tsar, in his view, is responsible to God not only for himself personally, but for every man
in his empire. Ivan IV expressed with extraordinary force the
ecclesiastical character of imperial power and its ecclesiastical
function. In the epistles of *Starets* Philotheus the Tsar is called the
'guardian of the orthodox faith', i.e. he has ecclesiastical functions
and ecclesiastical power. Metropolitan Makarius (a contemporary
of Ivan IV) went so far as to write, 'Thee, my lord, has God chosen
upon earth and raised up to the throne in His place, giving into
thy hands the grace and life of our great Orthodox faith.' We
shall not go into further detail, but shall simply point out that
Patriarch Nikon is the only writer to express sharp disagreement
with this traditional view of the Tsar's place in the Church. He is
close to the ideas of Western theocracy, which holds that the

1. This (and this alone) is the source of the doctrines of Russia's 'universally
human' mission which crowd the historiosophical theories of the first half of the
nineteenth century (continuing in individual thinkers to our own day). See
below, Chs. VI–VIII.

2. This was connected with the hope that Russia would free Constantinople
from Turkish domination. Here we see the roots of Russia's future claims to
Constantinople!

spiritual power is above the secular; this view is definitely alien to all other Russian ecclesiastical thought.

The doctrine that imperial power is a form of ecclesiastical service is usually characterized as 'caesaropapism' (as opposed to the 'papocaesarism' of the Roman doctrine). Of course, there are facts enough to support such a characterization; nevertheless, it fails to grasp the essence of this ecclesiastico-political ideology. Imperial power, although it is related to men's earthly life, appears in this ideology as a factor *within the Church*. The Church has an obligation to aid the Tsar in his service. It is especially interesting to note the principle of 'intercession' which developed in Russia— the pleading of the Church before the Tsar. Russian history gives a clear example of such an 'intercession' for justice in the person of St. Philip, Metropolitan of Moscow, who was martyred because he did not soften his harsh attitude toward Ivan IV. The exaltation of imperial power was not simply 'utopian', and it was not, of course, an expression of ecclesiastical 'servility' (for ecclesiastical circles themselves had created the ideology of imperial power); it expressed a *mystical conception of history*. If the meaning of history lies beyond the limits of history (preparation for the Kingdom of God) then the very process of history, although bound up with it, is bound up in a way that is *incomprehensible* to the human mind. Imperial power is the point at which history and God's will meet. The same Joseph of Volotsk who, as we have seen, exalted imperial power so highly, held firmly that an unjust Tsar is 'not God's servant but a devil'. This theory of the Tsar is not utopian or romantic; it is a special kind of historiosophy, toward the discovery of whose meaning a large number of nineteenth-century Russian thinkers devoted much effort. The solemn ceremony of anointing the Tsar included a number of specially composed prayers; and, of course, for the ecclesiastical consciousness, the Tsar was not a *bearer* of the principle of 'caesar': on the contrary, in him the opposition between the principle of caesar and the will of God was *overcome*. The Tsar expresses the 'mystical' harmony—inaccessible to reason—of the divine and human principles; in him historical being is *sanctified*. This ideology was the more valuable to the ecclesiastical consciousness in that it conceived the whole historical process as moving toward churchification, toward the transformation of earthly dominion into ecclesiastical dominion. Indeed, according to this ideology, 'Tsar' is a kind of 'ecclesiastical rank'.

It is interesting to note one ecclesiastico-theological dispute which came to a head in the late fifteenth century, providing a foundation for two types of religio-philosophical thought. I have in mind the dispute concerning *ecclesiastical property*—its admissibility or inadmissibility from the Christian point of view. Joseph of Volotsk solemnly defended ecclesiastical property in the name of the *social function* of the Church;[1] this was very closely connected with the *rapprochement* in principle of church and state, which we have seen in the doctrine of imperial power. Just as the Tsar serves the Church, so the Church serves the state, without separating itself from the state. The opposing point of view was developed by the so-called 'Trans-Volga *Startsy*' and especially by their leader, Nilus of Sorsk, who had visited Mount Athos and entered into the new theologico-mystical tradition of the 'Hesychasts'. At the same time, Nilus of Sorsk was close to the tradition of the Rev. Sergius Radonezhski. There is also a connection between Sergius Radonezhski and Joseph of Volotsk (through St. Pafnuti) but, of course, the most important of Sergius's views found expression in those of the 'Trans-Volga *Startsy*'.[2] The task of the Church with respect to the state was conceived as prayerful concern for the state, but, according to the ecclesiastical consciousness, these two institutions should not be brought *too close* together; the mystical nature of the Church should not be forgotten. Here the temptation which always hung over the basic theocratic temper of mind within the Church was decisively overcome. Of course, the tendencies of both the Rev. Sergius and of Nilus of Sorsk were completely opposed to Patriarch Nikon's doctrine that the Church should rule over the state at the *historical* level. The Church is above the state, not at the level of *history*, but on the mystical level. This was not a 'renunciatory' conception of Christianity for which the theme of history falls outside the religious consciousness. It is often said of this tendency that its 'predominant concern for the contemplative spiritual life was connected with a certain obliviousness of the world',[3] but this is a one-sided and hence erroneous characterization of this spiritual tendency, which did not isolate monastic

1. Florovsky (*op. cit.*, p. 18) justly remarks that Joseph 'looked upon, and lived, the monastic life itself as a kind of social burden, a special kind of earthly religious service'—that his ideal was a 'unique form of *going out among the people*' (an anticipation of nineteenth-century 'Populism').

2. Father S. Bulgakov says of this that 'the period which followed the age of the Rev. Sergius may be called the "Sergian" period in the history of the Russian spirit and Russian creative activity' ('Blagodatnyie zavety prep. Sergiya russkomu bogoslovstvovaniyu' ['The Rev. Sergius's Legacy of Grace to Russian Theology'], *Put*, No. 5, 1926).

3. Florovsky, *op. cit.*, p. 21.

from non-monastic life. The essence of this tendency is the preservation of the purity of the mystical life, not out of scorn for the
world, but in order to set the Church apart from the world. The
Church has the task of transfiguring the world; but in the untransfigured world the monk must hold himself aloof from worldly
vanity. Not without reason are the followers of this tendency called
'non-coveters'. Nilus of Sorsk had already faced the danger of
*secularization* of the Church, and for that reason he decisively
opposed the monasteries' owning property, engaging in agriculture, etc. The whole tendency which passed from Nilus of Sorsk
(and from the Rev. Sergius) through Paisius Velichkovski (see the
following chapter) into the Optina Cloister, was free of the church-
state ideology which we have described above. These were two
different spiritual tendencies, two different conceptions of the
Christian theocratic principle—although they agreed in rejecting
the conception of theocracy which was developed in Catholicism.

## 9. THE FIRST GERMINATIONS OF THE IDEA OF 'NATURAL LAW'

It is interesting to note, in connection with the tendency of Nilus
of Sorsk, the first germinations of the idea of 'natural law', which
began to develop markedly in Russia during the second half of the
eighteenth century, continuing into the nineteenth. Vipper considers that the idea of 'natural law', which is frequently encountered
among sixteenth-century Russian journalists and churchmen, was
'taken from the Roman juridical thesaurus'.[1] It is possible that
Vipper is right; however, with no less reason one may trace the
first germinations of the idea of 'natural' rights (as inherent in
every human being at birth) to the Christian world-view. In any
case, the idea of freedom as given by God to all men, runs persistently through sixteenth-century Russian literature. Prince Kurbski, a talented writer of the sixteenth century, in his polemic
against Ivan IV, charges him among other things with 'turning
the Russian land, that is to say, *free human nature*, into a hellish
fortress.' Similar thoughts are also to be found in one of the first
Russian 'freethinkers', Matthew Bashkin (sixteenth century) who
rebelled against slavery with extraordinary force (his writing ante-
dates the binding of the peasants to the land). Bashkin cites the
New Testament: 'Christ called all men brothers, and we have

1. Vipper, *op. cit.*, p. 19.

serfdom.' Peresvetov, a writer of the time, in defending political despotism in the interest of social justice wrote: 'God created man absolute in power and commanded him to be a master, not a slave.' We may note the Peresvetov spent a number of years in foreign countries (Poland, Hungary, and Bohemia) where he could have absorbed foreign ideas, but his original political ideology was combined with a very acute defence of popular rights.

## 10. THE RASKOL (SCHISM)

It remains for us to consider the last important phenomenon in the Russian ecclesiastical consciousness before the time of Peter the Great, namely, the *Schism* [*Raskol*]—only, of course, as it affects the differentiation of ideological trends. That the Schism is a part of the *ideological* quest within the ecclesiastical consciousness is no longer open to doubt. Most historians are still inclined to see the essence of the Schism in disagreements concerning matters of ritual and the correction of ecclesiastical texts; even these historians agree that the Schism revealed an *active* attitude of the people toward their faith. But the Schism is a much deeper phenomenon than is usually assumed. A. B. Kartashov, author of the best and most profoundly comprehensive characterization of the Schism,[1] remarks that the tension of the Russian spirit which became the pivot of its self-consciousness and led to the idea of a third Rome, i.e. the world mission of preserving the purity of Orthodox truth, was 'discharged' in the movement of the Old Believers. This 'preserving' mission was not at all *retrograde*, nor was it an expression of intellectual obscurity or ignorance. The leaders and supporters of the movement of the Old Believers were men of subtle minds. The remark of one historian—that the Old Believers' 'retreat into ritual' was a 'belated self-defence against the disintegration which had begun in everday life'[2]—is unjust. This same writer, contradicting himself, remarks that 'the theme of the Schism was not the old ritual but the problem of Empire' (understood as a sacred kingdom).[3] This is closer to the truth, and so is his further remark: 'Not ritual, but the Antichrist is the theme and secret of the Russian Schism.' Eschatological motifs, which had not yet been extinguished

1. See his article, 'Smysl staroobryadchestva' ['The Meaning of the Movement of Old Believers'], in the collection in honour of P. B. Struve, Prague, 1925. Concerning the Schism, see Pierre Pascal, *Avvakoum et les débuts du raskol*, Paris, 1938.

2. Florovsky, *op. cit.*, pp. 57f.        3. *Ibid.*, p. 67.

in the ecclesiastical consciousness, took on greater significance as the theocratic problem was more sharply posed by history itself. Kartashov, in the above-mentioned study, evaluates this most clearly and profoundly when he relates the basic theme of the Schism to the ideology of the Third Rome, and the profound belief that 'there will not be a fourth Rome', i.e. that the fate of the world and the end of history are bound up with the destiny of Russia. The Old Believers were solving a problem of world history, not a local or provincial problem; hence the theme of Antichrist was not accidental or superficial in their theological consciousness. The movement of the Old Believers was historiosophical in its tendencies; it feared an *unrighteous* secularization of the Church, an infection of the Church by the secular spirit. Its positive concern was not, of course, ritualism or the mere preservation of the old, but a safeguarding of the Church's purity. Kartashov is quite right when he says that 'the sharp division between the pure and the impure among the Old Believers has a precedent only in ancient Israel.' 'The Russian people', he notes, 'saw in Christianity a revelation of the coming of the Saviour upon earth and of the creation through the strength of *Christian piety* [1] of another world *completely holy*, in place of this sinful and impure world.' [2] This dream is the 'Russian *civitas Dei*, a paradise in all the fullness of life's variety, except for sin.' The utopian impasse is evident in all this, the impasse of the dream of a 'sacred kingdom', but the utopia itself grew out of the theocratic idea which is precious to all Christianity. The Russian ecclesiastical consciousness paid dearly for its dream, its utopian conception of the theocratic idea of Christianity, in the distressing history of the Old Believers, which was filled with religious inspiration, but was sometimes hysterical and tormented by a sense of the 'iniquitous mystery' of the Antichrist. This was a fateful and tragic dissipation of ecclesiastical energies. On the Orthodox side there was more historical sobriety and cautiousness; the Old Believers took over from Orthodoxy not the theocratic idea itself, but the temptation of 'naturalism', i.e. the identification of the 'natural' historical order—which, though sanctified by the Church, is not holy—and the mystical order of the Kingdom of God. In essence, the utopia of 'Holy Russia', conceived as a reality already embodied in history, was also taken over by the Old Believers. The theocratic idea remained precious for Orthodoxy, but only as an *ideal*, as a vision of future transfig-

1. These words reveal very aptly the root of the Old Believers' sacred dream.
2. Kartashov, *op. cit.*, p. 378.

uration; and this historical position restored a correct relationship between the mystical essence of the Church and its historical being. The dreadful ordeal of a secularized conception of state power (the period of Peter the Great) was at hand; for such a conception the idea of a Third Rome could have only a blasphemously imperialistic character. Orthodoxy did not recoil from the idea of a Third Rome; neither did it view secularized state power as the Antichrist. And this re-established the possibility of a spiritually sober combination of providentialism and historical realism.

All of these motifs were revived in philosophic form after a century and a half, and the work of Peter the Great ('secularized' state power) once more became the subject of historiosophical disputes.

II. DISINTEGRATION OF THE TRADITIONAL WORLD-VIEW

The Schism, as we have noted, contributed to the liberation of the creative energies accumulated in the Church. Any general characterization of this process must focus, not on the seventeenth century, although in the seventeenth century it was clearly marked, but the eighteenth. We shall turn to this theme in the following chapter; for the present we wish merely to corroborate briefly what was said at the beginning of this chapter—that there was neither emptiness nor silence in the Russian ecclesiastical consciousness. The work of the ecclesiastical Logos developed ever more strongly and diversely, but even in this period the primary importance of *historiosophical* problems, and of the moral problems connected with them, became quite clear. However, *together with* this basic orientation of *thought*, religious contemplation developed in icon-painting and iconolatry. This is an expression of the Russian spirit's extraordinary sensitivity to beauty, not remote or ideal, but concretely historical beauty. The icon captures the basic Christian idea of mystical realism—the recognition of two orders of being, harmoniously combined in the Lord Jesus Christ. The mystery of the incarnation of God, which lies at the foundation of iconolatry, is also the mystery of the historical process, which proceeds under the guidance of Divine Providence toward the Kingdom of God. The ecclesiastical consciousness did not, however, confine itself to preserving a proper equilibrium between the divine and the human principle. In the historiosophical poem of the Third Rome, of sacred imperial power and its universal mission, the ecclesiastical consciousness tended toward the kind of *rapprochement* of the two orders of being which would lead to their identification. The 'natural' historical process, when denied the character of a 'sacred kingdom', appeared as the kingdom of Antichrist. The enormous sacrifice which the Old Believers brought to the altar of their sacred dream is sufficient evidence of how much passionate energy, spiritual integrity, and whole-hearted devotion to the idea of the 'sacred kingdom' had accumulated in the ecclesiastical consciousness. The break with this intemperate attitude toward history was accomplished in torment and vain sufferings, but it made possible a new attitude toward the history that was yet to be. The period of 'secularization'—the eighteenth century—was at hand.

# CHAPTER II

## The Eighteenth Century. The Crisis in the Ecclesiastical Consciousness

### THE PHILOSOPHY OF G. S. SKOVORODA

#### I. THE BEGINNING OF SECULARIZATION

THE eighteenth century was the century of 'secularization' in Russia. During this period an independent secular culture arose, which had no connection with the ecclesiastical consciousness; simultaneously, there was a profound crisis in the ecclesiastical consciousness itself. The ecclesiastical consciousness renounced its dream of the state's sacred mission and intensified its search for a purely ecclesiastical truth and justice, freeing itself from the temptations of an ecclesiastico-political ideology. The former cultural unity was destroyed; creative effort, both within the Church and outside of it, flowed into not one, but two different channels. This twofold process, which proceeded in the eighteenth century at an extraordinary, even baffling, rate is baffling only at first glance; in fact, it merely brought to light what had long since occurred in the depths of Russian life—as early as the end of the sixteenth century and especially in the seventeenth.

We have already said that the Schism, in separating from the Church those elements which championed 'antiquity', had the beneficial effect of crushing the ecclesiastical dream of a 'sacred kingdom'. It thus liberated the Church's creative energies, which had been captured by an ecclesiastico-political theme; on the other hand, state power developed clearly toward 'secularization'. Bitterly and painfully, but in sober awareness of what it was doing, the ecclesiastical consciousness entered a new path, one long since pointed out by Nilus of Sorsk and the 'non-coveters'. It looked within itself, turning to purely ecclesiastical themes, and sought 'purity' in the life and thought of the Church. Some looked to the ecclesiastical thought of the past, others tried to find new paths;

but in both cases the spirit of freedom was evident. Theological education also increased: a 'Helleno-Greek School' was founded in Moscow in 1685, transformed in 1700 into a 'Slavo-Latin Academy', and in 1775 renamed 'Slavo-Greco-Latin Academy'. This development gradually made room within the ecclesiastical consciousness for philosophic thinking which started from Christian principles but was free in its creative activity and search for truth. This process reached its highest expression in the philosophic works of G. S. Skovoroda, in whom free Christian philosophy appeared for the first time. This was a *secularization within the ecclesiastical consciousness*, which did not break with the Church.

However, this same process, as was pointed out above, also went on outside the Church and independently of it, sometimes in conscious opposition to the ecclesiastical consciousness. A secular culture was born which left ample room for 'worldly' interests and diversions. There were two different streams of creative activity, two styles of thought. Thus, as early as the eighteenth century two basic cultural trends were clearly exhibited in Russia; they have developed in fatal separation to the present day.

## 2. THE MOSCOW THEOLOGICAL ACADEMY

In order to understand the crisis in the Russian ecclesiastical consciousness, we must recall what took place in the ecclesiastical life of the Ukraine during the sixteenth and seventeenth centuries. Until the middle of the seventeenth century the Ukraine was linked politically to Poland, and it was precisely this fact that gave impetus to the ecclesiastical 'renaissance' which began in the Ukraine during the sixteenth century. This renaissance bore precious fruits for the ecclesiastical life of South Russia. And when, in the mid-seventeenth century, the Ukraine became part of the Russian Empire, it was not only fused with Russia politically and economically; in the religious field as well it passed on to Moscow the fruits of Ukrainian experience. It is true that the Ukraine was not at once ecclesiastically united with Moscow, but by the end of the seventeenth century, Moscow was the ecclesiastical centre for the Ukraine as well; and the penetration of ecclesiastical education to Moscow from the Ukraine took on special significance. At the same time, all kinds of 'Latinisms', which were alien to the essence of Orthodoxy, penetrated into Russian ecclesiastical life. But this fact was not of primary importance.

The ecclesiastical renaissance in the Ukraine was related to the need for a defence against the aggressive gestures of Roman Catholicism. In the late sixteenth century a brisk programme of Orthodox book publication was started; a group of 'wisdom-lovers' (philosophers) gathered about Prince Ostrozhski; a plan was conceived for creating a centre of learning (with an orientation toward the Greeks). The idea of an 'Orthodox Academy' arose; translating activity developed vigorously. The growth of an ecclesiastical self-consciousness, with a clear conception of the essential differences between Orthodoxy and Catholicism, caused an incipient gravitation toward Protestantism in Church circles.[1] Kiev developed close ties with the German Protestant centres, and these ties inevitably spread far beyond the limits of pure theology. But the disruption created by the Union in the higher circles of Church and society in the Ukraine led to the important 'Fraternity' movement, which united the urban population in defence of Orthodoxy. The Fraternities established schools and organized a translation programme, in order to make use, in their struggle against the opponents of Orthodoxy, of the latter's weapons. Both Greek and Latin were studied in the Fraternities; the doors were thus thrown open for the penetration of Western theological and philosophic literature into the Ukraine. A large ecclesiastical publishing house was established in the Pecherski Abbey (in Kiev), simultaneously with the founding of an Orthodox Fraternity there (1615). In the school of the Kiev Fraternity Catholic books were studied intently; original works appeared which were permeated through and through with the spirit of Catholicism, even though they were directed against it. The figure of Cyril Stavrovetski is typical in this connection; he published a book called A Mirror of Theology (1618) in which the influence of Thomism could already be felt. This was also true of Sakovich's On the Soul (1625). Religious thought became philosophical; philosophy entered widely into theological education. When Peter Mogila transformed the Fraternity School into the Kiev-Mogila College (1631)—it was renamed 'Academy' in 1701—theology was included under philosophy. Peter Mogila himself studied in Paris;[2] he was acquainted with both Western scholasticism and Renaissance philosophy. There is no doubt that he was a 'westerner'; he even

1. In 1599 a congress of Orthodox and Calvinist representatives was held in Vilna with the object of uniting in the struggle against Catholicism.

2. Shchurat's surmise (Ukrainskiye materialy po istori filosofi [Ukrainian Materials on the History of Philosophy], Lwow, 1908) that Peter Mogila studied with Descartes's teacher, Varon, is entirely without foundation.

reorganized the Fraternity School on the pattern of the Jesuit schools.

The Kiev-Mogila College produced a number of scholars and writers. Their works show almost no independent thought, but the significance of this movement for the development of theological education and philosophic culture should not be underestimated. The relevant documents have scarcely been investigated as yet; however, there is no doubt that their textbooks [1] not only spread an elementary knowledge of philosophy but also trained minds in systematic thinking. It is true that almost all of this South-Russian scholarship existed in complete bondage to the West, tearing itself away from the basic Eastern sources of Christianity; but it would be an historical error to underestimate the positive contribution which this scholarship made to the intellectual life, first of the Ukraine, and then of all Russia. Although South-Russian scholarship was still very far from free, it is no accident that the first declaration concerning freedom of thought, and the inner strength which is inherent in thought, came from the eighteenth-century Moscow scholar, Theophilactus Lopatinski, a student of the Kiev Academy.[2] Not only did formal philosophic culture gradually develop in the Kiev Academy; there is no doubt that creative ideas were also generated. We shall soon become acquainted with the philosophy of Skovoroda, a philosophy which was on a par with the best of its time; but, in fact, it was merely the culmination of the philosophic movement which was connected with the Kiev Academy.

### 3. MOSCOW MOVES TOWARD SECULARIZATION

Moscow avidly absorbed all that the Ukraine had to offer, but the influence of the West penetrated into Moscow from the north as well (through Novgorod and Pskov). Ivan IV had considered establishing schools for the teaching of Latin and German; in 1560 the Russian monk Ivan Aleksandrov compiled a Dictionary of the Latin and Russian Languages at Tübingen University; and after

1. For example, the *Opus Totius Philosophiae* (1745–7) of Innocentius Giselus.

2. Here is his declaration: 'Although we respect all philosophers, and especially Aristotle [!], . . . in our desire to learn the pure truth we do not rest on anyone's words. It is the nature of philosophy to trust reason more than authority. . . . The truth is revealed to all, it has not yet been exhausted; much remains for future generations.' See Arkhangelski, *Dukhovnoye obrazovaniye i dukhovnaya literatura v Rossi pri Petre Velikom* [Theological Education and Theological Literature in Russia under Peter the Great], 1882.

the Time of Unrest the direct influence of the West upon Moscow and Muscovite culture grew with extraordinary rapidity, especially under Tsar Aleksei Mikhailovich. Numerous translations from foreign languages were made by immigrants from the Ukraine and Belorussia; and the suspicious attitude toward Kiev, which was still apparent in Moscow at the beginning of the seventeenth century, gave way during the second half of the century to an attempt to attract to Moscow as many South-Russian scholars as possible. Moscow was still zealous in its quest for Greek scholars (the brothers Lichud *et al.*) but 'the fashion for everything Little-Russian' prevailed.

However, we should remember that South Russia's shift to the West had a *religious* basis (which also explains the undoubted clouding of its ecclesiastical consciousness), whereas Moscow's interest in the West developed entirely *outside* the religious sphere, and was constantly opposed by ecclesiastical circles. This was already in essence a 'secularization', a gradual development of 'worldly' culture, wholly independent of the ecclesiastical consciousness. Of course, the ever-increasing number of foreigners in Moscow and other cities could not fail to have an influence on religion, the more so in that a decisive, if surreptitious, break with the ecclesiastico-political ideology had occurred deep within the ecclesiastical consciousness after the secession of the Old Believers. The ecclesiastical consciousness was laid bare, as it were, in one of its aspects—the point where the dream of the 'sacred mission' of the state had previously burned so brightly. Historiosophical agnosticism, rejecting concrete predictions as to the end of the world, liberated men's minds from fruitless providentialistic speculations. The disagreement on the question of the Church's participation in state affairs, the sharpening of the ecclesiastico-political ideology among the Old Believers (who went so far as to assert that state power was a servant of the Antichrist) levelled out the ecclesiastical consciousness and prepared it to grant considerable independence to reason. When a Theological Academy was established near Moscow, and a centre of theological and philosophic education was created, Moscow began to free itself gradually from South-Russian influence and to find its own path.

### 4. THE SECULARIZATION OF STATE POWER

To this was added an occurrence of extreme importance: the complete and decisive 'secularization' of state power, which reached its culmination under Peter the Great. The tragic circumstances in which he became sovereign of Russia left Peter with a permanent mistrust of the clergy. After the death of Patriarch Adrian, Peter opposed the election of a new Patriarch and established for the Church a Synodic Administration, in which a civil servant of the Tsar occupied a position which gradually became dominant. The Russian autocracy, whose ideology, as we have seen, was created by ecclesiastical circles, became wholly free of the Church's influence, following Aleksei Mikhailovich's conflict with Patriarch Nikon, and became absolute under Peter the Great. Thus the Church not only lost its influence, but was itself subordinated to the power of the Tsar; it gradually fell into a position of dependence on the sovereign power which was extremely humiliating and dangerous for the Church. This brought about a final break with the earlier ecclesiastical ideology. The ideology was appropriated by the state power, but in a new, secularized form. The theocratic dream of a 'sacred kingdom' was revived later in free philosophic thought. Another process—the secularization of the national consciousness—began at the same time; the idea of 'Holy Russia' became a rhetorical formula. The national consciousness was animated by the ideal of 'Great Russia'. All of these factors determined the new style of Russian culture which finally took shape in the nineteenth century.

The ecclesiastical consciousness, however, abandoning the ecclesiastico-political theme, expended its creative strength in an attempt to give meaning and vitality to the new path of Church activity. This path led 'within', focusing upon the mystical aspect of the Church; the result was what we have called a 'secularization within the ecclesiastical consciousness'. The spirit of freedom was evident in two currents of ecclesiastical thought. On the one hand, the Church began to take a new, free attitude toward the state; and, as a result of this, it made ample room for ecclesiastical thought. Concerning the first, we must recognize that, despite a resolute internal dissent from the ecclesiastical reform which was forcibly carried out by Peter the Great, *ecclesiastical circles offered no serious opposition to this reform*, which was a much less powerful movement than the Schism had been somewhat earlier. Why was this? It is often attributed to the servility of the higher clergy, which is true in part, but only in part. The basic cause was a profound crisis in the ecclesiastical consciousness, as a result of which ecclesiastical circles began to see in state power a sphere *alien* to themselves. The secularization of state power corresponded

to a new ecclesiastical consciousness, which yielded to external
power precisely because it was external and spiritually alien. The
sphere of the Church was the sphere of inner life; its relationship
to secular power touched the periphery but not the essence of
ecclesiasticism.

### 5. SAINT TYCHON OF ZADONSK

There is no need for us to go into the historical details of this
process, the tracing of which belongs to the history of the Russian
Church. But in order to come closer to an understanding of this
ecclesiastical tendency we shall consider two outstanding representatives of eighteenth-century Russian ecclesiastical life—St.
Tychon of Zadonsk and *Starets* Paisius Velichkovski.

St. Tychon of Zadonsk (1724–83) was born into the poor family
of a sacristan in the Government of Novgorod. At the age of sixteen
he entered the Theological Seminary, where he made such exceptional progress that even before completing the course he received
a commission to teach Greek in the Seminary. At the age of
thirty-four, St. Tychon became a monk, and was soon appointed
rector of the same Seminary. He also began to teach philosophy.
At the age of thirty-seven he became a bishop and was appointed to Voronezh, but after four and a half years he
retired to the monastery of Zadonsk, where he spent the rest
of his life.

St. Tychon was by nature inclined toward solitude and the
contemplative monastic life; he wished to withdraw completely
from the vanity of everyday life. This was not merely an individual
trait of St. Tychon's; it was a sign of the times. The impulses of the
spirit, the work of the religious consciousness were no longer
connected in any way with current historical life. Not only were
there no proud dreams of a 'sacred kingdom', but the ecclesiastical
consciousness was still, as it were, *outside* of history, absorbed in
questions of the spiritual life. This does not imply an *indifference* to
life, but only a spiritual freedom from life's hypnosis. The whole
world was conceived as so far outside the Church that not only
was there no thought of their 'organic fusion', but, on the contrary, the Christian living in the world was supposed to withdraw
spiritually from it. This is the basic idea of St. Tychon's remarkable
work, which bears the characteristic title A Spiritual Thesaurus
Gathered from the World. This work is marked by a new temper
of mind. The ecclesiastical consciousness does not turn away from

the world, but neither is it captivated by the world. It is not occupied with the problem of making the world better; in every place and on all occasions it strives spiritually to overcome the world. St. Tychon's book teaches Church people to see more deeply into the eternal truths within external events, to free themselves from bondage to vanity, from fascination with this transient life. 'There is an intoxication', St. Tychon wrote in one place, 'not from wine, when a man gets drunk on love of this world, on vain thoughts.' Everything in the outer world is *symbolic*; everything is mystically linked to the 'spiritual thesaurus' or, contrariwise, to the 'secret poison' within man. St. Tychon considers all the phenomena of life only to investigate their symbolism, to explore the secret meaning contained in the world. This, according to St. Tychon, is an 'evangelical and Christian philosophy', which differs sharply from 'external love of wisdom'. It is not a spiritualizing of the world; yet the 'genuine' core of events is to be sought behind the world's bright colours, behind its outward surface. Here, for the first time, a foundation was laid for the idea of *transfiguring* life by giving it mystical meaning; the light of the Church shone in a new way. Not the *sanctification* of life, but its *transfiguration*, was the new hope held out by the Church. At the same time, the recognition of the need for and value of 'assiduous and correct reasoning' runs through the whole of St. Tychon's book. He insists that 'reason without divine enlightenment is blind', but that in the light of Christ reason regains its sight.

The opinion has been expressed more than once [1] that St. Tychon was influenced by German Pietism, and specifically by Arnd (with whom St. Tychon was familiar). But it has also been said that St. Tychon's writings represent 'the first attempt at a vital theology',[2] that his works are 'original from beginning to end'.[3] St. Tychon's mysticism sometimes came close to that of the West (*e.g.* his living and deeply felt experience of the Passion of our Lord), but in essence it was illuminated by the characteristic feature of Eastern Christian mysticism: a living sense of the light of Christ in the world. Hence the extraordinary vividness of the Easter experience in St. Tychon. One feels here the freedom of the ecclesiastical consciousness from bondage to the world; this is

---

1. For example, in Florovsky, *Puti russkovo bogosloviya* [Paths of Russian Theology], p. 123.

2. *Ibid.*, p. 125.

3. A remark of Arch. Philaret of Chernigov in his *Istoriya russkoi Tserkvi* [History of the Russian Church], 1862.

the path of *spiritual* activity in the world, of transfiguration (not sanctification) of the world. This transition of the theocratic idea of Christianity from the 'sanctification' of history and the idea of the 'sacred mission' of secular power, to the preaching of a transfiguration of the world, expresses the fundamental nature of the crisis in the ecclesiastical consciousness, which was exhibited in full measure with the inner flowering of its energies in the eighteenth century.

## 6. STARETS PAISIUS VELICHKOVSKI

*Starets* Paisius Velichkovski (1722–94) went even further than St. Tychon. His name is connected with the whole history of the Russian *Startsy*, and especially with the famous Optina Cloister. He left Kiev Academy without completing his studies, and went, seeking guidance, to the monastic life of the Moldavian hermitages, and from there to Mount Athos, where he shared in the tradition of ancient mysticism. He studied Greek patristic literature with extraordinary zeal and planned a revision of the old Slavonic translations of those Fathers of the Church who were unknown in the Russian monasteries. *Starets* Paisius became a genuine scholar, a student of manuscripts. Scholarly conscientiousness was a characteristic feature of his spiritual make-up, which was in all things very sober, thoughtful, and profound. A large number of monks (as many as seven hundred) gathered around Paisius on Mount Athos, craving his spiritual guidance. Being unable to continue his activity as a scholar and *Starets* on Mount Athos, Paisius moved to Moldavia, where he remained for the rest of his life.

Paisius's extraordinary scholarly contributions give way before his exceptional influence in reviving monasticism in Russia. He combined enormous pedagogical talent with the wisdom of a *Starets*, a clear view of man, and a firm awareness that every man's primary concern is the proper ordering of his spiritual life. Paisius's many disciples went to all parts of Russia. We shall encounter the chief centre of the movement of Russian *Startsy*—the Optina Cloister—more than once in the sequel; its revival in the late eighteenth century, which bore exceptional fruits in the nineteenth, was due to disciples of *Starets* Paisius. What may be called the 'Optina' movement in nineteenth-century Orthodoxy, which was closely connected with the religious currents in Russian philosophy, is an even more important manifestation of a basic shift in the ecclesiastical consciousness. It had essential manifestations in all branches of philosophical analysis, and was connected with the whole religious movement in nineteenth-century Russia. The theocratic idea of the Church was finally perceived as a transfiguration through the inner renewal of man. Freeing itself once and for all from its captivity to the dream of the 'sacred kingdom', the ecclesiastical consciousness profoundly liberated man's creative energies, while preserving his spiritual wholeness. Russian philosophic thought in the nineteenth century was to suffer more than once, and often in tragic anguish, for what had already taken shape in the eighteenth-century ecclesiastical consciousness. But the elimination of the ecclesiastico-political temptation from this consciousness left ample room for a 'Christian philosophy', in the strict sense, i.e. for a philosophy inspired by Christianity. We find the first manifestation of this movement in G. S. Skovoroda.

## 7. G. S. SKOVORODA. BIOGRAPHY

Gregory Savvich Skovoroda (1722–94) is noteworthy as the first Russian philosopher in the strict sense of the word. A study of his philosophic activity is interesting in itself, but it is even more interesting historically. Skovoroda would be incomprehensible taken out of historical perspective, apart from the philosophic culture which developed in South Russia around the Kiev Academy. The appearance of Skovoroda is evidence that the study of Western thought in the Academy was not in vain; we see in his original and independent system the first germinations of what was to develop in the Russian religious mind when its intellectual energy was directed toward philosophic problems. Skovoroda was a profound believer, but at the same time he was marked by unusual inner freedom. His inner freedom, his bold, sometimes audacious, flights of thought, stood in opposition to traditional ecclesiastical doctrines; but he feared nothing in his burning desire for truth. Skovoroda's equilibrium of faith and reason—he himself did not separate one from the other—rested upon the 'allegorical' method of interpreting Scripture. He was very bold in this, often going so far as to reject completely the literal meaning of Scripture for the sake of an interpretation which seemed correct to him. In a sense he fell into a vicious circle: his thought carried him so far that he took refuge in allegorical interpretation in order to remain within the confines of Biblical Revelation; in other cases an allegorical interpretation was the source of his inspiration. He had the genuine insight of faith; he was a mystic, in the best sense of the word, but his reason was unconstrained in its free inspiration, and there were often rationalistic features in his thought.

Although Skovoroda's development was closely connected with the ecclesiastical life of the Ukraine, he went far beyond its boundaries and was essentially in harmony with the Russian spiritual life. He is universally Russian in importance and occupies a legitimate place in the history of Russian philosophy.

Skovoroda embodied his religio-mystical world-view in his own life with astonishing directness. His life was, in fact, extremely unusual. He is sometimes called the Russian Socrates; he himself wrote that 'I intended with my mind and desired with my will to be a Socrates in Russia.' [1] Skovoroda's personality is similar to that of Leo Tolstoy in his striving for simplicity and a life among the people, as well as his moralism.

Skovoroda was born into a simple Cossack family in the Poltava Government. From his childhood he was marked by religiosity, a predilection for study, and 'firmness of spirit', as his biographer Kovalinski puts it. At the age of sixteen he entered the Kiev Academy, but his studies were soon interrupted by a summons to the court chapel in St. Petersburg (the young Skovoroda had an excellent voice). After two years he returned to Kiev, where he graduated from the Academy at the age of twenty-eight. Refusing an appointment in the clergy, Skovoroda went as a church singer with a certain General Vishnevski who was on a diplomatic mission to Hungary. He visited Hungary, Austria, Poland, Germany and Italy, often travelling on foot. Wherever possible, he closely observed local life and attended lectures in the universities. His biographer tells us that he had a thorough command of Latin and German, and knew Greek and Hebrew well. Skovoroda had a very broad education. Ern, the author of the most comprehensive monograph on Skovoroda, points out that his knowledge of ancient authors was 'quite exceptional for eighteenth-century Russia'.[2] Among ancient authors Skovoroda knew Plato, Aristotle, Epicurus, Philo, Plutarch, and Seneca well; he also studied the Fathers of the Church very carefully (especially Dionysius the Areopagite, Maximus the Confessor, and Gregory of Nazianzus). It is harder to say anything definite about his knowledge of European philosophy, but there is no doubt that he knew many authors, for he carried on sharp polemics with several of them. It may be said without

1. Quoted by Zelenogorski, 'Filosofiya Skovorody' ['The Philosophy of Skovoroda'], *Voprosy filosofi i psikhologi*, No. 23 (1894).
2. V. Ern, *Skovoroda*, Moscow, 1912, p. 62.

exaggeration that Skovoroda's philosophic and theological erudition was very broad and well grounded. However, even a cursory acquaintance with Skovoroda's works makes one feel his unquestionable originality, not in the sense that he was subject to no influences, but in the sense that he always thought his ideas through independently, even if they came to him from outside. He was a genuine philosopher; [1] he did not expound his system until he was over forty, and, in general, this system remained unchanged to the end of his life.

Skovoroda's style is highly original and often hinders the reader; however, this should not be exaggerated, as it is by Chizhevski.[2] Skovoroda loved symbolism and was partial to antitheses. But the chief difficulty of his works results from the fact that Russian philosophic terminology had not yet been worked out—many terms which he coined have not been retained in Russian philosophy.[3]

Let us turn once more to Skovoroda's biography. When he returned from abroad after a stay of almost three years, he accepted a position as teacher in a provincial theological school; but as a result of a petty conflict with the ecclesiastical authorities (about the theory of poetry which he was teaching), he was forced to resign. He became a private tutor in the home of a wealthy landowner. However, Skovoroda's independent character and his abrupt directness resulted in his having to give up this position as well. Finding himself at leisure, Skovoroda went to Moscow and stayed in the Troitsko-Sergiyevski Abbey, where he was offered a position as teacher in the Theological Academy. However, he declined this offer and returned to the South, where he was once more invited to the home of the landowner where he had taught previously. The most cordial relations were now established and Skovoroda remained in the same place for four years. During this time, he evidently experienced a crisis, in which his religious and

1. Shpet (*Ocherk razvitiya russkoi filosofi* [Outline of the Development of Russian Philosophy], Part I, 1922, pp. 69–70) arrogantly denies that Skovoroda was a philosopher, asserting that 'in Skovoroda's works I find an extremely small amount of philosophy'. Shpet, who has written an excellent study of the history of Russian philosophy in general, denies the philosophic quality of the thought of almost all Russian thinkers. He is a fanatical follower of Husserl, and considers as philosophic only what corresponds to Husserl's views of philosophy.

2. In his valuable article 'Filosofiya Skovorody' ['The Philosophy of Skovoroda'], *Put*, XIX.

3. This is also true of the philosophic terminology created by Radishchev (see the following chapter).

philosophic position took definite shape. During this period he wrote a number of poems ('A Garden of Divine Songs'), of which we shall have further occasion to speak.

In 1759 Skovoroda accepted an invitation to teach in the Kharkov Collegium (founded in 1727). There he met young M. I. Kovalinski, whom he loved warmly and deeply throughout his life. This unique 'spiritual romance' filled Skovoroda's life with a great spiritual joy; to the end of his days he maintained the tenderest relations with this friend of his youth, who answered with equal affection and, after Skovoroda's death, wrote a remarkable biography of the latter.

Skovoroda did not remain long in the Collegium. However, after a short time he returned there again to give guidance to his young friend. His views once more provoked persecution, and in 1765 Skovoroda left the ecclesiastical service for good. This was the beginning of his period of 'wandering'; to the end of his days Skovoroda had no permanent residence. ' What is life?' he wrote in one place. 'It is a journey; I strike out upon the road, not knowing where I go or why.' In his wanderings Skovoroda travelled with a knapsack on his back (in which there was always a Bible in Hebrew), essentially as a mendicant. Sometimes he made extended visits in the homes of his many friends and admirers; sometimes he left his friends without warning. His asceticism assumed harsh forms, but this only emphasized his spiritual cheerfulness. Skovoroda always devoted a great deal of time to prayer.

Skovoroda's philosophic creativity flowered during the years of his wanderings. All of his dialogues were written during this period (his philosophic works are all in dialogue form). Not long before his death he went to the Government of Orlov to meet his friend Kovalinski, and gave him all of his manuscripts. Returning to the South, Skovoroda died within two months. Upon his grave was placed the epitaph which he had written: 'The world hunted me, but it did not catch me.'

## 8. SKOVORODA AS A RELIGIOUS THINKER

Turning to a study of Skovoroda's philosophy, let us point out first of all that there is as yet no generally accepted interpretation of this philosophy. Zelenogorski sees in Skovoroda primarily a moralist, and explains his system on this basis. Ern, who has written the only comprehensive monograph on Skovoroda to date, takes Skovoroda's anthropologism as the starting point for reconstructing his system. Finally, Chizhevski in his article 'The Philosophy of Skovoroda' [1] starts from the antinomies of Skovoroda's doctrine, the continual antitheses which lie at the basis of all his views. Zelenogorski's assertion is definitely not supported by Skovoroda's works; the moral problem is, of course, always present in him, but, as we shall convince ourselves in the sequel, this problem is not the focus of his creative activity. Essentially, Chizhevski offers a characterization of Skovoroda's *method* instead of an analysis of his philosophy; Chizhevski himself admits that Skovoroda's antitheses apply only to his method of thinking.[2] Only in Ern do we find a genuine attempt to reconstruct Skovoroda's system, and, if we do not accept his exposition, it is because Skovoroda's anthropologism, which is itself indubitable and indeed central, is nevertheless determined by his more general *epistemological* position, which in turn is determined by his religious perception of the world and man. Therefore, one must begin the study of Skovoroda with his religious world, his religious ideas. Skovoroda became a philosopher because his religious experiences demanded it; he moved from a Christian consciousness to an understanding of man and the world. In general, Skovoroda recognized no barriers to the movement of his thought. For him the spirit of freedom is a religious imperative, not the tumult of an incredulous mind. This conscousness of freedom is also evidence of how far secularization had gone within the Church, inspiring reason to bold and creative activity, without hostility or suspicion toward the Church. Skovoroda's personal relations to the Church have evoked the conjecture that he essentially left the Church;[3] however, this is untrue. Skovoroda was a *free ecclesiastical thinker*, who felt himself a member of the Church, but firmly preserved his freedom of thought. Every constraint upon inquiring thought seemed to him a falling away from ecclesiastical truth and justice.[4] All of his works speak decisively of his feeling toward the Church. Skovoroda's thought never broke away from the Bible, and the more his thought matured, the more profound did the meaning of the Biblical narratives appear to

1. *Op. cit.*, pp. 34ff.

2. *Ibid.*, pp. 28–9.

3. Such, for example, is the viewpoint of Ern (*op. cit.*, p. 325: 'Skovoroda, although he was not in principle hostile to the Church, nevertheless found himself in a position of mute, unconscious opposition to it.') Bonch-Bruyevich, the editor of Skovoroda's works, goes further and, on the basis of isolated expressions in Skovoroda, represents him as close to sectarianism.

4. Hence in Skovoroda we sometimes find sharp expressions against 'school theologians', ridiculing of the 'monkish masquerade', etc.

him. Is not this phrase from one of his last dialogues sufficient evidence of his closeness to the concrete life of the Church: 'How many times has the mystery of the Eucharist bound me to God.' [1] But, of course, his intense and brilliant thought separated him sharply from the average type of piety. We know from his friend and pupil Kovalinski how often Skovoroda experienced a spiritual exaltation, a specific kind of ecstasy. Skovoroda himself wrote to his young friend concerning one such mystical experience:

'. . . I went for a walk in the garden. The first sensation which I felt in my heart was a kind of release, a freedom and cheerfulness. . . . I felt within myself an extraordinary emotion, which filled me with incomprehensible strength. A momentary but most sweet effusion filled my soul, and everything within me burst into flame. The whole world vanished before me. I was animated by a single feeling of love, peace, eternity. Tears poured from my eyes and suffused a tender harmony through my whole being. . . .'

In another letter to Kovalinski he wrote, 'Do people ask what Skovoroda is doing? I rejoice in the Lord and find happiness in God my Saviour. The eternal Holy Mother nourishes my old age.' One has only to read Skovoroda's works to convince himself that this is not simply rhetoric, or an imitation of some other mystic, but a genuine experience. And if Skovoroda is to be compared with the mystics, it is not with those of the West—although there is an astonishing similarity between him and Angelus Silesius— but with those of the East.

Skovoroda lived by his faith, and he had not the least fear of losing that faith in the paths of free thought. 'The philosophizing of dead hearts', he wrote with a sigh, 'obstructs philosophizing in Christ.' [2]

In one of his poems he wrote:

> I want no new sciences, only a sound mind,
> And the *wisdom of Christ* in which the soul delights.
> . . . Oh, freedom! In thee I began to grow wise. . . .
> My nature longs for thee, in thee I wish to die.

Skovoroda says with conviction in one place that 'the truth is the Lord's, and not satan's',[3] i.e. he who has found truth has also found God. This idea (which is close to Malebranche in modern

---

1. *Sochineniya* [Works], ed. Bonch-Bruyevich, St. Petersburg, 1912, p. 445.
2. *Ibid.*, p. 313.          3. *Ibid.*, p. 328.

philosophy) gives Skovoroda a sympathy with paganism which was not to be found in any one else at the time—except, of course, those who adopted a position of relativism. For Skovoroda paganism contains an anticipation of the truth which was fully revealed in Christ.[1] In his free striving to penetrate the mystery of being, Skovoroda appears to fall into the rationalizing criticism of the Bible which first appeared in Spinoza and developed strongly in Europe during the eighteenth century. But this, as we shall see later, is only an apparent similarity.

### 9. SKOVORODA'S EPISTEMOLOGICAL DUALISM

From his religious concentration and his constant immersion in prayer, Skovoroda developed a new understanding of life and the world, a new perception of man. His theory of the ways of knowing took form. As a result of his mystical experiences, Skovoroda was haunted by the thought that 'the whole world sleeps'.[2] In his poems we find many references to the hidden life of the world, a life which can be felt only religiously. Skovoroda felt deeply the world's *secret sadness*, its *hidden tears*. Long before Schopenhauer, who felt the sufferings of the world so acutely (under the influence of Hinduism), Skovoroda was constantly concerned with the world's affliction.

> Oh, lovely world! Thou art an ocean, a chasm,
> Thou art darkness, whirlwind, yearning, sorrow. . . .

And again:

> This world hath a splendid look,
> But within it lies the *unsleeping worm*.
> Woe unto thee, world! Thou showest me laughter,
> But within thy soul thou *weepest secretly*.

Thus on the basis of religious feeling Skovoroda became *alienated* from the world. The life of the world appeared to him in a dual aspect. The reality of being was different on the surface and in the depths; and this led Skovoroda to the *epistemological dualism* which became central in his philosophy. There is cognition which glides over the surface of being, and there is cognition 'in God' (on this

---

1. See especially, *ibid.*, p. 355. This conviction was often expressed by Skovoroda.
2. This thought is found very frequently in Skovoroda. See his earliest work and his lost dialogue (*ibid.*, pp. 51, 520).

point Skovoroda again comes close to Malebranche).[1] Skovoroda
insists on the *psychological* priority of sensory knowledge, from which
it is necessary to rise to spiritual knowledge. 'If you wish to know
something truly,' he wrote, 'look first at the flesh, i.e. at its outward aspect, and you will see there the divine traces which reveal
an unknown and secret wisdom.' [2] This higher cognition, this be-
holding of the 'divine traces' comes from a spiritual illumination,
but it is accessible to anyone who can tear himself away from the
bondage of the senses. 'If the Holy Spirit [has entered into the
heart],' he wrote, 'if our eyes are illuminated by the spirit of truth, then
everything is seen *doubly*, all creation is divided into two parts. . . .
When thou beholdest God with a new eye, thou seest everything
in Him, as in a mirror; everything has always been in Him, but
thou hast never seen it before.' [3] 'One must see doubly everywhere',
Skovoroda asserts.[4] This implies the mutual irreducibility, and
consequently the independence, of sensory and nonsensory knowledge.

The path to such a deepened contemplation of being must be
found first of all in man's relation to himself. Self-knowledge, which
reveals in us two 'strata' of being, i.e. a spiritual life behind our
psychophysical experiences, permits us to see everything in this
duality of being. Epistemology becomes a doctrine of the duality
of being itself. We shall see this again in Skovoroda's philosophical
anthropology and his metaphysics. Self-knowledge, therefore, is
the beginning of wisdom: 'If you have not measured yourself first',
Skovoroda remarks, 'what benefit will you gain from measuring
other creatures?' 'Who can discover the design in the materials of
earth and heaven if he has not first been able to look into his own
flesh?' [5] 'The seeds of all the sciences are hidden within man',
Skovoroda asserts. 'He is their secret source.' [6] 'My body, I know,
is established on an eternal design; thou seest in thy self only the
earthly body, thou dost not see the spiritual body.' [7] This thesis is
wholly in the spirit of Platonism, i.e. the recognition of a 'world of
ideas' which 'duplicates' being. Skovoroda tends toward a mystical
interpretation of what is revealed to the 'spiritual eye'—'to know
oneself and to understand God is a single work'. But such a

---

1. However, there are absolutely no grounds for asserting that Skovoroda
was familiar with Malebranche, although he was somewhat acquainted with
contemporary French philosophy, as may be seen from his brief critical notes
on the spirit of the age.

2. *Ibid.*, p. 309.     3. *Ibid.*, p. 96.     4. *Ibid.*, p. 199.
5. *Ibid.*, p. 88.     6. *Ibid.*, p. 257.     7. *Ibid.*, pp. 89, 91.

conclusion would be premature. Skovoroda frequently identifies the 'true' man (who is revealed in us through spiritual knowledge) with Christ: 'When thou recognizest thyself, thou wilt in the same glance recognize Christ.' [1] We shall return later to an analysis of this theme.

## 10. SKOVORODA'S ANTHROPOLOGY

From Skovoroda's epistemology we must go first of all to his anthropology. The problem of man, his nature, his destiny, and the meaning of his life stood at the very focus of Skovoroda's reflections. The basic concept, which Skovoroda analysed exhaustively in his doctrine of man, is the concept of the *heart*. Here more than anywhere else, he stayed close to the Biblical doctrine.[2] What is central and essential in man, according to Skovoroda, is his heart. 'As a man's heart is, so is he', he wrote. 'The heart is the master of all else in man; it is the true man.'[3] The heart is so much the focus and centre in man that 'the essence of all our members is in the heart'.[4] Skovoroda goes even further: 'The whole external appearance of man is only a *mask* covering his members, which are hidden in the heart as in a seed.' [5] This is somewhat reminiscent of occult doctrines. But we should not forget that according to the principle of 'seeing all things doubly', Skovoroda teaches that 'there is an earthly body and a spiritual body which is mysterious, hidden, and eternal.' Accordingly there are also two hearts. Concerning the 'spiritual' heart, Skovoroda says that it is 'an abyss which embraces and contains all things', but which nothing can contain. We cite one more passage from Skovoroda's numerous utterances on this point:

'What is the heart, if not the soul? What is the soul, if not a bottomless abyss of thought? What is thought, if not the root, the seed and the grain of all our flesh and blood, and of all other appearance? . . . Thought is the secret spring of our whole bodily machine.'[6]

All of this is an original *metaphysics of man*, which is extremely close to Biblical anthropology, with unquestionable echoes of the

1. *Ibid.*, p. 131.
2. Biblical psychology has been analysed, to my knowledge, only in an early work—the only one up to the present time—Delitsch, *System der biblischen Psychologie*, 1856 (English translation Edinburgh, 1875). See also the first chapter in Wheeler Robinson, *The Christian Doctrine of Man.*
3. Skovoroda, *op. cit.*, p. 238.      4. *Ibid.*, p. 94.
5. *Ibid.*, p. 171.      6. *Ibid.*, pp. 238f.

anthropology of Philo,[1] but it is also close to those eighteenth-
century doctrines which culminated in the concept of an 'unconscious' sphere in man. Skovoroda is here an *investigator* of man's
nature, although in his various statements one continually finds
echoes of other thinkers. Thus there are echoes in Skovoroda of a
Platonic anthropology, specifically, of the doctrine of the 'erotic'
nature of our aspirations. 'The heart does not love unless it sees
beauty', Skovoroda remarks in one place.[2] To this aesthetic formula
is added a doctrine which is basic to Skovoroda's ethics: that we
love deeply only what is 'akin' to us. Skovoroda's ethics, as we
shall see, enjoins obedience to the 'secretly inscribed law of human
nature'. This comes very close to the Stoic principle of 'living
according to nature'.

But there are motifs in Skovoroda's anthropology which led him
away from his original Biblical basis. In characterizing the 'heart',
Skovoroda uses a conception which had come into use (first in
mystical, and then in general, literature) from Meister Eckhart:
the conception of a 'divine spark', which is 'buried in man'.[3] This
was not merely a figure of speech in Eckhart's anthropology and
ontology; it was connected with his whole doctrine of being, with
the *Seinsmonismus* which had such fatal consequences for his theology.[4] Skovoroda asserts that not only is there a 'divine spark'
(Eckhart's '*Fünklein*') in man, but 'the Holy Spirit is also hidden
there'. In his first dialogue, 'Narcissus', he asserts that empirical
man is a 'shadow' and 'dream' of the true man. In every man the
'Holy Spirit—a divine energy—is concealed', and often it seems
in reading Skovoroda that the 'true' man, whom we all have in
our depths, is 'one' in all men, as a single 'idea' of man with
respect to the many individual men. If this interpretation—for
which there is considerable evidence in Skovoroda—were correct,
it would imply that the individual human being is *phenomenal*. That
which is genuine and 'true', the 'essence' of every man, being
numerically one in all, would rob individuality of all meaning
beyond the limits of the phenomenal world. 'The true man, toward whom we ascend in our spiritual vision, is *one in all of us and
whole in each.*'[5]

This must be interpreted properly, or else one may be tempted

---

1. For a detailed analysis of Philo's anthropology see Helmuth Schmidt,
*Die Anthropologie Philons von Alexandreia*, Würzburg, 1933.
2. *Op. cit.*, p. 75.          3. *Loc. cit.*
4. On this point see Ebeling's study of Meister Eckhart.
5. Skovoroda, *op. cit.*, p. 112.

to see a deviation toward pantheism in Skovoroda's anthropology. Skovoroda does not teach that God is the 'substance' in every man. The above-quoted words refer to the *Son of God*—the *Logos*—*made flesh and man*. The Logos is individual in its being as man, and at the same time It is *everyman*. The 'true man' in each of us is the guaranty of our individuality, but it is not to be separated from the 'heavenly man', from the Lord. Skovoroda does not analyse the relationship of individual and universally human in the 'true man' which is in each of us. When he treats the problem of evil, especially in the later dialogues (see below), Skovoroda asserts firmly that in the depths of each man there is both a 'kingdom of God' and a 'kingdom of evil'. 'These two kingdoms', he writes, 'carry on an eternal struggle in every man.' [1] But this does not permit us to exclude the element of individuality from the concept of the 'true man', for each one, 'participating in' a single kingdom of God, can go from it into the 'kingdom of evil', which testifies to the supra-empirical stability of the individual principle. We must bear this in mind in order to interpret correctly such formulas of Skovoroda's as, for example: 'The tree of life is within our flesh. . . . The tree of life is the Lord, Jesus Christ. The Divine Incarnation connects *all mankind* to God; therefore, after this Incarnation the "true man" is "one in all and whole in each".' [2] The Lord is not divided, although He is in all; he remains 'whole' in each and at the same time He is in all. Skovoroda here approaches a most difficult problem, not only for anthropology but also for metaphysics, that of the relationship of the individual and universal components in being. But he only approaches the problem, he does not solve it. However, on the interpretation of Skovoroda's anthropology which we have adopted, every suspicion that his anthropology bogs down in the impasse of pantheism disappears. The essential duality in man, according to Skovoroda, runs through his *whole individuality*, i.e. is contained within its limits; individuality is a reality not merely on the empirical plane, but beyond its boundaries as well.

## 11. SKOVORODA'S METAPHYSICS

Let us now turn to Skovoroda's metaphysics. He defends dualism here too, but the phantom of pantheism now takes on a more definite character. 'The whole world', Skovoroda writes, 'consists of two natures: a visible one—creation, and an invisible one—God. God penetrates and contains all of creation.' And in another place

1. *Ibid.*, p. 417.                    2. *Ibid.*, p. 442.

we read: 'God is the being of all things; in the tree He is the true
tree, in grass the grass; . . . in our earthly body He is the new body.
. . . He is in all things.' [1] God is the 'foundation and eternal design
of our flesh',[2] there are 'two natures in everything, the divine and
the bodily'[3] and therefore, 'nothing can perish; everything is
eternal in its principle and incorruptible.' [4] How reminiscent of
Meister Eckhart! And how close this comes to pantheism (in a
form so frequent among the mystics)! In one place Skovoroda
directly identifies the concepts 'nature' and 'God'.[5] Here his
thought is extremely close to the vitalistic cosmology of the Stoics.

Despite a number of passages which give sufficient reason for
interpreting Skovoroda's metaphysics pantheistically, it would be
a serious mistake to do this. Skovoroda is essentially much closer
to *occasionalism* (of Malebranche's type). God is the source of all
energy in being; He is the 'secret spring of all things'.[6] If this is
taken into consideration, the element of *acosmism* which is unquestionably present in Skovoroda—the low appraisal of empirical
reality as a mere 'shadow' of true being—takes on its proper meaning. The idea of God's presence and activity in the world runs
persistently through Skovoroda. This is not idealism, for corporeal
being, the whole of visible nature, is not an illusion; however,
empirical reality is wholly 'sustained' and moved by God. 'God is
the eternal ruler and secret law in created things.' He is the 'tree
of life' and all things else are a 'shadow'.[7]

In one of his later dialogues, Skovoroda expresses his metaphysical dualism in Platonic terms, and even tends to the idea that
matter is eternal,[8] which leads him to neglect the idea of creation.
This was connected with Skovoroda's new doctrine of the internal
unity of good and evil; we shall turn to an analysis of this doctrine
below, and there we shall offer an appraisal of this aspect of
Skovoroda's metaphysics.

Chizhevski and Ern both insist that *symbolism* is a characteristic
feature of Skovoroda's metaphysics. However, it is necessary to
distinguish symbolism as a manner of thinking, as mental imagery,
from symbolism in the ontological sense. Both are present in Skovoroda, but ontological symbolism—especially in his doctrine of
the Bible as a special world—does not go deep in Skovoroda, nor
is it essential to his metaphysics.

1. *Ibid.*, pp. 86, 63.          2. *Ibid.*, p. 90.
3. *Ibid.*, p. 243.              4. *Ibid.*, p. 244.
5. *Ibid.*, p. 245.              6. *Ibid.*, p. 331.
7. *Ibid.*, p. 320.              8. *Ibid.*, p. 507.

## 12. SKOVORODA'S ETHICS

We have now to consider Skovoroda's ethics. In Skovoroda's world-view and in his own life, problems of morality occupied such an important place that he is sometimes regarded as primarily a moralist. This is not true, for Skovoroda's moral reflections did not in any way weaken his philosophic activity; nevertheless it is impossible not to feel Skovoroda's genuine moral passion, his constant moral seriousness. Perhaps the epistemological dualism which, in our opinion, marks Skovoroda's whole system, was itself a product of Skovoroda's moral aversion to the emptiness of external life and his craving for a deeper and more spiritual way of life. There is no evidence that Skovoroda's creative activity had such moral roots; it is impossible to deny that Skovoroda's moral views were determined by his anthropology and his metaphysics, rather than vice versa. If a moral approach to the problems of the world did psychologically determine Skovoroda's creative activity, this could have been only in the early stages of his work. Skovoroda's ethics is not an ethics of creative activity, but one of submission to the 'secret' laws of our spirit. This, of course, is not quietism; nevertheless, moral inspiration does not so much impel man forward as define the *struggle* with his own self. In man there lives a secret 'guide of the blessed nature' and 'one has only to refrain from hindering the wisdom which lives within us.' [1] Man's moral path, his internal structure, should give the victory to the mystical energy within him. The empirical energies in man (his will, primarily) hinder moral growth because they continually perplex him. 'Accuse not the world; this corpse is not to blame', Skovoroda exclaims; 'the root of sinfulness lies in man himself and in Satan.' Hence moral growth is the struggle of man's heart, of the spiritual principle in him, against his empirical impulses. 'The will is a hungry hell!' Skovoroda exclaims. 'Everything is poison to thee, thou art poison to all things. . . . Everyone who deifies his own will is an enemy of God's will and cannot enter into the Kingdom of God.' [2]

In the depths of every man is the secret law of his growth; therefore one must, first of all, 'find oneself'. All of the sufferings and torments through which man passes result from his living in opposition to that for which he was created. 'What torment it is', says Skovoroda, 'to labour in an *unnatural* work.' The concept of 'naturalness', or the following of one's vocation, becomes central

1. *Ibid.*, pp. 354, 364.     2. *Ibid.*, pp. 454, 449.

in Skovoroda's ethics. 'Nature and naturalness', he says, 'signify God's innate blessing, His secret law which governs all creatures.'[1] One must 'first of all seek out within oneself the spark of divine truth; this spark, sanctifying our darkness, will bring us to the sacred Siloam',[2] i.e. will purify us.

Skovoroda was sharply aware of the forces which bind us to the empirical world, obstructing our ascent to eternal truth and justice. Once, near the end of his life, these words broke from him: 'O my Father, it is hard to tear one's heart away from the world's *sticky elements!*'[3] Bondage to the world is not merely an infirmity of our sensuousness, riveting us to the world; it is more complex and profound, and is connected with the *reality of evil* in the world, which enmeshes man on all sides. Skovoroda perceived this realm of evil with anguish and torment. 'Let not the abyss of the world consume me with fire', he prayed.[4] But as time went on, Skovoroda reflected more and more on the problem of the reality of evil. At first he advanced the idea that 'darkness was impressed upon us in order that the light might be revealed',[5] but toward the end of his life, he modified this doctrine of the mysterious concomitance of good and evil, his final doctrine being that the sharp incompatibility of good and evil is a fact which applies only to the *empirical* sphere; in other words that the distinction between good and evil is obliterated beyond the limits of the empirical world. 'Know', he writes, 'that there is a serpent; know that he is also God.'[6] This surprising formula, so close to one of the branches of ancient gnosticism, is developed by Skovoroda into a complete theory. 'The serpent is harmful only when he crawls upon the earth', i.e. when he remains within the empirical sphere. 'We crawl upon the earth like infants [i.e. we are immersed in the world's injustice] and the serpent crawls after us.' But if we 'raise him up', '*his saving strength appears*'.[7] The overcoming of evil is thus effected through the overcoming of its empirical aspect. 'If we see in the serpent only maliciousness and the flesh, he will not cease to sting us.' The significance of this doctrine is not simply that evil reveals itself to us as the path to good, but that there is a certain *identity* of the two. 'These two halves', Skovoroda writes, 'make up a *single whole*; the Lord created death and life, good and evil, poverty and wealth, and *bound them into one*.'[8] In other words, the duality of the

1. *Ibid.*, p. 339.          2. *Ibid.*, p. 237.
3. *Ibid.*, p. 499.          4. *Ibid.*, p. 434.
5. *Ibid.*, p. 286.          6. *Ibid.*, p. 512.
7. *Loc. cit.*              8. *Ibid.*, p. 520.

empirical world does not extend beyond the world itself, but in order that the 'saving strength' within evil may be revealed it is necessary to escape the power of the empirical world, i.e. to overcome it spiritually. This is the 'path of *transfiguration*' (the title of the last chapter of this dialogue): 'Try', says Skovoroda, 'to make divine truth and justice shine out of thy false earth', to reveal the eternal aspect in the depths of the empirical. Holding fast to it, we emancipate ourselves from the falsity of empirical being and thus enter upon the path of transfiguration. Evil is an indubitable reality within the limits of the world; evil is not illusory, but the world itself is illusory in its present givenness. Ethical dualism is overcome by the transfiguration of visible into invisible, created into divine. There is a certain *mystical optimism* in Skovoroda, a turning toward the light which is hidden in the world, a striving to behold this light in the darkness, and to transfigure life. 'I love not life, stamped as it is with death', Skovoroda once exclaimed, and immediately added: 'It [i.e. empirical life] is itself death.' [1] The untransfigured world was gratuitous and tormenting to Skovoroda. His soul sought a transfiguration which, even in anticipation, gives strength to our spirit. 'Leave all of this physical corruption [i.e. the empirical world, which bears the stamp of death]', Skovoroda urges, 'and go thyself from earth to heaven . . . , from the perishing world to the *primordial* world. . . . This [visible] sun is not necessary to me; I go toward a better sun. . . . It satiates and delights my very self, my centre, my heart's abyss, an abyss which is not captured by anything visible or tangible. . . . Oh, my heart's God! My very sweetest part! Thou art my mystery; all flesh is Thy veil and shadow.' [2]

In concluding our account of Skovoroda's ethics, let us point out once more that the whole eighteenth century, with its complete absorption in historical experience, seemed petty and insignificant to Skovoroda. The idea of external progress and external equality was alien to him; he often made ironic comments on the subject. Here is one such passage: 'We have measured the sea, the earth, the atmosphere, and the heavens; we have disturbed the earth's womb for metals, discovered a countless multitude of worlds. We construct incomprehensible machines. . . . Every day brings new experiments and marvellous inventions. Is there anything that we cannot conceive or carry out! But the sad thing is that, in all of this, *greatness* is lacking.' [3]

1. *Ibid.*, p. 193.
2. *Ibid.*, p. 406.
3. *Ibid.*, p. 224.

## 13. APPRAISAL OF SKOVORODA'S PHILOSOPHY

From all that has been said the inner wholeness and unquestionable independence of Skovoroda's philosophy becomes clear. It is a philosophy of mysticism, which takes its departure from a firm feeling that the essence of being is to be found beyond the limits of sensory reality. Although Skovoroda does not call empirical being illusory, the hidden aspect of being so overshadows the empirical sphere for him that a strong mystical bias results. This is mysticism, precisely because 'genuine' being is revealed to our spirit only 'in Christ', in that mysterious life which is generated from living 'in Christ'. Skovoroda is not a pure phenomenalist; he does not declare the empirical world an illusion. But sensory being is for him only a 'shadow', a weakened, dependent reality. However, the 'flesh' is capable of opposing the spirit, which testifies to its reality.

Skovoroda's mystical metaphysics is unfinished, chiefly as the result of his failure to solve the problem of the inter-relationship of the universal and individual components in 'genuine' being. Although he is a theist, he very often comes close to pantheism; dreaming of the transfiguration of the individual, he sketches out a path for this transfiguration in which the very principle of individuality begins to lose metaphysical stability. At the same time, Skovoroda continues to hold firmly to a Christian metaphysics, and this remains the basic *point of departure* for his searchings. Skovoroda's strength, the valuable side of his creative activity, consists in the *overcoming of empiricism*, in the revelation of the incompleteness and falseness of sensory being. In this negative emphasis Skovoroda rested firmly on Christianity, on Biblical inspiration. The Bible actually *inspired* Skovoroda; for this reason his various critical remarks, directed against the literal interpretation of the Bible and persistently developing its allegorical interpretation, were completely free from the *rationalistic biblical criticism* which had already found clear expression in the West in the eighteenth century. We repeat: the Bible inspired Skovoroda; it sharpened his understanding of existence, deepened his understanding of man, and led him to an investigation of 'genuine' being. From Christianity Skovoroda went to philosophy, not departing from Christianity, but simply entering upon the path of free thought. It would be historically unjust to forget that Skovoroda, in tearing himself away from sensory being and entering upon the study of the 'genuine' world, moved forward as an *investigator*. His bold theory that the disintegration of being into opposites (good and evil, life and death, etc.) is true only for the empirical sphere, and does not entail a *metaphysical* dualism—in other words, that the empirical antinomies are 'resolved' in the mystical sphere —is a result of *analysis* and not mere peremptory assertion.

Skovoroda's philosophy was without question a product of his personal creative activity, but this does not preclude the possibility of a number of influences on him. With the present state of the materials it is quite impossible to assert anything categorical in this respect; it seems important to point out the extraordinary similarity of Skovoroda's theoretical constructions to those of Malebranche. In Skovoroda the mode of exposition is different and the idea of the Logos is not so clearly central as in Malebranche's system. The rejection of sensory being is motivated quite differently in the two philosophers; Skovoroda thinks biblically, Malebranche is everywhere the rationalist. Nevertheless, the similarity of the two philosophers' theories is often remarkable.

Skovoroda stood firm in his free creative activity, but rebellion was entirely alien to him. He was convinced that in his search for the truth he was remaining with Christ, for 'the truth is the Lord's and not satan's'. Skovoroda never broke away from the Church, but he was never afraid to follow the path of free thought. In the history of Russian philosophy he occupies a very important place, as the first representative of *religious philosophy*. At the same time, we see in Skovoroda an unquestionable *secularization of thought* within the Church. The medieval formula *'fides quaerens intellectum'*, is truly applicable in his case.

We proceed now to a study of this same process of secularization of thought outside the boundaries of the Church, in the secular intelligentsia, which became a definite force in Russian life after the coronation of Peter the Great.

# CHAPTER III

## The Beginning of Secular Culture in Russia

### PHILOSOPHIC TRENDS IN EIGHTEENTH-CENTURY RUSSIA

#### I. GENERAL FEATURES OF RUSSIAN LIFE IN THE EIGHTEENTH CENTURY

'SECULAR' culture both in Western Europe and in Russia grew out of the *disintegration* of an earlier ecclesiastical culture. That secular culture springs from religious roots is evident from the fact that within secular culture itself—especially as it becomes differentiated—there is always an elemental religious quality, a kind of extra-ecclesiastical mysticism. Secular cultural creativity is always inspired by a clear and definite ideal, that of establishing a 'happy' life on earth. Such creativity is essentially 'of this world', but it is strongly marked by 'religious immanentism'. The ideal which inspires secular culture is, of course, the Christian doctrine of the Kingdom of God, but a completely earthly kingdom, created by men without God. Precisely for this reason, the psychology of cultural creativity is inevitably *utopian* in spirit, hoping passionately for a complete, universal, free and joyous realization of the ideal on earth. Secular culture bears the ineradicable stamp of *romanticism*; it combines scientific, social, and other ideas with socio-political *dreams*.

A culture always creates a 'leading class', in which the creative energies and aspirations of the epoch are crystallized. In the representatives of this 'leading class', a specific psychology is gradually built up, one which differs deeply and essentially from that of ecclesiasticism. The cultural leaders are usually so remote from the Church in the depths of their creative life that friendly and hostile attitudes toward the Church are equally possible for them, without serious crisis. But, in *both* cases, secular culture moves spontaneously toward *exclusion* of the Church from daily life. This internal conflict of Church and culture can only be explained by the fact that the secularization of culture, at least in Western Europe, developed as a departure and break from the *Church*, but not from *Christianity*. Thus in the very dynamics of cultural creativity, the very motive forces of civilization, there burns, whether with visible or hidden flame, an age-long litigation with the Church.

In Russia the departure from an integral ecclesiasticism and the creation of a new mode of 'secular' life began as early as the end of the fifteenth century (under Ivan III). But even at that period it was soon complicated by the fact that the new mode of life took shape under the influence of Western secular life, the attraction and, later, fascination of which was very strongly felt by Russians. This process became clear, even 'acute', after the Time of Unrest (mid-seventeenth century) but it appeared with full and almost 'elemental' force at the time of Peter the Great and his successors. At first the way of life of the Tsars themselves and their retinues, and then gradually that of the circles which surrounded them, began to change sharply and rapidly. It was not merely the technological 'conveniences' of life, but even more the *aesthetics* of the Western way of life which captivated Russians with inconceivable force. As early as the seventeenth century a theatre was established, and in the time of Peter the Great various Western customs and mores (styles of clothing, shaving of beards, evening dances at which women were permitted to appear freely, etc.) were imposed under Peter's direct supervision and by his strict injunction.[1] These changes corresponded to inner upheavals which were taking place in the Russian soul, especially its internal secularization which demanded an external expression. The West also had its model (classical antiquity); but in the West the process took nearly two centuries. In Russia, however, the presence of a living and attractive 'model' made unnecessary—at least during the early period—any independent elaboration of a new mode of life. As a result, this mode of life took shape in the upper strata of Russian society so rapidly that within a few decades the old customs and mores were preserved intact only in the provinces, among the people and the Old Believers.

Of course, it was not merely the external forms of life that were altered; there was also an increasing demand for a new 'ideology' to replace the previous ecclesiastical ideology. Everywhere the thirst for education became intense, specifically for secular education as it existed at that moment in the West. Lomonosov's biography is typical in this respect: the son of a sacristan, he made his

1. On this point see the abundant material in E. Haumant, *La Culture française en Russie* (1700–1900), 2nd ed., Paris, 1913.

way to the Moscow Theological Academy, went abroad, and became a most remarkable scientist! The biographies of many
eighteenth-century Russians exhibit similar external features; one
is astonished everywhere by the early maturity, the rapid mastery
of everything significant in Western civilization. For example,
there was the young Princess Dashkova, who later became president of the Academy of Sciences. She was widely educated, knew
several languages, and during her stay in Western Europe enjoyed
the friendliest relations with outstanding writers of the time.[1] The
rapidity with which Russians mastered the most important products
of Western civilization, and emerged one after another upon the
path of independent creative activity is astonishing. But there was
another factor in this rapidity. In breaking away from the ecclesiastical mode of life, Russians in the early period fell into absolute
bondage to the West, finding in themselves no roots for the elaboration of an independent mode of life. This is why there was so much
*blind* imitation of the West in Russia for so long, so much 'comical
enthusiasm',—as Khomyakov later expressed it—carried to the
point of absurdity.

### 2. BASIC PHILOSOPHIC TRENDS IN RUSSIA DURING THIS PERIOD

Russians were also very receptive to the philosophic culture of the
West. The penetration into Russia of the philosophic ideas of the
West (predominantly from France, but also from Germany and
England) has long been studied, and there is an extensive literature on the subject. But there is as yet no complete picture of the
whole philosophic movement in eighteenth-century Russia. This
philosophic movement was complex and intricate. The naïve and
profound, the great and insignificant were interwoven in a spirit
of over-simplified eclecticism. But it would be a serious mistake to
characterize the whole eighteenth century in Russia as one of
philosophic eclecticism. At the same time, certain eighteenth-
century tendencies were *typical* for the whole future of Russian
philosophy; they exhibited traits which later received fuller and
more distinct expression.

We cannot make the present chapter a complete study of these
tendencies. We shall necessarily be brief, mentioning only the chief

1. Her biography was very vividly and interestingly written by Herzen,
whose work remains the best account of her life to date. Of particular interest
is Princess Dashkova's friendship with Diderot.

tendencies in the philosophic movement of the eighteenth century, and touching upon the representatives of these tendencies only in passing. Only in our exposition of Radishchev's views will we offer a somewhat more detailed analysis. In general, we may note the following basic tendencies in the eighteenth-century philosophic movement in Russia: (1) What we may call 'Russian Voltairism', in which scepticism and 'freethinking' must be distinguished from more serious 'Voltairism'. This term, which has become current in Russian literature (and life), is a very inadequate and one-sided indication of the nature of this tendency from which both intellectual radicalism and the essentially different 'nihilism' later developed. (2) The second tendency was determined by the need to create a new ideology of nationalism, with a view to the overthrow of the previous ecclesiastical ideology. Some sought a new foundation for nationalism in 'natural law', others in 'enlightenmentism' (eighteenth-century Russian humanism). (3) The third tendency, which was also secularistic, sought to satisfy religious and philosophic needs outside the Church; Russian freemasonry is a part of this tendency. Freemasonry, as we shall see, was marked not only by a religious and mystical orientation, but also by a persistent interest in nature-philosophy.

All of these were trends in secular thought which marked the beginning of free philosophic inquiry. A pupillary imitation of specific tendencies in Western thought did not preclude the beginnings of original thinking, but we are, of course, still only 'on the threshold' of philosophy. Let us note immediately that besides the above-mentioned philosophic movements, an 'academic' philosophy developed, in the Theological Academies (Kiev, Moscow) and in the University (at this time only in Moscow, where the University was founded in 1755), which contributed its share to the development of philosophic culture. We shall discuss this in subsequent chapters.

### 3. RUSSIAN 'VOLTAIRISM'

Let us turn first of all to what is conventionally called 'Russian Voltairism'. The mere fact that the Russians themselves labelled a whole trend of thought and temper of mind with Voltaire's name is very characteristic. As a matter of fact, Voltaire's name was a banner which brought together all who rejected, with merciless criticism and often with contempt, the 'old ways' in customs and mores, ideas and religion, ridiculing everything encrusted with tradition and defending the most daring reforms and innovations.

On the soil of this wholesale rejection of the past a taste for utopias gradually developed (beginning with an enthusiasm for Fénelon—see below). But in speaking of Voltaire's influence in Russia we must keep in mind his *artistic* works primarily, and especially his novels. This has been very well shown by Sipovski.[1] Scepticism, irony, criticism of the social order, mockery of superstitions, a worship of reason, a decisive rejection of miracles, a worship of everything 'natural', and finally the problem of evil—these were the basic motifs in that Russian literature which moved under the banner of the 'new ideas'. Voltaire was for Russians the chief representative of the 'new consciousness'. We should not forget the particularly deferential attitude of Catherine II toward Voltaire (in letters to Grimm she called him 'my teacher'). D. D. Yazykov has shown that 140 translations of Voltaire's works were published during the eighteenth and early nineteenth centuries.[2] To this we should add that, on the testimony of his contemporaries, 'Voltaire's works were at that time imported in large numbers and could be found in all the bookstores.' Also, as Metropolitan Eugene (Bolkhovitinov) tells us, 'Voltaire was just as well known in manuscript as in print.' [3] Voltaire was published even in the provinces; a Tambov landowner named Rakhmaninov published Voltaire's complete works (a second edition appeared in 1791). To be sure, after the French Revolution Catherine II ordered all of Voltaire's books in the stores to be confiscated—and a palace bust of Voltaire was banished to the cellar.

Russian Voltairism developed into radicalism, on the one hand, but it also had another expression. As Fonvizin tells us, the 'studies' in certain philosophic circles consisted of 'blasphemy and sacrilege'. 'Having lost his God', Klyuchevski remarks, 'the rank-and-file Russian Voltairian did not simply leave His temple as a man who had become superfluous there, but like a rebellious servant, went on a pre-departure rampage, trying to shatter, mutilate, and defile everything.' [4] It is not difficult to see here the first germinations of that unremitting nihilism which entered quite permanently

1. In his article 'Filosofskiye nastroyeniya i idei v russkom romane XVIII v'. ['Philosophical Moods and Ideas in the Eighteenth-Century Russian Novel'], *Zhurnal Ministerstva Narodnovo Prosveshcheniya*, 1905.
2. D. D. Yazykov, 'Volter v russkoi literature' ['Voltaire in Russian Literature'], in *Pod znamenem nauki* [Under the Banner of Science] (essays in honour of Prof. Storozhenko), 1902.
3. Aleksei Veselovski, *Zapadnoye vliyaniye v russkoi literature* [The Western Influence in Russian Literature], 4th ed., 1910, p. 76.
4. V. Klyuchevski, *Ocherki i rechi* [Essays and Speeches], Moscow, 1913, II, 255.

into the Russian way of life in the nineteenth century. Klyuchevski justly says of this current of 'Voltairism' in Russia: 'The new ideas were delightfully scandalous, like the illustrations in a suggestive novel. Our Voltairian's philosophical laughter freed him from divine and human laws, emancipated his spirit and flesh, made him inaccessible to any fear save that of the police. . . .' [1] Together with this 'nihilistic' current, we must consider the Russian dandies, inane persons who were blindly carried away by 'everything French'—language, manners, fashions, mode of living. This often assumed inconceivably comical forms; and when Russian journalism developed under Catherine II, Russian writers and journalists never ceased to ridicule and scourge this absurd yet passionate worship of 'everything French'. This is portrayed most strikingly by Fonvizin in his *Brigadeer*, where Ivan, the hero of the drama, declares passionately that 'though his body was born in Russia his soul belongs to the French crown.'

This break with everything native and national is rather incomprehensible at first glance, and seems to place eighteenth-century Russians in a bad light—the rupture continued until the middle of the nineteenth century. This is true, of course, but the situation is more complicated than it appears. The whole nihilistic temper of mind resulted from the loss of a previous spiritual soil, the absence—in the new cultural conditions—of a native environment precious to the soul from which it could draw sustenance. There was no longer any connection with the Church, which not long before had completely filled men's souls. Life was sharply 'secularized', separated from the Church; an abyss yawned between them. Certain Russians, passionately thirsting as before to 'confess' some new faith, entered wholeheartedly into the life of the West, but others adopted a cheap scepticism, or nihilistic freethinking.

### 4. THE GENESIS OF RUSSIAN RADICALISM

Russian Voltairism in its nihilistic aspects left lasting traces in Russian society, but it pertains rather to the Russian mode of life than to Russian culture. The serious wing of Voltairism, which laid the foundations of Russian intellectual and political radicalism, was much more important. Of course, Voltaire's was not the only significant influence; Russians were also carried away by Rousseau, Diderot, the Encyclopaedists, and the later materialists. In a Dictionary of Russian Writers (eighteenth century) we find

1. *Ibid.*, p. 256.

Diderot, Locke, Rousseau, and Shakespeare listed along with Voltaire. Among many Russians Bayle enjoyed enormous authority; among others it was Montesquieu. Metropolitan Eugene tells of a priest, a colleague of his at the Moscow Theological Academy, who was never without Rousseau's works, just as later Leo Tolstoy wore on his breast a portrait of Rousseau instead of a cross. The Encyclopaedia was translated both as separate articles and as a whole. It is known that the Russian journalist and historian Boltin completed a translation of the Encyclopaedia as far as the letter K. In 1767 a group of nineteen persons was formed for the publication of translations from the Encyclopaedia under the editorship of Kheraskov.[1] The Russian ambassador to France, Prince D. A. Golitsyn, a friend of Diderot (whose trip to Russia was arranged by the former) was so close to Helvetius that upon the latter's death he edited and published his *De l'homme*. Incidentally, Prince Golitsyn's son gave up his honours and secular life, embraced Catholicism, and went to America as a missionary teacher. He is an interesting prototype of another Russian who gave up faith and fatherland—Professor Pechyorin.

I. V. Lopukhin, one of the outstanding freemasons of the eighteenth century, tells us that he 'willingly read Voltaire's mockeries of religion, Rousseau's refutations, and similar works.' Reading Holbach's well-known *System of Nature*, in which materialistic ideas are combined with an unquestionably sincere moralism, Lopukhin was carried away to such an extent that he translated the conclusion of the book into Russian and resolved to distribute his translation. But, as he tells us, after he had finished transcribing the passage, he suddenly felt such pangs of conscience that he was unable to sleep or rest until he had burned the whole translation.

Russian radicalism, recognizing no authority, inclined to extremes and to a sharp statement of problems, began at this period. But because of this sharp break with history, this extremism, there began to develop in Russian minds a tendency toward day-dreaming, i.e. toward *utopias*. This is so characteristic, and left such a mark on the philosophic searchings of the eighteenth century, that it is worth considering in some detail.

## 5. THE RISE OF SOCIAL DOCTRINES

The first utopia to appear in Russian was Fénelon's *Adventures of Telemachus*. Tredyakovski translated this novel into verse (the

1. Veselovski, *op. cit.*, p. 67.

famous Telemachid). Tredyakovski modestly says of himself, 'I have no desire to vie with such a famous poet.' The *Adventures of Telemachus* actually was very much to the taste of the Russian public and called forth a number of imitations. It is interesting to note that toward the end of the eighteenth century a Russian translation of Thomas More's *Utopia* appeared, under the title A Picture of the Best Possible Government, or Utopia (1789). But, of course, it was Rousseau, with his sharp opposition of civilization and a 'natural' order of life, who gave especial impetus to the development of utopian thinking. The concept of a 'natural' order of things had an enormous fermentative influence on the development of utopian thinking. We shall see more than once how strongly Russians were influenced by the idea of a 'natural' life. It *dissipated* the enthusiasm for external order, for the aesthetics of living, for the achievements of the Enlightenment in the West, which had unquestionably had an enormous influence on Russians. The opposition of a fictitious 'natural' life to the actually existing order of Western life liberated Russians from the bondage into which they had fallen, seduced by the life and ideas of the West. At this point the first foundations were laid for a Russian critique of the West.[1] Haumant is partially right when he says that 'Russians did not yet realize that one could condemn civilization, especially that of Western Europe.'[2] In the West, too, the opposition of real life to a fictitious 'natural' order was a result not so much of dissatisfaction with contemporary life as a utopian orientation of thought, which was a *surrogate* for religious hope in a Kingdom of God. For Russians the spirit of utopianism was an original substitute for religious thought, the decline of which was compensated for by day-dreaming. One is struck by the fact that utopian day-dreaming developed markedly in eighteenth-century Russia, simultaneously with a passionate worship of the West. We must therefore conclude that this day-dreaming did not spring from criticism of European reality (on the contrary, the spirit of utopianism was one of the first indications of a critical attitude toward the West) but from another root. This root was *abstract*

1. The first manifestation of this criticism was probably contained in Fonvizin's letters from abroad. But Prince Vyazemski has shown that this criticism rested on Western sources. See Veselovski's just comments, *op. cit.*, pp. 87, 90. Haumant (*op. cit.*, p. 119) rightly connects the 'Gallophobia' of certain Russians with their Anglomania, and notes that the West itself suggested to Russians a critical attitude toward the West.

2. Haumant, *op. cit.*, p. 112.

*radicalism*,[1] which had nothing to oppose to the idea of the Kingdom of God except a utopia. It is interesting to note that Novikov's journal *Utrenni svet* [Morning Light]—which was permeated with religious and philosophic ideas—published a translation of the utopian legend of the troglodytes from Montesquieu's *Persian Letters*. The historian and journalist Shcherbatov of the time of Catherine, whom we shall meet below, wrote a utopia of his own, A Journey in the Land of Ophir, in which he painted his ideal of Russia's future. Shcherbatov, inspired by Fénelon, and by the utopias of Morelli (the *Basiliad*) and Mercier (2440 *A.D.*), drew up, as Florovsky correctly notes, 'a plan for a unique clerical police state',[2] in which the chief overseers were to be priests. Finally, there was the utopian legend of Radishchev's Journey, which we shall examine below.

We have digressed somewhat, but a familiarity with the utopian tendency in the general movement of thought of eighteenth-century Russia will be useful in what follows.

## 6. TATISHCHEV. SHCHERBATOV

From the nihilistic and radical varieties of Russian 'Voltairism', we turn to the intellectual tendencies which were bound up with the demand for a new national ideology.[3] During the reign of Peter the Great a new intelligentsia was formed in Russia, guided wholly by 'secular' interests and ideas. The centre of crystallization around which these interests and ideas clustered was not the idea of a universal religious mission (the preservation of the purity of Orthodoxy), as had been the case formerly, but the ideal of Great Russia. The very personality of Peter the Great, his ceaseless and many-sided creative activity, breathing new life into a state which until then had been somewhat flabby, dazzled men's minds and kindled their hearts with a proud consciousness of Russian strength and greatness. Alongside the 'Voltairians' there arose a new kind of intelligentsia—genuinely cultured, following with great responsiveness everything that happened in Western Europe, especially France, but striving to create a Russian national

1. This concept may be compared to Taine's well-known characterization of eighteenth-century French thought as a kind of 'classicism'.

2. G. Florovsky, *Puti russkovo bogosloviya* [Paths of Russian Theology], p. 534n.

3. 'Voltairism' continued in Russia into the nineteenth century, but it had no serious influence on the movement of Russian thought.

ideology which would be completely 'secular' and remote from ecclesiastical thinking. The figure of Kantemir is very interesting and characteristic in this respect. He lived as a diplomat in London and Paris, was very close to a number of outstanding writers, translated into Russian Montesquieu's *Persian Letters* and Fontenelle's *Conversations on the Plurality of Worlds* (which, by intercession of the Synod, was confiscated). He also wrote Letters on Nature and Man,[1] a popular exposition of the principles of natural science.

Of much more importance for us is the activity of Tatishchev, the first Russian historian. Tatishchev was a very well educated man; he drew his chief inspiration from Hobbes' theory of the state. In his attempt to provide a foundation for the 'new intelligentsia' Tatishchev took as his point of departure the popular eighteenth-century doctrine of 'natural law'. This doctrine rests on a recognition of the inviolable autonomy of the individual, which can be abridged by neither Church nor State. In his Conversation on the Utility of Schools and Sciences, Tatishchev wrote as an apologist for secular life, insisting firmly that 'man's desire for happiness is absolute and is implanted by God'. Tatishchev was the first in Russian literature to develop a system of utilitarianism, taking 'rational egoism' as its point of departure. In these doctrines Tatishchev sketched a theory of the secularization of life, its emancipation from ecclesiastical control. The opposition of God and Church, so frequent among defenders of 'natural religion', is typical of the whole eighteenth century. Tatishchev considers it an *abuse* on the part of the Church to 'forbid what is established for man by divine law.' He comes to a conclusion consonant with the temper of mind of the period: that the Church should be subordinated to state control. Ecclesiastical law may fail to coincide with divine law; in such a case the state power should limit the law of the Church 'for the sake of decency'. The very concept of sin reduces to that of acts 'harmful to man'. In order to avoid such acts it is necessary to know oneself, to give the intellect dominion over the passions. 'God', he writes, 'included a punishment in every crime against nature, so that each crime should be followed by natural punishments.' This idea, which is very close to what Spencer later erected into a doctrine of 'natural discipline', completes the outline of Tatishchev's moral theory, a theory resting wholly on the autonomy of 'secular' life. The very opposition of 'natural' laws, as divine in origin, to ecclesiastical laws, is a clear

1. *Pisma o prirode i cheloveke.* Veselovski (*op. cit.*, p. 57) reports that these letters are preserved in manuscript in the Public Library [in St. Petersburg].

expression of the 'new consciousness'. In the seventeenth century Russian readers took over from the translated stories of the time the idea of the freedom of the 'secular principle' from interference by ecclesiastical laws. Eighteenth-century journals continually emphasized that 'life is given to us in joy'. In Tatishchev's moral philosophy this doctrine took on finished form.

An appeal to the principles of 'natural law' (as opposed to ecclesiastical statutes) was an essential element in the new ideology. Works on 'natural law' were translated into Russian; in 1764 a certain Zolotnitski published a compilation called An Abridgement of Natural Law from Diverse Authors for the Use of Russian Society. We should also note that the idea of 'natural law' was basic for Theophanes Prokopovich, a passionate apologist for the reforms of Peter the Great, who openly preached the secularization of power and the 'justice of the monarch's will'. The personality of Theophanes Prokopovich has been largely discredited; historians have characterized him as a 'hireling and adventurer'.[1] But that he was one of the most enlightened and philosophically inclined men of his time cannot be denied. His opportunism was combined with malice toward his enemies, his assiduous conformity to the spirit of the time[2] with a placing of secular power above spiritual power. All of this is true, but it was just such men as Theophanes Prokopovich who expressed the 'new consciousness'.

In any case, the idea of 'natural law' served in principle as a foundation for constructing a secular ideology and justifying 'secular existence'. Tatishchev did not eliminate religion or the Church; this was not necessary for him. He merely wished to shift them somewhat, in order to give first place to everything 'natural'. Tatishchev, who was thoroughly familiar with contemporary philosophic thought, assured his readers that 'true philosophy is not sinful', but useful and necessary. This same position was held by another outstanding thinker of the period, Shcherbatov, who, by the way, departed from the doctrine of natural law on one point: he refused to recognize human equality. In his History he idealized old Russian life, and declared sadly that in modern times 'superstitions had decreased but faith had also decreased'. He demanded for Russia 'moral enlightenment' as well as intellectual progress. But Shcherbatov, too, rested on the doctrine of 'original' (i.e. natural) rights. His attitude toward the Church was marked by

1. See for example Florovsky, op. cit., pp. 89ff.
2. 'He wrote always with a carefully sold pen', Florovsky maliciously remarks(loc. cit.).

the mistrust typical of his time. 'Our priests and churchmen', he remarks, 'having little enlightenment and no morals, are the most harmful people in the state.' Shcherbatov wrote such treatises as The Rebirth of Morals in Russia, and Conversation on the Immortality of the Soul (in the spirit of 'natural religion').[1] He outlined a programme for the 'teaching of the diverse sciences', in which he expressed the idea that 'philosophy is valuable for what it can do to further the improvement of morals.'

The historical works of Tatishchev, Shcherbatov, Lomonosov, and Boltin—the first Russian historians—were inspired by a national self-consciousness which sought foundations for itself outside the previous ecclesiastical ideology. They stood in general for 'secular life', and they found satisfaction for their new patriotic feeling in a study of the Russian past. Resting on ideas of natural law, and coming close to contemporary philosophic currents in the West, they constructed a 'new consciousness' of secularized eighteenth-century man. This work went even further among those who may be called representatives of eighteenth-century Russian humanism.

## 7. THE RISE OF FREEMASONRY. NOVIKOV

The first important Russian poets of the eighteenth century— Lomonosov and Derzhavin—exhibit a secularized nationalism combined with humanism. 'Great Russia', not 'Holy Russia', inspired them; the national eros, the ecstasy at Russia's greatness, was directed wholly toward Russia's empirical being, apart from any historiosophical foundation. This turning to Russia was, of course, a reaction against the blind worship of the West and the contemptuous attitude toward everything Russian which appeared so strongly in Russian Voltairism. Lomonosov was a fiery patriot who believed that

> The Russian land shall bear
> Platos, its very own,
> And Newtons, swift of mind.

1. Certain historians of philosophy and writers on Russian philosophy confuse 'natural religion' with *deism*, the essence of which is the recognition that God created the world and a rejection of God's participation in the life of the world. 'Natural religion', on the other hand, entails no definite doctrines, except for a general admission of the reality of Deity. As Zielinski has shown (*Cicero im Wandel der Jahrhunderte*, 4th ed., Leipzig, 1929) all the theories of 'natural' religion in Europe go back to Cicero's *De natura deorum*.

Derzhavin, a true 'singer of Russian glory', defended the freedom and dignity of man. In verses written upon the birth of
Catherine II's grandson (the future Emperor Alexander I) he
exclaimed:

Be the master of thy passions,
Be a *man* upon the throne!

This motif of pure humanism became the centre of crystallization
of the new ideology. To keep from losing ourselves in the immense
material on this subject, we shall consider only two striking representatives of eighteenth-century Russian humanism—Novikov
(during the first period of his activity) and Radishchev.

N. I. Novikov (1744–1818) was born into the family of a landowner of modest means, and received a rather meagre education
at home, but worked hard to educate himself. At the age of twenty-
five, he undertook the publication of a journal *Truten* [The Drone]
in which he showed himself a man of great social sensitivity, a
passionate unmasker of the injustices of Russian life, and a fiery
idealist. Combating blind worship of the West, and ridiculing the
harsh morals of Russian life of the time, Novikov wrote with deep
sorrow of the difficult condition of the Russian peasants. In a later
journal *Zhivopisets* [The Artist] we find a fragment from his
Journey, a book in which the bitter lot of the peasants is strongly
emphasized. 'Oh, humanity!' he exclaimed, 'thou art unknown in
these villages.' This fragment anticipated Radishchev's famous
book, A Journey from Petersburg to Moscow.[1] The *social* problem
—the problem of introducing genuine humaneness into human
relationships—became central for Russian humanism from this
time on. Here is the image of the ideal man as sketched by Novikov: 'A rational and virtuous gentleman; he does good to everyone
he can. He thinks that reason was given him so that he might
serve the state, wealth so that he might help the poor, that he was
born a man in order that he might be useful to all other men.' In
defending the equality of all men, Novikov appealed not to the
ideas of natural law, as was usual at the time, but to Christianity.
Novikov's language becomes particularly enthusiastic when he defends the necessity of Russians' remaining spiritually true to their
homeland, while accepting whatever is of value from foreign
nations. This is why he undertook the publication of the Ancient

1. V. Bogolyubov (*N. I. Novikov i yevo vremya* [N. I. Novikov and his Time],
Moscow, 1916, p. 69) justly regards Novikov's article as 'the strongest statement
in the general press against serfdom before Radishchev's *Journey*'.

Russian Library (under the patronage of Catherine II) in order that Russians might, by learning about their past, recognize the 'greatness of spirit of our forefathers'. The work of thought moved under the aegis of reaction against the 'Westerners' of the time, and elaboration of a new national self-consciousness. But in eighteenth-century Russian humanism the fundamental importance of morality became more and more apparent, and there was even a preaching of the priority of morals over reason. Pedagogical dreams, which were so close in eighteenth-century Russia to the utopian project of 'creating a new race of men', emphasized the 'development of the most refined heart'—the development of a *'propensity to good'*—rather than reason. Fonvizin in The Minor uttered this aphorism: 'The intellect, if it be mere intellect, is a trifle; it is *good morals* that give real value to the intellect.' This is a typical expression of the moralism which was a new feature of the Russian consciousness.[1] There was some Western influence here; I have in mind not only Rousseau,[2] but also the English moralists. However, there was also a *native* tendency to give pre-eminence to morals (we shall see this constantly in the nineteenth century, right up to Tolstoy's 'panmoralism').

Novikov's publishing activity (he issued a total of 448 titles) was soon transferred to Moscow, but there it took on a different character. He joined the Moscow freemasons, and his spiritual interests shifted entirely from social to religious, philosophic, and purely moral themes. This went beyond the limits of pure humanism; therefore we shall return to Novikov when we characterize freemasonry. For the present, however, let us turn to another striking proponent of eighteenth-century Russian humanism, A. N. Radishchev, who was more of a philosopher.

## 8. RADISHCHEV. BIOGRAPHY

Radishchev's name is surrounded by an aura of martydom (as was also the case with Novikov), but, in addition to this, Radishchev became for subsequent generations of the Russian intelligentsia a kind of banner—a brilliant and radical humanist, a fiery partisan of the pre-eminence of social problems. However, despite numerous monographs and articles devoted to Radishchev, the legend con-

1. It is interesting that in the first student magazine, which appeared in Moscow in 1764, the preaching of Christian virtue was linked with the natural-law doctrine that all men are 'by nature' free and equal.
2. This is true of Fonvizin, who was sharply critical of the West.

cerning him has not yet stopped growing. He is sometimes seen as the initiator of socialism in Russia[1] or as the first Russian materialist.[2] There is, in fact, as little basis for such judgments as there was for Catherine II's sentencing of Radishchev to hard labour. His sharp criticism of serfdom was not at all new; there was a great deal of such criticism in the novels of the time and in magazine articles like the above-cited 'Fragment from a Journey' in Novikov's *Zhivopisets*. But that was before the French Revolution. Catherine II took a comparatively complacent attitude toward manifestations of Russian radicalism at that time and did not yet think of repressing them, much less of persecuting their authors. But Radishchev's book, appearing in 1790, fell at a very sensitive moment in the political life of Europe. French emigrants were already beginning to appear in Russia;[3] anxiety was felt everywhere. Catherine II was in a nervous state. She began to see manifestations of the revolutionary infection everywhere, and took quite extraordinary measures to 'suppress' it. At first only Radishchev suffered, his book being banned from sale. Later Novikov suffered; his enterprise was completely ruined.

Let us consider Radishchev's biography more closely. He was born in 1749 into the family of a well-to-do landowner; he studied first in Moscow and then in St. Petersburg. In 1766 he was sent to Germany to study, along with a group of young men. Radishchev remained in Leipzig for about five years, studying diligently and reading voraciously. In the brief fragment dedicated to the memory of Ushakov, his friend and comrade of the Leipzig seminar, Radishchev tells of their enthusiasm for Helvetius. Radishchev received his philosophic training under the guidance of the then popular Professor Platner, who was not distinguished by originality and in fact was an eclectic, but nevertheless taught the philosophic disciplines in a very clear and absorbing fashion. Radishchev studied natural science and medicine at length, and returned to Russia in 1771 with a large store of knowledge and habits of systematic thinking. His literary activity began with a

1. P. N. Sakulin, *Russkaya literatura i sotsializm* [Russian Literature and Socialism], Moscow, 1922, p. 63.

2. See Betyayev's article 'Politicheskiye i filosofskiye vzglyady Radishcheva' ['Radishchev's Political and Philosophic Views'], *Pod znamenem marksizma*, No. 8 (1938).

3. The history of the French emigration in Russia has been studied in detail by K. K. Miller (*Frantsuzskaya emigratsiya v Rossi* [The French Emigration in Russia], Vols. I and II). Unfortunately, only the first volume has appeared in print.

translation into Russian of Mably's book *Observations on the Greeks*. In his notes, appended to the translation, Radishchev passionately defended and developed the ideas of 'natural law'. In 1790 his first major work, A Journey from Petersburg to Moscow, appeared.[1] This book, which shows the influence of Sterne's *Sentimental Journey*,[2] immediately began to sell very rapidly, but within a few days it was withdrawn from sale and charges were preferred against the author. Catherine II herself read Radishchev's book carefully (her interesting notes on the book have been preserved) and immediately decided that it showed an obvious 'spreading of the French infection'. 'The author of this book', we read in her notes, 'is filled and infected with French errors; he tries in every way to undermine respect for authority.' Although the author's name did not appear on the book, it was soon discovered who the author was, and Radishchev was imprisoned. At the interrogation he pleaded guilty, admitting that the book was 'pernicious'; he said that he had written it 'in a fit of madness' and begged for mercy. The criminal court which tried Radishchev's case sentenced him to death for having 'plotted' against the Empress, but by Catherine II's decree the punishment was commuted to ten years' exile in Siberia. Radishchev was joined in Siberia by his family and was given the opportunity to send for his library; he was also permitted to receive French and German periodicals. In exile, Radishchev wrote several articles on economic problems as well as a long philosophic treatise entitled On Man, His Mortality and Immortality. In 1796 Paul I released Radishchev from exile and permitted him to return to his village; after the coronation of Alexander I all his rights were finally restored. He even took part in the work of the Commission for the Framing of Laws, writing a long report which, because of its radical views, was not only rejected but severely condemned by the chairman. Radishchev, exhausted and overworked, committed suicide in 1802.

Such was the melancholy life of this unquestionably gifted man. Radishchev was a serious thinker who might in other circumstances have contributed much of value in the field of philosophy, but fate was against him. Radishchev's creative work was viewed one-sidedly by subsequent generations; he was made the 'hero' of the Russian radical movement, a brilliant fighter for the emancipation of the peasants, a representative of Russian revolutionary nationalism. He was all of these things, of course. Russian nationalism,

1. This work has been translated into both French and German. *Trans.*
2. Radishchev himself admitted this.

which had already been secularized before Radishchev's time, adopted in his person the radical conclusions of 'natural law', and became a seedbed of that revolutionary ferment which had first appeared clearly in Rousseau. But today, 150 years after the publication of Radishchev's Journey, when we can permit ourselves to be primarily historians, we must recognize that this characterization of Radishchev is very one-sided. In order to evaluate Radishchev's Journey correctly, we must familiarize ourselves with his philosophic views. Although these views are very incompletely expressed in his works, the key to an understanding of Radishchev in general must be sought in them.

### 9. PHILOSOPHICAL INFLUENCES ON HIS THINKING

Let us say a few words concerning Radishchev's philosophic erudition. We have noted that Radishchev was a diligent auditor of Platner, who was a popularizer of Leibniz. In fact, Radishchev's works exhibit many traces of Leibniz's influence. Although Radishchev did not share the basic idea of Leibniz's metaphysics (the doctrine of monads) it should not be concluded from this—as Lapshin does[1]—that Radishchev was little influenced by Leibniz. Another historian goes even further, literally asserting that 'there is no basis for thinking that Radishchev was acquainted with Leibniz's own works.'[2] To this it may be objected briefly that neither is there any basis whatever for such an assertion as this. On the contrary, it would be strange to think that Radishchev, who had followed the courses of the Leibnizian Platner very carefully, was never interested in Leibniz himself. Just a year before Radishchev's arrival in Leipzig, Leibniz's chief work in epistemology (the *Nouveaux essaies*) was published. During Radishchev's stay in Leipzig, this work was a philosophic novelty, and it is quite impossible to imagine that Radishchev, who studied philosophy widely, did not know Leibniz's treatise (the influence of which is unquestionably evident in Radishchev's epistemological views). Echoes of the *Monadology* and even the *Theodicy* can be discovered in Radishchev's various polemical writings. Finally, the fact that Radishchev was thoroughly acquainted with Bonnet,[3] who, fol-

1. I. I. Lapshin, *Filosofskiye vzglyady Radishcheva* [Radishchev's Philosophic Views], Petrograd, 1922, p. 4.
2. P. N. Milyukov, *Ocherki po istori russkoi kultury* [Essays in the History of Russian Culture], III, 448.
3. Even Milyukov admits this. *Op. cit.*, pp. 451f.

lowing the Leibnizian Robinet, rejected Leibniz's pure dynamism (as does Radishchev) is indirect evidence of Radishchev's familiarity with Leibniz.

Among German thinkers, Radishchev was most attracted by Herder, whose name does not appear once in Radishchev's philosophic treatise. He was especially partial to the French thinkers. We know of his direct interest in Helvetius from the fragment dedicated to his friend Ushakov. Radishchev often polemicizes with Helvetius, but he always takes the latter's views seriously. He was familiar with eighteenth-century French sensationalism in its various forms, and, in general, he preferred those thinkers who acknowledged the *complete reality* of the material world. This alone does not, of course, make Radishchev a materialist, as Betyayev vainly attempts to show.[1] Radishchev's studies in natural science confirmed him in his *realism* (not materialism); it was precisely this that separated Radishchev from Leibniz in metaphysics.

Let us note finally that Radishchev studied closely certain works of English philosophy (Locke, Priestley).

## 10. RADISHCHEV'S EPISTEMOLOGICAL VIEWS.
### HIS ANTHROPOLOGY

We shall begin our exposition of Radishchev's views with his epistemology. His statements concerning the problem of knowledge are quite casual and are dispersed in various places, but they all bear the stamp of the synthesis of empiricism and rationalism which inspired Leibniz in his *Nouveaux essaies*. Radishchev first asserts categorically that 'experience is the basis of all natural knowledge'.[2] In the spirit of French sensationalism he remarks: 'You think with a bodily organ [the brain]; how can you conceive of anything extra-corporeal?' But this sensory foundation of knowledge must be supplemented by reason. Radishchev distinguishes sense experience from 'rational' experience.[3] Further on he says: 'Our cognitive powers are not distinct in their existence; the strength of knowledge is single and *indivisible*.' Here he is true to Leibniz, whom he follows in acknowledging the law of 'sufficient reason'.[4]

Radishchev also follows Leibniz in developing his thoughts concerning knowledge of the external world. 'Matter in itself is

1. Betyayev, *op. cit.*  2. *Sochineniya* [Works] ed. Kallash, 1907, II, 156.
3. *Ibid.*, p. 171.  4. *Ibid.*, p. 198.

unknown to man', he asserts, wholly in the spirit of Leibniz.[1] 'The inner essence of a thing', he continues, 'is unknown to us; we do not know what force is in itself nor do we know how an effect follows from a cause.' [2] Radishchev is equally close to Leibniz in his statement of the law of continuity: 'We consider it proven', he writes, 'that there is a manifest gradualness in nature.'[3] This 'stair-case law', as Radishchev called it in one place, is a principle asserted by Leibniz.

In these epistemological ideas, Radishchev was completely faithful to Leibniz. But he broke decisively with Leibniz as to the content of knowledge, particularly on the question of the nature of matter. For Leibniz, the assertion that matter in itself is unknowable was the foundation for philosophic spiritualism in his general theory of being and phenomenalism in his theory of matter (*phenomenon bene fundatum*). Radishchev, however, categorically defended realism with respect to matter, as did the French Leibnizian Robinet.[4]

Radishchev's treatise exhibits a clear taste for nature-philosophy and an excellent knowledge of the contemporary French and German literature of the subject (he considered himself especially indebted to Priestley).[5] But it was difficult for him to accept fully the dynamic theory of matter—which Priestley espoused, following the well-known physicist Boscovich. 'In analysing the properties of materiality', Radishchev remarks, 'we must take care that matter *does not disappear completely.*' [6] And further on, firmly asserting the reality of matter, he speaks of the 'groundlessness of the opinion that matter is inert'. Like Robinet, he conceives of matter as *living*. Radishchev is not polemicizing with occasionalism, but simply following Robinet. In his doctrine of man, he takes as his point of departure the vitalistic unity of nature: 'Man is kin—born of the same womb—to everything that lives on the earth; not only beast and bird . . . but also plant, fungus, metal, stone, earth.' [7]

Let us proceed to Radishchev's anthropology. He links man to the world as a whole, but he also recognizes man's specific capacities.

---

1. *Ibid.*, p. 182.    2. *Ibid.*, p. 279.    3. *Ibid.*, p. 275.

4. Lapshin sees here the influence of the English philosopher Priestley, whose works Radishchev in fact knew. But Radishchev's realism exhibits too clearly the *vitalistic* conception of matter held by both Bonnet and Robinet. Radishchev attributed to minerals, for example, traits of organic life (such as sexual differentiation!); in this he obviously followed Robinet. See Lapshin, *op. cit.*, pp. 8–10.

5. 'Priestley serves us as a guide in these reflections', he wrote. (*Op. cit.*, II, 205.)    6. *Ibid.*, p. 203.    7. *Ibid.* p. 149.

The most important of these is the ability to make value-judgments. 'Man is the only being on earth that knows evil', Radishchev writes.[1] And in another place: 'Man's special property is his limitless potentiality both to perfect and to degrade himself.' In opposition to Rousseau, Radishchev sets a high value on man's social impulses and decisively opposes isolating children from society (advocated by Rousseau in *Émile*). 'Man is a sympathizing and imitating creature', Radishchev writes. For him, natural sociality is the basis of morals; here he diverges sharply from the French moralists, who derived social impulses from 'self-love'. As a warm partisan of the idea of 'natural law', Radishchev justifies everything that is genuinely natural in man. 'The laws of nature can never wholly atrophy . . . in man', he says. 'Complete morti-fication of the passions is a mutilation. . . . The root of the passions is good: they produce a happy agitation in man. Without them he would fall asleep.' [2]

In defending the right of man's natural impulses, Radishchev protests heatedly against every suppression of 'nature'. This is the basis of his socio-political radicalism. His famous Journey from Petersburg to Moscow is as much an original *utopia*, inspired by a defence of everything natural in those who are socially oppressed as it is a radical critique of social inequality and political and bureaucratic arbitrariness. This utopian orientation is very clearly exhibited, for example, in the story of his dream of being Tsar. After describing the fawning and lying of the Tsar's retinue, Radishchev brings Truth into the story, and Truth, removing the film from the Tsar's eyes, shows him the terrible truth.

In his treatise on immortality, Radishchev sets in opposition the arguments of defenders and opponents of individual immor-tality. His own sympathies tend toward a positive solution. In religious matters Radishchev tended toward the *relativism* charac-teristic of the 'natural religion' of the seventeenth and eighteenth centuries (but not *deism*, as is often assumed by those who confuse deism with 'natural religion').[3]

## 11. GENERAL APPRAISAL OF RADISHCHEV'S IDEAS

Having completed our exposition of Radishchev's philosophic views, we can now offer a general characterization of his world-

1. *Ibid.*, p. 157.　　　　2. *Ibid.*, pp. 216, 261.
3. See, for example, Myakotin's article on Radishchev in the collection *Iz istori russkovo obshchestva* [From the History of Russian Society].

view and indicate his place in the history of Russian philosophy. Although Radishchev's rôle in the development of socio-political thought in Russia was an important, even a great one, it would be quite incorrect to limit our interest in Radishchev to this phase of his activity. Of course, Radishchev's harsh fate justifies the extraordinary attention paid him by historians of the eighteenth-century Russian national movement. He was, without doubt, the high point of this movement, a brilliant and passionate representative of radicalism. The secularization of thought proceeded very swiftly in eighteenth-century Russia, leading to a secular radicalism among the descendants of those who had earlier defended ecclesiastical radicalism. Radishchev, more clearly and completely than others, rested on the ideas of natural law which, in the eighteenth century, were fused with Rousseauism and a critique of contemporary injustice. But, of course, Radishchev was not alone in this. He simply expressed the new ideology more clearly, and asserted the pre-eminence of the social and moral theme in this ideology more fully than others. Radishchev should be thought of primarily in connection with this second task—the elaboration of a free, extra-ecclesiastical, secularized ideology. A philosophic foundation was needed for this ideology, and Radishchev was the first to attempt to construct such an independent foundation—resting on Western thinkers, of course, but synthesizing them in his own way. A nationalist and humanist, Radishchev was permeated with a burning passion for freedom and a restoration of the 'natural' order of things. He was not an eclectic, as is sometimes held.[1] There were germs in him of an original synthesis of the leading ideas of the eighteenth century. Basing himself on Leibniz in theory of knowledge, Radishchev cleared a path for future theoretical constructions in this field (Herzen, Pirogov, *et al.*). But in ontology Radishchev was a warm defender of realism, and this turned his sympathies toward the French thinkers. Radishchev had a strong propensity for bold, radical solutions of philosophic problems, but careful deliberation also occupied a large place in his thinking. His treatise on immortality shows how philosophically *conscientious* he was in examining such difficult problems as that of immortality. In any case, a reading of Radishchev's treatise convinces one of the imminence of philosophic maturity in Russia and of the possibility of independent philosophic creativity.

1. Lapshin (*op. cit.*, p. 37) also comes to the conclusion that in Radishchev we find 'not an eclectic attempt to combine the logically incompatible, but a work of keen and independent thought'.

## 12. LOMONOSOV

We turn from this trend in eighteenth-century Russian philosophy to a third important tendency, of a *religio-philosophic* character. This tendency also followed the line of secularization; without separating itself from Christianity it separated and estranged itself from the Church. We find the first manifestations of free religio-philosophic thought in the distinguished Russian scientist M. V. Lomonosov, who, it has been truly said, made 'the first Russian theoretical attempt to unite the principles of science and religion.'[1]

Lomonosov was a scientist of genius. Certain of his theories and discoveries (for example, the law of the conservation of matter) went far beyond his time, although they were not properly evaluated by his contemporaries. Lomonosov was also a poet, in love with the beauty of nature; and this he expressed in a number of remarkable poems.

Lomonosov (1711–65) received a rigorous scientific education in Germany, and became thoroughly acquainted with philosophy under the famous Wolff. He also knew Leibniz's works well.[2] Philosophically, Lomonosov leaned toward Leibniz, insisting that experience must be supplemented by 'philosophic cognition'. He was thoroughly familiar with Descartes's philosophy and accepted the Cartesian definition of matter. On one occasion he wrote: 'We are especially grateful to Descartes for having encouraged the scientists in their right to dispute with Aristotle and the other philosophers, and thus opened the way for *free philosophizing*.' Freedom of thought and inquiry was so 'natural' for Lomonosov that he did not defend this freedom, but simply put it into practice. Being naturally religious, Lomonosov refused to let science crowd out religion, insisting on *peace* between the two realms. 'The mathematician reasons incorrectly', he wrote, 'if he wishes to measure God's will with a compass, but the theologian too is wrong if he thinks that one can learn astronomy or chemistry from the Psalter.' The attacks on religion by French writers were alien

1. Popov, 'Nauka i religiya v mirosozertsani Lomonosova' ['Science and Religion in Lomonosov's World-View'] in a collection of essays in honour of Lomonosov, ed. by Sipovski, St. Petersburg, 1911, p. 2.

2. Tukalevski in his article 'Glavnyie cherty mirosozertsaniya Lomonosova (Leibnits i Lomonosov)' ['Principal Features of Lomonosov's World-View (Leibniz and Lomonosov)'], in the same collection, offers considerable evidence that Leibniz had a direct influence on Lomonosov, but he does not provide a definitive treatment of the problem.

and even abhorrent to Lomonosov,[1] but he had great respect for those scientists (Newton, for example) who recognized the existence of God. In his well-known formula: 'The investigation of nature is difficult, but it is agreeable, useful, and *sacred*.' Recognition of the 'sanctity' of free scientific inquiry is a basic thesis of secularized thought. Intellectual activity is 'sacred' in itself. Thought is acknowledged as 'autonomous' in principle, separate from the other powers of the spirit.

Lomonosov's religious world is extremely interesting. A careful study of 'Lomonosov's Borrowings from the Bible',[2] has shown very clearly that in his poetry on religious themes Lomonosov follows the *Old Testament* exclusively; New-Testament motifs are wholly absent. This, of course, is not accidental. It is connected with the general extra-ecclesiastical orientation of even religious people in eighteenth-century Russia. It is interesting to note in Lomonosov a religious aversion to the idea of chance:

> O ye who . . .
> Have grown accustomed to ascribe all to blind chance,
> Be assured . . .
> That the Providence of the Most High reigns in all things.

In general, Lomonosov had a predilection for the idea of 'pre-established harmony'. For him nature is full of life; on this point he agrees completely with Leibniz.

Lomonosov expressed his aesthetic delight in nature brilliantly and forcefully. For him this delight is inseparable from both scientific inquiry and religious meditation. He preferred chemistry to the other natural sciences, prizing it for 'opening the curtain of nature's inmost sanctuary'. Here Lomonosov anticipated the philosophical view of chemistry of another Russian genius, D. I. Mendeleyev.

In Lomonosov we find a religio-philosophic position, new for Russians, in which freedom of thought does not interfere with genuine religious feeling—but which is essentially extra-ecclesi-

1. The attempt by a recent author (Burmistenko, 'Filosofskiye vzglyady Lomonosova' ['Lomonosov's Philosophic Views'], *Pod znamenem marksizma*, No. 9 (1938)) to represent Lomonosov as an opponent of religion is based on such strained interpretations that it is not worth refuting.   Equally unfounded are the assertions of the recent author, Maksimov, 'O Lomonosove' ['On Lomonosov'], pp. 31–54 in *Ocherki po istori borby za materializm v russkom yestestvoznani* [Essays in the History of the Struggle for Materialism in Russian Natural Science], Moscow, 1947.

2. See Mme Darovatskaya's article in the collection ed. by Sipovski.

astical. The position is somewhat different in the case of those religious Russians who sought to satisfy their searchings in freemasonry, a movement which, in the eighteenth century, captured broad circles of Russian society with extraordinary force.

## 13. RELIGIO-PHILOSOPHIC SEARCHINGS IN FREEMASONRY

In the eighteenth and early nineteenth centuries Russian freemasonry played an enormous part in the spiritual mobilization of Russia's creative energies. On the one hand, it attracted people who were seeking a counterpoise to the atheistic tendencies of the eighteenth century. In this respect it was an expression of the *religious* needs of Russians of this period. On the other hand, freemasonry, which attracted men by its idealism and its noble dreams of service to mankind, was itself a manifestation of *extra-ecclesiastical religiosity*, free from all ecclesiastical authority. On the one hand, freemasonry led men away from 'Voltairism'; on the other, it led them away from the Church. For this reason, freemasonry in Russia furthered the fundamental process of secularization which was going on in the eighteenth century. Capturing important strata of Russian society, freemasonry undoubtedly awakened creative impulses. It was a school of humanism, but it awakened intellectual interests, too. Giving wide room to the free searchings of the spirit, freemasonry was a liberation from the superficiality and vulgarity of Russian Voltairism.

The humanism which was nourished by freemasonry is already familiar to us in the figure of N. I. Novikov. At its basis was a reaction against the one-sided intellectualism of the age. A favourite formula was that 'enlightenment without a *moral ideal* bears poison within itself'. This, of course, is close to Rousseau's preaching, to the exaltation of the feelings; but it also echoes the trend in Western Europe which was associated with the English moralists, and the formation of the 'aesthetic man' (especially in England and Germany),[1] i.e. with all that prepared the way for Romanticism in Europe. The various occult tendencies which arose at the height of the European Enlightenment also had an influence here.[2]

In the Russian humanism which was associated with freemasonry, purely moral themes played an essential part. Eighteenth-

1. See Obernauer's interesting book, *Die Problematik des ästhetischen Menschen und die deutsche Literatur*, 1923.
2. See A. Viatte's large and valuable work, *Les Sources occultes du romantisme*. Paris, 1928.

century humanism was closely connected in this respect to the moral passion of nineteenth-century Russian journalism. But for the moment it is more important for us to consider other aspects of Russian freemasonry—its religio-philosophic interests and its taste for nature-philosophy. Both of these elements were of very great importance in preparing for the philosophic creativity of the nineteenth century.

Turning to the religio-philosophical tendencies in freemasonry, let us note that the movement began to spread into Russia in the mid-eighteenth century, during the reign of Elizabeth. The Russian upper classes had already broken decisively with the old Russian ways. Some were carried away by a cheap 'Voltairism', others became absorbed in nationalistic interests, or in pure humanism, or occasionally in scientific studies—especially of Russian history. But there were people of a different temper of mind who, because of their spiritual needs, were distressed by the emptiness which followed their break with the ecclesiastical consciousness. The triumphs of freemasonry in Russian society showed that there were a *great many* such people. Freemasonry opened for them a path to an intense spiritual life, to a serious and genuine idealism, and even to a kind of religious life outside of the Church. Among Russian freemasons there were genuinely righteous men (the most remarkable was S. I. Gamaleya); there were also many sincere and profound idealists. The Russian freemasons were, of course, 'Westerners'; they looked to their Western 'brothers' for revelations and precepts. This is why the Russian freemasons expended so much effort in bringing Russians into contact with the enormous religio-philosophic literature of the West.

The translated and original masonic literature clearly exhibits a basic religio-philosophic theme: the doctrine of the *secret life* in man, of the *secret meaning* of life in general. Here theoretical and practical interests fused into one; this mystical metaphysics was especially attractive because of its independence of official Church doctrine, and its obvious superiority to the current philosophies of science. The esoteric character of this mystical anthropology and metaphysics, the fact that it could be approached only through stages of 'initiation', was no less impressive than the freemasons' assurance that truth was preserved in their traditions rather than in ecclesiastical doctrine. For Russian society, the doctrines of freemasonry were a manifestation of *contemporary* life at its profoundest depths. The legendary stories of the temple of Solomon, the symbolic embellishments of books and ceremonies, were impressive not because they

were considered to have originated in antiquity but because contemporary individuals defended them, often with a flourish of
mystery and power. Freemasonry, like all secularized cultural
movements, also believed in a 'golden age to come', in progress.
It summoned men to creative activity, to philanthropy. All of the
basic characteristics of the future 'progressive' intelligentsia took
shape in Russian freemasonry. First among these was the pre-
eminence of morality and the consciousness of a duty to serve
society, a practical idealism. This was the path of the intellectual
life and of effective service to an ideal. Science, questions of world-
view, and the 'inner' religious life (i.e. one free from conformity to
the Church), were all combined to create a specific mode of life
and thought.

A considerable number of freemasons were attracted by the
hope of penetrating to the 'esoteric' aspect of Christianity which
the 'external' Church screened from them. This path called for a
unity of faith and knowledge: reason without faith is incapable of
grasping the mystical dimension of being, and faith without reason
falls into superstition. Freedom is necessary in both cases; both
reason and the mystical life 'flower freely'. Freedom is also necessary in the reciprocal relationships of science and mystical knowledge. It is interesting to note that a translated article was printed
in Novikov's *Utrenni svet* (which was masonic in tendency), demon-
strating the absurdity of Rousseau's doctrines. If men reverted to
a 'state close to nature' they would not be happy and blessed, but
'wretches and scoundrels'. Another of Rousseau's ideas was refuted
with equal energy, namely that enlightenment (civilization) has
resulted in a 'deterioration of morals'. In their defence of culture
and enlightenment the freemasons exhibited a *gnostic* motif: one
must be enlightened—'truly' enlightened, of course—in order to
achieve moral maturity. The highest stages of the spiritual life are
revealed through a deepening of mystical knowledge, and this
ascending path is in principle infinite. One historian of this period
has used the felicitious phrase 'masonic *utopianism*'.[1] 'It is possible
for a finite creature to attain such perfection that he will have a
detailed conception of the whole world', wrote one of the most
profound of Russian freemasons, Schwarz. Shpet remarks quite
gratuitously and wrongly of Russian freemasonry that 'it stifled
philosophy in good morals'.[2] Just the opposite was the case: the

1. Milyukov, *op. cit.*, p. 428.
2. Shpet, *Ocherk razvitiya russkoi filosofi* [Outline of the Development of
Russian Philosophy], Petrograd, 1922, p. 61.

occult, mystical conception of morality required 'enlightenment', combined, of course, with the idea of the good. The moralistic orientation with respect to science and truth which followed from the anthropology accepted by freemasonry (see below), was especially close to the Russian consciousness. The doctrine of the inseparability of 'true' knowledge from the idea of the good extends in a continuous line to our own day.

Together with the call to 'true enlightenment' there is in freemasonry an 'awakening of the heart'. The ascetic tradition of occultism, which demanded the 'excision of the passions', the 'forcing of the will' (without which the 'inner man' could not be liberated), here flowed into freemasonry. Florovsky justly remarks that this is a 'characteristically acute feeling, not so much of sin as of impurity'—felt as an obstacle to the upward flights of the spirit.[1] In the mystical anthropology of freemasonry, immense importance was attached to the doctrine of original sin and the 'perfect' Adam. The 'restoration' of this 'primitive perfection' took on a more naturalistic colouring in the nineteenth century in the doctrine of the 'superman' and the idea of 'mangodhood'.[2]

There is no need for us to consider the details of the mystical doctrine of man and the cosmos as it was developed in the pages of Russian masonic publications. However we shall quote one characteristic passage, which exhibits the essential *anthropocentrism* of this whole temper of mind.

'Without *man* all of nature is dead; all order is chaos. The vine does not enjoy itself; flowers do not feel their own beauty. Apart from us the diamond lies valueless in the flint. Everything is united in *us*; wisdom, order, and precise beauty reveal themselves to *us* in all things . . . Man is an extract of all creatures.'[3]

The freedom of the questing spirit, which greedily seizes upon conjectures, 'revelations', and surmises, in order to penetrate the sphere of 'secret knowledge', is essential for this whole temper of mind. In certain cases this derived essentially from the religious life, but in others it was a baptism in modern 'Christian syncretism', which as early as the time of Sebastian Franck had begun to spread in Western Europe, as a kind of surrogate for Christianity (the most outstanding individual of this second type being I. V.

---

1. Florovsky, *op. cit.*, p. 119.
2. On this point see the above-mentioned book by Obernauer.
3. Quoted by Bogolyubov, *op. cit.*, p. 299.

Lopukhin).[1] The whole eighteenth century (and even the seventeenth) moved under the banner of a 'reconciliation' of the Christian confessions in the name of a 'universal Christianity'.

Such an 'inner conception of Christianity' was very much to the liking of eighteenth-century Russians, especially those with religious needs. The above-mentioned I. V. Lopukhin is an especially striking figure in this respect (it was not accidental that he called his book On the Inner Church). We have already noted how he broke with Voltairism. Having a marked tendency toward moralizing and sentimentality, he regarded the Church as a 'dying institution'. It is not surprising that, thanks to the freemasons, numerous translations of the Western mystics and occultists (including even the defenders of 'Hermetism') appeared in Russian. The most influential was Böhme, and also Count Saint-Martin (his book *Des erreurs et de la vérité*, which was published in 1775, appeared in Lopukhin's Russian translation in 1785), Mme Guyon, Poiret, Angelus Silesius, Arnd, Pordage, Valentin Weigel, *et al.*

## 14. ENTHUSIASM FOR NATURE-PHILOSOPHY IN FREEMASONRY

It remains to say a few words concerning nature-philosophy in Russian freemasonry. This is associated primarily with the name of I. G. Schwarz, who came to Russia in 1776 as tutor to the children of a wealthy landowner. In Moscow he joined the masonic lodge, and then settled there permanently, becoming a professor at Moscow University. The Moscow freemasons commissioned Schwarz to go abroad to establish connections with foreign lodges, and upon his return to Moscow he established (in 1782) the 'Order of the Rosicrucians [*Rosenkreuzer*]'.

Schwarz was an enthusiastic occultist, who infected those around him—except for Novikov, who was not interested in nature-philosophy—with his fiery enthusiasm. In the West occultism was continuous with natural science, and supplemented it with its own fantasies; this was also true in Russia. But just as in the West occultism preceded a more rigorous 'philosophy of nature' (cf. Schelling and his school, and the whole of romantic nature-philosophy), so in Russia occultism, with its persistent striving to grasp the 'secrets of nature', its presentiment of a living unity in nature,

---

1. On this point see Dilthey's excellent remarks in *Weltanschauung und Analyse des Menschen seit Renaissance und Reformation*, *Werke*, Berlin, 1922, II (especially on Sebastian Franck).

created a *philosophical* interest in the study of nature. Like the early Christian doctrine, occultism held that the present face of nature is *corrupt*: because of man's sin, nature too 'has been clothed in the rude garment of material elements'. The task of cognition is to elicit, by tearing aside the shroud of perishability woven by the Fall, the 'visible covering of the Spirit of Nature, the substance from which a new heaven and a new earth will be created.'

This occult nature-philosophy, with its fantastic theories, sometimes came into sharp conflict with science, denying, for example, the existence of Uranus, since this contradicted the doctrine of seven planets and the mystical conception of the number seven. But in general the fantasies of nature-philosophy prepared the way for those philosophic movements which, in the nineteenth century, found new and more serious expressions in Schellingism.

### 15. PHILOSOPHY IN THE THEOLOGICAL ACADEMIES OF THE EIGHTEENTH CENTURY

To complete our study of the philosophic tendencies in eighteenth-century Russia we must acquaint ourselves with the contributions of the Theological Academies and the University of Moscow to philosophic culture during this period. But it will be more convenient to do this in the following chapter. For the moment, let us sum up what has been said, and point out certain fundamental facts concerning the intellectual movement in eighteenth-century Russia.

1. The first and most important fact was the formation of a *secular* type of culture. In the eighteenth century this was only partially completed, but the assertion of intellectual freedom was its moving force.

2. This assertion of intellectual freedom developed differently in Russian Voltairism (in its nihilistic and purely radical form), in eighteenth-century humanism, and in freemasonry; but it was strengthened by this very diversity.

3. Philosophic interests were awakened in all of these directions, deriving their sustenance primarily from the rich philosophic literature of the West. But in gifted individuals these seeds began to grow, laying the foundations for future independent efforts in the field of philosophy.

4. With the exception of the nihilistic branch of Russian Voltairism, the other tendencies of thought, while remaining free and firmly defending 'free philosophizing', not only did not battle

against Christianity but, on the contrary, asserted the possibility and necessity of a peaceful reconciliation of faith and knowledge.

5. First place among the themes which especially inspired those Russians who inclined to philosophy must be assigned to problems of morals and society. There was also a general anthropocentrism of thought and a relatively slight interest in problems of nature-philosophy.

6. The decline of the ecclesiastical world-view left historio-sophical themes without an intellectual foundation; historiosophical questions began to be treated in the form of *utopias*. Thus there arose the utopian orientation of thought which was to be characteristic for the future.

# PART TWO

## The Nineteenth Century

# CHAPTER IV

## Philosophy and Its Fate in the Higher Schools. Early Nineteenth-Century Mysticism

### EARLY SCHELLINGISM. THE NEW HUMANISM

### 1. INFLUENCE OF THE THEOLOGICAL ACADEMIES

A SIGNIFICANT part in the development of philosophic culture in nineteenth-century Russia was played by the higher schools, both theological and secular, in which philosophy was taught. This was, of course, the usual *academic* teaching from textbooks. But it not only accustomed students to the terminology, and acquainted them with the history of philosophy; it also awakened philosophic needs. This activity of the higher schools, which was outwardly imperceptible, should be taken into consideration in a study of the development of the movement of philosophy in Russia.

Moscow University (founded in 1755) was the first higher school of a secular type; there was also a 'Collegium' in Kharkov, which was made into a university in the early nineteenth century, but during the eighteenth century differed very little from the Theological Academy.[1] But Moscow University, in the early period, was also dependent for its Russian professors on the Theological Academies from which these first university professors came. Thus the two Theological Academies in Kiev and Moscow were of fundamental importance for the development of philosophic thought in the higher schools in the eighteenth century. But, from the beginning of the eighteenth century, theological seminaries were also active in various other cities (there were 44 of them in Russia during the eighteenth century), in which philosophy was taught and from which outstanding seminarists were often sent abroad (to Germany) to be prepared for professorships.

1. Theology was introduced into the curriculum of the Kharkov Collegium as early as 1734.

The philosophy courses in the Theological Academies and seminaries were given in Latin for a long time; they were either translations or reworkings of foreign textbooks in philosophy. The content of these courses depended solely on whether Catholic or Protestant textbooks were taken as models. The theology textbooks compiled by Theophanes Prokopovich provided some of the most thorough and successful courses, and were very widely used in Russia.

The teaching of philosophy in the Theological Academies should not be undervalued. We know from our study of Skovoroda how thoroughly the history of philosophy was studied in the Kiev Theological Academy. Theophanes Prokopovich was thoroughly acquainted with both ancient and modern philosophy (from Descartes to his own contemporaries), although he himself followed Suárez in many respects. Somewhat later the textbooks of Baumeister, a follower of Christian Wolf, came into vogue in the theological schools. Through these schools the influence of German *Pietism* began to affect first the Russian students and then broad circles of Russian society. In this respect the figure of Simon Todorski (1701–54) is very interesting. He taught in the Kiev Theological Academy, and went from there to Halle, which was at the time a centre of Pietism. There he translated into Russian Johann Arnd's *On True Christianity*, which was very influential in Russia in the eighteenth and early nineteenth centuries. Even more remarkable and influential was Platon Levshin (Metropolitan of Moscow), who was thoroughly familiar with the French philosophic literature of his time (Voltaire, Rousseau, Helvetius, *et al.*), and concerning whom the Austrian emperor, Joseph II, on his visit to Russia, said that he was '*plus philosophe que prêtre*'. Florovsky remarks, not without irony, that he may be considered a representative of 'churchified Pietism.' [1] Pietism did actually attract Russian ecclesiastical circles, as was evident in the early nineteenth century when a 'Bible Society' was formed in Russia. The influence of Pietism was also evident in Metropolitan Platon's theology.

The development of philosophy in the theological schools was determined not only by their dependence on Western philosophic tendencies but also by their *ecclesiastical function.*. This gave direction to, but also obstructed, philosophic thought. It was no accident that Skovoroda, when he had freely and boldly developed his own Christian philosophy, refused an academic position—with

1. G. Florovsky, *Puti russkovo bogosloviya* [Paths of Russian Theology], p. 166.

the exception, as we have seen, of brief experiments. Creative philosophic movements did not begin in the theological schools until the nineteenth century. The first significant representative of such a movement was Professor Golubinski (1795–1854) of the Moscow Theological Academy. We shall speak of him below in connection with academic philosophy.

## 2. PHILOSOPHY IN MOSCOW UNIVERSITY

In Moscow University, of course, conditions for the development of philosophy were freer. It was not the case, as Shpet asserts, that university philosophy, 'having taken its first step, fell into a paralytic state'.[1] Such a judgment merely reveals Shpet's un-historical and tendentious approach to the history of Russian philosophy. The first *Russian* professors of philosophy in Moscow University (we shall speak of the foreigners later)—Popovski, Syreishchikov, Sinkovski, Anichkov, Bryantsev—actually gave their courses from Western text-books. But even among these men we find two different tendencies: some inclined toward Voltairism, which was popular at the time, others toward British philosophy, i.e. pure empiricism. We should note that teachers of philosophy usually taught other subjects; for example, Professor Anichkov taught mathematics in addition to philosophy. The teaching of 'natural law' was also very close to philosophy. We have already mentioned 'natural law' as one of the ideological foundations of the eighteenth-century Russian humanists. Toward the end of the eighteenth century the teaching of 'natural law' was viewed with suspicion as a hotbed of the 'revolutionary infection'. One of those to suffer was the scholar Desnitski, who had studied in England and was a follower of Hume and Adam Smith. He had been a student at the Moscow Theological Academy, and, when he returned from abroad, be-came a professor at Moscow University. Even before the French Revolution he had to quit his position. This happened later in the nineteenth century to Kunitsyn, another talented teacher of 'natural law', at St. Petersburg University.

The professors of philosophy named above were not distinguished by philosophic talent, but they do not deserve the scorn which is often heaped upon them by historians.[2] It is incorrect to say, as

1. G. Shpet, *Ocherk razvitiya russkoi filosofi* [Outline of the Development of Russian Philosophy], p. 88.
2. For example, the derogatory remarks in A. Koyré, *La Philosophie et le problème national en Russie au début du XIXᵉ siècle*, Paris, 1929, p. 47.

Shpet, for example, does, that 'the university professors of the eighteenth century merely diverted themselves [!] with philosophy.'[1] We should not forget that philosophic interests were highly developed in the broadest circles of Russian society during the second half of the eighteenth century; and the university professors were not beneath this level. We should recognize the truth of what Domashnev, the president of the Academy of Sciences, said in his speech of greeting to the Swedish king upon the latter's arrival in Russia (1777): 'Our age is honoured with the name "philosophic" because the philosophic spirit has become the *spirit of the time*, the sacred principle of laws and morals.'

Of course, this 'philosophic spirit' often suffered from over-simplified eclecticism, but at least there was no primitivism in the university professors whom we have mentioned. We should not forget that their teaching and writing were under constant and vigilant surveillance. When Anichkov published his dissertation (in 1769) on the theme of 'natural religion'—which corresponded to the prevalent tendencies of Western Europe—his book was burned as atheistic. We should realize that Russian society at this time enjoyed more freedom than the professors! This is paradoxical but true. Voluntary 'guardians' followed the professors' lectures constantly; the punishment meted out to Desnitski, the harsh measures taken against Anichkov's dissertation, were not isolated, and they were renewed from time to time. The teaching of philosophy in the Theological Academies was, it is true, protected by the ecclesiastical character of the Academy; the lectures were 'followed' comparatively little. But the university professors were constantly subject to vigilant surveillance, often with the participation of their own colleagues! This created very difficult conditions for creative work. We shall see below, for example, how the first Russian Schellingian, D. M. Vellanski, was forced out of the university by his own colleagues.

Nevertheless, it was impossible to halt the growth of philosophic thought. At the very beginning of the nineteenth century, translations of some of Kant's works (secondary ones to be sure) appeared.[2] Nadezhdin, who later became a professor, tells us that when he entered the Moscow Theological Academy (in 1820) a manu-

---

1. Shpet, *op. cit.*, p. 57.

2. A general survey of Kant's philosophy was given in a book translated from the French [!] in 1807. *The Foundations of the Metaphysics of Morals* and *On the Sublime and Beautiful* were translated from the original in 1803 and 1804 respectively.

script translation of Kant's *Critique of Pure Reason* was passing from hand to hand. That Kant was spoken of in Moscow as an outstanding philosopher as early as the 1780's is evident from Karamzin's 'Letters of a Russian Traveller'. But, though Russian society enjoyed a certain freedom in the choice of philosophic tendencies, the freedom of university professors was constantly limited by surveillance. As a result the philosophic temper of mind of those professors who did not follow modern German thinkers (these latter were often accused of atheism) could be expressed more freely. That is why Russians, from the end of the eighteenth century, were afraid to declare themselves openly as followers of Kant, although they knew and studied him. However, the followers of British empiricism could express their views freely and without fear. In fact, we have the example of Osipovski, a professor of mathematics at Kharkov University and an outstanding scholar, who criticized Kant in his works and openly ridiculed those who 'philosophize about nature *a priori*'.[1] Perevoshchikov, another mathematician and astronomer (at Moscow University), combated Kant's doctrines in his lectures, in the name of empiricism.

We must consider all of this in our appraisal of the development of Russian philosophic culture in the higher schools during the eighteenth and early nineteenth centuries. We should not be surprised to find so much eclecticism in the professors of philosophy of the period; this was much more 'comfortable' in the external sense. There were, of course, *bona fide* eclectics, but many thinkers simply 'insured' themselves by professing eclecticism. This is a very depressing aspect of the history of Russian philosophic movements, and it hung over philosophic thought for a long time, sometimes becoming genuine persecution. We shall encounter this more than once in the sequel. It also obliges us to be more cautious in our historical appraisal of university philosophy.

### 3. MYSTICISM IN RUSSIAN SOCIETY AT THE BEGINNING OF THE NINETEENTH CENTURY

The eighteenth century was, of course, only the prologue to the development of philosophy in Russia. However, the various tendencies which were evident in the eighteenth century (see the preceding chapter) were not accidental; they all appeared later—in the nineteenth century—in more mature and distinct form. In

---

1. Cf. the philosophic position of the celebrated Russian mathematician Lobachevski.

any case, the eighteenth century in Russia won for philosophy a definite place, at the same time that it reinforced its secular character. Kireyevski's description of the spiritual atmosphere of the early nineteenth century applies fully to the eighteenth: 'The word "philosophy" had at that time something *magical* about it.'[1] Philosophy awakened hopes which went far beyond the limits of its possibilities; men expected from it not so much answers to the theoretical problems of the mind as solutions to the problems of life. This was not an elimination of theoretical problems, but a demand for an *integral synthesis*, analogous to that provided by religion. Philosophy became the principal channel for creative searchings precisely because it was regarded as a *secular substitute* for an ecclesiastical world-view. However, we should note that the secular tendencies, the defence of an untrammelled freedom of philosophic thought, were not necessarily connected at this time with rationalistic trends. We find the same thing, for example, even in those who defended the primacy of *feeling* over reason. This is especially important to keep in mind if we are to understand why the word 'philosophy' had something 'magical' about it. A significant place was reserved in philosophic searchings for the demands of feeling (predominantly aesthetic feeling, as we shall see below). Hence the enthusiasm which was so characteristic of the philosophizing youth of early nineteenth-century Russia.

Let us consider first the manifestations of *mysticism* in Russian society at the beginning of the nineteenth century. The destruction of freemasonry during the last years of the reign of Catherine II was followed, during the short reign of Paul I, and especially of Alexander I, by a renaissance, even a flowering, of mysticism. Mysticism in general proved very stable. The stability of mystical tendencies in Russian society (we are speaking of extra-ecclesiastical mysticism throughout) cannot be attributed to foreign influences or external historical conditions. Evidently there was some need of the Russian soul which found satisfaction neither in the Church nor in general culture. I think that this was a psychological metamorphosis of that same religious trait which we have already encountered in the Old Believers, who gave it clearest expression, and which may be called *theurgical*. It is not a matter of knowledge of God, or of a 'sense' of God, but of *activity in God*, specifically, the *transfiguration of life*. It is precisely at this point that the theurgical idea borders closely upon *magic*, and may change imperceptibly into it. We have already noted that among the Russian Old Believers

1. Kireyevski, *Sochineniya* [Works], Moscow, 1911, II, 132.

—and, earlier, in the whole ecclesiastical society—the dream of transfiguring the natural order into a sacred order, into the Kingdom of God, rested on a faith in the 'force of piety' (see Ch. I, §10). In due course this dream of the transfiguration of life, which provided an outlet for accumulated energies, overflowed into the essentially theurgical idea of 'Moscow—the third Rome', of a sacred 'eternal kingdom'. But when, in the course of a single century (from the early seventeenth to the mid-eighteenth), this earlier dream of a 'sacred kingdom' died out in the Russian soul and new movements of a secular character kindled hopes in the 'force of piety', the resulting spiritual vacuum generated a torment of spirit and a passionate need for creative dynamism of *some* kind, even outside the Church. Was there not within the Church itself, in the silence of its monasteries, the same concentration of theurgical hopes which found its expression in the 'spiritual activity' that penetrated everywhere, thanks to Paisius Velichkovski (see Ch. II, § 6)? The theocratic idea—as a doctrine of 'sacred power'—definitely faded from the Russian ecclesiastical consciousness. As a result, this consciousness was wholly purged of the theocratic illusion. At precisely this period *Starets* Serafim Sarovski, with his stress on 'gaining the Holy Spirit' as the purpose of life, appeared upon the scene. There was a specific *polarization* of the theurgical idea; the dream of transfiguring historical being into the Kingdom of God through the 'force of piety' faded out of the ecclesiastical consciousness. But the theurgical demand made itself felt with new insistence in the secularized consciousness, no longer counting on the 'force of piety', but on other life forces which now began to take on the character of 'sacred' (though extra-ecclesiastical) energies. The various trends of early nineteenth-century mysticism here stand in a position of first importance. There were many of them at this time, but for us it is important to consider only two mystics, Labzin and Speranski.

### 4. LABZIN

A. F. Labzin (1769–1825) very early displayed outstanding talent, especially in mathematics (he studied higher mathematics to the end of his life). At the age of sixteen he came under the influence of Professor Schwarz, the freemason—founder of the Rosicrucian Order in Moscow—under whose guidance he studied philosophy extensively, feeling himself profoundly attracted to it. There is no definite evidence that Labzin was enthusiastic about Schwarz's occult ideas, although Pypin, for example, considers Labzin a 'continuer of Rosicrucianism in literature'.[1] Labzin undertook the translation and publication of mystical books, such as Eckartshausen's *Key to the Mysteries of Nature*, 1804, *Vital Hieroglyphics for the Human Heart*, 1803, etc. In 1806 he began to publish the *Sionski vestnik* [Zion's Herald], which was an immediate and widespread success. However, this journal was soon closed and did not resume publication until 1817, when Alexander I turned decisively toward mysticism. A branch of the British Bible Society was formed in Russia, and a kind of 'universal Christianity' was implanted from above. Criticism of Western sects was forbidden. The whole spiritual atmosphere of the time exhibited a triumph of 'nonecclesiastical Christianity'. This was strikingly represented by the Quakers, who had great success both with Alexander I and in the general religious movement of the time. In this atmosphere Labzin resumed publication of his *Sionski vestnik*, warmly developing the idea of 'inner Christianity', and calling upon Russians to 'awake'. But this 'awakening', according to Labzin, required no 'outward acts'; it is necessary, for the 'perfection of the soul and of the whole man', for 'union with the heavenly world', to combat the influence of the material world upon the soul. *Magnetism*, which frees the soul from the body, is, according to Labzin, the means for doing this.

Labzin was resolutely opposed to credal divisions; he even asserted that the faith of Christ 'does not separate believers from nonbelievers' or 'Old-Testament man from New', that 'Christianity existed from the creation of the world', that 'the Church of Christ is boundless, embracing the whole human race'. Labzin spoke of Holy Scripture as a '*mute* preceptor which points symbolically to the living teacher dwelling within the heart'. 'The outer church is a crowd of public, inferior Christians, like Job on the dung-heap.' Labzin, in this preaching of nonecclesiastical Christianity, which shows clear signs of a secularism verging on conflict with the Church, openly followed the Quakers. In his justificatory letter (when he decided, in view of the obstructions of censorship, to discontinue his journal) he wrote that his 'models' were Böhme, Stilling, and Saint-Martin.

It would be erroneous to conclude that Labzin gave no place to reason. His mysticism did not deny the importance of reason in the 'lower' stages of spiritual enlightenment. 'It is an offence to faith', he wrote, 'to say that faith demands the sacrifice of reason; on the contrary, reason is the *ground* of faith, . . . but faith asserts what

1. Pypin, *Religioznyie dvizheniya pri Aleksandre I* [Religious Movements under Alexander I], p. 99.

reason understands confusedly.' 'Reason leads man to the doors of the temple, but it cannot bring him within. Faith may be dispensed with; but reason is eternal, for man is a rational being.' [1] These statements are an interesting revelation of Labzin's closeness to the rationalistic tendencies of the time,[2] as well as to the first germination of the theurgical conceptions, which sought in a knowledge of the 'secrets of nature'—for example, magnetism, in which everyone was interested at the time—a key to higher revelations (outside the Church).

Labzin's life ended unhappily. He was exiled to a remote province—because of a sharp word concerning persons close to the Tsar. However, he found warm admirers there who made his last days easier.

### 5. SPERANSKI

The mysticism of M. M. Speranski (1772–1834), an outstanding political figure under Alexander I, exhibits different characteristics. His career was marked by strikingly abrupt changes. He came from the people, but began very early to manifest exceptional talents at school. Upon graduation from the Theological Seminary in St. Petersburg (later renamed 'Academy'), Speranski, who had worked very hard in school, went into government service rather than scholarly work, and as a young man became closely associated with Alexander I, as a kind of 'prime minister'. In 1812, because of slander, he was relieved of his positions and exiled to a remote province. He gradually rehabilitated himself, eventually returning to government work; under Nicholas I he carried out the immense and extremely important work of codifying the laws.

The philosophic education which Speranski received at the St. Petersburg Theological Academy did not provide him with a finished world-view. His mind, which inclined to mathematics and abstract theory, was at its best in juridical thought, to which he owed his extraordinary career, a career which took him from a lowly rank to the highest rung on the ladder of government service. However, his spontaneous religiosity was not suppressed. As in many other outstanding Russians of his time, religious needs were very strong in Speranski; but he was not much attracted by

1. Quoted by Kolyupanov, *Biografiya A. I. Koshelyova* [A Biography of A. I. Koshelyov], I, 170–6.

2. Labzin's friend Dmitriyev testifies to this in his memoirs. 'His reason', he wrote of Labzin, 'conceived everything clearly and simply, grounded everything on strict necessity and on the law which unites visible and invisible, earthly and heavenly. Such, I thought, is the *science* of religion. . . .'

the concrete life of the Church, and ecclesiastical doctrine seemed dry to him. He felt that it did not express the full profundity of Christian moralism.

'The inward path is very different', he wrote in a letter, 'from the outward path taken by many Christians. What I call the outward path is a *moral religion* from which secular theologians have crowded out the Divine teaching; what I call the outward path is a mutilated Christianity, *overlaid with all the colours of the sensuous world* [i.e. secularized!], and consenting in a policy of indulgence toward the flesh and the passions . . . , a weak, *deviating*, compromising Christianity which differs only verbally from pagan moral doctrine.'

These harsh words, which we will meet later in Herzen, for example, and to which many Russian radicals would willingly have subscribed, were written by Speranski even before he turned wholeheartedly to mysticism, and are thus the more interesting. Speranski's renunciation of the Church's conception of Christianity was motivated—as was the case with many of his contemporaries—by his search for a 'pure' Christianity (not 'deviating' or 'compromising'), i.e. an 'inner' Christianity. In 1804, the year in which the above-quoted letter was written, Speranski became friendly with a mystic whom we have already met, I. V. Lopukhin, author of The Inner Church and other books (see the preceding chapter), who undertook to direct Speranski's mystical self-education. From Böhme, Saint-Martin, and other occult mystics, Speranski turned to Madame Guyon, Fénelon, and the Church Fathers. He gradually developed a new mystical world-view, critical of the 'common sense' which blocks one's feeling for the 'mystery of life'. In a letter to his daughter, he even praised 'day-dreaming' for tearing us away from the 'calculations of life'.[1] 'We all live in a kind of madness', he wrote in another letter to his daughter, 'for we are wholly immersed in the passing moment, heedless of eternity.'[2] This longing for eternity does not entail a break with earthly life, but only with the superficial perception of life. To his friend Tseier he wrote: 'The Kingdom of God is within us, but we *ourselves are not*; thus it is necessary for us to return within.' Speranski went very far in distinguishing the 'true' and 'false' conceptions of Christianity. Here is a characteristic passage, full of sharp and bitter accusations against the Church.

1. *Pisma k docheri* [Letters to My Daughter] (1869 ed.), p. 130.
2. *Ibid.*, pp. 236f.

'The Anti-Christ has transformed his host; he has given them the outward aspect of Christian warriors, and assured *his* warriors that they are really warriors of Christ. . . . He has invented an ideal of Christ for them . . .; to inward fasting he has opposed outward fasting, to spiritual prayer prayer of many words, to resignation of spirit humiliation of the flesh. In a word, he has created a *complete system of false Christianity*.'[1]

This accusation of contemporary Church Christianity exhibits an interesting characteristic of the secular religious thought of the time, which considered itself the bearer of 'genuine' Christianity: it was ready to repeat with Speranski the ancient charges of the Old Believers, to view the Church as a product of the Anti-Christ! We shall find this theme more than once in Russian religio-philosophic searchings—for example, in Leo Tolstoy.

In criticizing the church as a 'system of false Christianity', Speranski did not reject the mysteries of the Church; here his consciousness was divided, and because of this certain scholars tend to conclude that his critique of the Church applied only to its perversions, not to its essence.[2] But this whole period, especially in Russia, moved under the sign of a kind of *universal* and *supraecclesiastical* Christianity. In this respect, Speranski was in complete harmony with his time. But it should not be thought that Speranski was concerned only with 'inner' Christianity. He put forward, for the first time in Russian (secular) religious thought, the idea of a *Christianization of social life*, later called 'social Christianity'. The tendencies of French religious thought which inclined toward social Christianity appeared later, so that Speranski was entirely original on this point. This aspect of his theories is interesting because it proved so very stable in Russian thought. Speranski's most important statements on this subject are to be found in his letters to Tseier. 'Those men', Speranski wrote, 'who assert that the spirit of the Kingdom of God is incompatible with the principles of political societies are mistaken.' And further: 'I do not know a single question of state which cannot be referred to the New Testament.' [3] Speranski forgets here the sharp distinction in the New Testament itself between that which is God's and that which is Caesar's. This is not naïveté, of course, nor an accidental

1. Note entitled 'The Anti-Christ' in the collection *V pamyat gr. M. M. Speranskovo* [In Memory of Count M. M. Speranski], St. Petersburg, 1872.
2. See Bishop Theophanes' very favourable opinion of Speranski, for example, p. 7, of the book *Pisma o dukhovnoi zhizni* [Letters on the Spiritual Life].
3. *Rus. Arkhiv*, 1870.

mistake. In defending the idea of the transfiguration of political life 'in the spirit of the Kingdom of God', Speranski essentially brought Russian (secular) thought back to a utopia with which we are already familiar, the utopia of the 'sacred Kingdom'. The dream of 'Moscow—the third Rome' included the expectation of an 'eternal' and hence righteous kingdom. From this conviction an autocratic ideology arose, permeated with the faith that the antinomy of God and Caesar is resolved in the Anointed Tsar. But the ecclesiastical inspiration of this dream had already slackened in the eighteenth century. At the end of the century—in Karamzin and others—there was a renaissance in secular historiosophy of the idea of 'sanctity' of state power. Karamzin developed this into a complete conservative programme, set forth in his Notes on the Old and New Russia.[1] The contradictions and disagreements of this first historiosophical attempt to defend the idea of the 'sanctity' of power are shown in great detail in Pypin's book. More 'harmonious' theories appeared later in Russian historiosophy. But in Speranski we find another variant of this renascent historiosophical utopia. He too tends to regard sovereign power as something sacred;[2] but this is not a programme of 'social quietism', nor a recognition of the state as sacred *quand même* (as in Karamzin); rather it is a search for methods of *transfiguring* the state. We should not forget the mystical expectations which were associated with the 'Holy Alliance'—and not by Alexander I alone. It has been justly pointed out that 'under Alexander the state once more felt itself holy and sacred'.[3]

Speranski's mysticism was more subtle and profound than that of Labzin; but both of them, in different ways, cleared the way for *secular religious thought*. In this spiritual movement there was much that was connected with the age itself—an age full of mystical excitement—but there was also something symptomatic of the inner spiritual dialectic of Russia. There was a profound ferment in the Church itself and around it; many high members of the hierarchy (for example, the well-known Filaret, Metropolitan of Moscow) and various circles of secular society were stirred by

---

1. *Zapiski o drevnei i novoi Rossi.* Pypin aptly characterizes Karamzin's views as a 'system of social quietism', *Obshchestvennoye dvizheniye pri Aleksandre I* [The Movement of Society under Alexander I], 2nd ed., 1885, p. 205.

2. Letter to Tseier, *Rus. Arkhiv*, 1870, p. 188.

3. Florovsky, *op. cit.*, p. 133. The mystical expectations connected with Mme. Krüdener's influence on Alexander I are very interesting for the characterization of this period. Cf. also Kotelnikov's sect.

religious searchings, either in the spirit of 'universal', i.e. supra-ecclesiastical, Christianity or the idea of the 'inner Church'. It is not surprising that a hostile attitude soon developed in the ecclesiastical consciousness toward this whole 'modern' movement. There was sharp reaction, which later became very strong and aggressive. This was the beginning of the division between 'progressive' and 'reactionary' tendencies—so fateful for the whole life of Russia—which continued throughout the nineteenth century.

### 6. WESTERN INFLUENCES IN RUSSIA

The mysticism of Labzin and Speranski exhibits more clearly than other Russian mystical tendencies of the time the connection of mystical searchings with the general spiritual crisis which followed the entry of Russian thought upon a path of free, i.e. extra-ecclesiastical, theorizing. This is revealed even more clearly in the purely philosophic searchings of the early nineteenth century; and of course it is not accidental that Russian thinkers were especially attracted to Schelling's *nature-philosophy*. This characteristic of Russian Schellingism, which later gave way to an enthusiasm for the aesthetics of Schelling and the German romanticists generally, linked the philosophic movements of the early nineteenth century to the interest in nature-philosophy of the Russian freemasons of the late eighteenth century (Schwarz and his friends).

In order to discover what Schelling's early nineteenth-century Russian followers took from him and how they did so, let us glance briefly at the way in which German philosophy of the late eighteenth and early nineteenth centuries penetrated into Russia. The growth of interest in *purely abstract* themes must be credited to the general growth of philosophic culture in Russia in the second half of the eighteenth century, and especially to the teaching of philosophy in the higher schools. We have already mentioned the translations (often in manuscript) of Kant and his followers. At the beginning of the nineteenth century, a number of serious, and —for their time—outstanding, representatives of German philosophy appeared in the Russian universities. After their appearance, Russian young people began to occupy themselves more and more with philosophy. Especially noteworthy were Professors Buhle in Moscow and Schad in Kharkov. Buhle was a very learned scholar whose exposition was clear and attractive; incidentally, in Russia he was concerned chiefly with literary questions. His student, Professor Davydov, whom we shall have occasion to meet again, characterized Buhle's doctrine as 'reasonable idealism', meaning that Buhle was not a fanatic adherent of transcendental idealism. Nevertheless, the study of Kant penetrated steadily, though slowly, through the University and the Theological Academies.

Schad [1] was a much more important and striking figure. He suffered from the purge of philosophy in 1816, which affected the universities of St. Petersburg, Kazan and Kharkov. Schad, who taught philosophy in Kharkov University for five years (1811–16), was a follower of Fichte [2] and left a considerable mark on philosophic culture in Russia, as can be seen from his students. It is especially noteworthy that Professor Pavlov, who played an enormous part in the philosophic movement in Russia during the 1830's (see below), began his philosophic education under Schad. During Schad's stay in Kharkov interest in philosophy was at a very high level. Osipovski, the mathematician, whom we have already mentioned, was also active at Kharkov during this period. His attitude toward German idealism was in general ironical and sharply critical; he specifically ridiculed Schad's 'naïve' assumption of the identity of thought and reality. From Osipovski's empirical point of view such an assumption was naïve.

But in Schad himself Fichteanism developed into Schellingian nature-philosophy. For the career of Russian philosophy this extraordinary and absorbing interest in Schelling (as a *nature-philosopher*) is extremely characteristic. Russian Schellingism has not yet wholly disappeared; we need only recall Schelling's enormous importance for the world-view of Vladimir Solovyov, whose influence is still alive in our day.

### 7. VELLANSKI. BIOGRAPHY. THEORETICAL CONSTRUCTIONS

The first clear manifestation of Russian Schellingism—and the closest to the original—was the work of D. M. Vellanski (1774–1847).[3] Of lowly origin, he entered the Kiev Theological Academy at the age of 15 but did not finish his studies there, going instead to the Medical Academy in St. Petersburg. Upon graduation, Vellanski was sent to Germany to complete his education. There

1. Concerning him see Koyré, *op. cit.*, pp. 52–65. On Schelling's influence in Russia see L. Müller, 'Schelling in Russland', *Arch. für Geschichte der Philosophie*, 1949.

2. In this connection see Ueberweg, *Geschichte der Philosophie*, 12th edition, 1923, IV, 35.

3. On Vellanski see Koyré, *op. cit.*, pp. 91–9.

he took up the study of philosophy with special enthusiasm and, upon his return to St. Petersburg, applied for a Chair of Philosophy. Because there was none in the Medical Academy, he took the Chair of Botany. His dissertation was devoted to the problem of The Reform of Medical and Physical Theories. There were no opponents—although public defence of the dissertation was scheduled three times—and Vellanski received his degree without defending the dissertation. He was an excellent lecturer; in the words of his pupil Rozanov, 'Vellanski's personality was all fire and flame.' This was connected with his passionate enthusiasm for Schelling's ideas, to which he remained true throughout his life. One historian[1] denies that Vellanski was a genuine Schellingian because he confined himself to Schelling's nature-philosophy and did not follow Schelling in his later works. This reasoning is more than strange; as though the acceptance of some of Schelling's doctrines must be accompanied by an avowal of all the others. Vellanski was a learned naturalist, but he warmly defended the philosophic formulation of scientific problems. Koyré now 're-bukes' Vellanski for not having accepted all of Schelling's doctrines, but the Academy of Sciences in St. Petersburg twice refused Vellanski the title of academician because he put 'too much philosophy' into his science. Vellanski wrote to Professor Pavlov (who was also a Schellingian): 'For thirty years I have been crying in the Russian scientific world like a voice in the wilderness.' He was indeed alone, despite the fact that Russians of his time were very much interested in nature-philosophy. This was a result partly of the very difficult language in which Vellanski wrote, partly of the fact that he was more interested in 'reforming' science (in the spirit of Schelling's philosophy) than in popularizing Schelling—which Pavlov did magnificently, thus playing a more important part in the development of Russian Schellingism. We should mention, by the way, that Vellanski had many warm followers. Kolyupanov testifies that as early as the 1840's his book Biological Investigation of Nature in its Created and Creative Aspects, published in 1812, 'was causing the students of the upper classes in the Gymnasium to rack their brains over it.'[2] Especially noteworthy among Vellanski's pupils was Dr. Yastrebtsev, who wrote in his Confession: 'Vellanski completely subdued me with his nature-philosophy.' From nature-philosophy Yastrebtsev moved to general philosophic questions (he was scornful of 'factomania' in science) and ended by defending faith.

1. Koyré, *op. cit.*, p. 98.     2. Kolyupanov, *op. cit.*, I, 445.

Vellanski was a *nature-philosopher*, but also a philosopher in the broad sense. In 1824 he wrote to Prince Odoyevski (concerning whom see the following chapter): 'I was the first to announce to the Russian public, more than twenty years ago, the new knowledge of the natural world based on the theosophical concept which, though it started with Plato, took shape and reached maturity in Schelling.' [1] In fact, Vellanski took from Schelling not only his nature-philosophy but also, to a considerable extent, his transcendentalism. However, the most influential aspect of Schelling was his *shift to realism*, not only for Vellanski, but for German and Russian Schellingism. Transcendentalism was annulled, as it were, by the Schellingians; this curious *deflation* of Schelling's basic philosophic position—for which Schelling himself, incidentally, provided ample grounds—had already taken place in Germany. Together with his realistic interpretation of Schelling, Vellanski gives prominent place to a realistically conceived philosophy of nature. However, we should not underestimate the importance of the general philosophic material in Vellanski; he is still essentially a transcendentalist—in the spirit of Schelling's 'system of identity'. At one time he thought of writing an outline of his general ideas in philosophy.[2] He did not do this, but not for want of a genuine philosophic education, as Shpet supposes; [3] this is difficult to imagine in a conscientious scholar like Vellanski, who had planned to take a Chair of Philosophy. Nevertheless, from his works one may gather quite a consistent outline of epistemology and metaphysics. Vellanski defended a synthesis of *speculation* and *experience:* 'Speculative and empirical knowledge', he wrote, 'are one-sided, and each alone is *incomplete* . . . ; speculation, for all its advantages, is *inadequate without experience.*' However, 'true knowledge consists of *ideas*, not sense-data. Although experience shows us many hidden aspects of nature, it has not explained the essential meaning of any of them. Experience and observation deal with the transient and limited forms of things, but do not touch their limitless and eternal essence.' In another place he writes that the task of science consists not in an empirical 'embracing of individual objects', but in a search for the general unity of nature. These epistemological theories are clearly determined by the metaphysical conception which Schelling developed in his philosophy of nature, and which strove to

1. See Bobrov, *Filosofiya v Rossi* [Philosophy in Russia], Pt. II, p. 221.
2. Vellanski's letter to Pavlov is evidence of this (quoted by Bobrov, *op. cit.*, Pt. II, p. 225).
3. Shpet, *op. cit.*, p. 126.

know nature as a living unity. 'Nature is a product of *universal life*,' Vellanski writes, 'acting in the capacity of creative spirit. All living and inanimate beings are produced by this same *absolute life*.' [1] Time, space, and matter are only 'manifestations' of an eternal and unlimited principle; hence 'universal life' is neither matter nor energy, but the ideal principle of both, which we grasp speculatively.

This general metaphysical conception, taken from Schelling, did not merely captivate Vellanski; it gave him a clear insight into the hidden creative mystery of the world. This insight inspired him in his scientific work. Vellanski was more than 'convinced' of the value of this conception; he was captivated and enraptured by it. Vellanski was a member of the *school* of Schelling; he worked out the problems of science and Nature in the spirit of Schelling's doctrines, accepting the doctrines of the world-soul, the principle of polarity in nature, the universal animation and organic structure of the world. The 'pan-substantial' principle, the Absolute, is the source of the inexhaustible vitality of the world. All empirical being is directly rooted in the Absolute. Vellanski's epistemological position flows from this basic conception of the world and its life; for him our reason 'is merely a reflection of Absolute Mind, the essence of universal life.'

In Schelling the order of ideas was reversed; he *started* from transcendental idealism, rather than proceeding to it. But Vellanski, like the other Schellingians, was inspired primarily by Schelling's metaphysics and accepted his transcendentalism for the sake of the metaphysics. Vellanski accepted transcendentalism seriously and unhesitatingly, well understanding its logical priority.[2] The anthology published in Germany under the title *Romantische Naturphilosophie*,[3] which clearly shows Schelling's influence on the

1. From the manuscript 'Zhivotny magnetizm' ['Animal Magnetism']. See Bobrov, *op. cit.*, Pt. III, p. 39.
2. Shpet says very crudely that Vellanski began with 'the tail of nature-philosophy rather than the head of philosophic principles' (*op. cit.*, p. 125). But Vellanski is no worse in this respect than other well-known Schellingians—Oken, Carus, *et al.* All of them, taking the principles of transcendentalism as their point of departure, were concerned to apply Schelling's principles to nature-philosophy, anthropology, etc. Shpet, in another place (*ibid.*, p. 132) speaks of Vellanski as 'insensitive to, and therefore heedless of, the purely philosophic significance of basic principles. . . . He was not able to exhibit the philosophic foundations of science and knowledge . . . *because he was not a philosopher*'. This is palpably unjust.
3. Edited by C. Bernoulli und H. Kern, Jena, 1926.

elaboration of the ideas of nature-philosophy by the romanticists, makes it plain that Vellanski's theories could take a legitimate and important place in this movement.

Vellanski's importance for the development of philosophic ideas in Russia is extremely great. His *direct* influence was not significant;[1] nevertheless, when Circles of 'Wisdom-Lovers' were formed in Moscow and St. Petersburg in the 1820's (see below), they all acknowledged Vellanski as the leader of Russian Schellingism. Pavlov, the leader of the Moscow Schellingians, was particularly interested in Vellanski. It is true that within a decade Vellanski seemed to the young people to represent a 'backward' trend of thought. But, in any event, the *first* place in Russian Schellingism —a trend which was extremely fruitful for Russian philosophic thought—belongs to Vellanski, not only chronologically, but because of his serious and persistent work in nature-philosophy.

## 8. MINOR RUSSIAN SCHELLINGIANS

Professor A. I. Galich (1783–1848), of the Pedagogical Institute and University in St. Petersburg, is often considered an early nineteenth-century Russian Schellingian. This is incorrect; Galich was not a Schellingian, nor did he espouse any particular system. In Koyré's cutting phrase, he was simply a 'professor of philosophy'. Nevertheless, his importance for the development of philosophic culture in Russia is such that he should not be ignored.

Galich graduated from the Theological Seminary (in the city of Sevsk) and became a pupil of Professor P. D. Lodi,[2] of St. Petersburg University, by whom he was sent abroad. Upon his return to Russia, Galich became a professor in the Pedagogical Institute and later in the University. His most popular works were A History of Philosophic Systems, Compiled From Foreign Texts, 1819; An Essay in the Science of the Beautiful, 1825; and An Image of Man (outline of a philosophical anthropology), 1834. Galich's fate was an unhappy one. When the fight against philosophy—chiefly against the followers of German idealism—began, Galich was one of the first to suffer. He was charged with 'having limited himself to expounding philosophic systems without refuting them'. After his dismissal from the University he was soon deprived of means of

1. We should mention in passing that Vellanski's lectures excited some of his hearers to the point of 'self-forgetfulness', even 'ecstasy' (Bobrov, *op. cit.*, Pt. II, p. 67), but his influence was severely limited by the fact that he taught in the Medical Academy.

2. P. D. Lodi was the author of *Logicheskiye nastavleniya* [Logical Precepts].

subsistence, and fell into extreme poverty. To round out his bitter fate, a manuscript of a work which he had prepared for publication was burned.

Galich's History of Philosophic Systems, although it is not an independent work, was of great service to Russian youth when (in the 1820's) they began to show a marked interest in philosophy. His book on aesthetic problems was of even greater importance. We have already noticed, in our study of the eighteenth century, the significance which aesthetics had for thinking Russians. The 'aesthetic humanism', of which we shall speak below, sent out deeper and broader roots. Beginning with the first years of the nineteenth century, translations of textbooks on aesthetics began to multiply. Aesthetic problems not only occupied a primary place; they also gave a colouring to other philosophic interests. This was in part a reflection of what was taking place in the West (predominantly in Germany), but the singular 'priority' of aesthetic problems had its own roots in the Russian soul. Sentimentalism, and later romanticism, not only brought with them a kind of 'delight'; they also left an imprint on the whole world-view. Among Russian Schellingians only Vellanski in the early period was concerned with problems of nature-philosophy; not until the 1830's did this aspect of Schellingism begin once more to attract the attention of broader circles. But romantic aesthetics—and especially Schelling's 'aesthetic idealism', his glorification of art, and his theory of artistic creation—captivated Russian thinkers from the very beginning of the nineteenth century. The literature —both in books and journals—devoted to aesthetic questions during the first decades of the nineteenth century has not yet been adequately investigated. In any event, these questions attracted universal attention, especially in connection with the literary disputes between the classical and romantic tendencies. Galich's book on aesthetics, although it is not notable for originality, and is sometimes rather foggy, nevertheless raised aesthetic questions to the level of philosophy. There is no doubt that it left its mark in the history of the aesthetic searchings of the 1820's and '30's. We may mention in passing that Galich's Image of Man—a first essay in philosophical anthropology—was not original either, although there was much valuable material in it. Especially important was a Spinozistically elaborated doctrine of the 'passions'.

Among the other Russian Schellingians we must mention first of all M. G. Pavlov (1793–1840), who graduated from the Theological Seminary in Voronezh, studied at Kharkov University (with Schad), and then went to Moscow University. After graduating, he was sent on a scientific mission to Germany and returned an enthusiastic follower of Schelling and Oken. Receiving a Chair of Agriculture and Physics, he began to lecture on these subjects and very soon gained extraordinary popularity, not only among the students of the various faculties but also among broad circles of Russian society. In his lectures Pavlov, who had a gift for clear and at the same time attractive exposition, invariably touched upon both theory of knowledge and the general principles of nature-philosophy. Pavlov's lectures were of great service in the development of philosophic interests among talented young people. (Concerning the philosophical circles of the 1820's see the following chapter.) In 1828 Pavlov began to edit a scientific and literary journal, *Athenaeum*, in which he published several articles on philosophy ('On the Interrelation of Speculative and Empirical Knowledge', 'On the Distinction between the Fine Arts and the Sciences').[1] He published several books in his special field, among which we should particularly note his Foundations of Physics.

In epistemology and especially in nature-philosophy Pavlov was a true follower of Schelling,[2] but he did not go beyond the general principles of transcendentalism in epistemology, being more audacious only in nature-philosophy. His article 'On the Distinction between the Fine Arts and the Sciences' was very important for the dialectic of the philosophic tendencies of the time. In this article Pavlov treated aesthetic problems in the spirit of Schelling. But Pavlov's articles, all of which show how deeply he was permeated with Schelling's philosophy, were not as important as his lectures.

Professor Davydov (1794–1863) is also numbered among the Schellingians—but always with reservations. He was a student of the above-mentioned Professor Buhle. Davydov's doctoral dissertation was devoted to Bacon, from which fact—without any further evidence—it has been concluded that he inclined toward empiricism. When admiration for Schelling became clearly evident among the young people especially interested in philosophy, Davydov

1. Pavlov had published an earlier article 'O sposobakh issledovaniya prirody' ['On the Methods of Investigating Nature'] in Prince Odoyevski's *Mnemosina*. Concerning Pavlov, see Koyré, *op. cit.*, pp. 126–36; Herzen, *My Past and Thoughts*, Vol. I.

2. Shpet considers Pavlov only 'approximately' a Schellingian (*op. cit.*, p. 127). Sakulin writes: 'We may consider Pavlov a Schellingian or, more precisely, an Okenian, only with very substantial reservations.' (*Russkaya literatura i sotsializm* [Russian Literature and Socialism], Moscow, 1922, I, 127.)

began to show a 'preference' for Schelling. He gave the students at the University Boardinghouse Schelling's works to read. Working together with Pavlov, who was a warm and sincere Schellingian, Davydov, who was essentially an eclectic, devoted much attention to Schelling and thus contributed significantly to the development of Schellingism in Moscow. It is sufficient to recall, for example, how enthusiastically the future historian N. Pogodin, whom we shall meet below, devoted himself to Schellingism. But Milyukov is right in his sharp judgment of Davydov when he writes: 'Davydov was the same kind of opportunist in philosophy as in everyday life; from the mere fact that Davydov considered it necessary to accommodate his views to Schelling's philosophy, we may conclude that Schellingism had become fashionable.' [1] When nationalism began to find official support in Russian government circles, Davydov wrote an article resolutely opposing the closeness of Russian philosophy to German idealism. We cannot deny Davydov a knowledge of the history of philosophy, and even a certain philosophical acumen,[2] but this failed to give valuable results in the sense of creative activity. Davydov's contribution was limited to his influence on the youth, which also defines his place in the history of Russian philosophy.

### 9. INDIVIDUAL PHILOSOPHERS OF THIS PERIOD IN RUSSIA

The material which we have examined thus far is not adequate for a general appraisal of Russian Schellingism. Only after we have acquainted ourselves with the Moscow and St. Petersburg philosophical circles, and with the works of Prince V. F. Odoyevski and other thinkers, will we be able to offer a general appraisal of Russian Schellingism. In concluding the present chapter, we shall mention only those representatives of early Russian Schellingism who were active in the first decades of the nineteenth century.

We must mention, first of all, K. Zelenetski (1802–58), who taught at the Lyceum in Odessa and was the author of an Essay in the Investigation of Certain Theoretical Problems. In the series of essays which make up this book, Zelenetski develops the ideas of transcendentalism in a way that is closer to Schelling than to Kant. In a special article devoted to logic he polemicizes with Hegel.

1. P. N. Milyukov, *Glavnyie techeniya russkoi istoricheskoi mysli* [Chief Trends of Russian Historical Thought], 3rd ed., 1913, p. 296.
2. For a detailed analysis of Davydov's views, see Koyré, *op. cit.*

Also in Odessa was Professor P. P. Kurlyandtsev (1802–38), who made himself known only as a translator: of Schelling's *Introduction to Speculative Physics*, of the well-known Schellingian Schubert's *Elements of Cosmology*, and of Steffens's (also a Schellingian) *On the Gradual Development of Nature.*

Vellanski's pupil, Kh. Ekebled (1808–77), published a book (in 1872) called An Essay in the Survey and Bio-Psychological Investigation of the Powers of the Human Spirit. The author himself admits that his main ideas were taken from Vellanski's lectures.

M. A. Maksimovich (1803–73), a pupil of Pavlov, first a botanist and then an historian of literature, was a professor at Kiev University. He wrote, in addition to a number of specialized works,[1] several studies in the philosophy of natural science—in the spirit of Schelling.

Professor Dudrovich of Kharkov (1782–1830), a pupil and follower of Schad, developed Schelling's ideas in his lectures. The same should be said of I. K. Kronneberg (1788–1838), Professor of Philology at Kharkov; he was also a popularizer of Giordano Bruno, and his studies in aesthetics were close to Schelling.

## 10. KARAMZIN

Schelling's *aesthetic* philosophy appeared in the foreground among the Schellingians of the generation after Vellanski; it was at the very focus of their philosophic thinking. Of course, the general influence of German romanticism was very strong here, but we should not forget that the aesthetic element played an important part in the philosophic tendencies of eighteenth-century Russia. Especial importance must be ascribed to what we may call 'aesthetic humanism', a movement closely connected with sentimentalism. Sentimentalism is not simply a phenomenon characteristic of eighteenth-century *belles lettres*, as is often assumed. Sentimentalism in literature was only an artistic manifestation of a broader phenomenon. Both in its roots and in its content, sentimentalism is a specific period in European culture, a product of the *religious movements* of the seventeenth and eighteenth centuries.[2]

The *aestheticizing* character of Russian sentimentalism is especially important. Western influences were at work here, especially

1. Concerning them, see Chizhevski, *Hegel in Russland.*
2. This is very well indicated in M. Weiser's work *Der sentimentale Mensch,* 1924.

Shaftesbury, who was the first in Western philosophy to associate moral feeling closely with the aesthetic sphere, a tendency which found expression in Schiller's well-known doctrine of the '*Schöne Seele*'.[1] But the aesthetic element in the Russian sentimentalists (I have in mind Karamzin and Zhukovski) is organically fused with their humanism. These two representatives of Russian sentimentalism are important because in them eighteenth-century humanism acquired a new foundation and a new character. The aesthetic element has such a large place in the intricate dialectic of Russian spiritual development that we must pause for a moment to consider aesthetic humanism as it first appeared in Russia with Karamzin and Zhukovski.

N. M. Karamzin (1766–1826) received a very thorough education in Moscow under Professor Schaden.[2] He was thoroughly familiar with German, French, and English literature, philosophic as well as artistic. Rousseau was his chief inspiration—Rousseau's flaming defence of the rights of feeling rather than his social and ethical passion. Karamzin was an 'enthusiastic' admirer of Rousseau in aesthetics. He even accepted republicanism, to which, we may say in passing, he remained true to the end of his life, despite the abrupt crisis in his ideas which converted him into an apologist for the Russian autocracy. Herzen said later that for him and his generation, the word 'republic' had a 'moral significance', i.e. it was not so much a political idea as a moral ideal. As to Karamzin, we should say that his republicanism had neither political nor moral content; he admired republicanism, as he says, 'sentimentally', for its aesthetic, formal harmony. He wrote to I. I. Dmitriyev: 'I remain a republican *in sentiment* but at the same time a loyal subject of the Russian Tsar.'[3] Karamzin once wrote to Prince Vyazemski: 'I am a republican at heart, and I shall die a republican.' And N. I. Turgenev testifies that when Karamzin learned of the death of Robespierre he burst out crying.[4]

It is clear that Karamzin's republicanism was not connected with historical reality; it was simply an *aesthetically coloured day-*

1. Concerning Shaftesbury's influence on German thought (in the sense indicated in the text) see especially Obernauer's interesting book *Die Problematik des ästhetischen Menschen und die deutsche Literatur*, 1923; also Unger, *Hamann und die Aufklärung*, 1911, p. 63, *passim*.

2. Karamzin was associated in Moscow with the German poet Lenz (a representative of the *Sturm und Drang* period or the so-called *Geniezeit*) who spent the rest of his life in Moscow.

3. Sipovski, *N. M. Karamzin*, 1889, p. 109.

4. See N. I. Turgenev, *La Russie et les russes*, Brussells, 1847, I, 326.

*dreaming*, which formed the basis of his aesthetic humanism—a humanism which was irresponsible not from frivolity but from lack of realism. This sentimental day-dreaming was not a *diversion*; if it included a 'sweet rapture' over one's own experiences, it was nevertheless turned toward reality. But the reality was judged only aesthetically. Thus Karamzin's philosophic eclecticism was 'natural'; it indicated not a lack of principle but a lack of responsibility, resulting from the pre-eminence of the aesthetic factor. In one place Karamzin expressed a thought which was often put forward in the West during the eighteenth century (e.g. by Hemsterhuis, Hamann, Jacobi): 'The sensitive heart is a rich *source of ideas*.'[1] 'All beauty gladdens me', he said frequently. Moral and intellectual responsibility was here stifled in 'panaestheticism' —and this was true of others besides Karamzin.

The aesthetic element remained in full force and unchanged throughout Karamzin's life—even when he devoted himself wholly to the writing of his *History of the Russian State*.[2] Karamzin must therefore be considered a representative of Russian *aesthetic humanism*.[3] It is impossible to doubt this, and prejudiced appraisals of Karamzin (for example, that of Pypin[4]) try in vain to obscure this fact. In an early article Karamzin wrote: 'We love Rousseau because of his *passionate love of man*.' But Karamzin himself displayed this same love of man, which he once characterized as 'tender morality'. This was the ideal that Schiller defined in the words *Schöne Seele*, an aesthetic optimism for which aesthetic experience supports a faith in the triumph of the good. 'The seed of good which is in the human heart never disappears', Karamzin repeats after Rousseau. But Karamzin's optimism derives from motifs of purely aesthetic humanism. His optimism cannot be separated from his dreamer's hope that 'the human race is approaching perfection' because 'Deity dwells in the heart of man'. Karamzin declares through the mouth of one of the protagonists in the 'Correspondence of Melidorus and Philaletus':[5] 'Heavenly beauty seduced my gaze and filled my heart with the most tender love; my spirit yearned

1. Karamzin, *Sochineniya* [Works], 1838, IX, 236.
2. The priority of the aesthetic principle even in Karamzin's historical research is well emphasized by Milyukov, *op. cit.*, p. 165.
3. Obernauer justly considers W. Humboldt the outstanding representative of aesthetic humanism because of his freedom from all historical 'admixtures'. There were enough of such 'admixtures' in Karamzin. (*Op. cit.*, p. 267.)
4. Pypin says ironically of Karamzin: 'In the realm of *abstract* concepts Karamzin was a most tender friend of humanity.' (*Op. cit.*, p. 199.)
5. 'Perepiska Melidora i Filaleta.'

for it in *sweet rapture*.' This is sentimentalism, of course, but behind it there is a definite spiritual orientation: the affirmation of an *aesthetic morality*. Karamzin once wrote: 'In the words of Rousseau, only what does not exist in reality is beautiful. This beauty, like a fleeting shadow, eternally evades us; but we possess it, at least in *imagination*.' The preservation of the enchantment of beautiful forms becomes an essential task before which the harsh truth of reality must give way.

Karamzin as an historian began to resurrect the idea of power as 'sacred', to revive the utopian ideology of the sixteenth century—but of course without ecclesiastical passion. In Karamzin's conservative patriotism, the ecclesiastical foundation of the doctrine of power is replaced by a concern for the glory, power, and greatness of Russia. This secularization of an earlier ecclesiastical idea substituted aesthetic admiration of Russian life and Russian history for ecclesiastical passion. Pypin is right in accusing Karamzin of having reinforced national self-delusion and furthered historiosophical sentimentalism, feasting his eyes upon Russian greatness while thrusting aside the real needs of Russian life. But Karamzin's historical contribution to the dialectic of the spiritual wanderings of his time was to add a new element to the ideology of the intelligentsia, by erecting a system of aesthetic humanism, and thus to take a new step toward the secular conception of life.

## 11. ZHUKOVSKI

The poet V. A. Zhukovski (1783–1852), another representative of aesthetic humanism, was active in a different way. Zhukovski had only the remotest connection with philosophy, but he has his place in the dialectic of Russian spiritual searchings. He exhibits, even more clearly than Karamzin, the pre-eminence of the aesthetic principle. At the same time, Zhukovski did more than anyone else to further the penetration into Russian life of the influence of German romanticism. Zhukovski admired Rousseau and Chateaubriand, Schiller and the early German romanticists. Schiller's aesthetic philosophy was alien to Zhukovski but his *rapprochement* of the aesthetic and moral spheres—the ideal of the *Schöne Seele*—was close to him.[1] In one of his articles (1809) Zhukovski wrote

1. The influence of Schiller's aesthetic philosophy on Russian thought continued throughout the nineteenth century. Unfortunately this influence has not yet been adequately studied. See Peterson's book, *Schiller in Russland*, Munich, 1934. We may note that Schiller's articles on aesthetic problems were translated

of the 'moral use of poetry' in the spirit of the doctrine of the *Schöne Seele*. The currents of German romanticism which aspired to penetrate beyond the limits of earthly reality, to reach the 'nocturnal aspect of the soul', and the 'inexpressible' in nature and man, were especially congenial to him. It is not accidental that (as early as 1806) he undertook the publication in Russian of a complete edition of Rousseau's works. 'The culture of the heart' was the constant focus of his experience and reflection. In Zhukovski the foundations were laid for a doctrine of man later to be developed by Kireyevski (see Ch. VII).

Zhukovski's frequent attribution of *religious significance* to art is very interesting. This was a feature of romanticism generally, but especially German romanticism—an emphasis on the aesthetic aspect of religion, morality, and social relations. Schiller's brilliant insights in this field undoubtedly mark the summit of this process in European civilization (a process which is not yet over). But the deification of art, the tendency to see in art a 'revelation', the attribution to art of a 'sacred' character, are all deeply connected with the process of *secularization*. In Zhukovski we find a characteristic formula:

> Poetry is God in the holy dreams of earth.
>
> (From the poem 'Camoëns')

This idea is expressed somewhat differently in the line: 'Poetry is the earthly sister of heavenly religion.' This formula is somewhat softer and vaguer than the first, in which poetry appears as *inherently religious*. The German romanticists—especially Novalis and Friedrich Schlegel—also identified poetry with religion; Zhukovski agrees with them in attributing to poetry an autonomous religious force, independent of the Church. Just as the natural historical order is inherently sacred for Karamzin,[1] so poetry, and art in general, are sacred for Zhukovski. This was in harmony with the fundamental processes of Russian culture, which consisted wholly in the crystallization of the new secular ideology.

From the aesthetic humanism of Karamzin and Zhukovski—a vague and essentially irresponsible doctrine—we turn to those currents in Russian thought in which the aesthetic element dominates completely, but where we find neither irresponsibility nor

into Russian several times, the first apparently being in 1813. At that time translations of German (and, later, also French) aestheticians filled the bookstores.

1. Karamzin once wrote: 'The revolution explained these ideas; we saw that the civil order is sacred, even in its most local and accidental inadequacies.'

vagueness. Here the influence of Schelling and of the deeper currents in German romanticism is also apparent. This new 'wave' of Schellingism appeared in the 1820's, primarily in the philosophical circles. Some of these were fructified chiefly by Schelling's philosophy, while for others Schelling's philosophy was only a transitional phase in the movement toward Hegel.

# CHAPTER V

## 'The Young Men of the Archives'

### D. V. VENEVITINOV, PRINCE V. F. ODOYEVSKI, P. YA. CHAADAYEV

### 1. INFLUENCE OF THE WAR OF 1812

THE war of 1812, subsequently known as the 'War of Liberation', gave a tremendous impetus to the development of intellectual and social life in Russia. An enormous number of Russians came into direct contact with European life as a result of the movement of the Russian army to the West, and this first-hand acquaintance with Western Europe had a much stronger influence on the Russian soul than the enthusiasm for the West which had developed in the eighteenth century. The consciousness of Russian political power served not merely to increase the sense of national dignity but also to formulate sharply the question of the introduction into Russian life of everything in the West which had impressed the Russians politically. Between 1812 and 1814 a process of increasingly marked crystallization of political movements began in Russia, culminating in the 'Decembrist' uprising of 1825. At the same time the theme of Russian 'cultural independence' flamed up with new force, no longer in the name of a return to the old Russian life, as had often been the case in the eighteenth century, but as a revelation of the 'Russian idea', of 'Russian principles' which had previously lain hidden in the 'depths of the national spirit'. In 1803 Karamzin had written: 'It seems to me that we are too *humble* in our ideas of our national dignity.' It is understandable that after the war of 1812–14 the demand for a clear expression of national self-consciousness increased very sharply. Liberals and conservatives were agreed on this; the consciousness of Russian power and 'maturity' was common to all groups.[1]

1. One of the Decembrists (A. A. Bestuzhev) expressed this mood very aptly: 'When Napoleon invaded Russia, the Russian people felt their strength for the first time. That was the beginning of freethinking in Russia.'

Even before the war of 1812 a political differentiation had begun in Russian society. At first it made itself felt only in the field of literature, but the basic meaning of the literary disputes of the first decade of the nineteenth century was determined by this political differentiation. Of great interest in this connection was the dispute between the group headed by Karamzin, who wished to enrich the Russian language with new words capable of expressing the new concepts and relationships, and the group headed by Shishkov, who wished to keep its development within the limits of the ancient forms. The basic differentiation in Russian life was already apparent in this dispute; after the war of 1812–14 this differentiation developed very rapidly, reaching full and clear expression. During these years two camps were formed, which differed not only on concrete questions of Russian life but also in the sphere of ideology. A place of very great importance in this process must be assigned to Alexander I himself, who delivered a number of striking speeches, marked by a warm defence of radical reforms [1]—including the abolition of serfdom—which greatly nourished and strengthened the growth of liberalism in Russian society. Nevertheless, Alexander I also strongly encouraged the mystical tendencies of which we have spoken in the preceding chapter. And the note of reaction often sounded very strongly in the mystical movements of the time.

The early tendencies of nineteenth-century Russia were all essentially continuous with the corresponding tendencies of the eighteenth century, although they perhaps assumed a more radical form. The chief influence during the 1820's came not from French but from German thinkers, as we have already seen (Ch. IV). German idealism was a forceful stimulant to the thinking young people; and, beginning in the 1820's, there was a formation of *philosophical circles*, which had great importance for the development of philosophic culture in Russia.

### 2. PHILOSOPHICAL CIRCLES IN MOSCOW

Two such circles sprang up simultaneously in Moscow in 1823. The first, which was purely literary, was headed by S. Ye. Raich,

1. For example, in his famous speech at the opening of the Polish Sejm (1818) Alexander I declared: 'The rulers of nations should voluntarily place decrees which are suggested to them before coercive decrees.' The future Decembrist, Lorer, hearing this speech, was moved to tears. (S. P. Melgunov, *Dela i lyudi Aleksandrovskovo vremeni* [People and Affairs of the Age of Alexander], Berlin, 1923, p. 267.)

translator of Tasso; the second, which was specifically philosophic, became known as the 'Society of Wisdom-Lovers' (i.e. Philosophers). In the first—literary—circle, papers on philosophic themes were sometimes read; but, of course, the second circle is of particular importance for us. Among its members were Prince V. F. Odoyevski (President), D. V. Venevitinov (Secretary), I. V. Kireyevski (the future Slavophile, concerning whom see Ch. VII), S. P. Shevyryov, M. P. Pogodin (the last two later became professors at Moscow University), A. I. Koshelyov, and several others. The Society of Wisdom-Lovers was active for only two years—until the end of 1825, when news of the Decembrist uprising impelled its members to close the Society as a precautionary measure. The Society was made up predominantly of young men who had met and become close friends in the service of the Archives of the Ministry of Foreign Affairs in Moscow, whence the name 'Young Men of the Archives'. They were all very young: Odoyevski was 20, Venevitinov 18, Kireyevski 17. All of them had received a thorough education at home, and almost all of them were highly gifted. After establishing mutual friendships, they soon found that they shared an interest in philosophy. From Koshelyov's journal we learn that he and Kireyevski (who was exactly his age) read Locke together and then proceeded to the German philosophers.[1] At this time the Schellingian Pavlov returned from abroad and began enthusiastically introducing his students at the University, and the residents of the University Boardinghouse, to Schelling's philosophy. Professor Davydov, whom we have already met, did the same. The Society of Wisdom-Lovers met secretly, according to Koshelyov.

'German philosophy predominated', he wrote, 'i.e. Kant, Fichte, Schelling, Oken, Görres, et al. We sometimes read our own philosophic works, but more frequently we discussed works of the German philosophers. The principles upon which all human knowledge must be founded were the chief subject of our discussions. Christian doctrine seemed to us suitable only for the masses of the people, not for philosophers like us. We prized Spinoza particularly highly and valued his works much above the New Testament and the rest of Holy Scripture. Prince Odoyevski presided; D. Venevitinov spoke at greatest length, often raising us to ecstasy with his words.'[2]

1. A. I. Koshelyov, *Zapiski* [Journal], 1889, p. 7.
2. *Ibid.*, p. 12.

The general mood of this whole period was very well depicted by Prince Odoyevski in his Russian Nights:

'My youth', he wrote, 'was spent in a period when metaphysics was as much in the general atmosphere as the political sciences are now. We believed in the possibility of an absolute theory, by means of which one would be able to order all the phenomena of Nature, just as today men believe in the possibility of a social order that will fully satisfy all human needs. . . . However that may be, at that time all of nature, all of human life, seemed very clear to us, and we rather looked down upon the physicists and chemists . . ., who rooted about in "vulgar matter".' 1

Let us first consider D. V. Venevitinov.

### 3. VENEVITINOV

It is generally agreed that D. V. Venevitinov was extraordinarily gifted. His personal charm, the direct sense of his talent, impressed his friends so profoundly that after his death (at the age of 22) they gathered annually for many years on the day of his death to honour his memory. In the Society of Wisdom-Lovers Venevitinov held a place of first importance; he was passionately devoted to philosophy and he infected others with this enthusiasm. In his own phrase: 'Philosophy is true poetry.' These words well express both the admiration for philosophy and the general mood which then prevailed among the university youth. It was almost a *religious* attitude toward philosophy which, indeed, completely replaced religion for many of them.

The fragments of Venevitinov's writings which have been preserved are too few in number to enable us to judge the philosophic ideas of a man who died in his twenty-third year; but even these fragments offer clear evidence that if he had lived his philosophic talent would have burned with a brilliant flame. Venevitinov studied the history of philosophy a great deal,2 and translated Oken into Russian (the translation has not been preserved).3 He felt, with the German romanticists, that 'the true poets have always been deep thinkers, philosophers'. He conceived the function

1. V. F. Odoyevski, *Russkiye nochi* [Russian Nights], 1913, p. 8.
2. These studies are mentioned in Venevitinov's letters to Kosh. For example he writes: 'I read Plato quite freely and I cannot admire him enough.' *Sochineniya* [Works], Moscow, 1934, p. 302.
3. *Ibid.*, pp. 308, 491.

of philosophy in the spirit of transcendentalism; philosophy's task, in his view, is 'theory of knowledge'.[1] At the same time, Venevitinov stressed the necessity of creating an independent *Russian* philosophy. He took a negative attitude toward blind imitation of the West, and was prepared to go so far as to break off relations with the West temporarily in order to find paths of Russian creative activity 'resting upon the firm principles of philosophy'. 'Russia will find its foundation, its guarantee of autonomy and moral freedom, in philosophy.'[2]

Aesthetics, as a theoretical discipline, is, according to Venevitinov, the connecting link between art and philosophy. In the very structure of the world he saw an aesthetic principle. His articles on aesthetics (for example, 'Sculpture, Painting, and Music') are so constructed that one can draw general philosophic conclusions from them. Venevitinov's verses may be applied to himself:

> He breathes the warmth of beauty,
> His heart and mind are one.

Not without reason does Venevitinov defend *intuition* as a source of ideas ('feeling generates thought').[3]

The priority of the aesthetic principle, which found its philosophic foundation in Schelling, was particularly congenial to the young Russian philosophers. We have only fragmentary hints of this in Venevitinov, but we find it expressed with much greater force and breadth in the philosophic theories of Prince V. F. Odoyevski, a member of the same Society of Wisdom-Lovers. We turn now to a study of his ideas.

### 4. ODOYEVSKI. BIOGRAPHY

Prince V. F. Odoyevski lived a comparatively long life (1803–69), and underwent a complex philosophic evolution. Three periods should be noted in his philosophic creative activity. He was an exceptionally fertile writer, who published many journals and collections of articles. His was a versatile and active nature; but, with all the variety of his interests and occupations, he remained a thinker at all times, striving always to make his theories rigorously

1. See his letter on philosophy (*ibid.*, p. 203).
2. *Ibid.*, p. 220.
3. Koyré gives a detailed exposition of Venevitinov's articles (without sufficient analysis, however) in his book *La Philosophie et le problème national en Russie au début du XIXe siècle*, pp. 139–45.

systematic. His importance in the development of Russian philosophy was formerly underestimated; but, since the appearance of Sakulin's detailed monograph,[1] we may consider it established that Odoyevski deserves a very important place in the development of Russian philosophy. Odoyevski astonishes one with the diversity of his interests. Like Herzen later, he was very much interested in natural science, from which—as he himself testifies [2]—he came to philosophy. We should bear in mind that he was interested in both *facts* and *general ideas* in the natural sciences. His interest in facts was manifested in a clear *realism* of principle, a firm and fearless following of the positive data of knowledge. His interest in the general ideas of natural science led him to philosophy, and he lived in a period of striking and triumphant development of nature-philosophy. Throughout his life Odoyevski was interested in philosophy and the exact sciences, but he was also a writer of *belles lettres*. Although he was not distinguished by great talent in the field of literature, Odoyevski nevertheless wrote a great deal, and his writings include some very able works. It is interesting to note that Odoyevski was a very good writer of children's stories— which, as is well known, requires a rare talent. His 'Wonder-Tales of Grandfather Irinei' preserve their value to the present day. His extraordinary interest in aesthetic problems should be especially stressed, particularly with respect to music, which he knew very well and to which he devoted a number of works. Finally, it should be pointed out that Odoyevski devoted a great deal of attention to social and economic problems. He felt very deeply the cardinal importance of these problems for the modern period, as is clear from the numerous tirades in his Russian Nights.

The breadth of Odoyevski's mind was manifested in the diversity of his interests, but at the same time he continually strove for *philosophic synthesis*—sometimes quite audaciously. Hence he is not to be charged with eclecticism. In all the periods of his development, the 'central' convictions around which he attempted to build his 'system' are plainly exhibited. It is not always clear how he unifies propositions which point in different directions, but there

1. P. N. Sakulin, *Knyaz V. F. Odoyevski. Iz istori russkovo idealizma* [Prince V. F. Odoyevski. From the History of Russian Idealism], Moscow, 1913. Sakulin's work, unfortunately, remained unfinished. Only Vol. I, Parts I and II—606 and 459 pages—have appeared. The [Russian] literature on Prince Odoyevski is quite extensive, but with the appearance of Sakulin's book (which made wide use of the manuscript works left by Odoyevski) the previous studies lost their significance.

2. Odoyevski, *op. cit.*, p. 9.

is an unquestionable tendency toward systematization in his work.[1]

Odoyevski entered the University Boardinghouse in Moscow very early—at the age of 13. The director of the Boardinghouse was Professor Prokopovich Antonski, a pupil of Schwarz, the eighteenth-century freemason, whom we have already met. Prokopovich Antonski was not himself a freemason; nevertheless, as Sakulin justly remarks, the *intellectual* traditions of freemasonry passed through him to the pupils of the Boardinghouse.[2] This historical continuity is not to be denied. Among the teachers was Professor Davydov, whom we have already met. Later the brilliant Schellingian Professor Pavlov also joined the teaching staff. In the Boardinghouse, Odoyevski began to study philosophy, and translated ancient and modern authors (including Chateaubriand: the *Génie du Christianisme*). He also studied music and musical theory a great deal, showing excellent taste in the subject.[3] Upon leaving the Boardinghouse, Odoyevski entered Raich's literary circle, where he read his translation of Oken and then, as we have seen, joined with other young men to form the 'Society of Wisdom-Lovers', of which he was President. In the same year Odoyevski —together with Küchelbecker—undertook the publication of *Mnemosina*, a kind of periodical almanac. In a statement 'From the Publishers', Odoyevski described *Mnemosina*'s task as 'setting a limit to our partiality for the French theorists',[4] 'disseminating certain new ideas which have flowered in Germany', and, at the same time, drawing the reader's attention 'to the treasures which lie close at hand'—i.e. to clear the way for independent Russian creative activity. When *Mnemosina* ceased publication, the Wisdom-Lovers began to publish *Moskovski vestnik* [Moscow Herald], a journal which continued to appear—under the editorship of M. P. Pogodin, who was at that time an enthusiastic

1. We must bear in mind that a *very* considerable number of Odoyevski's philosophic writings remained in manuscript form and have not yet been printed. We are acquainted with this material only through the excerpts which Sakulin gives in his book.

2. Sakulin, *op. cit.*, Pt. I, p. 14.

3. In his youth, Odoyevski wrote an ecstatic work—a genuine hymn—to music. See Sakulin, *op. cit.*, Pt. I, p. 92.

4. Concerning the waves of Gallomania and Gallophobia in Russia during the first decades of the nineteenth century see the above-mentioned book of Haumant, *La Culture française en Russie*. Haumant considers that French culture reached its greatest influence in Russia during the period between 1789 and 1815.

Schellingian—from 1827 to 1830. This journal, in which Odoyevski took an active part, contributed importantly to the development of philosophic culture in Russia, many articles on philosophy and aesthetics appearing in its pages.

Odoyevski soon moved to St. Petersburg, where he became very friendly with Vellanski; at this time he studied Oken, and then Schelling, with great thoroughness. In the last issue of *Mnemosina* Odoyevski defended the need for a 'knowledge of the living connection of all the sciences', in other words, the need to start from the 'harmonious structure of the whole' in studying particular aspects of being. He projected the publication of a Dictionary of Philosophy, and prepared some material for it; his study on the Eleatic School was published in the fourth issue of *Mnemosina*. In another issue he developed the idea of knowledge, an idea deduced from the concept of the Absolute, in the manner of Schelling. A number of unpublished studies, discovered and summarized by Sakulin, also relate to this subject.[1] In these studies, which are written in the spirit of Schelling, Odoyevski is concerned not with problems of nature-philosophy, but with problems of the human spirit—questions of ethics, aesthetics, and epistemology. His aesthetic ideas are particularly interesting. We must bear in mind that even before his acquaintance with Schelling, Odoyevski had attempted to construct an aesthetic theory.[2] He now took the concept of the Absolute as his point of departure in aesthetics as well; and, in his philosophy of music, he made special use of the principle of polarity.[3]

In his literary works of this period, Odoyevski took a negative attitude toward mysticism;[4] he was also very restrained in his attitude toward problems of social life. While remaining true to the principles of humanism, he reinforced them at this time with abstract ethical considerations.[5] Such was Odoyevski in the 1820's; this was the period of his enthusiasm for Schelling and his attempts to construct general theories in epistemology, ethics, and aesthetics on a foundation of transcendentalism. But, after his move to St. Petersburg (1825) and his marriage, a new period in his philosophic searchings began; he gradually drew away from Schelling and gave greater attention to mysticism.

1. Sakulin, *op. cit.*, pp. 144–76.
2. *Ibid.*, pp. 153, 155.
3. *Ibid.*, p. 168, Note 2. In Odoyevski's aesthetic views of this period there is much that is similar to those of Venevitinov.
4. *Ibid.*, p. 205.  5. *Ibid.*, pp. 297f.

## 5. ODOYEVSKI'S ANTHROPOLOGY

Sakulin, in his book on Odoyevski, notes three periods in the development of mysticism in Russia: 'In the period of Catherine mysticism was characterized chiefly by philanthropy, in the period of Alexander by religious contemplation; in the 1830's a social element was added.' [1] This rather neat scheme is true only with respect to the factors which *predominated* in Russian mysticism during the various periods; of course, all of the elements indicated were present in all of the periods, but in different proportions.

Odoyevski, in the early 1830's buried himself completely in the study of mystical literature: Arnd, Eckartshausen, Saint-Martin, Pordage, Baader. He also studied Ballanche, whom we shall meet later in our study of Chaadayev, as well as the writings of the Church Fathers—in the excerpts which are given in the well-known anthologies entitled *Dobrotolyubiye* [Love of Beauty]. He was particularly attracted by the mystical theologians, such as Simeon Theologus Novus and Gregorius Sinaites. The new theories and ideas which were maturing in Odoyevski at this time found expression in an article, 'Psychological Notes', and a book, Russian Nights. The materials and notes which remained unpublished, and which are quoted in excerpt in Sakulin's book, are also particularly important for the study of this period.

In this new period Odoyevski was occupied predominantly with problems of *anthropology* and *historiosophy*; and here Schellingism retained its importance as a foundation, or rather as a seed which, gathering nourishment from outside, grew into a new plant.

Odoyevski now took as his point of departure the proposition that 'three elements are fused together in man—the believing, the cognitive, and the aesthetic'. For this reason not only science, but *religion* and *art* as well, must be placed at the foundation of philosophy. Culture consists in their total integration; their development comprises the meaning of history. In this formulation of the basic problems, man himself appears in the place of primary importance, for it is in him that the three spheres are united. But in his theory of man Odoyevski followed primarily the Christian doctrine of original sin, which—even in the eighteenth century— had taken on new force in mystical writings, thanks to Saint-Martin, for whom this forgotten Christian doctrine of the 'corruption' of human nature was fundamental. The Russian secular

1. *Ibid.*, p. 342.

mystics [1] of the eighteenth and early nineteenth centuries (Labzin, Speranski), under the influence of Saint-Martin, placed in the foreground this doctrine of an original sin which entered into man and through him into all of nature. Odoyevski developed this idea persistently. Recalling the well-known words of the Apostle Paul (Romans viii: 22) that 'the whole creation groaneth and travaileth in pain together', he went on to emphasize that 'Rousseau's idea that man's nature is excellent in itself is partly a misunderstanding and partly false.' 'Man is only man when he goes against nature.' Man is called 'to aid the exhausted forces of nature . . . but, as a result of his sin, he is himself subordinated to them; this is the source of man's weakness and of the evil in him.' 'There is no evil in man's soul,' Odoyevski writes, 'for man is a part of Deity, and there would be none if man were not forced to take from nature the means for his life.' In other words, the dependence upon nature which resulted from man's fall is the source of his further corruption. 'The perpetual exaltation of nature, which the English so love,' Odoyevski remarks, 'destroys in man the idea of the *fall of nature* and of man.' 'Natural being', he continues, 'depends (nevertheless) on *man's will*.' 'If man should renounce his calling [i.e. his dominant place in nature] . . . the rude physical forces which he now barely keeps in check would throw off their chains, and nature would begin progressively to vanquish man.' Meditating further on this theme, and appealing to the observed fact that in certain diseases salt crystals are formed in the human body, Odoyevski asks the question: May it not be that the 'bodily organism is nothing but a disease of the spirit'? On the other hand, man, in knowledge and love, gradually frees himself from the condition created by original sin; and, in his 'aesthetic development, the life of the future is symbolically and prophetically prefigured, . . . a life which will provide that wholeness which existed in Adam before the Fall.' In this last thesis, which is close to Schiller's brilliant anthropological insights (Schiller saw in the aesthetic sphere a force for man's 'restoration'), Odoyevski expressed for the first time in Russian philosophy the idea, which was later to appear so frequently, of human 'wholeness' as an ideal task for inner effort.

Odoyevski's anthropological views,[2] in which he chiefly develops

   1. In Russian *spiritual* literature of the eighteenth century, of course, emphasis was always placed upon the doctrine of original sin.

   2. All of these quotations are taken from the manuscript material which Sakulin has reconstructed. *Ibid.*, pp. 444–61.

Saint-Martin's ideas,[1] must be related to his views of nature, as set forth in the treatise which was published in excerpt by Sakulin.[2] Odoyevski was inspired on this point by Pordage, as he himself points out, but we also find strong echoes of Schellingism. His doctrine of *symbolism* in nature, the law of the 'reflection' of certain phenomena in others, is especially important. 'In nature', Odoyevski wrote, 'everything is a *metaphor* of something else.' Here (as in the doctrine of a 'mother-idea' which is the reason of all reasons) Odoyevski comes close to Goethe's metaphysics.

### 6. MAN'S INNER WORLD

Odoyevski was most original and independent in what he wrote concerning man's inner world. Anticipating Bergson's theories, he asserted that culture weakens the instincts in man ('instinctual energies', in Odoyevski's term). Primitive man, according to Odoyevski, was endowed with strong instinctual energy. 'The ancients knew more than we', because of this instinctual insight; but with the development of rationality this energy began to fail. 'Reason left to itself could produce only syncretism; further than this it could not go.'

Odoyevski noted particularly the fact that the scientific research of his day was coming to conclusions which mankind had reached earlier through 'black magic', i.e. the 'occult' sciences. He also expressed the idea that 'false theory led the alchemists to many more discoveries than all the careful and prudent researches of contemporary chemists, because of the fact that formerly men possessed more instinctual energy.'

Odoyevski's 'instinctual energy' is a broader concept than Bergson's 'intuition', but both are specific manifestations of *Rousseauism* in the theory of man's cognitive powers: Man's 'Natural' state is here contrasted with what civilization has done for man's cognitive powers. We may mention, in passing, that in Odoyevski (as in Bergson) the concept of 'instinctual energies' goes beyond the limits of the cognitive function; it is also related to the biological sphere in man. Odoyevski, still following Schelling and

1. In Viatte's substantial work *Les Sources occultes du romantisme*, Saint-Martin's enormous influence on French literature of the late eighteenth and early nineteenth centuries is very well shown. But Saint-Martin's influence was also strong in German philosophic literature.

2. Sakulin, *op. cit.*, pp. 462–9.

the naturalists of the period, devoted special attention to the study of magnetism and somnabulism.[1]

The opposition of instinctual energy and reason is not so sharp in Odoyevski as it is in Bergson. According to Odoyevski we should strive to synthesize the two. 'It is a splendid thing', he wrote, 'to *understand* instinct' [i.e. to raise it to the form of rationality]. 'Reason must sometimes remain idle and cease to strive beyond itself, in order to penetrate deeply within itself, *to make room for "instinctual energies"*.' In this doctrine, too, Odoyevski touches a theme which was placed in the foreground by the Slavophiles and by a number of later Russian philosophers: the redintegration of the *ways of knowing*. Odoyevski's formula: 'intellect must be raised to the level of instinct', is close to the ecclesiastical doctrine which makes the task of the spiritual life 'to raise intellect to the heart'.[2] But in Odoyevski there is no place for the influence of grace; his mystical epistemology is *naturalistic*. Since there are innate ideas in every man (what Odoyevski calls 'pre-knowledge'),[3] the intellectual process consists for him in mastering this innate wealth. Moreover, Odoyevski held that there is a 'new world of ideas which suddenly opens before us' when we plunge deeply into ourselves.[4]

It is interesting to note that Odoyevski, in the order of intuition, defended the idea of deriving matter from energy. 'It may be', he wrote, in a kind of intuitive anticipation of twentieth-century ideas, 'that only a day separates us from a discovery which will show us how to *produce matter from nonmaterial energy*.' We quote one more remark of his on this same theme: 'If it is discovered some day that the action of electricity is sufficient to transform one body into another, what then will matter be?'

Related to these suggestions concerning the possibility of 'dematerializing' matter, is Odoyevski's conviction that, in general, contemporary natural science rests on an erroneous use of separate experiments, apart from their connection with the *whole*. Empiricism in general does not recognize the 'whole', which is revealed only by 'instinctual energy'.[5] For this reason, Odoyevski awaits a 'new science', which will overcome specialization and grasp nature

1. Cf. Odoyevski's extremely interesting theory of dreams, which was very close to that of the German romanticists. For a survey of the theories of the latter see Beguin, *L'Ame romantique et le rêve*, 1939.

2. In secular literature Speranski devoted special attention to this theme. Concerning him, see the preceding chapter.

3. Sakulin, *op. cit.*, pp. 573f.

4. *Russkiye nochi* [Russian Nights], p. 43n.

5. Cf. Theodor Gomperz's theory of the 'total impression'.

as a whole, as a living unity. He sees precursors of this 'new science' in Carus, Goethe, and Lomonosov. 'Science must become *poetic*', he asserts; and in support of this view he cites the fact that without artistic talent it is impossible to seize the mystery of the world. Just as a proof rests not merely on the data of reason, but requires a certain resonance of feeling, so, in mastering what has been won by science, we must be able to awaken a certain 'sympathetic' resonance, i.e. we must perceive scientific theories 'poetically'. Human language, for all its enormous richness, is inadequate if it does not awaken such 'poetic' resonance. The energy of expression which we find in art is an ideal for language. From this it is clear that the aesthetic element crowns all knowledge, all understanding; aesthetic perception is the summit of theory. For Odoyevski, poetic sensitivity, if it is not complicated by other elements, always leads us to truth; man never errs when he is guided by instinctual energy.

In aesthetics Odoyevski assigned the highest place to music. But all the arts, and everything that develops aesthetic culture, have a high value. In art, according to Odoyevski, an energy is operative which was perhaps possessed by *everyone* earlier, but which has been lost by mankind as a result of the development of rationality.[1] 'We seek to participate in art by means of this energy', Odoyevski writes. 'Poetic elementality is the soul's most precious force.'[2] In this formula, aesthetic humanism (the highest expression of the secular world-view), which was first expressed—as we have seen—by Karamzin and Zhukovski, achieves finished expression. The moral life too, according to Odoyevski, flows from the aesthetic principle. In this doctrine of the essential unity of the aesthetic and moral spheres—which is also a fundamental thesis of aesthetic humanism—Odoyevski remains close to Schiller's idea of the *Schöne Seele*. 'Morality is not the aim of poetry', Odoyevski wrote once, 'but I assert that the poet is always a moral man.'

Odoyevski's ethical views are related to this same 'instinctual energy', which provides the highest achievements in knowledge. Odoyevski recognized an 'instinctual knowledge of good and evil'; and, guided by this knowledge, he harshly condemned contemporary life for its bondage to material interests. He also harshly condemned the military character of contemporary states, sharply

1. These ideas were later defended by Vladimir Solovyov in his essays on aesthetics.
2. Here Odoyevski comes closest to Schiller's brilliant conception. Cf., in the following chapter, Gogol's doctrine of the primacy of the aesthetic principle in man.

flaying 'military education'.[1] But Odoyevski's doctrine of contemporary life, which was included among his historiosophical ideas, found its clearest expression in his book Russian Nights.

### 7. 'RUSSIAN NIGHTS'

In Odoyevski's own words, 'the period depicted in Russian Nights is that moment of the nineteenth century when Schelling's philosophy had ceased to satisfy seekers after truth, and they had begun to disperse in various directions.' Odoyevski's book contains many apt formulae on various philosophic themes, but we shall concern ourselves solely with an exposition of his historiosophy. It must be mentioned, to begin with, that Russian Nights offered, for the first time in Russian literature, a *critique of Western culture*. Up to this time, remarks critical of the West had appeared more than once in Russian literature, but Odoyevski was the first to treat this theme, which had so profoundly aroused Russian thought—and continues to do so—in a more systematic form. In the words of the hero of Russian Nights, who bears the characteristic name Faust,[2] Odoyevski expressed the idea of the 'ruin' of the West, of the internal disintegration of its former strength. Science, which has torn itself away from the 'all-uniting force of the intellect', has been broken up into a series of special disciplines; and comprehension of the 'whole' is impossible. Art has grown weak, since the poets, having lost faith in themselves, have lost their creative energy. Religious feeling is also perishing. 'We venture to say something which will perhaps seem strange to many people today, but in time will become all too plain: the West is perishing.'[3] Just as Christianity in its time brought new energies to the senescent world of antiquity and renewed its life, so now the salvation of Europe is possible only if a new nation with fresh energies enters the historical scene. The Russians, Odoyevski felt, were such a people, for 'we have been placed on the boundary between two worlds, the world of the past and that of the future. We are new and fresh; we are not a party to the crimes of old Europe. Before us its strange, mysterious drama is playing itself out, and perhaps the key to it is hidden in the depths of the Russian spirit.'[4] But,

1. Sakulin, *op. cit.*, pp. 573f.
2. The Russian Faust is very far from his German namesake; only the passionate search for truth justifies the identity of their names.
3. *Russkiye nochi* [Russian Nights], p. 341.
4. *Ibid.*, p. 344.

Faust asserts, we Russians must not save merely the *body* of Europe; we must also save its *soul*, for it is a question of the internal transformation of the very foundations of Western culture. Turning to the Russian people, the author says, 'In the Holy Trinity of faith, science, and art you will find the calm for which your fathers prayed. *The nineteenth century belongs to Russia.*' [1] As a matter of fact, these are not Faust's own thoughts, but are taken by him from a manuscript. Here are Faust's own remarks:

' My friend's thoughts concerning the West are exaggerated, but listen to the Western writers themselves . . ., listen to the cries of despair which resound in contemporary [Western] literature. . . . We see here the incurable anguish which prevails in the West— hope without conviction, negation without affirmation. . . . I see in the West an immense expenditure of energy. . . . The West, buried in the world of its spontaneous elements, has thoroughly elaborated them; marvellous was its work, and it has generated wondrous things. The West has produced everything that its spontaneous elements could produce, but in its restless, hurried activity it has developed one element and stifled the others: as a result, equilibrium has been lost. To achieve a full, harmonious development of the fundamental, universally human elements, the West has need of a Peter [the Great] to infuse it with the fresh, powerful saps of the Slavic East.'

Odoyevski frequently speaks of Russia—here called the 'Slavic East'—in the words later used by the Slavophiles, emphasizing the 'all-encompassing versatility of the Russian spirit', its spontaneous universality or, better, 'all-embracingness'. [2]

## 8. HUMANISM

This whole (second) period in the development of Odoyevski's world-view reveals in full force the basic features of his creative activity and personality, and at the same time defines his importance for the development of Russian philosophic thought. Odoyevski, first of all, continued the line of *humanism* which provided Russian intellectuals with the animating ideology previously furnished by the ecclesiastico-political dream of the sixteenth and seventeenth centuries. The eighteenth century, as we have seen,

1. *Ibid.*, p. 346.
2. These last quotations are from the 'Epilogue' to the Russian Nights.

was primarily occupied with this task: after Tatishchev, Shcherba-tov, and Lomonosov there was a period in which the ethical foundation of the new ideology was laid by Novikov and Radi-shchev. But ethical passion was insufficient; it was supplemented by the aesthetic principle, which crowned this system of secular ideology—first appearing in Karamzin. Odoyevski exhibits not only the priority of the aesthetic principle, but its foundation as well (in the theory of an 'instinctual energy', crowded out by reason, but concealing the source of aesthetic and ethical inspiration). This priority of the aesthetic principle, nevertheless, is part of a system of *genuine humanism*. But it does not simply bring the aesthetic and moral elements together; it fully identifies them.

One critic has expressed doubts as to the genuineness of Odoyev-ski's humanism. In his opinion, Odoyevski 'confined himself to the preaching of humanity in relations between landowners and serfs' and 'did not see the need for abolishing serfdom'. The critic points to the fact that, in his utopia (which was called '4338 A.D.'), Odoyevski 'accepted the existence of rich and poor, masters and servants', and 'rejected the absurd fictions of the eighteenth-century dreamers . . . of the possibility of equality among men'.[1] The only truth in this charge (*which Odoyevski does not at all deserve*) is that before the death of Nicholas I Odoyevski did not express himself in print concerning the need for abolishing serfdom. But, if one reads his diary,[2] it becomes clear the Odoyevski greeted the emancipation of the peasants with a joy and warmth of feeling which was rare in Russia at that time. To the end of his life he *celebrated* February 19th, the day of the emancipation of the peasants. His constant concern and intention was to bring the light of education and artistic enrichment to the people; he was a passionate 'populist'.[3] It was not without reason that Odoyevski for several years published a magazine for the people, called *Selskoye chteniye* [Rural Reading]. And we should note that Odoyev-ski's humanism was not an abstract programme but always found expression in real aid to those who suffered from the dislocations of the social order. The passionate thoughts—full of sincere indigna-tion—concerning the injustice of the contemporary order which

1. B. Kozmin (in a preface to 'Dnevnik V. F. Odoyevskovo' ['V. F. Odoyev-ski's Diary'] printed in *Literaturnoye nasledstvo* [Literary Heritage], No. 22-4, Moscow, 1935, pp. 81-3).

2. The part of the diary which appears in *Literaturnoye nasledstvo* covers the years 1859-69.

3. Concerning 'populism' [*narodnichestvo*] as a conspicuous element in the Russian humanistic ideology, see Chapter IX on Herzen.

are contained in *Russian Nights* are a clear expression of his humanism.[1] Although he belonged to a distinguished Russian family, Odoyevski never forgot those who bore the burden of social disorganization.

Odoyevski was noted for the diversity of his interests; his knowledge was encyclopaedic. He studied the natural, juridical, and historical sciences with equal devotion, and was continually occupied with art. Odoyevski's 'encyclopaedism' prevented him from devoting himself wholly to any single interest. In fact, his talent did not burn brightly in any one field, but the very fullness and diversity of his interests, his indefatigable curiosity, as he himself said, led him to constant striving for an *all-embracing synthesis*, for wholeness and inner harmony. This characteristic may, without exaggeration, be considered the result of his *inner aestheticism*, which tried to make a place for 'everything'—but in unity and harmony. Schelling captivated Odoyevski at one time because he provided an intellectual basis for the harmonious combination of his manifold tendencies. When his enthusiasm for Schelling had abated somewhat, and Odoyevski entered the second phase of his philosophic development, *anthropology* moved to the centre of his system.[2] The hasty survey of his ideas which we have given above is evidence that Odoyevski's creative activity tended toward the *investigation* of man's being, his many-sided life. Schelling was not forgotten here, but the centre of gravity shifted toward the study and investigation of man. Odoyevski entered upon the path of independent creative activity and put forth many remarkable ideas, often anticipating what the Slavophiles, Dostoevsky, and to some extent Solovyov said later. In this new path the central and all-uniting idea for Odoyevski was the reality and strength of man's aesthetic sphere, in which the flame of 'instinctual energy' burns most brightly. It was not the abstract problem of beauty which fixed Odoyevski's attention, but its anthropological aspect, the problem of the aesthetic principle in man. Science, morality, all of contemporary life, are valuable and important; but the final mystery of knowledge and the objective world, the mystery of man, is given in the aesthetic principle; and only through the triumph of the aesthetic principle can inner harmony and wholeness come to prevail in man. Humanism and aestheticism are the two foci

1. *Russkiye nochi* [Russian Nights], pp. 354–64.
2. We consider *anthropology* central for this period, not mystical idealism, as Sakulin insists. However, Sakulin speaks of Odoyevski's 'anthropocentrism' (*op. cit.*, p. 469).

of his personality, but they are not separated. Rather, they are hierarchically related through the ultimate centrality of the aesthetic sphere. This is 'aesthetic humanism'—with, of course, the colouring of mystical naturalism which gave a secular character to the whole ideology of the period.

## 9. THE THIRD PERIOD IN ODOYEVSKI'S LIFE AND CREATIVE ACTIVITY

Odoyevski's theoretical thought slackened somewhat in the third period of his creative activity;[1] he devoted himself extensively to various kinds of practical work—as his diaries eloquently testify—but strove, as before, to give philosophic meaning to his feeling for life. He became more and more enthusiastic about the development of natural science and the spirit of inquisitiveness and indefatigability in research which determined the success of the natural sciences during the nineteenth century. Odoyevski abandoned idealism and became a *realist* (elements of realism had always been strong in him); but now reality was for him primarily what is revealed 'in the facts', not in intuitions. In Russian Nights, Faust had still ridiculed 'factomania', but now Odoyevski placed high value on the accumulation of facts. This was not positivism, but realism. There was no rejection of metaphysics in Odoyevski, but he now tended to what Hartmann later called 'inductive metaphysics'.

Odoyevski had little renown during his lifetime, and even less after his death; but now, on the basis of the considerable body of material gathered by Sakulin from Odoyevski's papers (which were preserved in the Public Library in St. Petersburg), we must unhesitatingly assign Odoyevski a very important place in the development of Russian philosophy during the first half of the nineteenth century. By the example of Odoyevski, better than that of anyone else, we can explain the true meaning of Schelling's influence on Russian thought. From Schelling the Russians took not only his carefully constructed system of transcendental idealism, nature-philosophy, and aesthetics; they also received from him immense *philosophic stimulation*, which played its part even in those who did not follow Schelling. We turn now to a study of the philosophic activity of P. Ya. Chaadayev, who cannot be considered a Schellingian, but who—by his own testimony—owed a

1. Unfortunately, many works from this period are still unpublished, and Sakulin's study does not go beyond the second period.

great deal to Schelling. During the first period of his creative activity, Odoyevski was a warm admirer of Schelling, and the 'leaven' of idealism, especially in its aesthetic aspect, profoundly fructified Odoyevski's thought. Even in the second period, when his interests shifted from nature-philosophy to anthropology and he devoted himself extensively to profound investigation of man's inner world, Odoyevski relinquished neither his idea of the unity of nature nor his epistemological idealism, although he put forward the 'trinity of faith, knowledge, and art'. In his theory of the 'instinctual sphere in man', Odoyevski took a path *parallel* to that of the Schellingian school in Germany (especially Carus), although his investigations were independent. It should be noted that in the Russian philosophic literature of the 1830's and 1840's Odoyevski's term 'instinctual sphere' occurred frequently, which is evidence of his influence on Russian thought. His historiosophical views—the critique of the West, and the problem of an 'all-uniting synthesis'—cleared the way for the ideas of the Slavophiles, which received clear expression as early as the 1840's.

Schelling's influence will be encountered for some time yet in our survey of Russian philosophy. The first thinker upon whom his influence was reflected in one way or another is P. Ya. Chaadayev, to whom we now turn.

### 10. CHAADAYEV. BIOGRAPHY

P. Ya. Chaadayev (1794-1856) has always attracted wide attention on the part of historians of Russian thought. In this respect he has been luckier than anyone else. It is true that the interest in Chaadayev has usually been connected with only one aspect of his creative activity—his scepticism toward Russia, as expressed in the single 'philosophical letter' which was published during his lifetime. The tumult which arose around Chaadayev when this letter appeared in print (1836) was quite extraordinary. The journal which had published the letter was immediately suspended; Chaadayev himself was officially declared insane and subjected to compulsory medical supervision, which lasted about a year. Chaadayev's unusual fate and his generally remarkable personality gave rise to legends about him even during his lifetime. Herzen included Chaadayev among the 'revolutionaries', though without any reason; others have more than once considered him a convert to Catholicism. For some, Chaadayev is the outstanding representative of the liberalism of the 1830's and '40's; for others he is a mystic. Until very recent times not all of his 'philosophical letters' were known; in 1935 five previously unknown letters appeared, which reveal for the first time Chaadayev's religio-philosophic views (*Literaturnoye nasledstvo* [Literary Heritage] Vols. 22–4, Moscow). In any event, we now possess sufficient material for re-establishing Chaadayev's *system*.[1]

Let us turn first to his biography.

Peter Yakovlevich Chaadayev was born in 1794. Having lost his parents at an early age, he and his brother Michael remained in the care of his aunt, Princess A. M. Shcherbatova (daughter of the eighteenth-century historian and writer whom we have already met), who, together with her brother, Prince Shcherbatov, gave both boys a thorough education. In 1809 Chaadayev entered Moscow University. In 1812 he entered military service and took part in the Napoleonic War. In 1816 he met Pushkin—who was still a Lyceum student—and remained one of his closest friends until the end of Pushkin's life.[2] Chaadayev developed very rapidly; at an early age he displayed a firm and direct character and an extraordinary sense of his own dignity. Early in 1821 Chaadayev gave up military service; several legendary stories exist concerning this episode, the real basis of which has not yet been made completely clear. In the years before 1823 Chaadayev underwent his first spiritual crisis—in a religious direction. He had already read a great deal, and at this time he was carried away by mystical literature. Jung-Stilling's works had a particular influence on him. As a result of his extraordinary spiritual intensity his health broke down and he had to go abroad to recuperate. There he remained until 1826 —which saved him from destruction, as he was extremely close to the most prominent Decembrists. When Chaadayev returned from abroad, he was arrested but was soon released and permitted to return to Moscow. There he experienced a second crisis. He became a total recluse for several years, immersing himself wholly in complicated intellectual work. During these years of the most complete seclusion (to 1830), Chaadayev's whole philosophic and

1. Concerning Chaadayev see Charles Quénet, *Tchaadaeff et ses lettres philosophiques*, Paris, 1931 (a detailed biography); Eugene A. Moskoff, *The Russian Philosopher Chaadayev, his Ideas and his Epoch*, New York, 1937 (of very limited value); A. Koyré, 'P. Tchaadaeff and the Slavophiles', *Slavonic Review*, III (1927); T. G. Masaryk, *The Spirit of Russia*, New York, 1919, Vol. I; D. I. Chizhevski, *Hegel in Russland*, Reichenberg, 1934.

2. Pushkin wrote several superb poems dedicated to Chaadayev; their content is remarkable.

religious world-view took shape, finding expression in a series of studies (1829), which were written in the form of letters to a fictitious person. It was previously assumed that these letters were written to a Mme Panova, but it has now been shown that this was not the case. Chaadayev simply chose the epistolary form to expound his own views—a quite usual practice at the time. These letters had long passed from hand to hand; and finally N. I. Nadezhdin, an enterprising journalist and former editor of the magazine *Teleskop*, printed one of the letters. This was in 1836; the letter was not printed on Chaadayev's initiative, but with his consent. It created an impression like an exploding bomb. Chaadayev's harsh, relentless judgments of Russia and the dark pessimism of his appraisal of her historical fate astonished everyone. Although the letter had been passed from hand to hand for a long time, it had created no such reaction; but its appearance in print was like a 'shot ringing out in a dark night' (Herzen). A small group of radical young men—like Herzen—was inspired by the audacity of Chaadayev's charges, thrilled by their force and majestic menace; but the immense mass of Russian society took the letters differently. Even the liberal circles were shocked, and in the conservative circles there was extreme indignation. The government, as we have already noted, immediately suspended the journal, banished the editor from Moscow, and dismissed the censor. Chaadayev himself, as he later said, 'got off cheaply'; he was officially declared insane. A doctor came to examine him every day. He was considered under house arrest, and permitted to take a walk only once a day. Within a year and a half, all of these repressive measures were removed—on condition that he 'should not venture to write anything'. Chaadayev remained in Moscow to the end of his life, taking a most active part in all the ideological meetings which were convened by the most remarkable men of the time (Khomyakov, Kireyevski, Herzen, K. Aksakov, Samarin, Granovski, *et al.*).

'The melancholy and unique figure of Chaadayev,' Herzen wrote later [*My Past and Thoughts*, Pt. IV, Ch. 30], 'stood out sharply as a grievous rebuke against the dark background of Moscow "high life". . . . No matter how thick the crowd was, one's eye found him immediately; the years did not warp his upright bearing; his pale, delicate face was completely immobile. . . . An incarnate veto, a living protest, he gazed upon the whirlwind of faces that spun senselessly past him.'

'Perhaps he was most valued by those who considered themselves his opponents,' Khomyakov wrote after his death. 'His enlightened mind, his artistic feeling, his noble heart . . . attracted
everyone to him. At a time when thought seemed buried in a deep
and involuntary sleep, he was especially valuable, both in keeping
watch himself and in awakening others. . . . He was valued even
more by his friends for his constant melancholy, which was accompanied by the cheerfulness of a lively intellect.'

In his seclusion Chaadayev meditated continually on the same
themes—themes of general philosophy as well as historiosophy.
We find evidence of this in his correspondence, which was carefully
edited (although not completely, it is now clear) by Gershenzon.
New features gradually penetrated into his world-view, especially
in his views of Russia, although his fundamental ideas remained
firm as before. In 1856, after Alexander II had already ascended
the throne, Chaadayev died.

## II. INFLUENCES ON CHAADAYEV

Turning to a study and analysis of Chaadayev's world-view, let us
note first the influences which were reflected in his original system.

Chaadayev had, without doubt, very deep and essential connections with the Russian liberalism and radicalism of the first
decades of the nineteenth century. Those were years in which a
demand for changes in Russian life sprang up in Russian minds
with special force, one might say passion. It has already been
shown that before 1812 liberalism was even preached 'from above',
starting with Alexander I, himself. With Alexander's sharp turn
toward amystical conception of history and his own role in it—
which generated the theocratic enterprise of the 'Holy Alliance'
—the liberal and radical tendencies in Russian society began to
crystallize with irresistible force. There was much expansiveness
and freedom in the intellectual and spiritual atmosphere of the
time, and fiery young men gave themselves with passion and ardour
to dreams of rebuilding Russia. The surge of patriotism connected
with the war of 1812 strengthened this reformist mood. The
ecstasy at vanquishing a military strategist of genius brought with
it a sense of historic power. But, in addition to this ecstasy over
Russian power, the young men returning to Russia after 1814
brought back a lively need for *social* and *political* activity. On this
soil various groups began to develop. Ideologically, a part of the
youth was still nourished by the ideas of French enlightenment

literature, but the vast majority of the youth gravitated ideologically toward German romanticism, and through it to German philosophy. Schiller's influence on Russian philosophic searchings
during these years and after was especially important; unfortunately, it has not yet been adequately investigated.

Chaadayev was without doubt very deeply connected with this
whole movement. It is impossible to regard his closeness to the
Russian liberalism of the time as a 'misunderstanding', as Gershenzon does.[1] Of course, this connection with liberalism does not
in the least explain Chaadayev's inner world, but Pushkin has
justly noted Chaadayev's enormous potentialities for important
political activity. Pushkin's poem 'To a Portrait of Chaadayev' is
well known:

> By heaven's high will
> He was born to the shackles of the Tsar's service,
> He would have been Brutus in Rome, in Athens Pericles,
> But here he is a Hussar officer.

Pushkin also wrote a famous 'Epistle to Chaadayev':

> We await in the torment of hope
> The hour of *sacred freedom*. . . .

In any event, many aspects of Russian liberalism and radicalism
were close to Chaadayev, although he was later to condemn the
Decembrist uprising in harsh terms.

Turning to other influences on Chaadayev, we must mention,
first of all, that of Catholicism, which at the time was making
considerable progress in Russian upper-class society. Here we
must mention especially Joseph de Maistre, who stayed in St.
Petersburg for a very long time, as Sardinian minister plenipoten-
tiary. Many historians are inclined to accept de Maistre's strong
influence on Chaadayev. Of course, Chaadayev could not have
been ignorant of de Maistre's brilliant and powerful theoretical
constructions; but it was Bonald and Chateaubriand, rather than
de Maistre, who actually played a major role in Chaadayev's
intellectual evolution. There is no doubt that Chaadayev was
acquainted with the whole school of French traditionalists. It is
especially important to note the significance of Chateaubriand—
in his poetic, aestheticising description of the 'genius' of Christian-

1. Gershenzon, *Chaadayev. Zhizn i myshleniye* [Chaadayev. His Life and
Thought], St. Petersburg, 1908, Pt. III.

ity, and his transition to social Christianity [1]—and that of Ballanche, of which Chaadayev himself speaks.[2]

The German school was not without influence on Chaadayev. The 1935 edition of Chaadayev's rediscovered letters (in *Literaturnoye nasledstvo*) includes photographs of certain pages from books found in Chaadayev's library, with his notes. Kant is there: the *Critique of Pure Reason* and the *Critique of Practical Reason*. Of course, Chaadayev knew the works of both Schelling and Hegel. From his 'Philosophical Letters' it is evident that he studied modern philosophy very carefully. We must note especially Schelling's influence on Chaadayev. This question has been discussed many times in the Chaadayev literature.[3] Different authors settle it differently— some affirm, others deny, Schelling's influence. We shall have occasion to consider this question when we expound Chaadayev's system. For the present, let us note that, although Schelling's influence is little evident in the content of Chaadayev's doctrine,[4] the *inspiring* influence of Schelling's system of 'identity' is quite beyond dispute.

English philosophy, which Chaadayev knew and studied, left no traces in his work.

## 12. CHAADAYEV'S RELIGIOUS WORLD

We proceed to a study of Chaadayev's doctrines.

Most expositions of Chaadayev's doctrines place in the foreground his appraisal of Russia's past. Of course, this is the best known and perhaps most brilliant and acute of all that Chaadayev wrote, but his views on Russia are *not* at the centre of his teaching; on the contrary, they are logical deductions from his general ideas in the philosophy of Christianity. The focusing of attention on

1. See Viatte, *Le Catholicisme chez les romantiques*, 1922.

2. *Sochineniya* [Works], ed. Gershenzon, 1913, I, 188.

3. Chaadayev met Schelling personally in Karlsbad in 1825. According to Prince Gagarin, the first publisher of Chaadayev's works, Schelling spoke of Chaadayev as '*un des plus remarquables qu'il eût rencontrés*'. Concerning Schelling's influence on Chaadayev, see Quenet, *op. cit.*, pp. 165–72.

4. Chaadayev himself wrote of this in a letter to Schelling (1832): 'The study of your works has opened a new world to me. . . . This study has been a source of fruitful and delightful reflections; but I may be permitted to add that, in following your sublime paths, I have often been led to other destinations than your own.' (*Sochineniya*, I, 168.) [Original in French. Chaadayev, like many cultivated Russians of his time, wrote most of his personal letters in French. *Trans.*]

Chaadayev's sceptical view of Russia not only fails to elucidate his world-view, but hinders a correct understanding of it. It must be admitted that Chaadayev himself, when he chose the *epistolary* form for expounding his views, complicated the elucidation of his system for the reader; it has to be reconstructed—as Gershenzon first attempted to do. In our view, one may enter into Chaadayev's system only by placing his *religious* orientation at the centre of the whole; his religious experiences are the key to all of his views. In the literature on Chaadayev it is constantly pointed out that he was 'not a theologian'; Gershenzon considers it 'gross inconsistency' on Chaadayev's part not to have become a convert to Catholicism,[1] and Florovsky holds that 'the most obscure thing in Chaadayev is his religiosity', that 'there is less religiosity than anything else in his world-view', that he was an 'ideologist, not a churchman', that 'his Christianity shrivelled into an idea'.[2] Chaadayev himself wrote in a letter: 'I am, thank Heaven, neither a theologian, nor one learned in the law of the Church, but simply a Christian philosopher.'[3] In fact, Chaadayev strove to be a *philosopher*, basing himself on Christianity's contribution to the world; but, despite his own disavowal, he was also a theologian. He had no theological system, but he constructed a *theology of culture*. This is not Christian philosophy, as Chaadayev's system as a whole is, but a theological theory concerning questions in the philosophy of history and culture.

It is necessary, first of all, to elucidate Chaadayev's religious world. Gershenzon has discussed this very well and in great detail; from his book we learn that Chaadayev's 'conversion' took place as early as 1820—i.e. before he had begun to bury himself in mystical literature. Being of an intense and passionate nature, Chaadayev—as is evident from his letters and articles—experienced this 'conversion' with extraordinary profundity. In his early letters—written, from abroad, in 1823—we find repeated self-accusations which might even seem insincere if they were not corroborated by later letters. He once said very aptly: 'There is only one way to be a Christian, and that is to be one *completely*.'[4] The inner wholeness of Chaadayev's religious world had very deep roots; it did not spring from intellectual needs alone. There is *no* basis for suspicion of Chaadayev's ecclesiasticism, such as we find

1. Gershenzon, *op. cit.*, p. 104.
2. G. Florovsky, *Puti russkovo bogosloviya* [Paths of Russian Theology], p. 247.
3. *Sochineniya*, I, 236. [Original in French.]
4. *Ibid.*, p. 218. [French.]

in Florovsky. On the contrary, the theme of the Church filled Chaadayev's soul so deeply that in Russian philosophy only Khomyakov can be compared to him. We have said that Chaadayev constructed a theology of culture; but this is a part of his theology of the Church ('ecclesiology'). In practice, Chaadayev not only did not consider leaving Orthodoxy, but protested when one of his friends, A. I. Turgenev, called him a Catholic.[1] Chaadayev never broke with Orthodoxy, and in the last years of his life—on the testimony of Prince Gagarin, who was very close to him—he frequently partook of the Sacraments.[2]

Chaadayev himself felt that his religion 'was not exactly that of the theologians', and even called his religious world a 'religion of the future', 'to which all the flaming hearts and profound souls of the present are turned'.[3] These words reflect the feeling of (religious) solitude which never left Chaadayev; in order to understand it we must enter somewhat more deeply into his religious world. We have already said that his was a passionate and intense nature. We now add: a nature which sought activity—not external, trivial, or fortuitous activity, but activity *wholly inspired by Christianity*. One of the great mystics of Eastern Christianity, St. Isaac the Syrian, felt profoundly the 'flame of things'; these remarkable words may be applied to Chaadayev thus: he felt deeply the 'flame of history', its sacred flow, its mystical sphere. Chaadayev's originality and uniqueness lies wholly in his *theurgical* perception and understanding of history. We have spoken in preceding chapters of the theurgical element in Russian religious searchings. When the entire world-view of Russians was still ecclesiastical, this theurgical 'note' sounded in the Russian soul (from the fifteenth to the seventeenth centuries) in the dream of 'Moscow—the third Rome'. At that time Russians relied on the 'strength of piety' as a transfiguring principle, and fashioned the utopia of a 'sacred kingdom' and of the transfiguration of Russia into 'Holy Russia' on this foundation. The Kingdom of God, in the theurgical orientation, is built with the living participation of men; hence the 'limitlessness' of Russian piety and the trust in its transfiguring strength. With the decay of the ecclesiastical consciousness and the triumph of the processes of secularization, both within ecclesiastical society

1. Letter of 1835 (i.e. before the publication of the first 'Philosophical Letter'). *Ibid.*, p. 189.

2. Pr. I. S. Gagarin [S. J.], *Les Tendances catholiques dans la société russe*, Paris, 1860, p. 27.

3. The same letter to Turgenev (1835). *Sochineniya*, I, 189. [French.]

and outside it, this spiritual orientation did not disappear, but began to manifest itself in new forms. Eighteenth and nineteenth-century Russian humanism—in its moral or aestheticising form—grew from this *theurgical* root, from the religious need to 'serve the ideal of justice'. This same theurgical motif found expression in the occult searchings of the Russian freemasons, and in the mystical flurry of various spiritual movements during the reign of Alexander I; it was also expressed with exceptional force in Chaadayev. Chaadayev was born, it would seem, to be 'a hero of history'; and Pushkin (see the verses on Chaadayev quoted above) correctly sensed what Chaadayev might have been in a different historical setting. In a letter to Pushkin in 1829, Chaadayev wrote excitedly: 'It is my most ardent wish to see you initiated into the mystery of the age.' [1] These lines are very typical and important. Theurgical restlessness and torment, a craving to understand the 'mystery of the age'—i.e. to touch the sacred mystery which is being accomplished under the covering of external historical events—mastered Chaadayev completely, although it did not find expression in external activity. [2]

Chaadayev's basic theological idea was that of the Kingdom of God, understood not in *isolation from earthly life* but, in its *historical incarnation*, as the *Church*. [3] Therefore Chaadayev spoke constantly and insistently of the 'historicity' of Christianity. 'The Christian religion is not merely a moral system . . . but an eternal, divine force acting universally in the intellectual world.' [4] 'The purely historical aspect of Christianity, . . .' Chaadayev wrote in the same place, 'somehow contains the whole philosophy of Christianity.'

1. *Ibid.*, p. 73. [French.]

2. It did find expression at one point, in the abortive attempt to return to government service—before the publication of the first 'Philosophical Letter'. *Ibid.*, pp. 173–8.

3. Here are Chaadayev's characteristic words (at the end of the eighth letter, *Literaturnoye nasledstvo*, p. 62): 'The truth is one: it is the Kingdom of God, heaven on earth . . . [which is] the moral law realized. This is . . . the limit and goal of all things, the *final* phase of human nature, the resolution of the world drama, the great apocalyptic synthesis.' Chaadayev criticizes Protestantism for seeing in Holy Scripture the basis of all things; for Chaadayev the basis of all things is the Church with its mysteries and its world-transfiguring power.

4. First 'Philosophical Letter,' *Sochineniya*, I, 86f. [The full title of the eight 'Philosophical Letters' is 'Lettres sur la philosophie de l'histoire'. Four were published in 1862 in the original French, but one of these was later found to be spurious; the remaining five were published in 1935 in Russian translation. The celebrated 'First Letter' of 1836 originally appeared in a Russian translation. *Trans.*]

'The true meaning of the dogma expressed symbolically by faith in a universal Church is that . . . in the Christian world everything must necessarily facilitate, and in fact does facilitate, the establishment *on earth* of a *perfect order*, . . . the Kingdom of God.'[1]

Christianity's action in history remains mysterious in many respects, according to Chaadayev, for the operative force of Christianity is contained in its 'mystical unity'—i.e. the Church.[2] 'The mission of the historical Church', Chaadayev wrote later, 'was to civilize the world in a Christian way.' [3] This thought lay at the basis of his philosophy of history. The meaning of the historical process is not what it is usually thought to be; Chaadayev never tires of criticizing the historical science of his time. 'The reason of the age demands an entirely new philosophy of history.' [4] This 'new philosophy of history', of course, is *providentialism,* but it is understood more mystically and concretely than is ordinarily the case. Other passages in Chaadayev—as when he writes of the mysterious action of Providence in history—remind one of Hegel's doctrine of the 'craftiness of historical reason'. As an example I cite the following, from the first 'Philosophical Letter': 'Christianity transmutes all of men's interests into its *own*.' Chaadayev means by this that even where men seek 'their own', where they are concerned with personal and petty tasks, the sacred flame of the Church refines their activity for the benefit of the Kingdom of God. Deeply convinced that 'in the West everything was created by Christianity', Chaadayev explains: 'Of course, not everything in the European countries is permeated with reason, virtue, religion. Far from it, but everything is *mysteriously dominated* by the power which has been sovereign there for so many centuries.'

The attentive reader will not find it difficult to sense the theurgical motif in this whole theology of culture. Chaadayev resolutely defends man's freedom, his *responsibility for history*—although the historical process is also mystically impelled by Providence; therefore he objects strongly to the 'superstitious idea of God's daily intervention'. The more strongly he senses the religious meaning of history, the more insistently does he affirm man's responsibility and freedom. But here Chaadayev's philosophic theories are profoundly determined by his anthropology. We

1. *Loc. cit.*                          2. *Ibid.*, p. 117.
3. Letter to Princess Meshcherskaya. *Ibid.*, p. 242. [Original in French.]
4. Chaadayev's critique of historical science and his demand for a 'new philosophy of history' remained wholly uncomprehended by Milyukov (*Glavnyie techeniya* . . . [Chief Trends . . .], p. 379).

shall now turn to the latter, and then return to his philosophy of history.

### 13. ANTHROPOLOGY

'The life of [man as] a spiritual being', Chaadayev wrote in one of his 'Philosophical Letters', 'embraces two worlds, of which only one is known to us.' [1] One aspect of man belongs to nature, but another rises above nature; 'there cannot be an *evolution* from the animal to the rational principle in man.' Therefore, Chaadayev scorns the attempt of natural science to include man completely in nature: 'When philosophy concerns itself with purely animal man, it becomes—instead of a philosophy of man—a philosophy of animals, . . . the chapter on man in general zoölogy.' [2]

The higher principle in man is formed primarily through the social environment; this doctrine, which led Gershenzon to characterize Chaadayev's whole philosophy as 'social mysticism'—a false transference to the whole system of the feature of a part—is very close to that of the French traditionalists, chiefly Ballanche. Man is connected to society in the profoundest way, by innumerable threads; he lives society's life. 'The capacity to fuse [with other human beings]—sympathy, love, compassion . . . is the remarkable characteristic of our nature.' Without this 'fusion' and intercourse with others we would be deprived of reason from childhood, we would be no different from the animals: 'Without intercourse with other creatures we would quietly munch grass.'[3] Chaadayev draws extremely important conclusions from this recognition of man's deep and essential *sociality*. First of all, the 'origin' of human reason can only be understood by recognizing that social intercourse includes a spiritual principle. In other words, collectivity does not in itself create reason in new human beings, but the light of reason is preserved and transmitted through the social environment. 'On the day of man's creation, God conversed with him, and man heard and understood; this is the true origin of reason.' When the Fall erected a barrier between man and God, *memory* of the divine words was not lost; 'and God's word to man, transmitted from generation to generation, leads man into the world of consciousness and transforms him into a thinking being.' Man is not born into the world with his reason 'ready-made': individual reason depends on 'universal' reason (in

1. *Literaturnoye nasledstvo*, p. 27.
2. 'Otryvki' ['Fragments'] (*Sochineniya*, I, 160). Written in 1829!
3. This thesis is very often encountered in Chaadayev.

this case, social). 'If we do not agree that man's thought is the thought of the *human race*, then it is impossible to understand *what it is*.'[1] This remarkable formula, which anticipates Prince S. Trubetskoi's profound theories of the 'collective [*soborny*] nature of human consciousness', establishes the falseness of all *isolation* of consciousness and eliminates the doctrine of the *autonomy* of reason. On the one hand, the individual empirical consciousness—what Chaadayev calls 'subjective' reason—can, in the order of self-delusion, consider itself 'separate'; but such a 'pernicious ego', permeated with the 'individual principle, . . . merely separates man from all that surrounds him and beclouds all objects.'[2] On the other hand, that which actually enters into man from his intercourse with other men derives essentially from something higher than man—from God. 'All the powers of the intellect, all the means of knowledge', Chaadayev asserts, 'rest on man's *submissiveness*' to this higher world, for 'there is no truth in the human mind save that which was placed there by God.' In man 'there is no other reason than that which is subordinate [to God]', and 'all of our activity is only a manifestation [in us] of a force which places us at the universal level, the level of dependence.' In our 'artificial' (i.e. self-isolating) reason we wilfully replace that portion of the universal reason which has been allotted to us. The basic reality, therefore, is not the individual reason, nor a simple collective, but the 'world-consciousness', a kind of 'ocean of ideas', to which we are continually united. If man could 'carry his subordination [to the higher world] to the point of completely eliminating his freedom [of self-isolation], his present separation from nature would disappear, and he would fuse with nature; a sense of the world-will would awaken in him, and a profound consciousness of his actual involvement in the whole universe.'[3]

Man's dual dependence—on the social environment and on God—does not simply bring his reason into being; it is also in this that the roots of his moral consciousness are found. 'The light of the moral law glows from a remote and unknown realm', Chaada-yev asserts, in opposition to Kant. 'Humanity has always moved only in the glow of a *divine light*.'[4]

'An important part [of our thoughts and actions] is determined by something which is not ours at all; we do not produce what is best, most sublime, and useful in our inner life. Everything good

---

1. *Literaturnoye nasledstvo*, p. 53.   2. *Ibid.*, p. 34.
3. *Loc. cit.*   4. *Ibid.*, p. 45.

that we achieve is a direct consequence of our ability to subordinate ourselves to an unknown power. . . . [And this force],
which acts in us *without our knowledge,* is never mistaken; it leads the
*universe* itself to its predestined end. Thus the principal question is:
how can we reveal the operation of the supreme power in our
nature?' [1]

This supernaturalism does not become occasionalism [2] or pre-
determinism for Chaadayev; on the contrary, he asserts the full
reality of human freedom. To be sure, his doctrine of freedom, as
we shall see in a moment, is insufficiently clear, but freedom is
indisputably real for Chaadayev. He writes: 'Our freedom consists
only in our not being conscious of our dependence',[3] i.e. there is
really no freedom, only an 'idea' of freedom. However, a few lines
further on he calls human freedom a 'dreadful force' and says: 'We
become involved in arbitrary actions and each time we *rock the
whole universe.*' It is true that he also speaks of 'being dazzled by
deceptive self-confidence'. 'Man's own action', Chaadayev remarks in another place, 'proceeds from him only when it corresponds to law.' But, if order is maintained in the world only by
'law', freedom is not only real but is a dreadful force. 'If God did
not teach us', we read in the same place '[i.e. if He did not introduce
order into being], . . . surely *everything would revert to chaos.*' This
means that the freedom of created beings requires constant
influence from above to restrain its destructive force. 'Left to
himself, man has never taken any path except that of *indefinite
degradation.*' [4]

Chaadayev's doctrine of the 'dreadful' force of freedom is intimately connected with his doctrine of the corruption of man and
of nature as a whole—the doctrine of original sin and its reflection
in nature, first developed by St. Paul (Romans, viii: 20–2). The
whole of Christian anthropology is related to this doctrine; but
the doctrine had begun gradually to fade out of the European
consciousness, and this process went as far as anthropological
'idyllism'—the summit of which was Rousseau's doctrine of the
'radical goodness' of human nature. Although Protestantism has
held firmly and stubbornly to anthropological pessimism, optimism

1. *Ibid.,* pp. 24, 31.
2. In one place (*ibid.,* p. 43) Chaadayev himself seems to reduce human
activity to a '*principe occasionnelle*'; however, this idea does not imply a denial of
human activity, as in true occasionalism, but merely a recognition of its
weakness and impotence.
3. *Ibid.,* p. 44.                    4. *Sochineniya,* I, 104.

has been triumphant in the so-called neutral culture of the West until very recently. The revival of the doctrine of the corruption of man and of nature as a whole is associated, as we have pointed out, with the name of Saint-Martin. The Russian mystics (freemasons) of the eighteenth century held firmly to this principle, and it was profoundly shared by Chaadayev. That is why for him 'subjective reason' is permeated with 'deceptive self-confidence'. He considers the *ideology of individualism* essentially false and thus declares unhesitatingly (as Tolstoy did later): 'Man's mission . . . is the annihilation of his personal being and its replacement by a perfectly social or impersonal being.' [1] This is a conscious rejection of individualistic culture. 'Our present "ego" is not inflicted upon us by any inevitable law; we ourselves have placed it in our soul.' [2] Chaadayev asks:

'Can man ever acquire, in place of the personal and solitary consciousness which he now finds in himself, a *general consciousness*, which would make him constantly aware that he was a portion of a great spiritual whole?' [3]

Chaadayev answers this question in the affirmative: 'The germ of a higher consciousness is most definitely present in us; it forms the essence of our nature.' [4] This singular fascination with the hypothesis of a 'higher consciousness' is clearly an echo of *transcendentalism*, which, in general, views the empirical 'ego' as a mere condition for the manifestation of transcendental functions. In a way that is fully parallel to the dialectic of transcendentalism, which, especially in Hegel, assigned an 'instrumental' function to the individual, Chaadayev gives a place of chief importance to the 'higher consciousness'—always, however, distinguishing this 'higher' ('world' or 'universal') consciousness from the Absolute. On the one hand, there is a 'supernatural illumination' in man— which proceeds from God, 'descending from heaven to earth'; [5] on the other, there is in him an 'embryo of the higher consciousness', which is the deepest stratum of his nature. This 'natural', i.e. created, sphere of the 'higher consciousness' is strongly reminiscent of the 'transcendental sphere' of German idealism. This comparison makes intelligible such statements of Chaadayev as: 'God did not create time; He permitted man to create it.' It is not the empirical but the 'higher [transcendental] consciousness' which 'creates time'. 'The fusion of our being with the *universal being* . . .

1. *Ibid.*, p. 121        2. *Loc. cit.*        3. *Loc. cit.*
4. *Loc. cit.*        5. *Liter aturnoye nasledstvo*, p. 28.

promises a complete renewal of our nature, the ultimate limit of the efforts of a reasonable being, the predestined end of spirit in the world.' [1]

Thus the corruption of man—as a result of original sin—which finds expression in his false isolation from the 'universal being', i.e. from the *world as a whole*, leads to his 'separation from nature', creating the illusion of separateness of 'personal' being, and an ideology of individualism which is false through and through. By overcoming this phantom of isolation, the individual re-establishes his internal connection with the world-whole, renouncing isolation in order to find himself within the 'higher consciousness'. This is not mysticism, but a *metaphysics of man*, which in Chaadayev takes the form of an original amalgam of Schelling's doctrine of the world-soul with the social metaphysics of Bonalde and Ballanche.

'There is absolute unity', Chaadayev writes, 'in the total aggregate of beings; it is precisely this that we are attempting to the limit of our powers to demonstrate. This objective unity, existing completely apart from the reality which we perceive, throws extraordinary light on the great Whole. But it has nothing in common with the pantheism professed by a majority of contemporary philosophers.' [2]

In order to understand these ideas, we must emphasize that a few lines further on Chaadayev sharply and acutely criticizes metaphysical pluralism. For him, as for Pascal, whom he cites, mankind—in the continuous sequence of the generations—'is a single man', and each of us is a 'sharer in the work of the (higher) consciousness'. This higher (world) consciousness, which Chaadayev is ready to conceive on the analogy of world-matter [!],[3] is not a 'subject' but merely an 'aggregate of ideas', and this 'aggregate of ideas' is the '*spiritual essence of the universe*'.[4]

Here anthropology flows into cosmology, but it is clear at this point that the 'universe'—with its 'spiritual essence', its (universally-human) world-consciousness—is itself moved by a supramundane principle—by God. Chaadayev constructs his theory of being as follows: above the 'all' (with a small letter, i.e. above the created world) is God, from Whom creative emanations proceed into the world. The core of the world is the universally-human world-consciousness,[5] which receives these emanations. Lower

1. *Ibid.*, p. 35.      2. *Ibid.*, p. 46.      3. *Ibid.*, pp. 49f.      4. *Loc. cit.*
5. Chaadayev himself compares this concept—in his philosophy of history—with that of the *Weltgeist*. He wrote to Turgenev: 'There really is a universal Spirit, soaring above the world, the *Weltgeist* of which Schelling spoke to me.'

down comes the individual human being, who—because of original sin—has lost the consciousness of his connection with the whole and has torn himself away from nature. Still lower comes all of prehuman nature.

Chaadayev's epistemological views, which he expressed only in passing, were determined by his critique of Kantianism on the one hand (his polemic against the doctrine of 'pure' reason) and on the other by his critique of Descartes for halting at the empirical consciousness. This consciousness, according to Chaadayev, is a 'principle which is distorted, perverted, and mutilated by human arbitrariness'. At the same time Chaadayev resolutely combats the Aristotelian derivation of knowledge from the material of sense experience. For Chaadayev, knowledge results from a 'collision of consciousnesses', in other words, the interaction of men. He does not, of course, reject experience or empirical knowledge, but for him all sensory material is *controlled* by *rational ideas*, which are independent of experience. There is great subtlety in Chaadayev's remark that 'one of the secrets of the brilliant method of the natural sciences is that only what can actually become an object of observation is submitted to observation.' He distinguishes sharply between 'knowledge of the finite' and 'knowledge of the infinite'. In the former we always use the latter, for our ideas bring us light 'from the ocean of ideas in which we are immersed'. In other words, 'in knowing we make use of world-reason'. [1] And, since primary importance attaches to the 'mystical reality' which is hidden in the depths of spiritual nature, i.e. the 'ocean of ideas' which belongs to 'universally-human' ('universal', world) reason, all contemporary knowledge is greatly indebted to Christianity as a revelation of a higher reality in the world. Here Chaadayev writes, with typical anthropocentrism:

'Philosophers are not sufficiently interested in the study of purely human reality; their attitude toward it is too scornful. Because of their habitual contemplation of superhuman actions, they fail to note the *natural energies operating in the world*.'

Chaadayev's cosmology includes several interesting theoretical constructions, but we shall pass over them and turn to an

(*Sochineniya*, I, 183. [French.]) For Chaadayev's critique of the confusion of Creator and creation, see the forceful lines in *Literaturnoye nasledstvo*, p. 46.

1. N. I. Pirogov's remarkable doctrine of the human spirit comes very close to this. Of course, he could not have known Chaadayev's epistemology, which was first published in *Literaturnoye nasledstvo* in 1935. Concerning Pirogov see below, Ch. XIII.

exposition of his historiosophy. The latter will be sufficiently clear now, following our study of his anthropology.

### 14. PROVIDENTIALISM

If the reality of the 'higher consciousness' is above the consciousness of the individual, then the key to this consciousness is provided —apart from the metaphysics of man—by the existence of *history* as a *specific* form of being.

We are already familiar with Chaadayev's insistence that Christianity is revealed only in historical, not individual, being and cannot be understood apart from history. But he also asserts the converse: that historical being cannot be understood apart from Christianity. One must discard the passion for external historical facts which dominates science and turn to the 'sacred' process in history—to what is *basic* and *essential* in it. Only then, according to Chaadayev, will the true unity of history—its religious unity—be revealed. Chaadayev was concerned with the same problem as was Hegel: establishing the *basic* content of history, which is hidden under a wrapping of external facts. Of course, for Chaadayev there is a 'universal history', the 'subject' of which is mankind as a whole; however, its essence is not to be found in the mingling of peoples in a cosmopolitan jumble, but in the separate destiny, the special career, of different peoples. Each people is a 'moral individual'.

The meaning of history is realized by the 'divine will, which reigns in the ages and leads the human race toward its final goals.'[1] This conception is one of *providentialism*; hence Chaadayev speaks with sharp irony of the ordinary conception of history, which derives everything from the natural development of the human spirit, as though this spirit revealed no sign of the intervention of Divine Providence. He is even more ironic toward the theory of progress, which he characterizes as a doctrine of 'inevitable movement toward perfection'. To this superficial historiosophical determinism Chaadayev opposes his own doctrine that 'men are guided by mysterious promptings which operate apart from their consciousness.'[2]

But what is being created in history? How can one grasp the content of historical being more concretely? According to

1. See the whole of the Second Letter, devoted to the general philosophy of history. (*Sochineniya*, I, 94–119.)
2. *Literaturnoye nasledstvo*, p. 33.

Chaadayev, the *Kingdom of God* is being created, and therefore only providentialism can properly explain the historical process. But for Chaadayev, as we have seen, the Kingdom of God is being created *on earth*. Hence Christianity is essentially historical; it cannot be understood in 'other-worldly' terms. Thus Chaadayev's historiosophical conception demands that he exhibit his general idea in concrete historical material. Here Chaadayev, although he does not accept Chateaubriand's overemphasis on the aesthetic aspect of Christianity, nevertheless sketches the history of Christianity in the manner of Chateaubriand. But for Chaadayev the religious unity of history *presupposes* the *unity of the Church*—this is required by the logic of his historiosophy: since the divine energy penetrates into history through the Church, this very fact establishes the unity of the Church itself. Here Chaadayev's thought is influenced by his unconditional acceptance of the Christian West as that phase of history in which Providence is most fully realized. With unfeigned passion, genuine excitement, and warm feeling Chaadayev describes the 'miracles' of Christianity in the West— like Dostoyevsky in Ivan Karamazov's heated tirade, or Khomyakov, who spoke of the West as a 'land of holy miracles'. Chaadayev, more than any other Russian writer, perceived the West religiously, always following the course of history in the West with sympathy and emotion.

'In the West everything was created by Christianity . . .,' he wrote in the first "Philosophical Letter". 'Not everything in the European countries is permeated with reason, virtue, religion. . . . But everything is mysteriously dominated by the power which has been sovereign there for so many centuries. . . . Despite the emptiness, imperfection, and depravity of the European world, . . . it cannot be denied that the Kingdom of God has to a certain degree been realized there.'

Chaadayev's high appraisal of western Christianity, combined with the sharpest and most captious critique of Protestantism, is determined wholly by *historiosophical* rather than dogmatic considerations. This provides the key to what might be called his nonsectarian conception of Christianity. Catholicism inspired Chaadayev and aroused his enthusiasm—not its mystical and dogmatic side, but its influence on the historical process in the West. Chaadayev's defence of papism is wholly based on the fact that the Pope 'centralizes' Christian ideas (for history), that he is 'a visible sign of unity and at the same time a symbol of redintegration'. In studying Khomyakov we shall see that the logic of the concept 'unity of the Church' can lead to completely opposed conclusions, but we must admit that in Chaadayev this concept of 'unity of the Church' is motivated dialectically by *historiosophical*, not dogmatic, considerations. Recognizing that 'political Christianity' had already outlived its time, that now Christianity must be 'social' and 'more than at any other time must live in the realm of spirit and thence illuminate the world', Chaadayev nevertheless assumed that previously it had been 'necessary for Christianity to build its power and strength', without which the Church could not have given Christian civilization to the world. Chaadayev stands firmly behind this principle, which defines his theology of culture. It is not surprising that he measures the very *strength of Christianity* by its *cultural successes*. This is also the key to his critique of Russia.

Chaadayev's fiery and passionate accusations of Russia have *many* roots; they contain no *single* guiding idea. He could not include Russia in a scheme of providentialism which was suggested by the history of the West, and he candidly admitted a strange kind of *prejudice* in the very idea of providentialism: 'Providence', he wrote in one place, '*excluded* us [Russians] from its beneficent influence on the human mind . . ., leaving us *wholly to ourselves*.'[1] And even more sharply: '*Providence seems to have been wholly unconcerned with our fate.*' But how is this possible? First of all, the system of providentialism must be conceived as universal; but Chaadayev himself sees an influence of Providence even on non-Christian peoples. How are we to understand Chaadayev's remark that 'Providence seems to have refused to intervene in our [Russian] affairs'? The word 'seems' shows clearly that Chaadayev was well aware that there was something enigmatic in his judgments concerning Russia. Is it possible that peoples can evade Providence? Chaadayev's thinking tends *to some extent* to this conclusion; Russia, in his words, 'had *lost its way* on earth'. Hence his frequent bitter reproaches, directed at Russians: '*We* live only in the present, . . . without past or future', '*we* have taken nothing from the inherited ideas of the human race', 'historical experience does not exist *for us*', etc. These words ring with blame precisely because they assume that 'we'—the Russian people—*could have* taken a different path, but did not wish to. Therefore Chaadayev was in full harmony with his age: Russian radicalism had a similar

1. This and the following quotations are from the *first* 'Philosophical Letter'. (*Sochineniya*, I, 74–93.)

spiritual orientation; its accusations presupposed the freedom of Russians to choose better ways of life.

But Chaadayev offers another amendment to the enigma of Russia and to the discrepancies within the system of providential-ism. Is not Russian backwardness—'isolation from the universal education of mankind'—*also providential?* But, if so, then Russians are not to be reproached for their backwardness, since it conceals a *higher meaning*. In the first 'Philosophical Letter' (1829) Chaada-yev wrote: 'We are one of those nations which exist only to give the world some important lesson.' He later developed this motif in a number of new ideas about Russia. In 1835 (i.e. before the publication of his 'Philosophical Letter') he wrote to Turgenev:

'You know that in my opinion Russia has been summoned to an immense intellectual career: she must, one day, provide a solu-tion for all the questions which have been debated in Europe. Placed outside the swift movement which carries away men's minds [in Europe] . . ., the task has devolved upon her of one day providing the key to the human enigma.'[1]

These words indicate Russia's providential 'function'; but they also drain all meaning from the reproaches hurled against Russia in the 'Philosophical Letters'. Further on, Chaadayev's ideas become more definite; he reaches the conclusion that it is not yet Russia's turn to enter the arena of historical action. The new historic tasks facing the world, specifically, the solution of the *social* problem, are now conceived by Chaadayev as the *future* task of Russia. Earlier (i.e. before 1835) Chaadayev said of Russia with malicious irony that 'the general law of mankind is abrogated for her', that 'we constitute a gap in the moral order of the world', that 'in the blood of the Russians there is something inimical to true progress.'

'I cannot wonder enough at the extraordinary emptiness of our social existence. . . . We have sealed ourselves off in religious isolation . . .; we have not been equal to the great world-wide tasks . . . in which the social idea of Christianity was developed and formulated.'[2]

In the rediscovered letters we find sharp comments on Ortho-doxy:

'Why has Christianity not had the same consequences in Russia as in the West? Why is it that with us the action of religion is

1. *Sochineniya*, I, 181. [Original in French.]
2. First 'Philosophical Letter', *ibid.*, pp. 74–93.

reversed? It seems to me that this alone is ground for misgivings about the Orthodoxy on which we plume ourselves.' [1]

In 1835 there was a turn toward a new appraisal of Russia, as we have seen in the above-quoted passage from Chaadayev's letter to Turgenev. In another letter to Turgenev, in the same year, he wrote: 'Russia, if she *understands her mission*, must take the initiative for all generous ideas, since she does not have Europe's attachments, passions, ideas, or interests.' [2] It is remarkable that, even here, Russia has a special mission; she is not outside of Providence. 'Providence has made us too great to be egoists; it has placed us outside the interests of the nationalities [3] and charged us with the *interests of mankind*.'[4] In these last words, Chaadayev appropriates to Russia the high mission of a 'universally-human career'. But further on he develops this idea even more unexpectedly:

'We are destined to teach Europe an infinity of things which she could not understand without us. Don't laugh: you know that this is my *intimate conviction*. A day will come when we shall place ourselves at the intellectual focus of Europe. . . . Such is the logical result of our long solitude. . . . Our *universal mission* has begun.'[5]

In his unfinished work 'Apologie d'un fou', Chaadayev wrote (1837): '. . . We are summoned to solve a majority of the problems of the social order . . ., to settle the most serious questions that are preoccupying the human race.'[6] Now he admits: 'I am happy that I have occasion to make a confession: yes, there was exaggeration in the indictment which I brought against a great people [i.e. Russia]. . . . It was an exaggeration not to do justice to the [Orthodox] Church, so humble and sometimes so heroic. . . .'[7] In a letter to Count Sircour (1845) Chaadayev wrote: 'Our church is essentially ascetic, just as yours is essentially social. . . . These are the two poles of the Christian sphere, which turns on the axis of its absolute truth. . . .' [8] We quote a few more passages, which were dictated by the same wish to 'justify himself' and to cancel his earlier one-sided judgments. 'I have loved my country in my own way', he wrote in 1846, ten years after his conviction, 'and to have the reputation of a faithless Russian has been harder for me than I can tell you.' [9] But, however 'beautiful love of one's fatherland

1. *Literaturnoye nasledstvo*, p. 23.    2. *Sochineniya*, I, 185. [French.]
3. Thus something for which Russia had previously been rebuked was now regarded as the work of Providence.
4. *Loc. cit.*    5. *Ibid.*, p. 188.    6. *Ibid.*, p. 230.    7. *Ibid.*, pp. 232f.
8. *Ibid.*, p. 254. [French.]    9. *Ibid.*, p. 277. [French.]

is, there is something more beautiful—love of the truth. The path to Heaven leads not through one's *homeland* but through the *truth*.' This firm and convinced striving for the truth, and through it to heaven, best characterizes Chaadayev's basic spiritual make-up.

## 15. GENERAL APPRAISAL

It is time to sum up.

In appraising Chaadayev's philosophic theories it is necessary, as we have already indicated, to place his 'westernism' in a position of secondary importance. It is significant only as a concrete application of his general ideas. To be sure, before the appearance in print (in 1935) of five letters, out of eight, which were long considered lost, it was difficult to accept this view. But now, when we have before us all that Chaadayev wrote, it is clear that the centre of his system lies in his anthropology and philosophy of history. We have characterized Chaadayev's doctrine as a theology of culture precisely because he perceived deeply the complex of *religious problems of culture*, the 'mystery of the age', of which he spoke in his remarkable letter to Pushkin. Chaadayev was wholly concerned, not with the external aspect of history, but with its 'sacred mystery', the higher meaning which is to be realized in history. Christianity cannot be isolated from history, nor can history be isolated from Christianity. This is an attempt at a *Christocentric* conception of history, and one which is much better integrated than is Khomyakov's historiosophy. This provides the key to the passionate feeling for the 'unity of the Church' which defined Chaadayev's appraisal of the West and of Russia; but it is also a manifestation of his theurgical approach to history. Man possesses sufficient freedom to be *responsible for history*. And this acute sense of responsibility, this feeling for the 'flame of history', which so often passed into a singular historiosophical mysticism in Chaadayev, relates him—much more than his whole critique of Russia—to the radical Russian intelligentsia, which always felt so passionately and warmly its 'responsibility' for the destiny not only of Russia but of the *whole world*. The universalism of Chaadayev's thought, his freedom from narrow nationalism, his striving 'toward heaven through the truth, not through homeland'—not only give high value to Chaadayev's theoretical constructions, but also lead him to the elucidation of a 'theology of culture'. On this path Chaadayev developed his critique of individualism and of every 'isolating' orientation, generally. On this path he felt more deeply than others the social aspect of life; hence the idea of the Kingdom of God is for him the key to an understanding of history. History moves toward the Kingdom of God—and toward it alone: and this movement reveals the influence of Providence, the nature and operation of the 'mysterious force which directs the course of history'. But extreme providentialism is alien to Chaadayev: he leaves room for human freedom. However, man's freedom is not complete autonomy, or independence of the Absolute; freedom manifests itself creatively only when we follow a higher principle. If we do not follow God, freedom becomes a 'dreadful force', destructive in character. This is very close to the formula which Vladimir Solovyov advanced in a late period of his creative activity: man's freedom is manifested only in his impulse toward *evil*, not toward good. But the ultimate source of such a distorted manifestation of the 'dreadful force' of freedom ('which rocks the whole universe'), according to Chaadayev, is the injustice and falseness of all individualism, all isolation. The individual spirit is rooted not in itself but in a 'higher' (world) consciousness; therefore, when it isolates itself from this higher consciousness, the 'pernicious ego'— having torn itself away from its own spiritual womb and hence away from nature—becomes operative in it. This is a consequence of the radical corruption of human nature (original sin), which creates the mirage of the separateness of individual being. Only by renouncing the 'pernicious ego' and submitting to the voice of the higher consciousness, can man find his true path; and then he becomes a bearer of the higher principles which emanate from God.

It is not collectivism, which interprets this thesis too naturalistically, but the Church as sociality illumined by grace, that realizes God's designs in history. Hence only the subordination of external historical being to the idea of the Kingdom of God can initiate us into the 'mystery of the age'. This for Chaadayev is true realism, responsible participation in historical activity, union with the sacred aspect of history.

The importance for Russian thought of Chaadayev's theoretical constructions results from the fact that many of Russia's major thinkers have recurred to his themes, although his resolutions of these themes have had comparatively few adherents.

# CHAPTER VI

## The Return to the Ecclesiastical World-View

GOGOL

## The Beginning of 'Slavophilism'

A. S. KHOMYAKOV

### I. THE RETURN TO THE ECCLESIASTICAL WORLD-VIEW

THE break with the ecclesiastical world-view, which began in the second half of the seventeenth century and attained full expression in the eighteenth, raised the question—as we have seen—of the creation of a new ideology. The first theoretical statements of this new ideology advanced a programme of humanism, foundations for which were sought in pure morality, and frequently in 'natural law'. But toward the end of the eighteenth century moralistic humanism was complicated by the introduction of an aesthetic principle; and this form of humanism, which derived from Schiller's idea of the '*Schöne Seele*', long remained the dominant Russian ideology. The Russian intelligentsia, having broken away from the Church, sought inspiration in an aesthetic humanism, grounding its social movements in the latter. But the Russian intelligentsia, as we have seen, retained one feature of the former ecclesiastical consciousness—what we have called its 'theurgical idea'. 'Theurgical restlessness' kept thought and conscience at the height of historiosophical universalism; in this way a concern was developed and strengthened in the Russian intelligentsia for 'universally-human' themes, an intense and somewhat vacuous preoccupation with the problems of mankind 'in general'.

This historiosophical universalism, by its very nature, involved an inevitable return to religious questions; in any case, it awakened and nourished men's religious energies. In fact, despite the brilliant and triumphant development of the spirit of secularization, we find a return to a religious conception of the world even in the eighteenth century. And in the nineteenth century, Labzin, Speranski, and the various mystical tendencies of the period of Alexander I put forward religious ideas, as the basis for a new ideology, more and more insistently. Finally, in Chaadayev the idea of the Church took on such profound and fundamental importance that the meaning of history itself could no longer be revealed apart from it. But we must keep in mind that Chaadayev's theories—aside from the fact that his works (except for the first 'Philosophical Letter') remained unpublished—could have had no *direct* influence for the simple reason that, on his view, the Church, as the motive force of history, had made itself evident only in the West. Russia—in his early theories—was outside the action of Providence, excluded from the 'mystery of the age'. Thus Chaadayev's religious position provided nothing for the construction of a *Russian* ideology. We find the same thing in those Russians who embraced Catholicism: there was nothing for them to do in Russia.[1] But, after Chaadayev, other thinkers appeared who defended the primacy of the idea of the Church with just as much passion and inspiration, but found the 'true' Church in Orthodoxy, with which Russia was organically fused, rather than in Catholicism, which was historically alien to it. This made it possible for the religious position of these thinkers to fructify the ideological searchings of the Russian intelligentsia in a creative way. And, in fact, the religious thinkers who associated themselves with the Orthodox Church became the leaders and inspirers of a powerful, creative, and daring movement, which sought in the ecclesiastical consciousness an answer to all the complex and tormenting problems of life. This was also the beginning of a very deep and fruitful tendency in Russian philosophy.

We assign N. V. Gogol a position of first importance in this new group, not from chronological considerations, but because he expressed the disintegration of moral and aesthetic humanism more sharply than anyone else. Gogol may be called without exaggeration a prophet of Orthodox culture; this was his specific contribution to the development of Russian philosophic thought, and this explains his enormous significance for the dialectic of the spiritual life of nineteenth-century Russia.

1. In this connection the fate of Pechyorin's creative activity—which we have already mentioned in passing—is especially tragic.

## 2. GOGOL

Nikolai Vasilyevich Gogol (1809–52) was one of the creators of modern Russian literature and a writer of genius, but his religious searchings were no less remarkable. For a long time he was not understood by Russian society, or even by Russian ecclesiastical thinkers.[1] Indeed, his contribution to the treasury of Russian thought was not revealed until the twentieth century. Gogol's literary fame hindered the acceptance of his intellectual work for a long time.—Is there anyone who has not condemned Gogol for having strayed from the path of artistic creation! In the tragic burning of the second volume of *Dead Souls*, which is intimately bound up with Gogol's whole spiritual effort, most critics see an 'attack of mental illness'; they fail to notice the essence of the tragic collision of Church and culture which Gogol perceived so clearly, and the shock of which he took upon himself. There is no one in the history of Russian spiritual life who can be compared to Gogol in this respect; for he was tormented—not simply theoretically, but with his whole personality—by the theme of the interrelation of Church and culture. Chaadayev, who was closer to him than anyone else, was a man of 'solemn and intense' temperament. But, whereas Chaadayev saw nothing tragic in the problem of 'Church and culture', Gogol experienced this tragedy with exceptional force.

A great many critics refuse to accept Gogol as a thinker, but there is no question that he was one. The charge that his 'education was inadequate' must be finally repudiated as a result of S. A. Vengerov's work on Gogol. However, it is true that Gogol developed, in a sense, apart from his contemporaries, clearing his own path. Nevertheless, he was unquestionably influenced by German romanticism, which he knew through the numerous translations of German literary and philosophic works in the Russian journals.

Gogol's external biography is quite uncomplicated. He was the son of a Ukrainian writer, lost his father at an early age, and was brought up by his mother, a deeply and sincerely religious woman. After studying at home, Gogol entered the Lyceum at Nezhin and, following his graduation, went to St. Petersburg in search of fame. His first literary work, a long poem, was a failure; but when,

---

1. A place of first importance among the few ecclesiastical writers who really understood Gogol's basic ideas must be assigned to Archimandrite Bukharev (see his *Tri pisma k N. V. Gogolyu* [Three Letters to N. V. Gogol], St. Petersburg, 1861). Concerning Bukharev, see Ch. X.

somewhat later, he published *Evenings on a Farm Near Dikanka* he attracted universal notice. His literary creativity began to develop rapidly. Gogol was acknowledged as a first-class writer, and formed friendships with Pushkin, Zhukovski, and other literary men. At one point he developed scholarly interests, becoming a Professor of History at St. Petersburg University; but scholarly work was not to his liking and he soon left the University. Between 1831 and 1835 Gogol printed a few short stories and theoretical sketches, in which one of the central themes of his artistic and intellectual work was immediately defined: the problem of the aesthetic principle in man. Here, for the first time in the history of Russian thought, Gogol broached the question of aesthetic amoralism, posing with extreme sharpness the problem of the disparity of man's aesthetic and moral life. With Gogol, the ideology of aesthetic humanism began its disintegration; the complex of problems inherent in the aesthetic sphere was exhibited for the first time. Gogol was by nature heavily inclined toward a somewhat abstract and rigoristic moralism—a moralism that was almost obtrusively severe even toward himself. But, in addition to this moralism, he had a passionate and all-absorbing love of art. He loved art, so to speak, with invincible power. His consciousness of the specifically amoral quality of the aesthetic sphere (see below) led Gogol to the creation of an *aesthetic utopia*, which was manifestly unrealizable, dictated by the need to convince himself that art was 'useful'. The break-up of this utopia—externally connected with the staging of his brilliant comedy *The Inspector General [Revizor]*—produced an extreme trauma in Gogol's spiritual world. Revealing the precariousness and instability of all humanism, it cleared the ground for a religious crisis. And, in fact, Gogol began, in 1836 (when he was 27) to return deeply and passionately to religious life; and this religious interest never slackened. Gogol gradually began to work out a new conception of life and culture. He did a great deal of literary work, publishing the first volume of *Dead Souls*. But at the same time he was immersing himself with greater and greater intensity in religious life. He projected the publication of a theoretical work devoted to problems of Church and culture, and in 1847 he published Selected Passages from Letters to My Friends. This book —in which new, daring, and creative ideas are often expressed in naïve, sometimes very pretentious, and occasionally even unacceptable form—was not understood by Russian society. It aroused sharp and hostile criticism, the most striking expression of which was Belinski's famous letter to Gogol. Gogol took its failure extremely hard. He could not renounce his religious world-view, but the consciousness of the tragic incompatibility of Church and culture continued to oppress him with excessive power. In a fit of tormenting doubts he burned the second volume of *Dead Souls*, after which he lapsed into a state of extreme depression and soon died. Gogol lived only forty-three years, but during those years he not only enriched Russian literature with works of genius but introduced into Russian life the theme which to the present time has been one of the central themes of Russian searchings: that of the return of culture to the Church and the construction of a new ecclesiastical world-view—the theme of an 'Orthodox culture'.

Evidently the time has not yet come for a just historical appraisal of Gogol as a thinker—probably because the problems which he raised continue to agitate and disturb Russians in our own time. This in itself shows sufficiently the importance of the crisis which Gogol experienced. We shall not enter here into a detailed analysis of all of his ideas but shall treat only what is relevant to the dialectic of Russian philosophic searchings.[1]

### 3. THE CRITIQUE OF HUMANISM

Let us consider first of all Gogol's critique of moralistic humanism. His own moral consciousness was, as we have said, very acute and intense; in this respect he was close to the immense majority of Russian thinkers. But, with all the force and acuteness of his moral consciousness ('in the field of morality', one of his biographers remarks, 'Gogol was a genius'[2]), Gogol carried within him a kind of poison—or, more precisely, a profound sense of the whole tragic complex of problems inherent in the contemporary moral consciousness. He himself realized that the moral ideal which 'obsessed' him was unrealistic, even unnatural—a kind of rhetorical fiction without support in the natural structure of the soul. He experienced this most acutely and with greatest torment in connection with the theme which is so basic for all European and Russian humanism— that of one's relation toward men as brothers. 'But how can one love one's brothers?' Gogol writes. 'How can one love human beings? The soul wishes to love only what is *beautiful*, and the poor are so shabby; there is so little of beauty in them.' The moral principle is powerless, for in reality the soul is moved not by *moral*

1. The literature on Gogol as a thinker is not extensive. See my articles: 'Gogol als Denker' and 'Gogols ästhetische Utopie', *Zeitschrift für slav. Philologie* IX (1932). The French book by B. Schloezer, *Gogol*, 1932, is quite superficial.
2. K. Mochulski, *Dukhovny put Gogolya* [Gogol's Spiritual Path], p. 87.

but by *aesthetic* impulses. In other words, the human soul is wholly incapable, in its present condition, of truly moral action, i.e. of love. 'Nineteenth-century man rejects his brother. . . . He is ready to embrace all mankind, but he will not embrace his brother.' The moral ideal is thus merely a rhetorical fiction. However, all men are connected by such deep ties that in truth 'all are guilty for all'. This formula, which was forged later by Dostoyevsky, does not appear in Gogol—but its essence is there. He often expresses the idea that we are 'obliquely' (i.e. indirectly or imperceptibly) connected with all men, and that all of our actions and thoughts influence others.[1] In other words, the theme of morality and the good is inevitable, inescapable; it stands before every human being in fearful and threatening form, but it finds no support in the present structure of the soul. The dreadful thing, Gogol says in one place, is that we 'see no good in the good', i.e. even where genuine good exists, we are not in a condition to perceive it as good.[2]

The 'natural' amoralism of contemporary man is connected for Gogol with the dominance of the aesthetic principle. The problem of the nature of this principle and its relation to morality pre-occupied, even tormented, Gogol throughout his life. He was himself a warm and passionate admirer of art, but he laid bare the secret tragedy of the aesthetic principle with full and relentless honesty. Gogol here probed the very depths of that aesthetic humanism which, since the time of Karamzin, had become so deeply rooted in the Russian soul. In the short story 'Nevski Avenue' ['Nevski Prospekt'] Gogol tells of an artist whose soul is dominated by a profound faith in the unity of the aesthetic and moral principles. This faith is destroyed by his encounter with life. The artist meets on the street a woman of striking beauty, who turns out to be connected with a house of ill-fame. The artist is seized by despair; he tries to persuade the beautiful woman to give up her life, but she greets his words with mockery and scorn. The poor artist is unable to bear this dreadful discord between outward beauty and inner corruption. He loses his mind and, in a fit of madness, kills himself.

In another story, 'Taras Bulba', Gogol shows the discrepancy of

1. All of these quotations are from *Vybrannyie mesta iz perepiski s druzyami* [Selected Passages from Letters to My Friends]. [This work is available in a German translation by U. Steindorf, Munich, 1914. *Trans.*]

2. This theme underlies Leo Tolstoy's remarkable book *What Then Is to Be Done?*, which is in many respects a work of genius. Vladimir Solovyov wrote a well-known book on the theme of the 'justification' of the good.

the aesthetic and moral spheres from another perspective: the young Cossack Andri, overcome by love for a beautiful woman, gives up his family, his homeland, and his faith and goes over to the enemy camp without experiencing the least embarrassment or concern. In Andri the aesthetic principle, which is spontaneous and extramoral, dominates completely. He formulates the basic principle of the aesthetic attitude toward the world in clear terms: 'My homeland is where my heart is.' This is not only a renunciation of the very principle of morality but an assertion of the spontaneous force and fatal dynamism of an aesthetic impulse which throws down all moral barriers. Here we can detect the foundations of that anthropology which Dostoyevsky later expressed so forcefully in his doctrine of the chaotic and extramoral character of the human soul.

The more deeply Gogol realized the tragic incompatibility of the aesthetic and moral principles, the more problematical did the theme of beauty and art become for him. It was precisely for this reason that Gogol, who was boundlessly in love with art, constructed an aesthetic utopia by means of which he hoped to save himself from this collision. He was aflame with the faith that art can evoke in men a genuine impulse toward the good. In this faith he wrote his comedy *The Inspector General*, a work of genius, which was an enormous success on the stage but which, of course, brought about no moral upheaval in Russian life.[1] Gogol realized this; he understood clearly the utopian character of his hopes, and this realization was the point of departure for his further searchings. The separateness of beauty and the good means essentially that aesthetic humanism is *unrealistic*; only something deeper than either of them—i.e. religion—can genuinely unite them. Gogol's religious searchings developed around this theme: religion for him had the mission of transfiguring man's natural order, his culture, his creative activity. He did not turn to religion in isolation from culture; rather, he sought in it a solution to the ultimate problems of culture. He finally reached the point of relating all culture to the Church, thus posing the theme of ideology and introducing permanently into Russian thought the idea of an 'Orthodox culture'.

### 4. THE IDEA OF AN ORTHODOX CULTURE

We find in Gogol many deep and important critical reflections on Western culture; however, the fundamental meaning of his

1. See my study 'Gogols ästhetische Utopie', *op. cit.*

theoretical statements lies not in these, but in the assertion that the Orthodox Church 'has the potentiality of solving all the problems which have now been posed so sharply before all mankind.' This is a new idea, which became the point of departure for many Russian thinkers. The concept of culture was torn away from internal connection with its Western form. The thought appeared in Gogol for the first time (incidentally, it had also flashed across Russian thought earlier, in an obscure form) that Russia's path was essentially different from that of the West, since the spirit of Orthodoxy was different from that of Western Christianity. This idea of Russia's 'different' path appeared not only in the Slavophiles, in Herzen, and in Russian Populism, but also in a subsequent trend of socio-political thought—that of N. K. Mikhailovski *et al.* At the same time, return to the ecclesiastical idea no longer entailed a rejection of secular culture (as had been the case in the fifteenth and sixteenth centuries). Rather, it raised the question of the Christian *sanctification* and *transfiguration* of culture, toward which earlier Russian thought had moved, as we have seen—especially in Skovoroda. Gogol called for a reconstruction of all culture in the spirit of Orthodoxy; he was truly a prophet of 'Orthodox culture'. He thought through the question of the sanctification of art, and its Christian ministry, with special profundity and acuity. He was the first in the history of Russian thought to undertake an *aesthetic* critique of contemporary life, lashing its *vulgarity*. The trenchant critique of 'spiritual philistinism' which was later developed with such force by Herzen, Leontyev, and Dostoyevsky, was already expressed with enormous force in Gogol—beginning with his early ('Petersburg') stories, and including the novels *Rome* and *Dead Souls*. But Gogol also wrote constantly on how the aesthetic principle in man could be saved—how man could be directed toward the good, from which contemporary aesthetic tendencies had torn him. Hence Gogol's insistent emphasis on the *theurgical* function of art: 'We should not repeat Pushkin', he said, i.e. we should not create 'art for art's sake', 'however beautiful such a task might be'. Art is 'now faced with other tasks': to inspire mankind in the struggle for the Kingdom of God, i.e. to connect its creative activity with the Church's ministry in the world. Gogol always conceived the Church as a vital union of mystical energy and historical influence upon the world: 'A full and rounded view of life has survived in the Eastern Church; there is wide room in it not only for the soul and heart of man but for all the sovereign powers of reason.' For Gogol the 'highest court of appeal is the

Church'; 'only the Church has the power to resolve all our perplexities, quandaries, and problems.' [1]

'Within our land there is a conciliator who is not yet evident to everyone—namely, our Church. . . . In her is the rule and regulation of a new *incipient order of things*; and, the more I enter into her with heart, mind, and meditation, the more am I astonished at her marvellous potentiality for reconciling the contradictions which the Western Church . . .—a Church that has only turned mankind away from Christ—does not now have the power to reconcile.'

This, as we see, is a complete programme for the construction of a culture in the spirit of Orthodoxy, on the basis of *'wide room'*, i.e. a free turning to Christ. Gogol was aflame with a kind of 'luminous vision', to use Gershenzon's expression [2]—a vision of that 'new order of things', as Archimandrite Bukharev wrote, 'in which Orthodoxy is revealed to the world in the full light of its *universal*, regal significance.' [3] Gogol himself emphasized the 'universality of Christ's law of human love' [4]—its applicability in every situation, its sanctifying influence in every place, in all the phenomena of life. Thus Gogol's religious consciousness was free from the theocratic flavour; he accepted all the forms of culture, [5] taking into account the fact that mankind 'does not [now] have the power to encounter Christ directly'. And he saw the ecclesiastical function of art as the arousing of souls for this encounter.

This whole position not only lays new foundations for ideology, but in general marks—if not the opening—at least the approach of a period of new and free bringing together of cultural consciousness and Church. But, of course, the dialectic of the idea of Orthodox culture would have been sterile if this idea had remained merely a programme. The task of exhibiting it in a concrete system was undertaken primarily by the so-called 'senior Slavophiles' —headed by A. S. Khomyakov and I. V. Kireyevski—to whom we now turn.

1. See 'Avtorskaya ispoved' ['Author's Confession'], *Sochineniya* [Works], Berlin, 1921, X, 59.

2. *Istoricheskiye zapiski* [Historical Notes], 2nd ed., 1923, p. 175. Gershenzon, by the way, relates these words to Gogol's moral ideal; on his own admission Gogol's religious world remained closed to him (*ibid.*, p. 177).

3. Bukharev, *op. cit.*, p. 54.

4. 'Author's Confession', *Sochineniya*, X, 54.

5. See, for example, his especially ardent defence of the theatre (from a religious point of view), *op. cit.*, IX, 87–104.

## 5. GENERAL REMARKS ON SLAVOPHILISM. KHOMYAKOV.
### BIOGRAPHY

In studying the senior Slavophiles: Khomyakov, Kireyevski, K. Aksakov, Samarin, we must try in every way to avoid stylized characterizations. Although all of them were spiritually very close, and constantly influenced one another, we should not forget that each of them was a brilliant personality whose development was completely individual. For this reason we shall not speak of the 'philosophy of the Slavophiles' in general,[1] but of the philosophic ideas of each individual thinker.

The position of first importance must be assigned to A. S. Khomyakov; he was the leader of the whole group, and he brought to it both inspiration and intense activity. Although his fundamental philosophic articles were written more or less as a continuation and development of those of I. V. Kireyevski—as a result of which Kireyevski is often considered the creator of the philosophic system of the Slavophiles—Khomyakov's world-view had actually taken shape before Kireyevski experienced his religious conversion. Khomyakov's unquestionable priority will become clear when we consider Kireyevski's theories in the next chapter.

Aleksei Stepanovich Khomyakov (1804–60) was an extremely well-integrated, brilliant, and original human being, with very diverse talents and interests. He was a competent poet and dramatist, and was not without talent for social and political writing. Though not a 'professional' scholar, i.e. a professor, Khomyakov was an extraordinarily well-educated and well-informed person, with immense erudition in the most varied fields. As a theologian he was very well read in the works of the Church Fathers and in the history of the Church; as a philosopher he was acquainted with the most recent thinkers; as an historian (who wrote an interesting book called Notes on Universal History, in three volumes) his reading, one might say, was universal. At the same time, Khomyakov was a gentleman farmer who busied himself enthusiastically and intelligently about his farm, and was always inventing something new for the farm economy. Temperamentally, he was a 'warrior'—bold, straightforward, and strong.

Khomyakov's mother (née Kireyevskaya) occupied a place of great importance in his life; she was a person of deep religiosity, firm faith, and spiritual integrity. The strength and firmness of a

1. As even Gratieux does in his work devoted to Khomyakov (*A. S. Khomiakoff et le mouvement slavophile*, 2 vols., Paris, 1939).

faith illuminated by reason, which distinguishes Khomyakov among Russian religious thinkers (very few of whom failed to pass through a period of doubts), is connected with the spiritual atmosphere in which he lived from childhood. An interesting story has been preserved from his youthful period which testifies equally to his ardent character—sometimes reaching the point of extreme passion—and his acute observation. Khomyakov was studying Latin with a certain Abbé Boivin, and the two were translating a papal bull into Russian. The boy noticed a misprint in the bull, and jokingly asked the Abbé how he could consider the Pope infallible when he made mistakes in spelling.

When Khomyakov and his brother were taken to St. Petersburg, the boys thought that they had come to a pagan city and that they would be forced to give up their faith; they resolved firmly to suffer martyrdom rather than submit to an alien faith. These minor episodes depict very well Khomyakov's militancy and fearless readiness to defend truth and justice. At the age of seventeen he tried to run away from home in order to take part in the Greek war of liberation.

At the age of eighteen Khomyakov enlisted in the military service and within a few years saw active duty, conducting himself with outstanding bravery. While he was still a youth, and especially in later life, Khomyakov strictly observed all the fasts and attended services of worship on Sundays and holy days. He experienced no religious doubts, but there was neither sanctimoniousness nor sentimentalism in his faith. It burned always with a bright, strong, and steady flame. In order to characterize Khomyakov's personality, let us quote one or two testimonials written by persons who knew him well. Herzen, who was not particularly friendly toward Khomyakov, wrote of him:

'A powerful and active intellect, rich in resources and unscrupulous in their use, gifted with a fine memory and a quick mind—he disputed his way passionately and indefatigably through life. A tireless and relentless warrior, he struck and thrust, attacked and pursued, heaping his opponent with quotations and brilliant sallies. . . .' [1]

Further on we read: 'Khomyakov, like the medieval knights standing watch in the temple of the Mother of God, slept armed.' In the same passage Herzen calls him a 'dialectical swashbuckler'.

1. A. I. Herzen, *My Past and Thoughts*, Pt. IV, Ch. 30.

This is the opinion of a man who was not generally friendly to Khomyakov. Here is the opinion of his friend, M. P. Pogodin:

'What a gifted, lovable, and original nature was his! What an all-embracing intellect, what vitality, what a wealth of ideas (his head was a seemingly inexhaustible source of them)! How much knowledge of the most varied kind, joined with an extraordinary talent for words, which flowed from his mouth in a living stream! What was there that he did not know? There was no science in which Khomyakov did not have the widest knowledge, concerning which he was not able to carry on prolonged discussions with specialists. . . . And at the same time he wrote projects for freeing the peasants, laid out the boundaries of the American republics, indicated the route for the ships seeking [the arctic explorer] Franklin, analyzed Napoleon's defeat in minute detail, recited from memory whole pages of Shakespeare, Goethe, and Byron, expounded the theory of the Edda and Buddhist cosmogony.'

This diversity of knowledge and interests amounted almost to a dispersion of the intellect. Khomyakov did not neglect a single theme. This did not mean that he was superficial, but it did hinder intellectual concentration. We must also add that Khomyakov was a first-class dialectician, who loved to dispute and discuss; he was marked both by an unusual memory and by resourcefulness in dialectical skirmishes. Lively discussions absorbed him completely, but he did not particularly like to write. His philosophic views suffered especially from this, being expounded only apropos. The articles written during the last years of his life are the most systematic, but Khomyakov did not reduce his views to a finished system. There was a kind of chaotic quality in his very wholeness. Nevertheless he was a genuine philosopher, as well as a profound theologian, and one cannot help regretting that so much of his energy was expended on unimportant things.

Khomyakov had a family, and his family life was very happy. Being a true nobleman, he was never employed in government service except for his period in the army. Moreover, he was a true 'country gentleman', remaining cool and indifferent to political questions, although he was very much interested in social problems. His deep and whole-hearted loyalty to Orthodoxy was joined with an acute sense of what made Orthodoxy different from Catholicism and Protestantism. When the English theologian Palmer became interested in Orthodoxy—wishing at one time to become a convert—Khomyakov struck up a lively correspondence with him, which is theologically very interesting. In general Khomyakov followed the Western judgments of Orthodoxy closely, and wrote several remarkable articles on this subject. Incidentally, all of his theological writings—including his remarkable treatise, The Church Is One—were first published not in Russia but in Berlin (in 1867, after Khomyakov's death), and this volume was not admitted for sale in Russia until 1879.

Khomyakov, in N. A. Berdyaev's apt phrase, was a 'knight of the Church'. And, indeed, one feels in his straightforward, free, genuinely filial, and unservile attitude toward the Church not only strength and loyalty but a vital organic unity with it. Samarin, in his remarkable preface to Khomyakov's theological works, unhesitatingly assigns him the high title of 'teacher of the Church'. This characterization, though exaggerated, indicates correctly the fundamental character of Khomyakov's theological works. He introduced a new tendency into Russian theology—one might even say, a new method; [1] this is acknowledged by almost all Russian theologians.[2] In any case, Khomyakov has his place in the history of Russian theology; his works will not be forgotten.

Khomyakov's life was cut off suddenly—he died from an attack of cholera.[3]

## 6. INFLUENCES ON KHOMYAKOV

In studying Khomyakov, the question arises first of all of the influences to which he was exposed. We have already mentioned his broad and many-sided education. Throughout his life he read a great deal, both in the theological and philosophic disciplines. His articles and studies afford only *incidental* evidence of this; it would be rash to rely on them in establishing how and under what influences Khomyakov's world-view was formed. In view of the unquestionable wholeness of Khomyakov's own nature and the unquestionable unity of his views during the entire period of his

1. Florovsky (*Puti russkovo bogosloviya* [Paths of Russian Theology], p. 274) speaks of Khomyakov's 'ecclesiasticism' as a 'method' ('to be within the Church is a necessary prelude to theological knowledge'). This conveys Khomyakov's basic conviction accurately.

2. Florenski has produced the only sharp and unjust critique of Khomyakov. However, Florenski was himself an outstanding theologian. Concerning him, see Ch. XXX.

3. On Khomyakov see, in addition to the above-mentioned work of Gratieux, Arseniew, 'Khomiakov und Möhler,' *Una Sancta*, 1927. (Sonderheft 'Ostkirche.')

literary activity, we must assume that the basic and determining influences fell in the *early* period of his life, i.e. before 1840. Since Khomyakov's religious ideas were of central importance for his whole system, the basic and determining influences must be sought in this sphere.

We must first point out how extraordinarily well-read Khomyakov was in the works of the Church Fathers. He studied them very carefully, becoming permeated with their spirit; indeed, his basic theological views took shape under their influence. Of course, Khomyakov was self-taught in this field, but his not having attended theological school was actually favourable to his creative activity. His thought drew sustenance, not from textbooks or contemporary theological scholasticism, but from the works of the Church Fathers. His own deep and vital religiosity and his authentic life in the Church took on meaning for him in the light of what he discovered in patristic literature. Florovsky assumes that the works of St. Augustine influenced Khomyakov strongly, since he bases his polemic with the Western faiths on the same distinction between 'love' and 'discord' that St. Augustine insists upon.[1] This is possible, of course, but Khomyakov could not have found in St. Augustine his emphasis on the moral element in the knowledge of God—something which Khomyakov had unquestionably accepted prior to his polemical brochures; for St. Augustine's theory of the knowledge of God does not focus on this element. Thus we must seek the source of Khomyakov's theological inspirations not in any *individual* Church Father, but in patristic literature generally.

In addition to the Church Fathers, Khomyakov studied Church history very carefully; he also studied the history of religion in great detail, as is amply evidenced by his Notes on Universal History, in which an analysis of religious beliefs underlies the whole exposition. Khomyakov derives the basic generalization of his historiosophy—the system of freedom and the system of necessity—from this analysis. He also followed the religio-philosophic and theological literature of his time, as is evidenced by his theological polemics. We should not forget that Khomyakov was in constant touch with the most outstanding of his contemporaries: Chaadayev, the Kireyevski brothers, Odoyevski, Alexander Turgenev—and, later, Herzen, Pogodin, Shevyryov, *et al.*, all of whom followed the religio-philosophic literature of the West with unremitting attention. The question of the influence of the noted Catholic theologian Möhler, and his early book *Die Einheit der Kirche*

1. Florovsky, *op. cit.*, p. 278.

(1825),[1] on Khomyakov deserves special notice. Khomyakov was apparently familiar with all the works of this remarkable theologian; nevertheless we should not speak of Möhler's *influence* on Khomyakov. Although both of them based themselves essentially on the great Church Fathers, and although Möhler's definition of the Church (the central conception of Khomyakov's whole system) comes very close to Khomyakov's—nevertheless, though their similarity is great, their *differences* are unquestionable. What might be called Khomyakov's 'vision of the Church' is much more *internal*, more *spiritual*, so to speak. Florenski was wholly wrong to see traces or hints of a theory of 'panhuman sovereignty' in Khomyakov's doctrine of 'organic togetherness' [*sobornost*]. Even with respect to Möhler, such a suspicion would be out of the question. For him, as for Khomyakov, the Church is primarily an organism, but for Möhler it must also be an *organization*—whereas in Khomyakov one may find, by plucking individual phrases out of context, elements of an 'anarchic' approach to the definition of the Church.[2]

The question of purely philosophic influences on Khomyakov is much more complex and tangled. We must emphasize first of all the unquestionable influence of German romanticism, taken as a whole. The mystical tendencies in German romanticism were unquestionably alien to Khomyakov, but his cosmological ideas—which he developed in the last period of his life and, unfortunately, in a very fragmentary way—follow the outlines of romantic naturephilosophy. What is sometimes called Khomyakov's 'voluntarism'[3] is much closer to romantic cosmology than to the genuine voluntarism of Schopenhauer (whose works Khomyakov did not know; nevertheless, they have very interesting points in common). Schelling's influence was especially important—not only his *naturephilosophy* but his *transcendentalism* as well, a fact which is not generally noticed. Khomyakov follows Schelling essentially in his critique of Hegel, to whom Khomyakov devotes many pages. 'Organism'—the central category of Khomyakov's thought, which runs through his epistemology, anthropology, aesthetics, and philosophy of history—is unquestionably connected with Schelling's nature-philosophy. Berdyaev asserts, without any particular evidence, that Schellingism did not play a large role in Khomyakov's

1. A French translation of this book was published in 1938—in the collection 'Unam Sanctam'.
2. Khomyakov was very fond of Pascal and, according to Samarin, even called him 'his teacher'.
3. See N. A. Berdyaev, *Khomyakov*, Moscow, 1912.

development, since 'the motif of nature-philosophy was not basic for him'. [1] This last is incorrect, as will be shown below. Berdyaev himself rightly remarks that 'Khomyakov's philosophy of history grew in the atmosphere of the universal romantic spirit of the early nineteenth century.' [2] We must also point out Khomyakov's extraordinary closeness to Jacobi, especially on problems of epistemology; there is no evidence that Khomyakov was familiar with the writings of the 'philosopher of faith'; but, taking into consideration the extreme interest in Jacobi among Russian academic theologians and philosophers (see Ch. X), we must regard it as more than probable that Khomyakov owed something to Jacobi. The reader will see this for himself when we come to expound Khomyakov's epistemological theories.

In elucidating the genesis of Khomyakov's various theoretical constructions, we must bear in mind that many of his ideas became crystallized in the process of analysing and criticizing other men's ideas. This fact is beyond question, and it throws light on the peculiarities of Khomyakov's mind—a mind given to dialectic and, in a certain sense, motivated by the dialectical opposition of its own views to those of others. It is not accidental that almost all of Khomyakov's philosophic and theological articles and studies were written 'apropos of' someone else's articles or books. Evidently, there was a certain *sluggishness* in Khomyakov's philosophic temperament; external stimulation was needed to make him apply himself to the writing of philosophic works.

Let us turn now to a study of Khomyakov's theoretical constructions.

### 7. THE BASIC POINT OF DEPARTURE OF KHOMYAKOV'S PHILOSOPHY

We have already said that we find in Khomyakov no systematic outline, however compressed, of his philosophic ideas. In undertaking to present the reader with such an outline of his 'system', are we not running the risk of 'reconstruction' and arbitrary supplementation? We have already spoken of the impropriety of 'stylization'—of any attempt to represent Slavophilism as a single tendency. But, while avoiding such stylization in every possible way, we must exhibit the inner connectedness of the thought of a given thinker—assuming, of course, that there is a foundation for this in his work.

1. *Ibid.*, p. 142.      2. *Ibid.*, p. 146.

The first basic peculiarity of Khomyakov's philosophic creativity results from his having taken the *ecclesiastical consciousness* as a *point of departure* in constructing his philosophic system. This was a conscious principle with him; he saw in the Church a fullness of truth and a source of light which illumines us and all creation. He did not reach the light of faith by examining the world or studying philosophic interpretations of it; on the contrary, everything shone for him with a light radiated by the Church. Khomyakov was a 'Christian philosopher' in the true sense: he took Christianity as his point of departure. This, of course, is the 'premise' of his philosophic analyses; but we should not forget that in his very faith— which, though firm, was always illuminated by reason, or, more precisely, always appealed to rationality—Khomyakov was exceptionally *free*. There was no tinge in him either of sanctimoniousness or 'blind' faith; as we shall see below, he regarded the Church not as an authority but as a source of light. Faith took priority in Khomyakov's inner world; it was not an 'object' of thought or a 'subject' of discussion for him, but a basic prime-reality of his spiritual world. Khomyakov took his own Christian consciousness as a point of departure, and he saw its basis in the Church. But the idea of the Church is not the same for Khomyakov as for Chaadayev. For Chaadayev the Church is a force which acts in *history*, building the Kingdom of God on earth; for Khomyakov what is most basic and important in the idea of the Church as a prime-reality is its spiritual life. Khomyakov's whole theological doctrine is developed around this concept, which is also basic for his philosophic theories.

The Church, according to Khomyakov, is a 'spiritual organism' which is embodied in visible ('historical') 'flesh'. But the essence of the Church, its basis, is precisely this spiritual organism: 'a union in grace of the many reasonable creatures who submit to this grace'. The Church is 'poly-hypostatic', but all of its members are united with one another organically, not externally. The essence of the Church consists in the unity of the two elements, spirituality and organicity, as a 'legacy of spiritual life, inherited from the holy Apostles'.[1] Therefore, it is not simply a 'collective entity',[2] or a kind of abstract 'idea' concealed within the external life of the Church, but an integral, spirit-bearing reality, uniting

---

1. *Sochineniya*, Moscow, 1900, II, 237. In recent Russian theology, these same ideas, sharpened in the direction of extra-historism, have been developed by M. M. Tareyev—concerning whom see Ch. XIX.

2. *Ibid.*, p. 58.

its visible and invisible aspects in a living and concrete whole. 'Even on earth', Khomyakov writes, 'the Church does not live an earthly, human life but a divine life, a life of grace; . . . it does not live under the law of slavery, but under the law of freedom.'[1] The Church, as a single and integral organism, cannot be separated into visible and invisible aspects; it is 'not two Churches, but one and the same Church under different aspects'. Precisely for this reason the Church as a divine-human unity is an integral organism.

An essential point in this theological theory is that 'the visible Church exists [as a *Church* and not as an 'institution'] only in so far as it is *subordinated* to the *invisible* Church [i.e. the spirit of God] agreeing, as it were, to act as its manifestation'.[2] This is the basis of Khomyakov's doctrine—a daring and brilliant one—that 'the Church is not an *authority* . . ., for an authority is something external to us . . .; it is the truth'. 'It is extremely unjust', we read in another place, 'to assume that the Church demands forced unity or forced obedience. On the contrary, it *abhors* both the one and the other. Forced unity, in matters of faith, is a lie—and forced obedience is death.' This denial of the 'authority' of the Church leads Khomyakov to a decisive rejection of any kind of 'head of the Church' except Christ himself. But Khomyakov, least of all, is to be suspected of anarchism, on the basis of this doctrine of the freedom of the Church. The relation of the individual person to the Church is such that this ecclesiastical freedom serves in no sense as an *individualizing* function; it is not something given to the individual human being. Freedom belongs to the Church *as a whole*, rather than to each member of the Church separately. 'Although the believer's freedom is not subject to any external authority,' Khomyakov writes, 'it is justified by his oneness of thought with the Church.'[3] The individual human being is different outside the Church from what he is within it:

'Each human being finds himself within the Church, not in the impotence of spiritual isolation, but in the strength of spiritual oneness with his brethren and his Saviour. In the Church he finds his own self in its perfection or, more precisely, he finds there what is perfect in him.'[4]

We shall not go further into the details of Khomyakov's doctrine of the Church; we have considered it only because he bases his philosophic constructions upon it. He rejects both the exclusively spiritual conception of the Church and the overemphasis on its

1. *Ibid.,* p. 17.    2. *Ibid.,* p. 225.    3. *Ibid.,* p. 237.    4. *Ibid.,* pp. 111f.

visible, historical aspect. The Church is a prime-reality, and in union with it the individual person discovers himself for the first time—not in his contingent empirical manifestations, but in his true and profound principle.

## 8. ANTHROPOLOGY

Turning to Khomyakov's philosophic views, we shall first consider his anthropology, which for him is a mediating discipline between theology and philosophy and a foundation for epistemology. From his doctrine of the Church Khomyakov deduces a doctrine of the individual which decisively repudiates individualism. 'The isolated individual', Khomyakov writes, 'is marked by complete impotence and irreconcilable discord.' [1] He acquires strength only in a living and morally healthy relationship to the social whole. Chaadayev, we recall, related the individual to a 'world-consciousness'; for Khomyakov, the individual must be related to the Church in order to reveal himself in his fullness and strength. Khomyakov decisively rejects the theory of environment (the 'total aggregate of the accidents which surround human individuals' [2]); he also rejects individualism, which isolates and absolutizes the individual person. Only in the Church—a free union, permeated with brotherly love for others, in the name of Christ—does the individual find his talents and the fullness of his personal wealth. Reason, conscience, and artistic creation—although they may be manifested in the individual human being—are in fact a function of the Church; none of them is ever completely or perfectly realized outside it. Khomyakov was an enthusiastic admirer of the Russian 'obshchina' [village commune] precisely because it emphasized the primacy of the social whole so clearly.

Khomyakov's doctrine of the two root types of personality—which he placed at the foundation of his historiosophy—is very interesting. There is always a struggle of two opposed principles in the individual person, the one which predominates determining the basic type. These two principles are freedom and necessity. 'Freedom and necessity', Khomyakov wrote in one place, 'constitute the mysterious principle around which, in various forms, all human thoughts are centred.' This means that freedom is a gift which it is not easy to possess; and, as a result, our spirit may flee from it. Khomyakov (in his Notes on Universal History) calls the type of personality in which the quest for freedom predominates

1. *Op. cit.*, I, 161.                    2. *Loc. cit.*

'Iranian', and that in which subjection to necessity predominates 'Cushite'. In general, for Khomyakov, all history revolves around these two types. But this is, as it were, a 'natural' typology; it is not something immutable and absolute. However, the bondage of necessity cannot be overcome in the order of nature. The mere quest for freedom (by the Iranian type) has not yet revealed it fully. Only on the soil of Christianity—specifically, in the Church as an organism illumined by grace, in which the spirit of God is operative—does freedom triumph. At this point there is an important gap in Khomyakov's anthropology: he has no doctrine of the nature or origin of evil in man. He sees very well that unclarified freedom bears a principle of chaos within itself; but why, and how, the principle of freedom has come close to the paths of evil is something he never discusses.

The doctrine of the integral *wholeness* of man is put forward with special force in Khomyakov's anthropology. This doctrine, which found deeper and better-focused development in Kireyevski, forms the basic nucleus, as it were, of Khomyakov's anthropology. He deduces from it various theoretical constructions in the philosophy of history as well as in epistemology.

Man's wholeness results from the *hierarchical* structure of his soul: there are certain 'central powers of our God-like reason' around which all the powers of our spirit must be disposed.[1] This hierarchical structure is unstable; there is an antagonism between the central and peripheral powers of the soul. Khomyakov attaches particular importance to the *escape from freedom*, a phenomenon which gives rise to the paradox that, being destined for freedom and endowed with the power of freedom, men freely seek an order of life and thought in which necessity prevails. This is the tragedy of human life. Only in the Church are we able to find ourselves, but we constantly leave the Church to become slaves to natural or social necessity. This is not a matter of the 'passions'—as is usually thought—but a perversion of reason. 'Everything is directed by reason', Khomyakov once wrote in a letter, 'but everything lives by passion'. The fault is not in the passions, but in the loss of the 'inner organization' of reason, and the inevitable impairment of the healthy wholeness of the spirit.[2]

Such are the basic outlines of Khomyakov's anthropology. Let us turn now to a study of the subject which most attracted his attention—his epistemology.

1. *Ibid.*, p. 288.
2. Concerning the 'integral spirit' see *ibid.*, p. 272

## 9. EPISTEMOLOGY

Khomyakov's epistemological views disclose a very complex and tangled conflict in his spiritual world. On the one hand, in working out his epistemology, he took as his point of departure that to which his ecclesiastical consciousness summoned him. But at the same time—although he himself did not notice it, and students of his philosophy have failed to point it out—he was under the spell of *transcendentalism*, which he was unable to overcome or shake off. His insistent and sometimes captious, yet always important, critique of Hegel—with which his philosophic articles are filled—sprang from his profound opposition to the idealism of modern German philosophy. Firmly and with deep conviction, he cleared the way for *ontologism* in theory of knowledge. But his systematic epistemological ideas, and especially his doctrine of the fatal errors of 'rational knowledge', were bound up not only with the terminology but with the very spirit of transcendentalism. There is not only incompleteness and lack of basic agreement in Khomyakov's epistemology on this point, but also a profound disharmony, amounting to internal contradiction.

Khomyakov drew his inspiration, of course, from a theory of *religious* knowledge which was clearly bound up with the essence of his doctrine of the Church. But later, probably under Kireyevski's influence, he extended his ideas to knowledge generally, enunciating a doctrine of 'living knowledge', which became the germ of diverse and fruitful theories in Russian philosophy. The basic proposition of Khomyakov's epistemology flowed from his doctrine of the Church. It asserts that cognition and possession of the truth is not a function of *individual* consciousness, but is entrusted to the *Church*. This is not simply a sociological conception of knowledge— a question of supplementing the individual consciousness with what the social environment provides, but a matter of seeking a supplementation of individuality in the Church—a social organism illumined by *grace*. 'The truth is inaccessible to individual thinkers,' Khomyakov wrote. 'It is accessible only to an aggregate of thinkers, *bound together by love*.' [1] This means that 'ecclesiastical reason' [2] is the sole organ for the cognition of total truth. But, before elucidating the concept of 'integral reason', which is basic to Khomyakov's epistemology, let us note that, if 'total' truth is

1. *Ibid.*, p. 283.
2. 'The reasonableness of the Church', Khomyakov writes, 'is a higher potential of human reasonableness.' (*Ibid.*, p. 284.)

accessible only to 'ecclesiastical reason', then isolated individual reason is condemned to partial and incomplete knowledge, and its 'half truth' easily becomes untruth. The source of the partial truths attained by individual reason should not, strictly speaking, be sought in 'reason' at all—for 'reason' is necessarily 'total'. The isolated individual consciousness, unsupplemented by the Church, is to be conceived of as related not to reason but to 'rationality'. Khomyakov contrasts the concept of rational cognition current in his day to that of the 'integral spirit'; this explains why the theme of 'rational cognition', which was taken from popular contemporary theories, gained such a powerful hold on Khomyakov. Indeed, the idea of rational cognition stands at the centre of his critique of the West and of Western culture.

Let us note, to begin with, that the definition of Western culture as a triumph of 'rationalism', the accusation of rationalism brought against the whole West, arose in the West itself in the eighteenth century during the period of 'preromanticism' (both in Germany and in France), and was accepted by Russian thinkers as a 'self-evident truth'. But the *epistemological* distinction between 'rationality' and 'reason' which Kant placed at the foundation of his whole system—the distinction between *Verstand,* as a function of purely logical operations, and *Vernunft,* as a source of ideas—was of decisive importance. After Kant, chiefly as a result of Schiller's influence, this distinction preserved its fundamental importance in the transcendentalism of Fichte, Schelling, and Hegel.[1] But Russian thinkers *identified* rationalism as a *general cultural phenomenon* with *rational cognition.* Considering their closeness to Jacobi—whose popularity, as we have noted, began to spread in the Theological Academy in Moscow in the late eighteenth century, and could not have failed to attract the attention of thinking people who were connected in any way with ecclesiastical circles—it is understandable that the contrast which they made between rational knowledge and 'total reason' should have merged with their contrast of rational knowledge and 'faith'. This movement of thought was the more natural in that the chief object of Khomyakov's and Kireyevski's critique was the religious aspect of Western culture. Evidently Khomyakov very early identified *Western Christianity* with the entire system of rationalism, and this identification influenced the whole course of his own philosophic work, as well as that of Kireyevski later. In our view this is how the genesis of the epistemology of these two thinkers is to be understood. Let

1. See, for example, Justus Schwarz, *Hegels philosophische Entwicklung,* 1938.

us now turn to a systematic analysis of Khomyakov's theory of knowledge.

The higher truths are accessible to our reason only in the Church —but on condition that freedom is preserved in the Church, and is not replaced by authority. This means that the truth revealed to us in the Church must appear to us as truth, and must not be imposed upon us by the Church. In asserting this proposition, Khomyakov has in mind the overcoming of 'Latinism' [Roman Catholicism], which requires that the individual submit to and obey the Church, and which does not develop his cognitive powers but rather suppresses them. However, in asserting the rights of free investigation, Khomyakov no less forcefully repudiates the individualism to which Protestantism, which declares individual reason fully capable of knowing the truth, is inclined. For the attainment of true knowledge there must be a 'joining together' of 'many'—a common cognitive effort, warmed and illuminated by love. This 'organic togetherness' which is necessary for the attainment of true knowledge was later interpreted by Prince Serge Trubetskoi as characterizing *every* act of knowledge, even those which end in error. In any case, for Khomyakov it is not a matter of exalting collective cognition above individual cognition, but of insuring the presence of a 'communion of love', which gives evidence of the participation of the soul's moral forces in the cognitive effort. There must be an integral turning of the soul toward the theme of knowledge:

'To comprehend the truth', Khomyakov writes, 'rationality itself must conform to all the laws of the spiritual world, . . . and be related to all the vital and moral forces of the spirit. Therefore, the deepest truths of thought are accessible only to a reason which is harmoniously organized internally and in full moral conformity with the omniessential reason.'[1]

Thus, for Khomyakov the important thing is not the psychological wholeness that results in a subjective unity of the knowing spirit, but an objective wholeness—i.e. a wholeness related to moral needs which derive from the 'omniessential reason'. We shall see later that Khomyakov's chief indictment against 'Latinism', in connection with the ecclesiastical schism of the eleventh century, is precisely that the Western Church, having accepted a new dogma (Filioque)—without the consent of the Western Church— undermined the *moral* conditions of knowledge and thus isolated

1. *Sochineniya*, I, 281f.

themselves from the truth, falling under the dominion of rationalism. This idea was most clearly expressed by Samarin in his preface
to Khomyakov's theological works. 'Rationalism', he wrote, 'is
logical knowledge isolated from the moral principle.' [1] This corresponds fully to Khomyakov's basic doctrine and, at the same
time, shows us the extent to which his epistemological views on
this point were shaped by his religious critique of Western Christianity.

Wholeness of spirit, according to Khomyakov, is needed not
only to overcome the one-sidedness of rational knowledge, but
also in the initial stages of cognition—the primary acts which
initiate the process of knowing. Khomyakov calls these primary
acts *faith*; his idea of faith as the initial stage of knowledge has the
same broad sense as Jacobi's—it is not simply religious faith, but
total and 'immediate' union with reality. Khomyakov is extremely
close to Jacobi on this point, although their general philosophic
positions differ in many respects: Jacobi was a defender of irrationalism and epistemological emotionalism, and he was very
closely connected with the whole period of German preromanticism. However, we find in him a sharp polemic against rational
cognition, a sharp 'antinomism' of life and rationality. Khomyakov
—we must remember—opposes faith to rational cognition, not to
*reason*: faith itself, for him, is a function of (integral) reason. 'What
I call faith', Khomyakov writes, 'is that faculty of reason which
perceives actual (real) data and turns them over to the analysis
and consciousness of rationality.' [2] These data are the raw
material out of which all of our knowledge is built; they 'precede
logical consciousness'; they are a 'living consciousness which has
no need of proof or argument.' [3] This primary knowledge of faith

'is not *isolated* from experienced reality but permeated by it. . . . It
beats with every pulse of life, accepting all of life's multiplicity, and
penetrating it with its own understanding. It grasps the relation
of experienced reality to the as-yet-unmanifested first principle. . . .

1. *Op. cit.*, II, xxx.
2. Second Letter on Philosophy to Yu. F. Samarin. (*Op. cit.*, I, 327.)
Khomyakov himself here emphasizes that he is striving only 'to expound the
great step which was made by I. V. Kireyevski', trying only 'to continue
[Kireyevski's] intellectual exploit in the path which he indicated'.
3. This thought, like that which follows, coincides fully with the ideas of
Jacobi. Unfortunately, there is no evidence whatever as to Jacobi's direct
influence on Khomyakov (or Kireyevski). Nevertheless, their similarity, not
only of ideas but of terminology, is often astonishing. See the hint of acquaintance with Jacobi, *ibid.*, p. 179.

It does not usurp the province of rationality, but itself furnishes rationality with all the data for independent activity, and in turn is enriched by the latter's wealth. It is a knowledge which is *living* in the highest degree, and in the highest degree irresistible.'[1]

This 'living knowledge', Khomyakov writes in another place, 'requires the constant wholeness and unchanging harmony of man's soul.' [2] In itself, this 'living knowledge' is 'not yet *total reason*, for total reason also includes the whole realm of rationality.' [3] In other words, 'total reason' is the highest point of a cognitive process which *begins* in faith and *continues* in the rational processes, reaching its *culmination* in 'total reason'. If we bear in mind that faith is a function of this total reason, we shall also be able to understand Khomyakov's formula: 'Reason lives by faith in the perception of phenomena,[4] and it renounces itself [i.e. its 'totality'], turning back upon itself, in the processes of rationality.' From these quotations it is evident that the wholeness which 'living knowledge' requires is not identical with the 'total reason' which has reached its culmination. Clearly, the wholeness which is needed for these primary acts of faith cannot be shaken by the apparent separability of reason from the moral sphere. These acts, as we have seen, do not distinguish the knowing subject from the reality which is known; and this *ontological* quality of the primary acts of faith constitutes the wholeness of reason at this stage. Khomyakov himself, incidentally, is aware of the inappropriateness of the term 'faith' as applied to the primary acts of knowledge. The concept 'faith' is applied equally to the higher states of reason in which reason is turned toward the invisible world. In one place Khomyakov suggests that the concept 'faith' be applied to these higher states, and that the term 'inner knowledge' or 'life-knowledge' be applied to the primary acts of knowledge. [5]

After the soul has mastered this raw material of knowledge, the work of *rationality* begins. Here Khomyakov's terminology is not always sufficiently consistent. This applies primarily to the relationship of the concepts '*rationality*' and '*consciousness*'. 'Logical rationality', he writes, 'is one of the important aspects of consciousness.' [6] Logical analysis forms, as it were, an imprescriptible part of the concept of consciousness. In any case, Khomyakov speaks of different types of consciousness; at first there is simply an 'enjoy-

---

1. *Ibid.*, pp. 278f.      2. *Ibid.*, p. 254.      3. *Ibid.*, p. 279.
4. On the concept 'phenomenon' see below.
5. *Ibid.*, p. 282.                                  6. *Ibid.*, p. 252.

ment' of the object;[1] then come the higher degrees in ascending order. In one place he recommends that we 'look more deeply into the relation of consciousness to reason',[2] but he himself does not do this. 'Consciousness is reason in its reflectivity or passivity, or—if you will—receptivity.' This is the definition which we find in Khomyakov's last philosophic article.[3] Let us note in passing that, on his view, man's will belongs to the 'preobjective realm' and thus cannot itself be known. But the will distinguishes, in consciousness, that which originates 'in the self' from that which is 'not from the self'—i.e. it draws a basic line of demarcation between the subjective and objective worlds.[4]

In its initial (lowest) stage, consciousness is not separate from 'action'—although it is capable of separating itself from the latter. Such consciousness, fused with a simultaneous or subsequent action, Khomyakov calls 'complete consciousness';[5] yet the function of rationality has not yet appeared in it. This constitutes the 'wholeness' needed for the acts of 'life-knowledge': consciousness is not yet separate from that upon which it is focused. It is in this sense that Khomyakov says: 'Consciousness is not aware of phenomena'; i.e. 'phenomena as such are inaccessible to consciousness.' 'Consciousness can understand the law of the phenomenon, its relation to other phenomena, even its inner meaning'—but *nothing more*. What does this mean? It means first of all that reason, at the stage of 'life-knowledge' or perception, is not yet separate from the will, and that it is inseparable from the object, and even from what is beyond the object—which Khomyakov calls the 'unmanifested first principle'. This is a basic proposition of *ontologism*; and Khomyakov forcefully opposes it to idealism, which tears itself away from reality. But, since he goes on to speak of logical analysis as being concerned with 'phenomena', there is a retreat in his own terminology from a radical ontologism of knowledge, and a movement toward idealistic—in particular, transcendental—epistemology. In fact, as soon as rationality begins to operate, subject and object are contrasted; and the object is torn away, as it were, from the 'unmanifested first principle', becoming a 'phenomenon'—with all its illusory independence, its pure phenomenality, and its consequent loss of reality. Such a characterization of rational knowledge fails to explain its rupture with the reality behind the phenomenon. However, this thesis—that in rational analysis we are dealing with 'phenomena' and not with reality—

1. Is this not Jacobi's term *'Geniessen'*?    2. *Ibid.*, p. 249.
3. *Ibid.*, p. 345.    4. *Ibid.*, pp. 276–8.    5. *Ibid.*, p. 248.

forms the foundation of the whole critique of rationalism which is so essential to Khomyakov's theological writings. Here are his exact words: 'Rational cognition does not grasp the *reality* of what is known; the object of [rational] knowledge does not contain the *first principle* in the fullness of its powers.' [1] But why not?—Why does the initial ontological quality of cognition, in the primary acts of 'life-knowledge', evaporate as soon as rationality comes into play? For the idealists, beginning with Descartes, this was a consistent conclusion, since they interpreted even the primary acts of knowledge phenomenalistically, i.e. not ontologically. But Khomyakov, who stresses so forcefully the ontological quality of the primary acts of 'life-knowledge', goes on to appropriate the terminology of idealism, without noticing that he is abandoning the ground of the ontological quality of knowledge which he himself had established. Of course, this ontological quality must reappear somewhere; and it does—though there is as little reason for its reappearance as there was for its disappearance in the process of rational analysis—in the above-mentioned stage of 'total reason', with its synthetic function.

This is the basic inconsistency of Khomyakov's epistemology. On the one hand, he was the first in Russian philosophy to take a position of ontologism in epistemology, placing acts of faith ('life-knowledge')—in which knowing is not separated from the known —at the beginning of the cognitive process. On the other hand, because he wished to exhibit in the realm of epistemology the basic error of Western rationalism, which is traceable to religious roots (i.e. to the characteristics of 'Latinism'), Khomyakov vigorously emphasized the defects of a rationality which creates 'phenomena' from data of faith as yet unseparated from existence. He fails, we repeat, to notice how strange it is that in this rational process the connection with reality is somehow lost. In thus characterizing the function of rationality, Khomyakov moves wholly within the frame-work of *transcendentalism*. For not only did the contrast of reason and rationality [*Vernunft* and *Verstand*] develop historically in transcendentalism, but only in it did this contrast take on serious meaning. At the same time, in seeking a new philosophic position which would reflect the spiritual advantages of Orthodoxy—both in theology and the philosophy of culture—Khomyakov hoped to demonstrate the philosophic inadmissibility of transcendentalism, especially Hegelianism, which for him was the chief manifestation and culmination of rationalism. It was natural for Khomyakov,

1. *Ibid.*, p. 278.

in accepting ontologism, to reject transcendental idealism, especially Hegelianism; but it was unfortunate that he was unable to extricate *himself* from the meshes of transcendentalism. Khomyakov constantly praised Hegel's well-constructed schemes,[1] but he also found it necessary to exhibit the internal flaw of Hegel's whole system, to show that Hegel 'in his phenomenology accomplished the self-annihilation of philosophy'. *This* idea sprang from the very depths of Khomyakov's spirit—from his ontologism, his doctrine of the organic togetherness of cognition,[2] and from his aversion to theological and philosophic rationalism. But, in trying to demonstrate the internal flaw of idealism, Khomyakov himself took up a transcendentalist position; at least, his characterization of 'rational' cognition is close to the analogous assertions of the transcendentalists.[3] Thus Khomyakov's doctrine of rational cognition is bifurcated: he admits that rational cognition is an inevitable and necessary stage in the development of knowledge; [4] yet the fatal defect of rationalism consists precisely in this rational cognition, its isolation from existence, and its transformation of objects into 'phenomena'. To be sure, Khomyakov frequently says that rationality takes on a fatal significance when it 'severs the bond between cognition and the inner perfection of the spirit'. But then it is not rationality itself which is defective, but the fact of its isolation from 'spiritual wholeness'—and we cannot reproach Hegel with this. To criticize Hegel one must overcome transcendentalism *as such*, and Khomyakov did not do this, precisely because his characterization of rational cognition was in harmony with that of transcendentalism. In this respect, Khomyakov's epistemology is undoubtedly inconsistent; if he had carried through the doctrine of the ontological quality of cognition, it would have been evident that rationalism—against which he battled so persistently in the name of his basic theological views—is in no sense a *product of rational cognition*. Rationalism, as a fatal product of Western spiritual life and Western culture, is actually connected not with the prevalence of rationality or the abandonment of wholeness of spirit, but with a *disease* of the spirit. This has frequently been well

1. 'Hegel's *Phenomenology*', Khomyakov writes, 'will remain as a deathless monument to an inexorably rigorous and consistent dialectic; it will never be mentioned without reverence.' (*Ibid.*, p. 264.)

2. See, for example, his sarcastic remarks on the 'mystical concept of a collective spirit of collective mankind'. (*Ibid.*, p. 36.)

3. Especially Schelling, concerning whom see *ibid.*, p. 266 and *passim*.

4. In one place Khomyakov even says: 'Analytical work is inevitable; more than that, it is sacred.' (*Op. cit.*, II, 242.)

understood by Western thinkers, when they were aware of the defects of rationalism. To assert, as Khomyakov did—using Kireyevski's formula—that 'only [logically] possible, not actual, truths are open to the philosophy of rationality',[1] is to defend ontologism (the striving to know real being) *by means of the anti-ontological propositions of transcendentalism,* which reinterprets the material of knowledge as embracing 'phenomena', i.e. the 'shadow' of being, or its 'law', but not its 'actuality'—its logical structure rather than its reality.

In exhibiting the conflict of these two tendencies in Khomyakov's epistemological views, we do not intend to minimize in the least the value of the three basic and positive ideas which he elaborated. The doctrine of the general ontological quality of all cognition, and the rejection of idealism in epistemology; the characterization of the primary acts of knowledge ('life-knowledge') as acts of 'faith'; and finally, the assertion of the communal nature of cognition—all are theories of high value which found fruitful expression in the further development of Russian epistemology. But this shows Khomyakov's dependence on transcendentalism all the more clearly, a dependence which led to his captious criticism of rational cognition. Despite his numerous and valuable remarks on Hegel, it must be admitted that Khomyakov's critique of Hegel was not successful, primarily because, in repudiating Hegel's idealism, he himself was unable to go beyond the limits of transcendentalism. In any case, Khomyakov's epistemology is unquestionably a significant and valuable contribution to the development of purely philosophic speculation in Russia.

## 10. ONTOLOGY AND COSMOLOGY

Let us consider briefly some of Khomyakov's views on other philosophic themes, as expressed in his articles—first of all concerning questions of ontology and cosmology. Although these views were expressed briefly and apropos, they are all very interesting. For example, Khomyakov refuses to take *matter* as his point of departure in ontology, since it would have to be conceived as infinite, as the basis of the 'all'. But the concept of 'infinite matter' is an internal contradiction, because matter is divisible, measurable, always finite. Rejecting materialism as a doctrine of the nature of being, one must admit that the *'substratum'* of being—which must be conceived as infinite—cannot be material: 'Universal matter', Khomyakov writes, 'is an immaterial abstraction,

1. Khomyakov, *op. cit.,* I, 273f.

which does not have the character of matter.' [1] The dynamism of existence swallows up materiality, so to speak; the world must be conceived in terms of *energy*. If upon first view 'the world appears to reason as matter in space and energy in time', materiality soon ceases to be a primitive concept and becomes a function of energy. 'Time is energy in its development', Khomyakov says; 'space is energy in its combinations'. [2] 'Reason applies the general term "energy" to the principle of mutability of world-phenomena.' Khomyakov approved Taine's remark—which faithfully expresses the tendency of modern natural science—that 'energy is not independent, but is always a property of something else'. Further on Khomyakov reaches the conclusion—very forcefully expressed in his time and somewhat later by Lotze, in his *Mikrokosmos*—that the 'energy or cause of being of every phenomenon is contained in the "all." ' [3] But this 'all' is not a *sum* of phenomena, according to Khomyakov—and here he touches upon themes of extreme importance for cosmology: 'Particulars are not summed up in the infinite "all"; but, on the other hand, the principle of every phenomenon is to be found precisely in this "all." ' [4] Thus the 'all' (as a 'whole') is prior to particular phenomena. It is the root of all separateness, for every phenomenon is something 'snatched from the universal'. Authentic being transcends analysis; it is ontologically as well as cognitively prior to phenomena. 'Authentic being remains before us, freed from phenomena.' And further on: 'The phenomenon, as a reality, cannot be admitted as a factor in the movement of the "all." ' What then is the nature of authentic being? It is free, for necessity inheres only in phenomena, not in their 'root'. [5] It is also reasonable. It is 'free thought'—'freely-willing reason'. Khomyakov tends very definitely toward voluntarism in ontology. And here he anticipates in many respects the theoretical constructions of Eduard von Hartmann. Of course, Khomyakov's voluntarism clearly applies to the cosmos, to created being; it does not lead to an absolutizing of the world, i.e. to pantheism. But his utterances on this point are incomplete. Some of his cosmological ideas are very close to the theories which appeared in the twentieth century as Sophiological metaphysics (in

1. *Ibid.*, p. 306.        2. *Ibid.*, p. 326.        3. *Ibid.*, p. 335.
4. Here Khomyakov is extremely close to a metaphysical conception put forward by Nicholas of Cusa.
5. 'Necessity is only the freedom of another, and since every objectification is a free self-alienation of thought [from] freedom, necessity is *freedom made "manifest"*.' (*Ibid.*, p. 344.)

Florenski and Bulgakov). Nevertheless, in Khomyakov himself
these cosmological ideas remained fragmentary.

## II. HISTORIOSOPHY

We have already mentioned Khomyakov's view of the hierarchical
structure of the soul.[1] This structure, however, is unstable. To be
healthy the soul must exist in a 'communion of love' with other
souls. What, then, causes deviations from this norm?—Khomyakov gives no answer to this question. His doctrine of the two types
of spiritual structure, the 'Iranian' and the 'Cushite', is valid only
as a generalization from historical observations; it is not elaborated
from the viewpoint of philosophical anthropology. If the tendency
to worship necessity can be overcome, there would seem to be
some *single* foundation in man. But how and why individual human
beings and whole nations can exhibit a dichotomy of this single
spiritual foundation is not discussed or elaborated by Khomyakov.
It is interesting to note that he never treats the theme of *evil*. This is
the more strange in that Khomyakov had a deep sense of human
freedom; he regarded chance as *objectively real*, and in his historiosophical theories he never minimized the element of responsibility.
Yet all of these elements are essentially connected with the problem
of evil.

We shall not expound Khomyakov's utterances on questions of
aesthetics; they are too sketchy, and they are wholly bound up
with his doctrine of the primacy of the social whole over the
individual. Let us turn to the last division of Khomyakov's philosophic thought—his historiosophy. We must note that Khomyakov
approaches the problem of history very differently from Chaadayev. He too, like Chaadayev, meditated throughout his life on
themes of historiosophy, as his Notes on Universal History and his
individual articles on these themes testify. But Khomyakov
stressed the *natural conformity to law* of historical being. He did not
exclude the action of Providence in history, but his providentialism
was incomparably more modest than Chaadayev's. His generalization concerning the two types of historical development—the one
asserting the principle of necessity in every realm, the other the
principle of freedom—indicates the independent spiritual nature
of historical being. For Khomyakov 'the career and destiny of all
mankind'—not just that of individual nations—is being worked
out in history, although every nation 'is just as much a person as

1. See above, p. 190

is an individual human being'. But the comparison of a whole nation to an individual (which was common at the time) emphasizes the operation of natural 'laws' in history, the possibility of 'laws' of historical movement. This introduces limitations into the system of providentialism in the name of man's freedom and responsibility in his self-realization. Khomyakov's splendid poem, written before the Crimean War and addressed to the Russian people, is well known:

> Remember that to be an instrument of God
> Is a heavy burden for earthly creatures;
> He judges His servants severely,
> And alas! upon thee weigh
> So many dreadful sins.
>
> Then pray thou humbly in submission,
> Bathing the wounds of thy corrupted conscience
> In the healing ungent of thy tears!

Historical providentialism does not lessen men's responsibility or freedom; on the contrary, it rests precisely upon this freedom. For this reason history is moved by freedom and by the force which opposes it—the free striving for the chains of necessity. Thus the historical process is essentially a spiritual process, and faith, i.e. the religious impulse which springs from the depths of the national spirit, is the fundamental motive force of history. Berdyaev says of Khomyakov's philosophy of history that 'it includes moral and religious premises but no providential plan.' [1] This is an exaggeration, but Khomyakov actually gives some grounds for such a conclusion. For example, reading such a sentence as this: 'History [as a science] has thus far presented us with nothing but a *chaos of events*,' [2] one might at first think that this was a quotation from Herzen, an assertion of his historical alogism. But one has only to examine the context from which the sentence was taken to be convinced that Khomyakov is merely reproaching historical *science* for not having penetrated to the 'fate of mankind' (mankind being the *subject* of universal history) behind the 'chaos of events'. In another place Khomyakov writes: 'The *logic* of history is passing sentence on the spiritual life of Western Europe.' [3]

In the light of this statement, it becomes clear that, in accordance with the logic of historical development, a *judgment* of the free

1. Berdyaev, *op. cit.*, p. 154.          2. *Sochineniya*, I, 38.
3. *Ibid.*, p. 148.

creative activity of all nations and of mankind as a whole is being carried out in history. Here, of course, Khomyakov is closer to Hegel than to Chaadayev; indeed, Khomyakov's philosophy of history is extremely close, both in form and in spirit, to the Hegelian schemes. The *content* of history is different for Khomyakov, but his doctrine of the 'logic of history', and the conformity to law which is immanent in history, is in complete harmony with the principles of Hegelianism. He even uses the dialectical method in his interpretation of the historical process.

We shall not enter into a study of Khomyakov's concrete historiosophical theories—the critique of the West, and the setting up of Russia in opposition to the West. This is an important and creative theme for all the Slavophiles; but the important thing philosophically is not the concrete detail of his critique of the West, but the intense and passionate hope that through Russia Orthodoxy would be able to effect a reorganization of the whole system of culture. 'The universal development of history', Khomyakov asserts, 'requires of our Holy Russia that she express the manifold principles from which she sprang.' [1] 'History', we read in the same article, 'is summoning Russia to the forefront of universal enlightenment; and this is her historic right, as a consequence of the diversity and richness of her principles.' [2]

Khomyakov—who spoke of the West as a 'land of holy miracles', who wrote a very thoughtful letter concerning England, and who spent some time abroad—was not a 'hater' of the West. However, he was profoundly conscious, not only of Russia's special path, but of her universal task. This universal task was the liberation of mankind from the one-sided and false development which its history had taken under the influence of the West. [3]

Khomyakov's social philosophy rests on the principle of 'organic wholeness'; this was the source of his cult of the '*obshchina*' [village commune], and of his struggle with the individualistic tendencies of the nineteenth century, but it was also the source of his ardent defence of freedom. The Church provided his ideal of social life—a oneness in freedom, based on love. And this was the inner source of Khomyakov's firm and unshakable defence of freedom. His attitude toward the state also flowed from his organic conception of social life. There are no hints in his writings of an anarchistic

1. *Ibid.*, p. 169.  2. *Ibid.*, p. 174.
3. 'Western Europe', Khomyakov asserts, 'developed not under the influence of Christianity, but under the influence of Latinism, i.e., Christianity one-sidedly conceived.' (*Ibid.*, p. 148.)

rejection of the state, but we find in him something analogous to Rousseau's doctrine of popular sovereignty. At the level of historical reality the nation is more important and essential for Khomyakov than the state. The sovereign power rests on acceptance by the people: 'The obedience of the people', he wrote, is *'un acte de souveraineté'*. The people, being the source of power, entrust this power to the Tsar, who then bears the 'burden of power'. But the people retain their 'freedom of opinion'.

### 12. GENERAL APPRAISAL

Summing up what has been said above, let us note first that Khomyakov attempted to construct, with deeds rather than words, a 'Christian philosophy'. The living sense of the Church and the understanding of its meaning was of decisive significance for all of his thinking. He stood entirely apart from the tendencies of secularism, consciously and unhesitatingly taking what was revealed to him in the Church as his point of departure. However, the spirit of free philosophic inquiry was not suppressed in him at any point. His ecclesiastical consciousness was permeated with the spirit of freedom; and this internal freedom, which denied the necessity of authority in the Church, defined Khomyakov's spiritual make-up and the basic lines of his thought.

Khomyakov's ecclesiastical consciousness led him to a rejection of individualism as untenable; he was the first to elaborate a philosophical anthropology based on the idea of 'organic togetherness' [*sobornost*]. It may be said that the function of the Church in Khomyakov's doctrine is wholly analogous to that of the transcendental 'sphere' in German idealism, in which the individual 'finds himself'—in knowledge, morality, and creative activity—merely by rising to transcendental principles. There is a formal analogy here, of course, but there is also the essential difference that for Khomyakov the Church is a 'prime-reality'. The principle of 'organic togetherness', through which individualism is overcome—in epistemology as well as in morality and creative activity—is essentially *ontological*, precisely because this togetherness is not a 'collectivity' but a Church, i.e. a prime-reality rooted in the Absolute. Khomyakov's epistemological ontologism is inseparable from the Church as a 'divine-human unity'; this is the essential difference between his ontologism and similar theories in recent Russian philosophy.

Khomyakov's inner dualism—the combination of ontologism

and transcendentalism which we find in his prejudiced attitude toward 'rational' knowledge—shows that not everything in his philosophy flowed from his consciousness of the Church. He himself did not notice the bondage of his thought to the principles of transcendentalism; nor did he *fully understand* that transcendentalism in its ultimate depths was profoundly bound up with the religious tragedy of the West. Khomyakov *sensed* this keenly, and as a consequence he believed that an entirely different orientation from that in the West was possible in philosophy, based on the idea of the Church. But his critique of the West emphasized Western 'rationalism'; and he related this rationalism to 'rational' cognition, thus merely muddling and obscuring the problem before him. Khomyakov's basic endeavour was to ground philosophy, and culture as a whole, in the idea of the Church (in its Orthodox conception); but on this path he moved imperceptibly away from his ecclesiastical foundation and—in adopting the ideas of transcendentalism, which is in general the highest product of the secular consciousness—took up the position of a secular system alien to him. However, the internal incompleteness of Khomyakov's theories should not lessen in our eyes the immense step forward which he took in the elaboration of philosophic problems.

# CHAPTER VII

## I. V. Kireyevski, Yu. F. Samarin, K. S. Aksakov

### 1. THE BASIC THEMES OF SLAVOPHILISM

THE idea which dominated Khomyakov's philosophic activity—the construction of an integral world-view based on the ecclesiastical consciousness developed in Orthodoxy—was neither his personal creation nor his individual plan. Before, during, and after his lifetime—right up to our own day—many thinkers have developed the idea that Orthodoxy, whose perception and understanding of Christianity is different from that of the West, provides a basis for a new approach to the themes of culture and life. This idea has generated, and still generates, a *hope* and prophetic striving, as it were, toward a new 'era', an 'epochal' reconsideration of the whole of culture. This is the origin of the incurable dualism of this entire tendency. It seeks a new path of creative activity because it regards the old as obsolete. In this respect the positive task cannot be isolated from critical appraisal of the previous 'era'. The passion for building the new is inseparable from the passion for destroying the old. However, the power of the old often appears even after its solemn burial. The 'old' appeared most clearly at one time in the general spirit of secularism which reigned so powerfully in Western Europe; the proponents of 'Orthodox culture' were especially occupied with the struggle with this whole way of thought and life. Khomyakov's struggle with the spirit of secularism became a struggle with the spiritual world within which this movement had developed—i.e. a struggle with Western Christianity. And his method was to show that secularism was an *inevitable* result of the characteristic features of Western Christianity. The break with the East was considered a consequence of the disease of the West. We already know its name —rationalism. At this point, as we have already indicated, criticism of the previous 'era'—based on an overcoming of rationalism— merges into an attempt to construct a new 'foundation', not only for philosophy, but for the whole system of culture. However, a special emphasis on philosophy is characteristic of this tendency. In Kireyevski's words, 'the fate of philosophy becomes the fate of all intellectual life',[1] of all culture.

The group of which Khomyakov was the leader and inspirer received the name 'Slavophile' on the basis of an accidental characteristic. Its founders were not all 'Slavophiles'; indeed, Kireyevski in a letter once very seriously dissociated himself from 'Slavophilism',[2] preferring to characterize his position as 'Orthodox-Slovene' or 'Slavonic-Christian'.[3] It would be even better to call this tendency 'Orthodox-Russian'. The combination of Russia and Orthodoxy is the nodal point upon which all the thinkers of this group converge.

The 'senior' slavophiles included, besides Khomyakov, I. V. Kireyevski, Yu. F. Samarin, and K. S. Aksakov. Of the three, Kireyevski was most concerned with philosophy; we shall begin the present chapter with a study of his work.

## 2. KIREYEVSKI. BIOGRAPHY

The fate of I. V. Kireyevski, who was philosophically the most gifted of the whole group, was a very unhappy, even tragic one. Although he possessed lively literary talents, he was almost wholly deprived of the opportunity to publish his articles. He tried three different times to take up literary work, and three times the journal which published his articles was suspended because of it. This had an oppressive effect on Kireyevski: for many years he wrote nothing, or limited himself to rough drafts. At the same time, a need matured in him, demanding expression—a need 'to find new foundations for philosophy'. In fact, he was able to express himself on this theme only in passing. 'What a splendid, strong personality was Ivan Kireyevski,' Herzen wrote in his Diary. 'And how much perished in him, despite what he succeeded in developing. He was brought down as one might bring down a great oak. He withered away, and the struggle continued mutely within him, undermining his strength.'[4] Kireyevski's creative work, however, did not slacken until the day of his death.

1. Kireyevski, *Sochineniya* [Works], Moscow, 1911, I, 177.
2. 'I only partly share the Slavophile mode of thought; another part of Slavophilism I consider further from me than the most eccentric opinions of Granovski [the well-known Westerner].' Letter to Khomyakov (1844), *op. cit.*, II, 133.
3. *Op. cit.*, I, 161, 173.          4. Herzen, *Sochineniya*, 1875, I, 91.

Let us say a few words concerning his biography.

Ivan Vasilyevich Kireyevski (1806–56) was born into a highly cultured family. His father was a very well-educated man who was close to eighteenth-century masonic circles.[1] He had the reputation of a 'crank', but in fact he was merely marked by a keen and many-sided intellectual curiosity, being interested, incidentally, in philosophy. He was passionately opposed to Voltaire, and once burned all of the latter's works which were on his estate. He died when Ivan was still a boy, and the children's education (Ivan had a younger brother Peter—the well-known 'collector' of folk art and a person of great purity and integrity—as well as a sister) was supervised by their mother, a woman of remarkable religiosity and strength of character. She was on very friendly terms with the poet Zhukovski, who was a relative of hers. Under his influence she became an ardent admirer of German romanticism. Later she remarried; her second husband, Yelagin, was an admirer of Kant and Schelling, and translated the latter into Russian. In this environment, replete with intellectual and spiritual interests, Ivan Kireyevski grew up. When the family moved to Moscow he was tutored at home, mastering the ancient and modern languages. He attended public lectures given by university professors—in particular, the Schellingian Pavlov. After passing his examination, Kireyevski was given a position in the Archives of the Ministry of Foreign Affairs, where he met a number of talented young people, becoming especially friendly with A. N. Koshelyov. With them, as we know, he founded the 'Society of Wisdom-Lovers'. The members of this philosophical circle occupied themselves almost exclusively with German philosophy. After the circle was closed, in 1825, Kireyevski continued his studies in philosophy, and began to publish articles, in literary criticism, which attracted general notice. During this period he was fervently interested in the whole of Western culture; one may even speak with a certain justice of his enthusiasm for the West.[2]

In 1831 Kireyevski went to Germany; he attended the lectures of Hegel—whom he also met personally—and Schleiermacher in Berlin, and then went to hear Schelling in Munich. News of an outbreak of cholera in Moscow and concern for his loved ones caused Kireyevski to leave Germany and return to Russia. There

1. The freemason I. V. Lopukhin, whom we have already met, was Kireyevski's godfather.

2. See especially A. Koyré, *La Philosophie et le problème national en Russie au début du XIX<sup>e</sup> siècle*, Ch. VI.

he undertook the publication of a journal, with the very characteristic title *Yevropeyets* [The European], in which he set himself the task of furthering the *rapprochement* and interaction of Russian and Western culture. This was the period of his enthusiasm for the idea of universal synthesis which had inspired the early German romanticists. But Kireyevski's journal was suspended by the authorities because of his article 'The Nineteenth Century'. Kireyevski himself escaped punishment only because Zhukovski, who at the time was tutor of the heir apparent (the future Alexander II) interceded energetically on his behalf. For the next twenty years Kireyevski remained silent. In 1834 he married; his wife was a deeply religious person, who was also very well read in spiritual literature. (Her father-confessor, incidentally, was *Starets* Serafim Sarovski, who died in 1833.) Kireyevski began to establish contacts with Russian ecclesiastical circles in Moscow. His estate was situated less than five miles from the famous Optina Cloister, where at this time 'the movement of the *Startsy*' [1] was flourishing. Kireyevski developed a profound interest in the writings of the Church Fathers, and took part in the publication of their works by the Optina Cloister. In 1845 he returned briefly to literary activity, becoming the *de facto* editor of the journal *Moskvityanin* [The Muscovite], but he soon left it, owing to a dispute with the publisher, Professor M. P. Pogodin. During this same period Kireyevski tried to obtain a Chair of Philosophy at Moscow University, but nothing came of the attempt. In 1852 he published an article, 'On the Character of European Enlightenment and Its Relation to the Enlightenment of Russia', in the *Moskovski sbornik* [Moscow Miscellany]. Because of this article, which was held to be 'of doubtful loyalty', further publication of the journal was forbidden. Kireyevski took this very hard, but he did not give up his creative plans. In the same year he wrote to Koshelyov, 'I have not abandoned my intention of writing a text in philosophy, whenever it may be possible; . . . it is time for Russia to make its voice heard in philosophy.' [2]

After the death of Nicholas I, the journal *Russkaya beseda* [Russian Colloquy] began to appear in Moscow under the editorship of Kireyevski's close friend Koshelyov. The first number included Kireyevski's article 'On the Possibility and Necessity of New

1. The movement of the Russian *Startsy*, which is connected with *Starets* Paisius Velichkovski (see Ch. II) flourished particularly in the Optina Cloister. Concerning this movement see S. Chetverikov 'Das russische Starzentum' *Una Sancta*, 1927 (Sonderheft 'Ostkirche'); also I. Smolitsch, *Das Starzentum*.

2. Kireyevski, *op. cit.*, I, 74.

Principles in Philosophy', which was in fact a *posthumous* work. Kireyevski died of an attack of cholera before it appeared in print.[1]

Let us consider very briefly the question of the influences to which Kireyevski was exposed. We must mention, to begin with, the influence of German romanticism, which came to Kireyevski through his mother and Zhukovski. One of Kireyevski's earliest letters (1827, to Koshelyov) contains interesting lines, wholly in the spirit of the universal synthesis which had so captivated the German romanticists: 'We shall restore the rights of true religion, bring the exquisitely beautiful into harmony with morality [*Schöne Seele*], replace stupid liberalism with respect for law, and exalt purity of life above purity of style.' [2] This quest for synthesis, which was a kind of anticipation of the mature Kireyevski's central idea of 'wholeness' of spirit, is characteristic of his youthful dreams. In Herzen's Diary (November 1844) we read: 'Kireyevski is a Slavophile, but he also wants to come to terms somehow with the West; in general, he is both a fanatic and an *eclectic*.' [3] Of course, Herzen is quite wrong in calling Kireyevski an eclectic; but Kireyevski's craving for an all-embracing synthesis, in the spirit of the German romanticists, sprang from the very depths of his being. He was also close to romanticism in his high regard for *feeling*. In a remarkable letter to Khomyakov, written in 1840, he defended the 'ineffability' of feeling in the manner of the romanticists: 'The more of mystery a man finds in his soul, the more deeply has he comprehended himself . . . ; feeling which is fully expressed ceases to be feeling.' [4] In these lines we hear echoes of the cult of feeling which was so influential among the romanticists. We need only recall that, when Kireyevski later formulated his doctrine of the 'inner focus of the soul', much that was due to the early influence of romanticism flowed over into this doctrine.

Schelling's influence on Kireyevski is difficult to discuss. Scholars have produced considerable evidence against such influence,[5] but we must note that Kireyevski greatly admired

---

1. Concerning Kireyevski see I. Smolitsch, *I. V. Kireevskij, Leben und Weltanschauung*, Breslau, 1934; Koyré, *op. cit.*, Ch. VI; Masaryk, *The Spirit of Russia*, I, Ch. X; W. Setschkarew, *Schellings Einfluss in der russischen Literatur*, Leipzig, 1939; H. Lanz, 'The Philosophy of Kireevsky', *The Slavonic Review*, V (1925–6); Chizhevski, *Hegel in Russland*, Reichenberg, [Czechoslovakia], 1934, pp. 151–60.
2. Kireyevski, *op. cit.*, I, 8.
3. Herzen, *op. cit.*, I, 255.
4. Kireyevski, *op. cit.*, I, 67.
5. Setschkarew, *op. cit.*, pp. 57ff; Chizhevski, *op. cit.*, p. 155.

Schelling.[1] According to Kireyevski, Schelling's late system 'provides the most convenient step for passing from borrowed systems to independent love of wisdom'. In any case, he studied Schelling very carefully, pondering him deeply. He studied Hegel with equal attention. Recommending to his stepfather that he order Hegel's *Encyclopaedia*, Kireyevski wrote, 'You will find more of interest in it than in all the rest of modern German literature together. It is difficult to understand, but the game is worth the candle.' In general Kireyevski followed German philosophy very carefully,[2] pondering its most diverse tendencies. But this philosophy did not inspire him or stimulate his creative powers. It was the works of the Church Fathers, which he studied with great care, that were his source of inspiration. He noted with profound bitterness that the 'spiritual philosophy of the Eastern Fathers of the Church' was 'almost entirely unknown to Western thinkers'.[3] Recognizing that it was 'not possible to restore the philosophy of the Church Fathers in its original form',[4] Kireyevski nevertheless took this philosophy as the inspiration and point of departure for his own philosophic ideas.[5] Certain of his thoughts on this subject remained wholly undeveloped; others were expressed only in outline form. But, on the whole, Kireyevski's own theories represent a genuine attempt to exhibit and illuminate the basic patristic doctrines of man and the world in the light of contemporary knowledge and experience. Throughout his life Kireyevski prized the idea of a synthesis of the ecclesiastical consciousness with the highest and most valuable fruits of contemporary enlightenment—an ideal inherited from the romanticists. In this respect he was very close to the idea of Orthodox culture, a culture which was to replace that of the West. It is necessary for Russia, he wrote, that 'Orthodox enlightenment [6] should master the whole intellectual development of the contemporary world, so that, having enriched itself with secular

---

1. In his last article ('New Principles . . .') Kireyevski wrote: 'Schelling, with his inborn genius and extraordinary philosophic profundity, is one of those thinkers who are born not once in a century but once in a millenium.' (*Op. cit.*, I, 261.)

2. In this respect his article, 'Obozreniye sovremennovo sostoyaniya literatury' ['Survey of the Contemporary State of Literature'] (1845) is especially interesting. *Ibid.*

3. *Ibid.*, p. 199.          4. *Ibid.*, p. 253.

5. See, for example, his assertion that 'the direction of the first principles of philosophy depends on our conception of the Holy Trinity.' (*Ibid.*, p. 74.)

6. This expression corresponds completely to the concept of 'Orthodox culture'.

wisdom, Christian truth may the more fully and solemnly demonstrate its prevalence over the relative truths of human reason.' [1]

### 3. KIREYEVSKI'S RELIGIOUS WORLD

Kireyevski, even more than Chaadayev or Khomyakov, may be called a 'Christian philosopher'. He was a genuine philosopher who never at any point repressed the functioning of reason. But his idea of reason as an organ of cognition was wholly defined in terms of the deepened conception of reason which had found expression in Christianity.

Let us turn first to a study of Kireyevski's religious world.

Kireyevski grew up, as we have seen, in an extremely religious family. His mother was a sincerely religious person, not without tinges of Pietism. Zhukovski was no less sincerely and profoundly religious—also with tinges of Pietism—and he undoubtedly influenced Kireyevski's spiritual development. But apparently Kireyevski did not live an active religious life in his early years; at least, religion was not at the centre of his spiritual activity. We find interesting evidence on this point in a note entitled 'A History of I. V. Kireyevski's Conversion', which was found among his papers, and was apparently written by A. I. Koshelyov from the account of Kireyevski's wife. After Kireyevski married, he and his wife began to collide on questions of religion; his wife's ardent and intense religiosity seems to have been annoying to him. They made a mutual agreement that Kireyevski should not 'blaspheme' (!) in his wife's presence. When he suggested that his wife read Voltaire, she told him that she was willing to read any serious book, but that she would not tolerate blasphemy or mockery of religion. Later they read Schelling together, and she astonished him by saying that the thoughts expressed by Schelling 'had long been familiar to her from the works of the Church Fathers'. Gradually, under his wife's influence, Kireyevski himself began to read the works of the Church Fathers, and to form close ties with members of the clergy. The proximity of his estate to the Optina Cloister was a very important factor. We find in Herzen an interesting story, undoubtedly based on Kireyevski's own account, of the feeling which he experienced when standing in the chapel before the miracle-working icon: 'This icon', Kireyevski told him, 'century after century, has absorbed the currents of passionate exaltation, the prayers of grieving and unhappy people; it must have become

1. *Ibid.*, p. 271.

filled with energy . . ., become a living organ, a meeting-place of man and Creator. . . . I fell upon my knees and began to pray with sincere feeling.' [1]

Kireyevski actually lived not only by religious thought but also by religious feeling. His whole personality and spiritual world were shot through with the rays of religious consciousness. His was a genuine and profound religious *experience*, and in giving it meaning he drew very close to the immense spiritual wealth that was opened to him in the Optina Cloister. In this sense, Kireyevski, more than anyone else, must be looked upon as an exponent of what had been preserved within the ecclesiastical consciousness. If Khomyakov drew more from the depths of his own *personal* ecclesiastical consciousness, Kireyevski rested predominantly on what he found among the *Startsy* and in the monasteries. Kireyevski was, in a sense, closer to the Church than Khomyakov; he was in constant touch with people in the Church, especially the *Startsy* of the Optina Cloister. And, if the idea of the Church was central for Khomyakov—in philosophy as well as theology—the idea of *spiritual life* was central for Kireyevski. He started from this idea in his philosophic reflections. In a sense, his principal theoretical constructions were based on the concept of spiritual experience. But they were not excogitated, cerebral constructions. The unquestionable importance of Kireyevski's ideas consists precisely in their organic growth from an underlying reality. I do not mean to say that his ideas were adequate to the reality from which they grew. But the important thing is that they are not to be considered as merely 'constructions'. Though rooted in genuine spiritual *experience*, they were nevertheless subsequently transformed into a kind of theoretical construction: Kireyevski, like Khomyakov, interpreted religious experience in a way that set it in *direct opposition* to *Western Christianity*, which for both thinkers had been completely moulded into a system of rationalism. We have already noted that in the first period of Kireyevski's activity—i.e. up to his marriage—he was deeply immersed in the problems and ideas of the West. It would be no exaggeration to say that Western enlightenment lived in him. He spoke with good reason, in his last article, of the necessity 'for liberating the intellectual life of the Orthodox world from the distorting influences of foreign enlightenment'.[2] Kireyevski bore these influences within *himself*, just as Khomyakov, for example, retained features of transcendentalism to the end. But

1. Herzen, *Byloye i dumy* [My Past and Thoughts], Berlin, 1921, II, 319.
2. Kireyevski, *op. cit.*, I, 352.

Kireyevski was more extensively and deeply permeated with elements of the West than Khomyakov. Of course, this was highly apropos for the inner overcoming of the spirit of secularization, which was a pre-requisite for the construction of a 'Christian philosophy'. Kireyevski knew the West's 'distorting influences', not from the accounts of others, not from outside—but from within.

The setting up of genuinely Christian enlightenment in opposition to rationalism was in fact the axis around which Kireyevski's intellectual work revolved. This was not an opposition of 'faith' and 'reason'—but of two different systems of enlightenment. In general Kireyevski did not separate his philosophic consciousness from his theological consciousness—though he drew a sharp line between revelation and human thinking.[1] He did not accept a dualism of faith and reason, of Church and culture. He sought spiritual and intellectual wholeness, and this 'wholeness' was not merely an ideal for him; he viewed it as a basis for the theoretical constructions of reason. It was precisely at this point that Kireyevski raised the question of the mutual relationship of faith and reason: only their inner unity could provide a key to total and all-embracing truth. But this required a revision of the customary philosophic idea of reason; and Kireyevski found this in the clear and inspiring pages of patristic literature. The epistemological conclusions which he drew from this new doctrine of reason were not the *basis* of the doctrine; they were only *deductions*. Kireyevski's doctrine of reason is itself independent and basic. Therefore, for a proper understanding of his doctrine as a whole we must start with his philosophical *anthropology*.

### 4. ANTHROPOLOGY

We have already found a doctrine in Khomyakov—though devoid of details, to be sure—of the hierarchic structure of the soul and its 'central powers'. Khomyakov did not define exactly what he meant by this doctrine or what these 'central' powers of the soul were. Kireyevski connected this doctrine to patristic anthropology, placing the distinction between 'outer' and 'inner' man—the original Christian anthropological dualism [2]—at the foundation of his whole theory. Kireyevski formulates his doctrine as follows: 'There is in the depths of the soul a living common focus of all the separate powers of reason, a focus hidden from the ordinary

1. *Ibid.*, p. 247.
2. Even the Apostle Peter speaks of the 'hidden man of the heart' (I. Peter, iii: 4); and this is especially striking in the Apostle Paul.

condition of the human spirit.'[1] A few lines before this he speaks of the necessity of 'lifting reason above its ordinary level' and of 'seeking in the depths of the soul that inner root of understanding where all of its separate powers fuse together into one living and integral vision of the mind.'

Gershenzon, who was the first to draw attention to Kireyevski's doctrine of the 'inner focus of the spirit', interprets this doctrine in terms of emotionalism.[2] On our view this is incorrect and unacceptable. In fact *'spirit'* and not 'feeling' is the central concept in Kireyevski's anthropology. Here he simply continues the traditional Christian doctrine of man, with its fundamental distinction between the 'spiritual' and the 'psychic', the 'inner' and the 'outer' man. When Kireyevski speaks of the 'hidden common focus of all the separate powers of reason', he means by this 'inner nucleus' of man, as Gershenzon aptly calls it, the *whole spiritual sphere* in man. To put Kireyevski's ideas in the language of contemporary psychology: he distinguishes the 'empirical' sphere of the psyche, with its multiplicity of 'separate' functions, from the depths of the psyche, lying below the threshold of consciousness, the central point of which may be called the 'focal self'. The empirical sphere of the psyche is actually an *aggregate* of heterogeneous functions. The principle of wholeness—which conceals in itself the root of individuality and the condition of its specific quality—is hidden from us. We must *seek* it within ourselves in order to draw sustenance from it. It is not a question of the *'metaphysical'* aspect of man, but of those powers of the spirit which have been relegated by sin to the depths of man. The inner man is not separated from the outer as a result of any *ontological* heterogeneity. In *this* respect the two spheres are not separate; therefore one can and must 'seek' his own 'inner content' within himself. But the inner man is closed off as a result of the power of sin; therefore the character of man's cognitive life depends upon *whether or not sin is dominant in him*. Adopting patristic terminology. Kireyevski sees the path to regaining this lost wholeness, i.e. the prevalence of 'the inner focus' in us, in the *'concentration'* of the powers of the soul. The task of attaining this focus—of placing it at the centre of the whole empirical life—is, Kireyevski says, 'within the seeker's reach'.[3] But labour is necessary, and spiritual effort directed toward oneself, incessant disciplining of the 'natural' human inclinations,

1. *Op. cit.,* I, 250.
2. Gershenzon, *Istoricheskiye zapiski* [Historical Notes], 2nd ed., 1923, pp. 20ff.
3. *Op. cit.,* I, 250.

in the name of the spiritual tasks which are open only to the inner man. Thus Kireyevski's anthropology is not static but *dynamic*; man is not exhausted, or even characterized, by what he 'is' empirically. He can and must, in working upon himself, raise himself above his empirical constitution, subordinating it to the inner centre, the 'focal self'. In one place Kireyevski expresses his conception of man in these terms:

'The chief character of believing thought consists in the striving [1] to concentrate all the separate powers of the soul into a single power, to seek out that inner focus of being where reason, will, feeling, and conscience; the beautiful and the true; the wonderful and the desirable; the just and the merciful—and the whole sweep of the mind—are fused together into one living unity, thus *restoring* the essential personality in its *primitive indivisibility.*' [2]

In this remarkable passage—which, incidentally, is extremely close to patristic thought—Kireyevski establishes that the 'inner focus of man' conceals a unity uncorrupted by sin; the problem is simply to connect the empirical sphere of the soul with this 'inner centre.' [3] This, by the way, offers Gershenzon a pretext for the assertion that Kireyevski here displays a manifest naturalism, since he, apparently, does not relate the doctrine of wholeness of spirit to Christ.[4] It turns out, according to Gershenzon, that Kireyevski simply establishes the presence in man of spiritual powers which are hidden in his depths—the sort of thing that one finds in contemporary anthroposophy, for example. This, however, is a wholly false interpretation of Kireyevski's anthropology; the latter is saturated with the Christian view of man. Kireyevski's whole article 'On the Possibility and Necessity of New Principles in Philosophy' is based on a study of the relationship of faith and reason, with the intention of developing an Orthodox doctrine to counterbalance that of Western Christianity. At the same time Kireyevski relates all of his theoretical constructions to patristic thought. According to his doctrine,

1. The dynamism of Kireyevski's anthropology is here clearly expressed: man is not something immutable; he is 'in process of becoming' a new being— not through an evolution which is independent of his will, but as a result of voluntary regulation.

2. *Ibid.*, p. 275.

3. The closest approach to this conception in contemporary psychology is the law of mystical development established by Delacroix in his work *Les Grands mystiques chrétiens*, Paris, 1908.

4. Gershenzon, *op. cit.*, p. 34.

'the deep, living, and pure love of wisdom of the Church Fathers is the embryo of the higher philosophic principle. The simple development of this principle, in conformity with the contemporary state of science and the demands and problems of contemporary reason, would in itself comprise a new science of thought.' [1]

Kireyevski had interesting ideas on the contrasting impulses of the soul. In his letters to Khomyakov he expressed the idea that 'reason develops in inverse ratio to the development of will'.[2] The relation of will to reason, he remarked in the same place, 'harbours certain mysteries which have not yet been understood'. In another (very early) letter he expressed the idea, which he also held later, that 'he who has not grasped an idea with feeling has not grasped it at all, nor has he who has grasped it with feeling alone'.[3] Kireyevski's emphasis, which also expresses patristic ideas, on the special significance of the moral sphere in man is particularly important. It is not just 'one of the spheres' of his spirit; the *hierarchical primacy* of man's moral sphere is seen in the fact that the health of all his other aspects depends, in the first instance, on the 'health' of the moral sphere. Where there is no struggle with the 'natural' disunion of the psychic powers, moral health is *lost*. Kireyevski reproaches Western culture because its 'enlighten-ment, being based on the development of the disintegrated powers of reason, has no essential connection with man's moral disposi-tions'. He notes that, where such a disjunction of the cognitive powers from the moral powers exists, 'enlightenment does not rise or fall with inner elevation or baseness'.[4] This is a very interesting idea. But for Kireyevski the 'amorality' of enlightenment gives it a uniquely *stable* quality, resulting from a loss of the dynamism of spirit which makes the soul dependent on the sphere of morality.

'*Spiritual* enlightenment, on the contrary', Kireyevski writes in the same place, 'is *living* knowledge [and therefore unstable]: it is acquired in the degree to which one aspires inwardly to moral elevation and wholeness, and it *disappears* when this aspiration ceases, leaving in the mind only its outward, formal aspect.'

It is because spiritual enlightenment is 'unstable' that it can be lost. Kireyevski sees a kind of *play* in the 'amoral' orientation of

1. Kireyevski, *op. cit.*, I, 270.
2. Letter of 1840. (*Ibid.*, p. 67.) Kireyevski emphasizes that he is speaking only of 'logical reason'.
3. Gershenzon (*op. cit.*, p. 18) correctly relates Kireyevski's doctrine of feeling to Russian romanticism, particularly Zhukovski.
4. Kireyevski, *op. cit.*, I, 266.

'autonomous' reason. 'Thinking, separated from the aspiration of the heart [i.e. from wholeness of spirit],' we read in the 'Fragments', 'is a *diversion* for the soul; it seems that the more profound and important such thinking is, the more essentially thoughtless it makes the thinker.' [1]

In general we must 'rise' from 'natural' reason to spiritual reason. 'The chief distinction of Orthodox thought', Kireyevski writes, 'is that it seeks to raise reason itself above its ordinary level.' [2] 'Natural reason's whole chain of basic principles . . . is below the level of believing reason.' [3] 'The nature of the reason . . . which is experienced in the highest development of inner spiritual intuition is wholly *different in kind* from that of the reason which limits itself to the development of external life.' 'Reason is one', we read in the same article, 'and its nature is one; but its modes of action, like its conclusions, are different, depending on the stage at which it finds itself and the *powers* which are active and operative in it.' [4]

We have already made contact with Kireyevski's epistemology; but we must first consider one more theme in his anthropology —his doctrine of the relationship of individual personality to the social sphere.

'All that is essential in man's soul', Kireyevski writes, 'grows in him *socially*.' [5] This thesis is close to Khomyakov, as well as Chaadayev, and through Chaadayev to French social romanticism, especially Ballanche. But Kireyevski developed this theme only in passing. In the 'Fragments' we find such aphorisms as these: 'The forces of good do not grow in solitude—the rye is choked out by weeds.' And again: 'Each moral victory in the secret depths of a single Christian soul is a triumph for the whole Christian world; each spiritual power which has been formed within a single human being invisibly attracts to itself and advances the powers of the whole moral world.' [6] Kireyevski's consciousness of the spiritual interconnectedness of all men undoubtedly flowed from his idea of the Church. In these same 'Fragments' he expresses the thought that, when an individual human being labours to order his own spiritual life, 'he does not act *alone* or only *for himself*; he is furthering the common task of the whole Church'. From this proposition he draws the following conclusion: 'No special genius is needed for the development of independent and autonomous Orthodox thought . . .; the development of this thought must be the common task of all thinking and believing people.' [7] Here

---

1. *Ibid.*, pp. 280f.    2. *Ibid.*, p. 249.    3. *Ibid.*, p. 251.    4. *Ibid.*, p. 263.
5. *Ibid.*, p. 254.    6. *Ibid.*, pp. 273, 277.          7. *Ibid.*, p. 270.

Kireyevski comes very close to the doctrine or organic together-ness which we have discussed in connection with Khomyakov.

## 5. EPISTEMOLOGY

Kireyevski, like Khomyakov, devoted much attention to the problem of cognition. This was necessary for his position vis-à-vis the philosophy and culture of the West. Both men were *respectful*, so to speak, toward the philosophy of the West; but at the same time they sensed deeply and acutely that Russian thought, which was rooted spiritually in Christianity in a way quite different from the thought of the West, was fully capable of advancing 'new principles' in philosophy. This coincided with the idea held by many Russians at the time that 'the nineteenth century', as Odo-yevski put it, 'belongs to Russia'—i.e. through the creation of a new ideology and new philosophic principles, Russia would open up a new epoch in the development of the Christian world. Khom-yakov and Kireyevski were *disturbed* by the powerful theoretical constructions of German idealism. Both of these founders of 'autonomous and independent' Russian philosophy considered it very important that these constructions be critically overcome and that their internal connection with the whole system of Western culture be made clear.

Kireyevski, like Khomyakov, saw the chief defect of Western philosophy—or, more precisely, its basic disease—in its *idealism*, the loss of a living connection with reality, the view that 'the world's whole being is a shadowy dialectic of my own reason, and reason is the self-consciousness of universal being'.[1] Kireyevski's task, as he saw it, was to extricate himself from the meshes of idealism, i.e. to find a point of support for the construction of a theory of know-ledge which *would not isolate the knower from reality*. Such a point of support Kireyevski (as well as Khomyakov) found in epistem-ological *ontologism*, the assertion that knowledge is a part and function of our 'existential' penetration of reality, that we 'unite ourselves' cognitively with reality not by thought alone but with our whole being. The chief condition for the preservation of cognitive intimacy with being is the connection of man's cognitive processes to his whole spiritual sphere—i.e. wholeness of spirit. When this wholeness of spirit is weakened or lost, when the cognitive function becomes 'autonomous', there is a generation of 'logical thought' or 'rationality', which is fatally isolated from reality. 'Breaking up the

1. *Ibid.*, p. 244.

spirit's wholeness into parts,' Kireyevski writes, 'and abandoning higher consciousness of the truth to determinate logical thought, we tear ourselves away, in the *depths of self-consciousness*, from all connection with reality.' [1] This rupture occurs, as we see, 'in the depths of self-consciousness',[2] i.e. at man's inner focus. This means that union with reality is a function not of thought as such, but of the *personality as a whole*. 'In general, the substantial is inaccessible to abstract thought, for *only substantiality can attain to the substantial*.' [3] This means that, to the extent that logical thought becomes independent of the soul's other spheres, personal 'substantiality' is itself impaired. 'Only the freely reasonable personality possesses substantiality in the world,' Kireyevski writes, and only 'through the internal development of the understanding [within the] integral personality can we understand substantiality.' These somewhat obscure words formulate, in essence, the basic idea of ontologism in cognition. Loss of contact with reality in cognition is preceded by a kind of pathological process in the personality itself, a disintegration of its root wholeness. The 'power' of cognition, the possibility of 'possessing' reality, is determined not by cognition as such, but by the luminosity of the understanding, its realization in man's 'inner focus'. When we tear ourselves away from our original connection with reality, not only does thought become 'abstract' and sterile, but 'man himself becomes an abstract entity'. His original power of interacting with existence is lost. This fatal malady strikes most clearly and tragically in the realm of 'faith'—the mysterious connection of the human spirit with the Absolute. According to Kireyevski's formula: 'In the very depths of human reason [i.e. in the 'inner focus of the personality'], in its very nature, lies the possibility of consciousness of one's fundamental relationship to God,' i.e. faith. Faith rests on a profound union of the individual spirit—in its wholeness—with God. Therefore 'faith does not pertain to a separate sphere in man . . ., but embraces him in his wholeness. Thus the chief characteristic of believing thought is the striving to unite all the separate parts of the soul into one power.' This means that union with reality, as a function of personality, is *given* to '*believing thought*'. Why is this so?—Because 'the understanding with which man comprehends the divine also serves him for understanding the truth *in general*'.[4] The knowledge of reality is a function of the knowledge of God; and loss of contact with reality *begins* in the realm of faith, indicat-

1. *Ibid.*, p. 245.                    2. The terminology of transcendentalism.
3. *Ibid.*, p. 274.                    4. *Ibid.*, p. 246.

ing that faith itself is diseased. This means that the origin of 'abstract thought', of logical rationality and, in general, the whole system of 'rational' relationships to the world, is a secondary fact; the primary fact lies deeper. 'Logical thought, separated from the other cognitive powers, is the natural characteristic of a mind which has fallen away from its wholeness.' [1] The first impairment of the spirit's wholeness resulted from the Fall; but faith—being a manifestation of wholeness, in so far as the latter has been preserved in the 'inner focus of the spirit'—restores the natural functioning of the mind. 'Faith makes the mind understand that it has deviated from its moral wholeness,' [2] and this understanding helps us to rise above the 'natural' course of thought. Where faith is present, a 'dual activity' goes on in the thought of the believer:

'In following the development of his understanding, he simultaneously follows the *method* of his thinking, constantly striving to raise his reason to a level where it can sympathize with faith. An inner consciousness, or sometimes only an obscure feeling, of the primordial and ultimate limit of reason is *infallibly present* in its every movement.' [3]

The power of 'believing reason' results from the impulse of reason itself to rise to its highest form. This does no violence to the 'natural' functioning of the mind, which has already been impaired by loss of contact with the 'wholeness of its primary nature'; for faith reveals to us inwardly that the 'development of natural reason serves only as a series of stages' to higher activity. Thus, the corruption of our mind which resulted when it turned away from the 'wholeness of its primary nature' is repaired by what faith brings into our spirit. This is why,

'being at a higher stage of thought, the Orthodox believer can easily and *harmlessly* [!] understand all the systems of thought which arise at the lower stages of reason, see their limitations and their relative truth. But to the thought of the lower stages the higher is incomprehensible and appears as foolishness.'

Such is Kireyevski's solution of the basic problem of epistemology: the inner concord of faith and reason in the very sources of thought, the recognition of the inadequacy of the 'natural' course of thought, and the ascent to spiritual reason. Knowledge is not *qualitatively homogeneous* or identical, either in value or in its ability to get at reality, in the lower ('natural') and

1. *Ibid.*, p. 276.      2. *Ibid.*, p. 250.      3. *Ibid.*, p. 252.

the higher forms of thought. It is not a question of constraining reason or subordinating it to faith—this would not provide sufficient scope for spiritual vision—but of lifting thought inwardly to its highest form, where faith and reason are no longer opposed. In this ascent toward wholeness of spirit the danger of loss of contact with reality—the danger of idealism—disappears. Cognition which proceeds correctly leads us into reality and connects us with it.

How then are we to explain the origin of idealistic epistemology in the Western world, a world which originally lived by faith?— According to Kireyevski, there was an impairment of faith itself 'resulting in a development first of scholastic philosophy *within* faith, then of a Reformation *of* faith, and finally of philosophy *outside* faith'.[1] This scheme underlies Kireyevski's whole critique of Western culture: the fact that the Western Church substituted the outward authority of its hierarchy for the inner authority of truth (when, arbitrarily and without the consent of the East, it changed the Symbol of faith) has led to 'self-contained rational thought'—to rationalism, i.e. the victory of 'autonomous' reason. Transcendentalism, which represents the high point of this self-sufficient rationality, dissolves all reality in the dialectical self-movement of reason. Therefore we must distinguish 'hyperlogical knowledge', in which we are not torn away from reality but are immersed in it, from 'logical' knowledge. Idealism exhibits the *falseness* of all rationalism; and it is the inevitable result of rationalism, for logical rationality as such does not take us beyond the limits of what is *immanent* in consciousness. Living by logical thought, 'we live on a blueprint instead of in a house; and, having drawn the blueprint, we think that we have erected the building'.[2]

'The whole order of things [which arose with the triumph of rationalism],' Kireyevski writes in the 'Fragments', 'impels our thinking toward the isolation of logical thought. Faith surpasses natural reason precisely because the latter has sunk *below* the level of its primary nature.'[3]

'Of course', Kireyevski remarks, 'a thinking human being must subject his conclusions to the discipline of logic,'[4] i.e. we are not to reject but to overcome contemporary thought. The task of Russian philosophy is not to reject Western thought, but to supplement it with what is revealed in higher spiritual vision. The living experience of 'higher knowledge'—in which wholeness of spirit, which was lost

1. *Ibid.*, p. 226.    2. Letter to Khomyakov. *Ibid.*, p. 67.
3. *Ibid.*, p. 276.    4. *Ibid.*, p. 247.

in the Fall and impaired by the triumph of logical thought in Western Christianity, is recovered—this living experience of 'spiritual understanding' underlies Kireyevski's whole epistemology. Logical thought does not lead us into reality; it merely exhibits the logical structure of being. But true knowledge, like faith, unites us with reality.

Such is Kireyevski's epistemology.


## 6. HISTORICAL VIEWS

It remains to consider Kireyevski's views on problems of historiosophy.

Kireyevski was thoroughly familiar with Hegel's philosophy of history—perhaps the most attractive part of the latter's system—and, like Khomyakov, he rebelled at the idea of an immanent reason operating in history.

'We would form a false conception of the development of human reason if we considered it apart from the influence of chance,' he wrote. 'Nothing is easier than to represent real facts as unavoidable results of higher laws of reasonable necessity; but nothing so *distorts* a genuine conception of history as these *fictive* laws of reasonable necessity.' [1]

Kireyevski, without denying historical causality, places man's free will in the foreground. Rejecting historiosophical rationalism, he also rejects absolute providentialism—likewise in the name of human freedom; and he warns repeatedly against confusing the divine and the human.[2] He acknowledges not only human freedom but also the inner connectedness of history [3] and the subordination of this immanent causality to an 'invisible . . . tendency of the general moral order of things'; [4] i.e. he acknowledges Providence in history. Kireyevski emphasizes that the 'meaning' of history involves mankind as a whole:

'The enlightenment of each nation', he wrote in an early article, 'is not measured by the sum of its knowledge . . ., but solely by its *participation* in the enlightenment of *all mankind*, by the place which it occupies in the general course of human development.' [5]

1. *Ibid.*, p. 244.            2. *Ibid.*, p. 247.
3. 'We see . . . in history the indissoluble connection and successive movement of the human mind.' (*Ibid.*, p. 104.)
4. *Ibid.*, p. 242.            5. *Ibid.*, p. 104.

Kireyevski's ideas concerning the *continuity* of historical development are characteristic: each nation in turn advances to the foreground of history. And, although 'progress is achieved only by the combined forces of mankind', nations have their phase of historical flowering: they intercept 'on the run' (to use Milyukov's apt phrase [1]) the products of the life of other nations.

Of much greater importance and interest are Kireyevski's views on the problems of a concrete philosophy of history. Of particular significance here is his anticipation of a new historical 'era', a new age—a view which in general was highly developed in romanticism and was beginning to appear frequently in Russian literature. Here Kireyevski was not original; but he was 'in harmony' with an orientation which was united in him, as in other Russian thinkers, with a profound conviction that the new 'era' would involve a glorification of the 'Russian idea'. The beginning of this new 'era', however, meant the end of the previous one. To Kireyevski, as to many of his contemporaries, this seemed 'self-evident'. He combined a sincere love of the West—and the idea of a synthesis of European culture with Russian principles—with a harsh critique of the West and a recognition that it had reached a spiritual 'impasse'. But Kireyevski's critique of the West was his own—not borrowed from others, but developed in the name of the idea of 'wholeness' which was his cherished dream, an idea which had grown from romantic roots and had been consolidated under the influence of patristic anthropology.

'European enlightenment', he once wrote, 'has now achieved the plenitude of its development; . . . but the result of this plenitude has been an almost universal feeling of discontent and betrayed hope. . . . This feeling of discontent and unconsolable emptiness has seized men's hearts because the very triumph of the European mind has revealed the one-sidedness of its fundamental aspirations, . . . and because, with all the conveniences of life, and all of its superficial improvements, life itself has been deprived of substantial meaning. The cold analysis of many centuries has destroyed the foundations upon which—from the very beginning of its development—European enlightenment has rested. As a consequence, its own fundamental principles [i.e. those of Christianity] have become strange and alien to it. . . . And this analysis, which has destroyed its roots—this self-propelling knife of reason, recognizing nothing except itself and individual experience, this despotic

---

1. Milyukov, *Glavnyie techeniya* . . . [Chief Tendencies . . .], 1913, p. 373.

rationality, this logical activity, cut off from all man's other cognitive powers—is its very own doing.' [1]

Thus, according to Kireyevski's tirade—which has since become famous—the source of all the West's woes, and of its grave spiritual disease, is *rationalism* with its inevitable disintegration of spiritual wholeness.

'Western man', we read in the same article, 'breaks up his life into separate aspirations: religious feeling lives in one corner of his heart . . ., in another the powers of reason have their separate existence . . ., in a third the craving for sensuous pleasure, etc. Reason is easily transformed into shrewd cunning, genuine feeling into blind passion, beauty into a dream, truth into an opinion, substantiality into a pretext for imagination, virtue into self-righteousness; theatricality is life's obtrusive accompaniment . . . as daydreaming is its inner mask.' [2]

'Dualism and rationality are the ultimate expressions of Western culture. . . .' This one-sided, and in many respects unjust, conception of Western culture is focused essentially on Western philosophy—its unreligious character and its turning away from Christianity.

'It is difficult to imagine', Kireyevski wrote in his last article, 'where European culture will end, if there is not an inner change in the peoples. . . . Only one thing is still serious for Western man —industry, for which the physical individual has been spared. . . . One might say that [at the present time] the final age of philosophy and the unrestricted domination of industry are just beginning. . . .' [3]

As we see, the socio-economic problems of the West remained wholly foreign to Kireyevski—which fact, as we have seen, was well understood by Odoyevski. Therefore the new 'era', which is to begin with a flowering of Orthodox culture, is sketched by Kireyevski primarily in terms of 'culture' and the restoring of 'wholeness'. It is necessary, he thinks, 'for Orthodox enlightenment to master the *entire* intellectual development of the contemporary world, which has fallen to it as a result of the previous intellectual history of all mankind'.

1. From Kireyevski's article 'The Character of European Enlightenment . . .' (1852), *op. cit.*, I, 176.
2. *Ibid.*, p. 210.
3. *Ibid.*, p. 246.

## 7. GENERAL CHARACTERIZATION

We have already mentioned the repressive measures which greeted Kireyevski's ventures into print on several occasions. They were not fatal to his intellectual work, of course. We must, nevertheless, take into account the paucity of the materials which he left, and the extreme compactness of his exposition. There cannot be any doubt as to Kireyevski's genuine philosophic talent, or the value of his theoretical constructions, despite the brevity and compactness of their expression. This value is testified to by the way in which his ideas—in anthropology and epistemology—germinated in subsequent thinkers. His doctrine of the hierarchical structure of the soul, of man's 'inner focus' as his true centre in which the root unity of the human spirit is restored and the fragmentation of the spirit in the empirical sphere overcome; his doctrine of the special significance of the moral sphere, in the aspiration toward this 'inner focus'; the whole doctrine of the two 'stages' (not merely forms) of the life of the spirit ('natural' and 'spiritual' reason), and the resulting dynamism of principle in anthropology—all of this has been resuscitated more than once in Russian philosophy. Kireyevski's epistemological theories are connected with his doctrine of wholeness of spirit—especially his battle against the 'autonomy' of reason, and his struggle for the restoration of wholeness as a condition for realism in theory of knowledge. For Kireyevski the realism of cognition is inseparable from its ontological character. Consequently, the assertion of faith is a principle for him, since faith is the basis of the whole cognitive process. Cognition of God, for Kireyevski, is the inner foundation for cognition of the world; hence cognition of reality must be of the same type as that which characterizes faith. To know the truth must be to *dwell in the truth*, i.e. it involves not just the mind, but the whole life. Cognition is a function of the personality as a whole, not merely the mind. Kireyevski therefore mistrusts purely rational knowledge, considering it legitimate only within the framework of an integral union with the truth as prime-reality. There are undeniable *utopian* elements in Kireyevski's, and Khomyakov's, hope of restoring wholeness; this is not naturalism, as Gershenzon thinks, but epistemological utopianism. The restoration of wholeness and the triumph of the ontological element in cognition—i.e. not mere mental possession of the truth about being—transforms philosophy into wisdom, and brings about the universal 'restoration' which is the Kingdom of God. Carried away by his critique of rationalism, and sharply emphasizing its antithesis in 'Orthodox enlightenment', i.e. in the Orthodox culture of the future, Kireyevski, like Khomyakov, moved along the lines of historiosophical utopianism, as applied to the sphere of cognition. The romantic dream of universal synthesis was here transformed into the utopia of an integral Orthodox culture, which, in fact, would leave no place for development or history. Both thinkers, although they were very sober in their religious consciousness, each in his own individual way, were romanticists in their epistemological utopianism and their ardent worship of the 'integral spirit', through whose power the 'fragmentation' of contemporary culture was to be overcome.

In any case, there was no room in either thinker for the spirit of secularism; they conceived the Church itself as an assertion and authentic proclamation of freedom. The ecclesiastical consciousness of both thinkers strove to embrace all the themes and searchings of the spirit, giving them wide and ample room, but illuminating them inwardly through emancipation from 'this age' in ascetic activity and a living immersion in the Church. Illumination of the spirit comes through the Church's powers of grace; therefore the truth can only be attained 'ecclesiastically', i.e. in, with, and through the Church. This is the passion that underlay the theoretical constructions of both thinkers, but it also resulted in their being seduced by an 'epistemological utopia', and led them to a somewhat hasty condemnation of 'rationalism'. We are, in general, only on the threshold of 'Christian philosophy'; nevertheless, both thinkers were, in truth, Christian philosophers.

It is interesting to note another feature common to the two men: the 'theurgical restlessness' which we have seen in Chaadayev was alien to both of them. We shall find it germinating in Russian radicalism, beginning with Herzen (Ch. IX); but both Khomyakov and Kireyevski were strangers to it; and K. Aksakov, as we shall soon see, formulated a position of 'political indifference', one to which subsequent Russian thinkers frequently returned.

Kireyevski's influence as a writer and profound thinker is almost irresistible. If he is to be considered a 'failure' because external conditions interfered so strongly with his self-expression, nevertheless that which radiated from his thought and his spiritual world proved to be a genuine seed which later bore fruit.

It remains for us to examine the philosophic views of two of Khomyakov's and Kireyevski's associates—Yu. Samarin and K. Aksakov.

## 8. SAMARIN. BIOGRAPHY

Yuri Fyodorovich Samarin (1819–76), like K. S. Aksakov, brings us to a consideration of Russian *Hegelianism*. Both of them were virtually·uninfluenced by Schelling—a phenomenon which we find in other Hegelians of this period. They gave their 'first love' to Hegel, and he fructified their first philosophic searchings. Although for both of them, especially Samarin, Hegel's influence later faded out almost completely, theirs was actually a different type of philosophizing from that of the thinkers influenced by Schelling. Their neglect of problems of nature-philosophy, and the dominant importance of *historism* in their works, are characteristic in this respect. Nevertheless, both Samarin and Aksakov were essentially connected with 'Slavophilism': Khomyakov was extremely important—Kireyevski much less so—for the life and development of both of them.

Samarin received a thorough education at home, entering Moscow University at the age of fifteen. Upon graduation he began to prepare himself for the master's examination. At this time he became very friendly with Aksakov, and with the latter's help and encouragement freed himself completely from the influence of French culture, which had fascinated him in his early years. In 1840 Samarin began to associate himself with Khomyakov and Kireyevski, especially in their defence of the idea of a specifically Russian culture. His national consciousness was always very clear and strong; he was a passionate but very profound person. During this same period Samarin wrote a dissertation devoted to the history of Russian theology—on Stephan Yavorski and Theophanes Prokopovich. During the writing of his dissertation he was under Hegel's influence, and he asserted with characteristic decisiveness and radicalism that 'the question of the Church depends on philosophy; the Church's fate is indissolubly bound up with that of Hegel'.[1] 'Only by taking science' [i.e. Hegel's philosophy], we read in the same letter (to Popov), 'from a Germany which is powerless to hold it, can we effect the *reconciliation* of consciousness and life which will mark Russia's triumph over the West.' [2] During this period Samarin studied Hegel's works very thoroughly, as is evidenced by the outlines which have been preserved.

1. Samarin, *Sochineniya*, St. Petersburg, 1894, V, lv (letter to Popov, 1842).
2. *Ibid.*, p. liii.

'The Orthodox Church', he wrote Khomyakov, 'cannot exist apart from Hegel's philosophy. . . . We were born into a period of conflict between religion and philosophy—and this conflict is reaching its culmination in ourselves. . . . The relation of philosophy to religion must soon be defined: Orthodoxy, and Orthodoxy alone, is a religion which philosophy can recognize.' [1]

Samarin himself—doubtless under Khomyakov's influence—soon gave up this original idea of grounding (!) Orthodoxy in Hegel's philosophy. He entered gradually upon a path of independent philosophic work and dreamed of taking a chair of philosophy at Moscow University. However, upon his father's insistence he gave up scholarly work and entered government service at St. Petersburg. From there he was sent to Riga, where he collided for the first time with the problem of national minorities in Russia, and with the peasant question. With characteristic passion Samarin plunged into the study of these questions, writing long memoranda and reports. He took sharp exception to the Baltic policy which was then in force and wrote very frankly on this subject to his friends in Moscow. These letters, which exhibit his characteristically forceful and brilliant style, created a sensation, and were passed from hand to hand. Samarin was soon arrested and imprisoned in Petropavlovsk Fortress, but he was set free almost immediately and readmitted to government service. Somewhat later he took an active part in preparing for the emancipation of the peasants. During his last years he returned once more to theoretical work, writing a number of articles. 'I have often entertained the idea', he wrote, three weeks before his death, 'of dropping everything and plucking from the ground the thread of reflections which fell from Khomyakov's dying hands.' [2] But he was not able to carry out this plan.

Samarin cannot be left out of the history of Russian philosophy, although, owing to the limited scope of his writings on philosophic themes, his place is a modest one. He has a much more important place in the history of Russian *scholarship*: his dissertation and his writings on the problem of nationalities in Russia are of value even today. In passing, we may also note his outstanding polemical gifts, which were most brilliantly displayed in his remarkable letters to Fr. Martynov concerning the Jesuits. Herzen prized Samarin's dialectical talent especially, placing him even higher than Khomyakov in this respect.[3]

1. *Ibid.*, pp. lx, lxii.   2. *Op. cit.*, VI, xi.
3. Concerning Samarin, see Chizhevski, *op. cit.*, Pt. II, Ch. VII.

## 9. ANTHROPOLOGY

Samarin, under Khomyakov's influence, became a genuinely Orthodox thinker. His most remarkable work in this direction is the famous preface to Volume II of Khomyakov's Works (the theological writings), which is no less interesting for an understanding of Samarin himself and his religious world. Samarin wrote that Khomyakov 'prized faith as a *truth*'.[1] This was also characteristic of Samarin himself, whose religious world was the source of his philosophic views. This applies especially to philosophical anthropology—the philosophic discipline to which Samarin devoted most thought. In him, more clearly than in Kireyevski, anthropology comes before epistemology or metaphysics. This is connected, of course, with the mode of thought which in the twentieth century has christened itself '*Existenzphilosophie*'—as well as with a general ontological orientation in theory of knowledge.

Samarin insisted on distinguishing individual personality—the basic concept of philosophical anthropology—as an *organ of consciousness*, from personality as a *criterion of value*.[2] In contemporary terminology this root distinction may be expressed as the contrast between personalism and individualism. Samarin sharply opposed individualism, speaking frequently of its 'impotence' and the inevitability of the 'sad admission that the human personality is not independent'.[3] Christianity, according to Samarin, bids man *renounce* his individuality and subordinate it unconditionally to the whole. It must be admitted that this motif was strong in Samarin during his Hegelian period as well: 'Personality', he wrote in his dissertation, 'is a *translucent medium* through which pass the rays of eternal truth, warming and illuminating mankind.'[4] There is a higher court of appeal than individuality, namely, the community, which is based entirely on self-renunciation—the 'highest act of personal freedom and consciousness'.[5] Thus individualism is overcome through an act of free self-renunciation, from within and not from without. 'The communal order . . . is not based on an *absence* of personality, but on the free and conscious renunciation of its sovereignty.'[6] This means that individual personality is exhibited in its depths and creative force not when it is closed in upon itself, but when it exists in communion with others, subordinating itself to a higher whole—not for itself, but for higher principles. In other words, the power which helps the individual

1. Samarin, *op. cit.*, IV, 347.   2. *Op. cit.*, I, 42.   3. *Ibid.*, p. 38.
4. *Op. cit.*, V, 343.   5. *Op. cit.*, I, 52.   6. *Ibid.*, p. 64.

cast off the fetters of his natural self-isolation is the higher power of religion. The 'individual' principle, Samarin writes, is a principle of *disunion* rather than union; the individual as such provides no basis for the concept of *man*, for this concept refers to what *unites* all men and does not separate them from one another.[1]

'Only an artificial association can be based upon an individual person who makes himself the absolute measure of all things; no absolute norm, no law binding upon all men, can be logically deduced from the concept of individual personality, nor will history offer such a law.'

But the self-limitation of the individual person, being his free act, appeals to a principle higher than himself and opposed to individualism. The religious principle is such a higher principle, one to which the individual person can surrender himself freely and completely.

The relationship of each individual person to God is the primary and basic fact of his being; the direct experience of Deity is primordial and non-deducible—it is a 'personal revelation, illuminating the soul of each human being'.[2] Every human being comes into the world bearing this God-given light in his soul. Only by recognizing that God sustains an *individual* relationship, in the strict sense, with each individual human being—Samarin thinks—can we understand why our self-appraisals always include a search for the 'meaning' and 'reasonableness' of life.[3] If we reject the assumption of an individual Providence, its place will be taken by the myth of some magical 'necessity' which supposedly determines the course of human life. Furthermore, we construct and interpret our outward experience on the basis of this primordial spiritual experience, i.e. communion with God. 'All the material acquired from without is fused in the unquenchable flame [of inner effort]';[4] it takes on a new form, becoming a system of knowledge.[5]

Only by assuming such an individual 'Revelation' or primary and basic religious experience, i.e. a direct union of every soul with the first-source of life, can we explain man's ineradicable consciousness of freedom and responsibility, or even the fact of consciousness

---

1. *Ibid.*, p. 40.  2. *Op. cit.*, VI, 505, 515, 519.
3. *Ibid.*, p. 507.  4. *Op. cit.*, I, 140.
5. Gershenzon (*op. cit.*, p. 138) expounds Samarin's doctrine in these words: 'All thought and all knowledge are religious in their root.' This formula does not convey Samarin's thought precisely; Samarin insists on the reality of both extrasensory and sensory knowledge—but does not derive the latter from the former.

of oneself as 'an individual person'. On the other hand, if we do not recognize a religious experience in which man's whole soul is illumined by God, we cannot preserve our wholeness of soul. And without this an incorrect idea of the soul arises which inevitably degenerates into a false system of individualism.

The doctrine of wholeness of spirit, as we have seen, is the focal point of Kireyevski's anthropology, and it is more than fitting to recognize the decisive influence of Kireyevski on Samarin in this connection.[1] But Samarin's doctrine is completely free of the flavour of utopianism which we find in Kireyevski. According to Samarin 'our *task* is to create an integral image of the moral human being'.[2] Two elements in this formula invite attention: first of all, if the 'integral' image has to be *created*, wholeness must be *potential* rather than *actual*, i.e. it does not exist in reality—even in the 'inner focus', to use Kireyevski's term; one must realize it in oneself. The anthropological dynamism which we have found in Kireyevski is here expressed even more definitely. Of course, there is a *guarantee* of wholeness in the religious sphere of the soul (the 'image of God'), but this is only a guarantee. On the other hand, Samarin subordinates 'spiritual wholeness', even more emphatically than Khomyakov or Kireyevski, to the moral principle in man, which forms the very centre of his personality. Khomyakov and Kireyevski emphasize the importance of the moral element only with respect to cognition, but Samarin assigns a central place to the sphere of morality generally. He unhesitatingly relates the moral principle, its independence from the external world, and its creative power, to faith [3] and the soul's primordial religiosity. In his extremely interesting polemic with K. D. Kavelin, apropos of the latter's book The Tasks of Psychology, Samarin lays special stress on the dualism within the individual person, a dualism related to the autonomous and independent character of the moral principle. Kavelin, whom we shall discuss in Ch. XII, was a *semi-positivist*: he defended ethical idealism—holding, with philosophic naïveté, that idealism can be grounded in positivism. Samarin showed with great clarity the essential nonhomogeneity of these two groups of ideas. But Samarin's thoughts on this subject took on special precision in his remarkable letter to Herzen. The two men had been friends at one time in Moscow; but during the 1840's, when the break between the Westerners and the Slavophiles became final, they drifted apart.

---

1. Gershenzon asserts this categorically. (*Ibid.*, p. 119.)
2. Samarin, *op. cit.*, I, 137.  3. *Ibid.*, p. 141.

Shortly before his death Samarin—the initiative was his—being abroad, wished to see Herzen again; and the latter was sincerely delighted by Samarin's suggestion. The meeting of the former friends, which lasted for three days, was very cordial; but with each day, each discussion, their consciousness of the gulf which separated them grew stronger. After his departure, Samarin wrote Herzen a long letter, which is remarkable for its profundity and power. Like Kavelin, Herzen was a semi-positivist, but he was a much more brilliant and gifted man than Kavelin. Samarin exhibited with great clarity and precision Herzen's internal contradiction in combining ethical idealism and a cult of freedom with a purely naturalistic conception of the individual. Samarin emphasized that the individual person cannot be understood properly apart from his relation to the Absolute, and that his consciousness of freedom, his whole moral sphere, cannot be understood or taken seriously by a purely naturalistic doctrine of individuality.

## 10. EPISTEMOLOGICAL VIEWS. GENERAL APPRAISAL

Samarin treated in detail only problems of philosophical anthropology; in other fields of philosophy he expressed himself merely in passing and inadequately. On the question of the *sources* of knowledge, he decisively and very aptly criticized sensationalism, developing a doctrine of the direct cognition of the 'nonmaterial environment'. This refers both to social cognition and to the cognition of higher (religious, moral, and aesthetic) reality.[1] Samarin forcefully demonstrated the reality of religious *experience*—or better, he showed that the religious life rests on experience.

Following Kireyevski, Samarin insists that reality—higher reality and sensory reality alike—cannot be 'proven', i.e. cannot be rationally deduced. Reality is revealed to us only in *experience*, a living and operative union with the object of knowledge. This refers to sensory as well as spiritual experience;[2] Samarin calls both of these forms of experience 'external'. In his dissertation he advanced the thesis that 'the rupture between the knower and the known disappears only in the life of grace'.[3] This rupture indicates that existence and cognition are not identical, as rationalism asserts; indeed, this very rupture is *generated* by rationalism. Considerably later, in 1846, Samarin repeated this idea—but now the rupture is between 'life and consciousness'.[4] It is clear from the

1. *Op. cit.*, VI, 403.
2. *Ibid.*, p. 509.
3. *Op. cit.*, V, 458.
4. *Op. cit.*, I, 13.

context that Samarin has in mind the doctrine of the dependence of self-consciousness on social life which Khomyakov was developing during this same period. Therefore, we find no further development in Samarin of the ontological interpretation of cognition; he fully accepts the position of Khomyakov and Kireyevski, emphasizing the 'immediacy' of the soul's union with God. Precisely at this point, in union with God, cognition is inseparable from a living relation to God as the object of cognitive striving. Only by maintaining our religious impulses do we continue in a living (nonabstract) union with the reality of the world. We may say of religious experience that the 'heart of the concept of God includes a direct experience of His influence on each human being',[1] but this is also true of external experience. Hence Samarin's *realism* of principle in cognition with respect to both created and divine being.[2] Reason cannot reveal the reality of anything whatsoever; on the contrary, every reality must be given before thought can begin to operate on it. Let us repeat Samarin's words: 'The *reality* of a fact can only be perceived through personal experience.'[3] But he does not exclude criticism; indeed, he asserts flatly that it is possible that the organs of perception—sensory as well as non-sensory—'may modify objective fact, bringing *illusory* fact to our perception'.[4] He shows very astutely that realism in cognition can be asserted in principle only with relation to God.[5]

In 1861, on the initiative of a friend, Samarin began a new philosophic work, Letters on Materialism, which remained largely unfinished. It is a very interesting work, and one can only regret that Samarin gave up writing it. 'It strikes me', he wrote, 'that in the future strictly consistent materialism will be of enormous use,'[6] for the exhibition of its falseness will be accompanied by a disintegration of 'colourless, spineless, flabby humanism', making clear the truth of Christianity. Samarin reasserted the nondeducibility and primordial quality of personality with great force: 'There is a core in man—a focus, as it were—from which a native spring wells up.'[7] Personalism cannot, of course, be combined with materialism. Unfortunately, the Letters on Materialism only touch upon, but do not develop, the theme to which they were addressed.

Samarin's philosophic legacy, as we have seen, was not large; b ut his doctrine of personality extended the theories which had

1. *Op. cit.*, VI, 485.    2. *Ibid.*, p. 463.    3. *Ibid.*, p. 509.
4. *Ibid.*, p. 513.    5. *Loc. cit.*    6. *Ibid.*, p. 544.
7. *Ibid.*, p. 551.

been developed by Khomyakov and Kireyevski—in anthropology and, to some extent, in theory of knowledge. Personalism, as a denial of individualism, leads to the establishment of an inner bond between the individual person and the social whole. K. S. Aksakov, the last of the senior Slavophiles, added certain new features to the elaboration of this problem in Khomyakov, Kireyevski, and Samarin.

## II. K. AKSAKOV. GENERAL CHARACTERIZATION OF AKSAKOV

Konstantin Sergeyevich Aksakov (1817–60) belonged originally to the circle of N. V. Stankevich (see the following chapter), and he always preserved friendly relations with its members. As a student he became acquainted with Hegel's philosophy and, with characteristic enthusiasm, became a Hegelian—though not without some concessions to his early Schellingism. In the words of Chicherin, Aksakov was convinced at this period that 'the Russian nation is destined, before all others, to understand Hegel'—i.e. to provide wide room within itself for the self-consciousness of Absolute Spirit. Like Samarin, who was also a Hegelian at this time, Aksakov gave Hegelianism a Slavophile interpretation and application.

In his dissertation (on Lomonosov) as well as his historical and philological works, Aksakov showed himself a very meditative and original thinker. His theory of language is of particular interest. In view of the special character of this work, we shall not undertake an exposition of it here. Let us note only that Hegel's spirit was in fact laid to rest in Aksakov's historical schemes and philological reflections. We shall select from his various utterances only what is dialectically connected with the fundamental themes of Russian philosophic thought, especially the problem of personality —i.e. questions of anthropology. Although Aksakov introduced nothing new on this subject as compared to the other Slavophiles, he had his own special approach to these questions. Like Samarin, he saw a deadly duality in the principle of personality: it may take the path of self-separation, which is at the same time the path of self-destruction, or it may take the path of self-limitation in the name of a higher whole. The Russian *obshchina* [village commune] was such a higher whole, and Aksakov praised it in poetic language: 'In the Russian *obshchina*', he wrote, 'the individual person is not suppressed, but merely deprived of his tumultuousness, exclusiveness, and egoism. . . . Only the egoistical aspect of personality is swallowed up in the *obshchina*—but the individual person is *free* in it, as in a *chorus*.' The 'choral' life of the individual opens a special path before him, i.e. it preserves his uniqueness and gives it broad scope; but it subordinates the individual person to the whole, just as each singer in a chorus sings with his *own* voice but subordinates himself to the functioning of the chorus as a whole. In defending the freedom of the individual person within the limits of the life of the whole (*obshchina*), Aksakov sharply contrasts *society* and *state*; the first is a valuable and genuine supplementation of individual personality but the second is alien to its inner life. It is from this point of view that Aksakov criticizes Western culture; its excessive development of state apparatus has been connected with the legal expression of 'justice' as an inner principle. 'The West developed legality', Aksakov wrote, 'because it sensed the lack of justice within itself.' 'The *soul is on the wane* in the West; it is being replaced by the improvement of state forms and police-enforced public order; conscience is being replaced by law, inner impulse by regulation. . . .' Aksakov was ardent in his defence of human freedom precisely because the idea of freedom did not have an external meaning for him but was connected with the religious principle.

## 12. PHILOSOPHY AMONG THE SLAVOPHILES

In accordance with what was said in the preceding chapter concerning the incorrectness of treating Slavophilism as a whole, we shall not offer a general philosophic appraisal of Slavophilism. We wish to emphasize only two elements which were common to all the Slavophiles, and which we have frequently mentioned, in order to make clear the dialectical connection of the senior Slavophiles with the basic themes of Russian philosophy.

In Slavophilism Russian thought returned with extraordinary force to a religious—indeed, an ecclesiastical—orientation. Because they were aware of the internal logic of secularism in the West, the Slavophiles asserted all the more insistently that the inevitability of secularism in the West was connected not with the essence of Christianity but with its Western perversions. Hence their ardent and passionate striving to find in Orthodoxy a conception of Christianity which would not only preclude the possibility of secularism, but would fully satisfy and sanctify the basic and ineradicable searchings of the human spirit. On this basis they

*Save West w/o Orthodoxy*

asserted that the whole 'era' of Western culture was terminating from within, that culture henceforth must be reorganized in the light of Orthodoxy. All the Slavophiles saw in *Russia* the guiding creative force for this reorganization.

But it was not simply the need to return to an ecclesiastical world-view that defined the Slavophiles' theoretical constructions; secondary factors also entered which had first made themselves fully felt in Western secularism. The Slavophiles' position in this respect not only did not fuse with the traditional ecclesiastical world-view, as it had been consolidated in the seventeenth and eighteenth centuries; but, fully aware of what they were doing, they opened up new paths within the Orthodox consciousness itself. This was related to a genuine patristic tradition, but also to everything of value that had matured in modern science, philosophy, and general culture. The new 'era' was conceived not as a *synthesis* of Orthodoxy with Western culture, but as the construction of a new and creative cultural consciousness, growing organically out of the very foundations of the Orthodox ecclesiastical tradition. The Slavophiles lived in the faith—which was not without a utopian tinge—that all of the genuine values of the West had been 'saved' even though they were rooted in a wholly different spiritual tradition.

The return to an ecclesiastical orientation, and the anticipation of a new culture based upon it, was the Slavophiles' very important contribution to the work of Russian thought. But, before we can see how the seeds sown by the Slavophiles developed, we must study certain other manifestations of Russian thought during this same period. Let us turn first of all to a study of the early manifestations of Russian Hegelianism.

# CHAPTER VIII

## The Hegelian Circles

### N. V. STANKEVICH. M. A. BAKUNIN. V. G. BELINSKI

#### I. GENERAL REMARKS

WE turn now to a tendency of Russian thought which developed during the 1830's and '40's (i.e. simultaneously with Slavophilism) independently of the ecclesiastical idea, striving to consolidate and strengthen *aesthetic humanism* as the basis of a whole world-view. This 'resurrected' aesthetic humanism took on new creative force and displayed unquestionable vitality as the basic principle of Russian *secularism*; and this comprised the moving and inspiring force of aesthetic humanism and its attraction for those Russian thinkers who moved in the lines of secularism, decisively separating religion from ideology and philosophic thought. Many representatives of this tendency displayed a genuine and profound personal religiosity, which in some of them lasted throughout their lives. Nevertheless, they drew their inspiration from the principles of autonomism, developing their theoretical constructions in the spirit of secularism. It is significant in this connection that almost all the defenders of secularism were 'Westerners' ['*Zapadniki*']—i.e. men who openly and straightforwardly associated themselves with Western secular culture, attempting to link the paths of Russian thought to the problems of the West. Another characteristic of this tendency was *socio-political radicalism*, in which 'theurgical restlessness'—a sense of responsibility for history and a search for ways of intervening actively in its course—was resurrected and deepened in a new and original way. These features characterized the ideology of that part of the Russian intelligentsia whose thought moved outside the Church, a group which, in the apt expression of one writer, became a unique 'order'—with a stable intellectual tradition and a specifically sectarian psychology—both fanatical and intolerant.

All of this, of course, was very unfavourable for the development of philosophy as such. A number of writers of undoubted philosophic talent (Bakunin, Herzen, Chernyshevski, and Mikhailovski, later) devoted their energies not to philosophy, but to philosophical writing on social and political themes, a genre which was brilliantly represented in Western Europe as well. We shall see below that certain principles were involved in this tendency—in particular, the idea of the direct expression of intellectual effort in action, in concrete historical activity. This is not a random phenomenon in Russian thought; it simply exhibits in a new form the motif of *wholeness* with which we are already familiar. Even those thinkers who moved from transcendentalism to positivism remained in essence 'semi-positivists', since they introduced into their world-view elements of idealism which were not deducible from the principles of positivism, but were simply combined—overtly or covertly—with their positivism.

In the development of Russian Westernism and socio-political radicalism, German and French thought were operative in different ways, but aesthetic humanism rose above and composed all of their differences. For secularism and its construction of an 'independent' and autonomous system of thought, faith in 'truth', 'justice', and 'beauty' was the ultimate and sacred idea, not in the form given it by Schiller (the *Schöne Seele!*), but in somewhat different tones—which, however, remained essentially Schillerian. Both Schelling and Hegel inspired Russian thought within the *framework of Schiller's views*, as they themselves had originally been inspired by Schiller. Of course, not only the individual thinkers but the whole spiritual atmosphere in which they lived is important for an understanding of this tendency. It was an atmosphere of *philosophic culture*; broad circles of Russian society interested themselves in and lived by philosophic questions. Herzen wrote of this at length in his memoirs *My Past and Thoughts*; Turgenev also had much to say about it—in *Rudin*, for example, or the *Hamlet of Shchigrovsk*. From this point of view an intensive study of the Bakunin family, with which many outstanding people of the period were associated, would be very interesting.

The members of the philosophic circles (mainly in Moscow) [1] were chiefly young people; however, the influence of these circles was not limited to their youthful period, but carried over into their later years. We have already spoken of the circles with which

1. Concerning the philosophic circles, especially the Hegelian circles, see Chizhevski, *Hegel in Russland*, Pt. II, Ch. I.

Chaadayev, Khomyakov, the Kireyevskis, Samarin, and K. Aksakov were associated. We shall now consider two other circles, one headed by N. V. Stankevich and the other by Herzen—though the two circles sustained close personal relations. Let us turn first to a study of Stankevich's circle, to which K. Aksakov belonged at one time, and which included M. A. Bakunin, V. G. Belinski, V. P. Botkin, *et al*. We shall first consider N. V. Stankevich, their 'leader' and the most brilliant and remarkable member of the circle.

## 2. N. V. STANKEVICH

Nicholas Vladimirovich Stankevich (1813–40) wrote very little during his brief lifetime. His correspondence, as in the case of other thinkers of the time, is of chief importance.[1] But even this does not give an adequate idea of the man; one must read widely in the correspondence of Bakunin and Belinski, and in the various memoirs of the period, to feel Stankevich's full importance and understand his extraordinary influence.

Stankevich received his preliminary education in Voronezh at the so-called 'Nobleman's Boarding School'; at the age of seventeen he entered Moscow University, living at the home of the Schellingian Professor Pavlov. There Stankevich immersed himself completely in the world of German romanticism; Schiller's aesthetic world-view impressed him particularly. 'Art is becoming a God for me', he wrote at this time. Toward the end of his life this formula gave way to a somewhat different one: 'Art is the first stage in the knowledge of God.' This is in full harmony with the primacy of the aesthetic principle which was so deeply bound up with romanticism. Stankevich, of course, was a romanticist throughout his brief life, although rigorous thought later began to develop strongly in him.[2] In any case, feeling, for Stankevich—as for all the Russian thinkers of this period—was connected in the most intimate way with intellectual activity; and here he was an incorrigible romanticist.

Stankevich had poetic talent, of minor calibre, and his personality was marked by a constant animation which acted irresistibly

1. Concerning Stankevich, see Chizhevski, *op. cit.*, Pt. II, Ch. II; W. Setschkarew, *Schellings Einfluss in der russischen Literatur der 20–30 Jahre des XIX Jahrhunderts*, Leipzig, 1939. Stankevich is superbly portrayed in Turgenev's novel *Rudin* in the person of Pokorski.

2. A contrary view is expressed by Setschkarew (*op. cit.*, p. 75) and Chizhevski (*op. cit.*, p. 184). But neither writer documents his categorical denial of Stankevich's romanticism.

on everyone around him. He was wholly imbued with a unique poetic optimism; his favourite phrase was: '*Es herrscht eine allweise Güte über die Welt.*' This faith in an 'all-wise beneficence' which prevails in the world, this living sense of the world's harmony and beauty, flowed from the very depths of Stankevich's soul and defined the aesthetic humanism of which he himself was a highly refined representative. We must note that in Stankevich himself this faith was combined with a wonderful kindness and a very deep and vital religiosity which gave his personality an extraordinary charm.

Under the influence of Pavlov, and especially of the Professor of Literature N. I. Nadezhdin, Stankevich developed an enthusiasm for Schelling; but later, under the influence of his new acquaintance Bakunin, he shifted his enthusiasm to Fichte and then to Hegel. During this period Stankevich's philosophic interests moved decisively into the foreground. He went to Germany—a move necessitated by his failing health—and attended lectures in Berlin. While still in Moscow he had considered taking his master's examination in philosophy; in Berlin he deepened his philosophic studies, but his health became worse and worse. He went to Italy, still continuing his studies. In the summer of 1840 his life was cut short; his philosophic plans remained unfinished.

Philosophically, Stankevich was influenced first by Schelling, upon whom, in his own words, he 'came unexpectedly'. It is interesting to note that Stankevich himself felt that Schelling 'brought me back to my *earlier* path, to which aesthetics was about to lead me'.[1] Schelling brought Stankevich back to an integral perception of the world and of life: 'I wish to have complete unity in the universe of my knowledge,' he wrote, after mentioning Schelling's influence. '. . . I wish to see the connection of each phenomenon with the life of the whole world—its necessity, its role in the development of the one idea.'[2] From Schelling Stankevich learned, as he himself testifies, to understand the unity of history and nature, to bind the diverse aspects of being into a living whole. But he also took over Schelling's transcendentalism[3]

1. *Perepiska* [Correspondence], Moscow, 1914, p. 450.
2. It is thus incorrect to assert that 'the separate philosophic notes scattered through Stankevich's letters are *wholly within the framework of Hegelianism*'. (Chizhevski, *Gegel v Rossi* [Hegel in Russia], p. 79.) In fact, Schelling's influence never vanished from Stankevich; however, Hegel's closeness to Schelling on many points should not be forgotten.
3. Chizhevski (*Hegel in Russland*, p. 184) is thus wrong when he ascribes Stankevich's turn to 'real philosophic thought' to Hegel's influence. Stankevich's taste for 'rigorous' philosophy came from his study of Schelling.

and his conception of the cosmos. We find echoes of Schellingism in the fragment 'My Metaphysics', written *before* his acquaintance with Hegel, while he was still very young. But there is an essential difference between Stankevich, in this period, and Odoyevski, for example, in his Schellingian period. In the latter, motifs of nature-philosophy and aesthetic idealism are in the foreground, whereas in Stankevich there is a much stronger interest in transcendental-ism as such. This is shown most clearly by the fact that, after Schelling, Stankevich studied—Kant! It is also interesting to note the motifs of *impersonalism* in Stankevich during this period: he wanted to take as his point of departure not the transcendental Self, but *Reason*. 'Reason', he wrote, 'is prior to all things.' [1] For Stankevich it was possible to take the transcendental Self as one's point of departure only because 'the Self, having no beginning, is coeval with understanding'. (This was written before his study of Fichte.) Let us note one final element in Stankevich's early Schel-lingism: the setting of religion *above* philosophy. 'Only one stage is possible above [Schelling's system],' he wrote, 'the permeation of this system by religion: it is capable of developing into [!] pure Christianity.' Somewhat later he expressed himself differently: 'Only philosophy can make religion *durable*.' (He wrote this in 1835, a year before he began to study Hegel.) But we find just *before* this formula a sharper statement of the idea of the hierarchical primacy of religion: 'Only for the soul that is reconciled to God . . . is nature as a whole renewed; difficult moral questions, which are *insoluble* for the mind, resolve themselves without the least struggle; life once more becomes beautiful and lofty.' [2] For the believer in a wise Beneficence 'Blind Ananke does not rule existence.' [3] Even in these years Stankevich recognized the 'autonomy' of reason; but he also noted the inadequacy of autonomous reason—i.e. of philo-sophy alone—with respect to problems which only religion can solve.

After Kant, Stankevich proceeded (under the influence of M. Bakunin; see § 4) to a brief study of Fichte. The inadequacy of Stankevich's knowledge of Fichte has been justly noted.[4] But in him, as in Bakunin and Belinski, a temporary enthusiasm for Fichteanism was connected with an emphasis on the *primacy of ethics*; the need for such an ethicism, and the recognition of its truth and justice, were present in themselves. All of them valued Fichte's ethical radicalism, and the ethical motif which so strongly

---

1. Stankevich, *op. cit.*, p. 293.    2. *Ibid.*, p. 283.    3. *Ibid.*, p. 249.
4. Chizhevski, *Gegel* . . . [Hegel . . .], p. 78.

dominates his system, as a second basic element in aesthetic humanism. In any event, Stankevich, and especially Belinski, displayed moral passion throughout their lives; both of them gravitated essentially toward the 'pan-moralism' which was manifested later with such extraordinary force in Leo Tolstoy and, somewhat differently, in N. K. Mikhailovski. Stankevich and his friends valued especially Fichte's idea that the *individual* is rooted in the transcendental sphere; this doctrine made possible their emancipation from romantic subjectivism.

This element also explains a paradox in the dialectic of the development of Stankevich's whole group—the fact that they came to Hegel from Schelling *through* Fichteanism. This is actually less paradoxical than it might at first appear. Schelling's nature-philosophy and aesthetics had appealed to earlier Russian thinkers; but Stankevich's group—although they were mildly enthusiastic about Schelling's nature-philosophy, his relating of history to nature, and his aesthetics—were most attracted by his *transcendentalism*. However, a doctrine of the individual—this concept was very weak in Schelling generally—could not be developed on the soil of Schellingism; consequently, Stankevich placed religion above philosophy in this period. But Fichte's extraordinary moral passion provided Stankevich and his group with what they had not found in Schelling—an idea of the individual. In one of his late letters to Bakunin, Stankevich wrote: 'Reality is the arena of the genuine man; only a weak soul lives in the *Jenseits*.' [1] This shows Hegel's influence, of course, but Stankevich and his friends reached their assertion of real, concrete individual life through Fichte. This Fichtean motif also persisted during their enthusiasm for Hegel, leading in due course to a critique of Hegel. This was most strongly expressed by Belinski, but in Stankevich too we find a protest against the dissolution of individuality in the universal. [2]

Stankevich studied Hegel thoroughly and enthusiastically, and he felt the power of Hegel's synthesis deeply. He translated a rather competent article on Hegel by Wilm; [3] and, in addition to Hegel's own works, he studied the works of his followers, including Feuerbach and August Cieszkowsky, a Polish Hegelian whom we shall have occasion to mention in the chapter on Herzen. Stankevich himself wrote an article on 'The Possibility of Philosophy as a

1. Stankevich, *op. cit.*, p. 650.
2. *Ibid.*, p. 624.
3. This translation was published in his collected works (Moscow, 1890).

Science'. But for some reason it was not printed, and the manuscript was lost.

While he was still studying Fichte, Stankevich became absorbed in the idea of philosophy as a rigorous science; but he wrote his friend Neverov: 'Fichte has succeeded so subtly and satisfactorily in turning the whole world into a modification of thought that he has made thought itself a modification of some unknown subject. . . . He has constructed a whole world of phantoms out of the laws of the mind, and he has made the mind itself a phantom. . . .' 'In Fichte', he adds, 'I can already see the possibility of *another* system.' Stankevich found this new system in Hegel, whom he studied at great length. Chizhevski [1] has rightly pointed out that Stankevich was wholly exempt from the misinterpretations of 'reality'—one of Hegel's basic concepts—concerning which (as we shall see in our study of Belinski) misunderstandings were frequent. 'Reality—in the sense of immediate, external existence—is an accident,' Stankevich wrote; 'reality in its truth is reason, spirit.' Stankevich appraised the importance of the state, and of history generally, very subtly and accurately—'accurately' in the sense of being close to Hegel.

The statements in Stankevich's correspondence are fragmentary, of course, and do not permit a reconstruction of his theoretical views. But this correspondence makes it clear that, in his person, Russian philosophy lost a thinker of unquestionable talent, whose philosophic work would have been of considerable significance. However, Stankevich's importance as the lively and animated leader of a whole group of young thinkers is still very large. In studying the history of Russian thought, one should not forget his spiritual influence or his loyalty to philosophy. Nevertheless, his importance in the consolidation of aesthetic humanism as the basic characteristic of the Russian intelligentsia's new secular ideology is even greater. The combination of faith in progress with an enthusiastic worship of beauty and art lent the Russian intelligentsia an optimism and an operative idealism which satisfied, and at the same time moderated, their 'theurgical restlessness'. 'Faith in mankind', Stankevich once wrote, 'is one of my most precious beliefs.' [2] Rapture over the beauty of the new life to come was a characteristic expression of the new forms of secularism that had emerged throughout Europe under the influence of romanticism.

1. *Op. cit.*, p. 80.
2. Stankevich, *op. cit.*, p. 290.

### 3. M. A. BAKUNIN. BIOGRAPHY

Let us proceed to a study of M. A. Bakunin.[1] His philosophic writing, which is insignificant in extent and is contained chiefly in his letters, is nevertheless of great importance for a correct understanding of the development of philosophic thought in Russia. Stankevich's Hegelianism, which was quite close to the original, was joined peacefully and harmoniously with a basic aesthetic humanism; but Bakunin conceived Hegelianism wholly as a doctrine of *historical being* and of the dialectic of Absolute Spirit in its historical self-manifestation. This was the point at which Hegelianism exercised its powerful and creative influence, and here Bakunin was a pioneer and trail blazer. His own subsequent evolution to a preaching of universal destruction and an ardent defence of anarchism and nihilism based on philosophic materialism is not yet fully understood, but we find in Bakunin and Bakuninism many 'seeds' of what later found such forceful development in the philosophy of Lenin and his followers. Since we are here concerned with Bakunin's *philosophic* ideas and theories, we must pass over his revolutionary activity, his wanderings, and his adventures; however, to understand what is philosophically essential in Bakunin, we must touch upon his biography.

Michael Aleksandrovich Bakunin (1814–76) was born into a highly cultured and well-to-do family, a true 'noblemen's nest'. His father was very well educated for his time, having studied at the University of Padua in Italy, and had some poetic talent. The whole family—there were eleven children—was devoted to cultural interests. The village of Premukhino, in which the Bakunins lived, was for many years a gathering place for talented young people of the time, Stankevich, Belinski, Botkin, *et al.* At the age of fourteen young Michael entered a military school in St. Petersburg, upon graduation from which, at the age of nineteen, he was commissioned an officer. To save himself from the 'boredom and apathy, of military service (his own expression), Bakunin plunged into intense intellectual activity. In these early years the basic traits of his character—a very highly developed imagination, a need for exaltation, extremism, 'obsession' with some idea, a taste for abstract thought—had already appeared in full force. Bakunin

1. Chizhevski, *Hegel in Russland*, has a long chapter on Bakunin (Pt. II, Ch. III), which is based on wide knowledge of the pertinent material. See also Masaryk, *The Spirit of Russia*, I, Ch. XIII; B. Hepner, *Bakounine et le panslavisme révolutionnaire*, Paris, 1950; E. H. Carr, *Michael Bakunin*, London, 1937.

soon gave up military service and went to Moscow without his father's knowledge, attempting to establish himself independently there. In Moscow he met Stankevich, Belinski, and Herzen; and these meetings were of decisive importance for his later life. Bakunin suffered material hardship during this period (he was twenty-two when he went to Moscow), but bore it quite easily. Even before going to Moscow, Bakunin had made the acquaintance of Stankevich, who persuaded him to study Kant—the *Critique of Pure Reason*. In Moscow Bakunin studied Fichte, becoming for a time an ardent adherent of his doctrine; with his characteristic penchant for proselytism, he infected his friends—especially Belinski—with this interest. The extraordinary influence of Fichte's style and terminology—especially of his *Anweisung zum seligen Leben*—upon Bakunin's style has been justly noted.[1] In the following year (1837) Bakunin first studied Hegel and, to some extent, Schelling. (He returned to a study of Schelling when he was in Berlin.) During these years Bakunin read a great deal in philosophy, as well as history, theology, and even mysticism—Saint-Martin and Eckartshausen, for example. He developed an urge to go abroad and, after many trying experiences, finally reached Berlin in 1840 (at the age of twenty-six)—thanks to the material assistance of Herzen. At first Bakunin studied a great deal; then he associated himself with the left-wing Hegelians, and in 1842 printed in their journal a brilliant article called 'Reaction in Germany', under the pseudonym Jules Elysard. This article, which was powerfully and brilliantly written, created a strong impression in international circles;[2] it is, in fact, very important for the understanding of the dialectic of the philosophic development of Bakunin, as well as that of many of his contemporaries. This article contained Bakunin's famous phrase: 'The joy of destruction is a creative joy.'

Polonski has rightly noted that 'a romantic craving for extraordinary accomplishments drove Bakunin to the West'.[3] Bakunin needed exaltation and the flame of passion; when he had persuaded himself that 'reaction' (see below) had triumphed in Germany, he felt himself impelled to leave that country. At this time he came upon L. Stein's *Die Socialisten in Frankreich*, a book which made a very strong impression on him and acquainted him for

1. Chizhevski, *op. cit.*, p. 191.
2. A. Ruge, the editor of the *Deutsche Jahrbücher*, later wrote that Bakunin's article was 'remarkable'.
3. V. Polonski, *Bakunin*, Moscow, 1922, I, 87.

the first time with French social tendencies.[1] He went to Switzerland, then Belgium; his *'Wanderjahre'* had begun. We shall not retrace Bakunin's stormy political activity prior to 1848, his participation in the Slav Congress in Prague (in 1848), his arrest and imprisonment, his extradition to Russia and imprisonment from 1851–54 in Petropavlovsk Fortress—where his Confession was written—and in Schlüsselburg Fortress (until 1859), from which he was exiled to Siberia. We shall not discuss Bakunin's flight to America, in 1861, or his further wanderings in Europe. During this period he moved from an exultant religiosity to atheism, from projects of Pan-Slavic Federation to anarchism. This evolution has a special importance for the understanding of the fate of philosophy in Russia; we shall discuss this matter below.

Let us turn to a study of Bakunin's philosophic ideas during the various periods of his life.

#### 4. FICHTEAN PERIOD. STUDY OF HEGEL

Bakunin was a true romanticist. Apart from this, it is impossible to understand either his very complex and somewhat confused nature, his excessively adventurous life, or his philosophic development. Throughout his life, even when he was an atheist in principle, this romanticism was religiously coloured; but there was not an ounce of ecclesiasticism in Bakunin's religiosity, even in the period of his soul's most ardent turning to God. Chizhevski is not entirely wrong in speaking of Bakunin's religiosity as a 'pseudomorphosis of Christian mysticism',[2] but neither is he entirely right. In Bakunin we have a unique, brilliant, and creative manifestation of what may be called 'secular religiosity'—a religiosity which developed outside the Church. Bakunin's mystical utterances—which would fill dozens of pages—contain much that is similar to the 'speculative mysticism' of the Middle Ages (the latter was ecclesiastical, but its theories derived chiefly from pure speculation and pure thought). In this sense, K. Aksakov's observation, in his Memoirs, that (in the 1830's) Bakunin's 'chief interest was *pure thought*' is correct. However, Bakunin's religiosity was not merely cerebral; it caught up his whole being, filling him with genuine flame and passionate feeling. But it was confined wholly to

1. See Bakunin's 'Ispoved' ['Confession'], long unknown, which was published in *Materialy dlya biografi Bakunina* [Materials for a Biography of Bakunin], Moscow, 1923, I, 105.
2. Chizhevski, *Gegel* . . . [Hegel . . .], p. 86.

a framework of religious *immanentism*—which is the secret of 'secular, extra-ecclesiastical religiosity'.

Fichte's *Anweisung* . . ., as we have already said, had a very strong influence on Bakunin. 'The goal of life', he wrote in 1836, 'is God —not the God to whom men pray in the churches . . ., but the God who *lives in mankind* and is exalted with the exaltation of man.' Bakunin often combined this motif of religious immanentism with a preaching of Christianity, suffering, and self-sacrifice—for example, in his letters to his sister Varvara.[1] However, the motifs of immanentism gradually crowded out Christian terminology. 'Mankind is God clothed in matter'; 'man's mission is to bring heaven, to bring the God Who is enclosed within himself, to earth, . . . to raise earth to heaven' (letter of 1836). 'I feel God within me; I experience paradise in my soul,' Bakunin wrote at the same time. One has only to read his correspondence of this period to realize that these words express an authentic experience—though in exultant tones.

'My friends', he wrote in a letter of 1836, 'the earth is not our fatherland; our happiness is of heaven. . . . Our religion is infinite . . ., everything is sanctified by it; everything must manifest the infinite approximation of *divine mankind* to the divine goal. . . .'

'Bakunin's preaching', [during these years] Kornilov notes, 'won him many passionate followers—and not merely in his own family.'[2]
Bakunin derived from Fichte not only a mystically interpreted immanentism but also the principles of a personalistic ethics.

'All that is great, mysterious, and sacred is contained solely in the simple and impenetrable singularity which we call the individual person. The universal, taken in abstraction, is . . . dead. Only God, manifesting himself as person in revelation, and the immortal singularity and uniqueness—illumined by the Spirit of God—of the human person, is living truth.'[3]
But Bakunin became acquainted with Hegel's works, and was gradually carried away by the power of their philosophic inspiration. For the moment, however, he enclosed his *former* views in

1. Polonski (*op. cit.*, p. 33), rightly regards Bakunin's mysticism during this period as Christian; but it was an extra-ecclesiastical Christianity.
2. A. A. Kornilov, *Molodyie gody M. Bakunina* [The Youth of M. Bakunin], Moscow, 1915, p. 230.
3. Bakunin, *Sochineniya* [Works], Moscow, 1911, III, 49. The previous quotations are taken from Kornilov, *op. cit.*

Hegelian terminology. Scholars have said that Bakunin's study of Fichte was 'inadequate',[1] and this was even more emphatically true of his study of Hegel (while Bakunin was still in Moscow). With his characteristic passion and his predilection for proselytism, Bakunin spread Hegelianism—as he then knew it—among the talented writers and journalists of his circle. In this respect his place in the history of Russian Hegelianism is a very significant one. Bakunin worked on Hegel a great deal, but he did not complete his study. Later, however, he returned to it again. In Berlin he entered fully into Hegel's system; but at the same time, as we shall see below, his Hegelianism—in the strict sense of the word—ended there.

Hegel captivated Bakunin chiefly by the rigorous unity of his system, his consistent immanentism, his profound sense of concrete existence, and his idealistic interpretation of that existence. But of even greater importance is the fact that Bakunin's 'theurgical restlessness'—a responsible attitude toward the 'mystery of the age'[2] —took definite form under Hegel's inspiration. 'My individual self,' he wrote in 1837, 'now seeks nothing for itself; its life from now on will be a life in the *absolute*. . . . My individual self . . . has found the absolute . . .; my life has become identified in a certain sense with the absolute life.' This mystical and religious illumination of Bakunin's inner world in the light of the Absolute is in essence a continuation of the mystical interpretation of Fichte. The opposition of good and evil, which is essentially connected with the ethical orientation, disappeared completely. 'There is no evil; everything is good,' Bakunin wrote in a letter. 'The life of the spirit is all that truly *is*; there is nothing outside it.' 'Life is filled with dreadful contradictions . . .; but it is beautiful, and it is filled with mystical, sacred meaning—filled with the presence of the eternal living God.'[3] At the same time he broached the question of a 'new religion', which was to be wholly immanent—'a religion of life and activity . . ., a new revelation'.[4] 'Chance is a lie, an illusion—in true and actual life there is no chance; all is *sacred necessity*.' 'Finite man is separated from God; reality and good are not identical *for him*; there is a distinction between good and evil

1. Both Kornilov and Polonski agree on this.
2. In a letter to Ruge Bakunin wrote (1843): 'You are initiated into the mystery of an eternal power which is generating a new age within its womb.' (*Op. cit.*, III, 213.) Bakunin himself was constantly impelled by his sense of the 'mystery of an eternal power'; this was basic to his theurgical orientation.
3. *Ibid.*, p. 72.
4. *Ibid.*, p. 63.

*for him* . . ., but through consciousness man returns from finitude to his infinite being.' 'Evil does not exist for a religious man; he sees in it illusion, death, limitation—vanquished by Christ's revelation. Grace . . . dispels the mist separating him from the sun.'

Revelation and rationality are in conflict in this 'new' religion; thought operates between them, 'transfiguring rationality into reason, which knows no contradictions, and for which everything is good and beautiful.' '*Everyday life* is the most dreadful illusion, shackling us with petty, yet strong and invisible, chains.' The path to true reality lies in liberation from 'everyday life'. In this early period, while he was still in Russia, Bakunin was filled with a mystical ecstasy at Russian 'reality': 'We should draw close to our splendid Russian reality and, putting aside all empty pretensions, feel at last our legitimate need to be real Russians.' Echoes of these ideas appeared later in Belinski.

Bakunin's theoretical article 'On Philosophy' (printed in the journal *Otechestvennyie zapiski* [Notes of the Fatherland]) [1] dates from this same period (1840). This article, which is purely theoretical, exhibits the same motifs that we have just noted in Bakunin's religious orientation. The truth consists in a 'reasonable unity of the universal and the particular, the infinite and the finite, the one and the many . . ., the abstractly finite and the nonabstractly infinite'. Knowledge should 'explain the mystery of realization', deduce the singular and particular from the universal —'the one universal idea'—through 'the development of ideas independently of experience'. The leaven of Hegelianism had also begun to operate with respect to problems of knowledge. It made itself felt even more strongly in Bakunin's second theoretical article,[2] in which he expounded Hegel's *Phenomenology of Spirit*. This was not an independent work; but Hegel's basic idea that singular self-consciousness is impelled by a 'universal essence' found even more striking expression in it. In Bakunin's letters these general propositions are applied to anthropology: 'Death, the complete destruction of individuality', he wrote, 'is the highest fulfilment of personality . . .; that is why death occurs in the supreme moments of life.' [3] 'Individuality must pass away and disappear in order to become personality.' 'God, Who is rooted there', operates in the

---

1. For details see Chizhevski, *Hegel in Russland*, pp. 195ff.
2. *Ibid.*, pp. 196ff.
3. Bakunin, *op. cit.*, III, 90. Here we find the motif of 'self-negation' which became basic during the following period of Bakunin's creative activity.

depths of each human being's individuality.[1] However, 'the person of God, immortality, and human dignity can only be understood *practically*, through free *activity* . . .; activity is essentially an affirmation of God within ourselves'.[2] This is a new motif (common to a number of Russian thinkers; for details see Ch. IX on Herzen) which consistently transforms man into an 'instrument' of Spirit, so that the authentic life of Spirit in the singular human being cannot be conceived apart from 'activity'—i.e. 'the realization' of the universal in concrete reality. Bakunin's idea that the 'new religion' 'should operate in the realm of life ["activity"] and not theory' dates from this same period. 'Life [i.e. "activity"] . . . is filled with mystical meaning, filled with the presence of the eternal living God.' These passages show signs of a new period in Bakunin's philosophic development. He is already beginning to move away from Hegel, and this movement is soon to end in the disintegration of his Hegelianism. This process is so characteristic of the development of secularism on Russian soil that it cannot be passed by.

## 5. THE CRISIS IN BAKUNIN'S PHILOSOPHIC SEARCHINGS

The new motifs in Bakunin's philosophic development are dialectically connected with his basic ideas in historiosophy, but they undoubtedly had their purely psychological roots as well. When he wrote, in his article 'Reaction in Germany': 'Let us have confidence in the eternal Spirit Which destroys and annihilates only because it is the unsearchable and eternally creative source of all life,'[3] he was continuing—in a one-sided way—Hegel's approach to the 'historical mystery'. But, as he himself noted very truly in his Confession: 'In my nature there was always a love of the fantastic, of unusual and unheard-of adventures, undertakings which opened up boundless horizons.'[4] 'My political fanaticism', he wrote in the same place, 'lived more in my imagination than in my heart';[5] and he spoke of himself as a 'Don Quixote'.[6] As a matter of fact, Bakunin's personal traits—a need for exaltation and an excessive development of the imagination—did play their part; but their importance was instrumental. The 'essential thing', i.e. the genuine and profound upheaval which took place in Bakunin, was bound up—apart from the dialectic of his ideas and his personal qualities —with the internal movement of the secular spirit toward

1. *Ibid.*, p. 81.  2. *Ibid.*, p. 112.  3. *Ibid.*, p. 148.
4. 'Confession', *Materialy* . . . [Materials . . .], I, 175.
5. *Ibid.*, p. 138.  6. *Ibid.*, p. 132.

*utopianism.* We have already encountered utopianism repeatedly on Russian soil—even in the eighteenth century—and there it was obviously a surrogate for the religious conception of history. But, prior to Bakunin, Russian utopianism was purely theoretical. In a considerable number of Russian thinkers the utopian spirit remains purely theoretical—'armchair', so to speak, and 'literary'— to the present day. In Bakunin utopianism exhibited features of revolutionary dynamism for the first time. Certain of the Decembrists, to be sure, expressed a kind of revolutionary utopianism; but it was not manifested in genuine form until Bakunin. And since his day Russian thinkers have not abandoned this theme; it has flared up from time to time to burst into frightful flame. This revolutionary utopianism was bound up with the dialectic of Bakunin's ideas, and for this reason it enters into the history of Russian philosophy.[1] Let us therefore turn to a rapid survey of the evolution of his historiosophical thought.

This is not a matter of purely philosophic evolution, but of the development of historiosophical views. Chizhevski has justly noted that 'the Hegelian path to absolute truth was for Bakunin the path to God—his *own* God'.[2] This is true: the basic direction of Bakunin's thought remained religious not only in phraseology but in essence—within the framework of religious immanentism. As early as 1841 Bakunin wrote: 'Life is a beatitude, but one in which tempests rage and black clouds threaten, in order to combine in a higher harmony.' He now began to formulate a mysticism of *negation and conflict.* Not only did he accept Hegel's thesis concerning the dialectical value and inner inevitability of negation, but he began to give *priority* to negation as the sole bearer of the Spirit's creative principle. He saw *wholeness* in contradiction, i.e. in the negation of the positive—for negation 'includes' the positive value which it negates. 'The energy of the all-embracing essence [contradiction] springs from the incessant self-immolation of the positive in the pure flame of the negative.' This singular enthusiasm for negation was combined with the idea of the importance of 'activity' as a movement of the idea into 'reality'. 'O, Lord,' Bakunin wrote, in 1841, 'spare us from all miserable love of the world.' He hungered for 'real activity' which is 'possible only where there is real con-

1. Chizhevski (*Gegel . . .* [Hegel . . .], p. 112) considers that 'the antiphilosophical nihilism of Bakunin's late phase is irrelevant to the history of philosophy'; but Russian revolutionism had, and has, its own dialectic which has often burst with violent force into the development of Russian thought.

2. *Ibid.,* p. 101.

tradiction'. 'Away with these logical and theoretical daydreams of finite and infinite', he wrote later (1842); 'such things can only be grasped by *vital activity*.' These words are especially characteristic of Bakunin, who had a strong penchant for day-dreaming and exaggeration. He conceived his 'philosophy of activity' as a way of getting at genuine reality. And he combined it with a faith in his own *providential mission*. It is not surprising that he began to criticize 'pure' philosophy: 'Philosophy is merely theoretical; it develops solely within the framework of cognition.'[1] This comprises its limitation.

'Modern philosophy', Bakunin wrote in 1843, 'has perceived the unity of theory and practice; but there it has reached its limit, for beyond this limit lies a *this-worldly* realization—which flows from the divine nature, the primordial equality, and the communion of free men—of that which comprises the divine nature of Christianity.'

These last words exhibit religious immanentism in the form of utopianism with a wonderful transparency.

In his novel *Rudin* Turgenev—who undoubtedly portrayed Bakunin in the person of Rudin—very aptly characterized the latter's eloquence as 'impatient improvisation'. Bakunin's truly 'impatient inspiration' impelled him to the most unexpected steps. He saw the beginning of a new era, divining symptoms of its approach in the events of his time. 'The whole universe', he wrote in 1843, 'is suffering the birth pangs of a new and beautiful world. The great mysteries of humanity which were revealed to us and preserved for us in Christianity, despite all its [i.e. Christianity's] mistakes . . ., will now be a real truth.'[2] The words which we have already quoted (from a letter to Ruge) concerning the 'mystery of an eternal power which is generating a new age within its womb', also date from this same period.

Bakunin resolved not to return to Russia. 'I have been spoiled for her', he wrote, 'but here [in Western Europe] I can still act.'[3] He devoted his energies henceforth to advancing the 'birth of the new age'. We need not delve into his '*Wanderjahre*', but we must consider the result of his immersion in revolutionary activity. He devoted himself to it with such passion and such an indomitable nature that Caussidière, the Prefect of Paris during the Revolution of 1848, had reason to say of him: 'On the first day of a revolution

1. Bakunin, *Sochineniya*, III, 227.
2. *Ibid.*, p. 187.      3. *Ibid.*, p. 120.

he is a treasure; on the second he ought to be shot.'[1] Let us mention Bakunin's association (in 1847) with Proudhon, to whom he explained the subtleties of the Hegelian dialectic.[2]

In his article 'Reaction in Germany', which was a turning point in his philosophic development,[3] Bakunin extolled 'negation' and 'annihilation'. 'The eternal opposition of bondage and freedom', he asserted, '. . . has now reached its *ultimate* and supreme height; we are *on the eve* of a new era.'

'That old mole, Spirit, has completed its underground work and will soon appear as the judge of reality. Let us have confidence in the eternal Spirit which destroys only because it is the inexhaustible and eternally creative source of all life. The joy of *destruction* is at the same time a *creative* joy.'

These words, with which Bakunin concludes his article, clearly express the new mode of revolutionary utopianism. In them the preaching of a 'philosophy of negation' reaches its limit. Let us note in passing a motif from this same article which reappeared somewhat later with extreme force in Herzen, and a few decades later in K. Leontyev. Prophesying that the new era (of democracy)[4] would soon begin, Bakunin says:

'The triumph of democracy will not be merely a *quantitative* change—such a broadening would lead only to a *general vulgarization*—but a qualitative reform as well, a new, living, and genuine revelation, a new heaven and a new earth, a young and beautiful world, in which all contemporary dissonances will be resolved in a harmonious unity.'[5]

The fear of a 'general vulgarization', which found such brilliant expression in Herzen and Leontyev, and in Gogol earlier, exhibits

1. *Pisma Bakunina k Gertsenu i Ogaryovu* [Bakunin's Letters to Herzen and Ogaryov], ed. Dragomanov, St. Petersburg, 1896, p. 48. [French translation: *Correspondence de Michel Bakounine*, Paris, 1896.]

2. Herzen in *My Past and Thoughts* recounts an interesting story (told by Karl Vogt) that one evening, having grown tired of listening to everlasting discussions of the *Phenomenology*, Vogt left Bakunin and Proudhon, and the following morning when he called at Bakunin's he found the two men sitting beside the burnt-out fireplace: they were finishing their discussion of Hegel.

3. But not, of course, its 'culmination', as Chizhevski thinks (*Hegel in Russland*, p. 204).

4. 'Democracy marks a *complete turning point* in the world's whole way of life, and foretells a new life *never before known* in history. . . . *Democracy is a religion.*' (Bakunin, *Sochineniya*, III, 129.)

5. *Ibid.*, p. 137.

an *aesthetic* motif which in general was comparatively rare in Bakunin. During this period he was also an ardent defender of personalism against collectivism.[1]

The utopian orientation is essentially religious; in Bakunin, because of his typical religious phraseology, this is especially clear.

'We are on the eve of a *world-wide* historical turning point . . . which will not be *political*, but a matter of *principle* and *religion*. . . . Nothing less than a new religion is involved, the religion of democracy . . ., for God is present not in the individual but only in communion.'[2]

'You are mistaken', he wrote in 1849, 'if you think that I do not believe in God; but I have wholly given up comprehending Him through science and theory. . . . I seek God in men, in human freedom, and now I seek God in revolution.' This singular 'search for God in revolution' is not empty rhetoric; revolution—the awakening of hidden creative energies—is for Bakunin a revelation of Spirit. 'Away with all religious and philosophic theories,' he wrote in 1845, 'the truth is not theory but activity—life itself . . .; to know the truth is not simply to think, but to live—and life is more than thinking: life is a miraculous embodiment of truth.' When we come to consider N. F. Fyodorov's 'philosophy of the common task' (Ch. XX), we shall encounter these same motifs of singular pragmatic epistemology. Bakunin was gradually repudiating all 'theory' in his own life. Using very sharp words, in a late work called *State and Anarchy*, 1873, Bakunin said of Hegel and his followers that their 'world hung between heaven and earth, and the very life of its reflective inhabitants was transformed into a continuous file of somnambulant ideas'. Bakunin's shift toward ontologism in theory of knowledge—a position which we have already seen in Khomyakov, Kireyevski, and Samarin—was engulfed by his sudden shift to materialism and atheism.[3] His revolutionary activity had made him very hostile to the Church, and his extra-ecclesiastical religiosity passed violently into atheism.

1. 'Communism is not a real, living union of free men, but an intolerable coercion, a *herd of animals pressed together by violence*.' (*Ibid.*, p. 223).
2. *Ibid.*, p. 230.
3. Turgenev wrote Herzen in 1869: 'In 1862, when I saw him for the last time, he believed in a personal God . . . and condemned you for unbelief'. (*Pisma Bakunina* . . . [Bakunin's Letters . . .], p. 95.) But in 1864 Bakunin made atheism basic to the programme of the 'Union of Social Democracy'.

Masaryk speaks quite aptly of Bakunin's argument in defence
of atheism as an 'ontological proof of atheism'.[1] 'If God
exists,' Bakunin asserted, 'man has no freedom; he is a slave. But
man can and must be free, therefore God does not exist.' He now
felt 'sacred necessity', which in his Hegelian period had not interfered with individual freedom, as a denial of freedom. He did not
seek a foundation in transcendentalism—which he sharply
ridiculed, asserting that its world 'hangs between heaven and
earth'—but in materialism and positivism. In one of his late
articles, 'Anti-Theologism', Bakunin wrote: 'The existence of God
is logically bound up with the self-abdication of human reason; it
is the negation of human reason.' [2] He now regarded the fundamental nature of the world as 'an eternal and universal modifi-
ability . . ., which is a pure negation of Providence'. *Nature*
mysticism replaced religious mysticism—'universal causality . . . is
eternally creative and created. . . .' [3] Defending anarchism and
'universal destruction', Bakunin also sketched the foundation of a
'new ethics'. Since materialistic determinism entails a denial of
freedom of the will, the usual concept of responsibility—which
gives society the right to punish—also drops out. The ethics which
Bakunin worked out (if it may be called 'ethics') is, as Masaryk
justly notes, a monstrous combination of sophistry and Jesuitism
which is Machiavellian in principle.[4]

## 6. GENERAL APPRAISAL

With this we conclude our exposition of Bakunin's theoretical
views. The various stages of his intellectual evolution are not
exclusive or characteristic only of Bakunin; on the contrary, his
evolution is very significant as an anticipation of certain dialectical
'deviations' in Russian thought. It would be wrong to relate this
evolution completely to the spirit of secularism on Russian soil.
Nevertheless, the secular tendency was its foundation and its point
of departure. There was an unquestionable religious need in Bakunin, which was the basis of *all* of his spiritual searchings; it has often
been said of his revolutionary activity that it was permeated with
a unique (Slavophile) Messianism.[5] He remained a romanticist
throughout his life, even in the late period when he inclined toward
a narrow programme of 'enlightenment'; but his romanticism

1. Masaryk, *op. cit.*, I, 447.          2. Bakunin, *Sochineniya*, III.
3. *Ibid.*, p. 176.                       4. Masaryk, *op. cit.*, I, 453.
              5. *Ibid.*, pp. 458f.

was rooted in religiosity, a need to live in the 'infinite'[1] and Absolute. However, Bakunin, like other secular thinkers, conceived and experienced the Absolute as immanent and extra-ecclesiastical. In Russian radicalism, as we shall see repeatedly, a passionate religious need, which easily became fanatical and sectarian, often turned into utopianism—sometimes of the 'armchair', sometimes the revolutionary, variety—in the absence of ecclesiastical sustenance. Hegelianism was the defining element in Bakunin's turn to revolutionism; by sharpening Hegel's doctrine and interpreting it one-sidedly, he came to see creative force only in negation. 'The spirit of the modern period', he once wrote, 'speaks and acts only in the whirlwind.' In anticipation of the new—*wholly* new—era, Bakunin interred not only the state, but also 'bourgeois' science. 'Science must perish along with the world that it reflects.' [2] The 'search for God in revolution' is not an empty phrase. This revolutionary mysticism is dialectically connected with historiosophical and religious immanentism. A philosophy of 'activity' and a singular 'pragmatic' epistemology led Bakunin from his study desk into life, from theory to practice. But there it unexpectedly subordinated the individual to the objective flux of history, surrendering to the bondage of determinism. In general this combination of utopianism and determinism is very characteristic of nineteenth-century intellectual tendencies not only in Russia, but in Western Europe.[3]

Let us turn from Bakunin to V. G. Belinski, who was his close friend during the period of the Hegelian circles.

### 7. BELINSKI. THE DISPUTE CONCERNING HIS WORK

A heated dispute, which has not yet subsided, has long raged in Russian historical literature around the name of V. G. Belinski—primarily on the question of *evaluating* his importance in the history of Russian thought. Chizhevski states, in his large work, Hegel in Russia, that Belinski's reputation was wholly 'undeserved'.[4] It cannot, of course, be denied that Belinski was primarily a *writer on*

1. Bakunin later made fun of the period when 'it was thought that the eternally-sought-for absolute had been found, and that one could buy it wholesale and retail in Berlin'; but he himself was interested only in the 'absolute' to the end of his life.

2. 'Proclamation to the Youth' (*Rechi Bakunina* [Bakunin's Speeches], ed. Balashev, p. 235).

3. See Chapter XIII, which is devoted to Bakunin, in Masaryk, *op. cit.*, I.

4. *Gegel v Rossi*, p. 113.

*social and political themes* even more than a literary critic; but his writings on social and political themes were both grounded in and permeated by philosophic ideas. In studying Belinski one must study his *letters* primarily, for in them he expressed his thoughts and searchings freely. He is not wholly before us in his articles, which were always restricted by the limits and tasks of journalism, as well as by the conditions of censorship in his time. Any attempt to study Bakunin, Chaadayev, or any of the Slavophiles apart from their correspondence reveals a bare and often obscure spiritual world. On the other hand, historians of Russian thought should not forget that the philosophers who wrote on social and political themes included not only such major thinkers as Herzen and Berdyaev, but also thinkers of lesser calibre, such as Chernyshevski, Mikhailovski, and Merezhkovski. Vladimir Solovyov too, to some extent, and later Peter Struve and Fr. Sergius Bulgakov among many others, devoted a considerable portion of their creative energies to philosophic writing on social and political themes. Bakunin's expression of philosophy in 'action'—living historical activity—gradually drew him away from philosophy; and we observe in other thinkers a similar encroachment of 'concrete' life upon 'pure' philosophic interests. In the case of such Western writers as Nietzsche, Guyau, Scheler, and many others, it is not only difficult but incorrect to separate 'purely' philosophic theories from writing on social and political themes. This is a special *kind of philosophizing*—undoubtedly 'bound' and unfree as a result of the 'pressure' of problems of concrete life; nevertheless, it is a kind of philosophizing. This 'irregularity' is encountered very frequently among Russian thinkers; only very rarely is a Russian thinker completely free of it. This does not mean that philosophy is a 'handmaiden'; still, it is not a completely free 'mistress'. And, in so far as philosophic activity generally—especially in nineteenth- and twentieth-century Russia—has been connected with an open or concealed *struggle* against the *Church*, or else with an attempt to base itself on the Church, we do not find full and genuine autonomy of thought even in Europe. For Europe, too, was unable to turn its back upon the problems raised by Christianity. I do not wish to offer an apology for philosophic writing on social and political themes; I mean only to emphasize that, in so far as this writing is actually connected with and sustained by philosophic thought, it has a place in a history of philosophy. The history of Russian philosophy, in any case—a philosophy which was constantly occupied with the theme of the Church and its proclamation of freedom, and the theme of the Kingdom of God, although this was discussed within the framework of religious immanentism—exhibits in almost every thinker a transition from 'pure' thought to concrete problems. Let us stress one more point: 'theurgical restlessness'—the problem of direct influence on life and on the course of events, the problem of responsibility for history—plays an enormous role in Russian philosophic writing on social and political themes (in such writers as Belinski, Herzen, Chernyshevski, Mikhailovski, Berdyaev). This element, as we have seen, formed an essential ingredient of the ecclesiastical world-view of the sixteenth and seventeenth centuries. With the decline of this world-view and the purging of the ecclesiastical consciousness of false theocratic doctrines, the theurgical motif did not vanish from ecclesiastical thought, but was dissolved in the general idea of the Church. It emerged in pure form in the nineteenth century—having appeared only rarely and partially in the eighteenth—in the movement of Russian *secular* thought. In Belinski and Herzen this theurgical motif forms, as it were, the central nerve of their philosophic writing on social and political themes. We have considered it in some detail in our study of Belinski, for in him the theurgical motif found its way into the movement of Russian secular thought —and into Russian social and political radicalism—with full definiteness for the first time.

If we were to compare Belinski to one of the Russian thinkers with whom we are already familiar, our first choice would be *Chaadayev*—because of the intensity and passion of their search for total and unconditional truth and justice, 'the one thing that is needful'. In Belinski, as in Chaadayev, the search for the Kingdom of God and its truth and justice is a central theme. Both of them (and Herzen must be added to their number) were major representatives of Russian 'Westernism'—builders of culture along the paths laid out by the West. However, all of them were united by a passionate, captious, and severe, but also ardent love of Russia.

## 8. BIOGRAPHY

Vissarion Grigoryevich Belinski (1811–48) lived only a short lifetime.[1] His grandfather was a priest, his father a ship's doctor.

1. Concerning Belinski see P. N. Milyukov, *Le Mouvement intellectuel russe*, Paris, 1918, pp. 131–86; the memoirs of I. S. Turgenev; F. M. Dostoyevsky, *The Diary of a Writer* [trans. by B. Brasol], New York, 1949, Vol. I; Chizhevski, *Hegel in Russland*, Pt. II, Ch. IV; Setschkarew, *op. cit.*, pp. 85–92.

Belinski grew up in a difficult family environment and in conditions of extreme poverty, in a remote province. His chief interest manifested itself while he was still a lad—an interest in literature, which attracted him not so much by its art as by its constant preoccupation with man's inner world and his fate. Belinski was of an *unscientific* though *philosophic* turn of mind [1]—but he considered formal philosophy completely alien and unnecessary. He was interested in the truth about *man*, the study of man's soul in the light of a general world-view; and for such concrete philosophizing literature was an especially valuable aid.

After graduating from the Gymnasium, Belinski went to the University in Moscow. While still a student he wrote a play—in the romantic style—devoted to a critique of serfdom. It showed a very strong influence of Schiller, who in general left a deep mark on Belinski's searchings, and on the aesthetic humanism which, except for a brief period, he constantly served. During this period Belinski joined Stankevich's Circle; and we have already discussed Stankevich's enthusiasm for Schiller. Belinski suffered a severe blow, however; he was expelled from the University, because his play was too radical. He took up journalistic work, and in 1834 his first article, 'Literary Reveries', was published in *Molva* [The Report].[2] Written brilliantly and from a wide knowledge of Russian literature, it permanently defined the literary form of Belinski's work; all of his articles—with very rare exceptions—were devoted to literature, but they illuminated literary themes by means of general philosophic ideas. 'Literary Reveries' was based on Schelling's poetic nature-philosophy; however, it was not a popularization of Schelling's ideas, which were not expounded with sufficient accuracy in it, but an original *reworking* of Schellingian nature-philosophy, placing chief emphasis on man's inner world, the 'moral life of the eternal idea' (in man), and the conflict of good and evil which fills the life of the individual and mankind as a whole. The whole programme and passion of aesthetic humanism, an inspired summons to goodness and creativity, make up the general portion of this article; and even today it captivates one with its direct and ardent lyricism.

In 1836 Belinski came under Bakunin's influence, and became

1. It is interesting that Prince Odoyevski, for example, recognized in Belinski 'a man with an immense philosophic intellect'. (Setschkarew, *op. cit.*, pp. 86f.)

2. Concerning the strong impression created by this article, see I. I. Panayev, *Vospominaniya* [Memoirs]. [This article is translated in Belinski's *Selected Philosophical Works*, Moscow, 1948, pp. 3–97. *Trans.*]

absorbed in Fichte's ethical idealism. Bakunin explained Fichte to him, and later he and others did the same with Hegel: Belinski himself did not know German. He gave up Schellingism and devoted himself wholly to problems of personalism—accepting Bakunin's version of Fichteanism. At the same time he, like Bakunin, tore himself away from empirical reality into a world of 'ideas'. In 1837 Bakunin, with his characteristic predilection for proselytism, initiated Belinski into the mysteries of Hegel's system. During this same period—or rather, toward the end of 1839—Belinski moved to St. Petersburg, and this break with the Stankevich Circle made him more independent. While he was still in Moscow he had lapsed into an excessive historiosophical mysticism based on Hegel's well-known but constantly misinterpreted formula: 'all that is real is reasonable'. However, Belinski's turning to real historical life liberated him from the dreamy and abstract idealism of his former period; it was the beginning of a shift toward philosophic and practical *realism*, a sober recognition of the empirical sphere in individual and historical life. For Hegelianism, to be sure, the significance of the empirical sphere in history results from its embodiment and revelation of the dialectical movement of Absolute Spirit. But the motif of realism, a vital, intuitive gravitation toward *concrete* being—as a living union of the empirical and absolute components—is basic and decisive for Hegel. Belinski's enthusiasm for Hegel sobered him down and brought him back to historical reality. With his characteristic predilection for extreme and one-sided interpretations, Belinski gave a singular romantic twist to Hegel's realism. We shall consider this in detail below. But he soon came to realize that Hegel's system did not leave room for a true valuation of the *individual person*; Hegel's 'impersonalism'—although this characterization oversimplifies the Hegelian doctrine of the individual—repelled Belinski. He categorically rejected the formula that 'all that is real is reasonable'. Problems of personalism moved into the foreground for him; and this concern provides the key to his later enthusiasm for socialism.

In St. Petersburg Belinski married; but long years of semi-starvation and poverty had left a severe mark on his health. He contracted tuberculosis and was sent abroad to be treated, but the treatment was to no avail. Belinski returned home, where he soon died (in 1848) in the thirty-eighth year of his life.

## 9. THE HEGELIAN PERIOD

Belinski was not, of course, a philosopher in the full and strict sense of the word; but he cannot be left out of a study of Russian philosophy. This is not simply because his works found support in the philosophic tendencies of his time, but because he has his own place—and a significant one—in the dialectic of Russian philosophic searchings. These searchings, as we have frequently emphasized, must be interpreted as a manifestation of the spirit of secularism, or as a struggle against it. Religious themes—in the plenitude of the ideas brought into the world by Christianity—continued to define the basic searchings of Russian thought; but, in so far as they had a philosophic rather than a purely religious meaning, these searchings formed a system of ideology. In Russia the pulse of philosophic searchings throbbed (and still throbs today) with these themes. This does not in the least exclude or annul other philosophic problems, which emerged indirectly but were nevertheless bound up with these themes, because of the systematic quality of the ideas themselves.

Belinski—like Stankevich and Bakunin, as well as Herzen, whom we shall consider in the following chapter—was deeply and genuinely religious, but his religious needs did not draw their sustenance from the Church. Like many other representatives of the Russian intelligentsia, who still lived on the legacy of 'inner Christianity', he insisted on separating Christianity and the Church. Secularism was directed chiefly against the Church (as is the case everywhere); it not only did not exclude 'inner' religiosity but drew its sustenance precisely from the latter. However, as a result of this separation from the Church, Russian secularism—and not only Russian—treated the theme of the 'Kingdom of God' wholly within the framework of immanentism, transforming it into a 'utopia of the earthly paradise' realized through historical progress. Religiously, this theory was impelled by 'theurgical restlessness'.

The first period of Belinski's creative activity (1834–6) exhibits a combination of Schillerian aesthetic morality with Schellingian nature-philosophy and philosophy of art.

'God's whole boundless and beautiful world', so Belinski begins his first article ('Literary Reveries'), 'is the breath of one eternal idea, the thought of one eternal God. . . . This idea is endless, it lives perpetually. . . . All worlds are bound together by an electric chain of love. . . . The whole chain of consciousness is an ascending ladder of knowledge of the immortal and eternal Spirit Which lives in nature . . .; man is nature's organ of consciousness. . . .'

These lines exhibit Schelling's nature-philosophy in its *anthropocentric* aspect; the poetic colouring of the whole conception clearly reflects a romantic temper of mind. 'The young philosophers', Vengerov notes, 'took in Schelling's pantheism not with their minds but with their hearts.' [1] This exalted attitude toward man as the highest stage in nature was characteristic of the ideology of aesthetic humanism which already dominated Russian secularism. Belinski himself worked a good deal on its further elaboration, and in it we find the first rudiments of philosophic personalism.

Some scholars see the influence of Nadezhdin, a professor at Moscow University, whose influence on Stankevich we have already discussed, in Belinski's famous 'Literary Reveries'. This question has now been adequately explored, and Nadezhdin's influence must be acknowledged.[2] Belinski gave himself up with ardour to his poetic perception of the world and his faith in man— chiefly, of course, under Stankevich's influence; [3] but he also had his own source of moral inspiration. This was partly his profound —though non-ecclesiastical—religiosity and partly his own moral turn of mind.[4] The aesthetic element, however, dominated all others; and it was for this reason that Schiller's influence on Belinski was so strong in his early period. Later Belinski referred to this as a period of 'abstract heroism'. Pypin [5] is partly right in repudiating the charge that 'aesthetic quietism' dominated the Stankevich Circle during this period; nevertheless, 'abstract heroism' did dissipate their spiritual and intellectual energies, cutting them off from empirical life.

Belinski met Bakunin in 1836 and was infected by his enthusiasm for Fichte's idealism, which further intensified his 'abstract heroism'. 'Ideal life', he wrote at this time, 'is real, positive, concrete

1. Note to Vengerov's edition of Belinski's *Sobraniye sockineniya* [Collected Works], St. Petersburg, 1900–7, II, 417.

2. See especially Milyukov, *op. cit.*

3. 'I looked at Stankevich', Belinski once wrote, 'and fell in love with God.' (*Pisma* [Letters], ed. Lyatski, St. Petersburg, 1914, II, 85.)

4. Annenkov wrote aptly of Belinski: 'The moral force which underlay all of Belinski's thinking and writing was what gathered ardent friends and admirers about him. . . . An outline of Belinski's lifelong moral homily would comprise his true biography.' (*Vospominaniya* [Memoirs], 1881, p. 54.)

5. A. N. Pypin, *Belinski. Yevo zhizn i perepiska* [Belinski. His Life and Correspondence], 2nd ed., St. Petersburg, 1908, I, 112.

life; and what is called real life is a negation, a phantom—nothing-ness, emptiness.' This loss of contact with empirical life reinforced Belinski's religiosity, arousing outbursts of moral passion. He once wrote his close friend, V. P. Botkin: 'Spirit of eternal truth, I pray to thee and bow before thee. With trembling, with tears in my eyes, I commit my fate into thy hands: order it according to thy reasonable will.' Somewhat later he wrote, in an article: 'There is a book in which everything is said, everything resolved—an im-mortal and holy book, a book of eternal truth and eternal life: the New Testament.' One has only to read Belinski's letters, of this and the following period, to feel the full seriousness and sincerity of these words. In any event, 'abstract heroism', which in his Fichtean period took on a more intense and systematic form, left a very deep mark on his subsequent searchings.

In 1837 Bakunin introduced Belinski to Hegel, and this opened up a new chapter in Belinski's spiritual life. Plekhanov justly notes that, when, in 1841, Belinski freed himself from his indiscriminate enthusiasm for Hegel, he still remained faithful to Hegel in many respects.[1] In fact, Hegel exercised a very *lasting* influence on Belinski's thought: Belinski himself often told with great feeling how much his acquaintance with Hegel's system had meant to him. Belinski is often reproached for not having read Hegel's own works, for basing his knowledge on second-hand accounts and, occasionally, on specially-prepared excerpts.[2] But Hegel's system took *possession* of Belinski; it tore him sharply and irrevocably away from abstract idealism and impelled him toward philosophic realism.[3] This is the chief importance of Belinski's Hegelianism. The break with 'abstract' idealism was not easy; Belinski admitted in a letter to Bakunin that he 'wept bitterly' when he had renounced his earlier theoretical views. He considered writing a work entitled 'Correspondence Between Two Friends' (the plan was not carried out, however)—'the correspondence of a "beautiful

1. Plekhanov, *Belinski. Sbornik statei* [Belinski. A Collection of Articles], Moscow, 1923, p. 93. See the very interesting article in this collection entitled 'Belinski i "razumnaya deistvitelnost" ' ['Belinski and "Reasonable Reality" '], in which Plekhanov develops the idea that what is usually considered Belinski's mistake (in interpreting the doctrine of 'reasonable reality') in fact corresponded to the interpretation of Hegel which was prevalent in Germany at the time.
2. See, for example, the somewhat crudely ironical remarks in Chizhevski *op. cit.*, pp. 117ff.
3. I. I. Ivanov (*Istoriya russkoi kritiki* [A History of Russian Criticism], St. Petersburg, 1900, III, 149) speaks incorrectly of 'positivism' in Belinski's interpretation of Hegel; but it is clear that he means *realism*.

soul" [*Schöne Seele*] and a spirit', in which Belinski would reproach 'sentimental idealism' ('abstract heroism') for its insensitivity to the element of conflict and suffering in historical reality. He was attracted and excited by genuine, not 'ideal' reality: 'I gaze upon reality', he wrote, in 1837, 'which I formerly viewed with such contempt, and I tremble with mysterious ecstasy when I realize its reasonablness.'[1] 'You have shown me', he later wrote Bakunin, 'that thought is something whole, something single . . ., that everything emerges in it from a single common womb, which is God revealing Himself in creation.'[2] Belinski's religious interpretation of Hegel's concept of (Absolute) Spirit was an expression of new ideas in familiar religious terms: 'God's will', he wrote in a letter to Bakunin, 'is the same thing as necessity in philosophy; it is "reality".' Ivanov is partly, but only partly, right in saying that Belinski 'wished [during this period] to replace science with religion, knowledge with contemplation, investigation with revelation, human life and history with the dialectic of a self-developing idea'.[3] In fact, the 'sense of the infinite' and the pulse of the absolute idea in everyday reality became for Belinski the key to comprehension of man and the world. 'Now, when I contemplate the infinite', he wrote in a letter, 'I understand profoundly that everyone is right and no one is guilty, that there are no false or mistaken opinions, but that all things are *components of spirit*.'[4] These words convey very accurately the purely philosophic sense of the real concrescence of finite and infinite, the pervasiveness of the infinite in the finite, which is the fundamental mystery of being—a mystery bequeathed to us by ancient philosophy, which has passed, through Nicholas of Cusa, Leibniz, and Hegel, into modern philosophy. The whole of empirical existence was illuminated for Belinski in a new way. He once wrote very boldly—though, in essence, truly: 'Sense perception itself, which emerges from the fullness of life, seems mysterious to me.'[5] We shall not multiply quotations of this kind; they are innumerable in this period of Belinski's thought. Belinski, with Hegel's help, became aware of the full profundity of the mystery of reality. His 'acceptance' of the world, his 'acceptance' of history and empirical reality, and even his interpretation of Hegel's formula: 'all that is real is reasonable' (where 'reality' is identified with 'that which exists') grasps the essence of Hegelianism much more profoundly than is usually assumed. Hegel, of course—like

1. Belinski, *Pisma* [Letters], I, 228.  2. *Ibid.*, p. 176.
3. Ivanov, *op. cit.*, II, 133.  4. Belinski, *op. cit.*, I, 218.
5. *Ibid.*, p. 204.

Parmenides before him—finds what is 'illusory' and 'contingent' (though 'unreal') in existence the greatest mystery. Belinski's interpretation of Hegel was based on an inadequate knowledge of his system; but Belinski formulated Hegel's central idea of the uninvestigable concrescence of finite and infinite *correctly*. Chizhevski is right, of course, in making fun of Belinski's 'naïve transcriptions' of Hegel's dialectical method and epistemology.[1] But can these sneers at the awkwardness of Belinski's philosophic language conceal his unquestionable philosophic penetration—despite the paucity of his philosophic training?

'For me', Belinski wrote in 1839, 'there is no path to the *Jenseits*.'[2] Religious immanentism, which had taken possession of his religious consciousness earlier, now acquired new force. 'The grace of God', he wrote, 'is not given to us from *above*, but lies like a seed *within ourselves*.' This religious immanentism manifested itself primarily with respect to historical rather than contemporary existence. Belinski lapsed into 'conciliatory conservatism', as Pypin puts it; but this was because he sensed the *logos* and 'sacredness' (a favourite term of Belinski's) of past history. This appears most clearly in his doctrine of the state, which is considered sacred in its full reality; and here Belinski carried his logical development of Hegel's ideas to its extreme. He unexpectedly broached the theme, bequeathed by the sixteenth and seventeenth centuries, of the 'sacred' meaning of Tsarist power.[3] Belinski expressed his ideas very concisely, contrasting the sovereign power of the Tsars with a republican regime: 'The President of the United States is a respected, but not a sacred, person. . . .' Belinski gazed into the mystery of the historical process with fear and trembling,[4] but he posed the problem of individual and society with special urgency. The development of this problem resulted in a gradual disintegration of his Hegelian historiosophy and a transition to socialism. Belinski still asserted the primacy of *society*, but the theme of individuality was already troubling him. 'Man's *personality* is particular and contingent,' he wrote in an article, 'but his *spirit* is

1. *Hegel in Russland*, pp. 212–5.
2. Belinski, *op. cit.*, II, 5.
3. If one were to compile an anthology of quotations from Russian thinkers on the 'sacred' significance of the power of the Tsars, Belinski, because of the clarity and *profundity* of his thoughts on this problem, would occupy one of the most important places.
4. It would be very interesting to compare Belinski's various formulas with those of Chaadayev (as we have seen them), but this would carry us too far afield.

universal and necessary.' Man for him was a 'living part of a living whole', but within a very short time he wrote, in a letter: 'Human personality is a great and dreadful mystery.' [1] On this point Belinski overcame Hegel more subtly and deeply than any of his contemporaries.

## 10. THE CRITIQUE OF HEGEL. BELINSKI'S ETHICISM

At the height of his straightforward Hegelianism Belinski wrote: 'Either the world is something *fragmentary* and self-contradictory or it is a single whole.' The idea of monism is expressed with stubborn logic in these words. In one of his articles Belinski made fun of those persons who recognize contingency in being—not as an illusion but as the limit of necessity.[2] Gradually, however, he began to be sobered down by living reality, recognizing it as not only 'alogical' but also antimoral. 'The objective world', he wrote in a letter, 'is dreadful.' And, when the news of Stankevich's death reached him, he experienced the problem of individuality with great tragic force. 'The question of personal immortality', he now thought, 'is the alpha and omega of truth. . . . I shall run after Moloch, whom philosophy calls "the Universal", and I shall ask him what business it [philosophy] has with him [Stankevich].' [3] This motif gradually moved into the foreground; the question of the *metaphysical grounding* of personalism took on paramount importance. 'What is it to me', Belinski wrote somewhat later, 'that the universal should live when the individual suffers?' And in another place: 'For me human personality is now above history, society, and mankind.' 'The universal is the executioner of human individuality; it has bound the individual with dreadful chains.' 'The Saviour Himself walked upon the earth and suffered for individual man.' But this whole temper of mind received its sharpest and strongest expression in Belinski's famous letter to Botkin (March 1, 1841):

'Hegel's subject is not an end in itself, but a means for the ephemeral expression of the universal. . . . Laugh if you wish, but this is my opinion: the fate of the subject, the individual personality, is more important than the fate of the whole world . . . including Hegel's *Allgemeinheit*. I am told: develop all the riches of

1. Belinski, *op. cit.*, I, 323.
2. Apparently this is a polemic against Herzen, who at the time defended historiosophical *alogism*.
3. Belinski, *op. cit.*, II, 159.

your spirit for the free self-enjoyment of Spirit. . . . Thank you very kindly, Yegor Fyodorovich [1] [Hegel] . . ., but if I should succeed in climbing to the highest rung of this ladder of development, even there I would ask you to render me an account of all the victims of real life and history. . . . Otherwise I should hurl myself head foremost from the top rung of this ladder. I do not want happiness even as a gift if my conscience is not easy with regard to each of my brethren. . . . It is said that disharmony is the condition for harmony. Perhaps. This is very profitable and delightful for music lovers, but not for those who are condemned to express their fate in the idea of disharmony. . . .'[2]

From this first full, though overly passionate, assertion of the absolute value of the individual, a new world-view began gradually to develop in Belinski. There were still a great many echoes of *Hegelianism* in it, but its basic accent was on personalism. Themes of personalism were what inclined Belinski's thought toward *socialism*—utopian socialism, of course, for there was no other kind at the time; and even if there had been Belinski would not have accepted it. 'The utopia of the earthly paradise'—as P. I. Novgorodtsev characterizes nineteenth-century socialist theories in his book The Social Ideal [3]—absorbed Belinski, as well as Herzen, Botkin, *et al*. Belinski defended the socialist ideal in the name of the *individual* and his normal development, and the guaranteeing of the opportunity for this development to 'everyone'. Man is not *metaphysically* stable. This idea, which Belinski took from Hegel's system, constituted the first new step in his thinking. 'Are not man's birth and destruction an accident?' Belinski asked in a letter. 'Does our life not hang by a hair every hour, depending upon trifles? Dead, unconsciously reasonable nature treats the individual more shabbily than a wicked step-mother.' But if nature is merciless that is all the more reason for men to be concerned about each human individual. Annenkov justly points out that rudiments of 'Russian socialism' can be found in the Slavophiles—with their exaltation of the '*obshchina*'; [4] but socialist hopes began to seize Russian thought as early as the 1820's. The moving force of this whole movement of nineteenth-century Russian thought was the concern for 'every' individual, i.e. motifs of personalism. Belinski, too, after his break with 'conciliatory conservatism' developed a

1. This was the usual nickname for Hegel in Russian circles of the time.
2. *Ibid.*, p. 213.
3. *Ob obshchestvennom ideale*, 3rd ed., Berlin, 1921.
4. Annenkov, *op. cit.*, p. 127.

socialistic utopianism in the name of the individual's emancipation from the oppression of the contemporary social order. It is not surprising that Belinski's socialism was soon transformed into *liberalism*, with a tendency toward social reforms. Belinski and Herzen were the founders of Russian liberalism, a position which was often combined with a search for 'social justice'. In any case, the defence of the individual was the basis of Belinski's new world-view. He did not bury himself deeper in metaphysics after he had radically rejected the impersonalistic element of Hegel's meta-physics; all of his intellectual work was devoted to the sphere of ethics. This explains the softening of Belinski's social radicalism. 'I know', he wrote, toward the end of his life, 'that industry is a source of great evils, but it is also a source of great blessings. Strictly speaking, it is only the latter: the evil is in the domination of capital and its tyranny over labour.' [1] The purely ethical character of Belinski's personalism gradually degenerated into an *enlightenment humanism*; he began to extol Voltaire, turning away from Rousseau and his faith in the '*souveraineté du peuple*'. 'Where and when has a people liberated itself?' he asked: 'Everything has always been done by individuals.' 'Bakunin and the Slavophiles', Belinski confessed in a letter, 'were a great help to me in throwing off my mystical faith in the people.' Elements of enlightenment doctrine began to colour his historiosophical views very strongly. In 1845 he wrote Herzen: 'I see darkness, obscurity, chains, and the knout in the words "God" and "religion".' His famous letter to Gogol concerning the latter's Selected Passages from Letters to My Friends is the clearest expression of Belinski's enlightenment ideas. 'The Church', he wrote in this letter, 'has been and is a champion of inequality, a flatterer of authority, an enemy and persecutor of brotherhood among men.'[2] Belinski not only became an atheist himself; he even asserted that the Russian people were 'deeply atheistic'. His letter to Gogol is the real manifesto of the coming age of Russian enlightenmentism. Social and political themes wholly displaced needs of a philosophic character in Belinski, or, rather, his philosophic views now became an over-simplified materialism, like those of Bakunin during his last period.

Annenkov once wrote: 'The moral force which underlay all of Belinski's thinking and writing was what gathered ardent friends

---

1. See Sakulin, *Russkaya literatura i sotsializm* [Russian Literature and Social-ism], Moscow, 1922, Ch. III.

2. *Selected Philosophical Works*, p. 506.

about him.' Belinski, more than any other Russian philosopher, exhibited an *ethicism* of principle. The aesthetic humanism which had been elaborated by secular-minded Russian thinkers took on certain new features in his work during the last period of his activity, the period of realism. He placed the problem of the individual in the foreground, viewing the philosophic themes of his time in the light of this problem. His personalism degenerated into humanism; elements of enlightenmentism undermined even the aesthetic element, and during his last years this element was somewhat subordinated to the central ideas of humanism. But Belinski's significance in the dialectic of the development of Russian thought lies precisely in this process—the degeneration of personalism into humanism, the subservient status of art, angry attacks on the Church, a conversion to atheism—and at the same time an ardent and passionate defence of 'everyman', a flaming summons to the reform of social relationships. All of this was not incidental but a position typical of one tendency of Russian thought, for which secularism became the inspiration. Herzen's creative activity developed in a different way but in this same direction; we turn now to a study of his work.

# CHAPTER IX

## A. I. Herzen (1812–70)

### I. GENERAL REMARKS

EARLY Russian Hegelianism, as we have seen it thus far, was connected with circles under the influence of German culture; in Herzen, however, we meet another type of Russian Hegelianism, a type close to French, rather than German, culture. It is true that in his youth Herzen was very strongly influenced by Schiller, a fact which he mentions more than once in his memoirs (*My Past and Thoughts*); and German romanticism and mysticism were not alien to him. Nevertheless, the basic traits of Herzen's spiritual make-up were formed under the influence of eighteenth- and nineteenth-century French literature. His general revolutionary tendencies, his utopian religious striving to establish truth and justice *on earth*, his socialist dreams—all developed under French influence. It is thus no accident that Herzen's disillusionment with Western culture, which precipitated the crisis in his 'spiritual drama', was bound up with French impressions and related essentially to French culture. His acute aversion to bourgeois ('Philistine') psychology, a psychology which he painted with inimitable vividness in the works written during his residence abroad, was evoked chiefly by his French experiences.

Early Russian Hegelianism, as we saw in the previous chapter, neglected the general propositions of Hegel's philosophy almost completely, concentrating its attention on his philosophy of history. Nevertheless, the special attention which the Russian Hegelians devoted to the problem of the individual led them beyond the boundaries of history and induced them to raise questions of a general philosophic character. This was the case with Bakunin, and even more clearly with Belinski; it was also true of Stankevich during the last year of his life. We find essentially the same thing in Herzen. At first the philosophy of history was of primary importance for him; his critical attitude toward, and partial

271

overcoming of, Hegelianism was connected with the problem of the individual. This is very characteristic of the career of Russian philosophy, which gradually absorbed into itself specific elements from the systems of Western philosophers, rested on them, and then moved on to other problems in which all of its attention, all of its creative seeking, became concentrated. As far as Herzen is concerned, his original philosophic work and his authentic 'philosophic experience' were concentrated on ethical and social themes and on the problem of individuality. In his youth Herzen received a solid grounding in the natural sciences; he may even be regarded in a certain sense as the founder of Russian positivism, which was basically orientated toward the natural sciences, but his fundamental philosophic quest was *anthropocentric*. In this respect he is close to the great majority of Russian thinkers.

At the same time Herzen moves in the paths of Russian *secular* thought; he is one of the clearest and most passionate exponents of Russian secularism. And, as a result of the courageous honesty which is evident in all of Herzen's works, the impasse of secularism is exhibited more clearly in him than in anyone else. As we shall see, this explains the stamp of tragedy which lies on all of Herzen's intellectual creations produced during the period of his residence abroad.

Herzen's brilliant literary gifts, which place him in the group of first-rate Russian writers, helped him to find his own peculiar style, his own special way of expounding and developing his thoughts. For the historian of philosophy, however, this style is a hindrance rather than a help. In fact, even in developing the most abstract propositions, Herzen constantly turns from pure analysis to an artistic mode of expression; he interrupts his reasonings with a lively dialogue—which is nearly always both striking and felicitous—transforming his exposition into an 'exchange of opinions'. Herzen's philosophic ideas are often uttered in passing, and it is necessary to collect them, to systematize them, and sometimes to formulate his general propositions *for him*. We may note in passing that Herzen exhibits with full force—as was the case to some extent with Prince Odoyevski before him—the inner unity of philosophic and artistic thinking so frequent among Russians, which we find later in Tolstoy, Dostoyevsky, and Vladimir Solovyov, not to mention *dii minores* like Rozanov, Leontyev, *et al.* The artist in Herzen continually bursts into the work of the thinker and, so to speak, turns to its own account what has been acquired in the labour of pure thought. Although Herzen's artistic talent never reached the heights attained by the creative writing of Tolstoy and Dostoyevsky, there is no doubt that he was a genuine artist. This is evidenced by his short stories, and especially by his memoirs, *My Past and Thoughts*. With Herzen, as with other thinkers of the time, much valuable material is included in his correspondence.[1]

## 2. BIOGRAPHY

Herzen's personal life was very complex, both in its external and internal aspects, and the key to his philosophic ideas lies primarily in his biography. What has been called Herzen's 'spiritual drama'[2]—and this drama is deeply involved in the dialectic of the philosophic searchings of others besides Herzen—cannot be adequately understood apart from his biography. We shall therefore turn to a parallel study of his external and internal life.

Alexander Ivanovich Herzen was the illegitimate son of a wealthy and distinguished Russian nobleman, I. Ya. Yakovlev. The father worshipped his son while the child was still small, but later grew cool towards him; the boy soon became aware of the ambiguity of his position as an 'illegitimate' son. Influenced by the French literature which he found in his father's library, Herzen began at an early age to incline toward political and social radicalism.[3] His early republicanism was combined with an acute sense of the injustice of serfdom.[4] In extremely romantic circumstances, the fifteen-year-old Herzen made friends with the talented young Ogaryov, for whom he retained the warmest affection throughout his life. In keeping with the spirit of romanticism, Herzen cherished the ideal of friendship, and remained true to

1. For Herzen's biography see R. Labry, *Alexandre Ivanovič Herzen*, Paris, 1928. For a discussion of his work see D. I. Chizhevski, *Hegel in Russland*, Reichenberg, 1934, Pt. II, Ch. VIII; B. V. Jakovenko, *Geschichte des Hegelianismus in Russland*, Prague, 1938; A. Koyré, 'Herzen', *Le Monde slave*, 1931; T. G. Masaryk, *The Spirit of Russia*, New York, 1919, Vol. I.

2. S. Bulgakov, 'Dushevnaya drama Gertsena' ['Herzen's Spiritual Drama'], in the collection *Ot marksizma k idealizmu* [From Marxism to Idealism], St. Petersburg, 1903.

3. See especially *Byloye i dumy* [My Past and Thoughts], Berlin, 1921, Vol. I. ('Political dreams occupied me in my youth day and night', he confesses—*ibid.*, Pt. I, p. 94.) 'As a fourteen-year-old boy I vowed to revenge the victims [after the execution of the leaders of the Decembrist uprising] and dedicated myself to battle with the throne and altar. . . . Thirty years later I stood under the same banner.' (*Ibid.*, p. 92.) See also the Diary entry for June 17, 1843.

4. The development of early Russian radicalism—stimulated by aversion to serfdom—is described with great vividness by Prince P. Kropotkin in his *Memoirs of a Revolutionist*, New York, 1899.

this ideal to the end of his days. At the age of eighteen he entered the Faculty of Natural Science at Moscow University; there he experienced his first philosophic passion, and the awakening of philosophic needs, under the influence of the Schellingian, Professor Pavlov, whom we have already met. Even before this, Herzen, together with Ogaryov, had been carried away by Schiller, whom he mentions with enthusiasm during every phase of his creative work. First from Schiller and later from Schelling Herzen derived an ethical idealism, a philosophic approach to the understanding of nature and man—and at the same time the fundamental features of his secular thought. Herzen was a religious child; he himself testifies to this in his memoirs. 'In my early youth', he writes, 'I was often carried away by Voltairism; I loved mockery and irony; but I do not remember that I ever took the New Testament into my hands with cool feeling.' [1] The life of the *Church* did not touch young Herzen's spirit; but his religious consciousness was not extinguished, and later, under the influence of his fiancée, N. A. Zakharina, it flowered strongly.

During his student days Herzen made the acquaintance of a number of talented students; a circle gathered around him, parallel to Stankevich's Circle, but distinguished from the latter by its social and political interests. At the same time Herzen was studying diligently at the university. Upon completing his courses he presented an essay, on the Copernican system, but was not awarded a gold medal because there was 'too much philosophy' in his work. After leaving the university, Herzen continued his scientific studies, but he was suddenly arrested. When his friend Ogaryov was arrested—because of his closeness to students who had been accused of singing a revolutionary song—some rather sharp and strong letters from Herzen were found in his possession, and Herzen was also arrested (in 1834). After being detained for a considerable period he was sentenced to exile from Moscow—first to Perm, then to Vyatka, and, after two years, to Vladimir, which was nearer to Moscow. This exile decisively strengthened Herzen's opposition to the existing régime in Russia; but these same years were also marked by the development of his romance with his future wife, N. A. Zakharina. She was a very religious person, inclined to mysticism—an extra-ecclesiastical mysticism, in the spirit of the romantic religiosity of the period. Her religious exultation awakened kindred feelings in Herzen, and something from this period remained with him throughout his life. Herzen's remarkable

1. *Byloye i dumy* [My Past and Thoughts], Vol. I, p. 83.

correspondence, during the years of his exile, has justly been called 'one of the most remarkable documents of Russian romanticism'.[1] During this period Herzen's literary talent began to develop strikingly.

Herzen was permitted to return to Moscow in 1836. When he arrived, already married, he immediately assumed an outstanding position among the most distinguished people of that 'remarkable decade', to use Annenkov's felicitous expression. At this time he began to study Hegel. Thanks to his knowledge of German and, what is more important, his excellent philosophic preparation, Herzen mastered the basic principles of Hegel's philosophy more thoroughly and profoundly than his contemporaries. From Moscow he moved to St. Petersburg, but his stay there was soon interrupted; he was accused of spreading rumours unfavourable to the government. He then moved to Novgorod. At this period he made urgent requests for permission to go abroad, and when he finally reached Western Europe he remained there for the rest of his life. Even before his departure from Russia, Herzen experienced much grief. He lost three children, and this was reflected very strongly in his general temper of mind; it also began to undermine his Hegelian 'panlogism'. Nevertheless, he went abroad with great expectations. His romantic radicalism of this period is best characterized in a phrase which he himself used later: 'At that time', he wrote, 'the word "republic" had a *moral significance* for me.' In fact, for Herzen—and he was not alone in this—the concept 'republic' was connected not only with a particular political order, but even more with the establishment of a *social* order which, if it was not ideal, at least stood on the path to the ideal. Even at this time the *priority of the social factor* was clearly evident in Herzen's radicalism. Although he was engaged in politics all his life, politics had for him an *instrumental* significance. Herzen went abroad with a profound faith in Western Europe, in its bold and sincere attempt to establish a social ideal. But when he got abroad, tormenting doubts began to creep into his mind, and these gradually grew, especially after the outbreak of the Revolution of 1848. Herzen immediately hastened to Paris from Italy, where he had been staying. Having already broken with his sentimental idealization of Western Europe,[2] he was extremely agitated by the news of the

1. G. Florovsky, 'Iskaniya molodovo Gertsena' ['The Searchings of the Young Herzen'], *Sovremennyie zapiski*, XI (1929), p. 338.
2. We find the first evidence of disillusionment with Western Europe in the *Letters from France and Italy* (1847), *Sochineniya* [Works], V. Strakhov rightly

Revolution. But, when he reached Paris and experienced the events of June, he was seized by a profound abhorrence for the European bourgeoisie, which reduced him to despair. He felt himself 'on the brink of moral ruin'.[1] This was the final blow to Herzen's romantic idealism. It should be borne in mind that in the early 1840's he had abandoned the religious world-view which, under his fiancée's influence, had flowered in him during his exile. It is true that Herzen preserved certain elements of Christian faith throughout his life, in particular a serious attitude toward the New Testament;[2] and we shall see below that the basic and decisive elements in his ultimate world-view were completely determined by Christian ideas. Nevertheless, Herzen essentially abandoned the religious world-view and accepted fully the theoretical constructions of atheistic naturalism. His ethical idealism alone proved firm and durable, but it was connected in the most intimate fashion with his essential immanentism, his complete immersion in the world of 'here and now'. Precisely for this reason, social and political radicalism became the sole expression of Herzen's ethical idealism. This ethical idealism—as we shall see in greater detail below—was left wholly without a foundation; it rested entirely on a utopian faith in progress, in the Western European struggle for freedom and social justice. This is why the collapse of Herzen's faith in Western Europe led him 'to the brink of moral ruin'.[3] To renounce all faith in an ideal, in its truth and justice, meant for Herzen to deprive individual and historical life of all meaning. By his own admission, it was his 'faith in Russia' that saved him from 'moral ruin'. Herzen's creative powers were consumed in a passionate accusation of the spiritual order, the spiritual universe, of Western Europe—and there is, together with the demands of moral idealism, an *aesthetic* motif in his often captious criticism of Western Europe. This motif—as we shall see in more detail below—was

observes that 'Herzen was reduced to complete despair even before the Revolution of 1848.' (*Borba s zapadom* [The Struggle with the West], St. Petersburg, 1882, p. 31.)

1. *Pisma iz Frantsi i Itali* [Letters from France and Italy], *Sochineniya*, V, 110. [French translation: Geneva, 1871.]

2. See the above quotation from *My Past and Thoughts*. We reproduce the complete text here: 'I do not remember that I ever took the New Testament into my hands with cool feeling—and this stayed with me throughout my life; at all ages, in various circumstances I returned to a reading of the New Testament, and each time it brought peace and mildness into my heart.' *Byloye i dumy* [My Past and Thoughts], Pt. I, p. 83.

3. *Sochineniya*, V, 110.

always operative in Herzen's mind; and in his struggle with the *Philistinism* of Western Europe, in his passionate unmasking of the moral narrowness and spiritual insignificance of this Philistinism, aesthetic revulsion played a determining role. In this respect, too, there is a deep connection between Herzen and a number of other Russian thinkers—Gogol, especially, but also Leontyev, Mikhailovski, and to some extent Dostoyevsky, as well as Berdyaev in the modern period. In present-day Europe, according to Herzen, 'everything is run by the merchants'; the substitution of commercial values for spiritual values was for him a symptom of the profoundest spiritual impoverishment. His world-view now assumed a *tragic* colouring. Nevertheless, he still needed to believe in something large and luminous; his sole point of support in the 'transvaluation of values' which resulted from his disillusionment with Western Europe was the *defence of the individual*. This appears clearly in his remarkable book From the Other Shore, which, together with the Letters from France and Italy, marked the inner crisis of Herzen's 'spiritual drama'. In Herzen, personalism and an *alogism* of principle in historiosophy combined to form a unique tragic philosophy; and here as before he remained a romanticist. The attitude of tragic submission which appeared in Herzen after the collapse of his faith in European civilization was determined on the one hand by motives of *honesty* ('I will not lie to myself from fear of the truth'), and on the other by a pessimistic view of the cosmos as a whole, in which, he perceived, chance occupies a vast and frightening place. But it is precisely this 'unreasonableness' of being which promotes man's right to independence from the world. The ideal needs of the human spirit are in irreconcilable conflict with the blindness of nature and the power of chance. This isolation of the human spirit from nature reinforced Herzen's *affection* for man, for his needs and searchings, and at the same time created a certain *melancholy* love of art and beauty. The words which Herzen once wrote about the contemporary world ('. . . The world lives somehow . . . seeking not to build, but to *forget* itself' [1]) apply primarily to himself. 'Art', he wrote in a later period, 'and the summer lightnings of personal happiness, are our only goods.' [2] This is an example of the same aesthetic humanism with which Russian thinkers so often warmed their hearts when they had broken with the Church but were unable to suppress their ideal needs.

1. *Byloye i dumy* [My Past and Thoughts], Pt. V, p. 203.
2. *Ibid.*, p. 368.

We have seen that faith in Russia saved Herzen 'from moral ruin'. Of course, the ardent love which he always bore for Russia was operative here, but his faith in Russia, like his earlier faith in Western Europe, was determined much more by his *social searchings* than by *national feeling*. Herzen rested all of his hopes for society on the Russian village commune [*obshchina*]. (In this respect Herzen, even more than the Slavophiles, was a creator of *Populism* [*Narodnichestvo*]. See below, Ch. XI.) Together with Tolstoy, Dostoyevsky, and Leontyev, Herzen repudiated the previous 'era' of history— i.e. its European period—and devoted himself to thoughts about the 'new era'. Herzen's critique of European culture gradually became less captious and was characterized chiefly by reflection on the errors and injustices of the past. His literary activity was devoted entirely to social and political writing, but it was social and political writing of a philosophic character, imbued with new general views of history and the problem of progress. During his last period Herzen ranked himself among the 'nihilists'; [1] however, he used the word in a sense that set him apart from the Bazarovs of his time. His break with the new generation darkened the last years of Herzen's life, and this break had ample grounds. The new generation—which we shall discuss in Ch. XI, dedicated to Chernyshevski—defended realism (in a rather primitive form); but Herzen, although he was a positivist and inclined toward philosophic realism, remained to the end a *romanticist*. The spiritual orientations of the two sides, for all their closeness on particular points of world-view, were profoundly different—and Herzen was not the only one to feel the resulting rupture painfully.

The entire period of Herzen's residence abroad (1847–70) was devoted to editorial and journalistic work; he published one journal of Russian free thought after another. He was close to all the outstanding political figures of the time and stood at the very centre of international revolutionary activity. He himself has given an unsurpassed account of this in the volumes of *My Past and Thoughts*. He possessed considerable means and willingly subsidized publications of a radical character. At one time he was close to Proudhon, whose works he had valued highly while he was still in Russia. However, the friendship with Proudhon was soon broken off.[2] Herzen's personal life was marked by much grief and suffering, concerning which he has written with great candour in *My Past and Thoughts*. In 1870 Herzen died.

1. *Op. cit.*, Pt. V.
2. See Labry's special study, *Herzen et Proudhon*, Paris, 1928.

## 3. FIRST PERIOD IN THE DEVELOPMENT OF HERZEN'S WORLD-VIEW (MYSTICISM, SCHELLINGISM)

Turning to an analysis of Herzen's philosophic views, we note first of all that he himself never reduced his philosophic views to a system—although there is no doubt of their internal connectedness and unity.[1] Herzen's was a highly integrated nature and he constantly strove for integration in the realm of ideas, not sparing his own most precious convictions in the process; but the fact that he turned from pure philosophy to philosophic writing on social and political themes (while he was abroad) prevented him from systematizing his philosophic theories. The historian's task is to select what is fundamental in Herzen's utterances, not pedantically following the chronology of his creative activity, but of course never going beyond the limits of what we find in Herzen himself.

Herzen's philosophic views have thus far been investigated by only two writers—Plekhanov and Shpet (to some extent also by Masaryk). But Plekhanov is essentially concerned throughout to show that Herzen 'developed from Hegelianism towards materialism',[2] and Shpet prefers not to speak of Herzen's 'philosophy' in the strict sense of the word, but only of his 'philosophic world-view'. However, this opposition of philosophy and philosophic world-view, which remains basically unsupported, is typical of Shpet rather than of Herzen, who repeatedly put forward the idea of philosophy 'as a science', i.e. in the strict and precise sense of a system of fundamental ideas.[3] The fact that during the second half of his life Herzen turned to philosophic writing on social and political themes is theoretically connected with his 'philosophy of the act'— which is the equivalent of Bakunin's turning to 'practical action', the vital putting of ideas into practice. A philosophic term which one encounters repeatedly in Herzen is interesting in this connection (he did not take to Russian philosophic terminology): 'actualization' ['*odeistvoreniye*'], and 'to actualize' ['*odeistvoryat*']—which is probably a translation of the German '*verwirklichen*'. This embodying of ideas in practice lay along the path of development of Hegelianism, as was shown clearly by the Polish Hegelian Cieszkowsky in his book

---

1. 'I have no system whatever', Herzen wrote in *S tovo berega* [From the Other Shore] (1850), 'no interest whatever, except the truth, and I express the truth as it appears to me'. *Sochineniya*, V, 462. [French translation: Geneva, 1870.]

2. G. Plekhanov, *Sochineniya* [Works], XXIII, 368.

3. See, for example, the first article in the series On Dilettantism in Science.

*Prolegomena zur Historiosophie* (1838). The movement of thought from
theory to practice, from the idea to its embodiment, was connected
in the closest fashion with 'ontologism' in theory of knowledge—
something which we have repeatedly encountered. We shall consider
this point in due course during our study of Herzen. There was
another motif which was philosophically important in Herzen's
propensity for social and political writing—the indissoluble connection of the purely theoretical and *valuational* components in
the comprehension of being. The idea of 'pure' knowledge was
alien to Herzen; he constantly introduced the valuational element
into knowledge, and in this sense he is one of the forerunners of the
'subjective method' which came to flower in the theories of N. K.
Mikhailovski and the thinkers close to him. Herzen speaks frequently of 'unbribable reason', of the necessity of taking facts as
they are; but he could never actually free himself from passionate
and often prejudiced value judgments. Is this not perhaps the
reason why his views strike Shpet as a 'philosophic world-view'
rather than a philosophy? But this, if you will, is one of the basic
features of Russian thought in general—the intertwining of the
theoretical and axiological (valuational) approaches to being.
Herzen felt the *noncoincidence* of these two 'orientations' with
excruciating painfulness, but he felt their profound inseparability
no less acutely. This is, of course, merely an expression of the fact
that throughout his life Herzen remained essentially a *religious
thinker*,[1] for the inner inseparability of the theoretical and axiological components in the comprehension of being is characteristic
of the religious approach—*and of it alone*. Hence it is necessary in
studying Herzen and in reconstructing his ideas to begin with an
analysis of his religious consciousness and religious ideas.

In a letter to his fiancée Herzen wrote: 'Before 1834 I had no
religious ideas; in that year, which marks a new epoch in my life,
the thought of God became evident; the world began to appear to
me as something incomplete and inadequate.' [2] However, we have
considerable evidence that Herzen thought religiously even before
this. In a letter to Ogaryov (June 19, 1833) Herzen, carried away
by Saint-Simon's reflections on 'the new Christianity', wrote: 'We
feel that *the world awaits a renewal,* . . . it is necessary to lay other
foundations for European society.' [3] This same letter contains
a commentary on these words: 'Take the pure foundation of

1. This aspect of Herzen's creative activity is emphasized in the above-
mentioned study by S. Bulgakov.
2. *Sochineniya*, I, 407.                    3. *Ibid.*, p. 117.

Christianity—how exquisitely beautiful and lofty it is; but observe its adherents—dark and sombre mysticism'. It is clear from these lines that Herzen mistrusted *ecclesiastical* Christianity. And, in fact, with the exception of a brief period before his marriage, he was never really close to the Church. *Christian themes aroused his enthusiasm;* they were what he lived by, essentially, as we shall have occasion to convince ourselves more than once; but 'historical' Christianity (the Church) repelled him. He loved the New Testament, but there is no doubt that even in his early youth he absorbed the spiritual legacy of the eighteenth and nineteenth centuries, with their romantic religiosity, in which New-Testament ideas were intertwined with occultism, mysticism (from Saint-Martin) and 'inner' Christianity—all of which we have seen above in the Russian freemasons and mystics of the eighteenth and early nineteenth centuries.[1] During his exile Herzen was strongly influenced by his religiously exultant fiancée, and by the distinguished Vitberg, designer of the Church of Christ the Saviour in Moscow, who had also been a member of the Labzin Circle. From Saint-Simon, Herzen took over the idea of a 'new era' ('the renewal of the world'),[2] and he took his interpretation of this 'new era' from the mystics. While in Vyatka he wrote asking his friends to send him the works of Swedenborg, Paracelsus, and Eckartshausen.[3] At this time Herzen began to defend a dualism of principle. In a letter dated April 27, 1836, he wrote: 'Just now a religious thought interests me immensely—the fall of Lucifer as a vast allegory—and I have reached some very important conclusions.' [4] A few months later (in a letter to friends, September 22, 1836) Herzen wrote vehemently:

'All theories of humanity are rubbish. *Humanity is a fallen angel* . . ., [hence] there are two opposing tendencies in us which destroy and embitter us with their conflict: egotism, . . . obscurity are the direct legacy of Lucifer; and love, light, expansiveness are the direct legacy of God.'

1. See the above-mentioned work by Viatte, *Les Sources occultes du romantisme*, Paris, 1928.
2. 'His great words', Herzen wrote of Saint-Simon, 'contained a whole world of new human relations, a world of health, spirit, beauty, a world *naturally* moral and therefore morally pure.' The revival of the idea of 'natural' morality, which was so characteristic of Rousseauism, had a profound appeal for Herzen.
3. *Sochineniya*, I, 33, 341.
4. *Ibid.*, p. 271.

Herzen thinks that 'revelation has expressed this to us',[1] whereas it is in fact a direct expression of the *mystical anthropology* which flourished in eighteenth-century Europe. Man as a 'former angel' [2] languishes on earth: 'The angel does not wish to be a man.' [3] 'The body in respect to matter, egotism in respect to spirit—these are the weapons with which Lucifer opposes the incarnate Word.' A little later Herzen writes: 'I am sorry for my fallen brother; I see upon his brow the stamp, not wholly obliterated, of Lucifer's beauty. . . . How comely was Lucifer before his fall.' [4] For Herzen the whole cosmos shines with a double light:

'Look upon these mountains, these crags and scattered stones', he wrote to his fiancée, 'this is the exhausted body of the recalcitrant son; and yet from everywhere life strives toward the Father's sight. Trees and moss—this is the effort of life which culminates in a flower. In flowers the *stamp of despondency* [!] has already been obliterated, in them is the joy of being. And between the sight of the Father and the corpse of the son are thought and feeling, clothed . . . in the flesh of the fallen angel, man. *It is given him to know the exquisite beauty of the universe*; he has the capacity to rejoice in the sky, the sea, the glance of a friend, and he must not leave the earth *until he has comprehended all that it holds of beauty.*' [5]

The words which we have italicized show clearly that this is an interpretation in the spirit of *eighteenth-century mysticism* ('the re-establishment of primordial being') and Schellingian aesthetic idealism. 'Lovingly cleansing the heart, pressing the whole universe to our breast, we fulfil man's purpose', Herzen writes in the same place. And a few lines further on he speaks of 'the gathering of the exquisitely beautiful everywhere. . . .'

In Western Christianity generally, both Protestant and Catholic, during the eighteenth and nineteenth centuries, ideas derived from occult nature-philosophy were superimposed upon fundamental Christian ideas; similarly, in Herzen's religious ideas of this period, the ambiguous tones of occultism jar the pure melody of Christianity. Shortly after his enthusiasm for Saint-Simonism and the 'rehabilitation of the flesh', he wrote to his fiancée (June 17, 1837): 'You are right—*the body is a hindrance*. Room, more room, and I will fill the whole of infinite space with love alone. Away with the body!' [6]

1. *Ibid.*, p. 325.      2. *Ibid.*, p. 357.      3. *Loc. cit.*
4. *Ibid.*, pp. 409, 484.   5. *Ibid.*, p. 479.      6. *Ibid.*, p. 432.

We shall not multiply quotations; those we have given are sufficient for an appraisal of Herzen's early religiosity. Like the French and German romanticists, Herzen dipped into the muddy currents of occultism as well as into pure Christianity. The main point is that Christianity and the way of religion were presented to Herzen not in the purity of ecclesiastical doctrine, but in the framework of mystical tendencies deriving from the eighteenth century. It is not surprising that in his first work, On Man's Place in Nature, partly under the influence of Schellingism, partly in the spirit of mysticism, he bluntly rejected materialism, which he called 'frightful' and 'pallid'.[1] Schellingism gained a permanent place in Herzen's thought, with its affirmation of the metaphysical status of beauty ('nature is full of life and exquisite beauty', we read in this same article)—and this aesthetic motif is constantly repeated in his works. In 1837 Herzen wrote to his fiancée of the 'gathering of the exquisitely beautiful from far and near',[2] and to the end of his days he remained true to this aesthetic approach to life, derived at first from Schiller and later from Schelling. But in the early period this was fused with an exultant, mystically-coloured religiosity. 'Why did I open to this page [in Eckartshausen]?' he wrote to his fiancée. 'Chance? Nonsense! *There is no such thing as chance!* That is an absurdity which was invented by disbelief.'[3] These lines, written in 1836, are the more interesting since, with the collapse of his religious world-view, chance becomes one of the basic categories of Herzen's philosophy. In the same letter Herzen echoed the mystical ideas of the eighteenth century—with a direct reference to Eckartshausen—in another utterance, later very typical of him: '*It is not thought or study that is needed*—activity, love is the main thing.' We may note that this doctrine—that cognition must infallibly issue in 'action' (already familiar to us in Bakunin's philosophy)—had its roots in eighteenth-century mysticism. 'Literary activity alone is not enough', Herzen wrote to his fiancée later, 'it lacks flesh, reality, practical action.'[4] Just as the eighteenth-century mystics passed assiduously from theoretical knowledge of the 'mysteries of nature' and of history to 'magical' exercises, to 'deeds'; so in Herzen the demand for 'action', for the 'act'—and the impossibility of stopping at mere theorizing—stemmed from this occultism, which in general is a pseudomorphosis of the religious life. We stress the relation of Herzen's theme of 'activity' to occultism because we shall

1. *Ibid.*, p. 351.  
2. *Ibid.*, p. 402.  
3. *Ibid.*, pp. 76, 80.  
4. *Ibid.*, p. 480.

encounter variants of this theme many times on this same soil, most strikingly in N. F. Fyodorov (see Ch. XX).

It is interesting to note that Herzen in this period is already troubled by the theme of the *individual and his fate*. Asserting—in conformity with mystical nature-philosophy—that 'all of nature is a *return* from the fall', he considers that the 'general law' alone is incontrovertible : the 'particularity of the law is God's secret'. In the same passage Herzen asks what meaning there can be in the existence of individuals who are unable to realize their 'potentialities', and he ends thus: 'But their existence is not *in vain*. I believe firmly in the strict consistency and preciseness of Providence.'[1]

Even before the revocation of his exile, Herzen married N. A. Zakharina. When, a short time later, he met his close friend Ogaryov, who was also married, a mystical mood seized them all. A crucifix hung in Herzen's room, and all four of them knelt before it in grateful prayer. But Herzen's religious mood soon began to abate.[2] In 1839, before the birth of his son, he could still write: 'God entrusts this tiny creature to me, and I shall direct it towards God': [3] but within a year he felt otherwise. In a letter to Ogaryov, who had consoled him (there was much grief in Herzen's family at this time—premature births, the death of a child, his wife's severe illness) with the assurance that this was only a 'particular case', which did not disturb the general harmony of being, he wrote: 'Your consolations are a manifestation of *false monkish passivity*.' [4] However, there is still evidence of a religious resolution of Herzen's oppressive reflections on the terrifying power of death: 'The spirit is vanquished too at death, the irrational elements get the best of life. Here, indeed, religion—and religion alone—can offer any consolation. *Philosophy has not yet grasped the idea of the individual.*' This is said, of course, with reference to Hegel, but inquietude at the mystery of human fate constantly enveloped Herzen. And when three of his children died, a veritable revolt seized him. In his Diary (for April 1842) there is an ironic remark about 'childishly religious people'—'I cannot even envy them although I am astonished at the great mystery of healing hopeless

---

1. *Ibid.*, p. 384.

2. P. V. Annenkov relates in this connection that the 'monotony of triumphant notes' of his wife's religious exultation began to weary Herzen. *P. V. Annenkov i yevo druzya* [P. V. Annenkov and his Friends], St. Petersburg, 1892, p. 76.

3. *Sochineniya*, II, 263.          4. *Ibid.*, p. 415.

grief by a superstitious and *illusory* conviction.' In September of the same year powerful lines appear in the Diary concerning an 'oppressive grief which grows and grows—and suddenly one is seized by a mute anguish, and all the evil and tragedy of our life becomes clear. . . . It seems one is ready to die.' This is plainly a period of extreme spiritual crisis, which was to sweep away not only Herzen's complacent Hegelian panlogism, but also his religious faith. An acute sense of the tragedy of being seized him; and it was in this period that his own philosophic position took shape. This is the key to his later world-view, to the 'philosophy of chance', which was to undermine his earlier views. But before the 'philosophy of chance' had taken complete possession of Herzen's thought, he was subjected to the deep and powerful influence of Hegel. We shall now consider this period.

#### 4. HERZEN'S HEGELIANISM

Herzen studied Hegel very thoroughly—the entries in his Diary speak eloquently on this score—but his reception of Hegel was quite original. Chizhevski admits that Herzen, 'although he started from Hegelian premises, hardly ever ended with Hegelian formulations or schemes'.[1] Plekhanov constantly reproaches Herzen for his one-sided interpretation of Hegel, although he admits that there was no 'disparaging attitude' toward Hegel in Herzen.[2] Actually, a close study of Herzen convinces one that he was not a 'Hegelian' in the strict sense of the word; he treated Hegel's system 'freely', taking from it only what he needed. For Herzen, Hegel's system filled the void which was left by the collapse of his religious world-view. Religious immanentism, toward which Herzen had an inner propensity—dating from his early 'secular religiosity'—received a new formulation in the doctrine of an Absolute Spirit which lives in and through the world. This appears very vividly, even poetically, in Herzen's first article 'On Dilettantism in Science'. 'Substance tends to manifestation, infinite to finite', Herzen writes. 'Truth lives in the eternal movement *in which all being is caught up*; . . . in this is the universal dialectical throbbing of the pulse of life.' For the present Herzen accepts complacently the conception of the individual which corresponds to the system of immanentism. Philosophy develops in man 'universal reason, freed from individuality. . . . Reason does not recognize *this*

---

1. Chizhevski, *Gegel v Rossi* [Hegel in Russia], p. 195.
2. Plekhanov, *op. cit.*, XXIII, 359, 361, 356.

individual, it recognizes only the necessity of individuality in general. . . . In science the individual is lost, but this is a process of development from the immediately-natural to the conscious, freely-rational individual.'

This passage is wholly in the spirit of Hegel, but other passages in the same article limit or substantially modify this general position. Although he praises Hegel highly,[1] Herzen is *much closer to Schelling than to Hegel* in his interpretation of nature. True, his terminology is Hegelian; for him the development of nature takes place 'only through the logical movement of the concept', which does not, of course, answer to the realism of Schelling's nature-philosophy. But this Hegelian treatment is only a *covering* beneath which beats the pulse of Schellingian vitalism. Herzen himself writes that in the doctrine of the development of nature 'Schelling anticipated Hegel, but Schelling did not satisfy scientific standards.' [2] Actually, Herzen now clothes a purely Schellingian view of nature in Hegelian terminology, connecting it with the dialectical conception of processes in nature. Hegel's influence is also evident in Herzen's insistence that 'in science nature is restored, freed from the power of chance; in science nature is clarified in its logical necessity'. This, of course, follows from the idea that development knows 'no other agency than the logical movement of the concept'. Also in the spirit of Hegel are Herzen's frequent statements, in the articles 'On Dilettantism in Science', that reason 'does not recognize *this* individual, but only the necessity of individuality in general'. However, Herzen's general characterization of nature and of man's place in nature does not go beyond the limits of Schellingian vitalism. Nature for him is a vital flux of being, inexhaustible in its energy, and *not completely investigable*; irrationalism constantly erupts in Herzen's nature-philosophy *beneath* the wrapping of Hegelian rationalism. And at the point where the pulse of the irrational beats beneath his rationalism, the idea of *chance*, which is fundamental for Herzen, begins to crystallize. 'An attentive study', we read in the first article of the series Letters on the Study of Nature, 'will reveal, without any special

1. See the Diary entry for April 14, 1844. In the entry for April 19 of the same year we read: 'Hegel has made the first attempt to understand the life of nature in its dialectical development from *self-determining substance* to individualization, . . . to subjectivity, without introducing any agency *except the logical movement of the concept.*' Plekhanov is right, of course, from his point of view, in denying Herzen's materialism. Herzen, in Plekhanov's words, 'only moved toward materialism'. *Op. cit.,* XXIII, 368.

2. Diary entry for April 19, 1844.

exertion, a certain uncomfortableness in *all* branches of natural science. . . . Every branch of natural science leads to the oppressive awareness that there is something *elusive and incomprehensible in nature.*' This thought is absolutely incompatible with rationalism in nature-philosophy. A little further on there are even clearer lines: '*Everything that exists in time* has a random, arbitrary fringe which falls outside the boundary of necessary development, and does not follow from the concept of the object.' *This* conception of nature, which made itself felt beneath the wrapping of the 'logical movement of the concept', survived the crisis provoked by Herzen's awareness of the vast importance of chance. In Herzen's works, beginning with the book From the Other Shore, the idea of chance is essential not only for history but also for *nature*, which is now accepted as a mere flux of being, not determined by any 'movement of the concept'. When Herzen writes that 'life has its embryogeny, which does not coincide with the dialectic of pure reason',[1] or when in the same book he writes that 'reason is being produced, and produced with difficulty—it is found neither *in nature nor outside of nature, but must be achieved*',[2] there is no longer any trace of the Hegelian view of nature in the irrationalism of his nature-philosophy. The doctrine of a blind play of forces in nature corresponds precisely to that sense of nature, strong in romanticism generally, which found expression in Schelling. 'Life', Herzen writes in this same book, 'is both end and means, both cause and effect. . . . It is the eternal unrest of an active and intense substance, which seeks equilibrium only to lose it again.'[3] This is clearly not *materialism*;[4] there is no hint of it here—it is a vitalistic view of nature in the spirit of Schelling, and of Bergson's *Creative Evolution*. 'The naturalists know a great deal', Herzen wrote in his Diary, 'but in all things there is something which they do not know—and this something is more important than everything that they know.'[5]

The relatively slight importance of Hegel in the development of Herzen's thought becomes even clearer if we consider the latter's anthropology. For a long time, under Hegelian influence, Herzen regarded the basic function of the individual as a serving of

---

1. *Sochineniya*, V, 401.　　　2. *Ibid.*, p. 407.　　　3. *Ibid.*, p. 456.

4. In the works written during Herzen's residence abroad, phrases occur more than once which give reason for regarding him as a materialist (he frequently came under the influence of the vulgar materialism developed by his close friend K. Vogt). But in essence, if one does not cavil with words, Herzen always thought along the lines of *vitalistic* nature-philosophy—in the spirit of Schelling. See Plekhanov's study of Herzen (*op. cit.*, XXIII).

5. *Sochineniya*, V. Diary entry for October 29, 1844.

Absolute Spirit—through knowledge, which 'raises all existence to thought', as Herzen put the Hegelian formula in his Letters on the Study of Nature. Man's place in nature was the theme of one of Herzen's student works, written when he knew only Schelling. Schelling's general conception prevails in his thought now too, but it is clothed in Hegelian terms. The following lines, from the Letters on the Study of Nature, are clearly in the spirit of Schelling: 'All of nature's efforts and strivings culminate in man; they tend toward him, they flow into him as into an ocean.' 'Man's understanding is not outside of nature, it is nature's understanding of itself.' Further on we find lines written in the spirit of Hegel's nature-philosophy: 'Thinking frees the idea which exists in time and space into an environment of consciousness more appropriate to it.' Completely under Hegel's influence, Herzen now sees the central core of being in *historical* being as such: 'History connects nature and logic'; 'neither humanity nor nature can be understood apart from historical being'. From this point of view historical being has a unique ontological priority—and historiosophy becomes the central philosophic discipline. Such it was in Herzen, but Herzen's own historiosophical thought developed not in the framework of Hegelianism, but in *opposition* to Hegelianism. This opposition, or more precisely this essential rectification of Hegelianism, is introduced by Herzen's philosophy of the *act*. The article on 'Buddhists in science' was written on this theme. Herzen writes disparagingly of these Buddhists that 'you cannot induce them to enter into the world of real life'. The theme of activity, as we have seen above, was close to Herzen in the early period of his thinking —but at that time it was connected with religious ideas, in a framework of occultism. The 'act', in this framework, was essentially equivalent to magic; and it was in this form that 'theurgical restlessness'—a motif which had already been secularized and cut off from the previous (sixteenth-century) idea of a 'sacred kingdom'— developed, raising the question of responsible participation in the historical process. In Herzen more than anyone else this became a utopia, saturated with *historiosophical magic*. We have already heard his own testimony to the effect that the word 'republic' had a 'moral' significance for him. It was, more precisely, an ideal which contained 'magical' powers. This is the root of the uncritical faith in the magic of every kind of progress, in the magic of the revolutionary 'act', which, beginning with Bakunin and Herzen (in his early period), continues to inflame Russian hearts to the present day. In general, the theme of 'activity', which is usually traced to the influence of Cieszkowsky's ideas,[1] has its own deep roots in Herzen—let us stress this once more—and is internally bound up with his faith in the 'magical' power of historical forms ('republic'). This theme is *pre-Hegelian* in Herzen, but during his Hegelian period it crystallized around itself everything that did not fit into the Hegelian scheme. We learn that 'contemporary science has other pretensions [besides abstract knowledge]—it wants to descend from its throne into life. *And the scientists will not be able to hold it back;* there is no doubt about this'.[2] Further on we read: 'Man is destined not for logic alone, but also for the world of society and history.' 'Man realizes his individuality in intelligent, morally free and passionately energetic activity.' Properly understood, these lines imply a revolt against Hegelianism; this appeared with complete clarity in the conception of man which Herzen first worked out fully in his book From the Other Shore. 'Whole worlds of poetry, lyricism, and thought *slumber* in the soul of each of us.' [3] This treasure is in 'each of us', yet it stands *outside of* and *above* nature. The fate of this treasure is a matter of chance; yet by its inner strength it raises man above both the blind flux of natural being and the blind march of history. Herzen came to the conclusion that 'man is freer than is usually thought, . . . a large share of our fate lies in our own hands'.[4] 'Man's moral independence', he wrote in the same passage, 'is just as *unalterable* a truth and reality as is his dependence on the environment. . . . *Outside* of us everything changes, everything flows; *we stand at the edge of an abyss and watch it crumble,* . . . and we will find no haven except within ourselves, in the consciousness of our *unlimited* [!] freedom, our autocratic independence. . . .' This is a unique apotheosis of the individual, a hymn to humanity for its ability to oppose itself to all of being. It is clear that the individual also stands above historical being (which is blind and without purpose); and Herzen goes so far as to state that 'the subordination of the individual to society, to nation, humanity, or idea is a continuation of the practice of human sacrifice. . . .'

Hegelianism, with its subordination of the individual to the career of Absolute Spirit, gives way to the new conception of life which Herzen developed out of the philosophy of chance. Hegelianism is strongly evident in certain of Herzen's epistemological

1. By Shpet in particular, but also by Chizhevski.
2. See the articles 'On Dilettantism in Science' and the 'Letters on the Study of Nature'.
3. *Sochineniya*, V, 444.      4. *Ibid.*, p. 472.

views (in the articles 'On Dilettantism in Science' and the 'Letters on the Study of Nature'), and Herzen's Diary contains many expressions of profound admiration for Hegel, but the fact remains that Hegelianism dropped almost completely out of his thought. On the other hand, Herzen's alogism of principle took him back to his earlier doctrines, which had been formulated in the spirit of Schelling.

### 5. THE PHILOSOPHY OF CHANCE

Herzen once wrote vehemently that 'there is no such thing as chance'. In Hegel's panlogism chance occupies a very small place; it does not enter into 'reality'. But the idea of the fatal *power* of chance appeared early in Herzen. We should recall his numerous encounters with death, the cold breath of which filled his heart with terror. 'A mystery—a menacing and frightful mystery', Herzen wrote in his Diary (October 1842) on the occasion of his friend V. Passek's death. 'How clear it becomes that the *Jenseits* is an illusion, that only in the body and with the body are we anything.' The death of his own child (in December 1842) shook Herzen anew, and he wrote in his Diary: 'How outrageous is the power of chance'. He now found *alogism* rather than reasonableness in existence: '*The absence of reason* in the direction of *individual* life is obvious to me'. However, the riddle and mystery of human fate did not yet render all existence enigmatic for Herzen. In March 1843 he wrote: 'Melancholy and oppressive. . . . Is it possible that the whole of life should consist in torment and agony? A man lays up, grain by grain, with incalculable labour, even with his blood; *chance* strikes, and with one stupid blow destroys all that he has so painfully built.' In August 1844, when his oldest son was taken suddenly ill, Herzen wrote: 'What a frightful *slough of chances* envelops man's life. I feel myself powerless to struggle with the stupid and potent force in whose power are personality and *all that is individual.*' Still later: 'The precariousness of everything that is best and most sacred in life is capable of driving one mad' (November 1844). Within a month Herzen's statements had taken on a broader character:

'Not only the goods of life, but *life itself* is precarious; the least disequilibrium in this complex chemistry, in the desperate struggle of the organism with its constituent parts, and life is snuffed out. The highest manifestation of life is fragile, for its whole material strength is exhausted in achieving this height.'

Still later (in *My Past and Thoughts*) Herzen generalized his ideas in the following form:

'The absurdity of fact offends us. . . . It is as though someone had promised that everything in the world should be exquisitely beautiful, just, and harmonious. We have marvelled enough at the great abstract wisdom [!] of nature and historical development; it is time to consider that *in nature and in history there is much that is fortuitous, stupid, botched, and tangled.*' [1]

In these words Herzen's *alogism* is distinctly formulated; the fortuitous in nature and in history, if it does not negate, at least *limits* their rational order and harmonious arrangement at every point. Herzen's conviction of the reality of chance did not yet make him a sceptic, but it completely subverted Hegel's panlogistic system, as well as the more modest propositions of scientific and philosophic thought; and of course it completely demolished his religious view of life. When, before his departure for Western Europe, Herzen made the acquaintance of Feuerbach's *The Nature of Christianity*, this book merely summed up the destructive process which had been at work in his religious world.

But, precisely because inane chance occupies such an enormous place in all things, Herzen—true to his romantic orientation—was reinforced in his anthropocentrism. This anthropocentrism was tragically coloured, for it was built on the philosophy of chance, but it freed Herzen's thought from 'factolatry', from renunciation of self in the name of the 'laws of nature'. 'In man', Herzen wrote in 1848, 'there develops, along with consciousness, the need to save *something of his own* from the whirlwind of chance . . . a sense of his own dignity and a striving to preserve the moral uniqueness and autonomy of his personality.' [2] In these words his 'subjective idealism' (in the moral sense) appears clearly: in spite of the 'whirlwind of chances', man, standing among the ruins left by this whirlwind, can and must assert his 'moral uniqueness and autonomy'. This proud setting of man's 'moral uniqueness and autonomy' against the whirlwind of chances is incompatible with the positivistic view of knowledge which Herzen held at this time. [3]

1. *Byloye i dumy* [My Past and Thoughts], Pt. III, pp. 300, 339.
2. *Sochineniya*, V, 212f.
3. We have already noted (Ch. VII) the objections raised against Herzen by Samarin, who accused him of internal contradiction—of uniting a stubborn positivism with an equally stubborn assertion of man's 'moral uniqueness and autonomy'.

His affirmation of man's 'moral autonomy' had, of course, the effect of stressing more forcefully the fact that a 'whirlwind of chances' reigns in the world. Herzen's belief in immortality vanished completely.

'We know', he wrote later, 'how nature disposes of individuals— *it is all the same to her*, she continues about her own business. There is no escape. . . . I was troubled and unhappy when this thought [that there is no personal immortality] began to haunt me; I wanted to flee from it, but everything led me to submissiveness to this truth, to a self-abnegating acceptance of it.' [1]

We have seen that in his Hegelian period Herzen sought 'salvation' for the principle of individuality in the 'act'. 'Man has not only the capacity for understanding, but also *will*, which may be called *creative* reason.' The problem of individuality now became central. 'The individual is the *summit* of history', Herzen wrote in 1848. 'Everything abuts upon him, everything lives in him.' [2]

Personalism, the affirmation of the 'moral uniqueness and autonomy', the freedom and *independence* of the individual, nevertheless remained only a programme for Herzen. There is no *objective* basis for this affirmation in his philosophy. In the flux of natural being there is no place for the individual to consolidate himself; however substantial and profound his inner wealth may be, it will be carried away and destroyed by the blind torrent. All that Herzen can offer in opposition is the ethical value of the individual: 'There is nothing to be done with a man who goes voluntarily to his death—he is *incorrigibly* a man', [3] he wrote once. And in the same place we read: 'A free man *creates* his morality himself', i.e. he himself ascends to the summit which places him ethically, not metaphysically, above the blind flux. The divergence of real being and the realm of values nevertheless remains *unreconciled* in Herzen; escape from this intolerable dichotomy, which is possible only on the ground of religion, remained closed to him. He did not fall into either ethical relativism or illusory idealism, but remained always at the height of ethical awareness. However, the dualism of existence and value, if it is not resolved, leads to an abyss, to tragic pathlessness, to extreme pessimism. Herzen did not want to part company either with naturalism, the doctrine of nature's blindness, or with the categorical imperatives of the moral consciousness; and this doomed him inwardly to a barren

1. *Byloye i dumy* [My Past and Thoughts], Pt. III, p. 359.
2. *Sochineniya*, V, 213.
3. *Ibid.*, p. 225.

stand at the edge of the abyss. His anthropocentrism did not move from the ethical sphere to the plane of metaphysics. He still wanted to explain man in terms of nature, not nature in terms of man. This attitude reached its most acute form in Herzen's historiosophy, where the collapse of Hegelian logism was most profound.

## 6. HISTORIOSOPHICAL ALOGISM

From his early providentialism which, as we have seen, completely denied the possibility of chance, Herzen in the 1840's proceeded directly to a Hegelian conception of history, as the self-revelation of Absolute Spirit. Nature and history, for all their essential difference, are united in this 'substantial' foundation—and they are conceived by Herzen in their vital continuity and essential connectedness. Despite the fact that the idea of the 'whirlwind of chances'—not only in nature, but also in history—appears more and more persistently in Herzen, he still defends the idea of 'reasonableness' in history. He writes with conviction that 'science [and history is included here] . . . has developed the truth of reason which is inherent in reality: it has freed the thought of the world from the world's events, freed all existence from chance . . ., revealed the eternal in time, the infinite in the finite, and recognized their necessary existence'. In this formulation, which sets forth the career of scientific (including historical) knowledge in the Hegelian spirit, there is still no unreserved worship of facts ('facts, . . . taken in all the contingency of being, are of no force against the reason which glows in science'). There is, rather, a pervasive 'rationalistic fanaticism', as Herzen later expressed it.[1] 'Panlogism' still completely determined Herzen's thinking. But when various doubts led him to a recognition of *alogism* in history, this was the result of his viewing 'chance'—which he had previously admitted only in 'factual' being, considering that it vanished in the philosophic working over of facts—as a *genuine reality*. And this brought about the collapse of his 'panlogism'—a collapse which appeared most clearly to Herzen, as we have seen, in human fate, where 'the grievous *power* of chance' is evident at every step. 'Man can never reconcile himself', he wrote (in 1845), 'to the *extreme precariousness* and instability of all that is best in what he possesses.'[2] 'An all-destroying scepticism'. Herzen wrote to his friend Ogaryov in 1843, 'took root in my usually sunny world-view . . .; outwardly

1. *Byloye i dumy* [My Past and Thoughts], Pt. IV, p. 97.
2. *Sochineniya*, III, 433.

insignificant events marked an epoch within'. [1] Herzen's historio-sophical thought was slowly being undermined, but as late as 1847 he wrote sharply of the 'contradictions in the consciousness of contemporary man . . . which have mutilated his entire moral being'. These contradictions arise from the fact that there is both 'a desire to preserve science with all its rights, with its pretensions to *autonomy of reason* and reality of knowledge', and 'a romantic revolt against reason, based on vague feeling and obscure prompt-ings'.[2] We have already quoted Herzen's conclusion (of 1848) concerning man's 'need to save *something of his own* from the whirl-wind of chances'. This refers primarily to historical being, in which the 'whirlwind of chances' is continuous and unalterable. In a letter to friends in Moscow (also in 1848) Herzen spoke, with considerable restraint, of chance as 'an incomparably more important element in history than German philosophy thinks',[3] and within a year he wrote to Granovski: 'History differs from nature only in the development of consciousness, but *it has no purpose.*' [4] This is clearly a revolt against Hegel. In Herzen's book From the Other Shore the philosophy of alogism was developed in unequivocal form. Concerning the life of nature, Herzen wrote, in the passage already quoted, 'Life has its embryogeny, *which does not coincide with the dialectic of pure reason.*' But his chief blow fell on the theory of history. 'The future does not exist, it is formed by a combination of thousands of conditions, both necessary and *fortuitous,* and by the human will. . . . History *improvises* itself . . ., it makes use of every accident, it knocks *simultaneously* at a thousand doors. . . .' 'A part of every historical event is the result of physi-ology, of obscure cravings', Herzen wrote in the same place. He still believed in '*laws* of historical development', [5] and he believed firmly in the 'independence of nature'; but his scepticism gradually penetrated further. In the end he arrived at a unique historio-sophical *mysticism*, combined with a *naturalistic* view of the 'flux' of historical being; his new conception of history is reminiscent of a modern philosopher's formula, that history is 'the introduction of meaning into meaningless existence'. History moves by an enig-matic '*élan historique*'; historical being 'flows', it moves, but it *does not break up* into separate and independent 'particles'. The integra-tion of historical being remains enigmatic and unexplained in Herzen; he retained in essence the Hegelian view of history as an integral flux, merely severing its connection with the logos.

1. *Ibid.*, p. 238.     2. *Sochineniya*, V, 13–15.     3. *Ibid.*, p. 244.
4. *Ibid.*, p. 281.                                   5. *Ibid.*, p. 433.

Herzen's thought, having decisively recognized the power of chance, continued to move essentially in the framework of romantic nature-philosophy and historiosophy. Nature is a kind of whole; historical being is a kind of flux, blind yet mysteriously and integrally connected. 'Neither nature nor history', Herzen wrote, '*lead anywhere*, hence they are ready to go in any direction that is indicated to them, if it is a possible one.' These words contain the central idea of Herzen's alogism: 'History has no purpose', 'it goes nowhere', i.e. there is no 'logos' in it, only a mass of chances. In the article 'Ends and Beginnings' Herzen wrote of 'volcanic underground work [in history]'—which is equivalent to the function of Hegel's 'mole'. Herzen spares no pains to exhibit the alogical character of the historical flux; he loves to speak of the 'tousled improvisation of history'. But why does he cling to these romantic categories, reproaching historical being so fiercely for the 'improvisation' which reigns in it?—Because his secret *religious* dream, the dream of an ideal order which is to be realized in history, i.e. here on earth, is bound up with it. Herzen's religious immanentism—which completely crowded out his Christianity— is expressed in Hegelian categories, and it is for this reason that Herzen felt his disillusionment with the 'logicality' of history so poignantly. His historiosophical alogism had made too large a breach in his religious world, but he was not able to renounce religious immanentism; hence his philosophic system remained incomplete. All that was left for him was the tragic defeat of testifying to the 'tousled improvisation' of history. In *My Past and Thoughts* Herzen makes an interesting confession: 'We were distressed by a consciousness of the *impotence of ideas*, by the absence of any *compelling force of truth* in the real world. *A new kind of Manichaeism* took possession of us, we were ready to believe in rational [i.e. intentional] evil, as men once believed in rational good.' This 'consciousness of the impotence of ideas' reveals Herzen's secret striving: he is constantly seeking 'rationality', even in evil, i.e. he is seeking the Hegelian logos in history.

We cannot refrain from calling attention to the general significance of Herzen's historical alogism. It is not simply a *disintegration of Hegelianism*, but a *crisis of secular ideology*. Fr. S. Bulgakov rightly considers Herzen a 'religious seeker',[1] and Herzen remained such even when he became an *atheist*. His basic theme—the consolidation of the individual in an Absolute which defends him both from the power of death and the 'whirlwind of chances'—is a religious

1. Bulgakov, *op. cit.*, p. 163.

theme, which Herzen attempts to resolve on a foundation of secularism, i.e. rejection of the Church. Hegelianism provided a kind of resolution of this theme, in so far as it connected the individual to Absolute Spirit, seeing in man a revelation of an absolute principle. But Herzen had to admit that the fate of the individual found only *imaginary* resolution in Hegel. Like Belinski, and Tolstoy later, Herzen was unable to reconcile the fact of death with Hegel's religious immanentism. The disintegration of Hegelianism is the failure of an approach to philosophy which developed along the lines of secularism. Strakhov is right when he states that Herzen 'was reduced to complete despair even before the Revolution of 1848'.[1] Herzen's disillusionment with Western culture—first reflected with extraordinary force in his book From the Other Shore—served primarily to precipitate the crisis in his religious and philosophic searchings.

## 7. THE CRITIQUE OF WESTERN CULTURE. HERZEN'S TRAGIC WORLD-VIEW

Herzen's critique of western culture is marked throughout by partiality and even animosity. S. N. Bulgakov observes with justice that Herzen 'would not have been satisfied with any Europe, or in general with *any reality*, for no reality was capable of containing the ideal which Herzen sought'. There is no need for us to enter into the details of Herzen's critique of the West; but we must consider the position that Herzen reached as a result of the collapse of his ideas, a collapse which is depicted with such courageous honesty in his works. He himself characterized his general position as a form of *nihilism*, but he did not use the term in its usual sense. By 'nihilism' Herzen meant 'the most complete freedom. . . . Nihilism is *science without dogmas*, unconditional submission to experience and unmurmuring acceptance of the consequences'.[2] It is a rejection of all metaphysics, a denial of absolute morality, a relativism of principle—and at the same time a passionate seeking of at least partial significance, at least temporary triumph over the abyss which yawns before the mature human being. It is a philosophy of *despair, hopelessness, and disbelief*—a romantic revolt against tarnished reality, against the Philistine delight in external goods, a revolt dictated by the last remnants of a religious consciousness which could have found peace only in the Divine Kingdom, only in God.

1. Strakhov, *op. cit.*, p. 81.
2. *Byloye i dumy* [My Past and Thoughts], Pt. V, pp. 611f.

Nevertheless, something remained even in this revolt—elements from which, in the light of a vital religiosity, creative strength might have developed. Herzen himself had a foreboding of this, but his system lacked the basic factor for grounding such a position —the rooting of thought in the Transcendent. Herzen persistently sought to conquer for the individual a firm foothold in existence, but he was unable to go beyond the limits of man's inner world. He could have set his mind at rest with an assertion of the 'transcendentality' of man's higher aspects, but he was too much of a realist for this. The only thing that remained for him was a defence of the rights of 'independent and autonomous morality', with no hope of grounding this morality. In fact, as we have seen, Herzen argued himself into a doctrine of man's 'unlimited freedom', although he himself emphasized the 'grievous power of chance'. In the same book, From the Other Shore, we read: 'I do not advise you to quarrel with the world, but I do advise you to begin an autonomous, independent life, capable of finding salvation in itself even though the whole surrounding world should perish.' [1] And here is another passage from the same work: 'It is possible to halt the carrying out of one's fate *to a certain extent* [!]: history does not exhibit that strict, unalterable predestination of which philosophers preach; many *changeable* principles enter into the formula of its development, in the first place—individual freedom and power.' In the midst of the 'whirlwind of chances' Herzen grasped at the *category of possibility* like a straw, and held fast to it. This category of 'possibility', which is related essentially to the philosophy of chance, helped Herzen construct a theory of the 'possibility' of Russia's passing over the phase of capitalism and proceeding directly to the social ideal. Here Herzen opened to Russian thought fruitful and creative ground for various utopian theories (those of Mikhailovski and his group), although he himself made little use of the 'category of possibility' for general philosophy.

Such are the results of Herzen's philosophic quest. They are meagre and extremely pessimistic—and he himself found no escape from the tragic impasse. Relativism, scepticism and the diffuse mysticism, irrationalism and alogism which never left him, combined to destroy the harmonious order in his conception of nature, making abundant room for the philosophy of chance. The philosophy of chance, it is true, left room for a categorical assertion of the individual's right to a 'unique and autonomous morality',

1. *Sochineniya*, V, 483.

but no more than this. The moral world remained without relation to reality; it is *opposed* to reality precisely because it is *independent* of reality. The philosophy of chance provided Herzen with a ground for his affirmation of man's 'unlimited freedom' and the absoluteness of his ethical idealism. A philosophy of chance is an unsteady enough foundation for such an exalted anthropology: nevertheless, it was this that permitted Herzen to exhibit the basic problem of *individuality*. The individual's spiritual needs were an 'unalterable fact' for Herzen, and here he refused to yield an inch to positivism. Hence his general position is a 'semi-positivism', a paradoxical combination of positivism in ontology with a negation of positivism in the doctrine of man's spiritual 'independence' of real being. Let us add that Herzen united an ardent defence of freedom and an irreproachable observance of the demands of morality with a profound *aesthetic* sense. He sought in beauty not merely aesthetic enjoyment but also an answer to the romantic searchings of his spirit. Herzen thus reconstructed in a new form the same aesthetic humanism in which Russian secular thought had previously sought a substitute for religious truth and justice. In his person, a powerful and profound thinker attempted once again to eliminate the world of the 'beyond', while retaining Christian themes, and to find a resolution of these themes within the framework of religious immanentism. Herzen's failure, his 'spiritual drama', and his tragic perception of the impasse—all this, more than the facts of his personal life, afford a prophetic insight into the tragic pathlessness which awaited Russian thought in the future, when it had broken with the Church but was unable to renounce the themes bequeathed to it by Christianity.

# CHAPTER X

## The Philosophic Movement
## in the Russian Theological Schools
## during the First Half of the Nineteenth Century

GOLUBINSKI, SIDONSKI, KARPOV, AVSENEV,
GOGOTSKI, YURKEVICH, *et al.*

### I. PHILOSOPHY IN THE THEOLOGICAL SCHOOLS

WE have seen in an earlier chapter (Ch. II) that philosophic culture developed uninterruptedly in both of the Theological Academies (Kiev and Moscow) which existed in eighteenth-century Russia. Two more Theological Academies were opened in the nineteenth century (St. Petersburg and, later, Kazan), and they naturally depended for their teaching staff on the older Academies. A philosophic tradition became established in the Theological Academies of both Kiev and Moscow which was essentially very close to that of medieval philosophy in Western Europe. On the one hand, Orthodox dogmatics and patristic literature defined the fundamental limits and paths of reflection; on the other hand, the rich philosophic literature of Western Europe permitted a selection among various philosophic tendencies in constructing a 'Christian philosophy'. At the same time, as we have seen in our study of Skovoroda, it was in the Theological Academies that the idea first arose of a specifically *Russian* national philosophy, based upon the teaching of the Church, but utilizing the ideas of Western-European philosophy in a free synthesis. We know that at the beginning of the nineteenth century translations of current philosophic works—those of Kant and Schelling, for example—circulated in the Theological Academies. The type of philosophy created by Christian Wolf, which was expounded in numerous German textbooks, was generally accepted and, so to speak, officially approved—considered ecclesiastically reliable. However, this traditional Wolfianism did not in any sense preclude the study of other philosophic tendencies. Jacobi especially impressed the philosophers of the Theological Academies with his critique of rationalism and his assertion of faith as a special form of experience and 'direct' knowledge; but Kant, too—and transcendentalism generally—left a profound mark on their philosophic searchings. Nevertheless the problem of faith held a place of first importance, defining the basic orientation of these searchings. The question of the relationship of faith to reason took on the same decisive significance for all of their theoretical constructions that it had had for high scholasticism in the West. But in Russia 'Orthodox philosophy' was constantly discussed in *contrast* to Western Christianity. Material for this was frequently found in Western Christianity itself—in the Protestant thinkers and theologians against Catholicism, and in the Catholics against Protestantism. However, this should not close our eyes to the unquestionable *independence* of a number of Academic philosophers, even though philosophically they were often only on the *threshold* of systems. As we have already seen, this was characteristic of the whole of Russian philosophy at the time.

Above all the others, in force of philosophic talent, stands F. A. Golubinski, Professor at the Moscow Theological Academy, and creator of a school which, in the person of his gifted pupil, V. D. Kudryavtsev-Platonov, provided the first brilliant attempt at a philosophic system. In second place come the philosophers of the Kiev Theological Academy : V. N. Karpov, Archimandrite Theophanes Avsenev, S. S. Gogotski, and P. D. Yurkevich. Later, a tradition, if not a school, became established at the St. Petersburg Theological Academy, including Sidonski, V. N. Karpov, the Kiev Academy graduate who replaced Sidonski; later, Vladislavev, the highly gifted M. I. Karinski *et al.* Let us consider first the creative activity of F. A. Golubinski.

## 2. F. A. GOLUBINSKI. BIOGRAPHY

Fyodor Aleksandrovich Golubinski (1797–1854) was the son of a Kostroma sacristan who later became a priest. After graduating from the Kostroma Seminary, where his talents and knowledge made him outstanding, young Golubinski was sent—at the age of seventeen—to the Moscow Theological Academy, which at that time (1814) was a centre of great intellectual excitement. One of the manifestations of this excitement was the organization by the students of a 'scholarly colloquium', of which Golubinski became secretary. It is interesting to note that this occurred several years before the organization of the 'Society of Wisdom-Lovers' which we have already encountered and which, as we know, was the first manifestation of the philosophic searchings of nineteenth-century Russian society. While still a student, Golubinski became thoroughly acquainted with Kant and Schelling, as well as Jacobi. He was much indebted in this connection to V. I. Kutnevich, then Professor of Philosophy at the Moscow Academy. Golubinski, who had a good command of languages, translated several textbooks on the history of philosophy (those of Tannemann, Brücker, *et al.*). In 1827 Golubinski, who upon graduating from the Academy had become a teacher of philosophy there, married, and in 1828 became a priest. The maturity and clarity of his thought brought him early fame, and he was soon offered a chair of philosophy at Moscow University. However, Golubinski declined this invitation, not wishing to leave the Academy. He taught philosophy at the Academy to the end of his days.[1]

Golubinski is often characterized as a Platonist, and this of course is just, but his Platonism is coloured by patristic modifications of Plato. Golubinski knew the Neo-Platonists very well, especially Proclus; and he was acquainted with the religious tendencies of the seventeenth and eighteenth centuries, especially Poiret, Böhme, and Saint-Martin. Shpet, without any ground whatever, characterizes Golubinski as a Wolfian, although he also acknowledges that Golubinski was unquestionably influenced by Jacobi.[2] S. Glagolev stresses the influence of the French religious thinker Bautain.[3] Golubinski studied Baader thoroughly and was very fond of Schubert (he especially admired the latter's book *Ansichten von der Nachtseite der Natur*) as well as the other Schellingians—such as Steffens and Mayer.[4] He studied Hegel carefully and placed

1. Very few of Golubinski's works have been preserved, but one of his students, a priest named Nazarevski, has published detailed notes of his lectures (Moscow, 1884). Although these notes are in outline form, and rather dry in style, they accurately reproduce Golubinski's theoretical views. They include: (1) 'Lectures on Philosophy', (2) 'Ontology', (3) 'Lectures on Speculative Theology', and (4) 'Speculative Psychology'.

2. Shpet, *Ocherk razviti russkoi filosofi* [An Outline of the Development of Russian Philosophy], Petrograd, 1922, p. 176. Shpet's opinion concerning Golubinski's scepticism is equally unfounded (*ibid.*, p. 179).

3. S. Glagolev, 'Golubinski', *Bogoslovski vestnik* (1897), p. 458.

4. *Ibid.*, p. 461.

particular value on Hegel's interpretation of the various tendencies in the history of philosophy.[1]

Golubinski's philosophic erudition was very broad and substantial. He boldly took from all thinkers whatever he found in them that seemed correct, but he was not at all an eclectic. On the contrary, his thought exhibits considerable wholeness and a striking inner unity. He attempted to synthesize free philosophic thought and the data of Revelation.[2]

Let us turn to a study of his thought.

### 3. GOLUBINSKI'S FUNDAMENTAL IDEAS (EPISTEMOLOGY)

There is one central idea in Golubinski which is basic for the crystallization of all his other ideas and offers a point of support for the construction of a philosophic system, the plan of which is clear from the materials which he left. This is the idea of *Infinite Being*. A kind of basic vision or intuition, it illuminates for Golubinski the most tangled problems, accompanying him, like Ariadne's thread, in his explorations of the labyrinth of the world's mysteries. It is clear that this central idea is genetically connected with his religious consciousness. But, having once risen to the level of rationality, it becomes the basic point of departure for his philosophic analyses. He shows with exceptional clarity, by means of minute and rigorous analysis, that this idea is ineradicably present

1. We read in Herzen (Diary entry for Jan. 18, 1844): 'Metropolitan Philaret commissioned Golubinski to refute Hegel; Golubinski replied that he could not cope with the titan of Berlin and that he did not absolutely reject his doctrine. Philaret demanded that he should at least take issue with those points on which he disagreed. But Golubinski answered that Hegel was so consistent that one must either refute him completely or accept him completely.' This entry clearly reflects the *rumours* which were current in Moscow, but it is very difficult to say how much truth there is in them. There are many passages in Golubinski's lectures that are obviously directed against Hegel. Cf. Smirnov (*Istoriya Moskovskoi Dukhovnoi Akademi* [A History of the Moscow Theological Academy], p. 50): 'In Golubinski's opinion, Hegel did not solve the problem of the source of novelty [in development]. Novelty can only be explained by positing a fullness of being at the basis of development; but for Hegel, being is equivalent to non-being.' The report of Haxthausen—the well-known traveller who wrote a book on Russia—concerning Golubinski's judgments of Schelling and Hegel is very interesting. See Glagolev, *op. cit.*, pp. 485f.

2. Smirnov (*op. cit.*, p. 51) notes that 'Golubinski gave reason greater right to investigate the truth than Baader did', and that he 'did not turn philosophic doctrines into theological doctrines'.

in the human mind,[1] but the origin of the idea of the Infinite is wholly inexplicable on the basis of man's psychic life. In fact, the idea of the Infinite, as Golubinski shows,[2] is *logically prior to every particular cognition*. For this reason it cannot be deduced from anything,[3] but is 'innate' in man.[4] It is because this idea is present in us 'prior to experience' that cognition is possible, as an *ascent* from the finite to the Infinite, from the conditional to the Unconditional. In fact, the whole activity of cognition is motivated by the intention to know the 'Unconditional', to know total truth. And, of course, this intention, which constitutes the living strength and motive force of the whole cognitive process, cannot be deduced from sense perception. Moreover, we would never be able to distinguish ourselves, as the 'subject' of our perceptions, from their objective content if we did not have in us a striving for the Unconditional.[5] Why?—Because in sense perception the subjective and the objective, the 'self' and 'things', are inseparably fused together. But it is beyond question that our striving for the Unconditional separates the conditional—our 'self'—from the surrounding objective world in which the Unconditional appears before us. On the other hand, this gravitation toward the Infinite can have no root in the functions of reason, which elaborate the raw material of sense perception according to the categories,[6] since in themselves the categories, as applied to the raw material of sense, do not purge it of its contingent and conditional character. In general, the categories become conductors of the unconditional principle only

1. Golubinski's concept 'mind' corresponds fully to that of 'spirit', i.e. it is not to be interpreted in purely intellectualistic terms. See below.

2. 'The idea of the Infinite', we read in the 'Lectures on Philosophy' (p. 71), 'is the primary and immediate principle of all knowledge.' Cf. Golubinski's remark (*ibid.*, p. 68) that 'the idea of the Infinite is not a clear intuition, but only an obscure and mysterious presentiment, an idea of something unlimited which is prior to experience and is not exhausted by the definite concepts of reason'.

3. *Ibid.*, p. 71.

4. *Ibid.*, p. 82.

5. *Ibid.*, pp. 74f.

6. Golubinski takes Kant as his point of departure in his doctrine of categories, but he also criticizes him. The quest for unity in objective being, which underlies the categorical processes, is possible only because the soul 'has a consciousness of God as a self-subsistent unity' apart from experience and prior to experience. 'It does not appertain to the soul', we read in the 'Lectures' (p. 57), 'to be single'. 'The soul is conscious of itself as single only because it contains an image of the One.' Apart from this image 'we would have no consciousness of ourselves as the single centre of surrounding objects'. ('Lectures on Speculative Theology,' pp. 82, 87.)

when illuminated by the idea of the Infinite. Thus, our spirit's striving for unconditional knowledge, which is the motivation of cognition, can only be explained by recognizing a 'fundamental law in accordance with which our spirit strives toward the Infinite'.[1]

How then are we to understand the presence and action of the idea of the Infinite within us? Of course, it could not arise, much less exhibit its action and force, if the Infinite were not before our minds (=spirits) in its full immediacy. On this point Golubinski is in complete agreement with Jacobi's doctrine of 'direct' know-ledge ('faith'). 'True cognition', Golubinski writes, 'must be *living* cognition, a process in which the energies of the known object are appropriated by the spirit of the knower', so that there is in the knower a living 'sensation', an 'embracing of the known with one's *whole* being—not with reason only, but with will and feeling as well'.

Golubinski categorically defends epistemological *realism* and decisively repudiates epistemological idealism. He criticizes the arguments of epistemological idealism, beginning with Locke, very carefully and forcefully; and he defends the reality of the external world as it appears to us in sense perception with great persuasiveness. At the same time, he analyzes the problem of space and time in great detail and very minutely; asserting their reality, he defends the thesis that 'space, which is actually filled with matter, is *not infinite*'.[2]

### 4. ONTOLOGY AND ANTHROPOLOGY

As to the problems of ontology, in so far as one can judge from his lecture notes, we should point out to begin with that Golubinski regarded the world as a living whole—in a way different from Schelling, however, and closer to the vitalism of the Stoics. 'There is life in all of nature', we read in the Lectures, 'manifesting itself in different processes; for the wholly dead could not exist. . . . Being is the operation of energies.'[3] He further asserts that every finite being has a '*centre*'.

'In *every* organic being there is a concentrated inner principle which remains constant through changing external appearances; this is substance, an inner self-acting principle on which all appearances depend.'[4]

1. 'Lectures on Philosophy', p. 70.    2. *Ibid.*, p. 49.
3. *Ibid.*, p. 24.                     4. *Ibid.*, p. 89.

In another place we read: 'Finite entities operate arbitrarily through their own energies.' [1] This is superficially reminiscent of Leibniz; but Golubinski finds the latter's doctrine of matter as a *phenomenon* (even though '*bene fondatum*') unacceptable. Golubinski's doctrine is closest of all to the Stoic conception of the *logoi spermatikoi*. He once threw out an interesting remark concerning 'the universal energy of life',[2] which, he insisted, 'is not Infinite Being'. Still it 'exists' as a 'universal' fact. Here Golubinski came close to the Sophiological world-conception developed by Russian metaphysicians in the twentieth century, which, as we shall see, continually attracted Russian thinkers during the nineteenth century.[3] Let us quote a passage from Golubinski's lecture on being—which is more in the spirit of Leibniz than of Schelling:

'It is highly unlikely that only mechanical and chemical forces operate in the mineral realm, that it does not have its organisms. . . . The forces of attraction and repulsion sustain the whole heavens in uniform order. . . . Must there not be some common principle of activity at the centre of each planet and each star? If there is a constant centre even in a blade of grass, which maintains and reproduces its identical form, must there not be constant internal principles in the enormous [heavenly] bodies as well, upon which their other partial forces are based and sustained? We cannot fail to see organisms in the "inorganic" realm, on the earth's surface, for example. . . .' [4]

Golubinski, so far as one can judge from his Lectures, did not make a special study of anthropology. But isolated judgments on questions of anthropology (in the spirit of patristic thought) are scattered throughout his works. For him—and here he consciously opposed transcendentalism—'the soul's self-consciousness is *not primary*'; consciousness of God is the source of the soul's consciousness that it is single and distinct from its surroundings. Golubinski, as we have seen, calls the highest power of the human spirit, which makes possible direct communion with the sphere of Deity, 'mind'. 'Only the mind perceives the Infinite', Golubinski writes. '. . . Man's mind is a higher power, the foundation of all his other capacities. The living image of the Infinite Being is preserved *in us*.' [5] Golubinski distinguishes the 'mind' from the inferior power

---

1. *Ibid.*, p. 93.                    2. *Ibid.*, p. 85.

3. See Florenski's report that Golubinski 'bore the idea of Sophia deeply within himself'. (K. Mochulski, *Vladimir Solovyov*, Paris, 1936, p. 43.)

4. 'Lectures on Philosophy', Pt. III, pp. 110f.

5. *Op. cit.*, Pt. II, pp. 63, 66.

of *reason*, which is the capacity for forming concepts; but the activity of reason is directed by the mind. Our mind, in its striving toward the Infinite, similarly directs our will and our feelings. 'The hunger and thirst of our spirit can be satisfied only in the Infinite.'

We cannot deny that Golubinski's theoretical constructions are harmonious and internally complete. For him, as for his whole school—V. D. Kudryavtsev-Platonov, Archbishop Nikanor, and A. I. Vvedenski [1]—ontologism, and the rooting of man's spiritual impulses in God as 'Infinite Being', are typical. The doctrine of man's *direct perception of Deity* is another characteristic of Golubinski's theories, which follows logically from the first. Formally, this doctrine is closely connected with the influence of Jacobi, whose ideas greatly assisted Golubinski and his pupils in freeing themselves from transcendentalism; but in its essence it is bound up with his initial ontologism. Golubinski's doctrine of the direct perception of Deity is rooted in his ontologism.

## 5. F. F. SIDONSKI

F. F. Sidonski (1805–73), Golubinski's younger contemporary was a graduate of the Tver Seminary, who later studied at the St. Petersburg Theological Academy. After graduating from the Academy he began to teach English there, and soon received a chair of philosophy. In 1833 Sidonski, who was already a priest, published An Introduction to the Science of Philosophy (this book was crowned by the Academy of Sciences with a full Demidov Prize). Sidonski wrote a great deal on both theological and philosophic questions. He was forced to resign his chair of philosophy at the Theological Academy, but this disciplinary measure—which was undeserved—did not interrupt his scientific work. In 1856 the Academy of Sciences honoured him with the title of Academician, and in 1864 St. Petersburg University awarded him an honorary degree of Doctor of Philosophy, and offered him a chair of philosophy.

Sindonski was undoubtedly influenced by German idealism, but he always assigned an important place to experience in his theories; and this has caused some scholars—though without sufficient grounds—to consider him a follower of British empiricism. In fact, Sidonski conceived philosophy as 'empirical metaphysics', which is close to the contemporary idea of 'inductive metaphysics'. Philosophy should take experience as its *point of departure*—inner

1. See Pt. III of the present book.

experiences in particular—but it should rise from experience to reason. This procedure of 'empirical' metaphysics gives no ground, according to Sidonski, for fearing disagreement with the truths of faith, since revelation and reason are equally rooted in God. The 'verification' of religion by science, in his opinion, can never shake the truths of reason. The monistic tendency itself, which is characteristic of reason, is determined by the striving toward God as an all-embracing unity.

Sidonski distinguishes three basic themes in philosophy: (1) cosmological, (2) moral, and (3) epistemological. In his opinion, cosmology is central; epistemology is only a propaedeutic for cosmology. But external experience is not a basis for philosophy; it determines the 'content' of being, but not its 'source'. Reason, in order to operate, must be 'mysteriously united to real existence [i.e. nature] and to Primary Existence'. Philosophy, Sidonski thinks, wishes to *encounter Deity*. Reason offers a certain presentiment of what we find in Revelation; therefore reason must seek its support in Revelation. Reason should rise from abstract thought to religious intuition. Thought then becomes, in Sidonski's expression, 'implicit'—and reason is able to comprehend the 'mysterious image of being and the origin of objects'. These words are rather foggy, but we can see in them a reflection of *transcendentalism*. Sidonski reworked transcendentalism in his own way; he taught that 'reason passes into the life of the object'.[1] Reason is an 'abridgement of universal life and ideal being'. Incidentally, he constantly returns to the idea of 'verifying' the theoretical constructions of reason in experience.

Sidonski had unquestionable philosophic talent and great philosophic erudition, but he contributed very little to the Russian philosophic literature of the first half of the nineteenth century.

## 6. I. M. SKVORTSOV

Ivan Mikhailovich Skvortsov (1795–1863) was the son of a sacristan—who later became a priest—in the town of Arzamas in the Government of Nizhni Novgorod. Skvortsov studied at the Nizhni Novgorod Seminary until he was eighteen, and then was sent to the St. Petersburg Theological Academy. After graduating he was appointed professor in the Kiev Seminary (the Kiev Academy was closed at the time). When the Kiev Seminary was transformed into

---

1. This expression is in full harmony with the phraseology of transcendentalism.

an Academy in 1819, Skvortsov, who was already a priest, took a chair of philosophy there. He wrote many works on the history of philosophy, both ancient and modern, but in fact he had little to say on philosophic problems—being somewhat tinged with scepticism. For him, too, the first stage of cognition is given in faith, as a 'direct feeling of truth', but he sketches this doctrine in such broad and diffuse outlines that it is impossible to draw any conclusions concerning his epistemological views. Philosophy, in his opinion, should lead from 'natural' (direct) reason to Christianity; but its path is not free to begin with.

### 7. V. N. KARPOV

V. N. Karpov (1798–1867), Skvortsov's student, was much more talented and original; he earned an honourable reputation through his Russian translation of all of Plato's works—except the *Laws*. [1] Karpov was born into the family of a priest in the Government of Voronezh. Upon graduating from the Voronezh Seminary—where the Schellingian Zatsepin taught philosophy—Karpov entered the Kiev Theological Academy; after his graduation (in 1825) he became a teacher, first in the Seminary and then in the Academy. In 1833 he was invited to St. Petersburg Theological Academy, where he took the chair of philosophy which was left vacant by Sidonski's retirement. Karpov's chief work—his translation of Plato's dialogues—was carried out with great love and care. He wrote introductions to all the dialogues, briefly expounding and analyzing their contents. Karpov attempted a characterization and analysis of 'modern rationalism' (this is the title of his essay on the subject), i.e. the rationalism of Kant and the later transcendentalists, but the essay was not finished. [2] We quote one passage from this work:

'From the point of view of Kant's *Critique of Pure Reason* man is an entity (if only an entity) woven out of concepts, who ascends or descends the strands of his categorical spider web, immured in the pure forms of space and time, from which he cannot even look out, let alone escape. At the same time he is aware that, despite

1. The *Laws* had previously been translated into Russian by V. Obolenski (Moscow, 1827). Plato's complete works had been published in Russian translations by Pakhomov and Sidorovski (four volumes, St. Petersburg, 1780–85), but this edition was superseded by that of Karpov.

2. It was printed (unsigned) in *Khristianskoye chteniye* [Christian Reading], the journal of the St. Petersburg Theological Academy, in 1860.

the infinite expansibility of these forms, he is crowded and uncomfortable within them, like a caged bird.' [1]

We must acknowledge both the apt imagery and the essential accuracy of Karpov's critique; but what is there in Karpov himself behind this critique? It becomes clear from a study of his interesting Introduction to Philosophy (1840), Logic (1856), and Lectures on Psychology (1868) that Karpov had quite an integral system. There is no doubt that he was influenced by transcendentalism,[2] but he modified it considerably toward pure psychologism. In any case, he regarded consciousness, 'taken concretely' in the fullness of its content, as the point of departure for philosophic constructions. On Karpov's theory 'all the powers of the soul, *concentrated in faith* and illuminated by it', form an organ for cognition of the truth. 'One may discover in man laws applicable to the whole of being, overhear the harmony of life with which the whole universe is suffused, and contemplate in mystical symbols the bonds which unite the whole cosmos.' This is clearly a transformation of transcendentalism into anthropologism; but Karpov is free from the extremes of the empirical method. 'Psychology', he asserts, 'must begin its career with an investigation of man's *being*, not his *activity*.' He is enthusiastically and rather naïvely confident that an 'unbiased investigation of human nature' would be sufficient to free our mind from errors and to relate thought to the tenets of faith, since man finds in himself a living relationship not only to the external world but also to the higher world. Karpov calls this branch of psychology 'phenomenology'; and he goes on to make a number of interesting distinctions, which occasionally remind one of Husserl's analyses. Man reveals not only a path to external reality and the metaphysical environment—which, being 'supersensory', is known through 'ideas'—but also a connection, through his religious life, to a 'spiritual sphere' which is separate from supersensory or ideal being. Above the 'ideal-realism' of cognition [3] there is a realm inaccessible to cognition where 'spiritual intuition'—'the eye of the soul illuminated by faith'—is

1. *Khrist. chteniye* (1860), Pt. I, p. 414.
2. In one place (*Vvedeniye v filosofiyu* [Introduction to Philosophy], p. 133) Karpov himself spoke of the 'transcendental synthesis which should be the final fruit of a complete system'. This whole book is permeated with the idea of the primacy of consciousness, but Karpov decisively rejects the identification of concrete consciousness with the Absolute. (*Ibid.*, p. 128.)
3. Karpov prefers, however, to characterize his position as 'formal realism'.

operative. Only where faith is present, uniting us to God, does philosophy adhere undeviatingly to truth.

Thus, just as there are three ways in which man makes contact with the world (external sensations, which link us to sensory reality; 'ideas', which link us to the metaphysical realm of being—the 'conceptual' realm, in Karpov's terminology—and spiritual intuition, which unites us with Deity), so the world itself can be separated into three 'strata'—sensory being, metaphysical being, and Absolute Being. Only where these three principles are harmoniously joined in man's soul do 'all things form one infinite cosmorama, fusing into one chord, one sacred song to the All-High'.[1]

At this level of 'philosophic syntheticism', as Karpov calls it, the world itself—both sensory and 'conceptual', i.e. metaphysical—should appear, in the unity of its sensory and ideal aspects, as a *single whole*: we should discover the 'law of the harmonious being of the universe'. We have already quoted Karpov's words concerning the 'mystical symbols' of the 'bonds which unite the whole cosmos'. Here the stress is on the *symbolic* meaning of the unity of created being, for 'authentic' being is beyond the limits of the world. Karpov decisively rejects the 'absolute' character of human consciousness, i.e. he repudiates Hegel's immanentism of principle, and indeed that of all the German idealists. 'The thinking human spirit is in no sense an absolute being, nor is its thought absolute or creative.' Thus Karpov is confident—and here he is very close to Khomyakov and Kireyevski—that a 'philosophy which develops within the womb of Christianity cannot become a rationalistic philosophy'. And if rationalism has developed in the West, this can only be explained as a result of the consolidation of a *pagan* view in Western Christianity.

With this we conclude our exposition of Karpov's views.

### 8. AVSENEV

Peter Semyonovich Avsenev, Archimandrite Theophanes in monastic life (1810–52), was the son of a priest in the Government of Voronezh. Upon graduating from the Voronezh Theological Seminary he entered the Kiev Theological Academy (1829); after his graduation he was retained by the Academy to teach philosophy at Kiev University. In 1844 he took monastic orders. In 1851,

1. *Ibid.*, p. 133.

because of illness, he stopped teaching at the Academy and went to Italy, where he became Prior of the Russian Church in Rome; but he soon died (in 1852).

There was in Avsenev, in the words of his auditors, a marvellous 'harmony of thought and faith'. His lectures on philosophy won him renown far beyond the walls of the Academy and University. His erudition was extremely broad; his philosophic ideas gravitated toward Schellingism—specifically, the theories of the well-known Schellingian Schubert. Avsenev was viewed askance in the Theological Academy because of his philosophic ideas and his sympathy for Böhme and the Schellingians. We know of some of his ideas—in particular, his doctrine of the world-soul—only from the notes of his student, Bishop Theophanes Zatvornik.[1] Avsenev wrote very little, but parts of his lectures (chiefly on psychology) were published in the Jubilee Symposium of the Kiev Theological Academy. It is evident from these lectures that Avsenev defended the thesis that man's soul 'can communicate with the external world directly', i.e. apart from the organs of sense. This is not Jacobi, but an anticipation of the doctrine of intuition as it was developed in the late nineteenth century. Man's soul—Avsenev taught—is a part of the boundless ocean of spiritual being which engulfs the individual soul on all sides. The soul's 'openness' to external spiritual influences testifies to the reality of what exceeds the limits of the 'everyday life of the soul' (clairvoyance, somnambulism, etc.). Unfortunately, only a small sample of Avsenev's mature thought was preserved in his published articles.

## 9. S. S. GOGOTSKI

Sylvester Sylvestrovich Gogotski (1813–89) was a pupil of Avsenev's. The son of a priest, he studied originally in the Podolsk Theological Seminary; at the age of twenty he entered the Kiev Theological Academy, and upon graduation became a teacher there. He subsequently received the degree of Master of Philosophy from Kiev University, where he also became a teacher of philosophy. Gogotski wrote a great deal. His works on Kant and Hegel, his outline of the history of modern philosophy, and his five-volume Philosophical Lexicon deserve special mention.[2] He also wrote a great deal on pedagogical questions.

1. See the Collected Letters of Bishop Theophanes (Pt. II, pp. 109–11).
2. The best account of Gogotski is given in Chizhevski, *Hegel in Russland.*

Gogotski is usually considered a Russian Hegelian, but this is only partly correct. He placed high value on the connection of the separate phenomena in man with an integral historical process which has its own historical dialectic, effected by divine action on the human will. But this historical dialectic is not to be identified with pure logos. History does not exhibit the self-revelation of an Absolute Spirit which is beyond the limits of history, although operative in it. Gogotski thus repudiates Hegel's immanentism of principle and asserts a *theism*. But the dialectical method does not introduce us to the mystery of individual being; it exhibits only the *essence*, not the *being* or individual energy, of the subject. Dialectic has both upper and lower limits—God, and the individual human being ; but this does not weaken its power as an instrument for analyzing the historical process.

Gogotski valued Kant very highly, especially his *Critique of Judgment,* which he considered 'almost a prophetic book', because it linked the world of phenomena to the realm of unconditional being and established the principles of a teleological interpretation of being. However, he saw in Kant's theory of knowledge a root mistake: the restricting of the power of cognition to the phenomenal world. 'Reason, for Kant, lacks the capacity to penetrate to the essence of things; for him the essence of things is incapable of being understood.' Gogotski valued Hegel highly because he healed the rupture between being and cognition, treating the essence of the world as Spirit—a living Principle which brings life into the world.

Another member of the Kiev School was I. G. Mikhnevich, who became a teacher in the Odessa Lyceum, expounded Schelling very clearly, and was somewhat inclined toward Hegel. This school also included the more prolific O. M. Novitski (likewise a teacher of philosophy in the Odessa Lyceum), who developed a doctrine of reason as the capacity to intuit supersensory being—through ideas. These intuitions of reason are appropriated by the heart, and at this stage become feelings; then through the activity of the imagination they are transformed into rational knowledge, and rationality forms concepts. At this stage the intuitions of reason become 'easily understandable', but this only exhibits the more clearly their incapacity to grasp Infinite Being, the intuition of which was their point of departure. 'The Unconditional becomes inaccessible to knowledge', so that our spirit requires Revelation, which connects us to the genuine foundation of being—to God.

## 10. I. D. YURKEVICH

Let us turn to the most important representative of the Kiev school —Pamphilus Danilovich Yurkevich (1827–74). Upon graduating from the Poltava Seminary, Yurkevich entered the Kiev Theological Academy (in 1847), where he attended Avsenev's lectures. After his graduation (in 1851) he was retained by the Academy to teach philosophy. His various articles—especially his article 'From the Science of the Human Spirit', which was devoted to a criticism of Chernyshevski's study The Anthropological Principle in Philosophy (see the following chapter), as well as his brilliant article 'Against Materialism'—attracted wide notice. In 1861 he was offered a chair of philosophy at Moscow University, and he remained there for the rest of his life.

Yurkevich did not write a great deal, but all of his works are very significant. Let us mention first his article 'The Heart and Its Significance in Human Life' and his articles 'Materialism and the Tasks of Philosophy', 'From the Science of the Human Spirit', 'The Idea', and 'Plato's Doctrine of Reason and Kant's Doctrine of Experience'. Some of Yurkevich's articles and books were devoted to problems of education. His critique of materialism, incidentally, evoked sharp and ill-mannered articles and comments in the Russian journals; Russian radical circles associated Yurkevich's name for a long time—quite without reason—with the idea of 'obscurantism'; and this hindered the acceptance of his remarkable theoretical views. However, his critique of materialism is profound and important enough to retain its force even today. 'Philosophy can do more', he wrote, 'than simply define the validity, significance, and limits of experience.' Yurkevich showed magnificently that materialism does not grasp the real essence of being. He did not reject the reality of the material realm, but he justly emphasized that a 'new mythology' has often grown up around the study of matter. 'Is it not a myth', he asked, 'that there is a transition from quantity to quality in things?' This remark unquestionably falls on materialism's most sensitive point.

Let us consider first Yurkevich's anthropology, to which his remarkable study of the heart was devoted. He took as his point of departure the biblical doctrine of the heart as the focus of man's life, and attempted to illuminate this doctrine in a new way by means of the results of science. He decisively repudiated the one-sided intellectualism of modern times, which regards *thinking* as the central and basic power of the soul. Language itself (the Russian language, in any case) indicates that there is something in man which is 'intimate' [*zadushevny*, literally 'behind the soul', *Trans.*], i.e. a profundity 'behind' the soul, considered as a system of psychological processes including thought. This profundity, *for the sake of which* thought arises, is the heart—the focus of spiritual life. Thought, and all intellectual activity, draws sustenance from this spiritual focus. Man's heart as a physical organ is also a focal point; in it the central nervous system is connected with the sympathetic nervous system. The heart is directed both toward man's centre and his periphery. Thus it guarantees his wholeness as well as his individuality and uniqueness, which is expressed not in thought but in feelings and reactions. '*The tree of knowledge*', Yurkevich says, '*is not the tree of life*.' Not thought, but the life of the heart—the immediate and profound experiences which come from it—forms man's 'essence'. If reason is a light, the life of the spirit is generated prior to this light—in the darkness and obscurity, the very depths, of the soul. The light of understanding arises *from* the spiritual life; and for this reason the mind is the *summit*, not the *root*, of this life. The profound words of the Apostle Peter concerning the 'hidden man of the heart' [I. Peter, iii: 4] correctly point out the presence of a concealed but basic spiritual life, from which the 'higher' consciousness draws sustenance and inspiration. And this is why the key to the understanding of man and the elucidation of the most important and influential impulses of his soul lie in the heart.

In his article 'From the Science of the Human Spirit' Yurkevich carried his profound reflections on man's soul further, in order to show the utter superficiality of materialism. 'Spirit cannot be explained on the basis of matter', he wrote, 'because only in *interaction with our spirit* does this matter assume the form in which we know it in our experience.' To reject the non-material because it is 'nowhere evident' is to fail to understand the nature of introspection, which is genuine inner experience. Yurkevich's article, which was directed against Chernyshevski's work The Anthropological Principle in Philosophy, evoked a considerable stir—not, however, to the credit of Russian philosophy, for in this polemic superficial materialism showed itself as particularly shallow.

'Plato's Doctrine of Reason and Kant's Doctrine of Experience' is a very interesting work and one rich in ideas. Yurkevich moved decisively from Kant's transcendental idealism toward a metaphysical idealism in the spirit of Plato. However, an acceptance of the world of ideas is not a sufficient basis, according to him, for the movement from 'conceptual' being to 'substantial' being. Reality is not wholly grasped by logical ideas; the 'principle' which posits this reality is not 'essence' but 'existence'. The revelation which is provided by ideas cannot introduce us to the mystery of individual being, much less the mystery of Suprasistence, which translates the *possible* (idea) into the *actual* (reality). Here is a further remarkable idea, which we shall encounter in another version in V. D. Kudryavtsev (see Ch. XVIII): 'That which can be [=idea] becomes that which is [=reality] by means of that which *ought* to be.'

Yurkevich's idea that 'philosophy is the business not of man but of mankind' is also very interesting and important. (We have already seen this idea in Kireyevski.)

Yurkevich was far ahead of his time, and there was good reason for his influence on Vladimir Solovyov. It can only be regretted that Yurkevich's remarkable works are almost entirely inaccessible to the [Russian] reader, never having been reprinted. If his philosophic works are ever collected and reprinted, his profound views will take on new life for Russian thought. We wish especially to mention his theoretical constructions in the spirit of concrete idealism,[1] which were later developed by Prince Serge Trubetskoi (Ch. XXVII).

## 11. ARCHIMANDRITE BUKHAREV

The further manifestations of philosophic activity in the Theological Academies extend into the second half of the nineteenth century. Here we find philosophic systems appearing; we shall therefore defer their study to Pt. III. But we have yet to acquaint ourselves with the work of one of the most gifted and original thinkers of the Moscow Theological Academy—Archimandrite Feodor Bukharev, whose name is associated with the most profound and creative formulation of the question of 'Orthodox culture'. Secularism, as we have seen, split Russian thought in two at the same time that it facilitated a sharp formulation of the question of the relationship of Christianity to culture. An insistent attempt was growing in the Russian consciousness to tear culture away from the Church; this was a pure secularism. At the same time, an attempt developed—which was sometimes naïve, sometimes more profound—to establish peace between the

1. Yershov, *Puti razvitiya filosofi v Rossi* [Paths of Philosophic Development in Russia], Vladivostok, 1922, p. 27.

Church and culture. But from the time of Gogol, a positive appraisal of culture in the name of Christ began to be advanced from the very depths of the ecclesiastical consciousness. This Christian acceptance of culture, prophetically foreshadowed by Gogol, resulted in the comparatively minor and uninfluential theoretical constructions of 'Orthodox culture'. Among these the theories of Archim. Bukharev have a very special place.

Alexander Matveyevich Bukharev (1822–71), Archim. Feodor in monastic life, was born into the family of a deacon in the Government of Tver. Upon graduation from the Tver Seminary he entered Moscow Theological Academy, from which he graduated at the age of twenty-two. Not long before his graduation he took monastic orders, after some hesitation. He was a professor at the Academy (holding the Chair of Holy Scripture), but in 1854 he took the Chair of Dogmatics at the Kazan Academy, and at the same time became Inspector of the Academy. Within four years, as a result of friction with the Rector of the Academy, he resigned his professorship and took a position with the Commission of Religious Censorship in St. Petersburg. During this period he did a great deal of creative work on general as well as purely theological questions. He worked a great deal on a book devoted to the interpretation of the Apocalypse. But new clouds began to gather over him; his life was darkened by a harsh and unseemly polemic instigated by a certain Askochenski, a man who had attended the Theological Academy (in Kiev) and then become publisher of a journal *Domashnyaya beseda* [Domestic Conversation]. Bukharev had published several of his articles as a book, under the title Orthodoxy and the Contemporary World (St. Petersburg, 1860) —we shall discuss this work below—and it evoked an extremely violent critique on the part of Askochenski, who declared that every man who 'defends Orthodoxy and stretches out his hand to contemporary civilization is a coward, renegade, and traitor'. This polemic had unhappy consequences for Archim. Feodor: he was forced to give up his position as censor, and the religious journals refused to print his articles. When he was planning to publish his book on the Apocalypse, the Synod, on Askochenski's recommendation, forbade its publication. This was the last drop which filled his cup of torment to overflowing; he resolved to give up monastic orders, since it was impossible for him to observe the first monastic vow, that of obedience. He gave up monastic life in the name of religious freedom (in 1863), was soon married and lived, in very difficult circumstances, for eight more years, defending his ideas as fervently as before. His life was cut short in his forty-seventh year.

We shall not enter into a general characterization of Archim. Bukharev's theological views, but shall consider only his attitude toward the problem of 'secular' culture. The most remarkable thing about Bukharev is that, though he firmly accepted the essential distinction between the Divine and 'secular' realms (in the world's sinful condition [1]), he also deeply sensed the light of God *throughout secular life*. The contrast of Church and culture fell away, as something illusory or deliberately invented: to the extent that Christians are the agents of culture there can be no real opposition between the two. This opposition is exaggerated in order to obscure the rays of Christian strength and justice which illuminate culture. 'We should defend all aspects of humanity', Bukharev wrote, 'as the property of Christ. . . . The repression, constraint, and especially the repudiation of anything truly human, is an infringement of Christ's grace.' [2] 'Orthodoxy should shine like a sun in all civil life, in the whole circuit of our sciences, arts, and official relations.' [3] Thus Bukharev takes up arms against the tendency to isolate civil and everyday affairs completely from Christian principles.[4] He puts forth an interesting and profound thought concerning 'today's Arianism, which does not wish to see Christ as the true God. . . . in the whole realm of the sciences, arts, and social and private life'. [5] Bukharev sharply flays this 'timorousness before the divine', the refusal to recognize that 'creative forces and ideas are only a reflection of the Word of God'.[6] He especially reproaches ecclesiastical people on this score —men in whom 'spiritual consciousness of the truth in Christ is bound up with fearfulness and relentlessness toward everything that does not openly bear Christ's seal'.[7] Bukharev himself deeply sensed the 'hidden warmth' of Christ's Church, at just those points where there was no external evidence of Christ's presence. He attempted to re-establish the 'appurtenance to Christ' of these seemingly non-Christian phenomena. He spoke of a man (obviously himself) 'who had entered the dark depths of an idea which in modern philosophy had perverted Christ's truth'; and this man

1. *Tri pisma k Gogolyu* [Three Letters to Gogol], St. Petersburg, 1861, p. 58.
2. *O pravoslavi v otnosheni k sovremennosti* [Orthodoxy and the Contemporary World], St. Petersburg, 1860, p. 20.
3. *Ibid.*, p. 316.      4. *Ibid.*, p. 197.
5. *Ibid.*, p. 64.      6. *Ibid.*, p. 223.
7. *Tri pisma* . . . [Three Letters . . .], p. 5.

'was blinded by the *abundance of Christ's light which there revealed itself to believing thought*'.[1] The important thing is to view contemporary culture with believing thought; then the 'hidden warmth' of Christ's work will reveal itself even where there is apparently no trace of Christianity. In one passage, Bukharev interprets the development of thought from Fichte to Hegel as a one-sided, and therefore incorrect, assertion of the doctrine of Godmanhood.[2] This idea was subsequently developed, although in a different way, by Fr. Sergius Bulgakov in his outstanding work *Die Tragödie der Philosophie*. Bukharev was not afraid to express the idea that 'Christ as the Lamb of God also took philosophical sins upon himself'; [3] he even put forward the interesting theological idea of the 'mystery of Christ's grace with respect to human thought'.[4]

These propositions provide a foundation not only for the acceptance of contemporary culture but also for an indication of how the Christian should act in the circumstances of contemporary life. The spirit of freedom, which Bukharev felt with exceptional force, *undermines all secularism*. The contrast of Church and culture is seen as illusory and deliberately exaggerated. Every repression of free creative activity in culture is a 'halting of the divine worship of thought and heart'.[5] This is not to be interpreted as a complacent optimism that seeks to find Christian meaning in what is wholly alien to Christianity. On the contrary: Bukharev's fundamental emphasis is on the discernment of the *hidden* Christian meaning of modern culture; he does not deny its extra-Christian surface. He is *internally free* of the psychology of secularism—and this explains the inspiring force of his ideas. He believes that :

'a day will come when the intellectual and moral conflicts of our time will be exhibited and clarified on the same living foundations as those on which the Fathers of the Church refuted the ancient heretics; and then much that *now passes for Orthodox* will be seen as more akin to un-Orthodoxy.'[6]

For Bukharev the 'social ulcers and scars, whose uncovering is the usual subject of today's discussions and writing, are essentially the ulcers and scars of that spiritual leprosy with which *Christians themselves* are stricken'.[7] Both the miseries and the joys of contemporary life are ultimately derived from the Christian principles of the contemporary world: the miseries result from abandoning

1. *O pravoslavi* . . . [Orthodoxy . . .], p. 42.    2. *Ibid.*, pp. 43–5.
3. *Ibid.*, p. 45.          4. *Loc. cit.*          5. *Ibid.*, p. 65.
6. *Ibid.*, pp. 66f.                                7. *Ibid.*, p. 209.

these principles, the joys from accepting and following them. Our true humanity is revealed only when we are faithful to Christ: 'A man who is upright and faithful in his obedience to Christ, the Son of God, is also faithful to his own *human* dignity.' [1]

Bukharev opposed a supercilious attitude toward the Western world: 'It would be even more dangerous and disastrous for *us* if we renounced our brotherhood with the Western nations, so as not to have to make use of anything that is theirs.' [2] 'The Orthodoxy which we possess . . . is given to us for the whole world. . . . It makes us *debtors* to other nations.' Strong in his faith in the 'universal' meaning of Orthodoxy, Bukharev was able to make a bold approach to Western Christianity. [3]

Florovsky judges Bukharev's theoretical constructions very harshly, reproaching him with sentimentality, utopianism, 'unrestrained optimism', and, finally, with 'not having been able to solve the problem which occupied him throughout his life'. [4] These reproaches have a very strange and arbitrary ring. What Florovsky calls sentimentalism was in fact a deep insight into the 'hidden warmth', emanating from the Church, which suffuses contemporary culture. Gogol was a 'prophet of Orthodox culture', but Bukharev offered a positive exhibition of the Orthodox view of the contemporary world. The most important tendencies of subsequent Russian religious thought (Vladimir Solovyov, in a part of his theoretical constructions, and especially Fr. Sergius Bulgakov)— even in those who, like Rozanov, remained 'outside the walls of the Church'—are a direct continuation of Bukharev's 'theology of culture'. Chaadayev also constructed a theology of culture, but it was inspired by Western Christianity and influenced by the French 'traditionalists', whereas Bukharev's theology of culture was inwardly connected with Orthodoxy. His overcoming of secularism from within is an important contribution, and one for which he will always be remembered.

1. *Ibid.*, p. 307.     2. *Ibid.*, p. 317.     3. *Loc. cit.*
4. G. Florovsky, *Puti russkovo bogosloviya* [Paths of Russian Theology], pp. 347f.

# CHAPTER XI

## The Crisis in Russian Life. The Period of Alexander II

THE BEGINNINGS OF POSITIVISM AND MATERIALISM IN RUSSIAN
PHILOSOPHY. CHERNYSHEVSKI AND HIS FOLLOWERS. THE
FURTHER EVOLUTION OF RADICALISM IN THE 1870'S. N. V.
CHAIKOVSKI AND THE 'GOD-MEN'

### I. GENERAL REMARKS

WITH the death of Nicholas I (in 1855) a sharp external and internal crisis took place in Russian life. The last years of his reign had been marked by a tormenting gloom—the limits of patience and endurance within which the heart can still 'reconcile itself to life' had already been passed. The basic tendencies of Russian thought and life became fully crystallized in the stifling atmosphere of a police state—an atmosphere of political coercion and tormenting tension—in which University chairs of philosophy were abolished and the New Testament itself aroused doubts on the part of the censors as to its suitability for general distribution. During the last decade of the reign of Nicholas I Russian political and intellectual radicalism acquired its final hardening; with the change of regime this radicalism entered the scene with full clarity and decisiveness. But other tendencies of life and thought were also showing signs of inner maturity, and they were psychologically very close to radicalism in their dogmatism. Ideological searchings continued; their dialectic was not yet completed. But most of them were so mature and clearly formed as to be ready for systematic development. This development occurred slightly later—during the 1870's—but this was already, in essence, a period of systems. The 1860's did not yet offer finished ideological positions, but their foundations were clearly present.

The *religious* theme, which still preserved its central importance, was the basic watershed. Russian secularism, which Russian thinkers had been elaborating since the middle of the eighteenth century, was still clothed in the form of aesthetic humanism, a form which it had acquired during the first half of the nineteenth century. But in the 1840's the idea of socialism became an ingredient in Russian secularism, and henceforth it was to be the secular equivalent of a religious world-view. In conformity with the shift toward democratization in Russian life (with the emancipation of the peasants in 1861) secularism took on 'enlightment' features, but enlightenment in Russia did not find the pure expression that it had once had in Europe. With the exception of the liberal tendency, which was never really successful in Russian life, the various secular tendencies—although they defended the idea of enlightenment—did not find their motive force or creative meaning in this idea.[1] Their meaning was not to be found in the rudimentary doctrine of enlightenment, but in intense utopian searchings and a need to satisfy *religious* demands apart from Christianity, or at least apart from the Church. Secularism became either a theomachy or a search for God—and even when those who were called 'nihilists' tended toward atheism, it was a stormy and passionate atheism which merged into fanatical sectarianism. No one followed Herzen in his tragic deviation from the religious theme. Not only did this theme retain its central position in the spiritual searchings of Russian thinkers; it also subdued their minds. Secular theologians emerged one after the other. Two great Russian writers of the second half of the nineteenth century —Tolstoy and Dostoyevsky—aroused all Russian society religiously with their passionate language; and the Russian artists who devoted themselves to an oversimplified enlightenment doctrine continually and brilliantly reminded society of Christ (Kramskoi, Ge, Polenov, *et al.*).

## 2. THE GROWTH OF RADICALISM

Let us turn first to a study of the radical tendency, a tendency which left its imprint on the whole age. It had already taken substantial shape during the last years of the reign of Nicholas I. We need only mention the Petrashevski Circle—with its enthusiasm for Fourier and the other French socialists—of which Dostoyevsky,

---

1. It is thus a mistake to characterize the spiritual atmosphere of the period of Alexander II as one of 'enlightenment', as Chizhevski, for example, does (*Hegel in Russland*, p. 299).

among others, was a member. In addition to the Petrashevski Circle other groups of young people were being formed; and when the unsuccessful [Crimean] war of 1854–5 aroused Russian society, evoking a whole movement of self-accusation, the young people began to speak a language which had not previously been heard in Russia. Dostoyevsky and Tolstoy belonged to this generation, but it also included men of less renown, who soon entered the scene as representatives of a radical and even revolutionary temper of mind.

A sharp opposition to the previous generation and a struggle against its 'romanticism', its love of abstract thought, and its cult of art, were the characteristic features of this generation—which was between twenty and thirty years old in 1855. This new generation defended 'realism' and sought support in exact knowledge; hence their admiration, which often took the form of religious reverence, for the 'exact' (i.e. natural) sciences. The cult of art declined; in its place a demand arose that art should point out man's paths in life. This moralizing tendency corresponded to a general predominance of morality, and morality itself was discussed chiefly in terms of utilitarianism. However, a belief in the individual and his creative powers, a defence of the soul's 'natural' impulses, and a naïve faith in 'rational egoism', became the supreme principles of morality and of the whole world-view. All of this formed a kind of psychological unity which was felt as setting off the 'new people' from the previous generation. This new mentality was formed very rapidly, and it soon created a real gulf between the new epoch and the preceding ones. N. G. Chernyshevski—who, in his personality, his ideas, and his very style of writing, clearly expressed what was distinctive in the whole tendency of Russian radicalism during these years—was the intellectual leader and brilliant representative of this whole temper of mind.

### 3. N. G. CHERNYSHEVSKI. BIOGRAPHY

Nicholas Gavrilovich Chernyshevski (1828–89) was the son of a priest in the city of Saratov. His father intended him to take up a clerical life; but, seeing his son's outstanding abilities, he gave him a thorough education at home and, when he was sixteen, placed him directly in the senior class of the Theological Seminary. Chernyshevski astounded both his teachers and the other students with his vast learning—he had a thorough command of the modern languages, in addition to Latin, Greek, and Hebrew. His reading was quite exceptional, and set him off sharply among his comrades. Upon graduation from the Seminary he did not enter the Theological Academy but, with his parents' consent, entered the Faculty of History and Philology of St. Petersburg University (at the age of eighteen), graduating within four years. Chernyshevski's philosophic and socio-political convictions were formed during his student years; we should note especially his membership in the circle of Irenarch Vvedenski (1815–55), who was considered at the time the 'founder of nihilism'. In Vvedenski's circle discussion centred on socio-political, and sometimes philosophic, themes. Even at this time Chernyshevski's socialist sympathies were clearly defined. He followed socialist thought very carefully, especially that of the French writers.[1] In 1848 he wrote in his Diary that he had become 'a whole-hearted partisan of the socialists and communists'.[2] In 1849 he wrote: 'It seems to me that my loyalty is almost exclusively to Hegel . . .; I have a presentiment that I shall be enthusiastic about Hegel.' But very soon he changed his mind: 'Hegel is a slave of the present state of things, the present order of society. . . . His philosophy is remote from violent reforms and utopian reveries.' Chernyshevski's revolutionary mood, which had grown out of his study of socialist utopias, drew him away from Hegel. But in the same year (1849) he read Feuerbach's *The Nature of Christianity*. This book did not immediately shake Chernyshevski's religious views—concerning which see below— but he continued his study of Feuerbach and soon became an ardent and convinced adherent of the latter's anthropologism and materialistic tendencies.[3]

Upon graduating from the University, Chernyshevski became a Gymnasium teacher in his native city of Saratov. He spent a little more than two years in this position. During this time he married, and then went to St. Petersburg, where he devoted himself fully to journalistic work, and to science and philosophy to some extent. He passed his Master's Examination (for a chair of Russian literature) and set about writing his Master's Thesis on 'The Aesthetic Relations of Art to Reality'. The defence was conducted at the University before a very large audience, and

1. Despite the most severe measures, all the 'forbidden' books could be obtained in St. Petersburg. A raid on one bookstore brought to light more than 2,500 such books. (Yu. M. Steklov, *N. G. Chernyshevski*, St. Petersburg, 1909, p. 42, note 5.)

2. Chernyshevski, *Dnevnik* [Diary], Moscow, 1931.

3. Somewhat later (in 1850) Chernyshevski studied Helvetius's *De l'esprit* and found in it 'many ideas which I had reached with my own intellect'.

was declared satisfactory, but—upon the recommendation of Professor I. Davydov (the Schellingian whom we discussed in Chapter IV)—the Minister of Education did not certify Chernyshevski's degree. It is now clear [1] that within three years the new Minister certified the degree. But until very recently this fact remained unknown even to Chernyshevski's close relatives; [2] at this time journalistic activity absorbed his attention to such an extent that he did not even notify his relatives that he had received the degree.

In 1853 Chernyshevski began to write for two important journals of the time—*Sovremennik* [The Contemporary] and *Otechestvennyie zapiski* [Notes of the Fatherland], but after a short time he devoted himself exclusively to *Sovremennik*. His articles over a period of eight years fill eleven volumes of his collected works. Chernyshevski rapidly became the leader of the radical and socialist strata of Russian society. His notable critical studies, which later appeared under the general title Outlines of the Gogolian Period of Russian Literature, also date from this period. They were first published as a separate book in 1892, after Chernyshevski's death. His long philosophical essay The Anthropological Principle in Philosophy dates from this same period. [3] It was written in answer to P. L. Lavrov's philosophic essays (see the following chapter), and was also a retort to the criticism of P. D. Yurkevich, whom we have already met. Chernyshevski wrote a great deal on social and economic questions. In 1862 he was arrested, the reason for the arrest being a note from Herzen which was found when a certain Vetoshnikov was arrested: 'Chernyshevski and I are ready to publish *Sovremennik* either here or in Geneva.' (*Sovremennik* had been suspended for an eight-year period at the time.) The development of the revolutionary movement in Russia had already become very important, and Chernyshevski was generally regarded as its leader and inspirer. He was condemned, chiefly because of his writings—which had previously been passed by the censor. The court found Chernyshevski's relations with Herzen innocent, but declared him guilty of writing proclamations to the peasants, and sentenced him to hard labour. The court's

1. See Steklov, *op. cit.*, p. 142.

2. See Steklov, *op. cit.*, first edition, 1909; Plekhanov, *N. G. Tschernischewsky*, Stuttgart, 1894; and N. Kotlyarevski *Kanun osvobozhdeniya* [The Eve of the Emancipation], St. Petersburg, 1916.

3. All of Chernyshevski's philosophic works, including his Master's Thesis have been collected in one volume called *Izbrannyie filosofskiye sochineniya* [Selected Philosophic Writings], Moscow, 1938.

sentence created a very unfavourable impression even among conservative circles, not to speak of the radical youth. Chernyshevski was exiled to the province of Yakutsk in Siberia; he tried to escape from Yakutsk several times, without success, which merely made his situation worse. Finally, in 1883, he was permitted to return to European Russia. He was sent to Astrakhan, but within six years was permitted to return to his native city of Saratov. However Chernyshevski's strength was already failing. He died in Saratov in October 1889.

### 4. INFLUENCES ON CHERNYSHEVSKI

The question as to the influences under which Chernyshevski's philosophic views were formed is not yet sufficiently clear. Feuerbach is usually considered the basic influence,[1] and Chernyshevski himself provides sufficient evidence for this assertion—especially in the letters and articles written during and after his exile. In letters to his sons (1887) he wrote:

'If you wish to gain an idea of my opinion of human nature, you can do so by studying the one thinker of our century who, in my opinion, had wholly correct ideas about things. I have not read him for fifteen years, but in my youth I knew whole pages of his works *by heart*, . . . and I have remained his true follower.'[2]

In another place Chernyshevski, admitting the desirability of a new theory of man and of knowledge, wrote: '*To date* the best expositions of scientific ideas and the basic problems of man's love of knowledge have been provided by Feuerbach.'[3]

From these words one may conclude that Chernyshevski had a very high respect for Feuerbach, but nothing more. We shall see below that Chernyshevski, as Masaryk has justly noted,[4] was a *vulgar materialist*—whereas Feuerbach's materialism was only the limiting point of his anthropologism.[5]

---

1. This thesis is defended by Steklov, *op. cit.*, I, 55, 226; Plekhanov, *Sochineniya* [Works], V, 194; Kotlyarevski, *op. cit.*, p. 292, *passim;* Masaryk, *The Spirit of Russia*, II, 4; *et al.* Shpet takes decisive issue with this view—and with good reason—in his article 'Antropologizm Lavrova v svete istori filosofi' ['Lavrov's Anthropologism in the Light of the History of Philosophy'] in the volume on Lavrov (Petrograd, 1922), pp. 91–95.
2. Quoted by Steklov, *op. cit.*, I, 225.
3. Chernyshevski, *Sochineniya*, X, 196.
4. Masaryk, *op. cit.*, II, 5.
5. See Shpet's apt comments on Feuerbach's 'materialism', *op. cit.*

The question of the roots of Chernyshevski's positivism is no
less controversial. Masaryk declares that he was a positivist 'in
Comte's sense'.[1] Chernyshevski himself, in one of his early
political articles, said of Comte: 'the founder of positive philosophy—*the only philosophic system which is true to the scientific spirit*—is
one of the greatest geniuses of our time'.[2] To be sure, somewhat
earlier (in a Diary entry for 1848) he had decisively rejected
Comte's doctrine of the three periods in the development of
thought, but this entry referred only to the first volume of Comte's
*Positive Philosophy*; he did not read the other volumes until later.
Still, the above-quoted passage is very eloquent. However, in a
letter to his sons (1876) Chernyshevski wrote:

'There is another school which has almost nothing repulsive in
it, but which seems very *ridiculous* to me. That is Auguste-Comtism.
Auguste Comte, who fancied himself a genius, has spun out a
formula concerning the three stages of thought—a formula which
is completely absurd.' [3]

These words do not give sufficient grounds for asserting that
Chernyshevski was ever *enthusiastic* about Comte. Nevertheless, his
essential positivism is not open to question.

The main sources of Chernyshevski's views are to be found in
the general scientific and philosophic literature of his time—and
above all in the *cult of science* ('scientism') which was a general
characteristic of the nineteenth century. Chernyshevski—and to
some extent Herzen—was influenced by *French* ideas, including the
socialist ideas which completely captured his mind and heart. His
socio-economic ideas had a clear *ethical* root; [4] the primacy of
ethics over 'pure' science was essential for Chernyshevski. He had
a genuine *faith* in science, in its boundless possibilities and its
cognitive power. This faith was supported by a realism which had
begun to manifest itself clearly in Russian literature in the mid-
1840's as a counterbalance to the 'romanticism' of the 'fathers'.
Russian radicalism developed generally under the sign of 'realism';
it turned in naïve adoration to natural science as a guarantee of
truth and realism—at least during the 1850's and '60's. But it
would be wrong to conclude that romanticism disappeared
entirely from this new generation; a genuine romantic basis was

1. *Ibid.*, p. 38.
2. Chernyshevski, *op. cit.*, VI, 135.
3. Quoted by Steklov, *op. cit.*, p. 230.
4. This is correctly emphasized by Masaryk, *op. cit.*, II, 32.

retained under the cover of realism. Hence the 'scientism' of the Russian radicals was really a naïve *faith* in the 'power' of science. But in its ultimate foundation this unquenched romanticism manifested itself in a 'secular religiosity' which flourished under a cover of realism and even materialism. As Kotlyarevski has justly noted, 'for Chernyshevski and his adherents the cult of Feuerbach was a poetic cult, tinged with *religiosity*'. Kotlyarevski also notes aptly that 'Feuerbach's book [*The Nature of Christianity*] was one of the canonical books of the "religion of mankind" which arose in the early nineteenth century'. [1] In Chernyshevski, too, we find a growing cult of man and mankind.

Chernyshevski's religious life was never very intense—but, strictly speaking, it never subsided. [2] In fact, while his positivist and materialist views were developing, he not only long continued to meet the requirements of the Church, but he even retained his religious convictions for a considerable time.

'What if we are to expect a new religion?' he wrote in his Diary (1848). 'My heart is agitated and my soul trembles at the thought —I wish to preserve the old one. . . . I do not believe that there will be a new one, and I should be very, very sorry to part company with Jesus Christ, Who is so kind, so dear a person, and one Who loves mankind so much.'

When Chernyshevski began, very deliberately, to develop materialist views, he also, of course, turned his back on religious ideas; but he was not left without an object of religious worship. He accepted a religious immanentism, a faith in the 'sanctity of life', in 'nature'—a passionate loyalty to the utopian dream of establishing truth and justice on earth. In this respect Nekrasov's poem 'The Prophet', dedicated to Chernyshevski, is very interesting. The last two lines read as follows:

> The God of wrath and sorrow sent him
> To put earth's slaves in mind of Christ again.

### 5. THE ANTHROPOLOGICAL PRINCIPLE

Let us turn to a study of Chernyshevski's philosophic views. His basic article in philosophy: The Anthropological Principle in

1. *Op. cit.*, pp. 295–7.
2. Cheshikhin-Vetrinski notes correctly that 'the religiosity which Chernyshevski took from his parents' home changed nothing but its object with the breakup of his world-view'. (*N. G. Chernyshevski*, Petrograd, 1923, p. 55.)

Philosophy, was written as an answer to P. L. Lavrov. It was composed carelessly; there is no sustained or systematic development of its basic thought.[1] Chernyshevski scorns not only Fichte (the younger), whom Lavrov had quoted, but also Schopenhauer. His self-assurance that there is no truth except in his own trend of thought constantly spills over into jaunty familiarity, a contemptuous attitude toward everyone who does not share his views. Chernyshevski's previous works—both his articles, which were published in the book Outlines of the Gogolian Period of Russian Literature, and his Master's Thesis—showed much more respect for 'obsolete' philosophic positions. Now, however, he became intolerant and ill-humoured; his doctoral tone was insufferable. Under the title The Anthropological Principle he expounded only an outline of the 'new' anthropology—*with no relation to philosophy*— or more precisely with no substantial analysis of philosophic themes. The theory of man is a part of a philosophic system, of course, but only a part; however, for Chernyshevski the 'new' anthropology in essence eliminated all philosophic problems. He advances his theoretical constructions naïvely, but categorically, as the indisputable 'result of contemporary science', displaying a self-assurance and cavalier attitude toward those who do not share his views, which is usual in persons untouched by the critical orientation of science.

Chernyshevski struggled passionately against the 'philosophic' dualism of man, the contrast between 'spirit' and nature.

'Man must be viewed as a being with a single nature', he wrote, 'otherwise human life is sliced up into separate halves and each aspect of man's activity is viewed either as the activity of the whole organism or . . . as connected with the whole organism.' [2]

In the same place he speaks contemptuously of the 'majority of scientists, who work in a routine way, following the old fantastic [!] method of an unnatural splitting of man'. Chernyshevski defends the unity of man, and he conceives the principles of this unity in terms of *biologism*, supplemented by propositions of the most vulgar materialism, which are very close to those of the eighteenth-century French materialists. Briefly expounding the question of

1. Shpet rightly calls this article 'chaotic'. ('In this chaotic article', he remarks scornfully, 'you can find anything whatever, except philosophy.' *Op. cit.*, p. 93.)

2. *Antropologicheski printsip v filosofi* [The Anthropological Principle in Philosophy], Geneva, 1875, p. 100.

'man as a moral being' (he never recurred to this theme), Chernyshevski speaks of man 'as a being with a stomach and a head,
bones, veins, muscles, and nerves'.[1] He goes on to expound the
oversimplified doctrine of man which in the 1850's and 60's was
proclaiming itself, with naïve and cocksure jauntiness, as the
'achievement of science'. What would Chernyshevski have said if
he had lived to read the work of such an outstanding physiologist as
Alexis Carrel—for example his *Man the Unknown?* In his time the
'mystery' of man seemed so simple. We read in this same study,
for example, that 'sensation is like *any other chemical process* . . .', to
say nothing of his assertion that life is simply a 'highly complex
chemical process'.[2] It has been justly noted [3] that Chernyshevski
made no effort to prove his theses, but simply imposed his ideas on
the reader, expounding them as the 'results of the latest science'.
Strictly speaking, the Anthropological Principle . . . defends a
position of *materialistic biologism* rather than materialism. Chernyshevski considers this the 'scientific trend in philosophy',
contrasting it to all metaphysical systems, which are 'survivals of
a fantastic world-view'.[4] Later his thought began to tend distinctly
toward materialism; 'that which exists', he declared, 'is called
matter'.[5] In other words, only material being exists. In the
Anthropological Principle . . ., to be sure, Chernyshevski acknowledged the independent being of the psyche, merely emphasizing
that it is subject to the law of causalty,[6] but in his letters from
Siberia he asserted that 'sensations of light are simply undulations
of the ether which have reached the brain and continue to act
there'.[7] There is no 'transformation' of any kind: psychical processes
are simply physical undulations. Steklov, himself a materialist, says
that this vulgarly materialistic view carried the fundamental
principles of materialism 'to extreme logical conclusions'.

An assertion of naïve realism is characteristic of the oversimplified biologism which captured Chernyshevski's thought. He regards
the whole tendency of transcendentalism as 'illusionism' and, even
more harshly, as 'metaphysical nonsense'. He also sharply opposes
the assertion of the positivists that nothing can be known that is
beyond the boundaries of experience. He does not wish to set any

1. *Ibid.*, p. 66.                    2. *Ibid.*, p. 67.
3. Kotlyarevski, *op. cit.*, p. 303.          4. *Op. cit.*, p. 39.
5. These and other passages from the book *Chernyshevski v Sibiri* [Cher-
nyshevski in Siberia], which I was not able to consult, are quoted by Steklov,
*op. cit.*, I, 234.
6. *Op. cit.*, p. 54.                    7. Steklov, *op. cit.*, I, 243.

limits to knowledge whatever; and, of course, he is faithful to the spirit of a 'scientific theory of philosophy' in defending science's right to frame hypotheses. His positivism lies in his subordination of the 'moral' realm, i.e. all spiritual and intellectual activities, to physico-chemical principles. This is an oversimplification of the problems of the world which results in an elimination of philosophy. In a letter from Siberia Chernyshevski wrote: 'I am a thinker who holds unswervingly to the scientific point of view. My duty is to consider everything I think about from the scientific point of view.' [1] And he conceives this 'scientific point of view' as the subordination of every object of knowledge to physico-chemical principles. This unrestricted and uncritical subordination of all the themes of knowledge to the principles which prevail in the lowest realm of being, has been justly called an 'alogism'.[2]

Chernyshevski's realism, the striving to take 'reality' as his point of departure, is, of course, the strong side of his position. His follower Pisarev later expressed this realism in a celebrated formula: 'Words and illusions perish; *facts remain.*' The philosophic form of this 'factolatry' is positivism, an oversimplified and naïve doctrine, but one which corresponded to the general tendencies of the age.

## 6. ETHICS

We have already spoken of the central place of ethics in Chernyshevski's spiritual orientation; his was a deeply moral nature, with a predilection for moralizing and a radical insistence on principles. He was early carried away by socialism [3]—inspired by the idea of an essential change in the social order. Like Herzen and the Slavophiles, he believed deeply in the Russian *obshchina* [village commune]. He was, indeed, the leader of Russian socialist Populism. Chernyshevski's theoretical views in the field of ethics were distinguished neither by originality nor profundity. He was an admirer of utilitarianism and the system of 'rational egoism', which he regarded as a 'scientific foundation for morality'. This has a very naïve ring, but Chernyshevski, like the whole Russian radical tendency, spoke stubbornly and repeatedly of a 'scientific' foundation for ethics, a 'foundation' to be discovered in the data

1. *Ibid.*, p. 235.          2. Shpet, *op. cit.*, p. 93.
    3. Even before his acquaintance with Fourier—who left a very deep mark on Chernyshevski's ethics—he wrote in his Diary (July 1848): 'I am being more strongly confirmed in the maxims of the socialists.' Chernyshevski valued Considérant very highly, especially his *La Destinée sociale.*

of psychology. In the following chapter, which is devoted to the Russian 'semi-positivists', we shall find an echo of these ideas. 'The natural sciences', Chernyshevski wrote, 'have already developed to the point where they provide a great deal of material for the exact [!] solution of moral problems.' [1] By 'moral problems' he means not just ethics, but all problems of a spiritual nature. [2] Thus, after a long discussion of purely ethical themes, Chernyshevski haughtily announces that 'the method of analyzing moral concepts in the spirit of the *natural sciences* . . . provides the most unshakable foundation for these concepts'. [3]

Reasoning 'in the spirit of the natural sciences', he first of all ardently defends the complete freedom of everything 'natural' (here Fourier's influence is very strong). Rousseau's theorem concerning the 'radical goodness of human nature' made a very deep impression on Russian thinkers—both directly and through Fourier. This is particularly true of Chernyshevski—as of Herzen earlier, and especially of Pisarev, somewhat later (see below). Chernyshevski once sketched a very interesting image of the 'positive' man: he is a 'total man', i.e. one who is well integrated and inwardly harmonious. His 'positiveness' coincides with an absence of 'diseased imagination', but it 'does not weaken the force of his feeling or the energy of his demands'. [4] Further on he affirms, following the eighteenth-century French thinkers, that the root of *all* human impulses—unselfish as well as selfish—is the same (namely, 'self-love', the 'idea of personal advantage'), [5] adding that the egoistic root of all the impulses 'does not detract from the value of *heroism* or *nobility*'. [6] It is very important to take this into account if we are to interpret Chernyshevski's ethics correctly: his 'scientific' explanation of the ethical life does not eliminate the *autonomy of*

1. *Antropologicheski printsip* . . ., p. 52. In studying Chernyshevski's ethics one must keep clearly in mind that for him the word 'moral' ['*nravstvenny*'] corresponds to the *French* word '*morale*' (as distinguished from '*physique*'). Masaryk has carefully pointed this out, *op. cit.*, II, 39. Chernyshevski's *broad* sense of of 'moral' (=spiritual) is very clearly exhibited in all of his writings. Most of the authors—including Plekhanov and Steklov—who have written on Chernyshevski's philosophy have completely failed to note this.

2. Chernyshevski makes this clear when he places 'moral and metaphysical questions' on the same level. (*Op. cit.*, p. 65.)

3. *Ibid.*, p. 97.

4. *Ocherki gogolevskovo perioda russkoi literatury* [Outlines of the Gogolian Period of Russian Literature], 1892, p. 288.

5. *Antropologicheski printsip* . . . [The Anthropological Principle . . .], pp. 84–90.

6. *Ibid.*, p. 89.

*ethical valuations*. Like Herzen, he unhesitatingly accepts the value of 'heroism' and 'nobility'—not from the 'scientific' point of view, of course (for which, according to Chernyshevski, everything is determined by egoism), but from a purely ethical point of view, which is wholly *independent* of 'science'. He fictively grounds this *contraband* employment of a purely ethical criterion—its use is more open, as we have seen, in Herzen—by identifying the good with advantage. 'We have tried to show', Chernyshevski writes, 'that the concept of good is not destroyed—but, on the contrary, is strengthened—when we discover its true nature, when we find that good is advantage.'[1] 'The morally healthy man feels *instinctively* [!] that everything unnatural is harmful and burdensome.'[2] This reference to 'moral health' is only a mask for the ethical idealism by which Chernyshevski actually lived. There was good reason for the elimination of the idea of moral responsibility from his ethics. 'Human nature is not to be upbraided . . . or praised. . . . Everything depends on circumstances: . . . in some circumstances man becomes good, in others evil.'[3] But in such a case there is no basis for *ethical passion*, which nevertheless always remained strong in Chernyshevski. Steklov—following Plekhanov—sees Chernyshevski's error in his *rationalism* (in the analysis of the moral sphere), a tendency characteristic of the 'Enlightenment'.[4] But, of course, this is not simply a matter of overcoming a primitive ethical rationalism based on 'calculation', but of realizing that the so-called 'scientific' interpretation of the moral sphere cannot conceal the fact that ethical valuation is 'autonomous', i.e. wholly ungrounded.

In fact, Chernyshevski ardently and passionately defended the individual's right to freedom. Kotlyarevski has very aptly noted that the whole tendency of radicalism rested on a 'faith in the almost miraculous power of the individual'.[5] Chernyshevski's ethical passion was defined by his ardent love for all victims of oppression. He derived his socialism and ethical personalism quite artificially from the 'new' conception of man. Like Feuerbach, Chernyshevski moved essentially in the framework of *idealism*. Only the hypnosis of 'scientism' can explain how his ethical idealism could become clothed in this ill-fitting and narrow doctrine, which regards the reduction of all human activity to egoism as the 'result of science'.

1. *Ibid.*, p. 94.                    2. *Ocherki* . . . [Outlines . . .], p. 286.
3. *Antropologicheski printsip* . . ., pp. 6of.
4. *Op. cit.*, pp. 301, 304.            5. *Op. cit.*, p. 39.

## 7. CHERNYSHEVSKI'S AESTHETICS

Chernyshevski's aesthetics is an even more tangled, but at the same time more significant and interesting, part of his philosophy. Vladimir Solovyov, in his brief but very valuable article on Chernyshevski's aesthetics, called the latter's Thesis 'the first step toward a positive aesthetics'.[1] Chernyshevski himself, in the preface to a proposed third edition of his Thesis, wrote that his contribution consisted merely in having 'succeeded in conveying certain of Feuerbach's ideas to a Russian public'—although Feuerbach wrote practically nothing on aesthetics. It appears that Chernyshevski himself was not clearly aware of the real value of his aesthetic principles. In fact, he wrote in this same preface that 'even then' (i.e. when he was writing his Thesis) he considered his own aesthetic ideas 'not particularly important', and therefore shifted the centre of gravity to 'ideas of a broader scope' 'all [of which] . . . came from Feuerbach'.

To achieve clarity on these points we must elucidate the central idea of Chernyshevski's Thesis. It consists in a rejection of idealistic aesthetics—which places highest value on the artistic *idea*—and a recognition that concrete reality is above art. It was this last thesis that Solovyov praised so highly; for Solovyov was himself struggling against idealistic aesthetics, and defending the *real* meaning and importance of beauty.[2] Extolling living reality—in opposition to the idealists, who placed value not in concrete being but in the idea which is expressed in it—Chernyshevski was, of course, close to Feuerbach; but that is all that one can say. It would be much more accurate to compare Chernyshevski's views concerning the subordinate place of art with the doctrine of a 'return to nature' which was so sharply stated by Rousseau. Art is artificial; reality is the source of beauty and truth. In one place Chernyshevski speaks with great venom of the 'principle of trimmed hedges', opposing to these 'trimmed hedges' nature in its full freedom and naturalness. He does not oppose *day-dreaming*, but he opposes aesthetic sentimentalism. In so far as day-dreaming and even fantastic constructions occur in real life, they possess true value as a living part of reality. But, in so far as we cultivate dreams and *oppose* them to reality, in so far as we retreat into an *artificial* and invented world—i.e. retreat from reality—we lose contact with beauty. This is a carrying over of Rousseauistic motifs to the

1. Solovyov, *Sochineniya*, St. Petersburg, 1913, VI, 424–32.
2. Concerning Solovyov see Ch. XVI, XVII.

relationship between art and reality; there is so little of Feuerbach here that it is surprising that Chernyshevski himself credited his 'ideas of broader scope' to Feuerbach. Plekhanov [1] and Steklov [2] have even less ground for regarding Chernyshevski's aesthetics as a statement of the principles of historical materialism or a triumph of the 'anthropological principle'. Of course Chernyshevski was a follower of Feuerbach during the writing of his Thesis, and he undoubtedly tended toward materialism; but the Thesis itself—both in its theme and in its internal dialectic—shows very little evidence of this. It was a new and profound development of the *aesthetic humanism* which we have frequently had occasion to mention in the preceding chapters. But in Chernyshevski this aesthetic humanism broke sharply with philosophic idealism and associated itself with philosophic realism. Kotlyarevski aptly notes that 'the new aesthetics was created as a eulogy . . . of man . . ., who was recognized as nature's most artistic creation'. [3] This is true. And Feuerbach's influence was undoubtedly reflected both in Chernyshevski's humanism and in his religiously solicitous attitude toward human 'nature'. But the view expressed in his Thesis is broader and deeper than Feuerbach's religious cult of man. Solovyov was right in valuing this work so highly, despite the remoteness of his own philosophic position from Chernyshevski's views: Chernyshevski's aesthetics—which defended the reality of beauty or, more accurately, exalted the beauty of reality above artistic beauty—opened up new horizons for philosophical aesthetics. His aesthetic humanism contained motifs of religious immanentism which were to find rich and brilliant expression in the aesthetic searchings of Russian artists and thinkers in the twentieth century; but in other respects his aesthetic humanism was close to the position of Dostoyevsky and Solovyov.

In Chernyshevski's time there was much talk about the 'destruction of aesthetics' (in Pisarev, for example; see below), but he himself was in no sense a destroyer of aesthetics. It is incorrect to conclude—as Masaryk, for example, does—that 'aesthetics became an ancillary science to ethics' for Chernyshevski. [4] Is not the opposite the case? A hymn to reality and a rhapsody over 'nature' defined Chernyshevski's aesthetics; his ethics, in turn, was based on that in which he saw genuine and essential beauty.

1. Plekhanov (*op. cit.*, V, 190) regards Chernyshevski's Thesis as 'an attempt to construct an aesthetics on the basis of a materialistic philosophy'. This is an absolutely groundless assertion.

2. *Op. cit.*, I, 319.     3. *Op. cit.*, p. 316.     4. Masaryk, *op. cit.*, II, 18.

## 8. HISTORIOSOPHICAL VIEWS

To complete our characterization of Chernyshevski's philosophic views it would be necessary to consider his conception of historiosophical problems. But, if there is anything interesting in his writings in this field, it is simply that he expressed the historiosophical ideas of the Enlightenment very clearly and strongly.[1] Plekhanov and Steklov attempt to fit his views into the formula of economic materialism, but it must be admitted that they do not succeed—especially since propositions sometimes occur in Chernyshevski himself which are obviously idealistic. The strange combination of historiosophical determinism with a doctrine of the role of the individual in history is very important, not only for Chernyshevski, but for many of his contemporaries and successors. Incidentally, this is connected with his 'Blanquism' and his sympathies for revolutionary dynamism. It has been justly noted that no Russian intellectual movement exalted the importance of the individual as much as Russian nihilism did; [2] and Chernyshevski, with whom the jaunty and cocksure nihilism of the 1860's is genetically connected, undoubtedly did a great deal for the cult of the strong individual—bold and radical in the defence of his 'natural' rights—which was so characteristic of this period.

In surveying Chernyshevski's philosophic views as a whole, we must note once again the central importance of the religious theme in the dialectic of Russian philosophic development. Russian secularism continued to develop with extreme passion, exhibiting in this very passionateness an internal inseparability from the religious theme. Chernyshevski exhibited the 'anthropological principle' more clearly than his predecessors. It was not just a question of his oversimplified psycho-physical materialism (although this materialism entered into certain tendencies of Russian thought for a long time—right up to our own day), but rather of man's truly becoming the 'measure of all things'. In this respect Chernyshevski was very much in sympathy with Feuerbach's 'religion of the man-God' and his religious anthropologism. This is why Chernyshevski always respected and revered

1. *Ibid.*, p. 25. One author has correctly noted that Chernyshevski expounded his historiosophical views 'in a more seductively clear and decisive form than anyone before or after him'. (P. G. Struve, 'K istori nashevo filosofskovo razvitiya' ['On the History of Our Philosophic Development'], *Problemy idealizma* [Problems of Idealism], Moscow, 1902.)

2. Andreyevich, *Opyt filosofi russkoi literatury* [An Essay in the Philosophy of Russian Literature], 1922, p. 220.

Feuerbach, and Feuerbach alone. But in developing his aesthetics, Chernyshevski was motivated by a general gravitation toward 'reality', and thus followed Feuerbach in advancing ideas which were obviously related to other tendencies. Similarly, his philosophic legacy cannot be placed within the framework of pure Feuerbachianism, much less that of historical materialism—as Plekhanov and Steklov assert. Neither does Chernyshevski's philosophic legacy fit into an 'Enlightenment' framework, as other writers would have it. His aesthetic humanism is broader and deeper than Enlightenment doctrines, although enlightenment ideas occupy a considerable place in his thought. Chernyshevski is one of the most outstanding representatives of Russian secularism, a secularism which aimed to replace the religious world-view while preserving all the values revealed to the world in Christianity. The 'hidden warmth' of a genuine idealism suffuses Chernyshevski's cold and often shallow formulas: his aesthetic rhapsodizing over reality is unexpectedly pierced by the rays of that luminous cosmism which marks the metaphysical intuitions of Orthodoxy. (We have already seen this in Fr. Bukharev.) Chernyshevski has often been forced into stylized systems by various branches of Russian radicalism, but he himself was broader than their systems. We did not have an opportunity, and indeed it was unnecessary, to expound his economic ideas; but even here he does not fit into the schemes of economic materialism, despite frequent attempts to make him do so. He was broader even than his own obstinate assertions, which were so often determined by his social utopianism and political radicalism. Even in his stubborn and oversimplified utilitarianism, Chernyshevski, as we have seen, sometimes suddenly—and in spite of his own principles—defends the truth and justice of purely ethical valuations. Secularism *distorted* and *impoverished* his philosophic talent. The internal disharmony which runs through all of Chernyshevski's work is perhaps the most essential thing that we find in him. He became the founder of Russian positivism and materialism, serving these movements with all his energy and sacrificing his philosophic talent to them. But the inner disharmony of Chernyshevski's work shows clearly enough that he himself was crowded and uncomfortable within the narrow framework of positivism and materialism.

## 9. D. I. PISAREV

We cannot refrain from saying a few words about Dimitri Ivanovich Pisarev (1840–68)—a highly talented writer, in whom philosophic radicalism took on the militant features of nihilism.[1] Pisarev himself did not like the word nihilism,[2] preferring to call his tendency 'realism'. He eulogized the ideal of the 'critically thinking individual'. But, of course, he was a most brilliant and forceful exponent of *nihilism*. One of his brilliant (and very early) articles bears the characteristic title 'Nineteenth-Century Scholasticism'. For Pisarev all abstract questions are mere scholasticism; for example, the problem of the 'self' is a scholastic problem because, being insoluble, it is a 'vain play of the mind'. The shift toward realism and concrete reality which was the motive force in Chernyshevski's spiritual world, here reached its extreme limit, restricting the work of the mind to problems which are evoked by the 'immediate demands of life'.[3]

In his youth Pisarev was enthusiastic about Gogol's Selected Passages from Letters to My Friends, a book marked by an intense religious quest and an anxious asceticism. He joined a 'society of thinking people', which gathered for 'devout conversations and mutual moral support'. The mood of this circle has justly been compared to that of the mystical groups of the time of Alexander I.[4] We should also note that during this period Pisarev translated a canto of Klopstock's *Messiah*. Very soon, however, this religious mood subsided. He turned to another faith, devoting himself to it with the same omnivorous absorption—bordering on fanaticism—which he had earlier brought to his 'devout conversations'. The catechism of this new faith was made up of the secular myths typical of the 1860's in Russia: above all, an 'all-absorbing faith in the natural sciences'. Russian radicalism, up to and including the official Soviet philosophy of Titanism, has been organically united with a naïve, truly 'mystical' faith in the natural sciences; although in its essence Russian radicalism—including the Titanist tendency—has always been deeply idealistic. It is not surprising that Pisarev's new faith made him an uncritical admirer of

1. Masaryk (*op. cit.*, II, 53) justly characterizes Pisarev as the *enfant terrible* of the whole radical tendency of this period.

2. We have pointed out that Herzen willingly accepted this term, defending nihilism as freedom from authority and prejudice.

3. Pisarev, *Sochineniya* [Works], ed. Pavlenkov, 1897, I, 365. Concerning Pisarev see Masaryk, *op. cit.*, II, 79–92.

4. Florovsky, *Puti russkovo bogosloviya* [Paths of Russian Theology], p. 292.

materialism (he often spoke ecstatically of 'fresh [!] and healthy materialism').[1] Through this *faith* in materialism [2] Russian radicalism came close to Western Enlightenment doctrines, and Pisarev was one of their most ardent defenders. His works are filled with the historiosophical optimism which underlay the classical theory of progress. Pisarev never tired of summoning men to enlightenment and a 'reasonable world-view'. His ethical passion, which is extremely strong, was also connected with Enlightenment ideas. However, at this point features of neo-romanticism began to appear in Pisarev, and the Enlightenment doctrines began to decline. But his early death (Pisarev was drowned while swimming in the ocean at the age of twenty-seven) cut short this inner process.

Pisarev's ethical position, like that of Chernyshevski, is typical of the radical wing of Russian secularism: it is primarily a reduction of all human behaviour to egoism, an embracing of everything 'natural', and, at the same time, a faith in the 'natural' nobility and goodness of man. Motifs of Rousseauism are very strong in Pisarev, and no one else is as close intellectually as he is to that other nihilistic genius, Leo Tolstoy. Incidentally, even their attitudes toward science were identical—narrowly utilitarian. Tolstoy rejected all sciences that are not directly concerned with man and problems of human welfare; and Pisarev (for example in his article 'Nineteenth-Century Scholasticism') denied significance to scientific researches which are not related to 'living needs'. Like Tolstoy, Pisarev rebelled against 'intellectual aristocratism': 'What sort of science is it that is in its very essence inaccessible to the masses? What sort of art is it that can only be enjoyed by a few specialists?' [3] But—and this is extremely characteristic of the period—this attitude does not prevent Pisarev from defending an extreme individualism, for which reason Masaryk compares him to Nietzsche.

'We must emancipate the human individual', Pisarev wrote, 'from the various constraints which are laid upon him by the timidity of his own thought, the authority of tradition, the aspiration toward a common ideal, and all such obsolete rubbish— which prevents the living human being from breathing freely and developing himself fully.'[4]

1. *Op. cit.*, I, 356.
2. The views of M. A. Antonovich, a journalist who was very popular in radical circles of the time, were permeated with this same *faith* in materialism.
3. 'Nineteenth-Century Scholasticism', *op. cit.*, I, 366.
4. *Ibid.*, p. 339.

Such is the manifesto of this extreme individualist, who rejects alike the 'authority of tradition' and every *common* (i.e. not individual) ideal, while flaying the 'timidity of thought'. Pisarev's 'nihilism' is a consequence of his radical individualism, his passionate defence of absolute and total freedom for the individual. Therefore, although he was an extreme materialist,[1] Pisarev—like Herzen and Chernyshevski—defended man's total freedom, i.e. an autonomous freedom, independent of all 'necessity'. He did not notice the contradiction into which he, like all the other Russian positivists and semi-positivists, fell. Pisarev's ethics is an ethics of free creative activity in its extreme form; he constructed the kind of system that was later developed in France by Guyau with equal exquisiteness and inconsistency. 'The idea of duty', he wrote, 'should give way to free impulse and direct feeling.'[2] Pisarev defended ethical impressionism with youthful vehemence,[3] but at the same time he unexpectedly returned to the ideal of the integral personality,[4] giving a new interpretation to the searchings of the Slavophiles. He conceived this integration in purely psychological terms, as an absence of inner conflicts, an 'independent and completely *unartificial*[5] development': 'Try to live a *full* life.'

This summons to ethical creativity, which does not hesitate even at ethical impressionism, was united in Pisarev—as in Russian secular radicalism generally—with a very shallow rationalism. The 'critically thinking individual', concerning whom Pisarev wrote with great feeling in one of his best articles ('The Realists'), 'scorns everything that does not have essential use'.[6] He regards aspiration toward an ideal as 'aspiration toward a phantom'; but he assures us that 'prudent egoism coincides with the results of the most conscious love of man'.[7]

Pisarev was philosophically naïve, of course, but his illogical combination of idealistic passion and rudimentary materialism, sterile positivism[8] and a worship of freedom, uncritical

1. In an article on Moleschott's book, Pisarev even went so far as to assert that 'a microscope has *not yet* been invented which can follow the thought-processes in the brain of a living human being'(!).
2. Pisarev, *op. cit.*, I, 347.
3. 'I base everything on direct feeling. . . . I see in life only process; I eliminate purposes and ideals.' (*Ibid.*, pp. 368f.)
4. 'The fullest manifestation of humanity is possible only in the integral personality.' (*Ibid.*, p. 369.)
5. Rousseauistic motifs.     6. *Op. cit.*, IV, 95.     7. *Ibid.*, p. 65.
8. Pisarev constantly returns to the idea that direct obviousness 'is the only complete guaranty of reality'. (*Op. cit.*, I, 361, 369.) This is an expression of the primitive sensationalism with which Russian positivism has so often been joined.

relativism [1] and a 'conscious love of man'—remained typical of Russian secular radicalism.

Pisarev exhibits one other contradiction which is very characteristic of his, as well as a later, age: a 'destruction of aesthetics'— and at the same time a passionate search for the aesthetic aspect of life and an aversion to vulgarity and philistinism. Under the influence of Chernyshevski's defence of the primacy of reality over art, Pisarev took up arms against 'pure art'. One of his admirers assures us that Pisarev took up arms not against art as such but against its 'social foundations'.[2] This is true to some extent: in his article 'The Destruction of Aesthetics' we find such assertions as this: 'Art has converted itself with great readiness into a *lackey of luxury*.' 'Pure art is a parasitic plant which feeds constantly on the saps of human luxury.' Nevertheless, Pisarev's basic accent is not on the struggle against art's service of the rich, but on motifs of *Rousseauism*—a struggle with the artificial and essentially unnatural manifestations of civilization. Pisarev valued Heine's lyrical genius very highly, and he summoned poets to become 'Titans, shaking the mountains of age-old evil'; otherwise they would become 'tiny insects rummaging in flower dust'. Pisarev's conception of art was subtler and more profound than Chernyshevski's: his 'destruction of aesthetics' was not an elimination of the aesthetic element from the ideology of Russian humanism. On the contrary, it was a search for a *new art*, free from the baneful breath of an unrighteous social order. On this point, too, Pisarev was extremely close to Leo Tolstoy. Pisarev went to extremes in his struggle with the art of the dying nobility, for example, his struggle with Pushkin, whom he attempted to dethrone; but in essence he defended the *humanity* of art—the power of truth and justice which art must bear within itself. Here Pisarev—much more profoundly than Chernyshevski—approached the 'theurgical' conception of art which we find in Vladimir Solovyov.

However, we should not forget that primitive materialism suggested to Pisarev various absurdities in aesthetics, too—such as that 'aesthetics is [now] disappearing in physiology and hygiene' (!).

### 10. N. V. CHAIKOVSKI

Russian secular radicalism in the years immediately after Chernyshevski and Pisarev bore quite unexpected fruits. On the one

1. A struggle with 'absolute truths', and a defence of relativism, fills Pisarev's article 'Nineteenth-Century Scholasticism'.
2. Andreyevich, *op. cit.*, p. 236.

hand, it began to develop into so-called 'active Populism'; on the other, it put forward an extremely interesting philosophic tendency in the persons of P. L. Lavrov, N. K. Mikhailovski, and their followers. We shall, of course, omit the purely political trend which developed out of early radicalism; it contained nothing of value in the sphere of ideology.[1] Deferring our study of the philosophic activity of Lavrov and Mikhailovski to the following chapter, we shall consider in Russian Populism only what is directly connected with the inner dialectic of the ideas which we have analyzed above. We shall pause, though very briefly, with the most striking representative of this tendency—N. V. Chaikovski.

Nicholas Vasilyevich Chaikovski (1850–1926) was outstanding even in his student years as the leader of a circle of radical youth —in St. Petersburg—which included a number of revolutionary leaders who later gained fame. As a whole the circle of 'Chaikovskians' gravitated toward 'active Populism'. During these years (1867–70) the influence of Pisarev's materialism and 'rational egoism' was still strong—as Chaikovski himself testifies.[2] Influenced by the enthusiasm for natural science which was then fashionable, Chaikovski entered the Faculty of Natural Science of St. Petersburg University. At the same time he began to read the works of Auguste Comte, which corresponded fully to the general mood of the radical circles of the period. The members of Chaikovski's Circle made serious efforts to educate themselves; they read a great deal—Marx, among others. But their fundamental mood was defined by their consciousness of an 'unpayable historical debt to the people'.[3] This mood of the 'repentant nobleman', which was common in Russian circles of the period, did not flare up immediately after the emancipation of the peasants (in 1861), but in the early 1870's. N. K. Mikhailovski (see the following chapter) expressed this mood very well: 'We understood that we had attained a consciousness of universally human truth and justice . . . only as a result of the *age-long sufferings of the people.*' The idea of 'paying one's debt' to the people, and the consciousness of this debt, were no less strikingly expressed during this period by P. L. Lavrov (see the following chapter). Sensitive young people became deeply conscious of their debt to the people; this resulted in a 'going out to the people' and a passionate thirst to contribute

1. Concerning this trend see, for exam. 'e, Masaryk, *op. cit.*, II, §§ 111–13.
2. 'Vospominaniya' ['Memoirs'] in *N. V. Chaikovski* (a collection of articles), Paris, 1929, pp. 36f.
3. 'Open Letter to My Friends,' *ibid.*, p. 279.

their own energies to the service of the people. The Circle of 'Chaikovskians', on the testimony of Chaikovski himself, became a special kind of 'knightly order', marked by a striking ethical idealism—and an assertion of materialism and positivism.[1]

Within a few years, however, Chaikovski entered a period of acute ideological crisis. He was not alone in this; whole groups of young searchers after truth and justice, in his day and later, followed in his path. But we must bear in mind that the ideological crisis which led Chaikovski to a religious world-view did not affect all the strata of Russian radicalism; in fact it was soon submerged in the general movement of Russian radicals toward materialism. Nevertheless, Chaikovski's experience is important because it reveals the 'underground' religious need which was, and still is, alive in Russian secularism.

Atheism and materialism were the basic 'dogmas' of the Russian radicals of the 1860's; theirs was a genuine *faith* in science and progress. The more profound thinkers, including Chaikovski, soon saw that ardent enthusiasm and an active serving of the people do not follow from egoism or materialism; almost simultaneously a desire to 'create a new religion' flared up in various minds. It is interesting to note that this idea of a 'new religion' was always expressed in a framework of *religious immanentism* and *faith in man-kind*—as it was during this same period by Leo Tolstoy (see Ch. XIII). G. P. Fedotov has justly noted that Russian Populism, 'like all religious movements, is not completely explicable; it was an outburst of long-accumulated religious energy, compressed by strong pressure, and almost imperceptible in its latent state'.[2] A certain Malikov, who preached 'nonresistance' even before Tolstoy, had created a sect of 'God-men'; and it was to him that Chaikovski turned when he began to crave a religious foundation for his Populism. There were several phases in the development of Chaikovski's religious views. We shall not retrace this process, but shall merely quote a few passages from his writings, to show the direction in which religious energy moved within the boundaries of secularism. We say 'within the boundaries of secularism' because there was absolutely no question here of accepting the Church.

'Now, when my life of seventy-five years is drawing to a close', Chaikovski wrote in his 'Open Letter to My Friends' (1926), 'I

1. *Loc. cit.*
2. Fedotov (Bogdanov), 'Tragediya russkoi intelligentsi' ['The Tragedy of the Russian Intelligentsia'], *Vyorsty*, No. 2 (1927), p. 171.

ask the question: have I found an integral conception of the world, absolute Truth and Justice, absolute Good, and—what is most important—absolute Love? And I reply boldly and decisively: yes, I have. . . . It is impossible to live only by conditional values in the kingdom of Caesar when one does not possess the Kingdom of God and His absolute Good. . . .' [1]

Chaikovski's consciousness of God may be formulated in his own words as follows:

'The world is a single infinite and living organism. . . . Man is only a part—a sensitive and conscious organ—of this organism. Man's soul is only a part of the world-soul. . . . When our soul merges vitally with the soul of the whole universe, we hear God— first in ourselves, then in others, in nature, and in the heavens, i.e. we feel and conceive the cosmos as a single whole. . . . The universe is a living World-God. . . .' [2]

Chaikovski's *evolution* is not typical, but his religious searchings are typical, as is the disclosure of the religious thirst which existed in the depths of Russian secular radicalism. Even the fanatical Russian atheists were essentially animated by an ardent and purely religious enthusiasm. The history of Chaikovski's spiritual crisis is noteworthy because it reveals this hidden religious energy, not in radical Populism alone, but in Russian secularism generally.

1. *N. V. Chaikovski*, p. 284.
2. Quoted by T. I. Polner, 'Chaikovski i bogochelovechestvo' ['Chaikovski and Godmanhood'], *op. cit.*, p. 149.

# CHAPTER XII

## 'Semi-Positivism' in Nineteenth-Century Russian Philosophy

### K. D. KAVELIN. P. L. LAVROV. N. K. MIKHAILOVSKI. N. I. KAREYEV

### I. GENERAL CHARACTERIZATION OF 'SEMI-POSITIVISM'

RUSSIAN secularism reached its greatest intensity and creative influence during the second half of the nineteenth century; but at the same time it was passing through an extreme internal crisis. Without giving up its basic task of creating an integral world-view—apart from the Church, and the Church's root distinction between the Kingdom of God and the kingdom of this world—Russian secularism itself became *saturated to the limit with religious searchings*. Even the stormy force of Russian nihilism had a religious colouring; even those tendencies which professed materialism as a matter of principle exhibited strong religious strivings, and this applies not only to the nineteenth century but also to our own day. However, the germination of religious searchings within these secularistic tendencies appeared with special distinctness in a number of striking theoretical constructions which were almost all very brilliant and which, because of their fundamental dualism, we group under the heading of '*semi-positivism*'. All of them were more or less clearly oriented toward science and its positivistic tendencies; they were inspired by the idea of the 'earthly village', to use Herzen's expression, i.e. they moved within the lines of religious immanentism, and were almost always anti-metaphysical, very often basing themselves directly on Comte and his followers. Their struggle against metaphysical idealism, their rapture over the scientific spirit, and their unreserved faith in scientific relativism did not, however, prevent their moral consciousness from asserting its rights to absolute and unconditional significance—parallel to this relativism and often in

conscious opposition to the scientific spirit. The full force of
religious inspiration and an often mystical fervour found expression
in 'panmoralism', a passionate, omnivorous, inspiring, and triumphant manifestation of moral enthusiasm. The passion for freedom
cast out the idea of necessity which underlies the scientific conception of the world. An apotheosis of the individual and an assertion
of his absolute value do not take into account his subordination to
the inexorable forces of nature. This strange combination of barren
positivism and inspired ethical enthusiasm often made itself felt
with full force. Philosophizing thought was willing to reconcile itself
to such inner discord—so long as it did not have to give up
secularism. This inner drama was created and sustained by the
inner *bondage* of spirits which had forged their own chains, fearing
the Church, yet inspired solely by the themes of Christianity, and
burning creatively only for these themes. In the next few chapters
we shall examine various individual theories within this tendency,
a tendency whose fatal inner narrowness prevented so many
thinkers from freeing themselves from the 'spirit of the age'.

To begin with, we shall consider K. D. Kavelin, in whom
features of 'semi-positivism' were exhibited with full distinctness
for the first time. Strictly speaking, semi-positivism had already
appeared quite clearly in Herzen, but Herzen was still very much
bound up with idealism, and his tragic theoretical views lacked
the 'scientism' which injected so many false notes into the searchings of Russian thinkers. Kavelin's creative activity in the field of
philosophy was not large, but it affords the best possible introduction to the dialectic of 'semi-positivism'.

## 2. K. D. KAVELIN. PHILOSOPHIC VIEWS

Konstantin Dmitriyevich Kavelin (1818–85) entered Moscow
University at the age of seventeen, and in his youthful years was
close to the Kireyevskis and their associates. But at the same time
he was also close to Belinski, who was his tutor. Belinski's influence
was decisive; Kavelin remained a 'Westerner' throughout his life.
He soon became associated with Granovski and Herzen, and wrote
a series of remarkable articles on the history of Russia, which
display his characteristic defence of the idea of the individual. He
became a professor at St. Petersburg, and was soon invited to be
tutor to the Heir Apparent. His connections with the highest
circles became especially strong under Alexander II, when preparations for the emancipation of the peasants were being made.

Kavelin was one of the most outstanding and praiseworthy representatives of the Russian intelligentsia and, specifically, of Russian liberalism. For a long time he had no apparent connection with philosophy, but in the early 1860's he published a series of studies which were later collected into two books: The Tasks of Psychology and The Tasks of Ethics.[1] We have already had occasion to mention the first book in discussing Samarin's scientific polemic with Kavelin.

Kavelin's philosophic position was defined by a reaction, which was characteristic of the late 1840's, against the 'abstract' idealism of German philosophy, and a decisive turn toward 'exact' knowledge and the investigation of facts. Kavelin did not accept Comte, but he was wholly dominated by the general spirit of positivism. He was especially impressed by the principle of relativism. At every step, one might say, he assured himself and his readers that there are no unconditional principles—that everything is conditional and relative.[2] Strict and genuine necessity 'applies only in abstract thought'; there is no place for 'unconditional' necessity[3] in concrete thought, which is directed at reality. Kavelin, who was a very *cautious* thinker, opposed the categorical assertions of scientific positivism.[4] We even find in his writings such phrases as these: 'Nature and the individual human being are real, but the manner in which they are related is cloaked in impenetrable mystery. The higher forces which guide the destinies of the individual human being and of the whole world are even more mysterious.'[5]

This caution with respect to categorical judgments about the world and man is very characteristic of semi-positivism generally. Struggling against 'metaphysical mirages',[6] Kavelin wished to hold firmly to facts. He believed especially in the science of psychology, being confident that it would gradually lift the curtain of mystery which surrounds man. Of course, anthropocentrism is very characteristic of Kavelin: it is man that interests him, and man alone. His naïve faith in psychology is almost pathetic, and of course he did not escape the danger of 'psychologism'. However, the essential thing for his whole philosophic position is that he decisively accepts the reality of the creative principle in the individual.[7] 'Spontaneity and freedom', he declares,

1. *Zadachi psikhologi. Zadachi etiki.* Kavelin's philosophic works are grouped together in Vol. III of his *Sochineniya* [Works] (St. Petersburg, 1899).

2. Kavelin, *op. cit.*, III, 881.    3. *Ibid.*, p. 641.    4. Cf. *ibid.*, p. 631.

5. *Ibid.*, p. 929.    6. *Ibid.*, p. 568.    7. *Ibid.*, pp. 893, 982.

'are indubitable *psychic* facts.'[1] But, of course, man's freedom
is conditional too: 'Just as there is no unconditional necessity
in life, so there is no unconditional spontaneity.'[2] But the consciousness of freedom is not to be displaced or minimized in the
name of natural necessity, especially since the 'objectivity' of the
world is *illusory*, its source lying in man's psychic life.[3] 'Knowledge
arises in man; it exists only in and for him. To attempt to explain—
let alone deduce—psychic life from physical life, or *vice versa*, is to
fall into a vicious circle.'[4] Materialism and idealism are equally
unacceptable to Kavelin. The authentic reality of being remains
empirically dual: 'Psychic and material life rest on a single *common*
ground.'[5] This ground is man's inner world; hence 'psychology
alone can solve the problem to which neither philosophy nor
natural science provides an answer'.[6] Kavelin is ready to press
these assertions (which are close to Mach's epistemological position)
to their limit. The distinction between the subjective and objective
world loses its meaning for him: 'The world of external realities
is a continuation of the personal, individual, subjective world.'[7]

This philosophic position frees Kavelin from the blind worship
of natural science which characterized the basic tendencies of positivism. He recognizes the ineradicability and subjective truth and
justice of man's ethical sphere. To be sure, he believes naïvely in
a 'scientific foundation for ethics',[8] on the ground that now, as a
result of the progress of psychology, 'the innermost secrets of being
are accessible to investigation'. Actually, however, he is not in the
least cramped by 'scientific investigation' of the *facts* of the ethical
life. His lofty ethical inspiration is essentially *independent and
autonomous*. His subjection to science goes no further than a recognition that 'human freedom is possible only under certain conditions; it is not unconditional in itself'.[9] But, having made this
reservation, Kavelin goes on freely and boldly to construct an
*idealistic ethics*. 'The source and wellspring of man's ideal strivings',
he writes, appeasing his 'scientific' prudence, 'is his consciousness
. . ., for it is concerned not with real facts, but with our inner
state.' Kavelin seems to imply that such a statement is an adequate
foundation for ethical idealism. 'The true essence of ethics', we
read in another place, 'lies in the subjective ideals which ethics
sets for man's conscious life and activity.'[10] The recognition that

1. *Ibid.*, p. 919.    2. *Ibid.*, p. 920.    3. *Ibid.*, p. 1016.
4. *Ibid.*, p. 407.    5. *Ibid.*, p. 467.    6. *Ibid.*, p. 637.
7. *Ibid.*, p. 935.    8. *Ibid.*, p. 991.    9. *Ibid.*, p. 920.
                      10. *Ibid.*, p. 961.

these ideals are 'subjective' is a bow in the direction of science, but Kavelin considers the right of the ethical consciousness to set *its own* tasks for man—independently of external necessity—beyond question. 'Moral development and activity are just as much a real practical need as are the other aspects of human development and activity.' [1]

On the one hand, Kavelin's ethics is a 'hygiene of the spirit', based on the 'laws' of the psyche; but, on the other hand, he gives a high place to ethical inspiration and the purity and nobility of the moral consciousness. For him the 'aspiration toward truth, justice, and spiritual beauty' [2] is of primary importance. Incidentally, the aesthetic motif—an aversion to vulgarity and coarseness—defines the style of Kavelin's *aesthetic* humanism. 'We no longer fear the invasion of savage hordes', he once wrote, 'but barbarism steals in upon us in our moral depravation. . . . The tree [of culture] flourishes, but its roots are rotting.'

This severe moral appraisal of reality cannot be derived from Kavelin's 'scientific' ethics; in fact, it flows from his purely moral idealism, i.e. it is related neither essentially nor genetically to his pseudo-scientific ethical constructions.

### 3. P. L. LAVROV. BIOGRAPHY

Let us proceed to a study of the philosophic activity of P. L. Lavrov.

P. L. Lavrov had a very unhappy fate in Russia. His exile to Vologda, his flight to Western Europe, where he soon became head of a revolutionary publishing house, his membership in the 'International'—all of this caused the very mention of his name to be forbidden in Russia for a long time. His major works, when they appeared in Russia at all, did so only under various pseudonyms; his complete works did not begin to appear until after the Revolution of 1917. No substantial biography of Lavrov has yet been written. His philosophic work was unfavourably appraised for a long time: to many people it seemed wholly eclectic and unoriginal. Not until the appearance of a large volume on Lavrov (512 pp., Petrograd, 1922), which contained excellent articles on his philosophy by a number of authors, did opinion concerning him slowly begin to change. However, his work has still not been studied *as a whole*.

1. *Ibid.*, p. 982.          2. *Ibid.*, p. 961.

Lavrov grew up in approximately the same spiritual environment as Chernyshevski. For him, as for Chernyshevski, the 'scientific spirit' and scientific criticism provided the basic and defining principles of knowledge and creative activity. However, Chernyshevski very early devoted himself to writing on social and political themes, and this strengthened his tendency toward sharp and hasty criticism of the contemporary world, displacing his unquestionable philosophic talent; whereas Lavrov's brilliant revolutionary activity did not in the least diminish his scientific prudence or thoughtfulness. He was undoubtedly a true philosopher; and it was his scholarship, rather than his social and political writing, that constrained him. Lavrov was a genuine scholar, with immense erudition and manifold interests. In the breadth of his synthesis and the thoroughness of his knowledge he invites comparison with Herbert Spencer and Wilhelm Wundt. His philosophic talent is clearly exhibited in his 'semi-positivism'; it is cramped, but not suppressed, by his worship of science.

Lavrov's biography, as we have said, has not yet been worked out.[1] We shall touch only on the most important events of his life.

Peter Lavrovich Lavrov (1823–1900) was born into the family of a wealthy Russian landowner. His father was a military man, who sent his son to military school; young Lavrov attended Artillery School. Even in these early years (he graduated at the age of nineteen) Lavrov was distinguished by extraordinary erudition. During this period his interests tended chiefly toward mathematics and the natural sciences, but he also made a thorough study of the history of scientific thought. In 1844, at the age of twenty-one, Lavrov became a teacher of mathematics at the Artillery School, and within a few years a professor of mathematics at the Artillery Academy. Lavrov's scientific and historical studies were deeply bound up with his moral searchings. In this respect Lavrov, while sharing the moral orientation common to Russian philosophers, takes one of the most conspicuous places in the history of Russian ethical searchings. There is no doubt that Herzen's influence played an important part in his spiritual

1. Publication of Lavrov's works was begun after the Revolution, but apparently has not been completed. Lavrov's scholarly activity in the field of philosophy included the editing, with introduction and notes, of J. S. Mill's *System of Logic* (two volumes, St. Petersburg, 1865, 1867). Concerning Lavrov see Masaryk, *op. cit.*, II, 115–36.

development.[1] Lavrov is close to Herzen in a number of his basic ideas, although Herzen's tragic historiosophy was completely foreign to him. Lavrov's insistence on the primacy of ethics, an insistence which was both psychological and a matter of principle, persisted throughout his life, and constituted the real foundation of his trenchantly and systematically expressed secularism.[2]

Lavrov displayed philosophic interests very early, in connection with his study of the history of science. He was wholly carried away by the general atmosphere of positivism which prevailed in Europe after the late 1840's, but he also studied German idealistic philosophy thoroughly—his articles on Hegel are a testimonial to this.[3] The question as to what influences were decisive for Lavrov's philosophic development is very controversial. He himself speaks in his autobiography of the important influence of Protagoras, Comte, Feuerbach, and A. Lange; but it becomes clear from a study of his writings that several other philosophers had a considerable influence: especially Kant, but also Cournot, Ampère,[4] Spencer, and Marx.[5] These authors are so different that Lavrov must have been either a simple eclectic or a man with an original synthesis of his own. In fact, there can be no doubt that the latter was the case, but it is not easy to establish the centre or controlling basis of Lavrov's original theories. We shall return to this point later.

Lavrov was and remained throughout his life a scholar, but his lively sympathies for the 'progressive' tendencies of Russian life impelled him fatally toward the Russian revolutionary movements. Interestingly enough, he always published his articles not in the organs of Russian radicalism but in the more moderate, purely liberal journals. He was not close to Chernyshevski, the leader of Russian radicalism, despite their extreme similarity on many

1. This has been most aptly noted by Shpet in his article 'Antropologizm Lavrova v svete istori filosofi' ['Lavrov's Anthropologism in the Light of the History of Philosophy'], *P. L. Lavrov*, Petrograd, 1922, p. 100, *passim*. See also Masaryk, *op. cit.*, II, 130.

2. See especially Lavrov's concise formulas in the *Opyt istori mysli* [Essay in the History of Thought], Geneva, 1894, I, 1.

3. 'Gegelizm' ['Hegelianism'] and 'Prakticheskaya filosofiya Gegelya' ['Hegel's Practical Philosophy']. (*Biblioteka dlya chteniya*, V, IX (1858), III, V (1859).)

4. Concerning the influence of Cournot and Ampère see Shpet, *op. cit.*, p. 100. With respect to Lavrov's rationalism, a rationalism close to that of Cournot, see Masaryk, *op. cit.*, II, 122f.

5. Lavrov acknowledged himself a 'pupil of Marx'. ('Avtobiografiya' ['Autobiography']. *Vestnik Yevropy*, XI (1910), p. 90.)

points; Lavrov held himself somewhat apart from Chernyshevski and the radical movement generally.[1] Nevertheless, he was arrested in 1866 (in connection with Karakozov's attempt on the Tsar's life, an attempt with which he was wholly unconnected),[2] and was exiled to the Government of Vologda. In 1870, having given up hope of liberation, Lavrov fled Russia—wishing only to continue his scientific work, which had been quite impossible for him in the conditions of his exile.[3] In fact, once abroad, he occupied himself intensively with scientific work to the end of his life; but he very early became involved in revolutionary activity as well. During his stay in Vologda, Lavrov had written a series of Historical Letters—published under the pseudonym Mirtov—which had had an enormous influence (quite unexpected for Lavrov himself) on the radical Russian youth.[4] In 1872 a group of Lavrov's admirers sent their representatives to him in Paris with a proposal that he publish an émigré journal and assume the leadership of the social-revolutionary movement. Lavrov, who until then had refrained from direct participation in this movement (he had always hoped to be able to return to Russia to continue his scientific work) accepted this proposal—as a result of various circumstances—and founded the journal *Vperyod* [Forward], thus permanently precluding the possibility of returning to Russia. However he continued to publish in Russia, though always under pseudonyms. His participation in the International and his active involvement in revolutionary work made even the mention of Lavrov's name in the Russian press forbidden; his numerous purely scientific works remained either unknown or forgotten for wide circles of Russian society. In 1900 Lavrov died.

## 4. THE PRIMACY OF ETHICS

Turning to an exposition of Lavrov's theories, let us emphasize once more that he is not to be considered an eclectic. The fact that

1. Apparently Lavrov was not a member of the revolutionary society *Zemlya i volya* [Land and Liberty], as the authorities suspected. See *Materialy dlya biografi P. L. Lavrova* [Materials for a Biography of P. L. Lavrov], ed. Vityazev, Petrograd, 1921, p. 80, note 4. Lavrov was listed in the police files as early as 1861 (see *ibid.*, p. 84).

2. *Ibid.*, p. 89.

3. See Lavrov's extremely important letter to his son (*Materialy* ... [Materials . . .], pp. 34–9).

4. These Historical Letters [*Istoricheskiye pisma*] became a kind of gospel for several generations of Russians. [They have been translated into both French and German: *Lettres historiques*, Paris, 1903; *Historische Briefe*, Berlin, 1901.]

his views reflected the influence of Kant as well as that of the positivists, of Cournot as well as Feuerbach, indicates only the breadth of his 'critical realism'. In general, Lavrov's basic convictions sprang from his *faith in science*, his critical philosophy, and his rejection of metaphysics. This temper of mind was common to the whole period. Lavrov subscribed without hesitation or doubt to the spirit of secularism which pervaded the nineteenth century. This basic secular orientation remained with him to the end of his days; [1] he was always faithful to his critical rationalism. Positivism —as a search for truth exclusively within the limits of experience— deepened by the theoretical constructions of Kant and Cournot, predetermined Lavrov's intellectual work and left its imprint on his spiritual searchings. But in one sphere Lavrov recognized neither limits nor constraints; there his intellectual work proceeded freely, independently of his theoretical constructions—this was the sphere of ethics. Lavrov had a genuine passion for knowledge and critical investigation, but the flame of ethical passion burned in him with equal force and true inspiration. He was extremely loyal to his ideals. It has been justly said of him that 'his consciousness of moral duty was maintained at the ideal pitch of *religious worship* to the last moment of his life'.[2] This is something deeper than the humanism which we have frequently found as the basic content of Russian secularism. There is something in Lavrov—as there is to some extent but not so strongly in Mikhailovski—which is close to Leo Tolstoy's 'panmoralism'. Even in Herzen the independence and autonomy of moral inspiration set boundaries to a positivistic orientation of mind; we have also noted this feature in Chernyshevski. But in Lavrov the *primacy* of ethics is exhibited with special clarity. His anthropologism, which Lavrov himself considered the most characteristic feature of his system, is to be derived only from this. One of his earliest philosophic articles, 'Three Discussions on the Contemporary Significance of Philosophy', exhibits this very clearly. Other articles of the same period were written in similar tones. 'Philosophy', we read in this article, 'is the comprehension of all existence as a *unity*, and the *embodiment* of this comprehension in artistic images and moral actions.' [3] This

1. However, Lavrov's biographer notes that the death of Lavrov's wife upset his spiritual equilibrium for a time. He was especially agitated by the problem of immortality; but after a time his old rationalism regained the upper hand. (*Materialy . . .*, p. 21.)

2. *Pamyat P. L. Lavrova* [In Memory of P. L. Lavrov], Geneva, 1900, p. 29.

3. 'Tri besedy o sovremennom znacheni filosofi', *Otechestvennyie zapiski*, I (1861), p. 141.

formula makes it clear that the ethical (and aesthetic) spheres [1] are set *beside* knowledge, as independent realms of the spirit. We shall see below that, in a certain sense, ethical motifs predetermined all of Lavrov's basic theoretical constructions. But let us emphasize that neither epistemology—to which Lavrov assigned a place of first importance in systematic philosophic investigation—nor the critical history of reason—the favourite theme of his scientific researches—overshadowed for him the theme of the 'embodiment' of moral impulses. Lavrov regarded the idea of the 'integral man' as primitive and basic; it was this concept that defined his 'anthropologism'. The idea of the 'integral man' is a formal link between Lavrov, Khomyakov, and Kireyevski, but in the latter two its meaning is quite different from that which we find in Lavrov. In any case, Lavrov early perceived the specific quality of the ethical life,[2] and realized that the course of history becomes intelligible only if we admit the presence and efficacy of ethical ideals. Lavrov's 'semi-positivism' lies in his acceptance of the independence of the ethical sphere, a sphere which is unanalysable and non-deducible from 'facts'.

But let us turn to a more systematic analysis of his views.

## 5. LAVROV'S ANTHROPOLOGISM

Lavrov himself expressed the basic position of philosophic anthropologism in the three following principles: (1) the reality of individual consciousness—in other words, the 'individual principle of reality' (2) the principle of realism: 'we consider everything of which we are conscious, and which involves no contradiction either in the concept in question or in the combination of present and past consciousness, as real being'; and (3) the sceptical principle (with respect to metaphysics): 'the process of consciousness does not, in itself, enable us to decide whether it is the result of real being or whether real being is its product'.[3] But Lavrov goes on to make a characteristic addition: 'the sceptical principle has no place' in practical philosophy—i.e. in ethics.

1. It would be interesting to analyse the remarks on aesthetics which are abundantly dispersed through Lavrov's writings; but, of course, *ethical* motifs were of decisive significance in the formation of his system.

2. This is clearly exhibited in Lavrov's studies 'Ocherki voprosov prakticheskoi filosofi' ['Outlines of the Problems of Practical Philosophy'] and 'Sovremennyie ucheniya o nravstvennosti' ['Contemporary Moral Theories'].

3. *Stati po filosofi* [Articles on Philosophy], Pt. II, pp. 64–8.

'The absence of the sceptical principle in the theoretical constructions of practical philosophy gives the latter a special stability
and independence of metaphysical theories. . . . This reflects the
individual's independence. . . . The individual is conscious of himself as free, as wanting for himself, and responsible to himself.
This is the individual principle of freedom.'[1]

Let us note that Lavrov considers the (metaphysical) question
of freedom of the will insoluble; [2] but he asserts all the more forcefully the reality of the *consciousness* of freedom.

'It is impossible', he says, 'to eliminate man's obligation to himself or his judgment of himself. . . . I take as my point of departure
the fact of the *consciousness of freedom* and the fact of the *creation of
ideals*, and on the foundation of these facts I construct a coherent
system of moral processes.' [3]

In the final analysis, Lavrov, after making this fundamental
addition to his assertion of cognitive immanentism, develops an
ethical immanentism. Ethics retains all of its significance for him,
independently of the question of the 'metaphysical' reality of
freedom; this is not a shallow psychologism but *anthropologism*. For
him the whole man in the full manifestation of his life is the true
object of philosophy. And creative activity, which is always
purposeful, occupies an outstanding place in the individual's life.
We have just seen that for Lavrov the sceptical principle does not
apply in the sphere of ethics. Man is 'a unity of real and ideal'. We
must not forget the 'sceptical principle' with respect to cognition,
but in man's integral unity the centre of gravity evidently lies in
the *ethical sphere*. 'To philosophize', Lavrov once wrote, 'is to
develop a human being in oneself as a single harmonious entity.'
And, clearly, the moral consciousness, the capacity to be kindled
by an ideal and to direct one's activity in accordance with it, is the
stable foundation of such development.

At first Lavrov's anthropologism (in the three principles mentioned above) was directly related to his critical philosophy and
his positivism—a combination of the ideas of Kant and Comte;

1. *Ibid.*, p. 69.
2. 'Otvet Strakhovu' ['Reply to Strakhov'], *Otech. zapiski*, XII (1860), p. 102.
It is thus incorrect to say, as Radlov, for example, does ('Lavrov v russkoi
filosofi' ['Lavrov in Russian Philosophy']), that Lavrov considered freedom an
illusion. Lavrov considered the *metaphysical* question of freedom *insoluble*
(nothing more!), but he regarded the psychological reality of freedom as a firm
and central fact.
3. *Ibid.*, p. 107.

but, in the end, it unexpectedly appeared as an *ethical immanentism*. Only that *in which man is permitted to act* is *real*; therefore 'history is the essential characteristic which distinguishes the genus Homo from other zoological genera'.[1] History begins where there is a consciousness of freedom; prior to this man is only 'on the eve of freedom'. Man's reality is revealed only in the movement of history.[2] But if man's creative thought, determined by an ideal, is the motive force of history, there is ample scope in man's consciousness for freedom: the framework of simple necessity expands, revealing the realm of the 'possible'[3]—apart from which a consciousness of 'freedom' would be logically impossible. Thus it becomes clear why the mystery of all being is concentrated in man and, specifically, in his moral consciousness. The moral consciousness, beginning with simple 'desire', forms an ideal, motivating man's creative activity and tearing him away from the flux of unconscious being, and thus creates historical reality. Lavrov sums up his anthropologism as follows: 'Man is the source of nature (for he reconstructs "nature" from the data of experience), the source of history (for he fights for his ideals, and casts his seed into the soil of the surrounding world), and the source of his own consciousness (for he reorganizes his inner world).'[4] He thus makes it clear that he is speaking of man as a creative and moral being.

We have characterized Lavrov's anthropologism as an ethical immanentism. And, in fact, man's central significance is wholly defined by the presence of an ethical principle in him. However, this ethical sphere itself is conceived exclusively within the limits of immanentism.[5] The transcendent sphere, whose real significance for the ethical life was admitted even by Kant—in his brilliant doctrine of the 'primacy of practical reason' and man's ineradicable striving for the 'Unconditional'—is here completely dismissed. Lavrov's anti-metaphysical position prevents him from making the fundamental fact of the importance of the moral sphere intelligible—although he himself profoundly displayed this fact:

1. *Stati po filosofi*, Pt. II, p. 59.
2. This is the subject of Lavrov's immense unfinished work *Antropologicheskaya zhizn* [The Anthropological Life].
3. The category of 'possibility' also occupies a very important place in Mikhailovski's theoretical constructions, as was shown by B. Kistyakovski in his article 'Kategoriya vozmozhnosti' ['The Category of Possibility'], *Problemy idealizma* [Problems of Idealism], St. Petersburg, 1902.
4. 'Tri besedy . . .' ['Three Discussions . . .'], *op. cit.*, p. 140.
5. This was correctly pointed out by Archimandrite Bukharev in his note on Lavrov (*Tri pisma k Gogolyu* [Three Letters to Gogol], p. 72).

hence his 'semi-positivism'. Lavrov in fact is very close to Lange on this point, but his philosophic conception was wholly independent and original.

Having explained the essence of Lavrov's anthropologism, we will now be able to elucidate his basic philosophic views.

### 6. DOCTRINE OF THE INDIVIDUAL

Lavrov's anthropologism introduces nothing of importance into his conception of man. His anti-metaphysical position, of course, prevents this. Lavrov moves always in the tight circle of 'that of which we are conscious'; 'critical consciousness' is for him the most valuable product as well as the creative force of individual and historical movement. In this sense one may speak of Lavrov's one-sided *intellectualism*. He loves to speak of individual wholeness, but this wholeness is related to the impossibility of separating or isolating the sphere of morality from our cognitive relationship to the world. Lavrov's doctrine of man's inner structure is highly oversimplified; he does not take into consideration what Dostoyevsky contributed to anthropology, nor does he have a presentiment of the contributions of Freud and his school (Adler, Jung, *et al.*). He does not recognize man's inner 'complexity'. To be sure, he speaks frequently of the 'savages of higher culture', but this expression applies not to man's spontaneous impulses, but to those individuals who—although they belong to a nation which is living an historical life—are themselves outside of history. Participation in history, according to Lavrov, is created by uniting our *consciousness* to the movement of history—through a 'capacity to take pleasure in development'. Only the 'critically thinking individual' really enters into historical life. Man creates his own 'individuality'; individual personality is not an actuality but a potentiality, a task. The following idea is very interesting in this connection:

'Not only is the moral realm not innate in man, but by no means all individuals *elaborate* their moral promptings—just as [!] by no means everyone attains the level of scientific thinking. The *striving for pleasure* is all that is innate in man, and among his pleasures the intelligent human being elaborates the pleasure of the moral life, giving it the highest place in the hierarchy of pleasures.'

As we see, Lavrov oversimplifies the foundations of man's inner structure very much.[1] Although ethicism found forceful and

1. Cf. the corresponding views of Chernyshevski and Pisarev in the preceding chapter.

inspired expression in his theoretical constructions, as was indicated above, Lavrov's ethical ideas obviously did not *follow* from his anthropology at all. He was a relativist in anthropology; he recognized no 'nonderivative functions' in the soul (of which the moral realm is one). Human thought alone is a firm, nonrelative, truly unconditional point of support for Lavrov. And this comprises his intellectualism.

His concept of the individual is much richer—and even remarkable, in a sense—if we consider the individual's *moral* life. Strictly speaking, only an individual in whom the moral sphere has already been manifested and consolidated may be regarded as an 'indivisible whole'. The 'savages of higher culture', for example, who do not consciously participate in the movement of history— that is, do not further its 'progress'—have no moral life; they cannot achieve wholeness, for they do not possess the *two* spheres (cognitive and morally-evaluating) whose indissoluble wholeness is so essential. But the individual who has matured to the level of the moral life possesses an inner motif of wholeness. Thus man's 'wholeness' is not an *ontological* but an *historical* category. The narrowness of Lavrov's positivistic orientation appears most clearly in his transformation of the moral sphere, and of reason itself, into *products of evolution*, i.e. purely historical categories. The entire grandiose plan of his unfinished work An Essay in the History of Thought is based on this. Consciousness itself, the most precious attribute of individual personality, is a product ( ! ) of biological evolution.[1] But even here we find a contradiction:

'Whatever may be the *physical* source of awareness, the phenomena of consciousness are sharply isolated from all the phenomena . . . which we reduce, or attempt to reduce, to the motion of masses. *Consciousness cannot be reduced to motion*—even as an hypothesis.' [2]

But how, then, can one speak of the 'physical source of awareness'? Contradictions of this kind run through Lavrov's whole anthropology. For example, environmental influence is regarded as decisive for the psychic evolution of mankind, which evolution is very thoughtfully and profoundly sketched in this work; and

1. See Ch. III, 'Evolyutsiya soznaniya' ['The Evolution of Consciousness]' (Book I, 'Do istori' ['Prehistory'], Section I, 'Podgotovleniye cheloveka' ['The Preparation of Man']).
2. *Ibid.,* pp. 259f.

then suddenly the creative force of the 'self' appears, resting upon the consciousness of an ideal. This is the so-called secondary or ideal 'self', which takes on the character of a 'free agent'.[1] On the one hand, there is no place in evolution for freedom; everything is causally determined. On the other hand, the individual's feeling of freedom takes on the character of a vast creative force, which impels and transforms both man and history. Lavrov says in one place, anticipating Vaihinger's *Philosophy of 'As If'*: 'The point of departure [in history] is the individual's setting of goals for himself *as if* he were autonomous.' 'The moral ideal is the only beacon capable of giving history a perspective'—i.e. only what is *moral* is *historically real*. The moral sphere, on the one hand, is a purely subjective phenomenon; man sets himself goals 'as if' he were free. But at the same time the moral sphere is a factor of immense creative power, which produces historical being.

Such is the contradiction of Lavrov's anthropology, a contradiction which flows from his 'semi-positivism'—the combination of autonomous ethicism and a dogmatic fascination for scientific determinism. Man's illusory freedom reveals not an illusory but a powerful, real, and genuinely creative factor in being. And therefore Lavrov (very early) constructed a 'theory of the individual' in order to show that the consciousness of freedom includes the 'living and indestructible fact of creativity, and *responsibility* [!] for one's creation'.[2] When he advanced the ideal of the 'critically thinking individual', Lavrov ceased to be an investigator and became a 'preacher' in the name of ethical idealism. Philosophic as well as anthropological theories took on their full meaning at this height of ethical activity; necessity gave way to freedom, positivism to the 'consciousness of an ideal'. This was a system of 'ethical immanentism', and its author lived passionately in the light of the ideal of creative activity, but without a religious or metaphysical interpretation of this activity. In Lavrov secularism, saturated with profound contradictions, reached its highest point, remaining irreconcilable in its basic orientation.

## 7. PHILOSOPHY OF HISTORY

Lavrov's philosophy of history likewise flows from his ethics; it is wholly defined by the moral consciousness. Of particular import-

1. *Ibid.*, p. 249.
2. 'Ocherk teori lichnosti' ['An Outline of a Theory of the Individual'], *Otech. zapiski*, 1859, p. 232.

ance is the idea of 'paying off one's debt' to the people, which was first developed in Lavrov's Historical Letters:

'Mankind has paid dearly in order that a few thinkers in their cloistered studies might discuss its progress. If . . . one counted up how many lives have been lost . . . for every individual who now lives a genuinely human life, our contemporaries would be horrified at the thought of the capital in *blood and labour* which has been spent on their development. . . .'

In these words, which are extremely characteristic of the ideological searchings of the 1870's, Lavrov himself clearly exhibits some of the most profound motifs of his theoretical constructions. 'I shall release myself', he wrote in the same place, 'from responsibility for the *bloody price* of my development if I use this development to minimize present and future evil.' Hence the intense utopianism of Lavrov's thinking. It has been justly noted that there is a kind of asceticism in his 'preachings'.[1] The revolutionist in Lavrov gave way, in Ovsyanniko-Kulikovski's expression, to an 'ascetic enlightener'.[2] But Lavrov's 'enlightenment programme' was not like that of the Western Enlightenment; it was defined wholly by his ethical orientation. History provides ample scope for 'possibility' as well as necessity; thus it is important to 'be enlightened' as to what should be introduced into the historical process. History is a *creative transformation* of nonhistorical being; and, although it has its own inner laws, they are plastic enough to permit creative and fruitful participation in history—the more so, in that the motive force of history, as we know, is to be found in human thought. The elements of Rousseauism which we find in Mikhailovski were foreign to Lavrov: for him the ideal of history is in the *future*.

Lavrov's socialist convictions, which were very strong and deep-seated, were of course suggested by his moral consciousness; but it was necessary for him to *ground* his socialism rationally. It should not be forgotten that he was strongly influenced by Marx, as he himself has emphasized. And we must interpret Lavrov's general historiosophical rationalism in this light. He exhibits echoes of Hegelianism—taken up both through Marx and independently of

1. Andreyevich has collected a series of passages from Lavrov which deal severely and insistently with the 'obligations' of the critically developed individual. (*Opyt filosofi russkoi literatury* [An Essay in the Philosophy of Russian Literature], p. 299.)

2. D. N. Ovsyanniko-Kulikovski, *Istoriya russkoi intelligentsi* [A History of the Russian Intelligentsia], II, 243.

Marx—at a number of points. Unrestricted determinism is combined in Lavrov—as in Hegel and his followers—with a glorification of freedom as the operative force in history. This coincidence of necessity and freedom has a special character in Lavrov as a result of his use of the category of 'possibility', which was to become Mikhailovski's central historiosophical category. But for Lavrov the category of possibility is connected with the *psychological* reality of free action. We have seen that history begins for him where the 'natural' flow of processes is disturbed, as a result of man's consciousness of freedom. Lavrov recognizes the principle of determinism in historiosophy, but his summoning of the 'critically thinking individual' to free creative activity runs like a scarlet thread through all of his historical writings. Lavrov was much more an apostle of freedom—and this is why he became the leader of a large group of seeking young people—than a commentator on the historical necessity of progress. The passion of his ethicism directed its full inspiring force toward the free individual; Lavrov's fiery and incessant preaching of socialism has all the earmarks of utopian thought. Ovsyanniko-Kulikovski justly points out the *romanticism* in the thought of Mikhailovski and Lavrov.[1] The same romantic striving for social justice which is characteristic of Russian—and perhaps even non-Russian—romanticists manifested itself through a wrapping of positivism.

## 8. GENERAL CHARACTERIZATION OF LAVROV'S PHILOSOPHY

We have sketched the most important *original* features in Lavrov's theoretical constructions. We must now say something about his general philosophic views. Here he was not original, but merely expressed the general intellectual tendencies of his age. This is especially true of his epistemological views, which clearly exhibit the influence of Kant and modern critical philosophy. We are already familiar with Lavrov's 'individual principle of reality' and his 'sceptical' principle (only that which appears in consciousness is accessible to us). Although Lavrov unhesitatingly defends a realistic conception of the world, his sceptical principle prevents him from asserting this realism categorically. He saves himself from a debilitating epistemological relativism through his 'history of reason'; there he finds a firmness—illusory, of course, for here his thought moves wholly in the direction of a *petitio principii*—in the acceptance of realism, which he could not derive from his

1. *Ibid.*, p. 227.

relativistic anthropologism. However, Lavrov is aware that the scope of being is *diminished* for us in cognition, since abstract concepts crowd out the living material of knowledge. Kantian phenomenalism [1] early led Lavrov to an anti-metaphysical orientation, and even *before his acquaintance with Comte* he wrote of three stages in the development of human thought, which he characterized as: (1) 'popular belief'; (2) 'metaphysical myth'; and (3) 'scientific construction'.

Lavrov was a forthright opponent of both materialism [2] and idealism,[3] which he regarded as metaphysical theories. We have already noted his inconsistency on the question of the soul's dependence on the body. The 'nonderivativeness' of consciousness did not prevent him from speaking of the 'physical source of awareness'.

It remains for us to conclude our exposition with a general characterization of Lavrov's philosophy.

Lavrov undoubtedly had a highly original mind; however, the task of synthesis which he very early conceived for himself gave ample scope to the most varied influences. At the same time his philosophic searchings were greatly restricted by the spirit of secularism which completely dominated his thinking. His enthusiasm for 'scientism' precluded the themes which are dialectically connected with a philosophic interpretation of being as such. The only field in which Lavrov remained wholly unconstrained was ethics; but even there he tried stubbornly to remain within the boundaries of ethical immanentism, rejecting all metaphysics. The result was a flagrant contradiction in the system which Lavrov had very much wanted to make integral and whole. For Lavrov the ethical life was entirely defined and motivated by the consciousness of freedom, but the reality of this freedom was only psychological. His own ethical consciousness was passionate,

1. Shpet (*op. cit.*, p. 108) has aptly pointed out that Lavrov took up a Kantian position *before* the development of the 'back to Kant' movement in Germany during the second half of the nineteenth century.

2. 'Matter in general is an abstract construction of our thought. . . . Matter appertains to metaphysics.' ('Mekhanicheskaya teoriya mira' ['The Mechanical Theory of the World'], *Otech. zapiski*, IV (1859).) In this article we find such statements as: 'Materialism lies outside of science' (p. 483); 'Materialism is a metaphysical system' (p. 489); 'Matter has become a new idol' (p. 484).

3. For Lavrov idealism—as well as all religious theories—is a definite phase in the history of thought; for the contemporary consciousness it is a pathological phenomenon. (See especially *Opyt istori mysli* [An Essay in the History of Thought], p. 49.)

profound, and categorical; but his philosophic understanding was weakened to begin with by a positivistic temper of mind. He not only failed to achieve wholeness; he was not even able—because of his *a priori* rejection of everything 'metaphysical'—to exhibit the mystery of man with adequate profundity. This combination of a categorical and passionate ethicism with a relativism of principle condemned Lavrov to 'semi-positivism'. If he himself did not sense the inner discord of his system, this was because his taste for historical research blinded him to the disharmony of his principles. Lavrov's relativism of principle, which turned the mystery of man as well as all questions of meaning and value into 'historical categories', inwardly weakened his position. It is clear that the spirit of secularism only impoverished and narrowed what was contributed to his system by genuine philosophic inspiration, that of ethics in particular.

We find the same semi-positivism, the same inconsistent combination of categorical ethicism with a positivism of principle, in another major representative of this tendency—N. K. Mikhailovski, to a study of whom we now turn.

### 9. N. K. MIKHAILOVSKI. BIOGRAPHY. THE PRIMACY OF ETHICS

Nicholas Konstantinovich Mikhailovski [1] was born in 1842 into a noble family which was not well-to-do. He received his higher education at the Academy of Mines, but did not graduate. He began to publish in various journals at the age of eighteen. During this period the young scientist Nozhin (who died at an early age) influenced him greatly, stimulating his interest in biology. In 1869 Mikhailovski became a regular contributor to the journal *Otechest-vennyie zapiski* [Notes of the Fatherland]. His most important articles appeared in this journal over a period of fifteen years, attracting universal attention. When Lavrov founded the journal *Vperyod* in 1873 (see above), he invited Mikhailovski to join him abroad, but Mikhailovski was opposed to revolutionary activity at this time. Later, however, he joined the revolutionary group, becoming the ideologist of the Revolutionary Socialists. In the early 1890's, when the journal *Russkoye bogatstvo* [Russian Wealth] was founded, as the organ of this group, Mikhailovski became editor-in-chief. He died in 1904.

1. There is still no serious biography of Mikhailovski. Much biographical material is contained in his literary sketch 'V peremezhku' ['Taking Turns'].

Mikhailovski was a very energetic creative thinker, capable of broad generalizations and bold theoretical constructions; his was a profound and philosophically talented mind. But the intellectual atmosphere in which Mikhailovski lived from his early years was unfavourable for his scientific and philosophic work. Being of a *religious* nature—in the psychological sense of the word—he nevertheless fully shared the general orientation of secularism. We shall see below that on this foundation a profound inner rift developed in Mikhailovski. As with all religious natures who have believed in the truth and justice of secularism, Mikhailovski's religious impulses sought a way out in ethical passion. He became—like Dostoyevsky—one of the most brilliant and influential preachers of *personalism*. But his philosophic sensitivity did not permit him to halt with a mere 'professing' of personalism; the result of his reflections appeared in such remarkable articles as 'The Struggle for Individuality' and 'Notes of a Layman', as well as in Mikhailovski's remarkable sociological theories. In him personalism strove to become a world-view, to transform itself into a philosophic system; but we should not forget the ethical root, the basic ethical meaning of this personalism.

Mikhailovski's celebrated 'subjectivism' grew from this same ethical root. Like Herzen and Lavrov, he was essentially anthropocentric; he contributed significantly to the study of the 'mystery of man', but the positivism and relativism of the age deprived his anthropology—like that of the above-mentioned thinkers—of much of its creative power. However, just as Lavrov, although he was a relativist in principle, ascribed unconditional and categorical features to the ethical sphere—so Mikhailovski's ethical consciousness was unyielding and categorical. His anthropology, like Dostoyevsky's, shows the unquestionable and profound influence of Schiller. The ideal of inner wholeness was expressed much more concretely and brilliantly by Mikhailovski than by Lavrov. But Mikhailovski was not able to go beyond the limits of positivism to provide a metaphysical ground for man's moral searchings; hence his theoretical constructions, like those of Lavrov, are an expression of 'semi-positivism'.

Let us begin our study of Mikhailovski's theories with a consideration of the general principles of his ethical personalism, which contains the key to all of his theoretical constructions.[1]

1. For an analysis of Mikhailovski's fundamental ideas see Plekhanov, *In Defence of Materialism*, [trans. by A. Rothstein], London, 1947; Masaryk. *op. cit.*, II, 136–90.

## 10. PERSONALISM

Mikhailovski's personalism is close to the views of Herzen and Lavrov. Proudhon's influence is also clear; [1] but Mikhailovski's originality consists in his advancing with exceptional force—along with a basic ethical point of view—the rights of the individual in the struggle against the pressure of society, relating the themes of personalism to a metaphysics of nature. The individual has a deep-seated need for wholeness; he does not want to weaken or repress any aspect of himself. 'The individual must never be sacrificed', Mikhailovski wrote, 'he is sacred and inviolable, and all the efforts of our mind should be directed to following his destiny minutely, and establishing him at the point where he may triumph.' [2] This ethical imperative is the unshakable and creative basis of Mikhailovski's ideological searchings; he follows every discord between the theoretical and moral consciousness 'minutely' in order to defend the principles of individuality. Mikhailovski is convinced that in its depths theoretical truth can never undermine the truth of the moral consciousness; here the motif of human wholeness, and the wholeness of spiritual reality as such, is resurrected in a new form. Let us quote a well-known passage:

'Whenever the word "*pravda*" comes into my mind I cannot help admiring its striking inner beauty. It appears that no such word exists in any European language. Only in Russian, it seems, are "truth" and "justice" designated by the same word ["*pravda*"], fusing, as it were, into one great whole. *Pravda*—in this vast meaning of the word—has always been the *goal of my searchings*. To gaze without fear into the eyes of reality and its reflection in objective truth, and at the same time to preserve its subjective justice—such is the task of my whole life. . . . Everything has occupied me exclusively from the point of view of this great dual-unity of truth-justice.'[3]

'Throughout his life', Berdyaev remarks somewhat ironically, 'Mikhailovski was inspired by total truth-justice and strove for harmony, but he never attained truth-justice and he never knew harmony.' [4] This is true; but it is all the more remarkable that

1. This is correctly pointed out by Masaryk, *op. cit.*, II, 139.
2. *Sochineniya* [Works], St. Petersburg, 1906, IV, 451.
3. Preface to Vol. I, *op. cit.*, p. v.
4. N. A. Berdyaev, *Subyektivizm i individualizm v obshchestvennoi filosofi* [Subjectivism and Individualism in Social Philosophy], St. Petersburg, 1901, p. 18.

Mikhailovski actually did seek the *dual-unity* of truth-justice throughout his life. This proves beyond question that the quest for wholeness was the creative basis of his searchings. In any case, what he had to fear was not 'objective truth', the meaning of which cannot be disputed, since it appears in the form of unalterable facts, but subjective justice, i.e. moral justice, from which our consciousness so easily turns away. The 'subjectivism' of social cognition, upon which Mikhailovski insisted (see below), was defined precisely by the safeguarding of this 'dual-one' truth-justice, i.e. in the first instance, by moral justice, the significance of which is so often forgotten in studying social life. As a result of the obliviousness to this ethical element the 'individual' is threatened on all sides. Mikhailovski once said with good reason: 'I conceive the system of Truth-Justice as somewhat *broader* than philosophy.' [1] Philosophy, of course, takes ethical principles into account in its synthesis; but it usually *subordinates* them to the *understanding of reality*, deducing them from the latter. For Mikhailovski, this is an injurious limitation of ethics, which should not be 'subordinated' to theoretical truth in the system of 'truth-justice'. 'The mind which has habituated itself to an exclusive study of natural phenomena,' Mikhailovski wrote, 'tends to introduce the idea of iron necessity—and to neglect value judgments—in the realm of ethics as well.' [2] These words exhibit the most fundamental and important point of conflict between truth and justice; Mikhailovski does not question the idea of necessity in the sphere of cognition, but in the ethical sphere central importance accrues to the idea of freedom. However, the difficulties of safeguarding truth-justice are not limited to this conflict (concerning Mikhailovski's 'resolution' of which, see below). When Kavelin assured him that the theoretical and moral spheres can be united on the foundation of philosophy, Mikhailovski replied:

'I think that this is hardly enough. Philosophy, to be sure, brings together the ideas of what is and what ought to be . . ., but it unites them only in thought, not in life. It does not communicate the *religious devotion to an idea* which alone is capable of overcoming moral flabbiness.' [3]

Incidentally, Mikhailovski reacts harshly to the various latter-day attempts to 'create' 'new' religions: 'These attempts', he writes,

1. *Op. cit.*, IV, 405.  2. *Op. cit.*, I, 818.
3. In the remarkable 'Zapiski profana' ['Notes of a Layman'], *op. cit.*, III, 387.

'lack the essential characteristic of religion—the capacity to control human actions.' [1]

According to Mikhailovski, philosophy cannot make wholly intelligible the fact that '*in addition to* the need for knowledge there is a need for moral judgment'.[2] This 'dual-unity' evidently leads to a *religious* conception of truth-justice. Mikhailovski was clearly aware of the true (religious) meaning of his searchings, but he was too closely bound by the principles of secularism to accept ecclesiastical Christianity without fear.[3] Thus his religious searchings ended in an absolutizing of the individual—an unconditional and categorical personalism. The individual person, in the fullness and wholeness of his life, becomes the highest value; but he exhibits his genuine and irreplaceable force only in mastering his whole environment. Here Mikhailovski makes an unexpected leap toward relativism. The individual is absolute; all things are *for him*, not for themselves; they have value only in relation to the individual, who becomes a true 'measure of all things'. This position finds unique expression in Mikhailovski's original reworking of Comte's doctrine of the three phases of the development of mankind. First, according to Mikhailovski, comes the 'objectively anthropocentric' stage, in which man naïvely regards himself as the objective centre of the world; second the 'ex-centric' stage, in which central significance is ascribed to the objective world, to which man subordinates himself; and third the 'subjectively anthropocentric' stage, in which man and his ethical searchings are placed at the centre of the world.

'Man can say: yes, nature is ruthless toward me, it makes no distinction between me and the sparrow; but I will be ruthless toward her and subdue her with the labour of my blood, forcing her to serve me. I shall cancel out evil and create good. I am not nature's goal . . ., but I *have* goals and I shall attain them. . . . Nothing was created for man; but he himself, by the strength of his consciousness, places himself at the centre of nature.'[4]

Thus the concept of 'truth in itself' drops away. 'There is no absolute truth', Mikhailovski says. 'There is only truth for man;

1. *Ibid.*, p. 389.    2. *Ibid.*, p. 394.

3. See his remarkable 'fragments on religion' (1901). Concerning Mikhailovski's religious position, see Masaryk, *op. cit.*, II, 176. It would be interesting to compare Mikhailovski's views with the dreams of A. D. Mikhailov—the founder of the *Narodnaya volya* [People's Will] movement—concerning a 'new religion'.

4. Mikhailovski, *op. cit.*, I, 222.

and beyond the limits of human nature there is no truth for man.' [1]
This anthropologism narrows the concept of theoretical knowledge,
but on the other hand this knowledge takes on absolute significance
for man as a result of the absolute significance of man's ethical
sphere.

Mikhailovski's personalism led him inevitably to an *isolation* of
man from the order of nature and a struggle against nature and
the so-called 'natural course of things' [2]—which, according to
Mikhailovski, is found only where man does not intervene in
nature. In this struggle with nature we must be fully aware of the
individual's right to realize his goals, as well as the necessity of
overcoming the fragmentation of the individual which takes place
during the second period of history.

'Let anyone who wants to, look upon me as a part of something
greater than I am . . .; I do not cease to regard myself as a whole
man, an integral personality. I wish to live all the life that is
available to me, and no more. . . . I shall go consciously and
willingly wherever I am assured the wholeness, indivisibility, and
fullness of a total life.' [3]

'Man's good is his wholeness, his harmony.' [4]

Mikhailovski broadened his personalism into a specific metaphysics of nature in his remarkable studies devoted to the question
of 'The Struggle for Individuality'. He finds this struggle everywhere in the natural organic world; but in man it takes on a more
fatal character in proportion to the development of history.
Society suppresses the individual, turning him into a slave, a 'cog'
—depriving him of fullness and wholeness. Even the family, and
sexual differentiation in general, impairs the individual's wholeness. Mikhailovski shows in a series of studies how the higher
forms of individualization swallow up the lower. Human personality, although it is a high form of individualization, encounters
higher forms (with respect to the individual person) in the
family and, even more obviously, in society.

1. *Ibid.*, p. 121.
2. This is the title of the fifth article in a series entitled 'Teoriya Darvina i
obshchestvennaya nauka' ['Darwin's Theory and Social Science'], *op. cit.*,
Vol. I.
3. *Op. cit.*, III, 336.
4. *Op. cit.*, I, 125. Mikhailovski's motif of wholeness is very close to that of
Schiller, even containing elements of Rousseauism—the exaltation of 'natural'
wholeness. Concerning Rousseau see Mikhailovski, *Literaturnyie vospominaniya*
[Literary Memoirs], Vol. II.

'It may be that society is progressing', Mikhailovski wrote, 'but you must understand that the individual is retrogressing. . . . Society, by the very process of its development, strives to *split up* the individual, to give him some special function and to distribute the remaining functions to others, transforming the *individual* into an *organ*.' [1]

'I proclaim,' he wrote in another place, 'that I shall struggle with the higher individuality which threatens to swallow me up. I am not concerned with *its* perfection; I want to perfect *myself*.' [2] This motif—the struggle for the wholeness of the individual—is especially sharpened in Mikhailovski's discussions of the contemporary social order, which is based on a constantly developing differentiation of labour:

'Here the individual is trampled upon; individual freedom, interest, and happiness are sacrificed on the altar of a correctly or incorrectly understood system of "maximum production." . . . I *cannot rejoice* at the victory of the higher individuality [with respect to the individual].' [3]

Struggling for man's wholeness, and against the specialization and 'fragmentation' of the individual, Mikhailovski eulogizes the 'layman', i.e. the man who has not yet lost his wholeness. 'The layman is a man *par excellence*', he writes, 'and science must serve *him* if it wants to be worthy of its name.' [4]

### 11. MIKHAILOVSKI'S ANTHROPOLOGY

In his struggle for the wholeness and fullness of the individual, Mikhailovski—like Lavrov—bases himself on a quite pedestrian and superficial anthropology. He does not sense the metaphysical problems, the hidden depths in man. Thus the human will, the bearer of freedom and responsibility, is for him simply 'one of the links in a chain of causes and effects'. [5] Mikhailovski broadens his anthropological empiricism somewhat in his remarkable articles on collective psychology, especially in discussing the function of the imagination. But the recognition that man's freedom is a genuine and creative force comes all the more unexpectedly in Mikhailovski, as in the other semi-positivists. He does not simply note the fact that man possesses 'a *consciousness* of free choice in his activity'; he asserts that man really *can* and *should* struggle against

1. *Op. cit.*, I, 477.
2. 'Zapiski profana' ['Notes of a Layman'], *op. cit.*, III, 423.
3. *Op. cit.*, I, 454, 494.    4. *Op. cit.*, III, 354.    5. *Ibid.*, p. 14.

the 'natural course of things'. 'Only those for whom such struggle is unprofitable propose—and that in cases where it is unprofitable—that we should not struggle against the fatal course of things.' [1]

'In the *moment* of activity I am conscious that I freely set myself a goal. . . . This is the only basis for individual responsibility and moral judgment. . . . But the sense of responsibility, conscience, and the need for moral judgment are completely real phenomena of the psychic life.' [2]

Further on we read: 'We laymen regard the right to judge ourselves morally, to know good and evil, and to call a scoundrel a scoundrel, as a *sacred* and inalienable right. The fact that men's actions conform to law is a great truth, but it *should not* infringe upon this right.' But why not, since, a few lines before this, Mikhailovski says of freedom: 'Perhaps it is a delusion [!], but history is moved by it' [3]? As we see, Mikhailovski's anthropology provides too precarious a foundation for his ethical claims. Mikhailovski, as Ovsyanniko-Kulikovski justly notes, has a good deal of the romanticist in him,[4] and this romanticism breaks through in the categorical quality of his ethical searchings and claims. But Mikhailovski went even further; he was the most brilliant exponent of the so-called 'subjective method' in social science. This doctrine must be set beside the enormous and fertile tendency of German Protestantism and German philosophy, summed up under the title '*Das Problem der Werturteile*' ['The Problem of Value-Judgements'].[5] The term 'subjective method' is of course inept; but, as Masaryk has correctly noted, it is a 'bad name for an excellent thing'.[6] The essence of this 'subjectivism' is the recognition that *valuation* is a 'constitutive' rather than a 'regulative' factor in the cognition of human activity. As Mikhailovski puts it: '*Observation* of social phenomena is intimately and inevitably bound up with moral valuation.' [7] This formula contains the essence of the 'subjective method'. It is a matter of recognizing that a purely 'theoretical', i.e. *non-valuational* perception of man and his activity simply does not provide us with all the material that is contained in social facts. Valuation—from the point of view of 'interests', 'sympathies', or 'ideals',—is vital for 'observation', just as, in

1. *Ibid.*, p. 206.   2. *Ibid.*, p. 437.   3. *Loc. cit.*   4. *Op. cit.*, II, 227.
5. The chief philosophic work on this problem is A. Meinong, *Ueber Annahmen*, Leipzig, 1902. See also Heinrich Maier, *Psychologie des emotionale Denken*, 1908; T. Ribot, *La Logique des sentiments*, Paris, 1912; Reuschle, *Werturteile*, etc.
6. Masaryk, *op. cit.*, II, 187.   7. *Op. cit.*, I, 87.

general, 'emotional thinking' (fear, envy, faith, love, etc.) leads us for the first time into those aspects of man which are otherwise incomprehensible. This is a fact which is recognized today by a significant majority of psychologists. But Mikhailovski emphasizes its purely personalistic aspect ('I fully reserve the right to criticize God's great world from the point of view of my scrap of brain' [1]), stressing every individual's sovereign right to live and evaluate the world in accordance with his consciousness of the ideal. The important thing, according to Mikhailovski, is to introduce the viewpoint of the 'social ideal' into the understanding of the social world. The unity of theoretical truth and moral justice which is so essential for him, the valuation of the social sphere, should not be subjective in the strict sense; it should take as its point of departure the sovereign truth-justice of a 'higher 'ideal. But what is the origin of this higher ideal for Mikhailovski?—His 'Populism', of course. He himself expresses this very well in the words: 'Compassion lives in me and *consumes my soul.*' [2] It was Mikhailovski who gave currency to the expression 'repentant nobleman'—the equivalent of Lavrov's formula of 'paying off one's debt' to the people. Struve has justly remarked that 'Mikhailovski, in his moral doctrine, is virtually the most idealistic of the major writers on social and political themes of the 1860's and 70's.' [3] This accurately expresses the *passionate ethicism* which constituted the creative source of Mikhailovski's searchings. He was marked by that genuine 'primacy of ethics' which is characteristic of so many Russian thinkers. There is good reason for the presence in Mikhailovski of judgments that are very close to the extreme 'panmoralism'—or ethical anthropologism— which was most brilliantly expressed by Leo Tolstoy. 'Only that science which clears the path of life for me', we read in the 'Notes of a Layman', 'do I acknowledge as worthy of the sacred name of science.' [4] In his first long article 'What is Progress?' Mikhailovski repudiated 'pure' art; in another place he commented ironically that 'thought has ceased to be a means and has become a *Selbstzweck* [end in itself]'.[5] Further on, wholly in the spirit of the doctrine of 'class' ideologies, he wrote that what is called ' "justice", and "beauty", is nothing more than masked subservience to a given social order'. [6] This is a further expression of the inevitability of the subjective element in judgments concerning man and society. The highest stage of self-consciousness, as we have seen,

---

1. *Op. cit.*, III, 151.
2. *Op. cit.*, IV, 64.
3. Preface to Berdyaev, *op. cit.*, p. lxxxii.
4. *Op. cit.*, III, 336.
5. *Op. cit.*, I, 141, 221.
6. *Op. cit.*, II, 609.

is characterized, according to Mikhailovski, by the 'subjectively anthropocentric' point of view. And in this subjectivism of valuations central importance attaches—for Mikhailovski himself—to the ethical component.

Just as Mikhailovski combines a fiery personalism with an impoverished and meagre anthropology, so too he combines a passionate ethicism with a quite narrow conception of the ethical sphere. The pervasive contrast between Mikhailovski's meagre positivism and his profound spiritual searchings is striking. He constructed an ethics of 'conscience' and 'honour'—a system of secular ethics without a religious root, yet categorical and irreconcilable in its demands. He demanded the fusion and unity of theoretical truth and moral justice; and here his ethical passion, his ethical idea, attained extraordinary purity and force. The consciousness of freedom is the fundamental moving force of man's creativity, the basis of his indefatigable upward striving ('perhaps it is a delusion, but history is moved by it'—see p. 369). However, moral ideas have an 'empirical' origin for Mikhailovski; [1] he rejects all metaphysical grounding of morality, without reflection, considering that 'the moral law exists only in our consciousness'. [2] And from this proposition he draws a conclusion which permits him to defend (subjective) ethical absolutism: 'Since nature has no goals . . ., anyone who wishes to can impose any goal at all upon nature.' Ethics, on this precarious foundation, becomes a kind of free, 'poetic' creativity—in Aristotle's sense of the word—and no grounds remain for absolutism.

## 12. THE CATEGORY OF 'POSSIBILITY' IN THE PHILOSOPHY OF HISTORY

Such are the contradictions of semi-positivism at its deepest point —in ethics. It is not surprising that in his philosophy of history Mikhailovski puts forward very important and ethically valuable theories on this same precarious basis of subjectivism, without serious foundation. His whole philosophy of history, as has been shown in detail by Kistyakovski,[3] is built around the category of 'possibility'; and possibility itself is treated in terms of pure subjectivism. This category occupied a considerable place in Herzen's historiosophical theories—in the doctrine that it is *possible* for Russia to develop differently from Western Europe; and, strictly speaking, the whole school of sociological—or more accurately,

1. *Ibid.*, p. 273.     2. *Ibid.*, p. 151.     3. Kistyakovski, *op. cit.*

historiosophical—'subjectivism' must be traced back to him. This is an example of the intrusion of historiosophical principles into general philosophic theories. We shall see its culminating point in so-called 'Soviet philosophy'. In fact, the limitation or denial of historiosophical determinism requires a mitigation or rejection of general philosophic determinism. We have seen the origin of these theories in Herzen, where they were connected with the breakup of Hegel's 'panlogism'. In Mikhailovski the category of possibility is not connected with a critique of 'panlogism',[1] but flows from the general orientation of personalism and from an assertion of the *autonomy of ethical judgments*. For Mikhailovski's semi-positivism ethical judgments are connected with the consciousness of freedom; the psychological—and purely psychological—reality of freedom leads logically to a recognition of objective 'possibility' (indeterminism) in individual and historical reality. Thus ethicism bursts the framework of positivism.

We shall not go into the details of Mikhailovski's development of a philosophy of history on the basis of the category of 'possibility'; this has been well and thoroughly done in the above-mentioned work by Kistyakovski. But we must mention a series of Mikhailovski's excellent studies devoted to a struggle against the 'method of analogy' in sociology, against the carrying over of Darwinism into sociology, and in particular against the so-called 'organic school' of sociologists (Spencer *et al.*).[2] In these articles, which are brilliantly and often very profoundly written, Mikhailovski clears a path for personalism, and for the liberation of the moral consciousness from the fetters of a deterministic historiosophy. He persistently emphasizes the antagonism between the individual and society, and introduces a very fruitful distinction between 'type' and 'stage' of development. Nations whose life belongs to the 'higher' type may—as a result of their stage of development in this type—seem to be below nations which belong to a 'lower' type but have advanced much further in their stage of development. Defending a humanistic position, Mikhailovski is not afraid to say that 'it is very far from true that the struggle for existence is a law of nature'.[3] And, in conformity with his anthropologism, he

1. That Russian historiosophical thought of the 1870's no longer started from the collapse of panlogism is most obvious in the historiosophical theories of N. I. Kareyev, another representative of the 'subjective' school. See below.

2. Mikhailovski's critique of Spencer has been translated into French: *Qu'est-ce que le progrès?*, Paris, 1897. *Trans.*

3. *Op. cit.*, IV, 415. As is generally known, Prince Kropotkin wrote a remarkable work on this subject called *Mutual Aid, A Factor of Evolution*, London, 1902.

passes an even bolder judgment: 'The historical course of events is completely meaningless in itself.' [1] This assertion of historiosophical *alogism*—in the spirit of Herzen—is quickly supplemented by a personalistic thesis: 'The individual, and not some mystical force, establishes goals in history.' Thus the individual is not *constrained* by any fatal course of things; he has the 'logical and moral right to struggle' against the 'natural course of things', for 'the right of *moral judgment* is at the same time the right to intervene in the course of events'.[2] This intervention, which is objectively feasible because of the category of 'possibility', is motivated, as we see, by the 'right of moral judgment'. The primacy of ethical categories is here expressed with great clarity.

### 13. EPISTEMOLOGY

Nevertheless, Mikhailovski's general epistemological views remain on a foundation of oversimplified positivism. He fails to notice how desperately his basic world-view requires a different conception of being and knowledge. He 'accepts the basic propositions concerning the *limits* of knowledge',[3] and defends the 'exclusively empirical origin of all knowledge, its relativity, and the impossibility of penetrating into the hidden essence of things'.[4] With the naïve self-assurance which is so often characteristic of positivists, Mikhailovski echoes the peremptory words, 'Axioms themselves turn out [!] to be a result of experience and observation.' 'The most abstract ideas, in the final analysis, are rooted in sense experience; such [!] is the nature of man'; 'in all times and places men have acquired their knowledge from the external world'.[5] All of these propositions are asserted as beyond dispute—the results of 'scientific philosophy'. Mikhailovski was, in fact, an obedient disciple of Comte, Mill, and Spencer.[6] However he went even further than they did in his relativism and epistemological subjectivism. Here, for example, are typical words:

'For science . . . it is a matter of *indifference* whether knowledge of nature is itself true or illusory; it is only important that this knowledge should satisfy the demands of human nature. Therefore science places the question of the conditions of human life *above* the question of truth. . . . By substituting for the word "truth" the

1. Mikhailovski, *op. cit.*, III, 443.
2. *Ibid.*, p. 448.      3. *Op. cit.*, IV, 99.      4. *Op. cit.*, I, 24, 81.
5. *Ibid.*, p. 129; *op. cit.*, III, 359, 52.
6. To these must be added the influence of A. Lange and, to some extent, that of Proudhon. See Masaryk, *op. cit.*, II, 150–2.

phrase "satisfaction of man's cognitive need", we reach a criterion of truth which has guided man from time immemorial.' [1]

The important and interesting thing for Mikhailovski is not 'absolute' truth, but 'truth for man'.

Like Lavrov, Mikhailovski rejected relativism and sceptical agnosticism in ethics, becoming a fiery preacher of 'truth-justice'. Nothing is more interesting and typical of the inner dialectic of Russian positivism than this ethical passion, which is so inappropriate in a general relativism. The creative work of the mind is itself supported in secret by this ethical passion; the 'primacy of practical reason' dominates all intellectual effort.

## 14. N. I. KAREYEV. HIS PHILOSOPHIC VIEWS

It remains for us to say a few words, in our study of Russian semi-positivism, concerning N. I. Kareyev, a Professor of History at St. Petersburg University and an energetic and persistent defender of 'subjectivism' in social and historical knowledge.

Nicholas Ivanovich Karayev (1850–1931) was an outstanding historian, whose numerous writings and researches earned him great fame and popularity. He approached the problems of the philosophy of history, in which he always had great interest, as an historian—not from an abstract philosophic point of view, but in the light of concrete historical themes.[2] His large works, Fundamental Problems of the Philosophy of History and On the Role of the Individual in History, offer a very thorough critique of the historiosophical constructions of Hegel and his followers.

'History is not a straight line', he wrote, 'it is not a regular design traced out on a mathematical plane, but a living fabric of irregular and sinuous lines, which are intertwined in the most varied and unexpected ways. . . . The universal historical process is not *systematic.* . . . The march of world history is a chaotic concatenation of chances. . . . We must introduce the concept of chance into history.[3]

1. Mikhailovski, *op. cit.*, II, 347, 349.
2. His brief but eloquent study 'O svobode voli' ['On the Freedom of the Will'] (in the book *Etyudy sotsiologicheskiye i filosofskiye* [Sociological and Philosophic Studies]) is very valuable in this respect.
3. *Osnovnyie voprosy filosofi istori* [Fundamental Problems of the Philosophy of History], 1883, I, 153, 198, 203.

Since 'the individual is the supreme principle in the philosophy of history' for Kareyev, he naturally gravitates toward Mikhailovski's personalism (he himself acknowledged Mikhailovski's influence), as well as the latter's doctrine of 'subjectivism' in historical cognition. 'The whole philosophy of history', Kareyev concludes, summing up his critique of various historiosophical systems, 'is an application of the idea of progress to the destiny of mankind'; and the meaning of history lies not in its 'absolute' significance, but in its 'significance for man'.[1] Therefore, valuation cannot be dispensed with in the study of history. 'The philosophy of history', Kareyev wrote, 'is a *judgment* of history.' [2]

'Reason, thought, idea, do not pertain to the world as a whole, but to the world within the limits of *human knowledge*. . . . The world is not rational, it does not think; no idea underlies the universal process; thought and reason develop and ideas appear, in certain of the world's infinitely small creatures.' [3]

Kareyev, like Lavrov and Mikhailovski, bases his assertion of the individual's right to moral judgment of history on a recognition of the alogical nature of the cosmic process. To eliminate this element of subjective valuation, Kareyev thinks, is to 'risk having the meaning of phenomena remain closed to us. . . . In history itself we are dealing with [moral] consciousness . . .; and this consciousness, as one of the objects of our study, demands a subjective attitude toward itself.'[4]

The singular combination of scientifico-philosophic positivism and relativism with a categorical ethicism indicates, of course, the inadequacy of secularistic ideologies. Those thinkers who (as we shall see in Parts III and IV) did not hesitate to draw relativistic conclusions in the field of *morality* from their general philosophic relativism were much more consistent. But for the Russian consciousness, with its insistence on the primacy of the ethical sphere, to accept moral relativism was even more difficult than to remain within the limits of semi-positivism. It is not surprising that the inner dialectic of questing thought began to move toward an overcoming of the system of secularism. This process developed on diverse spiritual foundations; we shall turn first to those thinkers in whom it took place on a foundation of positivism and naturalism.

1. *Ibid.*, p. 246.  2. *Ibid.*, p. 242.
3. *Ibid.*, p. 326.  4. *Ibid.*, pp. 386, 393.

# CHAPTER XIII

## The Overcoming of the Secular Orientation on a Foundation of Naturalism and Positivism

### N. I. PIROGOV. L. N. TOLSTOY

### I. THE OVERCOMING OF SECULARISM ON RUSSIAN SOIL

WE have more than once emphasized that Russian secularism developed under Western influence. However, once it had arisen on Russian soil, it struck deep roots in the Russian consciousness and took on certain specific features. As a focus of struggle against the *Church*, secularism in the West, too, constantly developed into a specific kind of 'new religion'—pantheism, religio-philosophic immanentism, and even mysticism. But Russian secularism had an especially marked religious colouring, and was almost always clothed in some specific form of *sectarianism*. Even where it was organically connected with an extreme and consistent materialism, Russian secularism retained a specific religious psychology. Therefore it is not to be wondered at that the disintegration of a philosophical ideology connected with secularistic tendencies very often led on Russian soil to an acceptance of basic Christian ideas, and a reorganization of the entire world-view in the spirit of Christianity. This inner disintegration of secularism was a characteristic and creative movement in Russian thought, and one which has lasted to our own day. The essential point is that this return to Christianity took place on a foundation of declining secular tendencies.

This movement of thought first appeared strongly on Russian soil in the 1860's and '70's. We have already touched upon this subject to some extent in speaking of N. V. Chaikovski and the movement of the 'God-men' which was associated with his name. But the crisis which we find in two outstanding men of the time—N. I. Pirogov and L. N. Tolstoy—is the most striking characteristic of the period. The former was a world-famous surgeon and a man of genius who established, as it were, the type of the Russian doctor;[1] the other was an even more outstanding genius—an incomparable artist and a passionate moralist, whose searchings attracted not only Russians but people throughout the world. Both thinkers —although they had no personal connection—expressed, each in his own way and with extraordinary force, the internal rupture which was taking place in Russian secularism. One of them took the scientific world-view as his point of departure, the other the general cultural self-consciousness of the period. But as young men both of them were adherents of a positivistic and naturalistic world-view; both of them became profoundly disillusioned by it, and turned to a specific kind of religious world-view.

Let us turn first to a study of the philosophic evolution of N. I. Pirogov.

## 2. N. I. PIROGOV. BIOGRAPHY

Nicholas Ivanovich Pirogov (1810–81) was born into the family of a government official,[2] and received his primary education at home. Later he entered a private school, and at the age of fourteen passed the University entrance examination. At that time students had to be sixteen to enter the University; Pirogov's parents said that he was sixteen, although in fact he was only fourteen. At the age of seventeen Pirogov passed his final examinations at the University and was assigned to prepare himself for a professorship in Derpt. At the age of twenty-three he defended his doctoral dissertation, and went abroad for further study. At the age of twenty-six he was appointed to a chair of surgery at Derpt and soon gained a reputation as an outstanding surgeon, publishing a series of first-class works. He gained special fame with the publication of the Annals of a Surgical Clinic, in which, incidentally, he courageously and honestly described his own operating-room mistakes. In 1840 Pirogov was appointed Professor in the Academy of Military Medicine in St. Petersburg. During this period his scientific and civic activities developed strongly. When the Crimean War broke out he went to Sevastopol, but the disorder and abuses there depressed him so that he was unable to remain more than six months. Within a short time, however, he returned

1. Many memorials and institutions in Pirogov's honour existed in Russia. Especially noteworthy were the All-Russian 'Pirogovian' Medical Congresses —which were inaugurated in 1885.

2. Pirogov himself wrote a brief autobiography (printed in his *Sochineniya* [Works], Kiev, 1910, Vol. I).

to the Crimea (Simferopol), where he remained until the end of the war. Upon his return to St. Petersburg in 1856, Pirogov published a number of brilliant articles on pedagogical themes under the general title, Problems of Life [German trans: *Lebens-fragen*, Stuttgart, 1894]. These articles, which passionately defended the primacy of education over training, were permeated with a lofty humanism; they were extraordinarily successful in Russian society, going through numerous editions. Pirogov was offered a position as Superintendent of the Odessa Academic District; but his independent character, straightforwardness, and liberal views evoked a series of conflicts with the local administration. He was transferred to the same position in Kiev, but here too he was badgered by the local administration because of his bold and free statements. In 1861 Pirogov was relieved of his duties 'because of failing health'; he retired to his estate, where he remained almost continuously until his death. In May 1881 the fiftieth anniversary of Pirogov's entry into scientific and medical activity was celebrated throughout Russia; in November of the same year he died.

### 3. THE METAPHYSICS OF THOUGHT AND THE CRITIQUE OF MATERIALISM ACCORDING TO PIROGOV

Pirogov did not consider himself a philosopher nor did he pretend to be one,[1] but, in fact, he developed an integral and well-thought-out philosophic conception of the world. Before entering the University, he was thoroughly imbued with a religious world-view, but at the University he quite rapidly assimilated the views with which medicine was then saturated—those of a clear and consistent materialism. Although Pirogov had some contact with the doctrines of nature-philosophy current in his time, they did not influence him. Materialism impressed his young mind with the simplicity and clarity of its picture of the world. 'I am one of those', he wrote in his Diary, 'who, having scarcely left their student benches, devoted themselves with ardour to the empirical tendency of science, despite the fact that the labyrinth of nature-philosophy and Hegelianism extended all about.'[2] Throughout his life Pirogov remained an empiricist, a conscientious investigator of facts; but he soon widened his epistemological position into a 'rational empiricism', as he expressed it. We shall study Pirogov's epistemological views later—they are totally bound up with his doctrine of the metaphysics of thought—but let us

1. *Op. cit.*, II, 23, 76.                    2. *Ibid.*, p. 44.

point out now that his break with materialism occurred on *epistemological* grounds.

'I became convinced', he wrote, 'having served my term as an empiricist faithfully and honestly, that I could not remain . . . a positivist. . . . I was not destined to be a positivist. I could not command my thought not to go where it might be mistaken.' [1]

This unceasing intellectual activity, which did not permit him to rest permanently with any proposition, was characteristic of Pirogov. 'At every step', he wrote, 'we find a mystery hanging over us . . . [merely] hidden under scientific names. We are surrounded on all sides by the world's mysteries.' [2] The 'superficiality' of materialism became clear to Pirogov [3] and, what is most important, the *'worship of chance'* which reigns in science—as he expressed it [4] —became intolerable to him. Everywhere in science chance is assigned such an excessive place that man's mind cannot tolerate it. On the other hand, the atomistic theory of matter fails utterly to introduce us into the *mystery* of matter.

'It is now impossible for me', Pirogov wrote, 'to halt in thought at eternally moving and eternally existing atoms. . . . Matter is infinitely divisible, moving, and amorphous, and in some chance way it limits and forms itself. . . . *Atom* is an abstract concept. . . . Matter in general seems to me just as limitless as space, time, energy, or life.' [5]

Pirogov gradually inclined to the idea, which is such a commonplace in our time, that 'one may even admit the possibility of the formation of matter from an accumulation of energy'. [6]

But the inadequacy of pure materialism became even clearer to Pirogov when he had become convinced of the impossibility of reducing the concept of life to purely materialistic terms. The *nonderivativeness* of the concept of life made it one of the basic categories of Pirogov's thought, and he resolutely and boldly accepted a conception of the world which today is often termed *biocentric*.

'I picture to myself', he wrote, 'a boundless, amorphous, everflowing ocean of life, which contains the whole universe and permeates all of its atoms, continually combining and dispersing them and adapting them to the various purposes of being.' [7]

1. *Ibid.*, p. 76.    2. *Ibid.*, pp. 56f, 62f, 201.    3. *Ibid.*, p. 178.
4. *Ibid.*, p. 169.    5. *Ibid.*, p. 13.    6. *Ibid.*, pp. 21f, 39
7. *Ibid.*, p. 15.

Pirogov's doctrine of universal *life* illuminated epistemological problems in a new light; he developed a doctrine of the reality of '*universal thought*'.[1] In so doing, he not only broke completely with metaphysical materialism, but also developed a new conception of existence. 'Is not the reason why our mind finds teleological creativity outside itself', he asks, 'that the mind itself is a manifestation of a higher, universal life-principle, which pervades and manifests itself in the whole universe?' [2]

'It is unthinkable', he continues, 'that our brain is the only organ of thought in the whole universe, that everything in the world except human thought is irrational and meaningless. It is unthinkable that in the whole universe our brain is the only locus of manifestation of a "self", since this self wholly refuses to admit its oneness with its place of origin. . . . It seems more plausible to me that our "self" is introduced from outside. Is not our "self" universal thought, encountering in our brain an apparatus skilfully worked out for the purpose by life itself and intended for the particularization of the universal mind?'

This is a new metaphysics, constructed by Pirogov, according to which our 'self' is not a product of chemical and histological elements, but an embodiment of universal reason.

'The discovery of universal thought by my own cerebral thought . . .,' Pirogov writes, 'is the reason why my mind was not satisfied with atoms which achieve sensitivity and self-consciousness . . . through themselves alone, without the participation of any higher consciousness or thought. For me it is beyond question that the higher universal thought—which has chosen the universe for its organ, permeating and combining atoms in a certain form—has also made my brain an organ of thought.'

This new doctrine of universal thought now becomes the foundation for Pirogov's world-view.

'The universal consciousness becomes my own individual consciousness through a special mechanism contained in the nerve centres. We do not know, of course, how this takes place. But it is clear to me that my consciousness, my thought, and my mind's striving to find purposes and causes, cannot be something *fragmentary* or *solitary*, wholly unrelated to the universal life; it cannot be the culmination of the universe—with nothing above it.' [3]

1. *Ibid.*, p. 17.     2. *Ibid.*, p. 35.     3. *Ibid.*, p. 20.

## 4. THE DOCTRINE OF 'UNIVERSAL REASON'

This higher principle which is above the world, giving it life and rationality, was conceived by Pirogov for the time being as 'universal thought'—or 'reason'. Here he came very close to Stoic pantheism, with its doctrine of the universal Logos. But he gradually realized that 'to take the universe as a point of support is to build on sand. . . . My poor mind, dwelling upon the universe instead of God, revered it as a limitless and eternal principle.'[1] But the universe 'is only a manifestation and disclosure of creative thought. In other words, the world-consciousness, or universal reason, undergoes eternal motion and change; but an immutable and absolute foundation is necessary for the understanding of being.'[2] Pirogov concluded that it was necessary to recognize an Absolute *above* the world-consciousness—'we must acknowledge the sovereign reason and will of a Creator, a will which is teleologically manifested in matter *through* the universal life and universal mind'.[3] Thus Pirogov, step by step, re-established the foundations of a religious explanation of the world, assigning to faith a very large place *beside* knowledge. He had a decided and profound aversion for the 'worship of chance', which, he felt, holds questing thought in bondage. Chance, for Pirogov, is only an *asylum ignorantiae*.[4] In the strict sense of the word there is no 'chance'; nothing is uncaused. But in order to assert the principle of causality when everything appears to be a combination of chances, we must acknowledge the reality of a higher principle which rules the world—universal reason. The recognition of this 'universal reason'—*above* which stands God, as the Absolute—is very important for Pirogov's metaphysics. This concept is essentially the same as that of the world-soul. And here Pirogov anticipated the cosmological theories (beginning with Vladimir Solovyov and continuing to our day) which are connected with 'Sophiological' ideas. Pirogov's cosmology was actually very close to that of latter-day Russian Sophiologists.

## 5. EPISTEMOLOGICAL VIEWS

Pirogov, being a rigorous scientist, was fully aware of the hypothetical character of his theoretical constructions, but at the same time he clearly understood the impossibility of remaining on a foundation of mere facts.

1. *Ibid.*, p. 169    2. *Loc. cit.*    3. *Loc. cit.*    4. *Ibid.*, p. 175.

'Only a fact that *was*, *is*, and *will be*, would be the truth', Pirogov wrote, 'but we *do not know such a fact*. And if we are convinced of the necessity or possibility of the *nonfactual existence* of something which has always been, is, and will be, then this conviction is a truth for us, though obviously not a factual truth.' [1]

'It is no longer empiricism when we, who always and everywhere encounter spatial boundaries, begin to meditate on the *unbounded*.' This turning of our mind to the 'unbounded' is central for Pirogov's epistemology:

'We who are fated never to see or sense the immeasurable or unbounded, accept their factual existence; we are more convinced of the existence of the unbounded and measureless than was Columbus of the existence of America prior to its discovery. The difference is simply that we shall never discover our America as he did his.'

Experience—the perception of space, time, and life—is itself based on a primary sense of 'measureless and unbounded being', and this primary sense of space, time, and being, 'is deeply hidden in the nature of the life principle'. [2]
Our thought

'is always individual, for it is cerebral, organic . . .; but universal thought, because it is universal, cannot be organic. Our mind, being individual and organic, cannot rise to an understanding of the purposes of creation which belong to a nonorganic, unlimited, universal mind.'

This is why knowledge cannot be based only on facts; to ascend the path of knowledge 'speculation' is necessary. Pirogov characterizes his position as 'rational empiricism': all of our perceptions are accompanied by unconscious thinking—in the very moment of their origin—and this thinking is a function of our integral 'self'. [3] It is beyond dispute for Pirogov that all of our separate perceptions are in fact interconnected in the 'self' in which 'factual knowledge' lives. Therefore he distinguishes particular truths from single and total truth. [4] Pirogov's doctrine of 'total truth' recognizes the *limitedness* of a pure rationality which is isolated from the moral sphere; this limitedness is seen with special clarity in the fact that the consciousness of freedom, without which man cannot live or act, appears to the mind as an illusion. And, what is even more important, the mind leads us into the realm of the 'infinite, limit-

1. *Ibid.*, p. 52.   2. *Ibid.*, p. 29.   3. *Ibid.*, p. 49.   4. *Ibid.*, p. 57.

less, and eternal principle', whereas living feeling tears us away from this empyrean sphere, binding us to concrete existence. This focusing on real concreteness, a concreteness which is transitory and ephemeral, appears to the mind as error and illusion. However, all of man's creativity—and his whole moral sphere—is turned precisely toward concrete reality, at the same time that his mind leads him away from it. These 'illusions' [1] free us from the limitedness of the mind and bring wholeness into our spiritual world, as a result of which the inner unity of the cognitive and moral life is revealed to us.

Faith is the most important result of the freeing of our spirit from the 'consistency' of pure intellect. In a remarkable letter Pirogov even asserted that faith reveals and initiates the path of cognition. [2] To be sure, doubts are born from the womb of this primordial faith, generating the criticism which is so closely associated with science. But, having passed through the stage of doubt and having freed itself from the limitedness of 'consistent' reflection, our spirit returns to faith. [3] In this higher stage, faith becomes a force linking us to the sphere of the ideal, to God.

'The capacity to know, which is founded on doubt, does not accept faith; but, on the other hand, faith is not constrained by knowledge. . . . The ideal which serves as the ground of faith is placed higher than all knowledge and strives to attain the truth apart from knowledge.' [4]

Thus, when faith arises in this higher wholeness of the spirit, it gives ample scope and freedom to the spirit's cognitive activity; man achieves a free and creative harmony of faith and knowledge. Pirogov decisively rejects Deism as a theoretical construction of pure intellect, [5] and reverts to Christianity. Faith, for Pirogov, is a living sense of God. The mystical rather than the historical reality of Christ nourishes his spirit—and he thus defends complete freedom of religio-historical investigation, since the essence of Christianity is 'not in history'. [6]

Thus Pirogov moved from critical doubt to an awareness of the untenability of positivism and the need for metaphysics. And his metaphysics of thought produced an awareness that the 'consist-

---

1. The doctrine that 'illusions' restore integral truth is developed in the same place, *ibid.*, pp. 63–8.

2. Letter of 1850. *Russkaya starina*, No. 2 (1916).

3. *Ibid.*, p. 237.                4. *Sochineniya*, II, 182.

5. *Ibid.*, p. 185.                6. *Ibid.*, p. 187.

ency' of pure intellect does not lead to total truth. The 'illusions' of the spirit are the force which leads us to integral and single truth; through them the light of faith is kindled and the truth and justice of the religious conception of the world revealed.

## 6. DOCTRINE OF MAN

In Pirogov's complex and intense ferment of spirit, the traditional secular orientation crumbled away. He admitted candidly that it was difficult for him as a doctor, who dealt constantly with man's bodily functions, to accept the higher reality of the spirit, in particular the idea of immortality.[1] He began to regard the problem of materiality as even more remote from the oversimplified solutions of materialism. The 'impenetrable mystery' of existence appeared even more sharply; the very opposition of matter and spirit lost its unquestionable character.[2] Pirogov was ready to construct an original metaphysics of light, assimilating the principle of life to light.[3] He seems to have been on the verge of other metaphysical hypotheses; his Diary contains many notes which might have furnished a foundation for new theoretical constructions, but they are all very fragmentary.

Equally fragmentary, though extremely interesting, are Pirogov's ideas on problems of philosophical anthropology. He had a very deep sense of what Dostoyevsky called the 'underground'— the soul's hidden realm, in which diverse cravings have their roots. Pirogov even approached the anthropological position, which was stated so sharply by Klages in the twentieth century, that the soul *loses* a great deal from consciousness of its inner impulses. Pirogov treated the problem of 'self-stylization' with extraordinary profundity in his remarkable article 'Being and Seeming'.[4] This article was written in connection with a proposed children's theatre; in it Pirogov called into question the advisability of an early bifurcation of 'being' and 'seeming'. The intervention of consciousness in the life of the soul constantly introduces an element of 'self-stylization'; in children the distinction between 'seeming' to be and actually 'being' something has not yet appeared with full force. But adults exhibit a sharp inner duality, a separation of genuine from apparent being, i.e. falseness to others and to

1. *Ibid.*, p. 198.                    2. *Ibid.*, p. 199.
3. *Ibid.*, pp. 40, 200f. This is reminiscent in part of Schelling, in part of medieval ideas.
4. *Op. cit.*, I, 79–91.

*themselves.* This duality and falseness are deeply connected with the falseness, rhetoric, and theatricality of contemporary life. At the same time, according to Pirogov, 'base, evil, and miserable impulses' [1] may be concealed in the soul's 'underground' as in a deep pool. Evil lies in wait for man until he dominates his own consciousness and learns to direct his own life; [2] thus the spiritual life inevitably becomes an inner struggle against everything that may be hidden in man's 'underground'.

Pirogov, taking as his point of departure the hypothesis of a world-consciousness and universal thought, came face to face with the problem which was so sharply formulated by the transcendentalists: that of distinguishing the universally human component from the individual component in individual personality. According to Pirogov, our 'self' is only an individualization of the world-consciousness, but to the extent that we are conscious of ourselves (and this very consciousness is 'integral and indivisible' [3]), we reinforce our spiritual isolation. 'I am amazed', Pirogov wrote, 'by the inexplicable identity and wholeness of the "self".' [4] He was faced, as we see, with the problem of a personalistic metaphysics, but his thought did not go beyond a faith in individual immortality.

## 7. GENERAL APPRAISAL OF PIROGOV'S PHILOSOPHIC VIEWS

The most remarkable thing in Pirogov's theoretical constructions is, of course, his break with materialism and positivism and his movement beyond the limits of a secular ideology. The 'biocentric' conception of the world which he professed, the living sense of universal reason, and the interpretation of cosmological and anthropological themes in the light of these ideas—all turned Pirogov's consciousness toward the religious life. Traces of his former submissiveness to secularism remained throughout his life. Although he lived in a deep and ardent faith in the Godmanhood of Christ, his attitude toward the historical Church and the dogmas of Christianity was free and reserved. 'Despite the fact that my world-view is *different* from that of the Church', he wrote, 'I nevertheless acknowledge myself a son of the Russian Church.' [5] Pirogov distinguished between 'faith' and 'religion', [6] and he defended the compatibility of genuine faith in the God-man with freedom of conscience and thought.

1. *Op. cit.*, II, 207.  2. *Ibid.*, p. 209.  3. *Ibid.*, p. 83.
4. *Ibid.*, p. 114.  5. *Ibid.*, p. 216.  6. *Ibid.*, p. 221.

Pirogov's Diary remained unknown to Russian society until after his death; his original world-view was without direct influence on Russian thought. Nevertheless, his spiritual searchings, his overcoming of positivism, and his break with secularism are symptomatic and offer valuable evidence that Russian life was gradually overcoming the spiritual bondage to secularism in which it had remained for so long.

No less symptomatic, and perhaps more so, was the spiritual crisis of another outstanding figure of this period—Leo Tolstoy. Let us turn to a study of his thought.

## 8. L. N. TOLSTOY. GENERAL REMARKS

Tolstoy—like Dostoyevsky—has a special place in the history of Russian philosophy. An artist of genius who did not abandon artistic creation until the end of his life, Tolstoy was at the same time a profound, though one-sided, thinker. There is nothing comparable to the force and extraordinary vividness with which he succeeded in developing his ideas. His words are simple, but filled with a flaming strength; they always contain a profound and irresistible truth and justice. Like other Russian thinkers, Tolstoy subordinated everything to morality, but this was not a 'primacy of practical reason'; it was a genuine 'panmoralism'. Tolstoy dealt harshly with everything that did not fit into the Procrustean bed of his basic ideas, but his exaggerations and sharp formulations testify not only to his maximalism—which is rectilinear and often blind—but to the way in which he was consumed and tormented by the truth and justice which he expressed in his writings. Tolstoy's passionate search for the 'meaning of life' and his heroic opposition to age-old traditions are striking and, in a certain sense, unsurpassed and unrepeatable. Like some ancient hero, Tolstoy entered into single combat with the 'spirit of the age'; in this respect he belongs not only to Russia and Russian problems but to the whole world. Tolstoy was a 'world phenomenon', although he was completely and typically Russian—inconceivable and inexplicable apart from Russian life. He is incomprehensible apart from Russia and even, as we shall see, apart from Orthodoxy, although he struggled stubbornly and violently against the Orthodox Church. Tolstoy's inner antinomies—the perpetual incompleteness, one might say, *incompletability* of his thought—reveal the astonishing power of his spirit. An individualist to the marrow of his bones, a man who unhesitatingly rejected everything that was foreign to him, he was at the same time Russia's most forceful and brilliant exponent of philosophic impersonalism. An extraordinary artist and a passionate lover of music, he wrote a sharp and captiously unjust book against art. Following Rousseau's critique of culture and his rhapsodizing over the soul's 'natural' impulses, Tolstoy worked during the second period of his life at a purely rational solution of the problems of life, rejecting and scorning all 'natural' impulses. Neither in Russia nor in Europe did the nineteenth century produce another such remarkable man —another such powerful, passionate, and ardent 'seeker of truth and justice'. And the greatness of his personality was reflected in his thought.

Let us turn to a brief study of Tolstoy's biography.[1]

## 9. BIOGRAPHY

Leo Nikolayevich Tolstoy (1828–1910) was born into the family of Count N. I. Tolstoy. His well-known sketches *Childhood, Boyhood,* and *Youth* convey very well the family setting in which he spent his early years. He was only nine years old when his father died. On Tolstoy's own account this experience 'implanted in me for the first time a feeling of terror at death'. Tolstoy's mother died when he was only two. The boy grew up in a household of women who loved the children but had no influence over them. Tolstoy and his brother studied at home, preparing for the University entrance examination. Once enrolled at the University of Kazan, Tolstoy was bored by the lectures, and very soon—at the age of nineteen— left the University and went to his country estate, where he planned to prepare himself in two years for the final examination. However he did not remain in the country, but went to Moscow, living a purely worldly life. In 1851 Tolstoy gave up this life and went to the Caucasus, where he entered the military service and spent

1. The biography written by Tolstoy's disciple, P. I. Biryukov (*Leo Tolstoy, His Life and Work,* New York, 1906) is basic for the study of his life. Also important are: (1) the correspondence of Tolstoy and his wife; (2) T. A. Kuzminskaya, *Tolstoy as I Knew Him* [trans. by N. Sigerist *et al.*], New York, 1948; (3) the memoirs of Tolstoy's children: L. L. Tolstoy, *The Truth About My Father,* London, 1924; I. L. Tolstoy, *Reminiscences of Tolstoy* [trans. by G. Calderon], New York, 1914; A. L. Tolstaya, *The Tragedy of Tolstoy* [trans. by E. Varneck], New Haven, 1933; (4) A. B. Goldenveizer, *Talks with Tolstoy* [trans. by S. Koteliansky and V. Woolf], Richmond (England), 1933; (5) Tolstoy's Diaries. The chief biographical studies are: T. I. Polner, *Tolstoy and His Wife* [trans. by N. Wreden], New York, 1945; E. J. Simmons, *Leo Tolstoy,* Boston, 1946.

three years. From the Caucasus he went to Sevastopol, participating directly in military actions.

In 1852 Tolstoy published *Childhood*, and its success immediately
introduced him to literary circles. The stories which he wrote in
the Caucasus and at Sevastopol, especially his *Sevastopol Sketches*,
brought him extraordinary fame. When he arrived in St. Petersburg in 1855 he was immediately enveloped in an atmosphere of
such attention and admiration that it made his head swim. But
even at this time, as he himself recounts in his *Confession*, Tolstoy
felt himself a stranger to the literary environment with its artificiality and self-admiration. His relations with Turgenev became
especially strained. In 1856 Tolstoy went abroad, leaving as a
memento of this first trip a series of stories, among which the
brilliant sketch 'Lucerne'—which sounded the first notes of
accusation against contemporary culture—deserves special mention. Returning to his country estate, Tolstoy experienced several
enthusiasms—for music, forestry, etc. He became particularly
enthusiastic about pedagogical work, and built a model school on
his country estate Yasnaya Polyana [The Clear Glade]. Tolstoy
studied pedagogy a great deal, and made a special trip abroad to
observe the establishment of popular schools in Western Europe.
He even began to publish a special pedagogical journal, in which
he printed his own articles. These articles later evoked a whole
tendency of 'Tolstoyan pedagogy' in various countries—in Russia
last of all.

In 1860 Tolstoy's older brother Nicholas died abroad; his death
made an enormous impression on Tolstoy. ('This event tore me
away dreadfully from life . . .', he wrote in his *Diary*.) In his
*Confession*, where the problem of death has decisive importance for
Tolstoy's spiritual searchings, he wrote: 'Nicholas suffered for more
than a year, and died painfully, not understanding why he had
lived and still less why he had to die. No theories could give me,
or him, any reply to these questions during his slow and painful
dying.' [1]

In the fall of 1862 Tolstoy married Sophia Andreyevna Bers,
with whom he spent a long and happy life; their happiness was
troubled only during the last twenty-five years of Tolstoy's life.
During these first years of family life *War and Peace* was written, a
work that has taken a permanent place in world literature. Somewhat later Tolstoy wrote *Anna Karenina*. But toward the end of the
1870's he entered a period of severe spiritual crisis, which is

1. *Confession* [trans. by A. Maude], London, 1933, p. 13.

described with exceptional force in his *Confession*. The same problem of death stood before him, but now with irresistible force; and in the light of his reflections on death all of his dissatisfaction with the secular culture in which he had been completely immersed hitherto, came to a head. In the perspective of death, life appeared wholly insubstantial; the inevitable power of death drained life of meaning. Tolstoy was so tormented by the tragedy of the inevitability of death, he suffered so deeply from the absurdity of a life which is irrevocably cut off, that he almost committed suicide. There is hardly another document in world literature that is written as forcefully as Tolstoy's *Confession*, every word of which is full of flaming, elemental force. Tolstoy's spiritual crisis culminated in a complete break with the secular conception of the world, and an acceptance of a religious attitude toward life. Tolstoy himself says in the *Confession* that before his crisis he was a 'nihilist'—'in the sense of a complete absence of faith'. In any case, he strove to cut himself loose from the world in which he had lived and to return to the simple folk. 'I began to draw near', he wrote, 'to the believers among the poor, simple, unlettered folk: pilgrims, monks, sectarians, and peasants.' [1] He found in the simple folk a *faith* which gave their life meaning. With his characteristic passion and force, he now strove to draw sustenance from these believers, to enter into the world of their faith—and, first of all, following the people, he turned to the Church. His break with secularism was complete and decisive at this time. Tolstoy overcame all the difficulties which he encountered on this path by means of 'self-abasement and humility' (*Confession*). But he did not stay long in the world of ecclesiastical Christianity; remaining—as he thought—on the soil of Christianity, he broke with the ecclesiastical interpretation of Christ's teaching. *Dogmatics repelled him*, as did everything which was difficult for reason to accept. Theological rationalism, in a rather oversimplified form, dominated his consciousness. Tolstoy created his own metaphysics on the basis of a few propositions of Christianity. He rejected the Divinity and Resurrection of Christ, and resolved to rework the text of many passages of the New Testament in order to retain the basic teaching which, in his opinion, Christ had given to the world. He wrote a four-volume Critique of Dogmatic Theology, a large work entitled *What I Believe*, and a treatise *On Life*; and he meditated vigorously on themes of a philosophic character. There are clear traces of this in his published *Diaries*.

1. *Ibid.*, p. 56.

Tolstoy's spiritual world had now assumed a definite form: that of an original system of *mystical immanentism*, worked out by himself. Tolstoy's immanentism was in complete harmony with the spirit of modern rationalism, with its denial of everything transcendent. Nevertheless, it was a mystical doctrine of life and of man. This mystical element, which led Tolstoy to an acute and extreme immanentism, nevertheless divided him sharply from the contemporary world. Tolstoy's doctrine broke with both the *Church* and the *world*.

Disciples began to gather around Tolstoy, and his doctrine of nonviolent resistance to evil, in all countries of the world; 'Tolstoyan communities' sprang up. These new friends were often more fanatical and consistent than Tolstoy himself. Their meddling in Tolstoy's life and in his increasing family conflicts (neither Tolstoy's wife nor his children—with minor exceptions—wished to accept his renunciation of royalties for his literary works) began gradually to develop into a serious tragedy. This process continued for a long time, ending with Tolstoy's widely-known 'flight' from his family. On the road Tolstoy caught cold and soon died of pneumonia.

Tolstoy's religio-philosophic works are numerous, but they contain many repetitions. We shall treat chiefly his *Confession*, the treatise *On Life, What I Believe,* and *The Kingdom of God Is Within You.*[1]

### 10. THE QUESTION OF PHILOSOPHICAL INFLUENCES ON TOLSTOY

Before turning to an exposition of Tolstoy's philosophic theories, we shall consider the influences to which he was exposed. Tolstoy began to 'philosophize' very early, but he did not receive a systematic education in philosophy; and this was apparent throughout his life. There was much that was *accidental* in his philosophic enthusiasms during various period—accidental in the sense that he was influenced by books that happened to fall into his hands.

1. Concerning Tolstoy's religio-philosophic views see D. S. Merezhkovski, *Tolstoy as Man and Artist, with an Essay on Dostoievski,* New York, 1902; O. Lourié, *La Philosophie de Tolstoï,* Paris, 1899; G. Dwelshauvers, *Rousseau et Tolstoï,* Paris, 1912. To my knowledge there is no survey of the immense literature devoted to Tolstoy (see the very incomplete bibliography in Ueberweg, *Geschichte der Philosophie,* 12th ed., 1928, VI, 348).

But all of his enthusiasms corresponded to his own, distinct or indistinct, searchings.[1] When, at the age of sixteen, Tolstoy 'rooted out' his traditional views, he became passionately enthusiastic about Rousseau and wore a medallion with Rousseau's portrait around his neck instead of a cross. During these early years ethical problems were in the foreground of Tolstoy's attention. A 'striving for perfection', a constant dissatisfaction with himself, a struggle with the 'lower' impulses and passions, wholly filled his inner world even at this period. Tolstoy took from Rousseau a worship of everything 'natural', and a suspicious and mistrustful attitude toward the contemporary world, which gradually developed into a captious critique of all culture. Tolstoy's gravitation toward 'simplification' was not motivated by the psychology of the 'unpayable debt' to the people, which we have found in the various forms of Populism of the 1860's and 70's (see the preceding chapter on Lavrov and Mikhailovski). Tolstoy himself needed 'simplification' to enable him to throw off the weight of the conventions with which 'culture' was filled. In his need to give ample scope to the soul's 'natural' impulses, Tolstoy was not simply *influenced* by Rousseau; it was rather a congeniality of the two minds. The seeds sown by Rousseau bore abundant fruit in Tolstoy. There would be a certain justice in expounding all of Tolstoy's views as variations on his Rousseauism—so deeply did this Rousseauism influence him to the end of his life.

Of the other profound influences on Tolstoy's spiritual development we must note that of Schopenhauer.[2] In 1869 Tolstoy wrote Fet of his 'unceasing rapture over Schopenhauer and a series of intellectual pleasures such as I have never experienced before. . . . I don't know whether I will ever change my mind, but I am now convinced that Schopenhauer is the greatest genius among men'. We should note two basic motifs in Schopenhauer's system which were especially congenial to Tolstoy: his *phenomenalism* and the doctrine of the metaphysical illusoriness of individual being; and his *pessimism*—although in Tolstoy the latter soon became an optimistically coloured impersonalism. It is also interesting to note

1. Tolstoy's Diaries offer much for the study of the genesis of his various theories.

2. Tolstoy himself spoke a great deal—toward the end of the 1890's—of the influence on him of his younger contemporary, the Russian philosopher Spir, but in essence Spir's epistemological ideas did not carry Tolstoy beyond the boundaries of the phenomenalism which he had derived from Schopenhauer. Concerning Spir see Ch. XXVIII.

the coincidence of Tolstoy's and Schopenhauer's views on music; again this was not so much a matter of influence as of congeniality.[1]

Tolstoy experienced no other major *philosophic* influences, but he was an omnivorous reader who greedily absorbed the diverse spiritual influences of his time.

## 11. TOLSTOY'S PANMORALISM

The basic themes of Tolstoy's thought come to focus in his ethical searchings. His ideas may well be characterized as a system of 'panmoralism'. We have already frequently noted in the dialectic of nineteenth-century Russian searchings that ethics remained 'insoluble' for a number of thinkers—beginning with Herzen—in the prevalent positivism and naturalism. Tolstoy, who conceived knowledge in naturalistic and positivistic terms, did not dissolve ethics in a theory of being; on the contrary, he attempted to *reform* science and philosophy, subordinating them to ethics. This was not a 'primacy' of ethics, as in Kant, but a simple tyranny of ethics. Despite the sharp and obtrusive rationalism which deeply defined Tolstoy's religio-philosophic theories, there is something irrational and intractable in his 'panmoralism'. It is not a mere ethical maximalism but a kind of *self-crucifixion*. Tolstoy was a martyr to his own ideas; they tormented his conscience and destroyed his life—his relations to his family, his friends, and 'culture' as a whole. This was a genuine tyranny of one spiritual element over all the other spheres of life. It not only comprises the specific quality of Tolstoy's thought and work, but provides a key to understanding Tolstoy's quite extraordinary influence throughout the world. His preaching *shook* the world, attracting men not by the force of his ideas (which were shared by very few) but by the extraordinary sincerity and rare vividness of his writings, and by the fascination which radiated from a moral passion and a thirst for genuine and unconditional good which no one else has exhibited so profoundly.

Tolstoy's moral searchings were, of course, *religious* in character; he thirsted for an *unconditional* rather than a conditional good, for a good that was not relative but absolute. Although he was a 'darling of fate', in the expression of one writer—a man who had known everything that life can offer: the joys of family happiness,

1. See the very interesting study by S. L. Tolstoy 'Muzyka v zhizni L. N. Tolstovo' ['Music in the Life of L. N. Tolstoy'], in the jubilee volume ed. by Gusev, Moscow, 1928.

fame, and social advantage, and the joys of creation—Tolstoy longed for an eternal, absolute, and permanent good. Without such an 'eternal good' life was meaningless for him; and for this reason he became a preacher and a prophet of return to a religious culture. In the light of his searchings for an 'unconditional good', the utter instability and consequent meaninglessness of the irreligious life—a life unrelated to the Absolute—which the world has lived and lives, was revealed to him. Tolstoy's ethical position here appeared as a quest for a *mystical ethics*. Although he himself constantly uses the term 'reasonable consciousness',[1] which gives his ethics an outward appearance of rationalism and even intellectualism, he actually constructed a system of mystical ethics. The basic moral 'commandment' underlying Tolstoy's concrete ethics —that of nonresistance to evil—is wholly mystical and irrational. Although Tolstoy did not believe in the divinity of Christ, he gave His words a credence which only those who regard Christ as a God can give them. The 'reasonableness' of this commandment, a commandment which clearly contradicts contemporary life, is merely that it presupposes a different concept and criterion of reasonableness from that of our everyday life. Tolstoy himself recognizes that this 'higher' rationality *'poisons'* life for us.[2] It 'is always preserved in man as in a seed', and when it is aroused its first action is to deny ordinary life.

'It is terrible and strange to renounce a visible [i.e. ordinary] conception of life and yield to an invisible consciousness of it (as it would be terrible and strange for a child to be born if it were able to feel its birth), but it cannot be avoided, since it is *evident* that the visible conception of life leads to death, and the invisible consciousness alone yields life.'[3]

The mystical nature of this 'invisible consciousness', this higher reasonableness, is nowhere more clearly expressed than in Tolstoy's impersonalism. Possessed of an extraordinarily striking individuality, stubbornly and persistently following his own individual consciousness in everything, Tolstoy nevertheless categorically rejected individuality. This impersonalism became the basis of Tolstoy's whole doctrine—his anthropology, his philosophy of culture and history, his aesthetics, and his concrete ethics.

Let us consider first the new philosophical anthropology which Tolstoy developed.

1. This concept is most clearly exhibited in the treatise *On Life*.
2. *On Life* [trans. by A. Maude], London, 1934, p. 37.     3. *Ibid.*, p. 69.

## 12. THE PROBLEM OF THE INDIVIDUAL

'It is astonishing', Tolstoy wrote in his Diary, 'how we have become habituated to the illusion of our *separateness* and *isolation* from the world. But when you understand this illusion you are astonished that anyone can fail to see that man is not part of a whole, but only a temporal and spatial manifestation of something nontemporal and nonspatial.'[1]

The consciousness of our separateness—individual self-consciousness, in the strict sense of the word—is connected for Tolstoy only with the fact of our bodily separateness. But corporality itself, with its plurality and divisibility, is illusory and unreal. Tolstoy's phenomenalistic doctrine of the external world was strongly influenced by Schopenhauer, from whom the doctrine of the *principium individuationis* was also taken. But Tolstoy distinguishes the individual's *individuality* ('animal personality', in Tolstoy's expression) from his *personality* which lives by 'reasonable consciousness'.[2] However, Tolstoy does not wholly deny the element of uniqueness in this 'higher' concept of personality.

'*This most radical and particular self* . . ., this fundamental self . . . is . . . independent of the conditions of time and space, and is brought by us [?!] into the world from a sphere beyond time and space; and that *something* present in my particular relationship to the world . . . is my real and actual self.'[3]

Every human being exhibits a specific 'relationship' to the world, which is peculiar to him; this is manifested in 'animal personality' as a genuine and ultimate source of individual uniqueness. This doctrine is very close to Kant's and Schopenhauer's doctrine of 'intelligible character'; but, as Kozlov justly notes in this connection, 'character is not a substance'.[4]

There is no question but that Tolstoy's doctrine of 'reasonable consciousness' is somewhat *divided* between a personal and an impersonal interpretation. On the one hand, as we have just seen, 'reasonable consciousness' is a function of the 'real and actual self', a bearer of the specific quality of the spiritual person; on the other hand, for Tolstoy, reason, or reasonable consciousness—as

1. *Dnevnik* [Diary], Moscow, 1916, I, 137.
2. Tolstoy expounds his doctrine of man in the treatise *On Life*.
3. *Ibid.*, pp. 119, 121.
4. A. Kozlov, *Religiya Tolstovo i yevo ucheniye o zhizni i lyubvi* [Tolstoy's Religion and His Doctrine of Life and Love], St. Petersburg, 1888, p. 200.

Kozlov justly notes—has all the earmarks of a 'universal, impersonal force'. 'It is necessary', Tolstoy wrote, 'for man to renounce not his *animal personality* but its welfare. . . .' [1] 'The purpose of the world . . . is an infinite enlightenment and unity of all beings.' [2] But unity is not a merging together; it does not submerge the individual. Yet Tolstoy speaks, as we have seen, of a 'universal consciousness', a conception which is very close to the 'transcendental subject' of German philosophy. 'That which knows is *single* everywhere, in all things, and in itself', we read in the Diary; 'it is God, and the . . . *particle* of God which is our actual self.' [3] Tolstoy goes on to ask: 'Why did God divide Himself?' And he answers: 'I do not know'. Let us quote a few more interesting passages from the Diary:

'If a desire for the good has been aroused in man, he is no longer a separate bodily entity, but is the very consciousness of life, the desire for good. And the desire for good . . . is God. . . . The essence of life is not man's separate being, but *God contained in man*. . . . The meaning of life is revealed when man recognizes his *own* divine essence.' [4]

Thus Tolstoy has no doctrine of individual immortality. Resurrection, as a restoration of individuality, is even less acceptable to him. [5] Like Fechner and Wundt, he accepts the immortality of the spiritual life and, if you will, the immortality of mankind; Tolstoy speaks for example of 'eternal life in mankind'. [6]

Such is Tolstoy's anthropology. It is very close to Kireyevski's doctrines of 'spiritual reason', the struggle against 'spiritual fragmentation', and the restoration of man's 'wholeness'. But Kireyevski did not dream of denying the metaphysical status of the individual human being; his doctrine of the spiritual life was based openly and directly on the mysticism of the Church Fathers. Tolstoy, however, insists on calling his mystical doctrine of the 'true life' a doctrine of 'reasonable consciousness', attempting to sanctify and justify his theological rationalism with this label. He completely evades the question of why man's 'reasonable consciousness' is effaced and obscured by the consciousness of his illusory

---

1. *On Life*, p. 86.      2. *Ibid.*, p. 80.

3. *Dnevnik*, pp. 73, 75, 105.      4. *Ibid.*, pp. 28, 33, 58.

5. As is well known, in his exposition of the New Testament Tolstoy deleted all the passages which mention the Resurrection of the Saviour.

6. Tolstoy is sometimes inclined to ascribe a special being to 'mankind' as a whole. (See the philosophy of history in *War and Peace*, Epilogue, Pt. II.)

separateness, why 'reasonable consciousness' is revealed to us only through suffering, or why this consciousness, which is the source of all light in the soul,[1] though it summons man to good, tells him at the same time that it is unattainable. 'The sole good that reasonable consciousness discloses to man is hidden afresh by this very consciousness.'[2] We have already quoted Tolstoy's words that the higher consciousness 'poisons life for us'.

The key to these contradictions and omissions lies, of course, in Tolstoy's religious consciousness. He entered a path of religious mysticism, but he did not wish to acknowledge the mystical character of his experiences. He accepted the teaching of Christ, but denied Christ's divinity; yet he followed Christ as though he believed He was a God: he took Christ's words concerning the direction of life into the very depths of his soul. This strange combination of mystical excitement with an extremely shallow and meagre rationalism, an ardent, passionate, and sincere loyalty to Christ with a denial of His supramundane divinity, reveals Tolstoy's inner disharmony. It was once justly said that Tolstoy's doctrine 'parted company not only with the Church but even more with the world'.[3] But his break with the Church was a fatal *misunderstanding*, for Tolstoy was an ardent and sincere disciple of Christ, and his rejection of dogmatics, his denial of Christ's divinity and Resurrection, was connected with his rationalism, a rationalism which was internally incompatible with his mystical experience. However, Tolstoy's break with the world and with secular culture was genuine and profound; it was not based on a misunderstanding.

### 13. THE PHILOSOPHY OF CULTURE

Indeed, Tolstoy's whole philosophy of culture is a relentless, categorical, and uncompromising rejection of the system of secularism. Tolstoy, although he accepts *mystical* immanentism, completely rejects *secular* immanentism. The state, the economic system, social relations, juridical decrees, appear wholly without foundation or meaning in the light of his religious views. He adopted a position of mystical anarchism. But his destructive ideas were especially sharp and severe with respect to education, family

---

1. 'Our knowledge of the world *results from* the consciousness we have of our own aspiration towards good . . .,' i.e. from our 'reasonable consciousness'. (*On Life*, p. 58.)

2. *Ibid.*, p. 75.

3. V. A. Maklakov, *O L. Tolstom* [Leo Tolstoy], Paris, 1929, p. 27.

life, aesthetics, and science: here his ethicism was tyrannical in the extreme. So far as the evolution of Tolstoy's pedagogical ideas is concerned (we shall not expound these ideas here), he moved from an original denial of the right to educate children—a pedagogical anarchism—to the opposite extreme: not religious education 'in general', but an imposing on children of the specific doctrine which he himself professed. The rigoristic negativism of Tolstoy's attitude toward the family is well known to readers of his *Kreutzer Sonata*—especially the Epilogue. The inner intolerance which characterized his ethicism is especially evident in his attitude toward beauty. However, we must admit that Tolstoy here treated a thorny and difficult problem, which had long occupied Russian thought. Under the influence of German romanticism, but answering to deeply-felt needs in the Russian soul, a tendency of aesthetic humanism—which lived by faith in the inner unity of beauty and good, the unity of man's aesthetic and moral spheres— arose in Russia toward the end of the eighteenth century, flourishing in the nineteenth. Russian 'Schillerism', which entered so deeply and broadly into Russian creative activity, was wholly imbued with this idea. Gogol first raised the question of the inner discord of the aesthetic and moral spheres. Their unity now appeared as a mere dream; reality was a stranger to the aesthetic principle.[1] For a long time Gogol remained alone in his assertion— so tragically illuminated by the burning of Part II of *Dead Souls*— but this theme flared up anew, in a very sharp formulation, in the literary and philosophic writings of Tolstoy and Dostoyevsky.

Tolstoy's utterances on this theme are scattered everywhere—in his correspondence and in his Diary, but especially in the treatise *What Is Art?*. There he declared categorically and peremptorily that 'good has nothing in common with beauty.'[2] The fatal and demonic power of art—especially music, to whose influence Tolstoy himself was highly susceptible—tore him away from the good; art became for him a simple '*pastime*'.[3] 'Aesthetic pleasure,' he wrote in his Diary, 'is a pleasure of a lower order.' This is why he considers it '*blasphemy*' to place art and science on a level with the good.[4]

The plan of Tolstoy's *What Is Art?* also flows from this temper of mind, a temper very strange in a great artist. There is no need for

---

1. For details see above, Ch. VI.

2. Cf. *What is Art?* [trans. by A. Maude], 'World's Classics', London, 1930, p. 142.

3. *Dnevnik*, p. 52.     4. *Ibid.*, pp. 44, 55.

us to analyse this book here; it is wholly based on an insensitivity to beauty as such, and a setting up of universal intelligibility as the criterion of 'true' art—on the strength of which Shakespeare, Goethe, and Beethoven are rejected. It is not a question of these specific assertions, but of the tyranny of the ethical sphere. In the divergence of the paths of beauty and the good, which is itself an indisputable and fatal fact, Tolstoy does not see a tragic problem of culture; he merely throws out everything that has lost contact with the good.

Tolstoy is equally cold and relentless toward all science that does not subordinate itself directly to ethical principles. He regards contemporary science as false because it fails to place the problem of human conduct and the meaning of life at the centre of its researches.

'Science and philosophy', he once wrote, 'treat of almost everything, but not of how man can *perfect himself* and live a *better life*. . . . Contemporary science possesses a mass of useless information—concerning the chemical composition of the stars, the sun's motion toward the constellation of Hercules, the origin of species and the descent of man, etc., but it has nothing to say concerning the meaning of life; indeed, it considers this question outside its jurisdiction.'

In his critique of art and science Tolstoy touches the traditional foundations of secularism: following the lead of his 'panmoralism', subordinating everything to the idea of the good, Tolstoy lays bare the basic predicament of contemporary culture—its disintegration into a series of mutually independent spheres. He is seeking to build a *religious culture*; but his own religious position, although it rests upon the mystical idea of a 'reasonable consciousness', is treated one-sidedly, in exclusively ethical terms. Hence the paradox that in his critique of the contemporary world Tolstoy rests on a secular element—the 'natural' moral (reasonable) consciousness. He puts forward not a synthesis, nor an integral spiritual unity, as a counterbalance to contemporary life, but merely one of the powers of the spirit—the moral sphere.

## 14. TOLSTOY'S IMPORTANCE AS A THINKER

Nevertheless, Tolstoy's importance for the history of Russian thought is enormous. The extremes of his thought, his maximalism, his one-sided subordination of the whole of life to an abstract moral principle, carry one of the basic and determining elements of Russian thought to its limit. The theoretical constructions of Tolstoyan 'panmoralism' form a kind of limit beyond which it is impossible to go; but, at the same time, Tolstoy's contribution to Russian (and not only Russian) thought is a permanent one. His ethical scrutiny of secular culture from within was inspired by genuinely Christian experience. Although he did not believe in the divinity of Christ, Tolstoy followed Him like a God. But Tolstoy's strength is not merely in his *critique* and rejection of secularism. His return to the idea of a *religious culture*—a culture which is to offer a synthesis of spontaneous historical elements with eternal truth and justice, exhibiting the Kingdom of God in earthly life—is much more significant and influential. Hence Tolstoy's fundamental anti-historism and his specific shift toward theocracy, which reveals his *profound ties to Orthodoxy*; for Tolstoy, in accepting the theocratic idea, decisively and categorically rejects the element of statism, which is so typical of Western theocratic trends. Tolstoy rejected the historical reality of the Church, but he was seeking *only* a Church, a 'manifested' Kingdom of God, a divine-human unity of eternal and temporal. This is the key to Tolstoy's mysticism. His stubborn impersonalism must be ascribed to the influence and stress of his mystical experiences. It was not the case, as Lossky thinks, that Tolstoy's philosophic understanding was not equal to his artistic intuition of being—that he was a 'bad' philosopher.[1] Tolstoy's philosophic searchings followed their own specific dialectic, whose point of departure was an intuitive—intellectual—perception of the inseparability and indivisibility of temporal and eternal, relative and Absolute. The contribution which Christian theology might have made to Tolstoy's searchings remained remote from him; he grew up in an atmosphere of secularism and lived by secular interests. Tolstoy broke out of the cage of secularism, and destroyed it; and this triumphant exploit, together with his summons to rebuild culture on a religious foundation—comprises Tolstoy's immense *philosophic* importance, an importance which extends beyond the borders of Russia. The good must be Absolute or it is not good—such is the result of Tolstoy's searchings; such is his legacy to the Russian consciousness.

1. N. O. Lossky, 'Tolstoi kak khudozhnik i kak myslitel' ['Tolstoy as Artist and Thinker'], *Sovremennyie zapiski*, No. 37 (1928), p. 234.

# CHAPTER XIV

## The 'Pochvenniki'

### APOLLON GRIGORYEV. N. N. STRAKHOV. F. M. DOSTOYEVSKY

### 1. THE 'CULT OF PRIMITIVE IMMEDIACY' ('Pochvennichestvo') AS AN INTELLECTUAL TREND

WE turn now to a group of thinkers who developed their philosophic theories on the *foundation* of a religious world-view. The diversity of these tendencies, which developed especially during the subsequent period, is to be explained by the fact that the Orthodox faith has never entailed a mandatory world-view, or one recommended by Churchmen. The general gravitation of the Christian East toward Plato and Platonism, even in the golden age of Byzantine philosophy and theology, did not exclude a powerful Aristotelian influence. But in Russia a loyalty to the dogmatic foundations of Orthodoxy was readily combined with diverse philosophic sympathies—from acute rationalism to extreme mysticism. Even in the higher theological schools—as we have already seen in part—a strict loyalty to dogmatic principles was combined in various thinkers with wholly different philosophic constructions. But in F. A. Golubinski (see above Ch. X) and, somewhat later, in Khomyakov and Kireyevski, we find attempts to construct a 'Christian philosophy' on more categorical lines. These attempts to create a system of philosophic ideas corresponding to the 'spirit' of Orthodoxy did not preclude the use of Western philosophic ideas; indeed, it was often by means of such ideas that the guiding outlines of 'Orthodox philosophy' were discerned.

The period from the 1860's to the 1880's, with which we are now concerned, saw the appearance of a number of brilliant and original thinkers, who laboured at the task of deriving foundations for philosophy from the 'spirit' of Orthodoxy. This was still only the *threshold* of genuine systems—not from any lack of intention to build systems, but from various factors, chiefly external, which prevented the systematic development of theories and intuitions. However, the seeds which later grew into systems appeared for the first time in the 1860's and even earlier.

The thinkers with whom we are now concerned may, without violence to the facts, be divided into two groups. The first group clusters about the idea of 'primitive immediacy' [*pochvennichestvo*],[1] which, although it faded quickly, was at one time the slogan of a whole tendency, including Apollon Grigoryev, N. N. Strakhov, and F. M. Dostoyevsky. In the second group Christian principles were complicated—in different ways—by engraftings of 'naturalism'; its members include K. Leontyev and V. V. Rozanov. The philosophic trends in the Russian poetry of this period (Tyutchev, Alexei Tolstoy, Fet, *et al.*) deserve a special study, which we cannot undertake here.

Let us turn to the '*pochvenniki*', and first to A. A. Grigoryev.

## 2. APOLLON GRIGORYEV. BIOGRAPHY

Apollon Aleksandrovich Grigoryev was born in 1822 in Moscow into a cultured family which was not well-to-do. After being educated at home,[2] a process which he describes graphically in his autobiography, Grigoryev entered Moscow University, graduating in 1842. During this period he was carried away by Hegel; he was also active in student circles, and buried himself in romantic literature.[3] He lived for a number of years with A. A. Fet, one of the most brilliant Russian poets. Upon his graduation, Grigoryev was employed by the University (in the library), and somewhat later joined the editorial board of *Moskvityanin* [The Muscovite], a long-established journal headed by Professor Pogodin, a talented but second-rate Slavophile, whose thinking and writing exhibited a chronic boorishness. Pogodin remained only as publisher in the new ('young') editorial board of the *Moskvityanin*; the editors included such talented writers as A. N. Ostrovski, such cultured

1. A coinage from the Russian '*pochva*'=soil, foundation. Adherents of the doctrines of '*pochvennichestvo*' were called '*pochvenniki*', a word which is quite untranslatable in English. *Trans.*

2. Grigoryev's father studied at the Moscow 'Nobleman's Boarding School', and was a friend of Zhukovski and the Turgenevs. (*Moi literaturniye i nravstvennyie skitalchestva* [My Literary and Moral Wanderings], 1915, p. 55.)

3. In his early years Grigoryev was an enthusiastic admirer of E. T. A. Hoffman. (*Ibid.*, p. 32.)

figures as Edelson, the well-known church figure T. I. Filippov; such writers as Pisemski, Potekhin, *et al.* This 'young' editorial board, which had associated itself with the Slavophiles, stood for the development of an *'original and independent'* Russian culture. This new direction, which was free from anti-Westernism, found inspiration in Ostrovski's dramas depicting Russian commercial, middle-class, and rural life. For the editors of the *Moskvityanin* these dramas were a kind of revelation of Russian might—the unmanifested but powerful forces of the Russian soul. Grigoryev himself, who had been influenced by Hegel and was now becoming more and more enthusiastic about Schelling, felt that his generation stood 'between the transcendentalists [i.e. pure Schellingians] and the nihilists',[1] who appeared later as partisans of materialism. Grigoryev tended toward a rejection of transcendentalism in the name of psychologism (Beneke was temporarily influential in Russia at this time), but the 'transcendental leaven', as Grigoryev expressed it,[2] remained active in him. His inner tie with romanticism and the romantic sense of the profundity and mysteriousness of nature and man was a decisive influence. But the 'young editorial board' of the *Moskvityanin* combined this romanticism with a 'restoration in the soul of a new, or rather a renewed, faith in the *foundation*, the *soil* [*pochva*], the *people*—a restoration in the mind and heart of *everything immediate*'. In the cult of the 'soil' this unexpected resurrection—or rather germination—of the cult of 'immediacy' (cf. Jacobi) played a *decisive* role. We shall also find it in Dostoyevsky. But in Grigoryev, as he himself has vividly recounted,[3] wholly new experiences resulted from this enthusiastic and complete renunciation of life's false and artificial exterior in the name of its hidden, but infinitely deep, 'immediacy'. At this time he became a 'seeker of the Absolute', as he himself later put it. 'Enormous worlds, bound together into a single whole',[4] opened out before him. His basic ideas, his vision of the 'organic wholeness' of being in all of its living manifestations,[5] took shape; and finally —as Fet, who was living with Grigoryev at the time, testifies— religious feeling flared up. In this religious awakening national elements played a very large role, aesthetic elements a somewhat smaller one. Orthodoxy, which Grigoryev had come to value, was inseparable for him from elemental Russian spontaneity. 'By Orthodoxy', he once wrote, 'I mean a *spontaneous historical principle*

1. *Ibid.*, p. 106.  2. *Ibid.*, p. 108.  3. *Ibid.*, pp. 115f.  4. *Ibid.*, p. 116.
5. The idea of the 'organic' wholeness of being has been resurrected, under different influences, by the contemporary Russian philosopher, N. O. Lossky.

which is destined to live and create new forms of life.' [1] One must place this beside Grigoryev's assertion that 'the ideal is only the *fragrance* and *flower* of the *real*',[2] to feel the element of *naturalism* in his religious consciousness—an element which also inhered in Schelling's basic conception, as in that of the branch of romanticism which was most under his influence. For Grigoryev, the religious sphere is the most precious aspect of reality—its 'fragrance and flower'. Here the motif of immanentism is unquestionable. To be sure, we also find in his writings such lines as these: 'Wherever I begin I always come to the same thing—a profound and tormenting need to believe in an ideal and a *Jenseits*.' [3] Grigoryev rightly considered himself a seeker of the Absolute. However, Hegel too was a 'seeker of the Absolute' in the true sense of the word, but for him the Absolute was immanent in being. For Grigoryev, this ferment of immanentism, which so strongly pervaded romanticism in the West as well as in Russia, may have been an echo of his early enthusiasm for Hegel. But we shall see below that the element of 'Christian naturalism' was very strong in the 'cult of primitive immediacy' generally (especially in Dostoyevsky, see below). The combination of immanentism and striving 'toward the ideal', the *Jenseits*, sprang in both Grigoryev and Dostoyevsky from an *aesthetic* foundation.

Grigoryev's work on the 'young editorial board' of the *Moskvityanin* linked his thought more closely to Orthodoxy. His enthusiasm for Archimandrite Bukharev's articles (see above, Chapter X), in which the acceptance of the world and of history by the Orthodox consciousness was strongly expressed, was typical. In 1857 Grigoryev took advantage of an opportunity to go abroad—as a private tutor; he was depressed in Moscow, where he had experienced great unhappiness in his personal life. Returning to Russia, he was invited to write for the journal *Vremya* [Time], which was published by the Dostoyevsky brothers. The doctrine of 'primitive immediacy' had completely crystallized in the editorial board of this journal, and Grigoryev was an extremely welcome collaborator. But his relations with the editorial board soon deteriorated;[4] he

1. *Materialy dlya biografi A. Grigoryeva* [Materials for a Biography of A. Grigoryev], ed. V. Knyazhnin, Petrograd, 1917, p. 247.
2. *Sochineniya* [Works], ed. Strakhov, 1876, p. 202.
3. *Materialy* . . . [Materials . . .], p. 5.
4. After Grigoryev's death Dostoyevsky wrote: 'I suspect that Grigoryev would not have been happy on any editorial board in the world.' (Strakhov, *Biografiya, pisma i zametki iz zapisnoi knizhki Dostoyevskovo* [Biography, Letters, and Notes from Dostoyevsky's Notebook], 1883, p. 212.)

went to Orenburg and took a position as a teacher in the military college, where he died at the age of forty-two (in 1864).

### 3. PHILOSOPHIC VIEWS

Grigoryev was primarily a literary critic, but he was always enthusiastic about philosophy. Although he went from Hegel to Schelling, his searchings were original; his part in the elaboration of the ideology of 'primitive immediacy' is unquestionably a very significant one.

Although he took from Hegel a taste for philosophic interpretation of the world as a whole, Grigoryev remained a stranger to Hegel's *logism*. 'For me life is something mysterious', he wrote in a late article, 'something inexhaustible, an immense breadth in which logical conclusions often disappear like waves in the ocean.' [1] The hyperlogical quality of life led Grigoryev to a rejection of Hegelian rationalism; he spoke of his 'profound hostility to everything that grows out of the nakedly logical process'.[2] 'The logical status of [scientific] laws is beyond question', he wrote in another place; 'the world-wide work on these abstract laws proceeds quite correctly, but it proceeds in a *purely logical* world . . . which lacks the inexhaustible creativity of life.' [3] Schelling, as Grigoryev interpreted him, 'destroyed the *idol* of an abstract spirit of mankind and its development'. In a letter to Strakhov he wrote of the 'vague and mysterious muteness of sensations', i.e. the extralogical plenitude of immediate awareness.

We have already noted that there is in Grigoryev a specific cult of 'immediacy' as something broader and fuller than what the logical consciousness abstracts from it. This links his philosophic position very closely to that of Kireyevski—whom he respected highly, considering him a 'great philosopher'. Grigoryev especially admired Schelling's doctrine of 'intellectual intuition' as a direct union with the supersensory world; he also took over Schelling's ideas on art. 'Art alone', he asserted, 'brings something new and organic into the world.' [4] Let us recall the already-quoted words: 'The ideal is . . . the fragrance and flower of the real.' [5] And, since art realizes the concrete unity of ideal and real, only in art do we find the genuine creativity of life itself. Science grasps the ideal constitution of being, but it tears itself away from living reality; hence art is above science. 'When knowledge ripens into the

1. *Sochineniya*, p. 618.　　2. *Ibid.*, p. 469.　　3. *Ibid.*, p. 202.
4. *Loc. cit.*　　　　　　　　　　　　　　　　　　5. *Ibid.*, p. 615.

plenitude of life', Grigoryev wrote, 'it strives to take on artistic forms.' [1] Wholly in the spirit of Schelling, he assures us that 'art alone incarnates in its products that which is present, though unknown, in the atmosphere of the age'.[2] The basic idea of Grigoryev's philosophy of art follows from this: namely, the *'organic'* connection of works of art with the whole age and with the historical process. 'I believe with Schelling', he once wrote, 'that *unconsciousness* gives works of art their uninvestigable profundity.' [3]

This is also the source of Grigoryev's 'cult of primitive immediacy' [*pochvennichestvo*]. By 'soil' [*pochva*] he means the profound level of national life, the mysterious aspect of historical movement. His passion for 'independence and originality' moves toward an immersion in the depths of nationality; thus, the disagreement between the Westerners and Slavophiles was alien to him.[4] He sought a new historiosophical conception.[5] This new conception found the secret of Russian nationality in Orthodoxy. 'Life has become exhausted', he wrote, 'and a new life is beginning; it will proceed from Orthodoxy: this force contains a new world.' [6] Grigoryev repudiated Herzen's 'cynical atheism'. ('There is no *réhabilitation de la chair* in Orthodoxy', he retorted to Herzen's praise of Saint-Simon, 'but a triumph of the soul.') He was much impressed by Archimandrite Bukharev. Florovsky is wholly wrong in thinking that 'it was from Grigoryev that the *aesthetic reinterpretation of Orthodoxy*, which was later so sharply expressed by Leontyev, entered into the Russian world-view'.[7] The focus of Grigoryev's interests was not in aesthetics as such, but in an apology for the 'immediacy' which lives only in the organic wholeness of being, in the 'soil'. Orthodoxy was a revelation for him of the profound levels of the Russian spirit; and this is the source of the 'Christian naturalism', mentioned above, which was fully developed by Dostoyevsky.

Grigoryev's theories mark the highest point in the development of Russian *aesthetic humanism*. As a true romanticist, he believed in

1. *Materialy* . . . [Materials . . .], p. 150.
2. *Ibid.*, p. 288.
3. *Sochineniya*, p. 413.
4. *Ibid.*, p. 187.
5. *Ibid.*, p. 202.
6. *Materialy* . . . [Materials . . .], p. 220. Strakhov admits (*op. cit.*, p. 205) that 'the idea of a *new direction* occupied me especially under the influence of Apollon Grigoryev'.
7. Florovsky, *Puti russkovo bogosloviya* [Paths of Russian Theology], p. 305.

the essential unity of beauty and good, art and morality; [1] but in this position his religious consciousness, like that of many other Russian thinkers, did not diverge from his *secular* consciousness. The highest value of art, its 'theurgical' function (cf. Dostoyevsky and Gogol) was acknowledged by both of the hostile tendencies of Russian thought, though, of course, they interpreted the exaltation of beauty differently. What Grigoryev introduced into Russian thought was not primarily his romanticism or his worship of art, but a philosophy of the 'soil', a search for 'immediacy' through a restoration of 'organic wholeness' in man's intuition of the world and his historical creativity.

Let us turn to N. N. Strakhov.

## 4. N. N. STRAKHOV. BIOGRAPHY. INFLUENCE OF HEGEL

Nicholas Nikolayevich Strakhov [2] (1828–96) was born into the family of a priest; he studied in a theological seminary, and upon graduation entered the Faculty of Physics and Mathematics at St. Petersburg University. Because of a lack of funds he was unable to complete the University course; he transferred to the Pedagogical Institute, and upon graduation (in 1851) became a teacher of natural science, first in Odessa and than in St. Petersburg. In 1861 he gave up teaching and devoted himself exclusively to literary work. He became closely associated with Dostoyevsky as a regular contributor to the journals which the latter published. Somewhat later Strakhov became an ardent admirer of Leo Tolstoy; the two remained close friends to the end of Strakhov's life. His very interesting correspondence with Tolstoy makes it clear that he was influenced by the latter. In 1873 Strakhov again entered government service—first in the Public Library [in St. Petersburg] and then on the Scholarly Committee of the Ministry of National Education.

Strakhov wrote a great deal, and on the most diverse topics, early distinguishing himself as a literary critic. His articles on Russian literature retain their value to the present day. His series of articles (collected into two books) on the theme The Struggle with the West in Russian Literature, are very important. He wrote

1. See the article 'O pravde i iskrennosti v iskusstve' ['On Truth and Sincerity in Art'], *Sochineniya*, p. 137. See especially p. 178: 'Artistic intuition, by its nature, is inseparable from moral intuition.' In another place (*ibid.*, p. 576) he wrote: 'High artistic sensitivity is, perhaps, also the highest stage of humane feeling.'

2. Concerning Strakhov, see Chizhevski, *Hegel in Russland*, Pt. III, Ch. II.

a great deal on purely scientific problems; his book The World as a Whole, is especially significant, as are his works on psychology, philosophical anthropology, and pure philosophy. Let us note finally his articles on the philosophy of history.

The breadth and diversity of Strakhov's works makes him a genuine encyclopaedist; but his creative work is marked by a kind of 'incompleteness', as even his ardent admirer V. V. Rozanov expressed it. The lack of wholeness and completeness in Strakhov's theoretical constructions has long prevented a just appraisal of his works, and has constantly created misunderstandings about them. Thus, for example, Vladimir Solovyov—in the heat of polemic, to be sure—reproached Strakhov for 'indifference to the truth'. [1] This is wholly untrue, of course. But here are Rozanov's words (from his excellent article on Strakhov): 'Following the direction of Strakhov's thought . . . we discover two ideas which, although they are not central, are close to the centre; he almost never mentions the actual centre.' [2] Rozanov thinks that this centre is the *religious* problem, but this is only a guess, an hypothesis—not an unquestionable fact. However, when one reads the correspondence between Strakhov and Tolstoy—which Rozanov could not have known when he wrote his article—this hypothesis seems very close to the truth. Strakhov's admiration for Tolstoy, which was marked by a kind of rapturous feeling, is undoubtedly connected with what was basic and central in Strakhov's inner world; and Strakhov valued Tolstoy's ethical mysticism above everything else. Like Tolstoy, he placed unlimited value on free thought, and he evidently shared Tolstoy's free attitude toward the Church. But at the same time he bore a sense of God deep within his heart. He once reproached Russian thinkers for 'not being able to understand the *theological* character of the principal German thinkers'. (Cf. S. Bulgakov's analyses of German philosophy in his *Tragödie der Philosophie.*) Strakhov wrote in a letter to Tolstoy that 'Hegel was a pure mystic'.[3] This is important for the understanding of Strakhov.

Strakhov's books and articles exhibit a *duality* of interest and a twofold approach to philosophic themes. On the one hand, he built a system of 'rational natural science' (see especially his book

1. V. S. Solovyov, *Sochineniya*, V, 260.
2. V. V. Rozanov, 'O borbe s zapadom . . .' ['On the Struggle with the West . . .'], *Voprosy filosofi i psikhologi*, No. 4 (1890), p. 31.
3. Cf. I. A. Ilyin, *Die Philosophie Hegels als kontemplative Gotteslehre*, Berne, 1946.

The World as a Whole), in which he appears, at first glance, as a persistent defender of Hegelianism with respect to scientific cognition; and, on the other hand, Strakhov acknowledges—in the same book—that 'man for some reason is perpetually *hostile* to rationalism'. In the same place he remarks that 'the source of this dissatisfaction is not in the *mind*, but in the other needs of the human soul'. This is not simply an antinomy of mind and heart; the mind itself, according to Strakhov, exhibits the (partial) truth of irrationalism. This appears most sharply in Strakhov's historiosophical utterances and his judgments of Western culture. Essentially, he condemned the system of Western *secularism* as an attempt to grasp the secret of history in a purely rational way. 'The European Enlightenment', he wrote, 'is a powerful rationalism, a great development of abstract thought.' [1] But in the book On Eternal Truths he wrote, concerning the internal inadequacy and difficulties of rationalism: 'There can be no way out of rationalism *within rationalism itself.*' A strict defender of Hegel's theory of scientific knowledge, [2] Strakhov rejected rationalism in his appraisal of culture, developed an enthusiasm for Grigoryev's ideas, joined the *'pochvenniki'*, and accepted their exaltation of the 'unconscious' element in the historical process. During his period of enthusiasm for Tolstoy, he moved very far toward irrationalism, writing to Tolstoy: 'I have already *repudiated* Hegel'. [3] He accepted Schopenhauer's metaphysical voluntarism but neglected Schopenhauer's rational side so completely that he could write (to Tolstoy): 'Schopenhauer alone has taught me to *understand religion.*' [4] To be sure, Strakhov admitted that during the writing of The World as a Whole, he was a 'pantheist', and he adds (in the same letter to Tolstoy): 'Pantheistic science is the only science known to us.' [5] This religious interpretation of science did not provide an understanding of religion; it was simply taken over from Schopenhauer. But Strakhov's religious consciousness became permeated with Tolstoy's mystical ideas. His closeness to the latter is evident from such words as these.

'All life', he wrote in a letter to Tolstoy, 'comes from God. . . . The eternal spiritual principle, in which is the root of all being, is

1. Strakhov, *Borba s zapadom* [The Struggle with the West], St. Petersburg, 1882, I, xi.

2. Concerning his Hegelianism, see Chizhevski, *op. cit.*

3. *Sbornik Tolstovskovo Muzeya* [Collection of the Tolstoy Museum], Moscow, 1914, II, 23.

4. *Ibid.*, p. 22.        5. *Loc. cit.*

conscious of itself in our consciousness. Everything comes from God, everything leads to God, everything culminates in God.' [1]

'I now deny', he wrote in another letter, 'that mind controls history or that history is the development of an idea.' [2] This is pure historiosophical irrationalism. In the spirit of Tolstoy's impersonalism, he even speaks of the 'incomprehensibility' and 'absurdity' of personal immortality. [3]

Strakhov regarded Western culture as a 'triumph of rationalism', and his rejection of rationalism only strengthened his cult of Russian independence and originality. He became an ardent and passionate defender of Danilevski's ideas—as expressed in the book, *Russia and Europe*—concerning the differences of cultural-historical types; he was even 'troubled' by talk about the 'powerful development of European science'. In Strakhov the 'cult of primitive immediacy' culminated in a struggle against the whole system of Western secularism and an uncritical acceptance of Tolstoy's religio-mystical conception of culture.

Let us note one or two details of Strakhov's theoretical constructions.

### 5. STRAKHOV'S COSMOLOGY AND ANTHROPOLOGY

Strakhov's cosmological ideas, and especially his *anthropocentrism*, are of primary interest in his early period.

'The world', he wrote (in The World as a Whole), 'is a *coherent whole*; nothing in it exists "in itself".' This conception of the world differs both from the later developments of Sophiological metaphysics—Vladimir Solovyov and his 'school'—and the 'biocentric' conception which we have seen in Pirogov. The world's 'wholeness' is a consequence of its *unity*, according to Strakhov; and he conceives this unity in the lines of (Hegelian) transcendentalism. Nevertheless, if the world is a 'whole', it must have a centre which makes this 'connectedness' possible. The 'material' aspect of the world, subordinating itself to spirit, creates the forms of organic life. 'Organism', according to Strakhov, is an actual rather than a substantial category. An 'organism' is a process through which the spiritual principle, by 'educing itself', takes possession of matter. Thus, *man* is central in the world; he is the 'focus of the universe, its greatest mystery, but also its key'. 'Acting upon man, nature calls forth and displays his hidden essence. . . . But man constantly seeks a way out of the whole, striving to break the ties which connect

1. *Ibid.*, p. 341.  2. *Ibid.*, p. 23.  3. *Ibid.*, p. 249.

him with the world.' Man, who is the hierarchical crown of nature, and its living centre, reveals—in his centrifugal self-isolation from the world—the world's enigma and mystery. The key to this mystery is beyond the limits of the world—in the Absolute.

But if man's central position in natural being is not interpreted religiously it leads to a *dissolving* of man in nature. Apart from a religious and metaphysical anthropocentrism, the enigma of man is insoluble; man's existence is deprived of that toward which nature moves in man's development—is deprived of 'meaning'. The most precious impulses of the soul become a mere play of the imagination. Strakhov's reflections, as Chizhevski has justly noted, here exhibit a struggle against 'enlightenmentism'.[1] Strakhov's 'romanticism', his unwillingness to barter man's primogeniture for the illusory results of science, motivated his struggle against the rationalism and secular tendencies of Western culture. It was also the cause of his admiration for Tolstoy and for the latter's search for a religious foundation and interpretation of culture. But Strakhov went only halfway along this road; the mysticism which first burst through in his 'cult of primitive immediacy' continued to coexist with the remnants of his rationalism. Thus Strakhov himself was not completely consistent as to the 'centre' of his searchings.

All of this was clearer, deeper, and even fuller of antinomies in F. M. Dostoyevsky, the chief ideologist of 'primitive immediacy'.

### 6. DOSTOYEVSKY. HIS PLACE IN THE HISTORY OF RUSSIAN THOUGHT. BIOGRAPHY

Fyodor Mikhailovich Dostoyevsky (1821–81) belongs as much to philosophy as to literature. This is to be seen most clearly in the fact that he continues to inspire philosophic thought to our own day. Dostoyevsky's commentators are still reconstructing his ideas; the variety of their commentaries results not from any obscurity in Dostoyevsky's expression, but from the complexity and profundity of his ideas. Of course, Dostoyevsky was not a philosopher in the ordinary, familiar sense of the word; he wrote no purely philosophic works. He thought as an artist; the dialectic of his ideas was embodied in the collisions and encounters of his 'heroes'. The utterances of these heroes, although they often have independent value as ideas, cannot be isolated from their personalities. Thus Raskolnikov himself, apart from his ideas, attracts attention as an individual; he cannot be separated from his ideas, and these ideas

1. *Op. cit.*, p. 278.

cannot be separated from his experiences. Dostoyevsky belongs to Russian—indeed, to world—philosophy.

Dostoyevsky's creative activity centres about the philosophy of the human spirit: problems of anthropology, the philosophy of history, ethics, and the philosophy of religion. The abundance and profundity of his ideas in this area are striking. His was one of those creative minds that suffer from an overabundance rather than a dearth of ideas. Although he did not have a systematic training in philosophy, Dostoyevsky read are great deal, absorbing other men's ideas, and echoing them in his reflections. Even when he attempted to go beyond the limits of purely artistic creation (and he undoubtedly had immense talent, as well as temperament, for social and political writing) he always remained both thinker and artist. His *Diary of a Writer*, a work of original style, is filled with purely artistic studies.

Let us consider his biography.

Fyodor Mikhailovich Dostoyevsky was born into the family of a military doctor who lived in Moscow.[1] His childhood was spent in an auspicious environment. We quote Dostoyevsky's own words: 'I came from a devout Russian family . . .; in our family we knew the New Testament virtually from our first year. I was only ten years old when I knew almost all the main episodes of Russian history.' Upon graduating from Preparatory School, Dostoyevsky and his older brother entered the School of Military Engineering in St. Petersburg. During these years a sombre drama took place in his family: his father was killed by the peasants of his country estate—in vengeance for his atrocities. 'According to a family tradition', Dostoyevsky's daughter wrote, 'it was when he heard of his father's death that Dostoyevsky had his first epileptic fit.'[2] During his years at the School of Engineering, Dostoyevsky made friends with a certain I. N. Shidlovski, 'a romanticist who later returned to the path of religious searchings'—in the words of Dostoyevsky's biographer. Shidlovski had an unquestionable influence on Dostoyevsky. 'Reading Schiller with him', Dostoyevsky wrote his brother, 'I saw in him both the noble and fiery Don Carlos and Marquis Posa. . . . Schiller's name became to me a familiar and somehow magical sound, arousing many

1. For Dostoyevsky's biography see: *The Diary of a Writer* [trans. by B. Brasol], New York, 1949; D. S. Merezhkovski, *Tolstoy as Man and Artist, with an Essay on Dostoievski*, New York, 1902; E. J. Simmons, *Dostoyevsky, the Making of a Novelist*, New York, 1940.

2. *Fyodor Dostoyevsky, A Study*, London, 1921, p. 33n.

reveries. . . .' [1] During these years Dostoyevsky greedily soaked up the influences of romantic poetry, including that of Victor Hugo.[2]

In 1843 Dostoyevsky graduated in the officers' class of the School of Engineering and received a position in the Engineering Section, but he soon retired from government service. He lived in perpetual poverty, and, even when he received fairly considerable sums from home, spent them very quickly. In 1846 Dostoyevsky published his first work, *Poor Folk*, which immediately advanced him to the rank of a first-rate writer.[3] From this time on he devoted himself ecstatically to literary activity. However, the works which followed *Poor Folk* were a source of disillusionment and misunderstanding on the part of his admirers.

At the same time a major event was coming to a head in Dostoyevsky's life—his association with the Petrashevski Circle, which later led to his exile to hard labour in Siberia. This was a real crisis in Dostoyevsky's life. The second period of his creative activity—which opened with the *Notes from the Death House*, 1855— exhibits a different kind of thinking, a new tragic perception of life. We must bear in mind that after the publication of *Poor Folk* Dostoyevsky's early romanticism turned sharply in the direction of socialism. At this time the influence of George Sand and French utopian socialism was especially strong.[4] Dostoyevsky's early socialism was a very important, even decisive, factor in his spiritual searchings. It was a form of the same 'ethical immanent-ism' which underlay, and underlies, all theories of progress, including the philosophy of life which we have seen in Tolstoy. It is a faith in the fundamental 'natural' goodness of human nature, in the 'natural' possibility of a genuine and total 'happiness', brought about by 'natural' means. It flatly and decisively rejects the doctrine of the 'radical evil' of human nature—to use Kant's term— and the doctrine of original sin, atonement, and salvation through Christ. With respect to Dostoyevsky's spiritual searchings, this whole mode of thought may be called '*Christian naturalism*'; it is a doctrine which places all of its hopes in that Christian illumination of man which entered the world through the Incarnation and found its highest expression in the Transfiguration of the Saviour.

---

1. Strakhov, *Biografiya* . . . [Biography . . .], Pt. III, pp. 15f.

2. *Ibid.*, p. 16. Concerning Schiller's influence, see Chizhevski, 'Schiller und Die Brüder Karamazow,' *Zeitschrift für slav. Philologie*, 1929.

3. See Dostoyevsky's interesting reminiscences in *The Diary of a Writer*, January 1877, Ch. II, § 3.

4. Concerning the influence of George Sand, see *ibid.*, June 1876, Ch. I.

This is a *Christianity without Golgotha*, a Christianity of Bethlehem and Tabor. It is a specific combination of *Rousseauism* and *Schillerism*, refracted through the prism of Christianity, a faith in 'nature' and an acknowledgement of the natural nobility—even though it may be concealed under outer crusts—and hidden 'sanctity' of the human soul; or, as Dostoyevsky expressed it in an article on George Sand, a recognition of the *'perfection* of the human soul'.[1]

Dostoyevsky's idealistically tinged socialism linked him to the 'Petrashevskians'. 'In 1846 I was initiated (by Belinski)', Dostoyevsky wrote, 'into the whole "truth and justice" of the "regenerated world" of the future, and into the "sanctity" of the forthcoming communist society.'[2] 'At that time', he wrote in another passage, 'I passionately embraced this whole doctrine.'[3] As we shall see, Dostoyevsky never gave up his 'Christian naturalism' or his faith in the hidden and unmanifested, but genuine, 'perfection' of human nature. This is one of the two foci of his spiritual world. Dostoyevsky's association with the Petrashevski Circle ended tragically: he was arrested and condemned to exile at hard labour. Dostoyevsky—like the other prisoners—was told that he had been condemned to death. The prisoners were taken to the square and preparations were made for the execution, by firing squad, but when everything had been prepared it was announced that they had all been reprieved, and that the death penalty would be replaced by penal servitude. Dostoyevsky's closeness to death could not help shaking him [4]—but this shock was only the beginning of the horror which he still had to go through in penal servitude. At this point a profound internal and intellectual crisis took place in Dostoyevsky, a crisis which gave direction to all of his subsequent spiritual searchings.

After his release from penal servitude Dostoyevsky spent a few more years in Siberia, where he married, and then returned anew to literary work, writing the *Notes from the Death House* and a number of short stories. Within a few years he was permitted to return to European Russia (in 1859), first to the city of Tver, and within a few months to St. Petersburg. In 1861 he and his older brother began to publish a journal called *Vremya* [Time], the programme of which consisted in developing the new ideology of 'primitive immediacy' and abolishing the dispute between

---

1. *Ibid.*, June 1876.     2. *Ibid.*, 1873, § XIX.     3. *Ibid.*, 1873, § II.
4. For Dostoyevsky's reminiscences of what he experienced on the scaffold, see *ibid.* (1873), and the well-known passage in *The Idiot.*

Westerners and Slavophiles. The subscription blank for the journal stated:

'We have at last persuaded ourselves that we too are a separate nationality, independent and original in the highest degree, and that our task is to create for ourselves an indigenous form native to *our own soil*. . . . We forsee that . . . the Russian idea may well be a synthesis of all the ideas that have developed in Europe.' [1]

The chief collaborators on this journal were Dostoyevsky, his brother, Grigoryev, and Strakhov. In 1863 the journal was suspended because of an article by Strakhov on the Polish question which was written in a liberal spirit; but within a year Dostoyevsky's brother was given permission to publish a journal under a new name. In 1864 the Dostoyevskys began to publish *Epokha* [The Epoch], but the financial difficulties created by the closing of *Vremya* were so severe that *Epokha*, too, had to be closed. This period was important for the development of Dostoyevsky's creative activity in that it revealed his taste for *social and political writing*. He created his own special style of social and political writing (which was carried on chiefly by Rozanov). The *Diary of a Writer*—which he published during the last years of his life—remains to this day an invaluable source of material for the study of Dostoyevsky's ideas. Despite its closeness to current life, the *Diary* retains its significance because of the wealth of its ideas and the profundity of its analyses. Dostoyevsky's thought here often reached its greatest precision and expressiveness.

But, of course, literary work was the chief form of Dostoyevsky's creative activity during this period—i.e. after his penal servitude. Beginning with the first-rate work *Crime and Punishment*, Dostoyevsky wrote one novel after another—*The Idiot*, *The Raw Youth*, *The Possessed*, and finally *The Brothers Karamazov*. The extremely broad and philosophically important plan of these works is now known—and thorough analysis of their various versions has shown how much Dostoyevsky put into his artistic creation. It has been said that there is a level beneath the 'empirical' fabric of these works which, following Vyacheslav Ivanov, is often called 'metaphysical'. [2] In fact, Dostoyevsky's principal 'heroes' are not only living, concrete individuals; in their destinies, in the inner dialectic of

1. Strakhov, *Biografiya* . . . [Biography . . .], Pt. I, p. 279.

2. *Borozdy i mezhi* [Furrows and Boundaries], Moscow, 1916; see also Ivanov's *Dostoiewskij. Tragödie, Mythos, Mystik*, Tübingen, 1932, which includes all of his articles on Dostoyevsky. [English translation : *Freedom and the Tragic Life*, New York, 1952.]

their development, Dostoyevsky traces the dialectic of some specific idea. His philosophic and intellectual creativity finds expression in artistic creation.[1] And the power of his artistic talent is evident in the fact that his empirical portrayals are guided by a *purely artistic sensitivity*; he does not force artistic creation to conform to his ideas, as Tolstoy, for example, constantly did.

A most remarkable event in Dostoyevsky's life was his address at the 'Pushkin Celebration' in May 1880, at which the Pushkin memorial in Moscow was dedicated. All the major Russian writers, except Tolstoy, attended this celebration, which was actually a celebration of literature as such. The opening speeches were all interesting and delighted the audience, but Dostoyevsky's speech made such a deep impression that all previous intellectual differences seemed to vanish in a common surge of excitement. They were submerged and dissolved, so to speak, fusing into a new enthusiasm for the 'universally human' idea which Dostoyevsky had proclaimed with such extraordinary intensity. Later there was sharp criticism of this speech in various journals; but it was, if not the beginning of a new epoch in Russian intellectual life, at least a truly remarkable document. It marks an essential recurrence in Dostoyevsky's creative activity to the position which he had assumed immediately after his return from Siberia.

Unfortunately, death, which was to cut off Dostoyevsky's creativity, in the very flowering of his talent, was near. He died in 1881. The suddenness of his death shocked Russian society. A sincere and profound grief seized every heart. Dostoyevsky's funeral was a quite unprecedented event; it was attended by small children and students, as well as various literary, scientific, and civic groups.

## 7. DOSTOYEVSKY'S RELIGIOUS WORLD

Dostoyevsky's *religious* searchings provided the foundation for his intellectual life and theoretical constructions. His was always a religious nature; throughout his life he was 'tormented,' to use his own expression, by the idea of God. In Dostoyevsky, more than in anyone else, we see philosophic creativity *growing out of* the womb of the religious consciousness. But the extraordinary significance of his intellectual creativity consists precisely in the fact that he exhibited the complex of *religious* problems in anthropology, ethics,

1. But this should not be exaggerated, as Hessen most strikingly does in his articles on Dostoyevsky.

aesthetics, and historiosophy, with immense force and unsurpassed profundity. He was referring to his perception of these problems in the light of religion when he said that 'God tormented him'. 'Even in Europe', we read in Dostoyevsky's notebook, 'there is not and never was such power of atheistic expression. It is not as a child that I believe in Christ and profess His teaching; my hosanna has burst through a purging flame of doubts.' [1] But these doubts were generated in the depths of the *religious consciousness itself*; they were all clustered about a single theme: the mutual relationship of God and the world. Dostoyevsky never doubted God's *existence*, but he was always troubled by the problem (which he solved differently in different periods) of what God's existence *entails* for the world—for man and man's historical activity. Is a religious (and Christian) conception of, and participation in, culture possible? Can man *as he is in reality*, with all his activities and searchings, be justified and made intelligible in religious terms? Can human evil, the evil in history, universal suffering, be religiously justified and accepted? These are, in a sense, different expressions of the *problem of theodicy*. Not only did 'God torment' Dostoyevsky all his life; he *struggled against God* all his life—and this intimate religious process underlay the dialectic of his whole spiritual development.

Dostoyevsky bore, not as an outsider, but from within, all the *problems of culture*—its dreams and ideals, its inspirations and joys, its justices and its injustices. He did not assert that Christianity and culture were internally heterogeneous; on the contrary, he was profoundly confident that they could be truly and harmoniously combined. We never find in him the kind of hostility toward culture which we have seen in Tolstoy. But Dostoyevsky rejected secularism—the disunion of Church and culture, radical individualism ('isolation', as he liked to call it), and the 'atheistic' culture of the contemporary world—with even greater force. Secularism for him was a concealed or, more often, overt atheism.

During Dostoyevsky's enthusiasm for socialism, he accepted its doctrines 'passionately', [2] but even then he did not separate his 'passionate' faith in the establishing of justice on earth from his faith in Christ. He very soon parted company with Belinski—whom he first followed 'passionately', by his own admission—because Belinski 'reviled' Christ. It is no exaggeration to say that Dostoyevsky's enthusiasm for socialism was related to his *religious*

1. Strakhov, *Biografiya* . . ., Pt. II, p. 375.
2. See *The Diary of a Writer*, 1873, § II.

searchings. To be sure, in subsequent years his thought moved wholly in a framework of *antinomies*: his positive views were matched by sharp and decisive negations; but the *strength* and *loftiness* of his thought were such as to make this inevitable. Very few Russian writers have felt the dialectical zigzag in the movement of ideas as keenly as he did. But Dostoyevsky's antinomism was rooted in his religious consciousness, and apart from this consciousness it cannot be properly evaluated.

In any case, Dostoyevsky's early enthusiasm for socialism brought his religious consciousness directly to the basic problems of culture. Here is the key to what I have called his 'Christian naturalism' (see above)—his faith in the goodness of man and human 'nature'. During his last years Dostoyevsky wrote (in the *Diary* for 1877): 'Man's greatest beauty . . . and greatest purity are turned to no account, are of no use to mankind . . . solely because there has not been genius enough to direct the wealth of these gifts.' These words clearly express one pole of Dostoyevsky's basic historiosophical antinomy—a faith in 'nature' and its hidden 'sanctity', but also a recognition that there is not enough 'ability' to 'direct' this hidden wealth into fruitful action. We shall return to this theme in our systematic analysis of Dostoyevsky's philosophic ideas. For the moment, let us point out that his thought did not hold to the position of Christian naturalism, but came close, with extraordinary profundity, to the opposing thesis of the inner *ambiguity* of human nature, and the ambiguity of beauty—approaching a doctrine of the tragic quality of the 'natural' freedom which leads man to crime. It is wrong to assert, as Shestov, for example, does, that after Dostoyevsky's penal servitude his former views degenerated completely, that 'not a trace remained in Dostoyevsky of his former convictions'.[1] On the contrary, his thought moved in antinomies to the end of his days; specifically, a Christian naturalism, on the one hand, and a lack of confidence in 'nature' on the other, continued to coexist in him without reaching a culminating or integral synthesis. A 'cult of primitive immediacy'—as one of the manifestations of Christian naturalism—and at the same time the high ideal of a universal Christianity which transcends the boundaries of nationality; a passionate defence of the individual— ethical personalism in its highest and most intense expression—and at the same time an unmasking of the 'man from the underground'; a faith that 'beauty will save the world', and a bitter realization that

1. L. Shestov, *Dostojewski und Nietzsche* [trans. by R. von Walter], Cologne, 1924, p. 7.

'beauty is a dreadful and frightening thing'—these antinomies were not softened but, on the contrary, were heightened toward the end of Dostoyevsky's life. This was the dialectic of his religious consciousness. Dostoyevsky's philosophic significance, the influence of his ideas on the history of Russian thought, consists in his having exhibited the problems of a religious approach to culture with a wonderful force and profundity. In this sense, an historiosophical orientation dominates all of Dostoyevsky's thought; his profound insights in anthropology, ethics, and aesthetics are all internally related to his historiosophical reflections.

Let us turn to a systematic analysis of Dostoyevsky's ideas.[1]

## 8. DOSTOYEVSKY'S ANTHROPOLOGY

Dostoyevsky's philosophic creativity has not *one* but *several* initial points; however the most important and decisive is the theme of man. Like all Russian thinkers he is anthropocentric, and his philosophic world-view is primarily a personalism—with a purely ethical colouring, to be sure, but at the same time achieving extraordinary force and profundity in this colouring. For Dostoyevsky nothing is more precious or important than man, although nothing, perhaps, is more dreadful.[2] Man is an enigma, woven of contradictions, but at the same time—in the person of even the most insignificant human being—an absolute value. Indeed, Dostoyevsky was not tormented by God so much as by man—his reality and profundity, his fatal and criminal impulses, as well as his luminous impulses toward good. Dostoyevsky is customarily praised—and justly, of course—for the unsurpassed force with which he exhibits the 'dark' side of man, man's power of destruction and limitless egoism, the fearful amoralism which is hidden in the depths of his soul. It is true that Dostoyevsky's anthropology is devoted primarily to man's 'underground'. However, it would be very one-sided not to draw attention to the profundity with which he

1. The philosophic literature on Dostoyevsky is very extensive; however, the heritage of his ideas has not yet been completely assimilated. See N. A. Berdyaev, *Dostoievsky, An Interpretation* [trans. from the French edition by D. Attwater], New York, 1934; Merezhkovski, *op. cit.*; Shestov, *op. cit.*; L. A. Zander, *Dostoevsky* [trans. by N. Duddington], London, 1948; P. Evdokimoff, *Dostoievsky et le problème du mal*, Valence, 1942.

2. In this antinomy, too, Dostoyevsky is very close to Schiller. We need only recall the latter's words:

> *Aber das Schrecklichste der Schrecken*
> *Das ist der Mensch in seinem Wahn.*

reveals the luminous powers of the soul,[1] its dialectic of the *good*. In this respect, of course, he is close to ancient Christian (i.e. patristic) anthropology. Berdyaev is wholly wrong in asserting that 'Dostoyevsky's anthropology differs from patristic anthropology.'[2] Dostoyevsky exhibits not only the sin, corruption, egoism, and, in general, the 'demonic' element in man with unprecedented force; he exhibits *no less profoundly* the impulses toward justice and good in the human soul, the 'angelic' principle in man. The force and significance of Dostoyevsky's use of antinomies in philosophical anthropology derives from the fact that both of the opposites are presented in their highest form.

We have called Dostoyevsky's personalism 'ethical'; this means above all that the value, the unanalysable quality of human nature, is found not only in its 'flowering'—its highest creative attainments—but also inheres in the tiny infant which is still helpless, impotent, and wholly incapable of expressing itself.[3] Dostoyevsky's personalism is concerned not with the psychology, but the ontology of man—not with his empirical reality, but with his essence. However, Dostoyevsky's conception of man is internally pervaded by an *ethical* category. He not only describes the struggle of good and evil in man; he *seeks* it. Man, of course, is a part of the order of nature, and subject to its laws, but he can and should be independent of nature. In the *Notes from the Underground* the human spirit's independence from nature is expressed with wonderful power; Dostoyevsky declares that man's true essence consists only in his freedom.[4] 'The whole human enterprise', we read in the *Notes from the Underground*, 'consists exclusively in man's proving to himself every moment that he is a man and not a cog.' This

---

1. Dostoyevsky's anthropology is represented very one-sidedly in Shestov's book. But Fritz Lieb's special study ('Die Anthropologie Dostojewskis' in the collection of articles by various Russian thinkers entitled *Kirche, Staat und Mensch. Russischorthodoxe Studien*, Geneva, 1937) bears the stamp of this same one-sidedness, although it is somewhat mitigated. The two principles of Dostoyevsky's anthropology are more correctly noted by Berdyaev, *op. cit.*, pp. 57ff. See also Zander, *op. cit.*

2. Berdyaev, *op. cit.*, p. 62.

3. This was expressed with extraordinary force by Dostoyevsky in a letter written after the death of his first child. See also the mother's heart-rending confession to *Starets* Zosima of her inconsolable grief at the death of her son (in *The Brothers Karamazov*).

4. 'Great Heavens, what are the laws of nature to me! . . . Obviously I cannot pierce this wall with my forehead . . ., but neither will I reconcile myself to it just because it is a stone wall.' (*Notes from the Underground*.) Cf. the almost identical words in Mikhailovski (see above, Ch. XII).

self-affirmation is an assertion of man's independence from nature; it is in this that man's whole dignity consists.

But for this reason, only man's ethical life is genuinely human; only in it is man essentially a new, higher and incomparable being. In this sense we find, even in the *Notes from the Underground*, an *apotheosis* of man, which makes him, if not the centre of the world, at least its most important and precious phenomenon. The 'anthropologism' which we have seen in the Russian positivists and semi-positivists (Chernyshevski, Lavrov, Kavelin, and Mikhailovski) was wholly alien and repugnant to Dostoyevsky; he was closest to Herzen, with his passionate assertion of the human spirit's independence from nature. Dostoyevsky ridicules anthropological naturalism relentlessly in the *Notes from the Underground*. His whole doctrine of man is profoundly different from later doctrines which, while agreeing with Dostoyevsky concerning man's amoralism, treat this amoralism in the spirit of a primitive naturalism. For Dostoyevsky the amoralism which is concealed in man's depths is also man's *apotheosis*; it is a spiritual phenomenon, unconnected with his biological processes.

But the more categorical his ontological exaltation of man, the more relentless is Dostoyevsky's disclosure of the fatal disorganization and the dark impulses of the human spirit. The fundamental mystery of man consists for Dostoyevsky in his being an ethical creature, invariably and inevitably faced with the dilemma of good and evil, a dilemma *from which he can never retreat*. The man who fails to take the path of good necessarily places himself on the path of evil. Dostoyevsky does not *assume* that man's nature is ethical, or that man exhibits a fundamental ethical tendency; he *infers* this from his observation of men.

But here we find paradoxes which reveal not only man's basic ethical nature, but also the whole complex of human problems. First, Dostoyevsky caustically ridicules the superficial intellectualism in the conception of man which reached its shallowest expression in the theoretical constructions of utilitarianism. The *Notes from the Underground* demonstrate, in immortal pages, that 'man is an improvident creature' who acts least of all for his own advantage. 'When has there ever been a case in all the millenia of his existence in which man has acted from simple advantage?' The idea of man as a rational, and hence prudent, creature is a pure fiction, 'for human nature acts *as a whole*—unconsciously as well as consciously'. 'Desire may, of course, coincide with rationality . . ., but very often, and for the most part, it is completely and stubbornly at odds with rationality.' 'I wish to live', continues the man from the underground, 'in order to satisfy my whole capacity to live, not merely to satisfy my rational capacity. Rationality satisfies only man's rational capacity, but desire is a manifestation of his whole life.' The most precious thing for man is 'his own free desire, his own caprice, even though it be absurd'. The most precious and important thing for man is 'to live by *his own* stupid will', and therefore 'man always and everywhere, wherever he is, loves to act as he desires, and not as reason and conscience bid him'.

In Dostoyevsky, psychological voluntarism imperceptibly merges into irrationalism—a recognition that the key to the understanding of man lies deeper than consciousness, conscience, or reason—in the 'underground' where he 'himself' exists. Dostoyevsky's ethical personalism is clothed in the living flesh of reality: 'the nucleus' of man, his genuine essence, is given in his *freedom*, his thirst for individual self-assertion ('to live according to his own stupid will'). Man's ontology is defined by this thirst for freedom, this thirst to be 'oneself'. But, because Dostoyevsky sees man's hidden essence in his freedom, no one has had deeper insight into the mystery of freedom; no one has revealed its whole complex of problems or its 'disorganization' more clearly than he. Berdyaev has justly observed that for Dostoyevsky 'the freedom of the underground man contains the seed of death'. Freedom is man's most precious possession, comprising his ultimate 'essence'; nevertheless, it is a burden which is too heavy to bear. On the other hand, man's underground—and the 'genuine' man is precisely the 'natural' man, who has freed himself from all tradition and convention—in Dostoyevsky's words, harbours a stench, an internal chaos; it is full of evil, even criminal impulses, as well as impulses which are merely disreputable or petty. Consider Raskolnikov, for example: after rationally analysing all the precepts of traditional morality he comes to the tempting delusion that 'everything is permissible', and proceeds to an act of crime. Morality appears without foundations in the depths of his soul; freedom becomes amoralism. Even in penal servitude Raskolnikov for a long time *felt no repentance*. The turning point came later, when his love for Sonya burst into flower, but before that he found in his freedom no ground for moral hesitation. This reveals the enigma of man's soul: the *blindness of our freedom*, in so far as it is united only to naked reason. The path toward the good is not determined by *freedom alone*. It is irrational, of course, but only in the sense that it is not reason that moves us toward the good, but the will, the powers of the spirit.

Hence freedom as such, isolated from the living impulses of love, contains the seed of death. Why death?—Because man cannot in fact evade the Good; and if, having yielded to the free play of his passions, he turns his back on the good, a tormenting disease of the soul begins in him. Raskolnikov, Stavrogin, and Ivan Karamazov all suffered in different ways because they stifled the living sense of the Good (that is, of God) in themselves, remaining *with themselves alone*. Freedom, when it leaves us with ourselves alone, reveals only chaos in the soul, displaying our dark and ignoble impulses. It converts us into slaves of our passions, making us suffer torment. Man is an *ethical creature* and cannot cease to be one. Dostoyevsky points out forcefully and painfully that crime does not indicate any natural amorality, but on the contrary testifies (negatively) to the fact that, in turning his back on the good, man loses something without which he cannot live. In the *Notes from the Death House* Dostoyevsky wrote: 'So many great energies have perished here in vain! For it must be said that these were unusual men, perhaps the most gifted and strongest of the nation.' There is no doubt that these were men gifted not only with great strength but also with freedom; and this freedom tore them from the paths of 'traditional' morality, impelling them toward crime. This is the seed of death! In the *Diary of a Writer* for 1877 Dostoyevsky wrote: 'Evil is hidden more deeply in man than is usually thought.' [1] Shestov unjustly regards this as a 'rehabilitation of the underground man'; [2] on the contrary, in emphasizing the mysteriousness of evil in the human soul, Dostoyevsky points out the disorganization, or rather disintegration, of the human spirit, and at the same time the impossibility of abandoning an ethical orientation. 'The seed of death' which inheres in freedom shows that the disintegration of the spirit is not superficial but touches its ultimate depths, for nothing in man is deeper than his freedom.

The complex of problems of human freedom forms the summit of Dostoyevsky's ideas in anthropology. Freedom is not the ultimate truth about man; this truth is defined by the ethical principle in man, by the fact that in his freedom he moves either toward evil or toward good. Therefore freedom may contain the 'seed of death' and self-destruction, but it may also lift man to the height of transfiguration. Freedom gives ample scope to the demonic in man, but it may also exalt the angelic principle in him. The impulses of freedom comprise a dialectic of evil, but also a dialectic

1. *The Diary of a Writer*, July–August 1877, Ch. II, § 3.
2. *Op. cit.*, p. 91.

of good. Is this not the significance of the need for suffering which Dostoyevsky liked to emphasize, saying that the dialectic of good is set in motion through suffering—and often through sin?

This aspect of Dostoyevsky's anthropology is often neglected or undervalued; however, it affords a key to the explanation of the system of ideas which we have characterized as 'Christian naturalism'. The words which are quoted in passing (in *The Idiot*) that 'beauty will save the world' reveal the specific quality of Dostoyevsky's aesthetic utopia. All of his doubts concerning man, his disclosure of the chaos and the 'seed of death' in him, are neutralized by his conviction that hidden in man is a great force, capable of saving man and the world. The only misfortune is that mankind does not know how to make use of this force. In the *Diary of a Writer* Dostoyevsky once wrote (1877): 'Man's greatest beauty . . . and greatest purity . . . are turned to no account, are of no use to mankind . . . solely because there has not been genius enough to *direct the wealth* of these gifts.' Thus the key to man's transfiguration and harmony lies in man himself, but we do not know how to master this key. 'We do not understand', says *Starets* Zosima, 'that life is a paradise [at present], for we have only to wish to understand this and it will immediately appear before us in all its beauty.' The remarkable words of Versilov (in *The Raw Youth*), concerning a painting by Lorrain, express this same idea: light and truth are already in the world, but they remain unnoticed by us. 'A sense of *happiness*, such as I had never before experienced, pierced my heart to the point of pain.' This sense of the sanctity in man is conveyed in marvellous form in the brilliant 'Dream of a Ridiculous Man'. In the materials for *The Possessed* we find the following passage:

'Christ walked on earth to show mankind that even in its earthly nature the human spirit can manifest itself in heavenly radiance, in the flesh, and not merely in a dream or ideal—and that this is both *natural* and *possible*.'

It is clear from these words that Dostoyevsky's basic doctrine of man is closer to Rousseau's anthropology, with its basic principle of man's radical goodness, than to that of Kant, with his doctrine of 'man's radical evil'.

However, the dialectic of a 'natural and possible' good presupposes a religious life.[1] 'The whole law of human existence', Stefan Tromfimovich says in *The Possessed*, 'is that man should

1. See the doctrine of the 'mystical root' of man's impulses toward good in the *Diary of a Writer*, 1880, Ch. III, § 4.

worship something immeasurably great. The Immeasurable and the Infinite are just as necessary to man as is the tiny planet on which he lives.' The misfortune of mankind is that 'the aesthetic idea has become muddied' in man. Hence beauty has become a 'dreadful and frightening thing', 'something mysterious in which the devil wrestles with God—and the field of battle is the human heart'. (*Brothers Karamazov.*) This 'muddying of the aesthetic idea' —as a result of which the devil dominates the man who is aroused to aesthetic rapture—explains why men have lost the 'ability' to master the sanctity which is revealed to the heart.

Dostoyevsky's anthropology touches the ultimate depths of the human spirit, revealing the invincible power of the ethical principle in man, but also the muddying of the human heart as a result of which the direct path to the good is closed. Freedom has sucked up the 'seed of death'; there is a stench in the depths of the soul which is muddied by sin, but the force of good continues to live in man. Only through suffering, and often through crime, is man liberated from the temptations of evil, turning again to God. Hence Alyosha says of *Starets* Zosima: 'His heart contains the mystery of renewal for all men, the power which, in the end will establish justice on earth. . . .' The socialist dream of Dostoyevsky's earlier years, the romantic dream of 'restoring' the good in men (a term taken from Victor Hugo), remained to the end of his life. His anthropology stands halfway between a purely ecclesiastical and a secular idea of man. Dostoyevsky's views did not correspond completely to Church doctrine because he failed to give central importance to the Christian emphasis on the suffering and death of the Saviour as a necessary preliminary to His saving Resurrection. We have already said that, in Dostoyevsky's Christian conception of the world, emphasis falls on what was revealed about the world and man in the Incarnation and Transfiguration; but he neglects what was given in Golgotha. Nevertheless, Dostoyevsky's *faith in man* triumphs over his 'disclosures' of the chaos and foul-smelling underground in man. And at this point his anthropology is pierced with the rays of the Easter experience, an experience essential to the basic tonality of Orthodoxy.[1] Dostoyevsky retained the aesthetic humanism which was so characteristic of Russian thinkers, but he treated the nature of aesthetic experience in a new way (see below § 10).

It is often held that in the 'Legend of the Grand Inquisitor'

1. Concerning the Orthodox conception of man, see my book *Das Bild vom Menschen in der Ostkirche* [trans. by H. Strauss], Stuttgart, 1951.

Dostoyevsky shows man's insignificance especially harshly and cruelly, portraying him as a creature unequal to the 'burden' of Christian freedom. But it is forgotten that the words: Christ 'judged men too highly'; 'man was created weaker and lower than Christ thought'—are all spoken deliberately by the Grand Inquisitor to justify his conversion of churchgoing people into slaves. His mistrust of man is rejected by Dostoyevsky, although the 'Legend' contains many very profound thoughts concerning the problem of freedom. The fact that man cannot live without God and that the man who loses faith in God places himself on the path of Kirillov in *The Possessed* (although he may not go to the end of it), i.e. enters the path of mangodhood—remains for Dostoyevsky a basic truth about man. Whoever rejects Godmanhood as a revelation about man—a creature who finds his fullness in God—inevitably tends toward mangodhood.

### 9. ETHICAL VIEWS

We have already emphasized that the ethical category occupies the foreground in Dostoyevsky's anthropology and in his whole conception of man. In fact the ethical reflections which fill Dostoyevsky's works are defined by the initial *ethicism* of his thought. His ethical maximalism and the passionate intensity of his ethical searchings, which give such a profound significance to his basic artistic images, follow from the predominance in his thinking of the complex of problems of the good, and of the paths to it. Dostoyevsky was profoundly independent [1] in his ethical searchings, and it was in this field that his influence on Russian philosophic thought was especially great. Who among succeeding generations of Russian thinkers has not felt his profound influence? [2] Dostoyevsky was filled to overflowing with ethical passion; indeed, the chief root of his philosophic reflections is in the sphere of ethics.

1. S. Hessen in his articles on Dostoyevsky and Solovyov ('Borba utopi i avtonomi dobra v mirovozzreni Dostoyevskovo i V. Solovyova' ['The Struggle for Utopia and the Autonomy of the Good in the World-View of Dostoyevsky and V. Solovyov'], *Sovremennyie zapiski* (1931), 45 and 46), in pointing out the particular closeness of Dostoyevsky and Solovyov after the beginning of 1877, admits Solovyov's influence only in the careful reworking of *The Brothers Karamazov* (in the dialectic of the idea of the good). On the other hand, he is inclined to admit a reverse influence of Dostoyevsky on Solovyov.

2. Berdyaev speaks of this most directly ('Dostoyevsky has played a decisive part in my spiritual life,' *op. cit.*, p. 7). See also V. Ivanov, *Rodnoye i vselenskoye* [The Native and the Universal], Moscow, 1917, p. 147.

When Dostoyevsky, upon returning from penal servitude, began to express himself on ethical problems—both in articles on social and political themes and in his literary works—he first took issue with the oversimplified and shallow conception of man's moral sphere which we have seen in Chernyshevski, Kavelin, and other representatives of utilitarianism and semi-positivism. Dostoyevsky himself was to some extent—but only to some extent—close to these tendencies during the period of his enthusiasm for socialism. We need only recall the passionate pages devoted to this period in his reminiscences of the influence of George Sand (*Diary of a Writer*, June 1876, Ch. I). But the elements of naturalism, which he derived —through Fourier—from Rousseau, remained only in his *religious* views, in what we have called his 'Christian naturalism'. In his conception of ethical psychology these elements vanished completely after his penal servitude. In such an early work as the *Notes from the Underground* we find an extraordinarily sharp and relentless critique of utilitarianism and moral rationalism. In *Crime and Punishment* the ethical theme appears with a profundity which was new not only for Russian but for European thought. We have already seen, in our analysis of Dostoyevsky's anthropology, that he exhibits the decisive ineradicability of man's ethical orientation and the inner dialectic of good in the human soul.

Ethical maximalism attained exceptionally clear and strong expression in Dostoyevsky. Ivan Karamazov's revolt against God is defined by an ethical maximalism which refuses to accept the world because its 'future harmony' is based on suffering. Suffering, especially that of children—a theme which greatly agitated Dostoyevsky—is unacceptable to the moral consciousness. Was it not under the influence of Ivan Karamazov's passionate speeches that Vladimir Solovyov conceived his *Justification of the Good*? In any event, ethical maximalism reached its deepest and strongest expression in Dostoyevsky, entering as an essential element into the ethical theories of subsequent thinkers.

The theme of freedom, as man's ultimate essence, attains equal acuteness and unsurpassed profundity of expression in Dostoyevsky. The conception of freedom which is so vigorously repudiated by the Grand Inquisitor is in fact the deepest penetration into the mystery of freedom as revealed in Christ. Dostoyevsky is unsurpassed in this respect. No one else has exhibited the full range of the problems of freedom with such force as he; we have already discussed this sufficiently in the preceding section. It may be said that no one—either before or after Dostoyevsky—has equalled his profundity in the analysis of the impulses of good and evil, i.e. man's moral psychology. Dostoyevsky's faith in man rests not on a sentimental exaltation of man; on the contrary, it triumphs despite his immersion in the darkest impulses of the human soul.

We must admit that Hessen's interpretations of Dostoyevsky's ethical views are greatly exaggerated.[1] But it is true that Dostoyevsky repudiated not only the ethics of rationality, but also the ethics of *autonomism*, consciously defending a *mystical* ethics.[2] This means first of all that the moral impulses are not determined by feeling, rationality, or reason, but primarily by a living sense of God. Where this sense is lacking, the inevitable result is either an unlimited cynicism, leading to psychic disintegration, or mangodhood. On the other hand, Dostoyevsky—and here he accepted the doctrine of the Slavophiles—felt very deeply the injustice and falseness of self-enclosed individualism ('isolation', in his favourite expression). The formula 'all are guilty for all' is Dostoyevsky's: all men are connected in a mysterious unity which contains the potentiality of genuine brotherhood. Dostoyevsky warmly accepted the ideas of N. F. Fyodorov (see Ch. XX) concerning the spirit of 'nonbrotherhood' of contemporary life. We need only recall his merciless words in the 'Winter Notes on Summer Impressions': 'Who but an abstract doctrinaire could accept the *comedy of bourgeois unity* which we see in Europe as the normal form of human unity on earth?' The idea of *genuine* brotherhood was at the basis of Dostoyevsky's early socialism; and this idea remained strong in him throughout his life, determining the religious utopia with which his world-view was coloured, the utopian idea of converting the state—i.e. the whole earthly order—into a Church.

The mystical foundation of morality is expressed with great force and boldness in the words which *Starets* Zosima uttered before his death (*Brothers Karamazov*):

'God took seeds from other worlds and sowed them on this earth . . . and they germinated. . . . But that which grows lives and enjoys vitality only through its sense of contact with other mysterious worlds. . . . Much on earth is hidden from us, but in

1. See his articles 'Tragediya dobra v Br. Karamazovykh' ['The Tragedy of the Good in the Brothers Karamazov'] *Sovr. zapiski*, No. 36 (1928), and 'Tragediya zla' ['The Tragedy of Evil'], *Put*, No. 36 (1932). See also the above-mentioned article on Dostoyevsky and Solovyov.

2. We have already quoted Dostoyevsky's categorical opinion that the moral sphere in man draws its sustenance exclusively from a mystical root.

exchange we have been given a secret and hidden sense of our living bond with another world. . . .'

These words formulate Dostoyevsky's mystical ethics: our vital and genuine relationship to life is measured only by a love which exceeds the boundaries of both rationality and reason. Love becomes super-reasonable, rising to a sense of inner connection with the whole world, even with the dead, and with inanimate objects. ('Brethren, love each thing. Love each thing and you will *comprehend the mystery of things*.') This universalism of love is wholly sustained by a living sense of God.

### 10. AESTHETIC VIEWS

In his early years Dostoyevsky thought a great deal about the 'function of Christianity in art'. This preoccupation with problems of aesthetics shows the influence of Schiller, with his cult of the aesthetic principle in man and his deep faith in the unity of good and beauty. I think that the influence of A. Grigoryev, Dostoyevsky's one-time collaborator on *Vremya* [Time], was also strong. Dostoyevsky once wrote (*Vremya*, 1864):

'We believe that art has its own integral and organic life. . . . Art is just as much a human need as eating and drinking. The need for beauty and creation is inseparable from man. . . . Man thirsts for beauty, and accepts it without condition, simply because it is beauty.'

'Beauty inheres in everything healthy. . . . It is harmony, and it contains a guarantee of tranquillity.' 'Beauty', Dostoyevsky wrote in the same article, 'already exists in eternity. . . .' Let us note one more idea, later developed by Dostoyevsky in *The Possessed*: 'If a nation preserves an ideal of beauty, this means that it has a need for health and a norm, and this very fact guarantees the higher development of such a nation.' 'Mankind can live without science', the aged Verkhovenski declares (in *The Possessed*), 'and without bread; but he cannot live without *beauty*. The whole mystery is there, and the *whole of history*.' The incarnation of the ideal, the possibility of its attainment in historical reality, is 'guaranteed', according to Dostoyevsky, by the fact that there is beauty in the world. 'Nations are moved', we read in *The Possessed*, 'by a force whose origin is unknown and inexplicable. This . . . is what philosophers call the aesthetic or moral principle; I call it simply the quest for God.' Ethical experience appears as essentially mystical in so far as it impels our soul toward God. In the recently-published materials we find this thought: 'The Holy Spirit is a direct conception of beauty, a prophetic consciousness of harmony and hence a steadfast striving toward it.'

The religious interpretation of aesthetic experience overcomes all the temptations of the world, mitigates its injustice, and gives the whole content of culture a higher religious meaning. This is not simply an *acceptance* of culture; it is a religious consecration of culture, the first step in its transfiguration. In Russia only Archimandrite Bukharev expressed such views before Dostoyevsky's time, but after Dostoyevsky the problem of giving religious meaning to a culture which had grown out of the 'blind' processes of history—the problem of the consecration of culture—became a central historiosophical theme. Dostoyevsky himself exhibits a feature that is characteristic of these searchings—a recognition that the key to the transfiguration of culture is provided by *culture itself*, being contained in the depths of culture, and hidden from us only by sin. This is the 'Christian naturalism' which was such a powerful temptation to Dostoyevsky.

However, he began to doubt very early that 'beauty would save the world'. He himself wrote that 'the aesthetic idea has been muddied in mankind'. 'I am a nihilist', said the young Verkhovenski, 'but I love beauty.' He thus emphasized the ambiguity of beauty. And Dimitri Karamazov expresses similar doubts as to the creative power of beauty with extraordinary force: 'Beauty is a dreadful and frightening thing. . . . In it extremes meet and contradictions lie down together. . . . The dreadful thing is that what the mind [i.e. moral consciousness] regards as shameful seems unalloyed beauty to the heart.' The moral *ambiguity* of beauty, the internal discontinuity of beauty and the good, is at the same time a 'mysterious' thing, for in beauty 'the devil wrestles with God, and the field of battle is the human heart'. This struggle proceeds under the cover of beauty. We may truly say: beauty will not save the world, but the beauty in the world must be saved.

## 11. HISTORIOSOPHICAL VIEWS

Dostoyevsky's thought has great dialectical power. He exhibits antinomies at points where other men appease themselves with the illicit extension of a one-sided premise. Only after elucidating and sharpening the antinomies which are present in reality does he rise above them. The higher sphere in which contradictions are 'reconciled' is the 'empyrean sphere', the realm of religion. This constant ascent to religious heights made Dostoyevsky an inspiring force in Russian religious philosophy for subsequent generations (Berdyaev, Bulgakov, *et al.*). But Dostoyevsky's own religious searchings reached their greatest acuteness in his historiosophy.

We have already quoted the passage from *The Possessed* concerning the 'secret of history', the fact that nations are moved by an 'aesthetic' or 'moral' force, and that in the last analysis this movement is a 'search for God'. Every nation lives by this 'search for God'—'its own' God. Dostoyevsky's 'cult of primitive immediacy' is, of course, a specific form of Populism, but it is even more closely connected with the ideas of Herder and Schelling (in their Russian interpretation) concerning the special 'historical mission' of each nation. The secret of this mission is hidden in the depths of the national spirit; hence the motif of 'independence and autonomy' which was so insistently put forward by the 'young editorial board' of the *Moskvityanin,* and which Grigoryev brought home to Dostoyevsky. But Dostoyevsky's cult of primitive immediacy, as Berdyaev has justly emphasized,[1] goes much deeper: he is not bewitched by empirical history, but penetrates to the depths of the national spirit.

That Russia was destined for a special historical task was believed by Herzen and the Slavophiles, as well as by Dostoyevsky. The high point in the development of Dostoyevsky's ideas about Russia was his celebrated speech on Pushkin. But the idea of an all-embracing synthesis of the Western and Russian spirits, the idea that 'we Russians have two homelands—Europe and our Russia', runs through all of his works. This did not preclude his regarding Europe, in the words of Ivan Karamazov, as a 'precious cemetery'. Criticism of Europe occupies a very large place in Dostoyevsky's work; we need only recall Versilov's words on this theme. Russia's strength is in its Orthodoxy; hence, for Dostoyevsky, historiosophical themes lead directly to a religious conception of history. He wrote extensively and profoundly on these themes in the *Diary of a Writer*; but without doubt the 'Legend of the Grand Inquisitor' is the summit of his historiosophical reflections. This 'legend' is an **extra**ordinary attempt to exhibit the whole complex of historical problems from a Christian viewpoint. If Russian historiosophy, beginning with Herzen, shows a marked tendency toward alogism, it nevertheless acknowledges—as is most clearly

1. *Op. cit.,* p. 180.

expressed in Mikhailovski—that meaning is introduced into history by man. Both Christian providentialism and Hegelian panlogism are here categorically rejected.

In Dostoyevsky Russian historiosophical thought reverted to a religious conception of history: man's freedom, by divine intention, is the basis of the historical dialectic. The introduction of *human* meaning into history is represented in the grandiose project of the Grand Inquisitor. Dostoyevsky here emphasizes with great acuteness that to bring harmony into the historical process one must inevitably *suppress human freedom*; and he feels that this fact is profoundly related to all historiosophical rationalism. His insistence on the inadmissibility of such an approach to man, and his profound defence of the Christian gospel of freedom, do not throw Dostoyevsky into the embraces of Christian irrationalism. He, like Vladimir Solovyov, sees the answer in a free movement of the nations toward 'churchification' of the whole earthly order. Hessen justly criticizes Dostoyevsky's scheme as a form of *utopianism*, but Dostoyevsky (unlike the Marxists, and, to some extent, the proponents of Sophiological determinism [1]) does not assume that the ideal will *necessarily* be realized in history. On the contrary, he exhibits the dialectic of the idea of freedom with great profundity and acuteness: the figures of Stavrogin and Kirillov throw an ominous light on this dialectic. Dostoyevsky is utopian, not in retaining elements of philosophic rationalism—as the above-mentioned theories do—but in failing to take the problem of redemption into account. His conception of 'salvation', as we have frequently emphasized, neglects the mystery of Golgotha. Nevertheless, the grandiose and magnificent picture painted by the Grand Inquisitor is an attempt, unsurpassed in profundity to our day, to grasp the 'mystery and secret of history'. To be sure, Dostoyevsky's indications of the positive paths of 'Orthodox culture' are as diffuse as his critique of the 'Catholic idea' and of historiosophical rationalism, generally, is powerful; but it must be admitted that the 'metaphysics of history' is illuminated by Dostoyevsky with a force of genius found in no one else.

### 12. GENERAL APPRAISAL

Let us sum up our brief analysis of Dostoyevsky's ideas.

Dostoyevsky's philosophic activity found its deepest inspiration in the 'philosophy of the human spirit', but in this realm it achieved extraordinary significance. Anthropology, ethics, historiosophy,

1. I have in mind the theories of S. Bulgakov.

the problem of theodicy—all receive profound and acute treatment in Dostoyevsky. His contribution to Russian (and not only Russian) thought is very large. It is with good reason that the great majority of Russian thinkers in subsequent generations linked their creative activity to that of Dostoyevsky. Special importance attaches to the fact that Dostoyevsky forcefully formulated the problem of culture *within the religious consciousness itself*. The prophetic expectation of an 'Orthodox culture', which was first conceived by Gogol, and which marked out genuinely new paths of historical activity, became in Dostoyevsky for the first time a central theme of historiosophical searchings and constructions. Secularism, which the Slavophiles still conceived as the dialectically inevitable outcome of the religious process in the West, was viewed by Dostoyevsky as a permanent, though one-sided, orientation of the human spirit, *a specific religious orientation*. Raskolnikov incarnates the radical break of the human spirit with the religious consciousness, and Kirillov exhibits the inevitable religious reformulation of this break with God in the ideology of mangodhood. The forces which in Western philosophy had long since made secularism a kind of religious immanentism, arise in Dostoyevsky's heroes from the idea of reality—a reality dialectically inseparable from the religious principle. This reversion of thought from abstract radicalism to its primordial religious womb did not suppress or eliminate any of the profound problems of the human spirit; it merely placed the whole complex of problems on its basic foundation. Dostoyevsky, in fact, opened a new period in the history of Russian thought. Although Russian thinkers had always recognized the fundamental importance of the religious orientation, Dostoyevsky was the first to convert all the problems of the human spirit into religious problems. Of course, this immediately complicated the religious orientation, threatening a break with the classical formulations of the Church Fathers, but at the same time it formed the basis for an extraordinary and fruitful flowering of Russian religio-philosophic thought.

All of this is related to the modern period in the history of Russian thought, which is treated in Parts III and IV of this book. But we shall detain the reader in the following chapter with two brilliant thinkers—Leontyev and Rozanov—whose creative activity likewise introduces us to the modern period of Russian thought.

# CHAPTER XV

## K. N. Leontyev. V. V. Rozanov

### I. GENERAL REMARKS

WE are approaching the end of our study of the philosophic theories which preceded the appearance of
genuine systems. The period which began in the 1850's
with the accession to the throne of Alexander II was marked in its
inner style by a demand for the systematic formulation of ideological searchings, theories, and projects. If neither Chernyshevski,
Mikhailovski, nor the other thinkers of the period succeeded in
this formulation, the reason is hardly to be sought in a lack of
philosophic talent. Almost all the thinkers of this period had unquestionable and genuine philosophic talent. But the construction
of a system is not a matter of mere persistence in intellectual work.
There is an historical, as well as an individual, dialectic in philosophic development, as is evident in the ways in which thinking
proceeded during this period, within the conditions of Russian
culture. A materialist in his root convictions, Chernyshevski was
confident that his ethics and aesthetics were true to his fundamental principles, whereas in fact they were inspired by principles
wholly incompatible with materialism. This is not mere *inconsistency*; it is an inner constraint on thought which is too honest and
truthful to suppress what cannot be embraced by a scheme, merely
to save the scheme. Russian semi-positivism limped on both legs:
it held stubbornly to the meagre propositions of positivism, and
proceeded to advance a philosophy of freedom wholly incompatible
with positivist principles. The most rigorous and consistent thinker
of this period, P. L. Lavrov, hoped to find in his 'anthropologism' a
connecting principle between positivism and social idealism; but he
had little success, being unable to discover any systematic principle
in anthropology or psychology. All of these were *unsuccessful* attempts
—from the formal point of view—to construct systems, but even
failures may be dialectically valuable for subsequent constructions.

The thinkers with whom we are concerned in the present chapter also failed to give their fundamental theories a systematic form; but they tended toward a system, living inwardly by systematic principles—and this constitutes their dialectical significance.

Let us turn first to a study of the ideas of K. N. Leontyev.

## 2. K. N. LEONTYEV. BIOGRAPHY

Konstantin Nikolayevich Leontyev (1831–91) was born into the family of a landowner in the village of Kudinovo (in the Government of Kaluga).[1] His mother was an extremely religious person, and the life of the family took shape under her influence. From his mother Leontyev inherited a lively and profound religious feeling, which burned with a bright flame throughout his life; but together with this—and also under his mother's influence—he developed an aesthetic sense. The aesthetic approach to the world, life, and man also remained permanently with Leontyev as a specific and independent form of the life of the spirit. His aestheticism was so deeply rooted in his inner world that it became in a certain sense 'autonomous', tending to determine all the other spheres of the spiritual life. The hero of one of Leontyev's short stories once uttered words very characteristic of Leontyev himself as a youth: 'I fell in love with life, with all of its contradictions, and I began to consider my passionate participation in this marvellous drama of earthly existence almost as an act of *divine worship*. . . .'[2] Upon graduation from the Gymnasium, Leontyev entered the Faculty of Medicine at Moscow University;

1. The most complete biography of Leontyev is that of Berdyaev: *K. N. Leontyev* [trans. by G. Reavey], London, 1940. Since the publication of this book no new biographical material has appeared, to my knowledge, except Leontyev's very valuable autobiography ('Moya literaturnaya sudba' ['My Literary Fate'], *Literaturnoye nasledstvo*, Moscow, 1935, 22–24, pp. 427–96). Judging from the remarks in *Lit. nasledstvo* (p. 472, note 3) there is an unpublished biography, written by Leontyev himself, entitled 'Khronologiya moyei zhizni' ['A Chronology of My Life'].

Nine volumes of Leontyev's works were published in 1912–14; Vol. X was ready for the printer when the war broke out, halting publication. His letters have not yet been published in their entirety. For an appraisal of Leontyev see Masaryk, *The Spirit of Russia*, II, 207–20. P. Milyukov, 'La Décomposition du Slavophilisme' in *Le Mouvement intellectuel russe*, offers very little for a correct appraisal of Leontyev.

2. Leontyev, 'Egipetski golub' ['The Egyptian Dove'], *Sochineniya* [Works], III, 397.

without finishing the fifth course he was sent out as a doctor, taking part in the Crimean War. He very early became a writer (in the 1850's), and his short stories were quite successful. Turgenyev helped him a great deal, and Leontyev was an admirer of Turgenyev throughout his life. While still in the Crimea Leontyev planned a large novel, and when he was released from military service he took a position as a house physician with a nobleman named Rozen, in order to have more leisure for literary work. But he was uncomfortable there, and later he attempted to set himself up in St. Petersburg. During this period he suddenly married (in 1861) a semiliterate and beautiful woman of the lower middle class from Theodosia—who later became mentally ill. Finally, in 1863, he gave up his medical career entirely, and entered the diplomatic service. He was soon sent to the Near East. For ten years Leontyev served as consul in various Turkish cities, studying the Near East thoroughly. There his philosophic and political conceptions took final form. Giving up the diplomatic service because of disagreements on matters of principle with the makers of Russian foreign policy, Leontyev went to Mt. Athos, but soon returned to Russia. He was unable to find a place in the literary circles toward which his political views inclined him.[1] He tried working as a censor, but gave this up within a few years and entered a monastery—the Optina Cloister, famed for its '*Startsy*'. At this time the celebrated *Starets* Fr. Ambrose was active, and he gave his blessing to Leontyev's continued literary activity. Although Leontyev's wife, who became mentally ill very early, lived with him in the Optina Cloister, they were officially divorced on the initiative of Leontyev himself, who wished to become a monk.[2] In fact, in August of 1891 Leontyev secretly took monastic vows; in November of the same year he died.

Leontyev's life was full of failures; his singular ideas drew him toward the Russian reactionary circles (Katkov *et al.*), but his closeness to them was limited to political questions. The essence of Leontyev's religio-philosophic world-view made him a stranger to these circles. Hence he had very few friends or congenial acquaintances. Leontyev passed his life alone and in sorrow; the reason for this lay as much in his profound insistence on principles as in his ideas. His attitude toward his own theories and ideas was ardent and passionate. The most striking example of what

1. The autobiographical article mentioned above dates from this period.

2. Leontyev's wife survived him, dying after the revolution in 1917. (Cf. *Lit. nasledstvo*, p. 493, note 92.)

15*

disagreements of principle meant to him is afforded by the history of his relations with Vladimir Solovyov. Leontyev had an ardent affection for Solovyov, and was constantly influenced by him. Solovyov responded sympathetically, though somewhat coolly; however, he always had a high opinion of Leontyev. But, when Solovyov read a paper in Moscow on the theme of 'The Decline of the Medieval World-View' [1] in which he preached progress (in the spirit of Western democracy), Leontyev—who, as we shall see below, was decisively and categorically opposed to all 'egalitarian' movements—broke completely with Solovyov. Such an original and singular man as Rozanov (see below). valued Leontyev very highly; but Leontyev's antihumanism, which frequently took on the outward features of a genuine amoralism, was not only alien but incomprehensible to Rozanov.

### 3. INFLUENCES ON LEONTYEV

Before proceeding to a study of Leontyev's ideas, let us consider briefly the influences to which he was exposed. The question of Leontyev's relationship to the Slavophiles is of primary importance here. He is often considered a Slavophile; but, since he was profoundly repelled by Slavism—which he came to know well during his diplomatic service—he is considered a 'disillusioned Slavophile', and his theories are regarded as a 'disintegration' of Slavophilism. There is very little truth in this. Leontyev developed quite apart from the direct influence of the senior Slavophiles, although he grew up in the same strongly religious Russian environment— an environment of ecclesiastical traditionalism and genuine piety. Of course, one may find in Leontyev expressions of sympathy for the older Slavophiles, but his criticisms of them are equally numerous. Berdyaev, who has studied Leontyev very carefully and written the best monograph on him, categorically asserts that Leontyev, 'of course, was never a Slavophile and in many respects was the exact opposite of the Slavophiles'. [2] Florovsky characterizes Leontyev as a 'disillusioned romanticist',[3] and there is a good deal of truth in this. Leontyev reminds Masaryk of Hamann and Carlyle—original writers who fall into no easy classification.[4] The

1. See V. S. Solovyov, *Sochineniya*, Vol. VI.
2. Berdyaev, *op. cit.*, p. 8. Leontyev once called himself a Slavophile (*Sochineniya*, VI, 118), but only in the sense of 'a lover of the specific quality of Russian culture'.
3. Florovsky, *Puti russkovo bogosloviya* [Paths of Russian Theology], p. 305.
4. Masaryk, *op. cit.*, II, 214.

diversity of these judgments is characteristic of Leontyev's fate. His relation to Slavophilism cannot be judged solely on the basis of his critique of the West. The one indisputable influence testified to by Leontyev himself [1] is that of N. D. Danilevski, the author of the celebrated book, Russia and Europe. But this influence came after Leontyev's basic ideas had already taken shape. Danilevski only *reinforced* Leontyev in the historiosophical and political views which he had reached independently.

We have already mentioned Leontyev's admiration for Solovyov, who undoubtedly influenced him, and was one of his authorities; but Leontyev's closeness to Solovyov also came after the basic features of his world-view were already formed. We should also note Herzen's influence on Leontyev in the appraisal of Philistinism.[2] Leontyev kept Herzen's works with him even on Mt. Athos; but, of course, Herzen played no part in the *genesis* of Leontyev's ideas.[3]

From all of this only one thing is evident: Leontyev was a highly *original and independent* thinker. His *language* is one of the best evidences of this: it is always brilliant, original, permeated with ardent feeling, even passion. Leontyev always finds his *own* expressions. In his writing trenchant thought and ardent feeling are fused together into a musical harmony. 'Such an incisive, insolent, and extreme style', Berdyaev wrote of Leontyev, 'has been possessed by very few writers.' [4] This is quite true; the inner originality and independence of Leontyev's mind is manifested in the brilliant originality of his language.

### 4. THE DIALECTIC OF HIS RELIGIOUS CONSCIOUSNESS

Students of Leontyev's ideas often mistakenly regard his historiosophical theories, especially the doctrine of the 'triune process', as central and basic. However, Leontyev's historiosophical views took shape quite late and, what is more important, were not fundamental to his intellectual searchings. His intellectual activity was

1. Leontyev, *op. cit.*, V, 420n: 'Danilevski's book served as my chief foundation'. A little further on (*ibid.*, p. 433) he calls Danilevski's book 'truly great'.
2. See *Lit. nasledstvo*, p. 479n.
3. Bulgakov in his essay on Leontyev (*Tikhiye dumy* [Quiet Meditations], p. 117) justly notes that Leontyev 'was most successful and relentless in recognizing the features of triumphant middle-class Philistinism in the countenance of Europe'.
4. Berdyaev, article on Leontyev in the collection *Sub specie aeternitatis*, St. Petersburg, 1907, p. 309.

bounded by his *religious consciousness*, and the principal root of his theories must be sought in the latter. But, while Leontyev was a highly integrated person, his intellectual searchings did not develop from *a single root*—although they were *delimited* by his religious consciousness. We find in Leontyev during his early period a naïve and *uncritical* synthesis of religious and other ideas (see below). In middle life he experienced a profound and serious spiritual crisis. As a result of this his earlier complex of ideas disintegrated, giving way to a new, severe and morose conception, which defined the various views usually associated with his name. Such was the dialectic of his religious consciousness, a dialectic which underlay his intellectual constructions. Hence a study of Leontyev's ideas should be preceded by a study of his religious world.

Certain authors—most strikingly, Aggeyev—consider Leontyev's *aestheticism*, rather than his religious searchings, primary. Aggeyev, who devotes the first part of his book to a study of Leontyev 'as a religious individual', asserts categorically that 'Leontyev entered life as an aesthete'.[1] According to him, even during the flowering of his religious life, Leontyev distorted and decimated the content of faith 'in the name of aesthetics'.[2] In another place Aggeyev, offering a different interpretation of the relationship of aesthetics to the religious life in Leontyev, writes: 'Aesthetic feeling impelled Leontyev toward Orthodoxy.' He thus continues to assert the priority of the aesthetic principle in Leontyev.[3]

Berdyaev interprets this question somewhat differently: he considers *both* principles basic and radical in Leontyev, regarding them as mutually nonderivative. In his words, Leontyev's 'first religious experiences were *organically fused* with his aesthetic experiences.'[4] The testimony of Leontyev himself appears to favour Aggeyev's thesis. 'Unfortunately, my education was not strictly Christian . . .', he wrote in his late memoirs. 'I had to live forty years and experience an abrupt crisis in order to return to positive religion.' In the same place Leontyev recalls that, when as a medical student religious doubts assailed him, 'he appeased himself for a time with a kind of obscure deism—an aesthetic and free belief'. However, this was written in a late period, when Leontyev's religious life had assumed a severe and ascetic quality.

---

1. 'Khristianstvo i yevo otnosheniye k blagoustroyeniyu zemnoi zhizni' ['Christianity and Its Attitude toward the Harmonious Ordering of Earthly Life'], *Trud. K. Dukh. Akad.*, IV (1909), p. 579.

2. *Op. cit.*, VI, 323.        3. *Ibid.*, p. 301.        4. *Op. cit.*, p. 12.

In his recollections of his mother, Leontyev wrote of himself with sincere satisfaction: 'Later, as a young man, I too paid my tribute to European liberalism, but even in this fatuous period I never offended my mother's ideals by blasphemous mockery or the strident arguments of bad liberal philosophy.'

One thing is beyond dispute: when Leontyev experienced his 'crisis', he 'returned' to his early religious life, although after this crisis it took on a new character. But in essence this was only a transition from childish to adult religiosity. Leontyev himself says of this crisis that it was 'a passionate conversion to a *personal* Orthodoxy'.[1] This personal shock, which we shall discuss below, terminated a profound process which had been going on in Leontyev since his youth, closing a period of dualism in favour of religious firmness; but this was only the final stage in his religious development, not the 'origin' or 'birth' of his religious searchings.

From the time of Leontyev's childhood his spiritual world was nourished by religious experiences; but these experiences, although they touched the depths of his soul, were for the most part turned toward the 'outward form' of ecclesiastical life. Leontyev himself acknowledges this in the above-mentioned letter to Rozanov. While still a boy, he fell in love with the Orthodox service of worship, experiencing it aesthetically. The aesthetic perception of ecclesiastical life and the aesthetic attitude toward the Church were expressions of Leontyev's inner wholeness, a wholeness which, though uncritical and naïve, was genuine. In his youth Leontyev did not breathe the air of a culture poisoned by secularism; he absorbed the content of culture under the protection of his aesthetic admiration for the Church, still unaware of the inner dissonances of culture. We have seen that in his late memoirs he characterized his early religiosity as 'obscure deism'; but deism is characterized by an atrophy of the sense of Providence, the absence of an idea of God's direct participation in human life. And this was characteristic of Leontyev as a youth. Hence he experienced his crisis as a 'personal Orthodoxy', the consciousness of a personal tie with God.

The degree of 'naïveté' of Leontyev's youthful religious consciousness is especially clear from the crowding out and suppression of the moral orientation by the aesthetic element. Leontyev himself speaks of this in connection with his first artistic works: 'At that time the pernicious thought began to steal into my mind that nothing is unconditionally moral, but that things are moral or

1. Letter to Rozanov, *Rus. vestnik*, VI (1903).

immoral only in an aesthetic sense.' It would be terribly wrong to conclude that there was any personal 'amoralism' in Leontyev, any absence of moral impulses, although such conclusions are sometimes expressed by writers on Leontyev in discussing his 'antihumanism'. This antihumanism is not a matter of the absence of moral impulses,[1] but of the prevalence of the aesthetic element in the *religious* consciousness. Through this aesthetic temper, the culture of secularism flowed imperceptibly into Leontyev's soul, unperceived by the religious consciousness, i.e., without breaking with it. While remaining religious, Leontyev at a later period avidly absorbed the whole content of secular culture. The entire interval from his youth to his crisis is characterized by the disharmonious combination of extra-religious and antireligious culture with an outward loyalty to the Church. The impossibility of maintaining such a combination of heterogeneous principles led inevitably to a crisis—a choice between a genuinely religious and an irreligious attitude toward the world and culture.

Leontyev himself describes the period in which he was greedily absorbing the content of culture as a 'struggle of poetry and morality':

'I am aware that the former often gained the upper hand, not through any lack of *natural goodness or honesty* (they were naturally strong in me), but as the result of an exclusively aesthetic world-view. Goéthe, Byron, Béranger, Pushkin, Batyushkov, Lermontov . . . corrupted me in this direction in the highest degree. . . . Only the poetry of religion can eradicate in a man with a broadly and diversely developed imagination the *poetry of exquisite immorality*. . . .'[2]

These last, brief but brilliant, words convey accurately the very depths of the 'aesthetic orientation' which had begun to form in European culture in the mid-eighteenth century.[3] The aesthetic humanism which found expression in Humboldt and Schiller (the *Schöne Seele*) merely concealed an inner disintegration of morality. The poisonous but imperceptible stream of amoralism

1. Berdyaev speaks very truly of Leontyev's 'serious moral character' (*op. cit.*, p. 146, *passim*).

2. Correspondence of Leontyev with Aleksandrov, *Bogoslovski vestnik*, III (1914), p. 456.

3. See Obernauer's excellent work, mentioned above, *Die Problematik des ästhetischen Menschen und die deutsche Literatur*, 1923.

was actually much stronger where it was hidden by beauty and exquisiteness of form. After Gogol and Dostoyevsky—and to some extent Tolstoy, with his treatise on art—it was hardly necessary for a Russian writer to emphasize the *heterogeneity* of aesthetic and moral principles. But the root ethicism of Russian thinkers and artists in general has often concealed this heterogeneity behind a complacent optimism. Leontyev harshly characterized this whole spiritual atmosphere as the 'poetry of exquisite immorality'—but this was after his religious crisis. Before the crisis his religious feeling gave him no warning against the 'poetry of exquisite immorality'. In the same letter to Aleksandrov we find the following lines:

'I loved Orthodoxy very much (before my religious crisis)—its service of worship, its history, and ritual; and I also loved Christ. Even then, with all the profound corruption of my ideas, the New Testament moved me strongly. I also loved brotherly love, both in the sense of compassion, forbearance, and charity—and in the sense of *sympathy for all passions.* . . .'[1]

In this complacent combination of kindness and 'exquisite immorality', under the general cover of a love for ecclesiasticism, the purely aesthetic element still dominates over everything else. It is no exaggeration to say that the internal influences of secular culture changed Leontyev's whole spiritual life, although they were concealed beneath aestheticism and a complacent religiosity —'rose-coloured Christianity', as Leontyev later called the religion of Dostoyevsky and Tolstoy. The hero of one of Leontyev's early literary works, who is often thought to embody features of Leontyev himself, remarks: 'Morality is only a little corner of the beautiful—one of its poles.'

Leontyev's elimination of the moral principle from his general conception of life was simply a consistent carrying out of the primacy of aesthetics, a primacy preserved by the *authority of ecclesiasticism*. Without noticing it, Leontyev fell into substantial bondage to *secular aestheticism*, a position which had already separated itself from ethics and hence from the foundation of the religious sphere. The continuing dominance over Leontyev's soul of the outward covering of ecclesiasticism could not conceal the gradual necrosis of the religious sphere—as a result of the elimination of the moral principle. It was *this* that constituted the initial point of his religious crisis.

1. *Bog. vestnik*, III, 458n.

Leontyev himself describes this crisis in the following words:

'It was all based, on the one hand, upon a philosophic hatred of the forms and the spirit of modern European life (St. Petersburg, literary vulgarity, railroads, dinner jackets and top hats, rationalism, etc.) and, on the other hand, upon an aesthetic and childlike attachment to the outward forms of Orthodoxy. Add to this the accident of a very sudden and serious illness.' [1]

A 'personal faith' in God flared up in Leontyev at the time of his illness, a faith in the intercession of the Mother of God, to Whom he turned in ardent prayer. Within two hours he had recovered and by the third day he was on Mt. Athos, ready to take monastic vows. The fear of death brought his slumbering faith to the surface: 'I humbled myself', he wrote, 'and I understood at once the higher teleology of chance. Physical fear passed, but spiritual fear remained; from that time on I could not give up my fear of the Lord or my faith in Him.' This 'fear of the Lord' was a *return to morality*—a mystical morality, wholly defined by a religious conception of life. However, the triumph of the religious principle was combined from the very beginning with a suspicious attitude toward contemporary culture. Leontyev's own words are interesting in this connection: 'After my passionate conversion to a personal Orthodoxy my personal faith for some reason suddenly brought my political and artistic education to an end. This astonishes me and remains mysterious and incomprehensible to me to the present day.' This was a genuine crisis of the religious consciousness, a return to a genuine faith in God and to a mystical morality, a decisive break with the system of secular culture.

Now, with this religious crisis in mind, we will find it easier to understand the dialectic of Leontyev's ideas.

## 5. ANTHROPOLOGY

The key to the dialectic of Leontyev's ideas is to be found not in his historiosophical or political views, but in his *anthropology*, which —as a result of his new religious consciousness—was decisively opposed to the optimistic secular conception of man and faith in human nature. He repeatedly took sharp issue with 'anthropolatry'—

'the new faith in the earthly man and earthly mankind, in the ideal, independent, autonomous dignity of the individual. . . . [All

1. Quoted by Aggeyev, *op. cit.*, VI, 296.

of this is an expression] of the individualism, and the deification of the rights and dignities of man, which became dominant in Europe at the end of the eighteenth century.' [1]

'European thought now worships man simply because he is man.'[2] This revolt against the absolutizing of man in contemporary culture strikes at the *heart* of a secularism which repudiates the Church in the name of man's self-sufficiency. Leontyev finds neither an empirical nor a metaphysical basis for such an exaltation of man. 'If I humbled myself', he wrote in his 'Autobiography', 'it was not because I came to have less faith in my own reason, but in *human reason generally*.' [3] 'An inundation of rationalism (in other words, a diffusion of large pretensions to imaginary understanding) merely stimulates the destructive passions.' [4] 'The naïve man, who is submissive to authority', Leontyev wrote in the same place, 'appears, on careful examination, closer to the truth than the self-confident and presumptuous man.' 'Free individualism ['which in fact has given way to an execrable atomism' [5]] is destroying contemporary societies.' [6] Such passages could be multiplied; all of them reflect Leontyev's decisive opposition to the anthropocentrism which is so deeply connected with the system of secularism, and which is so strong in Russian thought and the Russian soul. Leontyev's distrust of man, human reason, and contemporary culture—with its 'poetry of exquisite immorality'—is all the stronger in that, as we have just seen, he experienced in his own life the action of 'mysterious and incomprehensible' forces. 'I now find', he wrote in his 'Autobiography', 'that the most profound and brilliant mind comes to nothing if its destiny is not decreed from above.' [7] 'Historical fatalism', the acknowledgement of 'invisible, mysterious, and superhuman forces' [8] now became Leontyev's favourite idea. 'The difficult and thorny heights of Christianity' [9] throw the first proper light on man and his career; for Leontyev Christianity is clearly incompatible with a cult of man or a faith in human nature. He broached the question of *salvation* with a force unprecedented in Russian literature. And, although he himself constantly emphasizes that he understands salvation in the transcendent sense, a careful reading of his works makes it clear that his intention is broader than his formula. Leontyev refuses to

1. Leontyev, *op. cit.*, VIII, 160.    2. *Op. cit.*, VII, 132.
3. *Lit. nasledstvo*, p. 467.    4. *Sochineniya*, V, 237.
5. *Op. cit.*, VII, 169.    6. *Op. cit.*, VI, 21.
7. *Lit. nasledstvo*, p. 467.    8. *Sochineniya*, VI, 121.
9. *Lit. nasledstvo*, p. 465.

treat the problem of man or man's life exclusively with respect to the fragment of his earthly life. He is profoundly conscious that man lives in a world beyond, and that his life *there* depends upon his life *here*. This central Christian conviction entered fully into Leontyev's thought after his crisis, determining his attitude toward current utilitarian morality and the bourgeois ideal. His abhorrence of spiritual Philistinism and external levelling was also determined, of course, by his aesthetic aversion to the contemporary world, but it was not *merely* a matter of aesthetics. It is often said that Leontyev's 'neo-romanticism' is an 'aesthetic reinterpretation of Orthodoxy' (deriving from Apollon Grigoryev),[1] and there is a *portion* of truth in this; but it is still more important to realize that Leontyev's aesthetic perception of the world and of life was *inspired* by his *religious consciousness*. This same historian compares Leontyev to Karl Barth, because the idea of salvation occupies the centre of his religious consciousness: 'Leontyev did not seek the truth in Christianity and faith, but merely salvation.'[2] This 'merely' is astonishing in a theologian, who seems to have forgotten that the soteriological motif has always been the chief criterion for the investigation of Christian truth.

In any case, Leontyev was truly afire with a 'philosophic hatred' of contemporary culture—not simply an aesthetic aversion, but a 'philosophic' rejection of it, i.e. a rejection of its 'meaning', a meaning constructed apart from the idea of salvation and eternal life. The contemporary world—which is anxiously preoccupied with the ordering of life on earth, and only on earth, tearing the spirit away from the idea of eternal life—became alien to Leontyev, primarily in a *religious* sense. The aesthetic *paltriness* of ecstasy over life here and now was evident only to a Christian consciousness. Leontyev, with his insistence on the primacy of the problem of salvation, has been little heeded, even to our own day; nevertheless, we must acknowledge the force and profundity of his religious consciousness. It is strange that almost no one—except Berdyaev—has sensed Leontyev's *ethical passion*. For the idea of salvation is essentially an ethical idea, but one that is concerned not merely with earthly life but with life beyond the grave. In Leontyev, to be sure, we constantly find the opposite extreme: for him everything in this life is trivial and empty. He readily falls into a seductive antihumanism. But in the light of Christianity—i.e. the idea of eternal life—even the aesthetic sphere pales for him. He repudiates the 'poetry of exquisite

1. Florovsky, *op. cit.*, p. 305.    2. *Ibid.*, p. 304.

·immorality'. In his 'Autobiography' he expressed himself very sharply to the effect that only the idea of God's image in man can reconcile us to the vulgarity of the 'multitude of prosaic, stupid, and nauseating people'. [1] Man's aesthetic paltriness is thus exhibited even more sharply and painfully in the light of religion.

Leontyev—like Nietzsche, to whom he is often compared—was not simply repelled by the contemporary world, and contemporary man, in the name of an aesthetic ideal; rather, his aesthetic 'captiousness' resulted from his unduly high religious conception of the 'true' man. Leontyev's anthropology exhibits the struggle of a religious conception of man with an everyday secular conception which fails to seek high tasks for man or measure his value in the light of eternal life, but simply worships man apart from his relation to the ideal. The ethical and aesthetic captiousness of Leontyev's anthropology results from his religious orientation. This will become clearer when we enter more deeply into Leontyev's ethical reflections.

## 6. ETHICAL VIEWS

Everyone who has written on Leontyev speaks constantly of his amoralism; however, there is a very serious misunderstanding here, for which Leontyev himself unfortunately provides a basis. Consider, for example, his series of articles 'Our New Christians' (on Tolstoy and Dostoyevsky), in which he sharply and harshly attacks 'sentimental, rose-coloured Christianity', asserting in various ways that 'modern European humaneness and Christian humaneness are clearly antithetical'.[2] Much evidence of Leontyev's 'amoralism' may be found in his works, and writers constantly speak of the 'complete atrophy of his moral feeling'.[3]

But what do we find in fact? Leontyev distinguished categorically (before Nietzsche!) between 'love for one's fellow man' and 'love for the far off'—mankind in general. The former is concerned with a real living human being and not a 'collective and abstract mankind' with 'varied and contradictory needs and desires'.[4] Leontyev ardently defends the first kind of love (for man), and passionately ridicules the second (for mankind), because of its artificiality, injustice, and failure to understand the

1. *Lit. nasledstvo*, p. 455n.      2. *Sochineniya*, VIII, 203.
3. L. A. Zander, 'K. Leontyev o progresse' ['K. Leontyev on Progress'] (reprint from *Rus. obozreniye*, 1921), p. 9. Bulgakov considers Leontyev an 'ethical monster' (*op. cit.*, p. 119).
4. *Sochineniya*, VIII. 207.

'irremediable tragedy of life'. The passages in Leontyev's works in which we find expressions of 'amoralism' actually refer only to the 'far off', to 'mankind in general'; and they are linked to his general historiosophical conception, which we shall consider below. However, even with respect to love for one's 'fellow man', 'myopic sentimentality' is alien to Leontyev. Like Dostoyevsky, he regards suffering as an inevitable and often health-giving element in life. He caustically ridicules the 'consoling childishness' which appeases itself with a complacent optimism, and calls for a return to 'severe and sorrowful pessimism, a courageous submissiveness to the incorrigibility of earthly life'.[1] He also rejects the 'irrational religion of eudaemonism'.[2]

Following Leontyev's own example, certain writers have spoken of his 'transcendent egoism',[3] i.e. asserted that his preoccupation with his personal fate beyond the grave displaced and suppressed his direct moral feeling. The only truth in this is that the problem of salvation, as we have already seen, took on central importance for Leontyev—but not in its purely egoistic aspect: for him the idea of salvation illuminated the basic problem of historiosophy and even of politics. We shall consider this below.

Leontyev's doctrine of love is very important for an understanding of his ethical views. While extolling *personal charity*, he categorically asserts that 'love of man which is not accompanied by fear of God and does not rest in Him is not purely Christian'.[4] Without fear of God, love of man loses its deep source, and is readily transformed into sentimentality and superficial compassion. This 'natural' kindness is subjective, and often limited; therefore, only the love of man which flows from a religious source is valuable and profound—and it is accessible even to the hardhearted, if they live by faith in God.[5] According to Leontyev, it is also essential to distinguish moral love from aesthetic love.[6] The former is genuine charity—the latter mere 'delight'. For him love of the far off, which underlies all European humanism, with its ideal of universal well-being, is a dreamy 'delight' in 'the idea of man in general', a worship of mankind which obligates us to nothing and summons us to nothing. There is no *goodness* in it. Hence, although there is much ardour in modern humanism, flowing over into revolutionism, there is no genuine goodness. Leontyev felt very deeply

1. *Ibid.*, p. 189.     2. *Op. cit.*, V, 251.     3. *Op. cit.*, VIII, 207.
4. *Ibid.*, p. 159.     5. *Ibid.*, p. 179.
6. This distinction is very important for the understanding of Leontyev. See *ibid.*, pp. 178–81.

the *dreamy* quality of the ideal of 'universal' well-being, and he denied it any genuinely *moral* value. Leontyev's corrosive critique of Dostoyevsky's speech on Pushkin is based on the view that a 'feverish preoccupation with the earthly welfare of future generations' [1] is an *oversimplification* of the tragic theme of history.[2] He sensed a 'psychologism', a sentimentality, in modern humanism; and he himself felt a 'need for a stricter morality'.[3] The inner severity which characterized Leontyev after his religious crisis did not mark an *elimination* of morality; it sprang from an awareness that the moral consciousness of modern times conceals much genuine—though 'exquisite'—immorality. On the other hand, the 'vociferous humanism' of the modern period is a direct product of religious and historiosophical immanentism—the intention to 'be good without God's aid'. If we wish to *understand* the dialectic of Leontyev's ideas, and not simply to heap accusations upon him —a practice common to almost everyone who has written on him —we must realize that moral justice for Leontyev, in the second period of his life, consisted not in eliminating the suffering of mankind, but in realizing God's mysterious will in life and history. The idea that the criterion of personal morality has little application in history is not something tangential for him, but one of the principles of his world-view. We shall turn to this presently; meanwhile, let us stress once more that Leontyev's moral ideas are permeated by an awareness of the *corruption* of contemporary man and contemporary culture, with its 'poetry of exquisite immorality'. He is much more the moralist than the aestheticizing thinker which he is often pictured, but his morality is severe, and coloured by a consciousness of the tragic quality of life which flows from his religious perception of the contemporary world.

## 7. HISTORIOSOPHICAL VIEWS

The fact that Leontyev was trained in biology was of immense importance for the genesis of his historiosophical views. The idea of a 'triune process', when it took final form in his consciousness, was a simple transfer of his views as a biologist to historical being. Yet, such an authority on Leontyev's views as Rozanov has characterized his historiosophical views as an '*aesthetic* conception of history'. Leontyev himself once wrote: 'Aesthetics saved the

1. *Ibid.*, p. 189.          2. *Ibid.*, p. 203.
3. Letter to Aleksandrov, *Bog. vestnik*, III (1914), p. 457.

civilized man in me'. [1] This means that there is no beauty in life without hierarchical structure, without 'power'. Leontyev had a keen interest in the *political* aspect of history; however, he did not accept 'statism', in the contemporary sense of the word. He neither subordinated the Church to the state [2] nor raised statehood to a supreme principle. His cult of statehood rested on the same principle of 'consolidation' which he ascribed to the element of 'form' in the ontology of beauty. 'Form is the despotism of an inner idea, which prevents the dispersion of matter.' [3] Statehood guarantees the life and development of a nation or nations, but its very power depends on the spiritual and ideological health of the people. The degeneration of statehood and the spiritual degeneration of nations proceed in parallel; and here the biologist in Leontyev suggested the idea of a *'cosmic* law of disintegration' [4] and the idea of a 'triune process'. Leontyev invites all men 'to examine the laws of life and of the development of statehood fearlessly, as the scientist examines nature.' In his opinion, a single law determines the stages in the development of the plant, animal, and human worlds—and the world of history.[5] Every organism ascends from an initial simplicity to a 'flourishing complexity', from which it moves through 'secondary simplifications' and a 'levelling interfusion' toward death. 'This triune process', Leontyev writes, 'characterizes not only the specifically organic world, but, it may be, everything that exists in space and time.' He considered it especially important that the 'triune process also occurs in historical being, i.e. in the life of races, state organisms, and entire cultured worlds.' [6] Leontyev had a very high opinion of this idea, and extended it far beyond the limits of the organic world from which it was derived. When he became seriously ill, he was 'seized by terror at the thought of dying at the moment when he had conceived but had not yet written down the hypothesis of the triune process as well as various artistic works.' [7] Leontyev's formula contains two equally important elements: on the one hand, an elucidation of the law which governs the development of all *individuality*—and here he stresses the theme

1. *Sochineniya*, VIII, 267.

2. Concerning the necessity of subordinating the state to 'mystical forces' see the striking formulas, *op. cit.*, V, 332. Leontyev broke sharply on this question with Katkov, a typical representative of 'statism' in Russian thought.

3. *Ibid.*, p. 197.                    4. *Ibid.*, p. 249.

5. For a more complete exposition see the chapter 'Chto takoye protsess razvitiya?' ['What Is the Process of Development?'], *ibid.*, p. 187.

6. *Ibid.*, p. 194.                    7. Quoted by Aggeyev, *op. cit.*, VI, 296.

of 'struggle for individuality' which was developed with such force by Mikhailovski—in other words, the theme of *personalism*.[1] On the other hand, Leontyev's formula carries to its limit the transfer of categories of organic life to historical being which had previously been developed with ample force by Danilevski in his book, Russia and Europe [German translation: Stuttgart, 1920.] Danilevski was the first in Russian philosophy to broach the theme of the subordination of historical being to the laws governing nature in the organic sphere; his unquestionable importance and influence [2] in Russian historiosophy is connected less with the doctrine of 'cultural types', than with the problem of the unity of natural and historical laws. When, somewhat later, Rickert clearly developed the distinction between the laws of nature and history, his doctrine was seized upon by a large number of Russian thinkers (see Parts III and IV). However, we find this same motif even in Herzen, with his assertion of the 'improvization' of history and his doctrine of the alogism of the historical process—and even more sharply in Mikhailovski, with his struggle against the 'analogical method' in sociology, i.e. the assimilation of historical to natural laws. But Leontyev, who was profoundly occupied with the problem of the flowering of individuality, and the laws of its development and decay, did not sense the *distinction* between nature and history; he completely subordinated man and history to the laws which prevail in the organic world.

This also provides a key to Leontyev's 'aesthetic' conception of history. The application of aesthetic rather than moral principles to historiosophical phenomena is an inevitable result of biologism in historiosophy. If there is no place in nature for moral valuation, then there is no place in the dialectic of historical being for a moral component. The moral principle—on such a view—is introduced into history from above, by God's power and Providence; but the spontaneous processes of history, its 'natural' conformity to law, stand apart from the moral principle. Leontyev, with characteristic boldness, drew the logical inferences from this principle, heedless of any possible shock to the moral consciousness. Thus he took up arms vigorously against the ideal of equality, since equality (the 'egalitarian principle') is foreign to nature. 'The egalitarian process is everywhere destructive.'[3] The 'naturalistic'

1. Of course, in the problem of the flowering and strength of individuality Leontyev's chief stress is on *man*. This is clear from the passages quoted below.
2. Leontyev repeatedly emphasized his dependence on Danilevski.
3. *Sochineniya*, V, 383.

and ethical points of view coincide for Leontyev. His historiosophical formulation of this view is as follows: 'Harmony is not a peaceful unison, but a fruitful conflict—pregnant with creativity, and sometimes cruel.' [1] The harmony in nature rests on conflict; harmony in the aesthetic sense is a 'despotism of form' which suspends centrifugal forces. There is no place in any of this for morality as such:

'Apparent social injustice', he wrote in one place, 'conceals an invisible social truth—a profound and mysterious organic truth of social health, which cannot be contradicted with impunity even in the name of the best and most compassionate feelings. Morality has its *own sphere and its own limits.*' [2]

It is not difficult to grasp the sense of these last words: morality is a genuine, even supreme, value in the *individual* consciousness, but that is as far as it goes; historical being is subject to its *own* laws—which may be divined by an aesthetically sensitive person— but it is not subject to morality.

Leontyev checked the general principles of his historiosophy against European experience and Russian problems, but 'politics', i.e. questions of what must be done or avoided in order to escape the process of withering and disintegration, also enter into his purely theoretical analyses. Leontyev's critique of contemporary European culture is sharp, relentless, corrosive, and severe. It includes two basic theses: democratization, on the one hand, and the development of nationalism, on the other, are manifestations of 'secondary simplification and simplifying interfusion', i.e. clear symptoms of the biological withering and disintegration of Europe. Leontyev notes all of the alarming symptoms of Europe's 'death' very sharply and maliciously; in Europe the passion for the 'diffusion of universal equality and the dissemination of universal freedom' has resulted in 'making human life completely impossible on this globe'. [3] Even more sharp and insistent is his aesthetic critique of contemporary culture; here Leontyev deepened and sharpened Herzen's views concerning the 'ineradicable vulgarity of middle-class Philistinism'. (Leontyev valued Herzen very highly and considered him an 'aesthete of genius'.) But the aesthetic criterion, Leontyev firmly believed, 'is the most valid one, for it

1. *Ibid.*, p. 223.          2. *Op. cit.*, VI, 98.
3. *Ibid.*, p. 47 (from an article characteristically entitled 'Sredni yevropeyets kak ideal i orudiye vsemirnovo razrusheniya' ['The Average European as the Ideal and Instrument of Universal Destruction']).

is the only criterion which is universal' with respect to all the aspects of historical being.[1] 'Culture is lofty and influential', Leontyev wrote, 'when there is abundant beauty and poetry in the historical picture as it develops before us; and the basic law of beauty is diversity in unity.' 'If there is diversity there will also be *morality*: universal equality of rights and equal prosperity would kill "morality".'

Leontyev 'fearlessly' defended the severe measures of the state; he became an 'apostle of reaction', exalting the 'sacred right of coercion' on the part of the state. 'Individual freedom has only led the individual to greater irresponsibility'; equality and universal well-being is a

'gigantic crowd which grinds everyone and everything in a single mortar of pseudohuman vulgarity and prosiness. . . . The methods of the egalitarian process are complex; its aim is coarse and simple in idea. The aim of everything is the average man, the bourgeois, comfortably settled among millions of equally average men, who are also comfortable.'

Leontyev's hatred and abhorrence of the 'grey' ideal of equal prosperity constantly suggests the sharpest and most uncompromising formulas. 'Should one not hate men', he asks in one place, 'who have gone astray, and are stupid—and likewise hate their future?'[2] 'Never before has history seen such a monstrous combination of intellectual pride before God and moral submissiveness to the ideal of the homogeneous grey worker, who is only a worker, and to the ideal of an atheistically apathetic panhumanity.'

## 8. GENERAL APPRAISAL

The dialectic of Leontyev's ideas culminates in an assertion of the primacy of a religio-mystical conception of man and history. In his religious crisis he plumbed the internal amoralism of the contemporary world to its ultimate depths—sensing the loss of the 'fear of God', i.e. of the consciousness of a supramundane source of life, truth, and justice. In his crisis he experienced a serious Christian revelation of the salvation of the world in Christ, but he faced with equal profundity the question of the Christian meaning of culture and history, the Christian paths in history. On *this* point he was close to Gogol, Chaadayev, Tolstoy, Dostoyevsky,

1. *Ibid.*, p. 63.                              2. *Ibid.*, p. 269.

and, indirectly, to the 'theurgical restlessness' of Russian socio-political radicalism. He anticipated the themes of Solovyov and those thinkers who were inspired by him; it is no accident that Berdyaev has written the best book on Leontyev, or that Bulgakov has made the best study of his work. Leontyev raised the question of the possibility, meaning, and content of culture from the Christian point of view with excessive but fruitful acuteness. It is ridiculous to reduce Leontyev's religious ideas to 'transcendent egoism', considering that Leontyev has entered so deeply into the dialectic of Russian historiosophical thought. In fact, he 'fearlessly' approached the most difficult and fundamental problems of the contemporary world; and his sharpening of the question of the incompatibility of Christianity and the whole of contemporary culture did not mean that he was not tormented by this basic theme of Russian philosophic searchings. If, on the other hand, he accepted 'craftiness in politics'[1] in the name of the living historical power of the state, he did not deny that Christianity, as he understood it, was 'itself indifferent to politics'.[2] He was tormented by the *problems of culture*, and politics is a most difficult sphere of culture. In the name of the 'fear of God' he repudiated the 'shallow' ideal of universal prosperity, declaring categorically that 'modern European humaneness and Christian humaneness are clearly antithetical';[3] at the same time he frequently repeated: *credo quia absurdum*.

The *incompleteness* of Leontyev's Christian consciousness prevented him from developing a positive programme of historical activity out of his religious principles. Once (in a letter to Rozanov) he expressed—among his 'mad aphorisms'—the following idea: 'A more or less apt and universal preaching of Christianity' will lead to the 'extinction of the aesthetic life on earth, i.e. the extinction of life itself.'[4] On this critical point Leontyev remained on the side of Christianity, in the name of its 'transcendent' truth; i.e. he remained in the tragic impasse to which he was brought by the incompleteness of his religious consciousness and his inability to accept the fact that Christianity is a salvation *of* life and not a salvation *from* life. Leontyev's sharp formulation of this root question constitutes his significance for the dialectic of Russian thought. His brilliant literary talent, keen mind, and 'fearless' disclosure of the radical impasses of contemporary life assure him a place of first importance in this dialectic.

1. *Op. cit.*, V, 333.    2. *Loc. cit.*    3. *Op. cit.*, VIII, 203.
4. Quoted by Aggeyev, *op. cit.*, VI, 315.

The inner complex of problems of the religious consciousness was no less dramatically exhibited in V. V. Rozanov, another remarkable thinker and writer, to whom we now turn.

## 9. V. V. ROZANOV. BIOGRAPHY

Characterization of the intellectual content of Rozanov's work is made extremely difficult by the fact that he was a typical *journalist*. Although he had an integrated world-view, and although there is a certain unity in his diverse creative activity, Rozanov's style of writing makes it very hard to exhibit this inner unity. He strikes one as a capricious impressionist who deliberately refuses to make his utterances logically coherent; but in fact he was a highly integrated man and thinker. The subtlety and profundity of his observations, and at the same time his 'respect' for all ideas, even those which simply happen to enter his head, results in an outward brilliance, as well as a motley effect, in his writings. But very few Russian writers have possessed the word-magic that Rozanov did. He subdues his reader primarily with the directness, and at times 'nakedness', of his ideas, which do not hide behind words or seek a verbal covering for their inner meaning.

Rozanov is probably the most remarkable *writer* among Russian thinkers, but he is also a genuine thinker, stubbornly and persistently cutting a path through the tangles of contemporary life and thought. The basic content of his incessant intellectual activity reveals Rozanov as one of the most gifted and powerful of Russian religious philosophers—audacious, widely educated, and sincere with himself to the ultimate degree. It was for this reason that he had such an enormous—though often not overt—influence on twentieth-century Russian philosophic thought. Like Leontyev, he was occupied with the question of God and the world, of their relationship and connection. It would be incorrect to regard Rozanov as a man who neglected God for the sake of the world; but he held his hopes and searchings so deep within himself that his religious consciousness was deformed and modified in order to prevent anything of value in the world from perishing. In the dispute between God and the world Rozanov (like Leontyev) remained on a religious plane, but if Leontyev was ready to repudiate the world—to 'freeze' it—for the sake of divine truth as he understood it, Rozanov on the contrary rejected Christianity for the sake of the truth of the world, because of Christianity's 'inability', as he thought, to accept this truth. Leontyev and

Rozanov were polar opposites on this point, but at the same time they were very close to one another. Interestingly enough, each of them has frequently been called a 'Russian Nietzsche', and in fact both of them exhibit features which invite comparison (although at different points) with Nietzsche.

Rozanov's biography is uncomplicated. Vasili Vasilyevich Rozanov was born into a poor provincial family in Vetluga in 1856.[1] His childhood was spent in difficult surroundings; as a small child he did not have a family environment. After graduating from the Gymnasium, Rozanov entered the Faculty of History and Philology at Moscow University; upon graduation he took a position as a teacher of history in a remote provincial city. There he conceived a philosophic work upon which he laboured for five years. His large book, On the Understanding (737 pp.) was published in 1886, but it remained quite unnoticed in the Russian press. At this time Rozanov took up journalistic work, which later became his chief concern. His article 'The Twilight of Enlightenment', which painted a harsh and caustic picture of the academic world, evoked repressive measures against him and made it very difficult for him to combine academic work with a free literary profession. Finally, thanks to the efforts of N. N. Strakhov, whom Rozanov ardently admired,[2] he obtained a position in St. Petersburg in 1893, in the Department of State Control. There he fell into the midst of the 'epigones of Slavophilism', or, more precisely, of journalists and writers who were struggling against the radicalism which then prevailed in Russian society. Rozanov's large book on Dostoyevsky (The Legend of the Grand Inquisitor) dates from 1903–4; this work won him universal notice. A number of his articles brought him enormous fame; and his material situation began to improve. He began to write for the newspaper *Novoye vremya* [New Times], which provided him with sufficient means. Collections of his articles appeared one after another: Religion and Culture, Nature and History, and later The Family Question in Russia (two volumes), and The Place of Christianity in History. Of his other works we should note especially his book, The Metaphysics of Christianity (Pt. I, The Dark Face of Christianity,

1. There is as yet no biography of Rozanov except for a small book by E. F. Gollerbakh, *V. V. Rozanov. Lichnost i tvorchestvo* [V. V. Rozanov. The Man and His Work], Petrograd, 1918 (50 pp.).

2. Of great importance for Rozanov's biography are Strakhov's letters to Rozanov with the latter's notes to these letters. (See Rozanov, *Literaturnyie izgnanniki* [Literary Exiles], St. Petersburg, 1913.)

which includes the article 'Sweetest Jesus', and Pt. II, Men of the Moonlight); By the Walls of the Church (two volumes) and still later, In Solitude, and Fallen Leaves (in two parts). During the revolution Rozanov lived in the Suburb of Sergiyevsk, where the Troitsko-Sergiyevski Abbey is located, and there he published his remarkable Apocalypse.[1]

Rozanov had enormous influence on the religio-philosophic searchings of D. S. Merezhkovski, to some extent on N. A. Berdyaev—in his anthropology—and Fr. P. Florenski, with whom he became acquainted long before his move to the Suburb of Sergiyevsk, where Florenski lived as a Professor in the Moscow Theological Academy. But besides his friends, Rozanov had many literary enemies—partly as a result of his manner of writing, which made many readers highly indignant, and partly as a result of his frequent lack of principle.[2]

Rozanov died in the Suburb of Sergiyevsk near the Troitsko-Sergiyevski Abbey in 1919 in extreme poverty and severe distress.

## 10. HIS SPIRITUAL EVOLUTION

Rozanov's spiritual evolution was very complex. He started from a specific kind of rationalism—with echoes of transcendentalism—in his first philosophic work, On the Understanding; but he soon abandoned this, although isolated traces of his earlier rationalism remained to the end of his life. From the very beginning (i.e. in his first book) Rozanov showed himself a *religious thinker*, and such he remained throughout his life. His entire spiritual evolution took place, so to speak, within his religious consciousness. In his first phase, Rozanov belonged wholly to Orthodoxy, evaluating the themes of culture in general, and the problem of the West in particular, in its light. The most striking documents of this period are The Legend of the Grand Inquisitor and the articles in the collections: In the World of the Obscure and Unresolved, Religion and Culture, etc. However, even at this time ideas appear in Rozanov which show that doubts were flaring up in his soul. On

1. There is no edition of Rozanov's collected works.
2. Solovyov's article on Rozanov is an example of such a sharp polemic. In connection with Rozanov's article on Leo Tolstoy, which was written in a rather 'unpleasant' tone and aroused strong indignation in literary and social circles, P. B. Struve suggested 'excluding Rozanov from literature'. Rozanov was barred from the Religio-Philosophical Society in St. Petersburg because of his sharp utterances on the Jewish question.

the one hand he sharply contrasted the East and the Christian West: Western Christianity seemed to him 'far from the world', an 'anti-world'.[1] In Orthodoxy 'all is more luminous and joyful'; in the West the spirit of the Church 'is still that of the Old Testament, but in the East it is already that of the New Testament'.[2] In the light of Orthodoxy Christianity appeared to Rozanov as 'full of gaiety and a wonderful lightness of spirit—without melancholy or oppressiveness'.[3] A little further on he writes: 'It is impossible to insist too much that Christianity is joy—nothing but joy and joy always.' However, during these same years he wrote the remarkable article 'Nominalism in Christianity', which asserted sharply that *all* Christianity 'has been turned into a doctrine', that 'nominalism' and rhetoric are not an incidental phenomenon in Christianity but 'Christianity itself, as it has been expressed in history'.[4] 'Christianity', he wrote, 'has not yet been started; *it does not exist at all*, yet we worship it like a legend.'[5] 'The whole torment and task of religion on earth is to become *real*, to *realize* itself.'[6] This defence of Christian *realism* contains the motive force of the dialectic of Rozanov's religious searchings. We are already on the threshold of the second period of his creative activity; he is already seized by doubts with respect to 'historical' Christianity, to which he opposes true and genuine Christianity. To be sure, we still find echoes of his earlier opposition of East and West. Here, for example, is a passage which appears almost beside the above-quoted defence of Christian realism: '*No one* has yet attained the depths of Christianity; and this task, which has not even dawned upon the West, is perhaps the original task of Russian genius.' However this may be, Rozanov began to be sceptical about 'historical' Christianity—and new theological ideas occurred to him. To the 'religion of Golgotha' he opposed a 'religion of Bethlehem',[7] which includes 'Christianity, but expressed in such a vitally joyous way that beside Golgotha, its ascetic phase, it seems a new religion'.[8]

We are now well within the second period of Rozanov's creative activity, in which Golgotha is *opposed* to Bethlehem. Rozanov began to criticize 'historical' Christianity in the name of 'Bethle-

1. Rozanov, *Religiya i kultura* [Religion and Culture], St. Petersburg, 1901, p. 64.

2. *Ibid.*, pp. 65f.     3. *Ibid.*, p. 243.

4. *V mire neyasnovo i nereshonnovo* [In the World of the Obscure and Unresolved], St. Petersburg, 1901, p. 47.

5. *Ibid.*, p. 267.     6. *Ibid.*, p. 103.     7. *Ibid.*, p. 57.     8. *Ibid.*, p. 61.

hem'; the problem of the family moved to the centre of his theological and philosophic reflections. He did not yet leave the
Church; he was still '*by* the walls of the Church' (the title of a
two-volume collection of his articles). But in the 'dispute' between
Christianity and culture, Christianity gradually grew dim, losing
its 'vitally joyous' strength, and gradually giving way to a 'religion
of the Father', to the 'Old Testament'. It is interesting to note
that the first article in Vol. I of Rozanov's book, By the Walls of
the Church (which bears the characteristic title 'Religion as
Light and Joy'), contains the sentence: 'A thorough inspection
convinces one that among all the philosophic and religious
doctrines there is no world-view more luminous and full of the joy
of life than that of Christianity.' [1] But even here Rozanov speaks of
the 'great misunderstanding which has arisen around the element
of Golgotha in the development of Christianity'. 'An indefatigable
search for suffering has sprung from the element of Golgotha in
the imitation of Christ.' Hence 'the whole act of atonement has
*evaded man* and thundered into an abyss, a wasteland, without
saving anyone or anything'.[2] These words exhibit dialectically
the transition to the second period, except that Rozanov's critique
is directed not at Christianity itself but at the Church's misconcep-
tion of Christianity. 'The essence of the Church, and even of
Christianity, has been defined', he wrote in another article, 'as a
*worship of death*'.[3] 'Nothing in Christ's existence', he continues, 'has
become such a great and constant symbol as his death. To become
like a relic, to cease to live, move, or breathe, is the Church's great
and universal ideal.'

But Rozanov's critique of the Church developed into a forceful
*struggle* against it when his reflections focused on the problem of
the family. 'To devote my whole life to the destruction of the only
thing in the world that I love', he once wrote '—has anyone had
a more grievous fate?' [4] This is very true: Rozanov could not tear
himself away from the Church; he even went to die 'by the walls
of the Church'—near the Troitsko-Sergiyevski Abbey. But the
inner dialectic of his thought led to a sharp and relentless struggle
with the Church, and later with Christ as well. In order to understand this dialectic and to evaluate the full significance of Rozanov's ideas, we must study his conception of man. For Rozanov's

1. *Okolo tserkovnykh sten* [By the Walls of the Church], St. Petersburg, 1906,
I, 15.
2. *Ibid.*, p. 18.    3. *Op. cit.*, II, 446.
4. *Uyedinyonnoye* [In Solitude], St. Petersburg, 1912, p. 213.

philosophical anthropology contains the key to his entire spiritual and intellectual evolution.

## II. ROZANOV'S ANTHROPOLOGY

We say Rozanov's *anthropology* as a whole, and not simply his 'metaphysics of sex', because, although the latter is the most important part of his anthropology, it is not the whole of it.

The fundamental intuition underlying Rozanov's searchings and theoretical constructions in the field of anthropology is a faith in human 'nature' and a tender love of man. He loved 'nature' in general, and this feature was so prominent in his world-view that the latter is often characterized as a 'mystical pantheism'; [1] however, this is incorrect. 'Nature is a friend, but it is not edible', Rozanov once wrote sarcastically. [2]

'Everything in the world loves everything else with a kind of blind, unconscious, stupid, and indefensible love. . . . Each thing reflects its external environment in itself . . . and this mutual "mirrorness" of things extends even to civilization; something enters into its features from the landscape of nature.' [3]

Rozanov's sense of the life of nature is in fact extraordinary —though not at all *pantheistic*. His remarkable article 'The Sacred Mystery of Being' contains passages close to the sense of nature which is frequently found in pantheism: 'There is, in fact, a certain *mysterious foundation* for accepting the whole world, the whole universe, as a mystical maternal womb in which we are born—and in which our sun was born, and from it our earth.' [4] I think that this 'mysterious foundation' is a *Sophiological* conception; but, to my knowledge, Rozanov mentions it nowhere except in this passage. However, we are not now concerned with this, but with the sense of the *life of the world* and the *connection of man and nature* which appears so frequently in Rozanov.

'From every humble cottage', he wrote, 'at the birth of every new self, our earth emits a tiny ray, and the whole earth glows

1. See especially A. S. Volzhski, 'Misticheski panteizm' ['Mystical Pantheism'] in the collection *Iz mira literaturnikh iskani* [From the World of Literary Searchings], St. Petersburg, 1906, This is the best existing work on Rozanov.

2. *Okolo* . . . [By the Walls . . .], I, 12.

3. *Ibid.*, pp. 77–9.

4. *Semeiny vopros v Rossi* [The Family Question in Russia], St. Petersburg, 1903, II, 53.

with a limited radiance, which does not reach heaven, but *is its very own*. The earth, when it gives birth, floats firmly—a radiant body, one that is religiously radiant.' [1]

'The world was not merely created rationally', Rozanov wrote in another place, 'but also sacredly, as much according to the Bible as according to Aristotle. . . . The whole world is warmed and united by love.' [2]

Rozanov came to various conclusions on the basis of his profound 'sense of nature'. His *biocentrism* of principle—which is evident even in his first book, On the Understanding—did not lead him to a 'mystical pantheism', as is often assumed, but to a conclusion which he himself formulated thus: 'All metaphysics is a deepening of our knowledge of *nature*.' [3] This is a cosmocentrism; but, since Rozanov's sense of the Creator was always acute, the idea of the createdness of the world remained essential for him. His cosmocentrism did not merge into pantheism.

Rozanov's whole anthropology is *cosmocentrically* oriented. I do not share Volzhski's opinion that 'Rozanov's love of life is unconnected with the *personality* of man or God.' [4] On the contrary, Rozanov's sense of (human) personality is extraordinarily strong, but it is cosmocentrically coloured. His whole metaphysics of man focuses on the mystery of *sex*; but this is very far from a Freudian pansexualism. Rozanov *humanizes* everything about the mystery of sex. We shall have further occasion to discuss his remarkable formula: 'That which man has lost in the cosmos he finds in history.' [5] At present the essential thing for us in this formula is the indication that man 'loses' something in the cosmos. But he does not lose *himself* in it; he is 'included' in the order of nature, and the point of this inclusion is sex, the mystery of the generation of new life. This 'creative' function of sex is what Rozanov finds necessary and valuable; sex, according to him, 'is man's *soul*'. [6] He even asserts that man in general is a 'transformation of sex.' [7] This is not an anthropological 'materialism'; quite the contrary: 'There is not a single atom in us—not a fingernail, a hair, or a

1. *Op. cit.*, I, 54.
2. Rozanov's comment on a letter from Strakhov, *Literaturnyie izgnanniki* [Literary Exiles] p. 248.
3. *Rus. vestnik*, VIII (1892), p. 196.
4. Volzhski, *op. cit.*, p. 363.
5. *Religiya* . . . [Religion . . .], p. 21.
6. *V mire* . . . [In the World . . .], p. 7.
7. *Lyudi lunnovo sveta* [Men of the Moonlight], St. Petersburg, 1911, p. 71.

drop of blood that does not contain a spiritual principle.' [1] The appearance of an individual is a vast event in the life of the cosmos, for every self contains something isolated from and opposed to all that is not the self.[2]

Conceiving sex as the sphere in man which mysteriously connects him with all of nature, i.e. conceiving it metaphysically, Rozanov regards everything else in man as an expression and development of the mystery of sex. 'Sex transcends the boundaries of nature; it is extra-natural and supernatural.' [3] In general, 'a person comes into being only where there is sex'. But in its depths sex is man's 'second, dark, noumenal aspect'[4]—'an abyss which leads to the antipodes of being, an image of the other world'.[5] 'Sex in man is like an enchanted wood, i.e. a wood filled with magic charms. Man flees from it in terror, and the enchanted wood remains a mystery.' [6]

The remarkable article 'Family and Life'—in the collection Religion and Culture—contains many of Rozanov's characteristic reflections on these same themes. 'Sex is not a function or an organ', he writes, opposing superficial empiricism in the theory of sex. To regard sex as an organ is '*to destroy man*'.[7] These profound words clearly reveal the *humaneness* of Rozanov's metaphysics; no one has had a deeper sense of man's 'sacredness' than he, precisely because he sensed the sacred mystery of sex. His books are intoxicated with a love of the 'infant' (his writings on 'illegitimate' children are especially remarkable). It is not accidental that Rozanov sees the ultimate source of the 'corruption' of contemporary civilization in the disintegration of the family, a process which is undermining this civilization.

Rozanov's deep reflections on problems of sex fit into the general framework of a system of *personalism*; and this comprises their significance. He elucidates the metaphysics of man through a recognition of the metaphysical centrality of the sphere of sex. 'Sex is not the body', Rozanov once wrote, 'the body merely whirls about it and out of it. . . .' [8] This and analogous formulas in Rozanov are immeasurably more profound than the 'mystical vision of the flesh' which Merezhkovski extolled so highly in

---

1. *Ibid.*, p. 70.                          2. *Ibid.*, p. 28.
3. *V Mire* . . . [In the World . . .], p. 110.
4. *Ibid.*, p. 5.                           5. *Ibid.*, p. 110.
6. *Iz vostochnykh motivov* [Eastern Motifs] (Notebooks), p. 24.
7. *Religiya* . . . [Religion . . .], p. 173.
8. *V mire* . . . [In the World . . .], p. 123.

Tolstoy: no one has felt the 'mystery' of sex and its connection with the transcendent sphere more profoundly than Rozanov. ('The relation of sex to God is stronger than the relation of intellect to God—stronger even than the relation of conscience to God.' [1])

## 12. HISTORICAL VIEWS

Meditating on the fate of the family in the development of Christianity, Rozanov was at first inclined, as we have seen, to charge the Church and 'historical Christianity' in general with a one-sided tendency toward an ascetic 'abhorrence' of the world. But his view gradually changed; he began to transfer his doubts to the *essence* of Christianity. 'Christianity long ago ceased to be a leaven and a ferment', and 'established itself'. [2] Hence 'we see about us the spectacle of a Christian civilization which is essentially *frozen* . . ., in which everything is nominal'.[3] The reason for this, Rozanov now thinks, is that 'monasticism is the only natural inference from the text of the New Testament'.[4] 'The Church', he asserts in another place, 'has no feeling for children'. [5] These doubts reached their highest point in the article 'Sweetest Jesus' (in the collection, The Dark Face of Christianity), which created a great stir. Rozanov here asserts that 'in Christ the world has become rancid'.[6] He now entered a period of Christomachy, turning decisively toward the Old Testament—the 'religion of the Father'. It now appeared that he 'had never liked to read the New Testament, but could not get enough of the Old Testament'.[7] 'Monasticism', he wrote, 'constitutes the metaphysics of Christianity.' [8] Rozanov now called Christianity 'Christo-theism', asserting that it contained 'only one-third of the truth of theism'. [9] His Christomachy took on special force and sharp emphasis in the Apocalypse of Our Time, written just before his death. This is a strange and terrifying work containing extremely sharp and

1. *Uyedinyonnoye* [In Solitude], p. 169.
2. *Okolo* . . . [By the Walls . . .], I, 91.
3. *Religiya* . . . [Religion . . .], p. 150.
4. Letter to Gollerbakh. See Gollerbakh, *Pisma Rozanova* [Rozanov's Letters], Berlin, 1922, p. 44.
5. *Semeiny vopros* . . . [The Family Question . . .], I, 35.
6. *Tyomny lik khristianstva* [The Dark Face of Christianity], St. Petersburg, 1911, p. 265.
7. *Opavshiye listya* [Fallen Leaves], St. Petersburg, 1913, I, 255.
8. *Lyudi* . . . [Men . . .], p. 194.
9. *Iz vostochnykh* . . . [Eastern . . .], p. 15.

dreadful formulas. 'Christ has intolerably burdened human life'; Christ is a 'mysterious Shadow which has caused the withering of all grains'; Christianity, with the 'narrow truth and justice of its New Testament', is 'powerless to order human life'. We even find such words as: 'The evil of Christ's coming. . . .' [1]

Christianity, Rozanov once wrote, is 'true but it is powerless'.[2] And the historical 'powerlessness' of the Church, its failure to dominate the historical process or to illuminate and transfigure it in every respect—all of this for Rozanov is the Church's 'sin'. We can now see Rozanov's historiosophical conception, which he never fully expressed. We have already quoted his profound thought: 'that which man has lost in the cosmos he finds in history'. However, this does not exalt man as an *historical agent*: the regal significance which man has lost in the cosmos and rediscovered in history is not created by man. 'Man does not make history; he lives and stumbles about in history without knowing why or whither.' [3] This is more than agnosticism; it is an historiosophical mysticism, which often comes close to Herzen's historiosophical alogism or Leo Tolstoy's impersonalism in the philosophy of history. Rozanov speaks in this same book of '*false* waves of history' which break about the monasteries. But the power of history over man's personal consciousness is much greater than it seems to us.

'To be *deceived* in history is the perpetual lot of man on earth. Hopes are suggested to man in order that, being guided by them, he may accomplish certain things which are needed to bring him to a condition which has *nothing to do with these hopes*, but is extremely harmonious and clearly necessary in the general order of universal history.' [4]

The only 'locus' for the manifestation of man's *individual* creativity is the family and child-bearing. Rozanov, as we have seen, goes to great lengths to exhibit the sacred significance of the family and child-bearing. He repeatedly emphasizes the mystical profundity which inheres in the family, its supra-empirical nature. 'The family cannot be rationally constructed. . . . The family is an institution which is essentially irrational and mystical.' [5]

1. 'Apokalipsis nashevo vremeni' ['The Apocalypse of Our Time'], *Vyorsty*, No. 2 (1927), pp. 336, 307, 316, 345. (Reprint.)
2. *Ibid.*, p. 305.
3. *Religiya* . . . [Religion . . .], p. 126.
4. *Ibid.*, p. 126.
5. *Semeiny vopros* . . . [The Family Question . . .], I, 75, 78.

## 13. 'MYSTICAL PANTHEISM'

We turn now to the purely philosophic premises on which Rozanov's theories rest. His whole world-view, which was formed apropos of the 'incidental' themes to which his journalistic duties committed him—with all his extraordinary 'honesty' (which often exceeded the bounds of 'decency')—remained faithful to the original intuition which underlay his first book. This book, which is permeated throughout with *rationalism* and a confidence in the 'rational predetermination' of being, presents a highly original *mystical* interpretation of rationalism. Being is reasonable, and its reasonableness is revealed to our reason; everything knowable is contained in our understanding, held in its forms, but still hidden. This 'parallelism' of being and reason appeared to Rozanov, by his own admission,[1] in a vision; and it determined the whole plan of his book, On the Understanding. Just as a plant grows from a seed, so all knowledge develops out of the depths of the mind. This image of the 'seed', which is basic to Rozanov's book, remained basic throughout his life. 'All sensation', he wrote in one article, 'is unilluminated and obscure, and its meaning is impenetrable to man, until it is associated with the meaning of something else which is *already* present in the soul.'[2] 'We should understand the phenomena of external nature', he continues, in the lines of transcendentalism, 'as mere *repetitions* of the processes and states of our *primary* consciousness.'

But Rozanov now interpreted rationalism, which is very close to transcendentalism, in terms of transcendental realism. 'Reality is higher than reasonableness or truth.'[3] And he goes on to interpret this realism theistically, which flatly and categorically refutes the assumption that Rozanov was a pantheist. 'Just as there is a conceived world which corresponds to the conceiving reason, so there is a duty which answers to moral feeling, and an *intuited* Deity answering to religious intuition.'[4] This is not a random expression in Rozanov; he lived by a sense of God throughout his life. But he felt more deeply than other men the divine light of the cosmos and its direct contact with the transcendent sphere. This, however, does not give us the right to speak of Rozanov as a

1. Note on a letter from Strakhov, *Lit. izgnanniki* [Lit. Exiles], pp. 342f.
2. 'Ideya ratsionalnovo yestestvoznaniya' ['The Idea of Rational Natural Science'], *Russki vestnik*, VIII (1892), pp. 196f.
3. *Literaturnyie ocherki* [Literary Sketches], 1899, p. 39.
4. *Ibid.*, p. 42.

pantheist; we may say only that he approached a *Sophiological* conception, which, in its intention (but not in its actual expression, for example, in Vladimir Solovyov), was free from pantheism. However, the *mysticism* of Rozanov's world-view appears clearly in his constant sense of the transcendent sphere beneath the illusory surface of 'rationalism'.

### 14. GENERAL APPRAISAL

Rozanov's *cosmocentrism* had an extraordinary influence on a number of Russian thinkers—not only those who were congenial to him but many who were hostile. The positive contribution which is indissolubly connected with Rozanov's name in the dialectic of Russian thought lies not in the problem of sex or the family—despite the importance of Rozanov's writings in this field—but in his cosmocentrism. Does this not explain why he is so often considered a pantheist? Rozanov did his part for a future *Sophiology* —which has not yet been completed by Russian philosophers— that is meant to interpret philosophically the content of the living religious perception of the cosmos characteristic of the Orthodox faith.

No less important is Rozanov's contribution to the theme of 'secularism', and the construction of a system of culture based on the Church, which is fundamental to the dialectic of Russian philosophy. Like Leontyev, he always took Christianity as his point of departure, remaining 'by the walls of the Church'; he was, like Leontyev, a conscious opponent of secularized Europe, but this did not prevent him from giving expression to the tragic fact that the heme of culture remained unsolved within the Church. On this path Rozanov, without giving way to secularism, nevertheless developed a sharper critique of the Church than even secularism has provided. The outcome of his complex and intense creative activity gives no comfort to secularism; it remains essentially *positive*. The positive influence of Rozanov's acute ideas on the renewal and renaissance of Russian religious searchings cannot be denied; and this influence tended toward a religious interpretation and sanctification of the 'spontaneous' processes of cultural creativity. It is impossible to solve the problem of an ecclesiastical culture without considering Rozanov's themes and his cosmocentrism. More than this: Russian personalism, which has often leaned excessively toward pure ethicism, must make room for Rozanov's themes if it is to rise to a Sophiological formulation. On this path toward a future Sophiology the heritage of Rozanov's ideas is especially valuable.

## 15. CONCLUDING REMARKS ON THE SECOND PERIOD IN THE DEVELOPMENT OF RUSSIAN PHILOSOPHY

With this we conclude our study of the second period in the history of Russian philosophy. We have made certain omissions in studying this period: we have not considered the individual philosophic works which began to appear more and more frequently after the 1860's. But it will be more convenient to postpone our general survey of these works until the chapter on 'university philosophy', which falls within the period of 'systems'. Furthermore, we should have made a special study of the philosophic tendencies in Russian poetry; but this theme requires a separate book.

We have come directly to the period of 'systems'. Essentially, almost all of the theoretical constructions with which we have been dealing in the period of Alexander II were capable of providing 'systems'; some of them—for example, those of P. L. Lavrov—were almost on the threshold of system-building. That this did not occur was due to various historical circumstances rather than to any absence of necessary talent. But such are the inevitable 'stages' in historical maturation.

C66276